The Seventh-day Adventist Hymnal

The Seventh-day Adventist Hymnal

REVIEW AND HERALD PUBLISHING ASSOCIATION

Washington, DC 20039-0555

Hagerstown, MD 21740

Printed in U.S.A.

Fourth printing, 1986

ISBN 0-8280-0307-6

INTRODUCTION

The Scriptures echo with the sound of singing. At Creation "the morning stars sang together, and all the sons of God shouted for joy" (Job 38:7). The psalmist declared, "I will sing unto the Lord as long as I live: I will sing praise to my God while I have my being" (Ps. 104:33). The apostle Paul wanted the members of the church at Colossae to encourage one another in the faith with "psalms and hymns and spiritual songs" (Col. 3:16). The first angel of Revelation 14 asks God's people to "give glory to him; . . . and worship him that made heaven, and earth, and the sea, and the fountains of waters" (verse 7).

This hymnal can be used to lead congregations into more creative and significant ways of praising God, a deeper love for Jesus Christ, a keener awareness of the church's place and mission in the world, a fresh knowledge of God's will for each life, and a preparation for our Lord's second coming.

James White recalled that in the early days of the Advent movement in America "there was . . . a power in what was called Advent singing, such as was felt in no other."—*Life Incidents*, p. 94. From their beginning, Seventh-day Adventists have been a singing people. The very first book they published was the 1849 collection of *Hymns for God's Peculiar People That Keep the Commandments of God and the Faith of Jesus*. James White published five hymnals and four supplements even before the church was formally organized in 1863. White drew freely from the musical heritage of the Methodists, Baptists, and other denominations. He also carried forward some of the "white spirituals" from the *Millennial Harp* of Joshua V. Himes, and added a few new hymns by Adventist authors Uriah and Annie Smith and Roswell F. Cottrell. Hymns such as "Gracious Father, Guard Thy Children" and "Jesus, I My Cross Have Taken" have survived in every hymnal since the first.

A few of the spiritual songs from this early period have been included in the Early Advent section of the hymnal to provide a resource for the celebration of the church's heritage. While they may not always reach the musical standard of the great hymns of the church, they nevertheless remind us of the fervent faith of our pioneers.

The first "official" Seventh-day Adventist hymnal was *Hymns and Tunes for Those Who Keep the Commandments of God and the Faith of Jesus*, issued in 1869. This served until *The Seventh-day Adventist Hymn and Tune Book (Hymns and Tunes)* was issued in 1886. Even though James White had died in 1881, the influence of his family was still felt in Adventist hymnody. His son J. Edson White set the musical type for the new hymnal and his nephew Franklin Belden served as musical editor, along with Edwin Barnes, an expatriate Englishman who served as organist in the denomination's largest church, the Battle Creek Tabernacle.

In 1908 Franklin Belden produced *Christ in Song*, a "tuneful" and rhythmic collection much loved by congregations. Indeed, popular demand has led the Church Hymnal Committee to restore some selections from Belden's hymnal. The next major collection, *The Church Hymnal*, appeared in 1941. Professor H. B. Hannum played a major role in that collection. In retirement, he offered encouragement and practical advice that enriched this new hymnal as well.

Although the average life of a church hymnal is about twenty-five years,

5

Seventh-day Adventists have waited far longer to replace their 1941 volume. Meanwhile, we have issued a number of smaller collections for special purposes. At length it was clear that the church would profit from a new hymnal. Old favorites from many sources needed to be recovered. Hymns that had not achieved acceptance needed to be set aside in favor of fine new compositions. New tunes, wedded to familiar texts, promised to revitalize some hymns, while in other cases the reverse was true—new poems accompanied by familiar music could give fresh expression to the church's faith. Church services needed the energy and meaning that additional worship aids could provide.

In response to these needs the General Conference Music Committee supported the Review and Herald Publishing Association in the development of *The Seventh-day Adventist Hymnal.* As plans progressed, the General Conference Committee, in Annual Council, endorsed the project. A nineteen-member Church Hymnal Committee was appointed under the direction of C. L. Brooks, chairman, and Wayne Hooper, executive secretary. The committee included music teachers, choir leaders, organists, composers, writers, editors, soloists, evangelists, pastors, and church administrators. The broad diversity of the Seventh-day Adventist Church was represented by men and women, black and white, clergymen and laypersons, academics and administrators. In addition, members of a large advisory committee reviewed the work and offered suggestions as it progressed.

How Hymns Were Chosen

The committee has sought hymns well suited for congregational singing and examined each one for scriptural and doctrinal soundness. They prized music that would be attractive both to old and young worshipers, and texts that recognized the diversity of cultures among the English-speaking church members who will use the hymnal. They mined the treasures of Christian hymnody past and present. They selected favorites from our Adventist heritage and gospel songs both old and new. They sought hymns that affirm the distinctive beliefs of Seventh-day Adventists as well as those that express points of faith we hold in common with other Christian bodies.

The selection process did not rely, however, on the tastes of the committee members only. Hundreds of pastors and laypersons sent suggestions to the committee. More than three thousand ministers in North America and Australia were asked to rate each hymn in the 1941 *Church Hymnal* according to whether they would retain or delete it. In response, the committee retained widely used hymns along with those that bore important spiritual messages or enjoyed hallowed associations. In order to make room for hymns of greater merit and beauty, they omitted some of marginal poetic or musical value. The international character of the Seventh-day Adventist Church dictated that patriotic hymns tied to a single nation be passed over. Hymns well adapted to congregational singing were given precedence over compositions intended for choirs or soloists.

New hymns were drawn from many sources. Hymnals old and new provided texts and tunes of enduring value from other churches. Sometimes it was necessary to alter the text of these hymns to eliminate theological aberrations or awkward, jarring expressions. With great caution, the text committee replaced archaic and exclusive language whenever this could be done without disturbing familiar phrases, straining fond attachments, or doing violence to historical appropriateness.

Musically the hymnal was improved with the addition of a number of American folk hymns and Negro spirituals as well as German chorales and old psaltery tunes. The hymnal includes a few modern gospel songs along with several striking new works by Adventist authors and composers.

How to Use the Hymnal

A survey of a typical hymnal page will aid the worshiper in the use of the hymnal. The title is the first line of the hymn-poem, except for those gospel songs in which a phrase from elsewhere in the text is more familiar. Both first line and familiar title are listed in the alphabetical index. To the left is found a Bible reference if the hymn is based on a specific passage. Below that appear the author's name, the date the hymn was written, and the author's birth and death dates. Occasionally the source of the text is given instead of the author.

On the right is the name of the hymn tune if it has a name. Next on the right of the page is a set of numbers indicating the metrical pattern of the poem, which is simply the number of syllables in each line (such as LM for long meter, or 8.8.8.8.). By referring to the Metrical Index one can find other tunes in the same meter that might fit the text and add interest to the singing. Where the same tune is actually printed with different texts elsewhere in the hymnal, the tune is sometimes written in a different key or with a different harmonization, and a cross-reference is noted at the bottom of the page. Cross-references are also used to suggest alternative tunes that are especially well adapted to a particular text. Just above the musical staff on the right of the page is the known information about the composer or source of the music.

Sometimes the word *unison* is printed above the staff to indicate music that is best interpreted if all sing the melody together. Of course, hymns written in four-part harmony can be sung in unison whenever desired. Nevertheless, to make unison singing more enjoyable for all, the pitch of many familiar hymns has been lowered.

To the left, below the music, is the copyright information if the hymn is still protected by copyright. This means the publisher has the right to print the hymn in this book only. For any other use of the hymn one must secure permission from the owner of the copyright. Any errors or omissions in the printing of copyright information will gladly be corrected in future printings.

Throughout the hymnal, gospel songs and great hymns stand together in topical clusters. The worship aids in the back of the hymnal offer readings, calls to worship, words of assurance, offertory sentences, and benedictions, all drawn from the words of Scripture. The hymnal includes suggestions for using these worship aids, and congregations will enjoy exploring new applications of their own.

In addition to the standard indexes, the "finding aids" include a list entitled Hymns Suitable for Young Worshipers, a canonically arranged index of scriptural allusions in hymns (with special thanks to Edward E. White), a scripture index to the worship aids, and an extensive topical index.

Purpose of the Hymnal

Ellen White, cofounder and spiritual leader of our church, noted that "the soul may ascend nearer heaven on the wings of praise."—*Steps to Christ*, p. 104. "Singing," she said, ". . . is as much an act of worship as is prayer."—*Patriarchs of Prophets*, p. 594. This hymnal is designed to help Seventh-day Adventists continue this chorus of praise that cheered God's ancient people, encouraged the early church, powered the Reformation, and brightens the fellowship of those who share the "blessed hope."

The Hymnal Committee

Chairman:
Charles L. Brooks
Executive secretary:
Wayne H. Hooper
Subcommittee chairmen:
Charles I. Keymer, *Organization and Indexes*
E. Harold Lickey, *Texts*
Melvin K. West, *Tunes*
Merle J. Whitney, *Worship Materials*

Members

James T. Bingham	Samuel D. Meyers
Alma M. Blackmon	John W. Read
Robert E. Cowdrick	J. Robert Spangler
Allen W. Foster	Ottilie F. Stafford
Ronald D. Graybill	Michael H. Stevenson
Frank B. Holbrook	Raymond H. Woolsey
Rochelle D. LaGrone	

CONTENTS

Numbers in italics refer to Scripture Readings

9

Praise to the Lord

1

Psalm 103:2-5
Joachim Neander (1650-1680)
Tr. by Catherine Winkworth, 1863 (1827-1878)

LOBE DEN HERREN 14.14.4.7.8.
Chorale Book for England, 1863
Harm. by Wm. S. Bennett

1. Praise to the Lord, the Al - might - y, the King of cre - a - tion! O my soul, praise Him, for He is thy health and sal - va - tion! All ye who hear, Now to His tem - ple draw near; Join ye in glad ad - o - ra - tion!

2. Praise to the Lord, who o'er all things so won - drous - ly reign - eth, Shield - eth thee un - der His wings, yea, so gen - tly sus - tain - eth! Hast thou not seen How thy de - sires e'er have been Grant - ed in what He or - dain - eth?

3. Praise to the Lord, who doth pros - per thy work and de - fend thee; Sure - ly His good - ness and mer - cy here dai - ly at - tend thee. Pon - der a - new What the Al - might - y can do If with His love He be - friend thee.

ADORATION AND PRAISE

2 All Creatures of Our God and King

Francis of Assisi, 1225 (1182-1226)
Para. by William H. Draper, 1926 (1855-1933)

LASST UNS ERFREUEN 8.8.8.8.8.8. Ref.
Geistliche Kirchengesänge, *Köln, 1623*
Arr. by Ralph Vaughan Williams, 1906 (1872-1958)

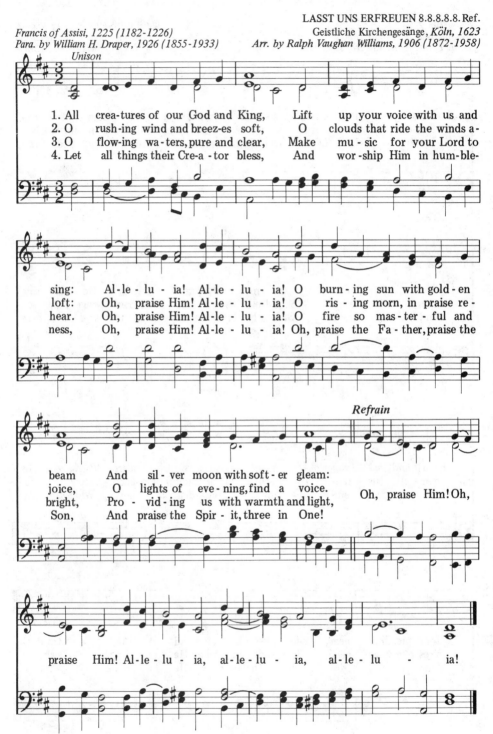

1. All crea-tures of our God and King, Lift up your voice with us and
2. O rush-ing wind and breez-es soft, O clouds that ride the winds a-
3. O flow-ing wa-ters, pure and clear, Make mu-sic for your Lord to
4. Let all things their Cre-a-tor bless, And wor-ship Him in hum-ble-

sing: Al-le-lu - ia! Al-le-lu - ia! O burn-ing sun with gold-en
loft: Oh, praise Him! Al-le - lu - ia! O ris-ing morn, in praise re-
hear. Oh, praise Him! Al-le - lu - ia! O fire so mas-ter-ful and
ness, Oh, praise Him! Al-le - lu - ia! Oh, praise the Fa-ther, praise the

Refrain

beam And sil - ver moon with soft - er gleam:
joice, O lights of eve - ning, find a voice.
bright, Pro - vid - ing us with warmth and light, Oh, praise Him! Oh,
Son, And praise the Spir - it, three in One!

praise Him! Al-le-lu - ia, al-le-lu - ia, al-le-lu - ia!

Higher key, No. 228

ADORATION AND PRAISE

God Himself Is With Us

3

Gerhard Tersteegen, 1729 (1697-1769)
Tr. by Hymnal 1940

WUNDERBARER KÖNIG 6.6.8.6.6.8.3.3.6.6.
Joachim Neander, 1680 (1650-1680)

1. God Him-self is with us; Let us all a - dore Him, And with awe ap-
pear be - fore Him. God is here with - in us; Soul, in si - lence
fear Him, Hum - bly, fer - vent - ly draw near Him. Now His own
who have known God, in wor-ship low - ly, Yield their spir - its whol - ly.

2. Come, a - bide with-in me; Let my soul, like Ma - ry, Be Thine earth-ly
sanc - tu - ar - y. Come, in-dwell-ing Spir - it, With trans-fig-ured
splen - dor; Love and hon-or will I ren - der. Where I go
here be - low, Let me bow be - fore Thee, Know Thee and a - dore Thee.

3. Glad - ly we sur-ren - der Earth's de-ceit-ful trea - sures, Pride of life, and
sin - ful plea - sures: Glad - ly, Lord, we of - fer Thine to be for-
ev - er, Soul and life and each en - deav - or. Thou a - lone
shalt be known Lord of all our be - ing, Life's true way de-cree - ing.

ADORATION AND PRAISE

4   Praise, My Soul, the King of Heaven

Psalm 103
Henry Francis Lyte (1793-1847)

LAUDA ANIMA 8.7.8.7.8.7.
John Goss (1800-1880)

This hymn has three settings. The second setting (four-part) may be used for all stanzas.
First setting: Unison

1. Praise, my soul, the King of heav - en; To His feet thy trib-ute bring;

Ran-somed, healed, re - stored, for-giv - en, Who like thee His praise should sing?

Praise Him, praise Him, al - le - lu - ia, Praise the ev - er - last-ing King.

Second setting: Harmony

2. Praise Him for His grace and fa - vor To our fa - thers in dis - tress;
3. Ten - der - ly He shields and spares us; Well our fee - ble frame He knows;

ADORATION AND PRAISE

Praise Him, still the same for-ev-er, Slow to chide and swift to bless;
In His hands He gent-ly bears us, Res-cues us from all our foes:

Praise Him, praise Him, al-le-lu-ia, Glo-rious in His faith-ful-ness.
Praise Him, praise Him, al-le-lu-ia, Wide-ly as His mer-cy flows.

Third setting: Unison

4. An-gels, help us to a-dore Him: Ye be-hold Him face to face;

Sun and moon bow down be-fore Him: Dwell-ers all in time and space,

Praise Him, praise Him, al-le-lu-ia, Praise with us the God of grace.

Alternate tune, REGENT SQUARE, No. 119

ADORATION AND PRAISE

5

All My Hope on God Is Founded

Joachim Neander (1650-1680)
Tr. by Robert Bridges (1844-1930)

MICHAEL 8.7.8.7.3.3.7.
Herbert Howells, 1936 (1892-1983)

Unison

1. All my hope on God is found-ed; He doth still my trust re-new,
2. Pride of man and earth-ly glo-ry, Sword and crown be-tray his trust;
3. God's great good-ness aye en-dur-eth, Deep His wis-dom, pass-ing thought:
4. Still from man to God e-ter-nal Sac-ri-fice of praise be done,

Me through change and chance He guid-eth, On-ly good and on-ly true.
What with care and toil he build-eth, Tower and tem-ple fall to dust.
Splen-dor, light, and life at-tend Him, Beau-ty spring-eth out of naught.
High a-bove all prais-es prais-ing For the gift of Christ His Son.

God un-known, He a-lone Calls my heart to be His own.
But God's power, hour by hour, Is my tem-ple and my tower.
Love doth stand at His hand; Joy doth wait on His com-mand.
Christ doth call one and all: Ye who fol-low shall not fall.

O Worship the Lord

6

SOUTHAMPTON 12.10.12.10.
Edwin Barnes, 1886 (1864-1930)

J. S. B. Monsell (1811-1875)

1. O worship the Lord in the beauty of holiness,
Bow down before Him, His glory proclaim;
With gold of obedience, and incense of lowliness,
Kneel and adore Him; the Lord is His name.

2. Low at His feet lay thy burden of carefulness;
High on His heart He will bear it for thee,
Comfort thy sorrows and answer thy prayerfulness,
Guiding thy steps as may best for thee be.

3. Fear not to enter His courts in the slenderness
Of the poor wealth thou wouldst reckon as thine.
Truth in its beauty and love in its tenderness,
These are the offerings to lay on His shrine.

4. These, though we bring them in trembling and fearfulness,
He will accept for the name that is dear;
Mornings of joy give for evenings of tearfulness,
Trust for our trembling, and hope for our fear.

ADORATION AND PRAISE

The Lord in Zion Reigneth

Fanny J. Crosby (1820-1915)

Hart P. Danks (1834-1903)

1. The Lord in Zi - on reign - eth, Let all the world re - joice,
2. The Lord in Zi - on reign - eth, And who so great as He?
3. The Lord in Zi - on reign - eth, These hours to Him be - long;

And come be - fore His throne of grace With tune - ful heart and voice;
The depths of earth are in His hands; He rules the might - y sea.
O en - ter now His tem - ple gates, And fill His courts with song;

The Lord in Zi - on reign - eth, And there His praise shall ring,
O crown His name with hon - or, And let His stand - ard wave,
Be - neath His roy - al ban - ner Let ev - ery crea - ture fall,

To Him shall princ - es bend the knee And kings their glo - ry bring.
Till dis - tant isles be - yond the deep Shall own His power to save.
Ex - alt the King of heaven and earth, And crown Him Lord of all.

ADORATION AND PRAISE

We Gather Together

8

KREMSER Irregular
Netherland Folk Song, 1625
Arr. by Edward Kremser (1838-1914)

Anonymous, 1625
Tr. by Theodore Baker, 1917 (1851-1934)

1. We gath - er to - geth - er to ask the Lord's bless - ing;
2. Be - side us to guide us, our God with us join - ing,
3. We all do ex - tol Thee, Thou Lead - er tri - um - phant,

He chas - tens and has - tens His will to make known;
Or - dain - ing, main - tain - ing His king - dom di - vine;
And pray that Thou still our De - fend - er wilt be.

The wick - ed op - press - ing now cease from dis - tress - ing,
So from the be - gin - ning the fight we were win - ning;
Let Thy con - gre - ga - tion es - cape trib - u - la - tion;

Sing prais - es to His name; He for - gets not His own.
Thou, Lord, wast at our side; all glo - ry be Thine!
Thy name be ev - er praised! O Lord, make us free!

ADORATION AND PRAISE

9 Let All the World in Every Corner Sing

George Herbert (1593-1632)

LUCKINGTON Irregular
Basil Harwood (1859-1949)

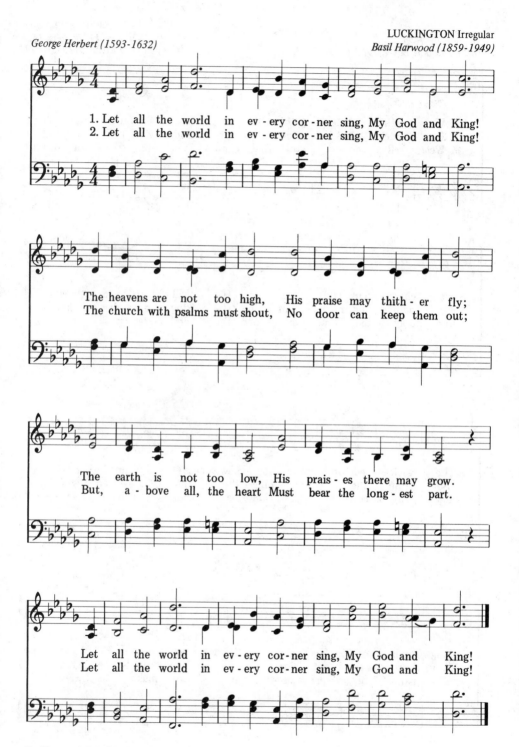

1. Let all the world in ev-ery cor-ner sing, My God and King!
2. Let all the world in ev-ery cor-ner sing, My God and King!

The heavens are not too high, His praise may thith-er fly;
The church with psalms must shout, No door can keep them out;

The earth is not too low, His prais-es there may grow.
But, a-bove all, the heart Must bear the long-est part.

Let all the world in ev-ery cor-ner sing, My God and King!
Let all the world in ev-ery cor-ner sing, My God and King!

ADORATION AND PRAISE

Come, Christians, Join to Sing

MADRID 6.6.6.6.D.
Source unknown
Arr. by David Evans (1874-1948)

Christian Henry Bateman (1813-1889)

1. Come, Chris-tians, join to sing, Al - le - lu - ia! A - men!
2. Come, lift your hearts on high; Al - le - lu - ia! A - men!
3. Praise yet our Christ a - gain; Al - le - lu - ia! A - men!

Loud praise to Christ our King; Al - le - lu - ia! A - men!
Let prais - es fill the sky; Al - le - lu - ia! A - men!
Life shall not end the strain; Al - le - lu - ia! A - men!

Let all, with heart and voice, Be - fore His throne re - joice;
He is our Guide and Friend; To us He'll con - de - scend;
On heav - en's bliss - ful shore His good - ness we'll a - dore,

Praise is His gra - cious choice: Al - le - lu - ia! A - men!
His love shall nev - er end: Al - le - lu - ia! A - men!
Sing - ing for - ev - er - more, Al - le - lu - ia! A - men!

Music from the *Revised Church Hymnary 1927* by permission of Oxford University Press.

ADORATION AND PRAISE

11 The God of Abraham Praise

Ex. 3:14,15
Thomas Olivers, c. 1770 (1725-1799)   Arr. from a Jewish Melody by Meyer Lyon, 1770 (1751-1797)
LEONI 6.6.8.4.D.

1. The God of A-braham praise, Who reigns en-throned a - bove;
2. The God of A-braham praise, At whose su - preme com - mand
3. The whole tri - um-phant host Give thanks to God on high;

An - cient of ev - er - last - ing days, And God of love;
From earth I rise, and seek the joys At His right hand;
"Hail, Fa - ther, Son, and Ho - ly Ghost!" They ev - er cry;

Je - ho - vah! Great I AM! By earth and heaven con - fessed;
I all on earth for - sake, Its wis - dom, fame, and power;
Hail, A-braham's God and mine! I join the heaven-ly lays;

I bow and bless the sa - cred name, For - ev - er blest.
And Him my on - ly por-tion make, My shield and tower.
All might and maj - es - ty are Thine, And end - less praise.

ADORATION AND PRAISE

Joyful, Joyful, We Adore Thee

12

Henry van Dyke, 1907 (1852-1933)

HYMN TO JOY 8.7.8.7.D.
Melody from Ninth Symphony
Ludwig van Beethoven, 1824 (1770-1827)

1. Joy - ful, joy - ful, we a - dore Thee, God of glo - ry, Lord of love;
2. All Thy works with joy sur - round Thee, Earth and heav'n re - flect Thy rays,
3. Thou art giv - ing and for - giv - ing, Ev - er bless - ing, ev - er blest,

Hearts un - fold like flow'rs be - fore Thee, Hail Thee as the sun a - bove.
Stars and an - gels sing a - round Thee, Cen - ter of un - bro - ken praise;
Well-spring of the joy of liv - ing, O - cean-depth of hap - py rest!

Melt the clouds of sin and sad - ness, Drive the dark of doubt a - way;
Field and for - est, vale and moun - tain, Bloss-'ming mea - dow, flash-ing sea,
Thou the Fa - ther, Christ our Broth - er— All who live in love are Thine:

Giv - er of im - mor - tal glad - ness, Fill us with the light of day!
Chant-ing bird and flow-ing foun - tain Call us to re - joice in Thee.
Teach us how to love each oth - er, Lift us to the joy di - vine.

ADORATION AND PRAISE

13 New Songs of Celebration Render

Psalm 98
Erik Routley (1917-1982)

RENDEZ A DIEU 9.8.9.8.D.
From La Forme des Prieres, Strasburg, 1545
Harm. adapt. from C. Goudinel by Russell Schulz-Widmar

1. New songs of cel - e - bra - tion ren - der To Him who
2. Joy - ful - ly, heart - i - ly re - sound - ing, Let ev - ery
3. Riv - ers and seas and tor - rents roar - ing, Hon - or the

has great won - ders done. Love sits en-throned in age - less splen-dor:
in - stru-ment and voice Peal out the praise of grace a - bound-ing,
Lord with wild ac - claim; Moun-tains and stones look up a - dor - ing,

Come, and a - dore the might-y One. He has made known His great sal-
Call - ing the whole world to re - joice. Trum-pets and or - gans, set in
And find a voice to praise His name. Righ-teous, com-mand-ing, ev - er

va - tion Which all His friends with joy con - fess: He has re-
mo - tion Such sounds as make the heav - ens ring; All things that
glo - rious, Prais - es be His that nev - er cease: Just is our

ADORATION AND PRAISE

vealed to ev - ery na - tion His ev - er - last - ing righ-teous-ness.
live in earth and o - cean, Make mu - sic for your might-y King.
God, whose truth vic - to - rious Es - tab - lish - es the world in peace.

Let Us Praise the Name of the Lord   14

8.6. Amens

Ursula Schlenker, 1949 (1930-   )
Tr. composite, 1984

Canon for 4 voices, Alfred Stier, 1949 (1880-1967)
Accomp. by Melvin West, 1984 (1930-   )

1. Let us praise the name of the Lord! Give Him glo ry, A - men.
2. Go ye in - to all the world, A - le - lu - ia, A - men.

*Accomp.

A - men, a - men, A - men, a - men.

* Accompaniment may repeat either or both scores for the duration of the canon.
Copyright Verlag Merseburger.

ADORATION AND PRAISE

15 My Maker and My King

Anne Steele (1716-1778)

EL KADER S.M.
Unknown

1. My Mak-er and my King, To Thee my all I owe;
2. The crea-ture of Thy hand, On Thee a-lone I live;
3. Lord, what can I im-part When all is Thine be-fore?
4. O! let Thy grace in-spire My soul with strength di-vine;

Thy sov-ereign boun-ty is the spring Whence all my bless-ings flow;
My God, Thy ben-e-fits de-mand More praise than I can give.
Thy love de-mands a thank-ful heart; The gift, a-las! how poor.
Let ev-ery word and each de-sire And all my days be Thine.

Thy sov-ereign boun-ty is the spring Whence all my bless-ings flow.
My God, Thy ben-e-fits de-mand More praise than I can give.
Thy love de-mands a thank-ful heart; The gift, a-las! how poor.
Let ev-ery word and each de-sire And all my days be Thine.

16 All People That on Earth Do Dwell

Psalm 100
William Kethe (? -c. 1593)

OLD HUNDREDTH L.M.
Louis Bourgeois, 1551 (c. 1510-1561)

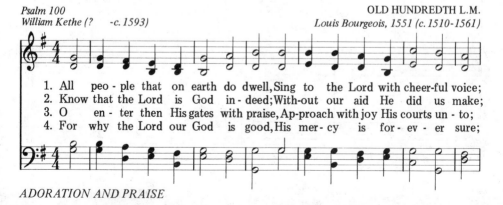

1. All peo-ple that on earth do dwell, Sing to the Lord with cheer-ful voice;
2. Know that the Lord is God in-deed; With-out our aid He did us make;
3. O en-ter then His gates with praise, Ap-proach with joy His courts un-to;
4. For why the Lord our God is good, His mer-cy is for-ev-er sure;

ADORATION AND PRAISE

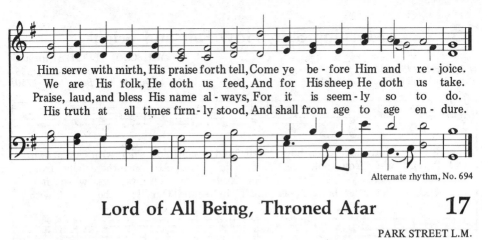

Him serve with mirth, His praise forth tell, Come ye be - fore Him and re - joice.
We are His folk, He doth us feed, And for His sheep He doth us take.
Praise, laud, and bless His name al - ways, For it is seem - ly so to do.
His truth at all times firm - ly stood, And shall from age to age en - dure.

Alternate rhythm, No. 694

Lord of All Being, Throned Afar — 17

PARK STREET L.M.

Oliver Wendell Holmes, 1848 (1809-1894)   Arr. from Frederick M. A. Venua, c.1810 (1788-1872)

1. Lord of all be - ing, throned a - far, Thy glo - ry flames from
2. Sun of our life, Thy quick - ening ray Sheds on our path the
3. Our mid-night is Thy smile with-drawn; Our noon-tide is Thy
4. Lord of all life, be - low, a - bove, Whose light is truth, whose
5. Grant us Thy truth to make us free, And kin - dling hearts that

sun and star; Cen - ter and soul of ev - ery sphere, Yet to each
glow of day; Star of our hope, Thy soft-ened light Cheers the long
gra - cious dawn; Our rain - bow arch, Thy mer - cy's sign; All, save the
warmth is love, Be - fore Thy ev - er - blaz - ing throne We ask no
burn for Thee; Till all Thy liv - ing al - tars claim One ho - ly

lov - ing heart how near! Yet to each lov - ing heart how near!
watch - es of the night, Cheers the long watch - es of the night.
clouds of sin, are Thine, All, save the clouds of sin, are Thine.
lus - ter of our own, We ask no lus - ter of our own.
light, one heaven - ly flame! One ho - ly light, one heaven - ly flame.

ADORATION AND PRAISE

18   O Morning Star, How Fair and Bright

WIE SCHÖN LEUCHTET Irregular

Philip Nicolai (1556-1608)
Tr. by Lutheran Book of Worship, 1978

Philip Nicolai (1556-1608)
Arr. by J. S. Bach (1685-1750)

1. O Morn-ing Star, how fair and bright! You shine with God's own truth and light, A-glow with grace and mer - cy! Of Ja - cob's race, King Da-vid's Son, Our Lord and Mas - ter, You have won Our hearts to serve You on - ly! Low - ly,

2. Lord, when You look on us in love, At once there falls from God a-bove A ray of pur - est plea - sure. Your Word and Spir - it, flesh and blood Re - fresh our souls with heav-'nly food. You are our dear-est trea - sure! Let Your

3. Al - might-y Fa - ther, in Your Son You loved us, when not yet be - gun Was this old earth's foun - da - tion! Your Son has ran-somed us in love To live in Him here and a - bove: This is Your great sal - va - tion. Al - le -

4. O let the harps break forth in sound! Our joy be all with mu - sic crowned, Our voic - es gai - ly blend - ing! For Christ goes with us all the way— To - day, to - mor - row, ev - ery day! His love is nev - er end - ing! Sing out!

ADORATION AND PRAISE

ho - ly! Great and glo - rious, all vic - to - rious,
mer - cy Warm and cheer us! O draw near us!
lu - ia! Christ the liv - ing, to us giv - ing
ring out! Ju - bi - la - tion! ex - ul - ta - tion!

Rich in bless - ing! Rule and might o'er all pos - sess - ing!
For You teach us God's own love through You has reached us.
Life for - ev - er, Keeps us Yours and fails us nev - er!
Tell the sto - ry! Great is He, the King of glo - ry!

O Sing a New Song to the Lord   19

Psalm 98   ST. MAGNUS C.M.
Scottish Psalter, 1650, alt.   *Attr. to Jeremiah Clarke (c. 1669-1707)*

1. O sing a new song to the Lord For mar - vels He has done;
2. With harp, with harp and voice of psalms Un - to Je - ho - vah sing;
3. Let seas with all their crea - tures roar, The world and dwell-ers there,
4. Be - fore the Lord: be - cause He comes, To judge the earth comes He;

His right hand and His ho - ly arm The vic - to - ry have won.
Let trum - pets and the ech - oing horn Ac - claim the Lord our King!
And let the riv - ers clap their hands, The hills their joy de - clare.
He'll judge the world with righ - teous-ness, His folk with eq - ui - ty.

Alternate harmony, No. 199

ADORATION AND PRAISE

O Praise Ye the Lord

Psalm 150
Henry W. Baker (1821-1877)

LAUDATE DOMINUM 5.5.5.5.6.5.6.5.
Charles H. H. Parry, 1894 (1848-1918)

1. O praise ye the Lord! Praise Him in the height;
2. O praise ye the Lord! Praise Him up - on earth,
3. O praise ye the Lord, All things that give sound;
4. O praise ye the Lord! Thanks - giv - ing and song

Re - joice in His word, Ye an - gels of light;
In tune - ful ac - cord: Ye sons of new birth;
Each ju - bi - lant chord, Re - ech - o a - round;
To Him be out - poured All a - ges a - long:

Ye hea - vens, a - dore Him By whom ye were made,
Praise Him who hath brought you His grace from a - bove,
Loud or - gans His glo - ry Forth tell in deep tone,
For love in cre - a - tion, For hea - ven re - stored.

And wor - ship be - fore Him, In bright - ness ar - rayed.
Praise Him who hath taught you To sing of His love.
And sweet harp, the sto - ry Of what He hath done.
For grace of sal - va - tion, O praise ye the Lord!

ADORATION AND PRAISE

1 Tim. 1:17
Walter Chalmers Smith, 1867 (1824-1908)

ST. DENIO 11.11.11.11.
Welsh Melody, c. 1839

1. Im - mor - tal, in - vis - i - ble, God on - ly wise,
2. Un - rest - ing, un - hast - ing, and si - lent as light,
3. To all life Thou giv - est to both great and small;
4. Great Fa - ther of glo - ry, pure Fa - ther of light,

In light in - ac - ces - si - ble hid from our eyes,
Nor want - ing, nor wast - ing, Thou rul - est in might;
In all life Thou liv - est, the true life of all;
Thine an - gels a - dore Thee, all veil - ing their sight;

Most bless - ed, most glo - rious, the An - cient of days,
Thy jus - tice like moun - tains high soar - ing a - bove
We blos - som and flour - ish, like leaves on the tree,
All laud we would ren - der: O help us to see

Al - might - y, vic - to - rious, Thy great name we praise.
Thy clouds, which are foun - tains of good - ness and love.
Then with - er and per - ish; but naught chang - eth Thee.
'Tis on - ly the splen - dor of light hid - eth Thee.

ADORATION AND PRAISE

22 God Is Our Song

Psalm 118:14
Fred Pratt Green, 1974 (1903-   )

OLD 124th 10.10.10.10.10.
Genevan Psalter, 1551

1. God   is   our Song,   and   ev - ery sing - er   blest   Who   prais-ing
2. God   is   our Song,   for   Je - sus comes to   save;   While prais-ing
3. This   is   the Song   no   con-flict ev - er   drowns; Who   prais-es
4. God   is   our Si - lence   when no songs are   sung,   When ec - sta-

Him   finds en - er - gy and   rest.   All   who praise God with
Him   we   of - fer all we   have.   New   songs we sing, in
God   our   hu - man wrath dis - owns.   Love   knows what rich com-
·sy   or   sor - row stills the tongue. Glo - rious the faith which

un - af - fect - ed   joy   Give back to   us   the   wis - dom
ven - tures new u - nite, When Je - sus leads us   up - ward
plex - i - ties of   sound God   builds up - on   a   sim - ple
si - lent - ly   o - beys   Un - til we   find a - gain the

we de - stroy, Give back to us   the wis-dom we de - stroy.
in - to light, When Je - sus leads us up-ward in - to light.
com-mon ground, God builds up - on a sim-ple com-mon ground.
voice of praise, Un - til we find a - gain the voice of praise.

ADORATION AND PRAISE

Now the Joyful Bells A-Ringing

23

Welsh Carol
Para. by K. E. Roberts (1879-1953)

NOS GALAN 8.7.8.7.D.
Arr. by Wayne Hooper, 1984 (1920-   )

1. Now the joy-ful bells a-ring-ing, All ye moun-tains, praise the Lord!
2. Dear our home as dear none oth-er; Where the moun-tains praise the Lord!
3. Cold the year, new white-ness wear-ing, All ye moun-tains, praise the Lord!

Lift our hearts like birds a-wing-ing, All ye moun-tains, praise the Lord!
Glad-ly here our care we smoth-er; Where the moun-tains praise the Lord!
Peace, good will to us a-bear-ing, All ye moun-tains praise the Lord!

Now our fes-tal sea-son bring-ing Kins-men all to bide and board,
Here we know that Christ our broth-er Binds us all as by a cord:
Now we all God's good-ness shar-ing Break the bread and sheath the sword:

Sets our cheer-y voic-es sing-ing: All ye moun-tains, praise the Lord!
He was born of Ma-ry moth-er Where the moun-tains praise the Lord!
Bright our hearths the sig-nal flar-ing, All ye moun-tains, praise the Lord!

Words from *Oxford Book of Carols* by permission of Oxford University Press.
Arrangement copyright © 1984 by Wayne Hooper.

ADORATION AND PRAISE

TSDAH-2

24 Every Star Shall Sing a Carol

1. Ev - ery star shall sing a car - ol; Ev - ery crea - ture,
2. When the King of all cre - a - tion Had a cra - dle
3. Ev - ery star and ev - ery plan - et, Ev - ery crea - ture,

high or low, Come and praise the King of heav - en
on the earth, Ho - ly was the hu - man bod - y,
high or low, Come and praise the King of heav - en

By what - ev - er name you know.
Ho - ly was the hu - man birth. God a - bove,
By what - ev - er name you know.

Man be - low, Ho - ly is the name I know.

ADORATION AND PRAISE

Praise the Lord, His Glories Show

25

LLANFAIR 7.4.7.4.D.

Psalm 150
Henry Francis Lyte, 1834 (1793-1847)

Robert Williams, 1817 (c. 1781-1821)
Arr. by John Roberts, 1837 (1822-1877)

1. Praise the Lord, His glo-ries show, Al - le - lu - ia!
2. Earth to heaven and heaven to earth, Al - le - lu - ia!
3. Praise the Lord, His mer-cies trace, Al - le - lu - ia!

Saints with-in His courts be-low, Al - le - lu - ia!
Tell His won-ders, sing His worth, Al - le - lu - ia!
Praise His prov-i-dence and grace, Al - le - lu - ia!

An-gels 'round His throne a-bove, Al - le - lu - ia!
Age to age and shore to shore, Al - le - lu - ia!
All that He for man hath done, Al - le - lu - ia!

All that see and share His love. Al - le - lu - ia!
Praise Him, praise Him ev - er-more! Al - le - lu - ia!
All He sends us through His Son. Al - le - lu - ia!

ADORATION AND PRAISE

26 Praise the Lord! You Heavens Adore Him

Psalm 148
Sts. 1, 2, anon., ca. 1801; alt.
St. 3, Edward Osler, 1836 (1798-1863); alt.

AN DIE FREUDE 8.7.8.7.D.
Anon. setting of Schiller's
Hymn to Joy, *Berlin, 1799*

1. Praise the Lord! you heavens, a-dore Him; Praise Him, an-gels in the height;
2. Praise the Lord! for He is glo-rious; Nev-er shall His prom-ise fail.
3. Wor-ship, hon-or, glo-ry, bless-ing, Lord, we of-fer as our gift.

Sun and moon, re-joice be-fore Him, Praise Him, all you stars of light.
God has made His saints vic-to-rious; Sin and death shall not pre-vail.
Young and old, Your praise ex-press-ing, Our glad songs to You we lift.

Praise the Lord, for He has spo-ken; Worlds His might-y voice o-beyed;
Praise the God of our sal-va-tion! Hosts on high, His power pro-claim;
All the saints in heaven a-dore You, We would join their glad ac-claim;

Laws which nev-er shall be bro-ken For their guid-ance He has made.
Heaven and earth and all cre-a-tion, Laud and mag-ni-fy His name.
As Your an-gels serve be-fore You, So on earth we praise Your name.

Alternate tunes, HYMN TO JOY, No. 12
AUSTRIA, No. 423

ADORATION AND PRAISE

Rejoice, Ye Pure in Heart!

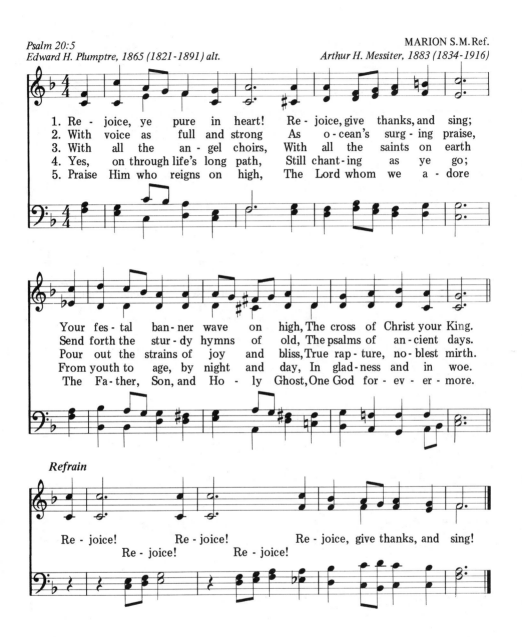

Psalm 20:5
Edward H. Plumptre, 1865 (1821-1891) alt.

MARION S.M.Ref.
Arthur H. Messiter, 1883 (1834-1916)

1. Re - joice, ye pure in heart! Re - joice, give thanks, and sing;
2. With voice as full and strong As o - cean's surg - ing praise,
3. With all the an - gel choirs, With all the saints on earth
4. Yes, on through life's long path, Still chant - ing as ye go;
5. Praise Him who reigns on high, The Lord whom we a - dore

Your fes - tal ban - ner wave on high, The cross of Christ your King.
Send forth the stur - dy hymns of old, The psalms of an - cient days.
Pour out the strains of joy and bliss, True rap - ture, no - blest mirth.
From youth to age, by night and day, In glad - ness and in woe.
The Fa - ther, Son, and Ho - ly Ghost, One God for - ev - er - more.

Refrain

Re - joice! Re - joice! Re - joice, give thanks, and sing!
Re - joice! Re - joice!

28 Praise We the Lord

FRAGRANCE 9.8.9.8.9.8.
French carol melody
Arr. by Martin Shaw (1875-1958)

J. Steuart Wilson, 1928 (1889-1966)

1. Praise we the Lord, who made all beau - ty For all our sens - es to en - joy; Owe we our hum - ble thanks and du - ty That sim - ple plea - sures nev - er cloy; Praise we the Lord, who made all beau - ty For all our sens - es to en - joy.
2. Praise Him who loves to see young lov - ers, Fresh hearts that swell with youth - ful pride; Thank Him who sends the sun a - bove us, As bride-groom fit to meet his bride; Praise Him who loves to see young lov - ers, Fresh hearts that swell with youth - ful pride.
3. Praise Him who by a sim - ple flow - er Lifts up our hearts to things a - bove; Thank Him who gives to each one pow - er To find a friend to know and love; Praise Him who by a sim - ple flow - er Lifts up our hearts to things a - bove.

Words and arrangement from the *Oxford Book of Carols* by permission of Oxford University Press.

ADORATION AND PRAISE

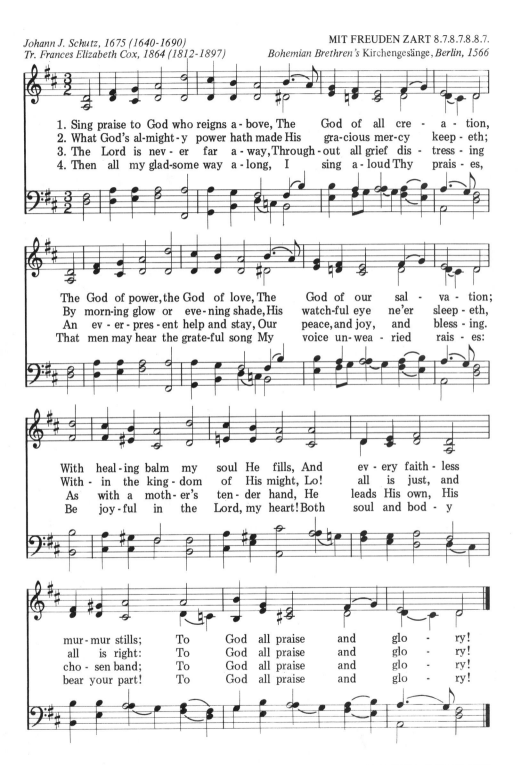

Johann J. Schutz, 1675 (1640-1690)
Tr. Frances Elizabeth Cox, 1864 (1812-1897)

MIT FREUDEN ZART 8.7.8.7.8.8.7.
Bohemian Brethren's Kirchengesänge, Berlin, 1566

1. Sing praise to God who reigns a-bove, The God of all cre - a - tion,
2. What God's al-might-y power hath made His gra-cious mer-cy keep-eth;
3. The Lord is nev-er far a-way, Through-out all grief dis-tress-ing
4. Then all my glad-some way a-long, I sing a-loud Thy prais-es,

The God of power, the God of love, The God of our sal - va-tion;
By morn-ing glow or eve-ning shade, His watch-ful eye ne'er sleep-eth,
An ev-er-pres-ent help and stay, Our peace, and joy, and bless-ing.
That men may hear the grate-ful song My voice un-wea-ried rais-es:

With heal-ing balm my soul He fills, And ev-ery faith-less
With-in the king-dom of His might, Lo! all is just, and
As with a moth-er's ten-der hand, He leads His own, His
Be joy-ful in the Lord, my heart! Both soul and bod-y

mur-mur stills; To God all praise and glo - ry!
all is right: To God all praise and glo - ry!
cho-sen band; To God all praise and glo - ry!
bear your part! To God all praise and glo - ry!

ADORATION AND PRAISE

30 Holy God, We Praise Your Name

German, 18th century
Tr. by Clarence A. Walworth (1820-1900)

GROSSER GOTT 7.8.7.8.7.7.
Katholisches Gesangbuch, *Vienna*, 1774

1. Ho - ly God, we praise Your name; Lord of all, we
2. Hark! the loud ce - les - tial hymn An - gel choirs a -
3. Ho - ly Fa - ther, Ho - ly Son, Ho - ly Spir - it,

bow be - fore You! All on earth Your scep - ter claim,
bove are rais - ing, Cher - u - bim and ser - a - phim,
three we name You; While in es - sence on - ly one,

All in heaven a - bove a - dore You; In - fi - nite Your
In un - ceas - ing cho - rus prais - ing; Fill the heavens with
Un - di - vid - ed God we claim You; And a - dor - ing

vast do - main. Ev - er - last - ing is Your reign.
sweet ac - cord: Ho - ly, ho - ly, ho - ly, Lord.
bend the knee, While we own the mys - ter - y.

ADORATION AND PRAISE

Tell Out, My Soul

31

Luke 1:46-55
Timothy Dudley-Smith, 1961 (1926-   )

MORESTEAD 10.10.10.10.
Sydney Watson (1903-   )

1. Tell out, my soul, the great-ness of the Lord:
Un-num-bered bless - ings give my spir - it voice;
Ten - der to me the prom - ise of His word; In
God my Sav - ior shall my heart re - joice.

2. Tell out, my soul, the great-ness of His name:
Make known His might, the deeds His arm has done;
His mer - cy sure, from age to age the same; His
ho - ly name, the Lord, the Might - y One.

3. Tell out, my soul, the great-ness of His might:
Pow'rs and do - min - ions lay their glo - ry by;
Proud hearts and stub-born wills are put to flight, The
hun - gry fed, the hum - ble lift - ed high.

4. Tell out, my soul, the glo - ries of His word:
Firm is His prom - ise, and His mer - cy sure.
Tell out, my soul, the great-ness of the Lord To
chil - dren's chil - dren and for - ev - er - more.

ADORATION AND PRAISE

32 When in Our Music God Is Glorified

ENGELBERG 10.10.10.4.

Fred Pratt Green (1903-   )

Charles V. Stanford (1852-1924)

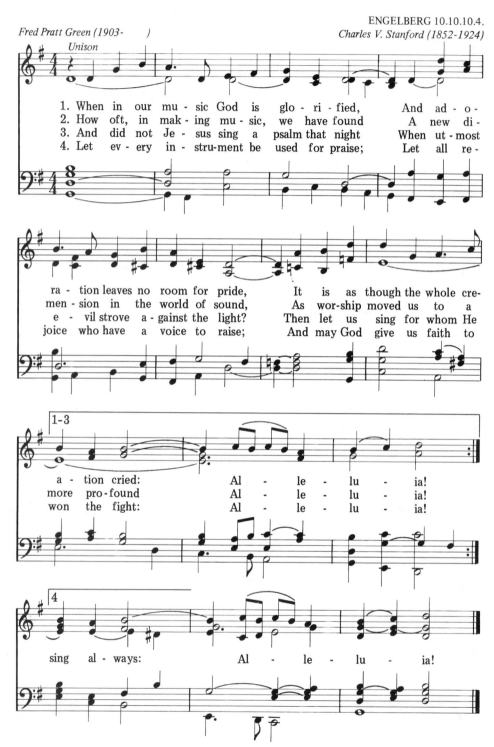

1. When in our mu - sic God is glo - ri - fied, And ad - o -
2. How oft, in mak - ing mu - sic, we have found A new di -
3. And did not Je - sus sing a psalm that night When ut - most
4. Let ev - ery in - stru - ment be used for praise; Let all re -

ra - tion leaves no room for pride, It is as though the whole cre-
men - sion in the world of sound, As wor-ship moved us to a
e - vil strove a - gainst the light? Then let us sing for whom He
joice who have a voice to raise; And may God give us faith to

a - tion cried: Al - le - lu - ia!
more pro-found   Al - le - lu - ia!
won the fight: Al - le - lu - ia!

sing al - ways: Al - le - lu - ia!

ADORATION AND PRAISE

Sing a New Song to the Lord

Psalm 98
Timothy Dudley-Smith (1926-   )

7.7.6.5.8.
David G. Wilson (1940-   )

Unison

1. Sing a new song to the Lord, He to whom won-ders be-
2. Now to the ends of the earth See His sal-va-tion is
3. Sing a new song and re-joice. Pub-lish His prais-es a-
4. Join with the hills and the sea, Thun-ders of praise to pro-

long. Re-joice in His tri-umph and
shown. And still He re-mem-bers His
broad. Let voic - es in cho-rus with
long. In judg - ment and jus-tice He

tell of His power. O sing a new
mer - cy and truth, Un-chang - ing in
trum - pet and horn, Re-sound for the
comes to the earth. O sing a new

1,2,3   4

song to the Lord.
love to His own.
joy of the Lord.
song to the   Lord.

ADORATION AND PRAISE

34 Wake the Song

ANNIVERSARY SONG 8.7.8.7.D.Ref.
W. F. Sherwin

W. F. Sherwin (1826-1888)

1. Wake the song of joy and glad - ness; Hith - er bring your no - blest lays;
2. Joy - ful - ly with songs and ban - ners, We will greet the fes - tal day;
3. Thanks to Thee, O ho - ly Fa - ther, For the mer - cies of the year;

Ban - ish ev - ery thought of sad - ness, Pour - ing forth your high - est praise.
Shout a - loud our glad ho - san - nas, And our grate - ful hom - age pay.
May each heart, as here we gath - er, Swell with grat - i - tude sin - cere.

Sing to Him whose care has brought us Once a - gain with friends to meet,
We will chant our Sav - ior's glo - ry While our thoughts we raise a - bove,
Thanks to Thee, O lov - ing Sav - ior, For re - demp - tion through Thy blood.

And whose lov - ing voice has taught us Of the way to Je - sus' feet.
Tell - ing still "the old, old sto - ry," Pre - cious theme—re - deem - ing love!
Breathe up - on us, Ho - ly Spir - it, Sweet - ly draw us near to God.

ADORATION AND PRAISE

Wake the song, wake the song, the song of joy and glad-ness,
Wake the song, wake the song,

Wake the song, wake the song, The song of Ju - bi - lee.
Wake the song, wake the song,

With Songs and Honors

35

Psalm 147
Isaac Watts, 1719 (1674-1748)

BEDFORD C.M.
William Wheale, c. 1723 (? -1727)

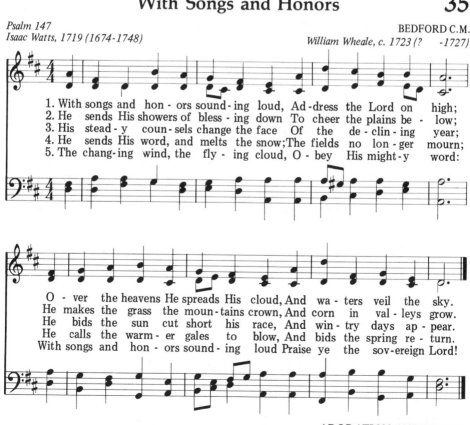

1. With songs and hon - ors sound-ing loud, Ad -dress the Lord on high;
2. He sends His showers of bless - ing down To cheer the plains be - low;
3. His stead - y coun-sels change the face Of the de - clin - ing year;
4. He sends His word, and melts the snow; The fields no lon - ger mourn;
5. The chang-ing wind, the fly - ing cloud, O - bey His might-y word:

O - ver the heavens He spreads His cloud, And wa - ters veil the sky.
He makes the grass the moun-tains crown, And corn in val - leys grow.
He bids the sun cut short his race, And win - try days ap - pear.
He calls the warm - er gales to blow, And bids the spring re - turn.
With songs and hon - ors sound - ing loud Praise ye the sov-ereign Lord!

ADORATION AND PRAISE

36   O Thou in Whose Presence

BELOVED 11.8.11.8.

Song of Sol. 7:10
Joseph Swain (1761-1796)

Attrib. to Freeman Lewis, 1813 (1780-1859)
Arr. by Hubert P. Main, 1869 (1839-1926)

1. O Thou in whose pres - ence my soul takes de - light, On whom in af - flic - tion I call, My com - fort by day and my song in the night, My hope, my sal - va - tion, my all!

2. His voice, as the sound of the dul - ci - mer sweet, Is heard through the shad - ows of death; The ce - dars of Leb - a - non bow at His feet, The air is per - fumed with His breath.

3. His lips, as a foun - tain of righ - teous-ness flow, To wa - ter the gar - dens of grace; From which their sal - va - tion the Gen - tiles shall know, And bask in the smiles of His face.

4. He looks, and ten thou - sands of an - gels re - joice, And myr - i - ads wait for His word; He speaks, and e - ter - ni - ty, filled with His voice, Re - ech - oes the praise of the Lord.

O Sing, My Soul, Your Maker's Praise 37

Psalm 34
Julius Krohn (1835-1888)
Tr. by E. E. Ryden (1886-1981), Toivo Harjunpaa, 1962

FINLAND 8.7.8.7.8.8.7.
Traditional Finnish melody

1. O sing my soul, your Ma - ker's praise In grate - ful hymns as - cend - ing; Whose stead-fast love has crowned your days With heav-'nly gifts un - end - ing. I sought the Lord, He heard my cry; His ho - ly an - gels hov - er nigh The tents of those who love Him.

2. The Lord is good to those who seek His face in time of sor - row, Pro - vid - ing com -fort to the weak And grace for each to - mor - row. Though grief may tar - ry for a night, The morn shall break in joy and light With bless - ings from His pres - ence.

3. The Lord will turn His face in peace When trou-bled souls draw near Him; His lov - ing-kind - ness shall not cease To those who trust and fear Him. Our God will not for-sake His own; E - ter - nal is His heav - 'nly throne; His king - dom stands for - ev - er.

ADORATION AND PRAISE

38 Arise, My Soul, Arise!

Johan Kahl (1721-1746)
Tr. Ernest Ryden (1886-1981) alt.
Unison

NYT YLÖS, SIELUNI Irregular
Finnish Folk Tune

1. A - rise, my soul, a - rise! Stretch forth to things e - ter - nal And
2. Now hear the harps of heav'n! Oh, hear the song vic - to - rious, The

has - ten to the feet of your Re - deem - er God. Though hid from mor - tal
nev - er - end - ing an - them sound - ing through the sky! To mor - tals is not

eyes, He dwells in light su - per - nal; Yet wor - ship Him in hum - ble - ness and
giv'n To join in strains so glo - rious; Yet here on earth we too can sing our

call Him Lord. His ban - quet of love A - waits you a - bove; Yet
prais - es high! He bought with His blood The ran - somed of God; To

ADORATION AND PRAISE

here He grants a fore-taste of the feast to come! Re-joice, my soul, re-joice, To
Him be ev-er-last-ing pow'r and vic-to-ry. And let the great a-men Re-

heav'n lift up your voice: Al-le-lu-ia, al-le-lu-ia, al-le-lu - ia!
sound through heav'n a-gain.

Lord, in the Morning   39

Psalm 5
Isaac Watts, 1719 (1674-1748)

MEAR C.M.
Aaron Williams (1731-1776)

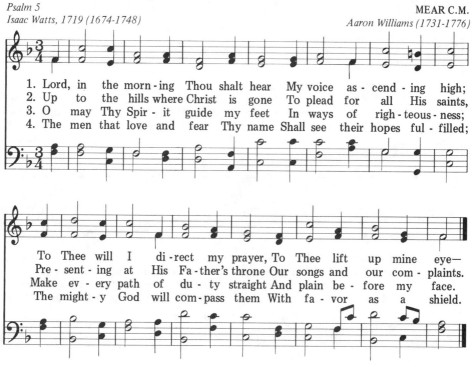

1. Lord, in the morn-ing Thou shalt hear My voice as-cend-ing high;
2. Up to the hills where Christ is gone To plead for all His saints,
3. O may Thy Spir-it guide my feet In ways of righ-teous-ness;
4. The men that love and fear Thy name Shall see their hopes ful-filled;

To Thee will I di-rect my prayer, To Thee lift up mine eye—
Pre-sent-ing at His Fa-ther's throne Our songs and our com-plaints.
Make ev-ery path of du-ty straight And plain be-fore my face.
The might-y God will com-pass them With fa-vor as a shield.

The Dawn of God's Dear Sabbath

ST. GEORGE'S, BOLTON 7.6.7.6.D.

Ada Cross, 1866 (1844-1926)

J. Walch, 1875 (1837-1901)

1. The dawn of God's dear Sab - bath Breaks o'er the earth a - gain,
2. Lord, we would bring for of - fering, Though marred with earth-ly soil,
3. And we would bring our bur - den Of sin - ful thought and deed,
4. And with that sor - row min - gling, A stead-fast faith, and sure,

As some sweet sum - mer morn - ing Af - ter a night of pain;
A week of ear - nest la - bor, Of stead - y, faith - ful toil,
In Thy pure pres-ence kneel - ing, From bond-age to be freed,
And love so deep and fer - vent, For Thee to make it pure,

It comes as cool - ing show - ers To some ex - haust - ed land,
Fair fruits of self - de - ni - al, Of strong, deep love to Thee.
Our heart's most bit - ter sor - row For all Thy work un - done—
In Thy dear pres - ence find - ing The par - don that we need,

As shade of clus-tered palm trees 'Mid wea - ry wastes of sand.
Fos - tered by Thine own Spir - it, In true hu - mil - i - ty.
So ma - ny tal - ents wast - ed! So few bright lau - rels won!
And then the peace so last - ing— Ce - les - tial peace in - deed.

O Splendor of God's Glory Bright

41

Heb. 1:3
Ambrose of Milan (c. 340-397)
Tr. by Robert S. Bridges (1844-1930) and others

GONFALON ROYAL L.M.
Percy C. Buck (1871-1947)

1. O splen-dor of God's glo-ry bright, From light e-
ter-nal bring-ing light; O Light of life, light's liv-ing spring,
True day, all days il-lu-min-ing.

2. O Thou true Sun, on us Thy glance Let fall in
roy-al ra-di-ance; The Spir-it's sanc-ti-fy-ing beam
Up-on our earth-ly sens-es stream.

3. O joy-ful be the pass-ing day With thoughts as
clear as morn-ing's ray, With faith like noon-tide shin-ing bright,
Our souls un-shad-owed by the night.

4. Dawn's glo-ry gilds the earth and skies; Let Him, our
per-fect morn, a-rise, The Fa-ther's help His chil-dren claim,
And sing the Fa-ther's glo-rious name. A - men.

42 Now That Daylight Fills the Sky

Latin hymn, 7th or 8th century
Tr. by John M. Neale (1818-1866) alt.

LAUREL L.M.
Dale Wood (1934-   )

1. Now that the daylight fills the sky,
We lift our hearts to God on high,
That He, in all we do or say,
Would keep us free from harm today;

2. Would guard our hearts and tongues from strife;
From anger's din would shield our life;
From evil sights would turn our eyes,
And close our ears to vanities;

3. So we, when this new day is gone
And night in turn is drawing on,
With conscience by the world unstained
Shall praise His name for vic't'ry gained.

4. "All praise to You, creator Lord!
All praise to You, eternal Word!
All praise to You, O Spirit wise!"
We sing as daylight fills the skies.

*When sung as a canon, 2nd part begins here.
Music copyright © by Lutheran Church Press and Augsburg Publishing House. Used by permission.

MORNING WORSHIP

When Morning Gilds the Skies

43

Psalm 150:6
From the German, c. 1800
Tr. by Edward Caswall, 1858 (1814-1878)

LAUDES DOMINI 6.6.6.6.6.6.
Joseph Barnby, 1868 (1838-1896)

1. When morn - ing gilds the skies, My heart a - wak - ing cries,
2. When - e'er the sweet church bell Peals o - ver hill and dell,
3. The night be - comes as day, When from the heart we say,
4. Ye na - tions of man - kind, In this your con - cord find,
5. In heaven's e - ter - nal bliss The love - liest strain is this,
6. Be this, while life is mine, My can - ti - cle di - vine,

May Je - sus Christ be praised! A - like at work and prayer,
May Je - sus Christ be praised! O hark to what it sings,
May Je - sus Christ be praised! The powers of dark - ness fear,
May Je - sus Christ be praised! Let all the earth a - round
May Je - sus Christ be praised! Let earth, and sea, and sky
May Je - sus Christ be praised! Be this th'e - ter - nal song

To Je - sus I re - pair; May Je - sus Christ be praised!
As joy - ous - ly it rings, May Je - sus Christ be praised!
When this sweet chant they hear, May Je - sus Christ be praised!
Ring joy - ous with the sound, May Je - sus Christ be praised!
From depth to height re - ply, May Je - sus Christ be praised!
Through all the a - ges long, May Je - sus Christ be praised!

MORNING WORSHIP

44   Morning Has Broken

BUNESSAN 5.5.5.4.D.
Traditional Gaelic Melody

Eleanor Farjeon, 1931 (1881-1965)
Arr. by Melvin West, 1984 (1930-   )

1. Morn-ing has bro - ken   Like the first morn - ing,
2. Sweet the rain's new   fall   Sun - lit from heav - en,
3. Mine is the sun - light!   Mine is the morn - ing

Black-bird has spo - ken   Like the first bird.
Like the first dew - fall   On the first grass.
Born of the one   light   E - den saw play!

Praise for the sing - ing!   Praise for the morn - ing!
Praise for the sweet - ness   Of the wet gar - den,
Praise with e - la - tion,   Praise ev - ery morn - ing,

Praise for them spring - ing   Fresh from the Word!
Sprung in com - plete - ness   Where His feet pass.
God's re - cre - a - tion   Of the new day!

MORNING WORSHIP

Open Now Thy Gates of Beauty

Benjamin Schmolck (1672-1737)
Tr. by Catherine Winkworth (1827-1878) alt.

UNSER HERRSCHER 8.7.8.7.7.7.
Joachim Neander (1650-1680)

1. O - pen now Thy gates of beau - ty, Zi - on, let me en - ter there,
2. Gra - cious God, I come be - fore Thee; Come Thou al - so un - to me;
3. Here Thy praise is glad - ly chant - ed, Here Thy seed is du - ly sown;
4. Thou my faith in - crease and quick - en, Let me keep Thy gift di - vine;
5. Speak, O God, and I will hear Thee, Let Thy will be done in - deed;

Where my soul in joy - ful du - ty Waits for God who an - swers prayer.
Where we find Thee and a - dore Thee, There a heav'n on earth must be.
Let my soul, where it is plant - ed, Bring forth pre - cious sheaves a - lone.
How - so - e'er temp - ta - tions thick - en, May Thy Word still o'er me shine
May I, un - dis - turbed, draw near Thee While Thou dost Thy peo - ple feed

Oh, how bless - ed is this place, Filled with so - lace, light, and grace!
To my heart, oh, en - ter Thou, Let it be Thy tem - ple now!
So that all I hear may be Fruit - ful un - to life in me.
As my guid - ing star through life, As my com - fort in all strife.
Here of life the foun - tain flows; Here is balm for all our woes.

Alternate harmony, No. 418

46 Abide With Me, 'Tis Eventide

WELCOME GUEST C.M.D.Ref.

M. Lowrie Hofford

Harrison Millard (1830-1895)

1. A - bide with me, 'tis e - ven-tide! The day is past and gone;
2. A - bide with me, 'tis e - ven-tide! Thy walk to - day with me
3. A - bide with me, 'tis e - ven-tide! And lone will be the night,

The shad - ows of the eve - ning fall; The night is com - ing on!
Has made my heart with - in me burn, As I com-muned with Thee.
If I can - not com-mune with Thee, Nor find in Thee my light.

With - in my heart a wel - come guest, With - in my home a - bide;
Thy ear - nest words have filled my soul And kept me near Thy side;
The dark - ness of the world, I fear, Would in my home a - bide;

Refrain

O Sav - ior, stay this night with me; Be - hold, 'tis e - ven - tide!

O Sav - ior, stay this night with me; Be - hold, 'tis e - ven - tide.

EVENING WORSHIP

God, Who Made the Earth and Heaven   47

Reginald Heber (1783-1826), st. 1
William Mercer (1811-1873), sts. 2,4
Richard Whately (1787-1863), st. 3, alt.

AR HYD Y NOS 8.4.8.4.8.8.8.4.
Welsh Melody

1. God, who made the earth and heav - en, Dark - ness and light:
2. And when morn a - gain shall call us To run life's way,
3. Guard us wak - ing, guard us sleep - ing, And, when we die,
4. Ho - ly Fa - ther, throned in heav - en, All - ho - ly Son,

You the day for work have giv - en, For rest the night.
May we still, what - e'er be - fall us, Your will o - bey.
May we in Your might - y keep - ing All peace - ful lie.
Ho - ly Spir - it, free - ly giv - en, Blest Three in One:

May Your an - gel guards de - fend us, Slum - ber sweet Your mer - cy send us,
From the pow'r of e - vil hide us, In the nar - row path - way guide us,
When the trum - pet call shall wake us, Then, O Lord, do not for - sake us,
Grant us grace, we now im - plore You, Till we lay our crowns be - fore You

Ho - ly dreams and hopes at - tend us All through the night.
Nev - er be Your smile de - nied us All through the day.
But to reign in glo - ry take us With You on high.
And in wor - thier strains a - dore You While a - ges run.

48 Softly Now the Light of Day

SEYMOUR 7.7.7.7.

George W. Doane, 1824 (1799-1859)

Arr. from Carl M. von Weber, 1826 (1786-1826)

1. Soft - ly now the light of day Fades up - on our sight a - way:
2. Thou, whose all - per - vad - ing eye Nought es - capes, with - out, with - in,
3. Soon from us the light of day Shall for - ev - er pass a - way;

Free from care, from la - bor free, Lord, we would com - mune with Thee.
Par - don each in - fir - mi - ty, O - pen fault, and se - cret sin.
Then, from sin and sor - row free, Take us, Lord, to dwell with Thee.

49 Savior, Breathe an Evening Blessing

EVENING PRAYER 8.7.8.7.

James Edmeston, 1820 (1791-1867)

George C. Stebbins, 1878 (1846-1945)

1. Sav - ior, breathe an eve - ning bless - ing, Ere re - pose our spir - its seal;
2. Though the night be dark and drear - y, Dark - ness can - not hide from Thee;
3. Though de - struc - tion walk a - round us, Though the ar - row past us fly,
4. Should swift death this night o'er - take us, And our couch be - come our tomb,

Sin and want we come con - fess - ing; Thou canst save, and Thou canst heal.
Thou art He who, nev - er wea - ry, Watch - est where Thy peo - ple be.
An - gel guards from Thee sur - round us, We are safe if Thou art nigh.
May the morn of glo - ry wake us, Clad in light and death - less bloom.

EVENING WORSHIP

Abide With Me

Luke 24:29
Henry F. Lyte, 1847 (1793-1847)

EVENTIDE 10.10.10.10.
William H. Monk, 1861 (1823-1889)

1. A - bide with me; fast falls the e - ven - tide;
2. Swift to its close ebbs out life's lit - tle day;
3. I need Thy pres - ence ev - ery pass - ing hour;
4. I fear no foe, with Thee at hand to bless;

The dark - ness deep - ens; Lord, with me a - bide!
Earth's joys grow dim, its glo - ries pass a - way;
What but Thy grace can foil the tempt - er's power?
Ills have no weight, and tears no bit - ter - ness:

When oth - er help - ers fail, and com - forts flee,
Change and de - cay in all a - round I see;
Who like Thy - self my guide and stay can be?
Where is death's sting? where, grave, thy vic - to - ry?

Help of the help - less, O a - bide with me!
O Thou, who chang - est not, a - bide with me!
Through cloud and sun - shine, O a - bide with me!
I tri - umph still if Thou a - bide with me!

EVENING WORSHIP

Day Is Dying in the West

CHAUTAUQUA 7.7.7.7.4. Ref.

Mary A. Lathbury, 1877 (1841-1913)

William F. Sherwin, 1877 (1826-1888)

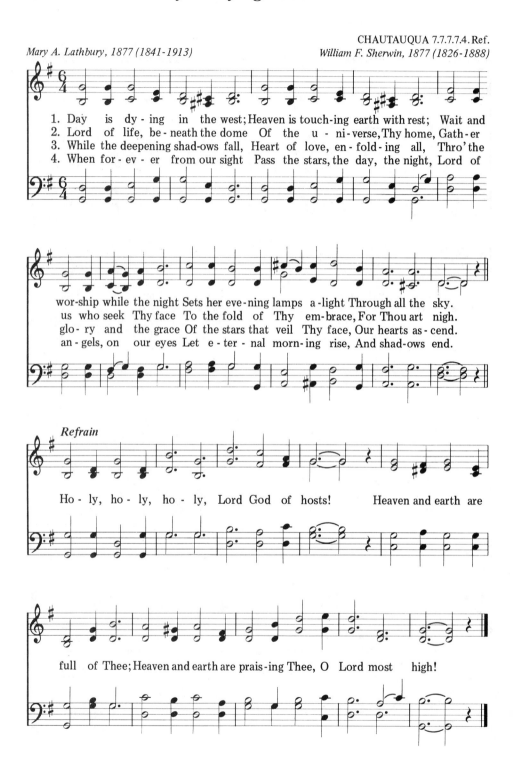

1. Day is dy-ing in the west; Heaven is touch-ing earth with rest; Wait and
2. Lord of life, be-neath the dome Of the u-ni-verse, Thy home, Gath-er
3. While the deepening shad-ows fall, Heart of love, en-fold-ing all, Thro' the
4. When for-ev-er from our sight Pass the stars, the day, the night, Lord of

wor-ship while the night Sets her eve-ning lamps a-light Through all the sky.
us who seek Thy face To the fold of Thy em-brace, For Thou art nigh.
glo-ry and the grace Of the stars that veil Thy face, Our hearts as-cend.
an-gels, on our eyes Let e-ter-nal morn-ing rise, And shad-ows end.

Refrain

Ho-ly, ho-ly, ho-ly, Lord God of hosts! Heaven and earth are

full of Thee; Heaven and earth are prais-ing Thee, O Lord most high!

EVENING WORSHIP

Now the Day Is Over   52

MERRIAL 6.5.6.5.

Sabine Baring-Gould, 1865 (1834-1924)

Joseph Barnby, 1868 (1838-1896)

1. Now the day is o - ver, Night is draw-ing nigh,
2. Fa - ther, give the wea - ry Calm and sweet re - pose;
3. Through the long night watch - es, May Thine an - gels spread

Shad - ows of the eve - ning Steal a - cross the sky.
With Thy ten - derest bless - ing May our eye - lids close.
Their white wings a - bove me, Watch - ing round my bed.

All Praise to Thee   53

TALLIS' CANON L.M.

Thomas Ken, 1674 (1637-1711)

Thomas Tallis, c. 1567 (c. 1505-1585)

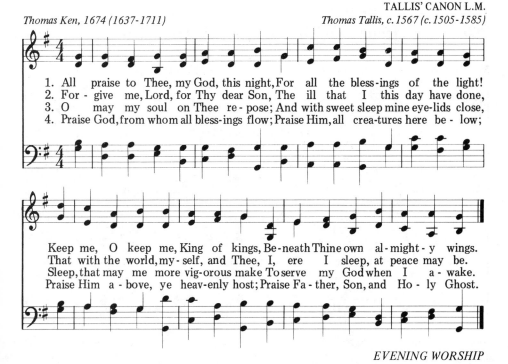

1. All praise to Thee, my God, this night, For all the bless-ings of the light!
2. For - give me, Lord, for Thy dear Son, The ill that I this day have done,
3. O may my soul on Thee re - pose; And with sweet sleep mine eye-lids close,
4. Praise God, from whom all bless-ings flow; Praise Him, all crea-tures here be - low;

Keep me, O keep me, King of kings, Be-neath Thine own al - might - y wings.
That with the world, my-self, and Thee, I, ere I sleep, at peace may be.
Sleep, that may me more vig-orous make To serve my God when I a - wake.
Praise Him a - bove, ye heav-enly host; Praise Fa - ther, Son, and Ho - ly Ghost.

EVENING WORSHIP

54 O Gladsome Light

Anon. Greek 3rd century
Tr. by Robert S. Bridges (1844-1930)

PHOS HILARON 6.6.7.6.6.7.
James Bingham, 1984 (1945-   )

1. O glad-some light, O grace Of God the Fa-ther's face, The e-
2. Now e'er day fad-eth quite, We see the ev-'ning light, Our
3. To Thee of right be-longs All praise of ho-ly songs, O

ter-nal splen-dor wear-ing; Ce-les-tial, ho-ly, blest,
wont-ed hymn out-pour-ing; Fa-ther of might un-known,
Son of God, life-giv-er; Thee there-fore, O most high,

Our Sav-ior, Je-sus Christ, Joy-ful in Thine ap-pear-ing.
Thee His in-car-nate Son, And Ho-ly Spir-it a-dor-ing.
The world doth glo-ri-fy And shall ex-alt for-ev-er.

Music copyright © 1984 by James Bingham.

55 Jesus, Tender Shepherd, Hear Me

SHIPSTON 8.7.8.7.
English traditional melody
Mrs. Mary Duncan, 1839 (1814-1840)
Arr. by Ralph Vaughan Williams (1872-1958)

1. Je-sus, ten-der Shep-herd, hear me, Bless Thy lit-tle lamb to-night;
2. All this day Thy hand has led me, And I thank Thee for Thy care;

Through the dark-ness be Thou near me; Watch my sleep till morn-ing light.
Thou hast clothed me, warmed and fed me; Lis-ten to my eve-ning prayer.

Music from the *English Hymnal* by permission of Oxford University Press.
Lower key, No. 544

EVENING WORSHIP

The Day Thou Gavest

56

ST. CLEMENT 9.8.9.8.

John Ellerton, 1870 (1826-1893)

Clement C. Scholefield, 1874 (1839-1904)

1. The day Thou gav-est, Lord, is end-ed, The dark-ness falls at Thy be-hest; To Thee our morn-ing hymns as-cend-ed, Thy praise shall hal-low now our rest.
2. We thank Thee that Thy church, un-sleep-ing, While earth rolls on-ward in-to light, Through all the world her watch is keep-ing, And rests not now by day or night.
3. As o'er each con-ti-nent and is-land The dawn leads on an-oth-er day, The voice of prayer is nev-er si-lent, Nor die the strains of praise a-way.
4. So be it, Lord; Thy throne shall nev-er, Like earth's proud em-pires, pass a-way; Thy king-dom stands, and grows for-ev-er, Till all Thy crea-tures own Thy sway.

EVENING WORSHIP

57   Now All the Woods Are Sleeping

Psalm 3:5
Paul Gerhardt (1607-1676)
Tr. by Catherine Winkworth (1827-1878)

INNSBRUCK 7.7.6.7.7.8.
Attr. to Heinrich Isaak (c. 1450-c. 1527)
Arr. by J. S. Bach (1685-1750)

1. Now all the woods are sleep - ing, And night and still - ness creep - ing O'er cit - y, man, and beast; But thou, my heart, a - wake thee, To pray'r a - while be - take thee, And praise thy Mak - er ere thou rest.

2. My Je - sus, stay Thou by me, And let no foe come nigh me, Safe shel - tered by Thy wing; But would the foe a - larm me, O let him nev - er harm me, But still Thine an - gels round me sing!

3. My loved ones, rest se - cure - ly, From ev - ery per - il sure - ly Our God will guard your heads; And hap - py slum - bers send you, And bid His hosts at - tend you, And gold - en - armed watch o'er your beds.

EVENING WORSHIP

Hark, the Vesper Hymn Is Stealing

58

RUSSIAN AIR 8.7.8.7.8.6.
Adapt. by Max V. Exner
Accomp. by Melvin West, 1984 (1930-   )

Thomas Moore (c. 1710-1792)

1. Hark! the ves-per hymn is steal-ing O'er the wa-ters soft and clear;

2. Near-er yet, and near-er peal-ing, Soft it breaks up-on the ear.

**Ju-bi-la-te, Ju-bi-la-te, Ju-bi-la-te, A-men.

*Accomp. A

*Accomp. B

*Accompaniment may play either A or B or both for the duration of the canon. This canon may be sung by from 2 to 18 voices. Enter at any measure.
**Jubilate means "Be joyful;" pronounced, "You-bee-lah-tay."
Arrangement copyright © 1984 by Melvin West.

EVENING WORSHIP

59 Great Our Joy as Now We Gather

MICHAEL 8.7.8.7.3.3.7.

Fred Pratt Green, 1972 (1903-   )
Unison

Herbert Howells, 1936 (1892-1983)

1. Great our joy as now we gath - er Where the Mas - ter
2. Pre - cious is the tie that binds us To our God when
3. May we learn from Christ's ex - am - ple How to use this
4. Lord, in - spire us with Your vi - sion Of a world which

makes us one: Where we wor - ship God the
faith grows cold; Pre - cious all that now re -
house of prayer: He who loved and cleansed His
must be won! Glo - rious is the church - 's

Fa - ther Thro' the Spir - it of His Son. All who
minds us He is still our safe strong - hold. Faith - ful
tem - ple Wants us all to wor - ship there. God the
mis - sion, Long en - deav - ored, scarce be - gun! Faith - ful

search for His church Find it where His will is done.
love serves to prove Here the Shep - herd has His fold.
Son shuts out none: In His King - dom all may share.
now— this is how God's e - ter - nal will is done.

OPENING OF WORSHIP

Blessed Jesus, at Thy Word

60

Tobias Clausnitzer, 1671 (1619-1684)
Tr. by Catherine Winkworth, 1858 (1827-1878)

LIEBSTER JESU 7.8.7.8.8.8.
Johann Rudolph Ahle, 1664 (1625-1673)

1. Bless - ed Je - sus, at Thy word We are gath - ered
2. All our knowl-edge, sense, and sight Lie in deep - est
3. Glo - rious Lord, Thy - self im - part! Light of light, from

all to hear Thee; Let our hearts and souls be stirred
dark - ness shroud - ed, Till Thy Spir - it breaks our night
God pro - ceed - ing, O - pen Thou our ears and heart,

Now to seek and love and fear Thee; By Thy teach - ings
With the beams of truth un - cloud - ed. Thou a - lone to
Help us by Thy Spir - it's plead - ing, Hear the cry Thy

sweet and ho - ly, Drawn from earth to love Thee sole - ly.
God canst win us; Thou must work all good with - in us.
peo - ple rais - es, Hear, and bless our prayers and prais - es.

OPENING OF WORSHIP

61 God Is Here!

ABBOT'S LEIGH 8.7.8.7.D.

Fred Pratt Green, 1977 (1903-)

Cyril V. Taylor, 1941 (1907-)

1. God is here! As we His peo-ple Meet to of - fer praise and prayer, May we find in full - er mea-sure What it is in Christ we share. Here, as in the world a-round us, All our var - ied skills and arts Wait the

2. Here are sym-bols to re - mind us Of our life - long need of grace; Here are ta - ble, font, and pul - pit; Here the Word has cen - tral place. Here in hon - es - ty of preach-ing, Here in si - lence, as in speech, Here, in

3. Here our chil-dren find a wel-come In the Shep - herd's flock and fold, Here, as bread and wine are tak - en Christ sus-tains us as of old. Here the ser - vants of the Ser-vant Seek in wor-ship to ex - plore What it

4. Lord of all, of church and king-dom, In an age of change and doubt Keep us faith - ful to the gos - pel, Help us work Your pur - pose out. Here, in this day's ty of ded - i - ca-tion, All we have to give, re - ceive, We, who

OPENING OF WORSHIP

com - ing of the Spir-it In - to o - pen minds and hearts.
new - ness and re - new-al, God the Spir - it comes to each.
means in dai - ly liv-ing To be-lieve and to a - dore.
can - not live with-out You, We a - dore You! we be - lieve!

Lower key, No. 583

How Lovely Is Thy Dwelling Place 62

MCKEE C.M.

Psalm 84
Scottish Psalter, 1650

American Negro Spiritual
Arr. by Harry T. Burleigh, 1939 (1866-1949)

Unison

1. How love - ly is Thy dwell-ing place, O Lord of hosts to me!
2. My thirst - y soul longs ar - dent - ly, Yea, faints Thy courts to see;
3. Be - hold the spar-row find-eth out A house where-in to rest;
4. Ev'n Thine own al - tars, where she safe Her young ones forth may bring,
5. Blest are they in Thy house that dwell, They ev - er give Thee praise.

The tab - er - na - cles of Thy grace How pleas - ant, Lord, they be!
My ver - y heart and flesh cry out, O liv - ing God, for Thee.
The swal-low al - so, for her - self Pro - vid - ed hath a nest.
O Thou, al - might - y Lord of hosts, Who art my God and King.
Blest is the man whose strength Thou art, In whose heart are Thy ways.

63 O Come, Let Us Sing to the Lord

Psalm 95:1-6
Scottish Psalter, 1650

IRISH C.M.
From A Collection of Hymns and Sacred Poems, Dublin, 1749

1. O come, let us sing to the Lord, Come let us ev - ery one A joy - ful noise make to the Rock Of our sal - va - tion.
2. Let us be - fore His pres - ence come With glad and thank - ful voice; Let us sing psalms of praise to Him, And make a joy - ful noise.
3. For God, a great God and great King, A - bove all gods, He is; The depths of earth are in His hand, The strength of hills is His.
4. To Him the o - cean vast be - longs, For He the sea did make; The dry land al - so from His hands, Its form at first did take.
5. O come, bow down and wor - ship Him, And kneel - ing, hum - bly pray, Come to our Mak - er and our God, And hear His voice to - day.

Lord, Dismiss Us With Thy Blessing

64

John Fawcett, 1773 (1740-1817)

SICILIAN MARINERS 8.7.8.7.4.7.
Tattersall's Improved Psalmody, 1794

1. Lord, dis - miss us with Thy bless - ing; Fill our hearts with
2. Thanks we give, and ad - o - ra - tion, For Thy gos - pel's

joy and peace; Let us each, Thy love pos - sess - ing,
joy - ful sound. May the fruits of Thy sal - va - tion

Tri - umph in re - deem - ing grace. O re - fresh us,
In our hearts and lives a - bound. Ev - er faith - ful,

O re - fresh us, Trav - eling through this wil - der - ness.
ev - er faith - ful To the truth may we be found.

CLOSE OF WORSHIP

65 God Be With You

2 Cor. 13:11
Jeremiah E. Rankin, 1880 (1828-1904)
9.8.8.9.Ref.
William G. Tomer, 1880 (1833-1896)

1. God be with you till we meet a-gain; By His coun-sels guide, up-
2. God be with you till we meet a-gain; 'Neath His wings pro-tect-ing
3. God be with you till we meet a-gain; When life's per-ils thick con-
4. God be with you till we meet a-gain; Keep love's ban-ner float-ing

hold you, With His sheep se-cure-ly fold you; God be with you till we
hide you, Dai-ly man-na still pro-vide you; God be with you till we
found you, Put His arms un-fail-ing round you; God be with you till we
o'er you, Smite death's threatening wave be-fore you; God be with you till we

Refrain

meet a-gain.
meet a-gain. Till we meet, till we meet, Till we
meet a-gain. Till we meet, till we meet a-gain,
meet a-gain.

meet at Je-sus' feet, Till we meet,
till we meet; Till we meet,

CLOSE OF WORSHIP

till we meet, God be with you till we meet a - gain.
till we meet a - gain,

God Be With You

66

RANDOLPH 9.8.8.9.

Jeremiah E. Rankin (1828-1904)
Unison

Ralph Vaughan Williams (1872-1958)
Harmony

1. God be with you till we meet a - gain; By His coun - sels
2. God be with you till we meet a - gain; Neath His wings se -
3. God be with you till we meet a - gain; When life's per - ils
4. God be with you till we meet a - gain; Keep love's ban - ner

guide, up - hold you, With His sheep se - cure - ly fold you:
cure - ly hide you, Dai - ly man - na still pro - vide you:
thick con - found you, Put His arms un - fail - ing round you:
float - ing o'er you, Smite death's threat-ening wave be - fore you:

Unison

God be with you till we meet a - gain.
God be with you till we meet a - gain.
God be with you till we meet a - gain.
God be with you till we meet a - gain.

Music from the *English Hymnal* by permission of Oxford University Press.

CLOSE OF WORSHIP

67 O Lord, Now Let Your Servant

NYLAND 7.6.7.6.D.
Luke 2:29-32
Ernest E. Ryden (1886-1981) alt.
Traditional Finnish Melody
Arr. by David Evans, 1928 (1874-1948)

1. O Lord, now let Your ser - vant De - part in heav'n - ly peace,
   For I have seen the glo - ry Of Your re - deem - ing grace:
   A light to lead the Gen - tiles Un - to Your ho - ly hill,
   The glo - ry of Your peo - ple, Your cho - sen Is - ra - el.

2. Then grant that I may fol - low Your gleam, O glo - rious Light,
   Till earth - ly shad - ows scat - ter, And faith is changed to sight;
   Till rap - tured saints shall gath - er Up - on that shin - ing shore,
   Where Christ, the bless - ed Day - star, Shall light them ev - er - more.

CLOSE OF WORSHIP

On Our Way Rejoicing

68

HERMAS 6.5.6.5.D.Ref.

J. S. B. Monsell, 1863 (1811-1875) alt.

Frances R. Havergal, 1871 (1836-1879)

1. On our way re - joic - ing Glad - ly let us go; Con - quer'd hath our
2. Un - to God the Fa - ther Joy - ful songs we sing, Un - to God the

Lead - er, Van - quish'd is the foe. Christ with - out, our safe - ty; Christ with -
Sa - vior Thank - ful hearts we bring, Un - to God the Spir - it Bow we

in, our joy; Who, if we be faith - ful, Can our hope de - stroy?
and a - dore, On our way re - joic - ing Now and ev - er - more.

Refrain

On our way re - joic - ing As we for - ward move,

Hear - ken to our prais - es, O blest God of love!

CLOSE OF WORSHIP

69   Lord, Make Us More Holy

6.6.6.6.6.6.

American Negro Spiritual

Arr. by Alma Blackmon, 1984 (1921-   )

1. Lord, make us more ho - ly; Lord, make us more ho - ly;
2. Lord, make us more faith - ful; Lord, make us more faith - ful;
3. Lord, make us more hum - ble; Lord, make us more hum - ble;
4. Lord, make us more lov - ing; Lord, make us more lov - ing;

Lord, make us more ho - ly   Un - til we meet a - gain.
Lord, make us more faith - ful   Un - til we meet a - gain.
Lord, make us more hum - ble   Un - til we meet a - gain.
Lord, make us more lov - ing   Un - til we meet a -

gain.   Like Je - sus, the Sav - ior,   Un - til we meet a - gain.

2 Cor. 13:14
Elizabeth Rundle Charles, 1859 (1828-1896)

FLEMMING 11.11.11.5.
Friedrich F. Flemming, 1811 (1778-1813)

1. Praise ye the Father for His lov-ing-kind-ness,
2. Praise ye the Sav-ior, great is His com-pas-sion,
3. Praise ye the Spir-it, Com-fort-er of Is-rael,

Ten-der-ly cares He for His err-ing chil-dren; Praise Him, ye
Gra-cious-ly cares He for His cho-sen peo-ple; Young men and
Sent of the Fa-ther and the Son to bless us; Praise ye the

an-gels, praise Him in the heav-ens; Praise ye Je-ho-vah!
maid-ens, ye old men and chil-dren, Praise ye the Sav-ior!
Fa-ther, Son, and Ho-ly Spir-it, Praise the E-ter-nal Three!

71   Come, Thou Almighty King

ITALIAN HYMN 6.6.4.6.6.6.4.

Anon. from George Whitfield's
... Hymns for Social Worship, 1757

Felice de Giardini (1716-1796)
Harm. by V. Earle Copes (1921-)

1. Come, Thou al-might-y King, Help us Thy
2. Come, Thou in-car-nate Word, Gird on Thy
3. Come, ho-ly Com-fort-er, Thy sa-cred
4. To Thee, great One in Three, E-ter-nal

name to sing, Help us to praise! Fa-ther all
might-y sword, Our prayer at-tend; Come, and Thy
wit-ness bear, In this glad hour: Thou who al-
prais-es be, Hence, ev-er-more: Thy sov-ereign

glo-ri-ous, O'er all vic-to-ri-ous,
peo-ple bless, And give Thy Word suc-cess;
might-y art, Now rule in ev-ery heart,
maj-es-ty May we in glo-ry see,

Come, and reign o-ver us, An-cient of Days!
Spir-it of ho-li-ness, On us de-scend!
And ne'er from us de-part, Spir-it of power!
And to e-ter-ni-ty Love and a-dore!

Alternate harmony, No. 370

TRINITY

Creator of the Stars of Night

72

Anon. Latin, 9th century
Adapt. from John M. Neale (1818-1866)

Sarum Plainsong
Arr. by C. Winfred Douglas (1867-1944)

1. Cre - a - tor of the stars of night, Thy peo - ple's ev - er - last - ing light, O Christ, Thou Sav - ior of us all, We pray Thee, hear us when we call.
2. At the great name of Je - sus, now All knees must bend, all hearts must bow; And things ce - les - tial Thee shall own, And things ter - res - trial, Lord a - lone.
3. To God the Fa - ther, God the Son, And God the Spir - it, Three in one, Laud, hon - or, might, and glo - ry be From age to age e - ter - nal - ly. A - men.

TRINITY

73 Holy, Holy, Holy

Rev. 4:8-11
Reginald Heber, 1826 (1783-1826)

NICAEA 11.12.12.10.
John B. Dykes, 1861 (1823-1876)

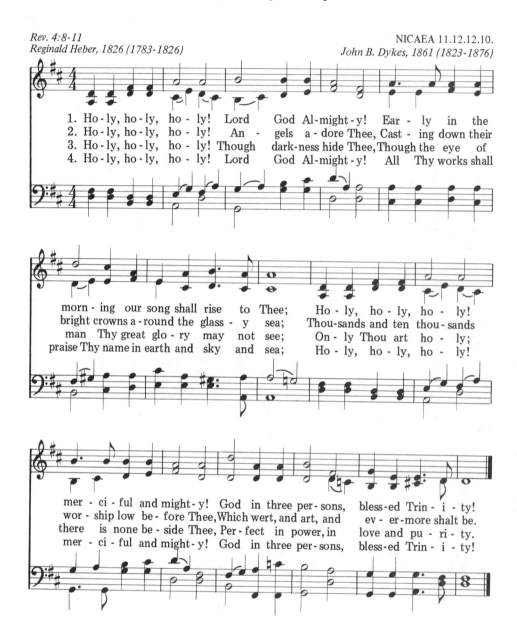

1. Ho-ly, ho-ly, ho-ly! Lord God Al-might-y! Ear-ly in the
2. Ho-ly, ho-ly, ho-ly! An-gels a-dore Thee, Cast-ing down their
3. Ho-ly, ho-ly, ho-ly! Though dark-ness hide Thee, Though the eye of
4. Ho-ly, ho-ly, ho-ly! Lord God Al-might-y! All Thy works shall

morn-ing our song shall rise to Thee; Ho-ly, ho-ly, ho-ly!
bright crowns a-round the glass-y sea; Thou-sands and ten thou-sands
man Thy great glo-ry may not see; On-ly Thou art ho-ly;
praise Thy name in earth and sky and sea; Ho-ly, ho-ly, ho-ly!

mer-ci-ful and might-y! God in three per-sons, bless-ed Trin-i-ty!
wor-ship low be-fore Thee, Which wert, and art, and ev-er-more shalt be.
there is none be-side Thee, Per-fect in power, in love and pu-ri-ty.
mer-ci-ful and might-y! God in three per-sons, bless-ed Trin-i-ty!

Like a River Glorious

74

Isa. 48:18
Frances R. Havergal (1836-1879) alt.

WYE VALLEY 6.5.6.5.D.
James Mountain (1844-1933)

1. Like a riv-er glo-rious Is God's per-fect peace, O-ver all victorious In its bright in-crease; Per-fect, yet it flow-eth Full-er
ev-ery day, Per-fect, yet it grow-eth Deep-er all the way.

2. Hid-den in the hol-low Of His bless-ed hand, Nev-er foe can
fol-low, Nev-er trai-tor stand; Not a surge of wor-ry, Not a
shade of care, Not a blast of hur-ry Touch the spir-it there.

3. Ev-ery joy or test-ing Comes from God a-bove, Giv-en to His
chil-dren As an act of love; We may trust Him ful-ly All for
us to do— Those who trust Him whol-ly Find Him whol-ly true.

Refrain

Trust-ing in Je-ho-vah, Hearts are ful-ly blest—
Find-ing, as He prom-ised, Per-fect peace and rest.

LOVE OF GOD

75 The Wonder of It All

WONDER OF IT ALL Irregular Ref.

George Beverly Shea (1909-   )

George Beverly Shea

1. There's the won-der of sun-set at eve-ning, The won-der as
2. There's the won-der of spring-time and har-vest, The sky, the

sun-rise I see; But the won-der of won-ders that thrills my soul
stars, the sun; But the won-der of won-ders that thrills my soul

Is the won-der that God loves me.
Is a won-der that's on-ly be-gun.

Refrain

O, the won-der of it all! The

won-der of it all! Just to think that God loves me. O, the won-der of it

LOVE OF GOD

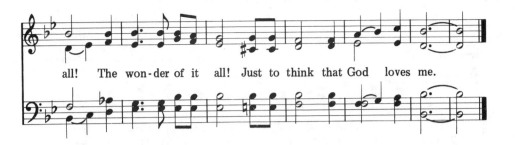

all! The won-der of it all! Just to think that God loves me.

O Love That Wilt Not Let Me Go 76

ST. MARGARET 8.8.8.8.6.

George Matheson, 1882 (1842-1906)

Albert L. Peace, 1885 (1844-1912)

1. O Love that wilt not let me go, I rest my wea-ry soul in Thee; I give Thee back the life I owe, That in Thine o-cean depths its flow May rich-er, full-er be.

2. O Light that fol-lowest all my way, I yield my flick-ering torch to Thee; My heart re-stores its bor-rowed ray, That in Thy sun-shine's blaze its day May bright-er, fair-er be.

3. O Joy that seek-est me through pain, I can-not close my heart to Thee; I trace the rain-bow through the rain, And feel the prom-ise is not vain That morn shall tear-less be.

4. O Cross that lift-est up my head, I dare not ask to fly from Thee; I lay in dust life's glo-ry dead, And from the ground there blos-soms red Life that shall end-less be.

LOVE OF GOD

77

O Love of God Most Full

VANDEMAN S.M.
From an anthem by
Oscar Clute (1837-1902)
Gordon Young, 1963 (1919-   )

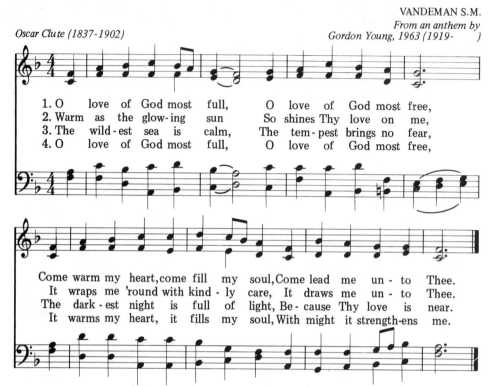

1. O love of God most full, O love of God most free,
2. Warm as the glow-ing sun So shines Thy love on me,
3. The wild-est sea is calm, The tem-pest brings no fear,
4. O love of God most full, O love of God most free,

Come warm my heart, come fill my soul, Come lead me un-to Thee.
It wraps me 'round with kind-ly care, It draws me un-to Thee.
The dark-est night is full of light, Be-cause Thy love is near.
It warms my heart, it fills my soul, With might it strength-ens me.

78

For God So Loved Us

August D. Rische, 1856 (1819-1906)
Paraphrase composite, 1956 and 1960

GOTT IST DIE LIEBE 10.9.Ref.
Thüringer Melody, c. 1840

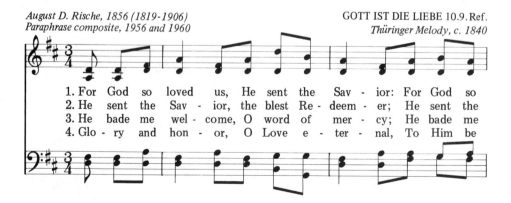

1. For God so loved us, He sent the Sav - ior: For God so
2. He sent the Sav - ior, the blest Re - deem - er; He sent the
3. He bade me wel - come, O word of mer - cy; He bade me
4. Glo - ry and hon - or, O Love e - ter - nal, To Him be

LOVE OF GOD

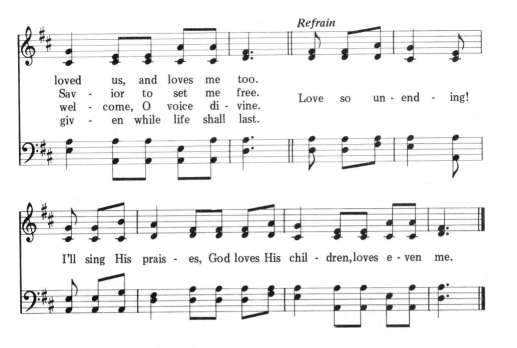

loved us, and loves me too.
Sav - ior to set me free.
wel - come, O voice di - vine.
giv - en while life shall last.

Refrain

Love so un - end - ing!

I'll sing His prais - es, God loves His chil - dren, loves e - ven me.

O Love of God, How Strong and True! 79

OMBERSLEY L.M.

Horatius Bonar, 1861 (1808-1889)

William H. Gladstone, 1872 (1840-1891)

1. O love of God, how strong and true! E - ter - nal, and yet ev - er new;
2. O love of God, how deep and great, Far deep - er than man's deep - est hate;
3. We read thee best in Him who came To bear for us the cross of shame;
4. We read thy power to bless and save, E'en in the dark - ness of the grave;
5. O love of God, our shield and stay Through all the per - ils of our way!

Un - com - pre - hend - ed and un - bought, Be - yond all knowledge and all thought.
Self - fed, self - kin - dled like the light, Changeless, e - ter - nal, in - fi - nite.
Sent by the Fa - ther from on high, Our life to live, our death to die.
Still more in res - ur - rec - tion light We read the full - ness of thy might.
E - ter - nal love, in thee we rest, For - ev - er safe, for - ev - er blest.

LOVE OF GOD

80

O World of God

JERUSALEM L.M.D.

R. B. Y. Scott (1899-   )

Charles H. H. Parry (1848-1918)
Arr. by Gordon P. S. Jacob (1895-   )

Introduction

Piano

Unison

1. O world of God, so vast and strange, pro-found and
2. O world of man where life is lived, so strange-ly
3. O world of time's far-stretch-ing years! there was a

won-der-ful and fair, Be-yond the ut - most reach of
min-gling joy and pain, So full of e - vil and of
day when time stood still, A cen-tral mo - ment when there

thought, but not be-yond a Fa - ther's care! We are not
good, so need-ful that the good shall reign! It is this
rose a cross up - on a cru - el hill; In pain and

LOVE OF GOD

LOVE OF GOD

81 Though I Speak With Tongues

1 Cor. 13
Fred Pratt Green (1903-   )

JANELLE 10.7.10.7.8.7.10.7.
James Bingham, 1984 (1945-   )

Unison

1. Though I speak with tongues of men and an - gels,
2. Love is pa - tient, knows no en - vy,
3. Though there'll be an end to hid - den knowl - edge,

Though I have the proph - et's gift,
Nev - er gloats when oth - ers sin;
Vi - sions, rap - tures, proph - e - cy:

Though I hold the keys to hid - den knowl - edge,
Love is nev - er glad to see in - jus - tice,
Faith and hope and love shall last for - ev - er,

Though my faith can moun - tains shift:
Al - ways wants the truth to win.
Love the great - est of the three.

LOVE OF GOD

With - out love   I am   no   bet - ter,
There's   no end   to love's   en - dur - ance,
With - out love   I am   no   bet - ter,

With - out love   it's   all   for   naught;
There's   no test   it   can - not   face;
With - out love   it's   all   for   naught;

Lord,   You spent   Your life in lov - ing oth - ers:
Lord,   You spent   Your life in lov - ing oth - ers:
Lord,   You gave   Your life in sav - ing oth - ers:

What   this   means   I   would   be   taught.
I   shall   fail   with - out   Your   grace.
What   this   means   I   would   be   taught.

LOVE OF GOD

82 Before Jehovah's Awful Throne

Psalm 100
Isaac Watts, 1719 (1674-1748) alt.

DUKE STREET L.M.
John Hatton (c.1710-1793)

1. Be - fore Je - ho - vah's aw - ful throne, Ye na - tions,
2. His sov - ereign power, with - out our aid, Made us of
3. We'll crowd His gates with thank - ful songs, High as the
4. Wide as the world is His com - mand, Vast as E -

bow with sa - cred joy; Know that the Lord is
clay, and formed us men; And when like wan - dering
heavens our voic - es raise; And earth, with her ten
ter - ni - ty His love; Firm as a rock His

God a - lone; He can cre - ate, and He de - stroy.
sheep we strayed, He brought us to His fold a - gain.
thou - sand tongues, Shall fill His courts with sound - ing praise.
truth shall stand, When roll - ing years shall cease to move.

Alternate harmony, No. 227

MAJESTY AND POWER OF GOD

O Worship the King

Psalm 104
Robert Grant, 1833 (1779-1838)

LYONS 10.10.11.11.
Wm. Gardiner's Sacred Melodies, 1815

1. O worship the King, all - glo - rious a - bove,
2. O tell of His might, O sing of His grace,
3. Thy boun - ti - ful care, what tongue can re - cite?
4. Frail chil - dren of dust, and fee - ble as frail,

O grate - ful - ly sing His won - der - ful love;
Whose robe is the light, whose can - o - py space;
It breathes in the air, it shines in the light;
In Thee do we trust, nor find Thee to fail;

Our shield and de - fend - er, the An - cient of days,
His char - iots of wrath the deep thun - der - clouds form,
It streams from the hills, it de - scends to the plain,
Thy mer - cies, how ten - der! how firm to the end!

Pa - vil - ioned in splen - dor, and gird - ed with praise.
And dark is His path on the wings of the storm.
And sweet - ly dis - tills in the dew and the rain.
Our Mak - er, De - fend - er, Re - deem - er, and Friend!

MAJESTY AND POWER OF GOD

84 God the Omnipotent

Henry F. Chorley, 1842 (1808-1872)
John Ellerton, 1870 (1826-1893)

RUSSIAN HYMN 11.10.11.10.
Alexis Lwoff, 1833 (1799-1870)

1. God the Om - nip - o - tent! King, who or - dain - est
2. God the all - mer - ci - ful! earth hath for - sak - en
3. God the all - righ - teous One! man hath de - fied Thee;
4. So shall we ren - der Thee thank - ful de - vo - tion,

Great winds Thy clar - ions, the light - nings Thy sword;
Thy pre - cepts ho - ly, and slight - ed Thy word;
Yet to e - ter - ni - ty stand - eth Thy word;
For Thy de - liv - erance from per - il and sword,

Show forth Thy pit - y on high where Thou reign - est,
Bid not Thy wrath in its ter - rors a - wak - en;
False - hood and wrong shall not tar - ry be - side Thee;
Sing - ing in cho - rus from o - cean to o - cean,

Give to us peace, O most mer - ci - ful Lord.
Give to us peace, O most mer - ci - ful Lord.
Pros - per the right, O most mer - ci - ful Lord.
"Thine is the power and the glo - ry, O Lord."

MAJESTY AND POWER OF GOD

Eternal Father, Strong to Save

William Whiting (1825-1878)

MELITA 8.8.8.8.8.8.

John B. Dykes (1823-1876)

1. E - ter - nal Fa - ther, strong to save, Whose arm hath bound the
2. O Christ, whose voice the wa - ters heard, And hushed their rag - ing
3. O Ho - ly Spir - it, who didst brood Up - on the wa - ters
4. O Trin - i - ty of love and power, All trav - 'lers shield in

rest - less wave, Who bid'st the might - y o - cean deep Its
at Thy word, Who walk - edst on the foam - ing deep, And
dark and rude, And bid their an - gry tu - mult cease, And
dan - ger's hour; From rock and tem - pest, fire and foe, Pro -

own ap - point - ed lim - its keep; Oh, hear us when we
calm a - midst its rage didst sleep; Oh, hear us when we
give, for wild con - fu - sion, peace: Oh, hear us when we
tect them where - so - e'er they go; Thus ev - er - more shall

cry to Thee For those in per - il on the sea.
cry to Thee For those in per - il on the sea.
cry to Thee For those in per - il on the sea.
rise to Thee Glad hymns of praise from land and sea.

MAJESTY AND POWER OF GOD

How Great Thou Art

Stuart K. Hine, (1899-   )

Stuart K. Hine

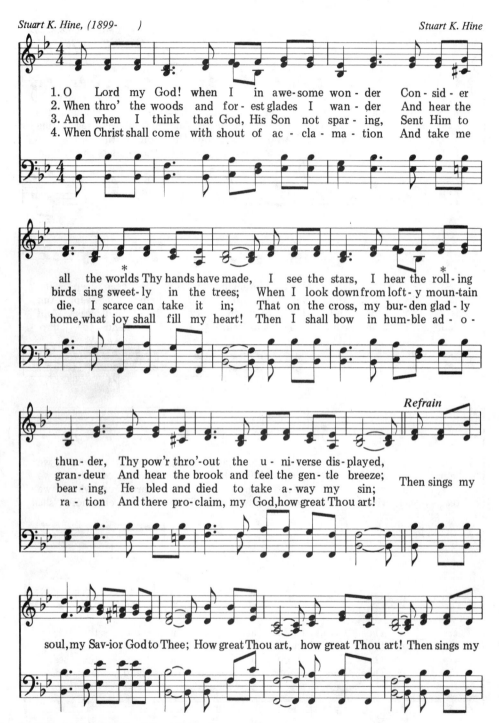

1. O   Lord my God! when I   in awe-some won - der   Con - sid - er
2. When thro' the woods   and for - est glades I   wan - der   And hear the
3. And when I   think   that God, His Son   not spar - ing,   Sent Him to
4. When Christ shall come   with shout of ac - cla - ma - tion   And take me

all   the worlds Thy hands have made,   I   see the stars, I hear the roll - ing
birds sing sweet-ly   in   the trees;   When I   look down from loft - y moun-tain
die,   I scarce can take it   in;   That on the cross, my bur - den glad - ly
home, what joy shall   fill   my heart!   Then I   shall bow   in hum-ble ad - o -

Refrain

thun - der,   Thy pow'r thro'-out   the u - ni-verse dis-played,
gran - deur   And hear the brook and feel the gen - tle breeze;   Then sings my
bear - ing,   He bled and died   to take a - way my   sin;
ra - tion   And there pro-claim, my God, how great Thou art!

soul, my Sav-ior God to Thee; How great Thou art,   how great Thou art! Then sings my

MAJESTY AND POWER OF GOD

soul, my Sav-ior God to Thee; How great Thou art, How great Thou art!

God Who Spoke in the Beginning 87

NEW MALDEN 8.7.8.7.8.7.

Fred Kaan (1929-) *David McCarthy (1931-)*

1. God who spoke in the be-gin-ning, Form-ing rock and shap-ing spar,
2. God who spoke thro' men and na-tions, Thro' e-vents long past and gone,
3. God whose speech be-comes in-car-nate—Christ is ser-vant, Christ is Lord—

Set all life and growth in mo-tion, Earth-ly world and dis-tant star;
Show-ing still to-day His pur-pose, Speaks su-preme-ly through His Son;
Calls us to a life of ser-vice, Heart and will to ac-tion stirred;

He who calls the earth to or-der Is the ground of what we are.
He who calls the earth to or-der Gives His word and it is done.
He who us-es man's o-be-dience Has the first and fi-nal word.

Alternate tune, REGENT SQUARE, No. 119

MAJESTY AND POWER OF GOD

88   I Sing the Mighty Power of God

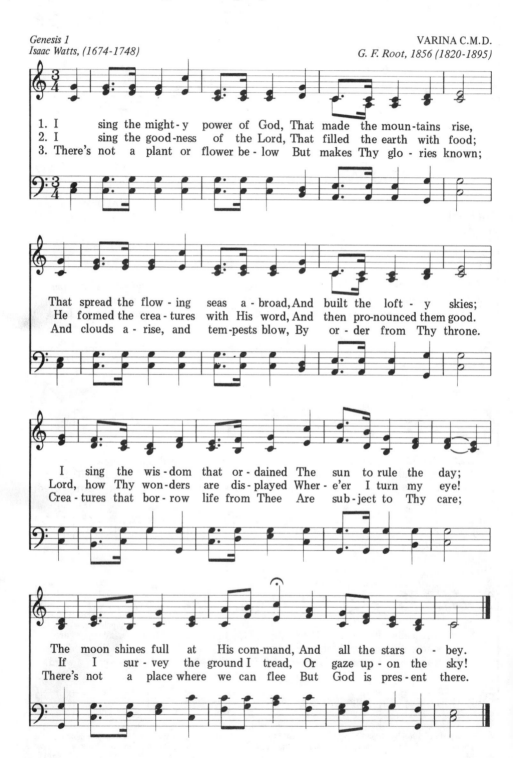

Genesis 1
Isaac Watts, (1674-1748)

VARINA C.M.D.
G. F. Root, 1856 (1820-1895)

1. I sing the might-y power of God, That made the moun-tains rise,
2. I sing the good-ness of the Lord, That filled the earth with food;
3. There's not a plant or flower be-low But makes Thy glo-ries known;

That spread the flow-ing seas a-broad, And built the loft-y skies;
He formed the crea-tures with His word, And then pro-nounced them good.
And clouds a-rise, and tem-pests blow, By or-der from Thy throne.

I sing the wis-dom that or-dained The sun to rule the day;
Lord, how Thy won-ders are dis-played Wher-e'er I turn my eye!
Crea-tures that bor-row life from Thee Are sub-ject to Thy care;

The moon shines full at His com-mand, And all the stars o-bey.
If I sur-vey the ground I tread, Or gaze up-on the sky!
There's not a place where we can flee But God is pres-ent there.

MAJESTY AND POWER OF GOD

Let All on Earth Their Voices Raise

OLD 113th 8.8.6.D.

Psalm 96
Isaac Watts (1674-1748)

Attr. to Matthäus Greiter (c. 1500-1552)
Arr. by V. Earle Copes (1921-   )

1. Let all on earth their voic - es raise, To sing the great Je - ho - vah's praise, And bless His ho - ly name: His glo - ry let the peo - ple know, His won - ders to the na - tions show, His sav - ing grace pro - claim.

2. He framed the globe; He built the sky; He made the shin - ing worlds on high, And reigns in glo - ry there: His beams are maj - es - ty and light; His beau - ties, how di - vine - ly bright! His dwell - ing place, how fair!

3. Come, the great day, the glo - rious hour, When earth shall feel His sav - ing power, All na - tions fear His name; Then shall the race of men con - fess The beau - ty of His ho - li - ness, His sav - ing grace pro - claim.

MAJESTY AND POWER OF GOD

TSDAH-4

90   Eternal God, Whose Power Upholds

FOREST GREEN C.M.D.
Trad. English Melody

Henry H. Tweedy, 1929; alt., 1972 (1868-1953)   *Arr. by Ralph Vaughan Williams, 1906 (1872-1958)*

1. E - ter - nal God, whose power up - holds Both flower and flam - ing star,
2. O God of truth, whom sci - ence seeks And rev - erent souls a - dore,
3. O God of beau - ty, oft re - vealed In dreams of hu - man art,
4. O God of righ - teous - ness and grace, Seen in the Christ, Your Son,

To whom there is no here nor there, No time, no near nor far,
Il - lu - mine ev - ery ear - nest mind Of ev - ery clime and shore:
In speech that flows to mel - o - dy, In ho - li - ness of heart:
Whose life and death re - veal Your face, By whom Your will was done;

No a - lien race, no for - eign shore, No child un - sought, un - known:
Dis - pel the gloom of er - ror's night, Of ig - no - rance and fear,
Teach us to ban all ug - li - ness, And all dis - har - mo - ny,
Help us to spread Your gra - cious reign Till greed and hate shall cease,

O send us forth, Your proph - ets true, To make all lands Your own!
Un - til true wis - dom from a - bove Shall make life's path - way clear!
Till all shall know the love - li - ness Of lives made fair and free!
And kind - ness dwell in hu - man hearts, And all the earth find peace!

Music from *The English Hymnal* by permission of Oxford University Press.

MAJESTY AND POWER OF GOD

Ye Watchers and Ye Holy Ones

91

LASST UNS ERFREUEN 8.8.8.8.8.8. Alleluias
Geistliche Kirchengesänge, *Köln, 1623*
Arr. by Ralph Vaughan Williams (1872-1958)

Athelstan Riley, 1906 (1858-1945)

1. Ye watch-ers and ye ho-ly ones, Bright ser-aphs, cher-u-bim and thrones,
2. O high-er than the cher-u-bim, More glo-rious than the ser-a-phim,
3. O friends, in glad-ness let us sing, Su-per-nal an-thems ech-o-ing,

Raise the glad strain, Al-le-lu-ia! Cry out, do-min-ions, prince-doms, powers,
Lead their prais-es, Al-le-lu-ia! Thou bear-er of the e-ter-nal Word,
Al-le-lu-ia, Al-le-lu-ia! To God the Fa-ther, God the Son,

Vir-tues, arch-an-gels, an-gels' choirs,
Most gra-cious, mag-ni-fy the Lord. Al-le-lu-ia, Al-le-
And God the Spir-it, Three in One.

lu-ia, Al-le-lu-ia, Al-le-lu-ia, Al-le-lu-ia!

Words and music from *The English Hymnal* by permission of Oxford University Press.   Lower key, No. 2

MAJESTY AND POWER OF GOD

92   This Is My Father's World

Maltbie D. Babcock, 1901 (1858-1901)

TERRA BEATA S.M.D.
Franklin L. Sheppard, 1915 (1852-1930)

1. This is my Fa-ther's world, And to my lis-ten-ing ears, All
2. This is my Fa-ther's world, The birds their car - ols raise; The
3. This is my Fa-ther's world, O let me ne'er for - get That

na - ture sings, and round me rings The mu - sic of the spheres.
morn - ing light, the lil - y white, De - clare their Mak - er's praise.
though the wrong seems oft so strong, God is the Rul - er yet.

This is my Fa - ther's world; I rest me in the thought Of
This is my Fa - ther's world; He shines in all that's fair; In the
This is my Fa - ther's world; Why should my heart be sad? The

rocks and trees, of skies and seas; His hand the won-ders wrought.
rus - tling grass I hear Him pass, He speaks to me ev-ery-where.
Lord is King; let the heav-ens ring! God reigns; let the earth be glad.

POWER OF GOD IN NATURE

All Things Bright and Beautiful

ROYAL OAK 7.6.7.6.Ref.
English traditional melody
Adapt. by Martin Shaw, 1915 (1875-1958)

Cecil F. Alexander, 1848 (1823-1895)
Unison

*1. All things bright and beau-ti-ful, All crea-tures great and small,

Fine

All things wise and won-der-ful, The Lord God made them all.

2. Each lit-tle flower that o-pens, Each lit-tle bird that sings;
3. The pur-ple-head-ed moun-tain, The riv-er run-ning by,
4. The cold wind in the win-ter, The pleas-ant sum-mer sun,
5. He gave us eyes to see them, And lips that we might tell

D.C.

He made their glow-ing col-ors, He made their ti-ny wings.
The sun-set, and the morn-ing That bright-ens up the sky,
The ripe fruits in the gar-den, He made them ev-er-y one.
How great is God Al-might-y, Who has made all things well.

*Stanza 1 to be sung as refrain after stanzas 2 to 5.
By permission of J. Curwen & Sons, Ltd. Used by permission of G. Schirmer, Inc., U. S. A. agents.

POWER OF GOD IN NATURE

94   Nature With Open Volume Stands

ANGELUS L.M.

Isaac Watts (1674-1748) alt.

Georg Joseph, 17th century, adapt.

1. Nature with open volume stands, To spread its Maker's praise abroad; And every labor of His hands Shows something worthy of our God.

2. But in the grace that rescued us His brightest form of glory shines; 'Tis fairest drawn upon the cross In precious blood and crimson lines.

3. Here His whole name appears complete. Nor wit can guess, nor reason prove, Which of the letters best is writ, The pow'r, the wisdom, or the love.

4. We would forever speak His name In sounds to mortal ears unknown, With angels join to praise the Lamb, And worship at His Father's throne.

POWER OF GOD IN NATURE

Spring Has Now Unwrapped the Flowers

95

TEMPUS ADEST FLORIDUM 7.6.7.6.D.
From Piae Cantiones, *1582*
Arr. by Ernest MacMillan (1893-1973)

From Oxford Book of Carols, *1928*

1. Spring has now un-wrapped the flowers, Day is fast re-viv-ing,
2. Herb and plant that win-ter long, Slum-bered at their lei-sure,
3. Through each won-der of fair days God Him-self ex-press-es;

Life in all her grow-ing powers Towards the light is striv-ing:
Now be-stir-ring, green and strong, Find in growth their plea-sure:
Beau-ty fol-lows all His ways, As the world He bless-es:

Gone the i-ron touch of cold, Win-ter time and frost time,
All the world with beau-ty fills, Gold the green en-hanc-ing;
So, as He re-news the earth, Art-ist with-out ri-val,

Seed-lings, work-ing through the mould, Now make up for lost time.
Flowers make glee a-mong the hills, Set the mead-ows danc-ing.
In His grace of glad new birth We must seek re-viv-al.

Words from the *Oxford Book of Carols* by permission of Oxford University Press.
Music used by permission of Ernest MacMillan.

POWER OF GOD IN NATURE

96 The Spacious Firmament

Psalm 19
Joseph Addison, 1712 (1672-1719)

CREATION L.M.D.
Arr. from F. J. Haydn, 1798 (1732-1809)

1. The spa-cious firm-a-ment on high, With all the blue, e-the-real sky, And span-gled heavens, a shin-ing frame, Their great O-rig-i-nal pro-claim. Th' un-wea-ried sun from day to day Does his Cre-a-tor's power dis-play, And pub-lish-

2. Soon as the eve-ning shades pre-vail, The moon takes up the won-drous tale; And night-ly to the lis-tening earth Re-peats the sto-ry of her birth; While all the stars that round her burn, And all the plan-ets in their turn, Con-firm the

3. What though in sol-emn si-lence all Move round the dark ter-res-trial ball? What though no re-al voice nor sound A-mid their ra-diant orbs be found? In rea-son's ear they all re-joice And ut-ter forth a glo-rious voice, For-ev-er

POWER OF GOD IN NATURE

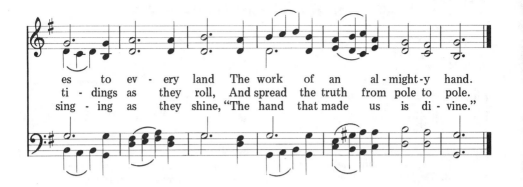

es to ev - ery land The work of an al - might-y hand.
ti - dings as they roll, And spread the truth from pole to pole.
sing - ing as they shine, "The hand that made us is di - vine."

Lord of the Boundless Curves of Space 97

SAN ROCCO C.M.

Albert F. Bayly (1901-1984)

Derek Williams (1945-   )

Unison

1. Lord of the bound-less curves of space And time's deep mys - te - ry,
2. Your mind con-ceived the gal - ax - y, Each at - om's se - cret planned,
3. Yours is the im - age stamped on man, Though marred by man's own sin;
4. Give us to know Your truth; but more, The strength to do Your will;

To Your cre - a - tive might we trace All na-ture's en - er - gy.
And ev - ery age of his - to - ry Your pur-pose, Lord, has spanned.
And Yours the lib - er - at - ing plan A - gain his soul to win.
Un - til the love our souls a - dore Shall all our be - ing fill.

Words by permission of Oxford University Press. Music copyright by Derek Williams. Used by permission.

Alternate tune, AZMON, No. 250

POWER OF GOD IN NATURE

98   Can You Count the Stars?

Wilhelm Hey (1789-1854)
Tr. H. W. Dulcken, vs. 1, 3
v. 2, anon.

8.7.8.7.8.8.7.7.
German Folk Tune

1. Can you count the stars that bright-ly Twin-kle in the mid-night sky?
2. Can you count the wings now flash-ing In the sun-shine's gold-en light?
3. Do you know how man-y chil-dren Rise each morn-ing blithe and gay?

Can you count the clouds, so light - ly O'er the mead - ows float-ing by?
Can you count the fish - es splash-ing In the cool - ing wa - ters bright?
Can you count their jol - ly voic - es, Sing-ing sweet - ly day by day?

God, the Lord, doth mark their num-ber With His eyes that nev - er slum-ber;
God, the Lord, a name hath giv - en, To all crea-tures un - der heav - en;
God hears all the hap - py voic - es, In their mer - ry songs re - joic - es;

He hath made them ev - ery one, He hath made them ev - ery one.
He hath named them ev - ery one, He hath named them ev - ery one.
And He loves them, ev - ery one, And He loves them, ev - ery one.

POWER OF GOD IN NATURE

God Will Take Care of You

1 Peter 5:7
Civilla D. Martin (1869-1948) alt.

C.M.Ref.
W. Stillman Martin (1862-1935)

1. Be not dis-mayed what-e'er be-tide, God will take care of you;
2. Through days of toil when your heart doth fail, God will take care of you;
3. All you may need He will pro-vide, God will take care of you;
4. No mat-ter what may be the test, God will take care of you;

Be-neath His wings of love a-bide, God will take care of you.
When dan-gers fierce your path as-sail, God will take care of you.
Noth-ing you ask will be de-nied, God will take care of you.
Lean, wea-ry one, up-on His breast, God will take care of you.

Refrain

God will take care of you, Through ev-ery day, o'er all the way;

He will take care of you, God will take care of you.

FAITHFULNESS OF GOD

100   Great Is Thy Faithfulness

Lam. 3:22,23
Thomas O. Chisholm, 1923 (1866-1960)

FAITHFULNESS 11.10.11.10. Ref.
William M. Runyan, 1925 (1870-1957)

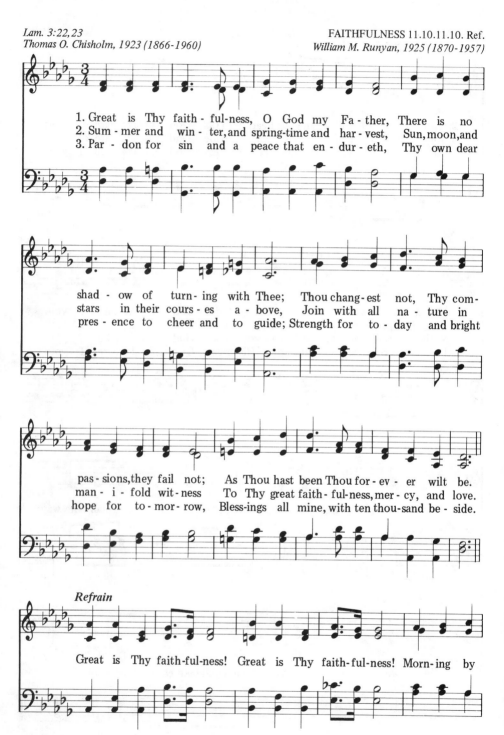

1. Great is Thy faith - ful-ness, O God my Fa - ther, There is no
2. Sum - mer and win - ter, and spring-time and har - vest, Sun, moon, and
3. Par - don for sin and a peace that en - dur - eth, Thy own dear

shad - ow of turn - ing with Thee; Thou chang - est not, Thy com-
stars in their cours - es a - bove, Join with all na - ture in
pres - ence to cheer and to guide; Strength for to - day and bright

pas - sions, they fail not; As Thou hast been Thou for - ev - er wilt be.
man - i - fold wit - ness To Thy great faith - ful-ness, mer - cy, and love.
hope for to - mor - row, Bless-ings all mine, with ten thou-sand be - side.

Refrain

Great is Thy faith-ful-ness! Great is Thy faith-ful-ness! Morn - ing by

FAITHFULNESS OF GOD

morn-ing new mer-cies I see; All I have need-ed Thy
hand hath pro-vid-ed, Great is Thy faith-ful-ness!Lord un-to me!

Children of the Heavenly Father 101

Carolina Sandell Berg, 1858 (1832-1903)
Tr. by Ernest W. Olson, 1925 (1870-1958)

TRYGGARE KAN INGEN VARA L.M.
Swedish Folk Melody

1. Chil-dren of the heaven-ly Fa-ther Safe-ly in His bos-om gath-er;
2. God His own doth tend and nour-ish, In His ho-ly love they flour-ish;
3. Nei-ther life nor death shall ev-er From the Lord His chil-dren sev-er;
4. Praise the Lord in joy-ful num-bers, Your Pro-tec-tor nev-er slum-bers;
5. Though He giv-eth or He tak-eth, God His chil-dren ne'er for-sak-eth;

Nest-ling bird nor star in heav-en Such a ref-uge e'er was giv-en.
From all e-vil things He spares them, In His might-y arms He bears them.
Un-to them His grace He show-eth, And their sor-rows all He know-eth.
At the will of your De-fend-er Ev-ery foe-man must sur-ren-der.
His the lov-ing pur-pose sole-ly To pre-serve them pure and ho-ly.

FAITHFULNESS OF GOD

102 Unto the Hills

Psalm 121
John Campbell 1866 (1845-1914)

YOU YANGS 10.4.10.4.10.10.
James Bingham, 1984 (1945-   )

Unison

1. Un - to the hills a - round shall I lift up my long - ing
2. He will not suf - fer that thy foot be moved; safe shalt Thou
3. Je - ho - vah is Him - self thy keep - er true, thy change-less
4. From ev - ery e - vil shall He keep thy soul, from ev - ery

eyes? O whence for me shall my sal - va - tion come, from whence a -
be. No care - less slum - ber shall His eye - lids close, who keep - eth
shade. Je - ho - vah thy de - fense on thy right hand Him - self hath
sin; Je - ho - vah shall pre - serve thy go - ing out, thy com - ing

rise? From God the Lord doth come my cer - tain
thee. Be - hold our God, the Lord, He slum-bereth
made. And thee no sun by day shall ev - er
in. A - bove thee watch - ing, He, whom we a -

aid, | From God | the Lord, | who heav'n and earth hath | made.
ne'er, | Who keep - eth Is - | rael in His ho - ly | care.
smite, | No moon | shall harm | thee in the si - lent | night.
dore, | Shall keep | thee hence - | forth, yea, for - ev - er - | more.

O God, Our Help

103

Psalm 90
Isaac Watts, 1719

ST. ANNE C.M.
William Croft, 1708

1. O God, our help in a - ges past, Our hope for years to come,
2. Un - der the shad - ow of Thy throne Still may we dwell se - cure;
3. Be - fore the hills in or - der stood, Or earth re-ceived her frame,
4. A thou-sand a - ges, in Thy sight, Are like an eve - ning gone;
5. O God, our help in a - ges past, Our hope for years to come;

Our shel - ter from the storm - y blast, And our e - ter - nal home!
Suf - fi - cient is Thine arm a - lone, And our de - fense is sure.
From ev - er - last - ing Thou art God, To end-less years the same.
Short as the watch that ends the night, Be - fore the ris - ing sun.
Be Thou our guide while life shall last, And our e - ter - nal home!

FAITHFULNESS OF GOD

104 My Shepherd Will Supply My Need

RESIGNATION C.M.D.

From Southern Harmony, *1835*
Harm. by Virgil Thomson (1896-)
Adapt. by Melvin West, 1984 (1930-)

Psalm 23
Isaac Watts, 1719 (1674-1748)

1. My Shep-herd will sup-ply my need, Je-ho-vah is His name.
2. When I walk through the shades of death, Thy pres-ence is my stay;
3. The sure pro-vi-sions of my God At-tend me all my days;

In pas-tures fresh He makes me feed Be-side the liv-ing stream.
A word of Thy sup-port-ing breath Drives all my fears a-way.
O may Thy house be mine a-bode And all my work be praise.

He brings my wan-d'ring spir-it back When I for-sake His ways,
Thy hand in sight of all my foes Doth still my ta-ble spread;
There would I find a set-tled rest While oth-ers go and come;

And leads me, for His mer-cy's sake, In paths of truth and grace.
My cup with bless-ings o-ver-flows, Thine oil a-noints my head.
No more a strang-er or a guest, But like a child at home.

FAITHFULNESS OF GOD

Sing to the Great Jehovah's Praise

LOBT GOTT IHR CHRISTEN C.M.

Charles Wesley (1707-1788)

Nikolaus Herman (c. 1485-1561)

1. Sing to the great Je - ho - vah's praise! All praise to Him be - longs; Who kind - ly length - ens out our days, In - spires our choic - est songs, In - spires our choic - est songs.

2. His prov - i - dence hath brought us through An - oth - er var - ious year; We all, with vows and an - thems new, Be - fore our God ap - pear, Be - fore our God ap - pear.

3. O God, Thy mer - cies past we own, And Thy con - tin - ued care; To Thee pre - sent - ing through Thy Son What - e'er we have and are, What - e'er we have and are.

GRACE AND MERCY OF GOD

106   Give to Our God Immortal Praise

Psalm 136
Isaac Watts (1674-1748)

DUNEDIN L.M.
Vernon Griffiths (1894-   )

Unison

1. Give   to   our   God   im - mor - tal   praise;   Mer - cy   and
2. Give   to   the   Lord   of   lords re - nown,   The King   of
3. He   sent   His   Son   with power to   save   From guilt and
4. Thro' this vain   world   He guides our   feet,   And leads us

truth   are   all   His   ways: Won - ders of grace   to   God be -
kings   with   glo - ry   crown: His mer - cies ev - er   shall en -
dark - ness and the   grave: Won - ders of grace   to   God be -
to   His heav'n - ly   seat: His mer - cies ev - er   shall en -

long,   Re - peat His   mer - cies   in   your   song.
dure   When lords and   kings are   known   no   more.
long,   Re - peat His   mer - cies   in   your   song.
dure,   When this vain   world shall   be   no   more.

Alternate tune, DUKE STREET, Nos. 82, 227

107   God Moves in a Mysterious Way

John 13:7
William Cowper (1731-1800)

DUNDEE C.M.
Scottish Psalter, 1615

1. God moves in   a   mys - te - rious way His won - ders to per - form;
2. Ye   fear - ful saints, fresh cour - age take; The clouds ye   so much dread
3. Judge not the Lord   by   fee - ble sense, But trust Him for His   grace;
4. His   pur - pos - es   will rip - en fast, Un - fold - ing ev - ery   hour;
5. Blind un - be - lief   is   sure to   err, And scan His work in   vain;

GRACE AND MERCY OF GOD

He plants His foot-steps in the sea, And rides up-on the storm.
Are big with mer - cy, and shall break In bless-ings on your head.
Be - hind a frown-ing prov - i - dence He hides a smil-ing face.
The bud may have a bit - ter taste, But sweet will be the flower.
God is His own in - ter-pret - er, And He will make it plain.

Amazing Grace

108

1 Chron. 17:16,17
John Newton, 1779 (1725-1807)
St. 5, John Rees, c. 1859

NEW BRITAIN C.M.
Virginia Harmony, *1831*
Arr. by Robert J. Batastini (1942-)

1. A - maz - ing grace! how sweet the sound, That
2. 'Twas grace that taught my heart to fear, And
3. The Lord has prom - ised good to me, His
4. Through man - y dan - gers, toils, and snares, I
5. When we've been there ten thou - sand years, Bright

saved a wretch like me! I once was lost, but
grace my fears re - lieved; How pre - cious did that
word my hope se - cures; He will my shield and
have al - read - y come; 'Tis grace hath brought me
shin - ing as the sun, We've no less days to

now am found, Was blind, but now I see.
grace ap - pear The hour I first be - lieved!
por - tion be As long as life en - dures.
safe thus far, And grace will lead me home.
sing God's praise Than when we'd first be - gun.

GRACE AND MERCY OF GOD

109 Marvelous Grace

Julia H. Johnston, 1911 (1849-1919)

Daniel B. Towner, 1911 (1850-1919)

9.9.9.9.Ref.

1. Mar-vel-ous grace of our lov-ing Lord, Grace that ex-ceeds our
2. Sin and de-spair, like the sea-waves cold, Threat-en the soul with
3. Mar-vel-ous, in-fi-nite, match-less grace, Free-ly be-stowed on

sin and our guilt! Yon-der on Cal-va-ry's mount out-poured—
in-fi-nite loss; Grace that is great-er— yes, grace un-told—
all who be-lieve! You that are long-ing to see His face,

There where the blood of the Lamb was spilt. Grace, grace,
Points to the Ref-uge, the might-y Cross.
Will you this mo-ment His grace re-ceive? Mar-vel-ous grace,

Refrain

God's grace, Grace that will par-don and cleanse with-in; Grace,
in-fi-nite grace, Mar-vel-ous

grace, God's grace, Grace that is great-er than all our sin!
grace, in-fi-nite grace,

GRACE AND MERCY OF GOD

God's Free Mercy Streameth

110

Eccl. 11:7
William W. How, 1871 (1823-1897)

RUTH 6.5.6.5.D.
Samuel Smith, 1865 (1821-1917)

1. God's free mer-cy stream-eth O-ver all the world,
2. Sum-mer suns are glow-ing O-ver land and sea;
3. Lord, up-on our blind-ness Thy pure ra-diance pour;.
4. We will nev-er doubt Thee, Tho' Thou veil Thy light;

And His ban-ner gleam-eth, By His church un-furled;
Hap-py light is flow-ing, Boun-ti-ful and free;
For Thy lov-ing-kind-ness We would love Thee more;
Life is dark with-out Thee, Death with Thee is bright.

Broad and deep and glo-rious, As the heaven a-bove,
Ev-ery-thing re-joic-es In the mel-low rays;
And when clouds are drift-ing Dark a-cross the sky,
Light of light, shine o'er us On our pil-grim way,

Shines in might vic-to-rious His e-ter-nal love.
Earth's ten thou-sand voic-es Swell the psalm of praise.
Then, the veil up-lift-ing, Fa-ther, be Thou nigh.
Go Thou still be-fore us To the end-less day.

GRACE AND MERCY OF GOD

111 It Took a Miracle

John W. Peterson (1921-   )

MONTROSE L.M.Ref.
John W. Peterson, 1948

1. My Fa - ther is om - nip - o - tent, And that you can't de - ny;
2. Though here His glo - ry has been shown, We still can't ful - ly see
3. The Bi - ble tells us of His power And wis - dom all way through,

A God of might and mir - a - cles— 'Tis writ - ten in the sky.
The won - ders of His might, His throne—'Twill take e - ter - ni - ty.
And ev - ery lit - tle bird and flower Are tes - ti - mo - nies too.

Refrain

It took a mir - a - cle to put the stars in place, It took a
mir - a - cle to hang the world in space; But when He saved my soul,

GRACE AND MERCY OF GOD

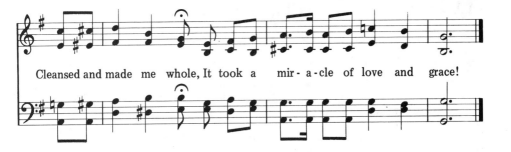

Cleansed and made me whole, It took a mir-a-cle of love and grace!

Let Us With a Gladsome Mind 112

MONKLAND 7.7.7.7.
John Antes (1740-1811)
Arr. by John B. Wilkes, 1861 (1785-1869)

Psalm 136
John Milton, 1623 (1608-1674)

1. Let us with a glad-some mind Praise the Lord, for He is kind:
2. He, with all-com-mand-ing might, Filled the new-made world with light:
3. All things liv-ing He does feed; His full hand sup-plies their need:
4. Let us then with glad-some mind Praise the Lord, for He is kind:

For His mer-cies shall en-dure, Ev-er faith-ful, ev-er sure.

113

As Pants the Hart

Psalm 42:1-5
Nahum Tate (1652-1715)
and Nicholas Brady (1659-1726)
in the New Version, 1696

MARTYRDOM C.M.
Hugh Wilson (1766-1824)
Adapt. by Robert A. Smith, 1825 (1780-1829)

1. As pants the hart for cool-ing streams When heat-ed in the chase,
2. For Thee, my God, the liv-ing God, My thirst-y soul doth pine:
3. Why rest-less, why cast down, my soul? Hope still, and thou shalt sing
4. To Fa-ther, Son, and Ho-ly Ghost, The God whom we a-dore,

So longs my soul, O God, for Thee, And Thy re-fresh-ing grace.
O when shall I be-hold Thy face, Thou Maj-es-ty di-vine?
The praise of Him who is thy God, Thy health's e-ter-nal spring.
Be glo-ry, as it was, is now, And shall be ev-er-more.

114

There's a Wideness

WELLESLEY 8.7.8.7.
Frederick W. Faber, 1854 (1814-1863)
Lizzie S. Tourjee, 1877 (1858-1913)

1. There's a wide-ness in God's mer-cy, Like the wide-ness of the sea;
2. There is wel-come for the sin-ner, And more gra-ces for the good;
3. For the love of God is broad-er Than the meas-ure of man's mind,
4. If our love were but more sim-ple, We should take Him at His word;

There's a kind-ness in His jus-tice, Which is more than lib-er-ty.
There is mer-cy with the Sav-ior; There is heal-ing in His blood.
And the heart of the E-ter-nal Is most won-der-ful-ly kind.
And our lives would be all sun-shine In the sweet-ness of our Lord.

GRACE AND MERCY OF GOD

O Come, O Come, Immanuel 115

From the Latin, 9th century
Stanza 1 tr. by John M. Neale (1818-1866)
Stanzas 2, 3 tr. by Henry S. Coffin (1877-1954)

VENI EMMANUEL 8.8.8.8.8.8.
French Processional, 15th century

1. O come, O come, Im - man - u - el, And ran - som cap - tive
2. O come, Thou Wis - dom from on high, And or - der all things,
3. O come, De - sire of na - tions, bind All peo - ples in one

Is - ra - el That mourns in lone - ly ex - ile here
far and nigh; To us the path of knowl - edge show,
heart and mind; Bid en - vy, strife, and quar - rels cease;

Refrain

Un - til the Son of God ap - pear.
And cause us in her ways to go. Re joice! Re joice! Im -
Fill the whole world with heav - en's peace.

man - u - el Shall come to thee, O Is - ra - el!

FIRST ADVENT

Of the Father's Love Begotten

Aurelius Clemens Prudentius (348-c.413)
Tr. by John M. Neale, stanza 1 (1818-1866)
Tr. by Henry W. Baker, stanzas 2,3 (1821-1877)

DIVINUM MYSTERIUM 8.7.8.7.8.7.7.
13th century plainsong, Mode V

1. Of the Fa - ther's love be - got - ten, Ere the worlds be - gan to be,
2. O ye heights of heaven a - dore Him; An - gel hosts, His prais - es sing;
3. Christ, to Thee with God the Fa - ther And, O Ho - ly Ghost, to Thee,

He is Al - pha and O - me - ga, He the source, the end - ing He,
Powers, do - min - ions, bow be - fore Him, And ex - tol our God and King;
Hymn and chant and high thanks - giv - ing And un - wea - ried prais - es be.

Of the things that are, that have been, And that fu - ture
Let no tongue on earth be si - lent, Ev - ery voice in
Hon - or, glo - ry, and do - min - ion, And e - ter - nal

years shall see, Ev - er - more and ev - er - more!
con - cert ring, Ev - er - more and ev - er - more!
vic - to - ry, Ev - er - more and ev - er - more! A - men.

The Advent of Our God 117

Charles Coffin (1676-1749)
Tr. by John Chandler (1806-1876) and others

FESTAL SONG S.M.
William H. Walter (1825-1893)

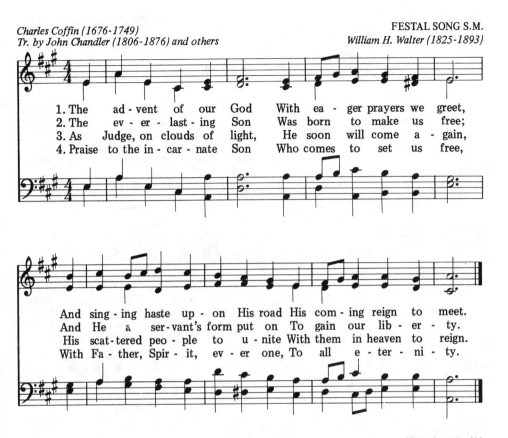

1. The ad-vent of our God With ea-ger prayers we greet,
2. The ev-er-last-ing Son Was born to make us free;
3. As Judge, on clouds of light, He soon will come a-gain,
4. Praise to the in-car-nate Son Who comes to set us free,

And sing-ing haste up-on His road His com-ing reign to meet.
And He a ser-vant's form put on To gain our lib-er-ty.
His scat-tered peo-ple to u-nite With them in heaven to reign.
With Fa-ther, Spir-it, ev-er one, To all e-ter-ni-ty.

Higher key, No. 615

FIRST ADVENT

118 The First Noel

THE FIRST NOEL Irregular Ref.
Wm. Sandy's Christmas Carols, *1833*

Traditional English carol, c. 1823

1. The first no - el the an - gel did say Was to cer - tain poor
2. They look - ed up and saw a star Shin-ing in the
3. And by the light of that same star, Three wise men
4. This star drew nigh to the north - west, O'er Beth - le -
5. Then en - tered in those wise men three, Full rev - er - ent -

shepherds in fields as they lay; In fields where they lay keep-ing their sheep,
east, be - yond them far, And to the earth it gave great light,
came from coun - try far; To seek for a king was their in - tent,
hem it took its rest, And there it did both stop and stay,
ly up - on the knee, And of - fered there, in His pres - ence,

Refrain

On a cold win-ter's night that was so deep.
And so it con - tin -ued both day and night.
And to fol- low the star wher - ev - er it went. No - el, No -
Right o - ver the place where Je - sus lay.
Their gold, and myrrh, and frank - in - cense.

el, No - el, No - el, Born is the King of Is - ra - el.

BIRTH

Luke 2
James Montgomery, 1816 (1771-1854)

REGENT SQUARE 8.7.8.7.8.7.
Henry Smart, 1867 (1813-1879)

1. An - gels from the realms of glo - ry, Wing your flight o'er
2. Shep - herds, in the field a - bid - ing, Watch - ing o'er your
3. Sag - es, leave your con - tem - pla - tions, Bright - er vi - sions
4. Saints, be - fore the al - tar bend - ing, Watch - ing long in

all the earth; Ye, who sang cre - a - tion's sto - ry,
flocks by night, God with man is now re - sid - ing;
beam a - far; Seek the great De - sire of na - tions;
hope and fear, Sud - den - ly the Lord, de - scend - ing,

Now pro - claim Mes - si - ah's birth; Come and wor - ship,
Yon - der shines the In - fant Light; Come and wor - ship,
Ye have seen His na - tal 'star; Come and wor - ship,
In His tem - ple shall ap - pear; Come and wor - ship,

Come and wor - ship, Wor - ship Christ, the new - born King.
Come and wor - ship, Wor - ship Christ, the new - born King.
Come and wor - ship, Wor - ship Christ, the new - born King.
Come and wor - ship, Wor - ship Christ, the new - born King.

BIRTH

120   There's a Song in the Air

Josiah G. Holland, 1872 (1819-1881)

CHRISTMAS SONG 6.6.6.6.12.12.
Karl P. Harrington, 1904 (1861-1953)

1. There's a song in the air! There's a star in the sky!
2. There's a tu - mult of joy O'er the won - der - ful birth,
3. In the light of that star Lie the a - ges im - pearled;
4. We re - joice in the light, And we ech - o the song

There's a moth - er's deep prayer And a ba - by's low cry!
For the vir - gin's sweet boy Is the Lord of the earth.
And that song from a - far Has swept o - ver the world.
That comes down through the night From the heav - en - ly throng.

And the star rains its fire while the beau - ti - ful sing,
Aye! the star rains its fire while the beau - ti - ful sing,
Ev - ery hearth is a - flame, and the beau - ti - ful sing
Aye! we shout to the love - ly e - van - gel they bring,

For the man - ger of Beth - le - hem cra - dles a King!
For the man - ger of Beth - le - hem cra - dles a King!
In the homes of the na - tions that Je - sus is King!
And we greet in His cra - dle our Sav - ior and King!

BIRTH

Go, Tell It on the Mountain

121

American Negro Spiritual
Adapt. by John W. Work (1901-1967)

7.6.7.6.Ref.
Arr. by John W. Work

Refrain
Unison

Go, tell it on the moun - tain, O - ver the hills and ev - ery-where:

Fine

Go, tell it on the moun - tain That Je - sus Christ is born!

Harmony

1. While shep-herds kept their watch-ing O'er si - lent flocks by night, Be -
2. The shep-herds feared and trem-bled When lo! A - bove the earth Rang
3. Down in a low - ly man - ger The hum - ble Christ was born, And

D. C.

hold through-out the heav - ens There shone a ho - ly light.
out the an - gel cho - rus That hailed our Sav - ior's birth.
brought us God's sal - va - tion That bless - ed Christ-mas morn.

BIRTH

122   Hark! the Herald Angels Sing

MENDELSSOHN 7.7.7.7.D.Ref.
Arr. from Mendelssohn, 1840 (1809-1847)
By William H. Cummings, 1856 (1831-1915)

Luke 2:14
Charles Wesley, 1739 (1707-1788)

1. Hark! the her - ald an - gels sing, "Glo - ry to the new-born King;
2. Christ, by high - est heaven a - dored, Christ the ev - er - last - ing Lord;
3. Hail! the heaven - born Prince of Peace! Hail! the Sun of Righ - teous-ness!

Peace on earth, and mer - cy mild, God and sin - ners rec - on - ciled!"
In the man - ger born a king, While a - dor - ing an - gels sing,
Life and light to all He brings, Risen with heal - ing in His wings.

Joy - ful, all ye na - tions, rise, Join the tri - umph of the skies;
"Peace on earth, to men good will;" Bid the trem - bling soul be still,
Mild He lays His glo - ry by, Born that man no more may die,

With th'an-gel - ic host pro-claim, "Christ is born in Beth - le - hem!"
Christ on earth has come to dwell, Je - sus, our Im - man - u - el!
Born to raise the sons of earth, Born to give them sec - ond birth.

BIRTH

Refrain, after each stanza.

Hark! the her-ald an-gels sing, "Glo-ry to the new-born King."

As With Gladness Men of Old 123

DIX 7.7.7.7.7.7.

Matt. 2:1-11
William C. Dix (1837-1898)

From Conrad Kocher, 1838 (1786-1872)
Arr. by Melvin West, 1984 (1930-   )

Unison

1. As with glad-ness men of old   Did the guid-ing star be-hold,
2. As with joy-ful steps they sped   To that low-ly man-ger bed,
3. As they of-fered gifts most rare   At that man-ger rude and bare,
4. Ho-ly Je-sus, ev-ery day   Keep us in the nar-row way;

As with joy they hailed its light,   Lead-ing on-ward, beam-ing bright,
There to bend the knee be-fore   Him whom heav'n and earth a-dore,
So may we with ho-ly joy,   Pure, and free from sin's al-loy,
And, when earth-ly things are past,   Bring our ran-somed souls at last

So, most gra-cious Lord, may we   Ev-er-more be led to Thee.
So may we with will-ing feet   Ev-er seek Thy mer-cy seat.
All our cost-liest trea-sures bring, Christ, to Thee our heav'n-ly King.
Where they need no star to guide, Where no clouds Thy glo-ry hide.

Harmony setting, No. 565

BIRTH

124   Away in a Manger

CRADLE SONG 11.11.11.11.

Anon. from Little Children's Book, *1885*

William J. Kirkpatrick (1838-1921)

1. A - way in a man - ger, no crib for a bed,
2. The cat - tle are low - ing, the ba - by a - wakes,
3. Be near me, Lord Je - sus; I ask Thee to stay

The lit - tle Lord Je - sus laid down His sweet head.
But lit - tle Lord Je - sus no cry - ing He makes.
Close by me for - ev - er, and love me, I pray.

The stars in the bright sky looked down where He lay,
I love Thee, Lord Je - sus! look down from the sky,
Bless all the dear chil - dren in Thy ten - der care,

The lit - tle Lord Je - sus a - sleep on the hay.
And stay by my side till the morn - ing is nigh.
And fit us for heav - en, to live with Thee there.

Arr. from the *Australian Hymnal* by permission of the Australian Hymn Book Co.

BIRTH

Joy to the World

125

ANTIOCH C.M.

Psalm 98:4-9
Isaac Watts, 1719 (1674-1748)

Arr. from Handel's Messiah, 1742 (1685-1759)
by Lowell Mason, 1830 (1792-1872)

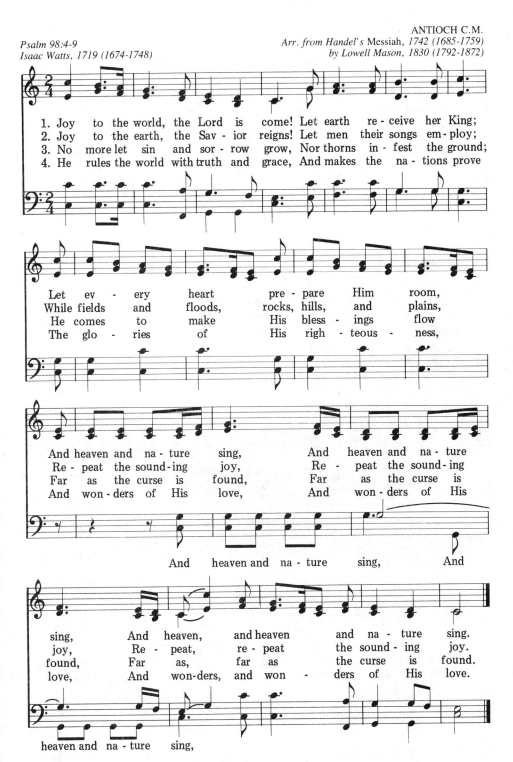

1. Joy to the world, the Lord is come! Let earth re-ceive her King;
2. Joy to the earth, the Sav-ior reigns! Let men their songs em-ploy;
3. No more let sin and sor-row grow, Nor thorns in-fest the ground;
4. He rules the world with truth and grace, And makes the na-tions prove

Let ev-ery heart pre-pare Him room,
While fields and floods, rocks, hills, and plains,
He comes to make His bless-ings flow
The glo-ries of His righ-teous-ness,

And heaven and na-ture sing, And heaven and na-ture
Re-peat the sound-ing joy, Re-peat the sound-ing
Far as the curse is found, Far as the curse is
And won-ders of His love, And won-ders of His

And heaven and na-ture sing, And

sing, And heaven, and heaven and na-ture sing.
joy, Re-peat, re-peat the sound-ing joy.
found, Far as, far as the curse is found.
love, And won-ders, and won-ders of His love.

heaven and na-ture sing,

BIRTH

126 In the Bleak Midwinter

UINTA Irregular

Christina Rossetti, (1830-1894) alt.

Wayne Hooper, 1964 (1920-   )

1. In the bleak mid - win - ter Frost- y wind made moan;
2. An - gels and arch - an - gels May have gath- ered there,
3. What can I give Him, Poor as I am?

Earth stood hard as i - ron, Wa - ter like a stone;
Cher - u - bim and ser - a - phim Thronged the air:
If I were a shep - herd I would bring a lamb;

Snow had fall - en, snow on snow, Snow on snow,
But His moth- er on - ly In her maid-en bliss,
If I were a wise man I would do my part;

In the bleak mid - win - ter, Long a - go.
Wor-shiped the be - lov - ed With a kiss.
Yet what can I give Him? Give my heart.

Music copyright © 1984 by Wayne Hooper.

Alternate tune, CRANHAM, No. 224

BIRTH

Infant Holy, Infant Lowly

127

Luke 2:7-11
Polish carol
Tr. by Edith M. Gellibrand Reed, 1921 (1885-1933)

W ZLOBIE LEZY Irregular
Polish carol melody, c. 13th century

1. In - fant ho - ly, in - fant low - ly, For His bed a cat - tle stall;
2. Flocks were sleep - ing, shep-herds keep-ing Vig - il till the morn-ing new;

Ox - en low - ing, lit - tle know-ing Christ the babe is Lord of all;
Saw the glo - ry, heard the sto - ry, Tid - ings of the gos - pel true;

Swift are wing-ing an - gels sing - ing, No - els ring - ing, tid - ings bring-ing,
Thus re - joic - ing, free from sor-row, Prais - es voic - ing greet the mor-row,

Christ the babe is Lord of all, Christ the babe is Lord of all.
Christ the babe was born for you, Christ the babe was born for you.

BIRTH

128 Break Forth, O Beauteous Heavenly Light

Johann Rist (1607-1667)
Norman E. Johnson, st. 2 (1928-1983)

ERMUNTRE DICH 8.7.8.7.8.8.8.7.7.
Johann Schop (1590-1664)
Arr. by J. S. Bach (1685-1750)

1. Break forth, O beau-teous heaven-ly light, And ush-er in the morn - ing; Ye shep-herds, shrink not with af - fright, But hear the an - gel's warn - ing. This Child, now weak in in - fan - cy, Our con - fi-dence and joy shall be, The power of Sa - tan

2. Break forth, O beau-teous heaven-ly light, To her - ald our sal - va - tion; He stoops to earth—the God of might, Our hope and ex - pec - ta - tion. He comes in hu - man flesh to dwell, Our God with us, Im - man - u - el, The night of dark-ness

BIRTH

break - ing, Our peace e - ter - nal mak - ing.
end - ing, Our fall - en race be - friend - ing.

As It Fell Upon a Night   129

PUER NOBIS NASCITUR 7.6.7.7.
From Piae Cantiones, *1582*
Arr. by Geoffrey Shaw (1879-1943)

Katherine K. Davis, 1942 (1892-1980)

1. As it fell up - on a night   In the win - ter weath - er,   An - gels bright in star - ry height Be - gan to sing to - geth - er
2. Shep - herds sleep - ing on the plain   Woke to see the glo - ry,   All a - mazed they stood and gazed And heard the an - gels' sto - ry.
3. Un - to you a child is born   In a man - ger low - ly,   Hum - ble, He, yet born to be The King of Love most ho - ly.
4. Hap - py an - gels from a - far,   Cease your sing - ing nev - er!   In ex - cel - sis glo - ri - a! For - ev - er and for - ev - er.

BIRTH

130 It Came Upon the Midnight Clear

Luke 2:13,14
Edmund H. Sears, 1849 (1810-1876)

CAROL C.M.D.
Richard S. Willis, 1850 (1819-1900)

1. It came up-on the mid-night clear, That glo-rious song of old,
2. Still through the clo-ven skies they come, With peace-ful wings un-furled,
3. And ye, be-neath life's crush-ing load, Whose forms are bend-ing low,

From an-gels bend-ing near the earth To touch their harps of gold:
And still their heav-enly mu-sic floats O'er all the wea-ry world;
Who toil a-long the climb-ing way With pain-ful steps and slow—

"Peace on the earth, good will to men, From heaven's all-gra-cious King;"
A-bove its sad and low-ly plains They bend on hov-ering wing,
Look now! for glad and gold-en hours Come swift-ly on the wing;

The world in sol-emn still-ness lay, To hear the an-gels sing.
And ev-er o'er its Ba-bel sounds The bless-ed an-gels sing.
O rest be-side the wea-ry road, And hear the an-gels sing.

BIRTH

Lo, How a Rose E'er Blooming

131

ES IST EIN ROS 7.6.7.6.6.7.6.

15th century
Tr. by Theodore Baker (1851-1934)

15th century
Arr. by Michael Praetorius, 1609 (1571-1621)

1. Lo, how a rose e'er bloom - ing From ten - der stem hath
2. I - sa - iah 'twas fore - told it, The Rose I have in

sprung, Of Jes - se's lin - eage com - ing As men of old have
mind, With Ma - ry we be - held it, The vir - gin moth - er

sung. It came, a flower - et bright,
kind. To show God's love a - right

A - mid the
She bore to

cold of win - ter When half spent was the night.
them a Sav - ior, When half spent was the night.

132   O Come, All Ye Faithful

Anonymous. Latin, 18th century
Tr. by Frederick Oakeley, 1841 (1802-1880), and others

ADESTE FIDELES Irregular, Ref.
John F. Wade's Cantus Diversi, *1751*

1. O come, all ye faith-ful, joy-ful and tri-um-phant, O come ye, O come ye to Beth-le-hem! Come and be-hold Him, born the King of an-gels!

2. Sing, choirs of an-gels, sing in ex-ul-ta-tion, O sing, all ye cit-i-zens of heaven a-bove! Glo-ry to God, all glo-ry in the high-est!

3. Yea, Lord, we greet Thee, born this hap-py morn-ing, Je-sus, to Thee be all glo-ry given; Word of the Fa-ther, now in flesh ap-pear-ing!

Refrain

O come, let us a-dore Him, O come, let us a-dore Him, O come, let us a-dore Him, Christ, the Lord!

BIRTH

Now Is Born the Divine Christ Child 133

IL EST NÉ 8.10.8.8.
18th century French carol
Arr. by Wayne Hooper, 1984 (1920-   )

Traditional French carol

Now is born the di-vine Christ child, Play the mu-sette, play the tune-ful o-boe, Now is born the di-vine Christ child, Sing we all and re-joice this day.

1. He was born in a sta-ble bare, On bed of straw how He sleeps so sound-ly, He was born in a sta-ble bare, Let us wor-ship and to Him bow.
2. Ag-es long since are past and gone, When the wise men fore-told His com-ing, Ag-es long since are past and gone, When the wise men fore-told His birth.

Fine

D.C.

BIRTH

134   O Jesus Sweet

O JESULEIN SÜSS 8.8.8.8.8.8.

Valentin Thilo? 1650
Tr. E. Harold Geer, 1933 (1886-1957)

Auserlesene...Kirchengesänge, *1623*
Harm. by J. S. Bach (1685-1750)
Arr. by E. Harold Geer, 1953

1. O Je - sus sweet, O Je - sus mild, Thy Fa - ther's
2. O Je - sus sweet, O Je - sus mild, With joy hast
3. O Je - sus sweet, O Je - sus mild, Thou art love's
4. O Je - sus sweet, O Je - sus mild, Help us to

will hast Thou ful - filled; For Thou hast left Thy
Thou the whole world filled; Thou com - est down from
im - age un - de - filed. In - flame our hearts with
do as Thou hast willed. What - e'er we have be -

heaven - ly throne Our low - ly state to make Thine
heav - en's hall To com - fort us whom tears en -
love's pure fire, That we may share Thy heart's de -
longs to Thee: O may we ev - er faith - ful

own. O Je - sus sweet, O Je - sus mild.
thrall. O Je - sus sweet, O Je - sus mild.
sire. O Je - sus sweet, O Je - sus mild.
be. O Je - sus sweet, O Je - sus mild.

BIRTH

O Little Town of Bethlehem 135

Luke 2:13,14
Phillips Brooks, 1868 (1835-1893)

ST. LOUIS 8.6.8.6.7.6.8.6.
L. H. Redner, 1868 (1831-1908)

1. O lit-tle town of Beth-le-hem, How still we see thee lie!
2. For Christ is born of Ma-ry; And gath-ered all a-bove,
3. How si-lent-ly, how si-lent-ly The won-drous gift is given!
4. O ho-ly Child of Beth-le-hem, De-scend to us, we pray;

A-bove thy deep and dream-less sleep The si-lent stars go by;
While mor-tals sleep, the an-gels keep Their watch of won-dering love.
So God im-parts to hu-man hearts The bless-ings of His heaven.
Cast out our sin and en-ter in— Be born in us to-day.

Yet in thy dark streets shin-eth The ev-er-last-ing light;
O morn-ing stars, to-geth-er Pro-claim the ho-ly birth!
No ear may hear His com-ing; But in this world of sin,
We hear the Christ-mas an-gels The great glad ti-dings tell—

The hopes and fears of all the years Are met in thee to-night.
And prais-es sing to God the King, And peace to men on earth.
Where meek souls will re-ceive Him still, The dear Christ en-ters in.
Oh, come to us, a-bide with us, Our Lord Im-man-u-el!

Alternate tune FOREST GREEN, No. 90

BIRTH

136 Good Christians, Now Rejoice

IN DULCE JUBILO 6.6.7.7.7.8.5.5.

14th century melody

Tr. by John M. Neale, 1853 (1818-1866)

Arr. by C. Winfred Douglas, 1918 (1867-1944)

1. Good Chris-tians, now re-joice, With heart, and soul, and voice;
2. Good Chris-tians, now re-joice, With heart, and soul, and voice;
3. Good Chris-tians, now re-joice, With heart, and soul, and voice;

Give ye heed to what we say: Je-sus Christ is born to-day;
Now ye hear of end-less bliss: Je-sus Christ was born for this!
Now ye need not fear the grave: Je-sus Christ was born to save!

Ox and ass be-fore Him bow, And He is in the man-ger now.
He hath ope'd the heav-'nly door, And we are bless-ed ev-er-more.
Calls you one and calls you all To gain His ev-er-last-ing hall.

Christ is born to-day! Christ is born to-day!
Christ was born for this! Christ was born for this!
Christ was born to save! Christ was born to save!

BIRTH

We Three Kings

KINGS OF ORIENT 8.8.8.6.Ref.
John H. Hopkins, 1857

John H. Hopkins, 1857 (1820-1891)

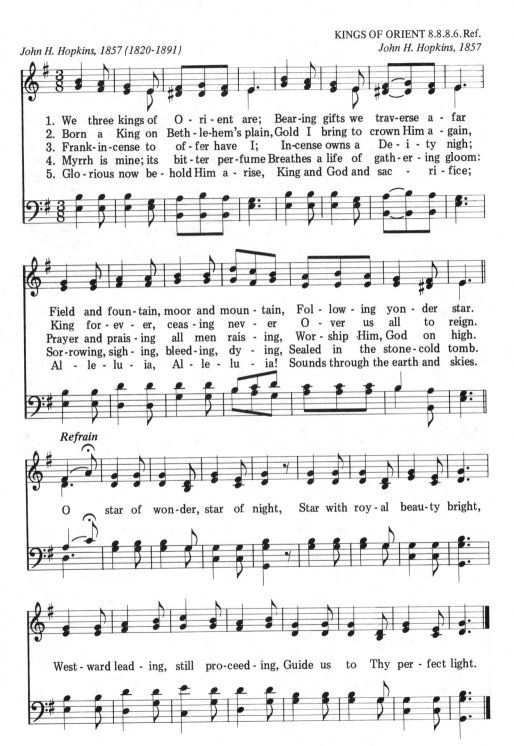

1. We three kings of O - ri - ent are; Bear-ing gifts we trav-erse a - far
2. Born a King on Beth - le-hem's plain, Gold I bring to crown Him a - gain,
3. Frank-in-cense to of - fer have I; In-cense owns a De - i - ty nigh;
4. Myrrh is mine; its bit - ter per-fume Breathes a life of gath - er - ing gloom:
5. Glo - rious now be - hold Him a - rise, King and God and sac - ri - fice;

Field and foun-tain, moor and moun - tain, Fol - low - ing yon - der star.
King for - ev - er, ceas - ing nev - er O - ver us all to reign.
Prayer and prais-ing all men rais - ing, Wor - ship Him, God on high.
Sor-rowing, sigh - ing, bleed-ing, dy - ing, Sealed in the stone-cold tomb.
Al - le - lu - ia, Al - le - lu - ia! Sounds through the earth and skies.

Refrain

O star of won-der, star of night, Star with roy - al beau-ty bright,

West - ward lead - ing, still pro-ceed - ing, Guide us to Thy per - fect light.

BIRTH

Rise Up, Shepherd, and Follow

10.7.10.7.Ref.

American Negro Spiritual

Arr. by Alma Blackmon, 1984 (1921-   )

1. There's a star in the east on Christ-mas morn. Rise up, shep-herd, and fol-low. It will lead to the place where the Sav-ior's born,
2. If you take good heed to the an-gel's words, Rise up, shep-herd, and fol-low. You'll for-get your flocks, you'll for-get your herds,

Refrain

Rise up, shep-herd, and fol-low. Leave your sheep and leave your lambs,

Rise up, shep-herd, and fol-low. Leave your ewes and leave your rams,

Rise up, shep-herd, and fol-low. Fol - low, Fol - low,

BIRTH

Rise up, shep-herd, and fol-low. Fol-low the star of

Beth-le-hem, Rise up, shep-herd, and fol-low.

While Shepherds Watched Their Flocks **139**

Luke 2:8-14
Nahum Tate, 1700 (1652-1715)

WINCHESTER OLD C.M.
Este's Psalter, 1592

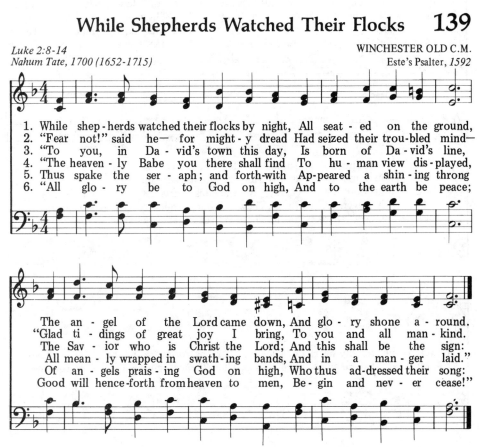

1. While shep-herds watched their flocks by night, All seat-ed on the ground,
2. "Fear not!" said he— for might-y dread Had seized their trou-bled mind—
3. "To you, in Da-vid's town this day, Is born of Da-vid's line,
4. "The heaven-ly Babe you there shall find To hu-man view dis-played,
5. Thus spake the ser-aph; and forth-with Ap-peared a shin-ing throng
6. "All glo-ry be to God on high, And to the earth be peace;

The an-gel of the Lord came down, And glo-ry shone a-round.
"Glad ti-dings of great joy I bring, To you and all man-kind.
The Sav-ior who is Christ the Lord; And this shall be the sign:
All mean-ly wrapped in swath-ing bands, And in a man-ger laid."
Of an-gels prais-ing God on high, Who thus ad-dressed their song:
Good will hence-forth from heaven to men, Be-gin and nev-er cease!"

BIRTH

140 Thou Didst Leave Thy Throne

Emily E. S. Elliott, 1864 (1836-1897)

MARGARET Irregular Ref.
Timothy R. Matthews, 1876 (1826-1910)

1. Thou didst leave Thy throne And Thy king-ly crown When Thou cam-est to earth for me; But in Beth-le-hem's home Was there found no room For Thy ho-ly na-tiv-i-ty.

2. Heav-en's arch-es rang When the an-gels sang Pro-claim-ing Thy roy-al de-gree; But of low-ly birth Didst Thou come to earth, And in great-est hu-mil-i-ty.

3. The fox-es found rest, And the birds their nest In the shade of the for-est tree; But Thy couch was the sod, O Thou Son of God, In the des-erts of Gal-i-lee.

4. Thou cam-est, O Lord, With the liv-ing word That should set Thy peo-ple free; But with mock-ing scorn, And with crown of thorn, They bore Thee to Cal-va-ry.

5. When the heav-ens shall ring, And the an-gels sing, At Thy com-ing to vic-to-ry, Let Thy voice call me home, Say-ing, "Yet there is room, There is room at My side for thee."

Refrain

1-4. O come to my heart, Lord Je-sus, There is room in my heart for Thee.

5. My heart shall re-joice, Lord Je-sus, When Thou com-est and call-est for me.

BIRTH

What Child Is This?

141

BIRTH

142 Angels We Have Heard on High

French carol, Luke 2:13-17
Tr. in Crown of Jesus, 1862, alt.
Adapt. by Earl Marlatt, 1937 (1892-   )

GLORIA 7.7.7.7.Ref.
French carol
Arr. by Edward Shippen Barnes, 1937 (1887-1958)

1. An - gels we have heard on high, Sing - ing sweet - ly through the night,
2. Shep - herds, why this ju - bi - lee? Why these songs of hap - py cheer?
3. Come to Beth - le - hem and see Him whose birth the an - gels sing;
4. See Him in a man - ger laid Whom the an - gels praise a - bove;

And the moun - tains in re - ply Ech - o - ing their brave de - light.
What great bright - ness did you see? What glad ti - dings did you hear?
Come, a - dore on bend - ed knee Christ, the Lord, the new - born King.
Ma - ry, Jo - seph, lend your aid, While we raise our hearts in love.

Refrain

Glo - - - ri - a in ex - cel - sis De - o, Glo - -

BIRTH

ri - a   in ex - cel - sis De - o.

Silent Night, Holy Night 143

Joseph Mohr, 1818 (1792-1848)
Tr. by John F. Young, 1863 (1820-1885)

STILLE NACHT Irregular
Franz Gruber, 1818 (1787-1863)

1. Si - lent night, ho - ly night, All is calm, all is bright;
2. Si - lent night, ho - ly night, Dark-ness flies, all is light;
3. Si - lent night, ho - ly night, Son of God, love's pure light;
4. Si - lent night, ho - ly night, Won-drous star, lend thy light;

Round yon vir - gin moth-er and Child! Ho - ly In-fant, so ten-der and mild,
Shep-herds hear the an - gels sing, "Al - le - lu - ia! hail the King!
Ra - diant beams from Thy ho-ly face, With the dawn of re-deem - ing grace,
With the an - gels let us sing, Al - le - lu - ia to our King;

Sleep in heav-en-ly peace, Sleep in heav-en-ly peace.
Christ the Sav - ior is born, Christ the Sav - ior is born."
Je - sus, Lord, at Thy birth, Je - sus, Lord, at Thy birth.
Christ the Sav - ior is born, Christ the Sav - ior is born.

144　O Sing a Song of Bethlehem

KINGSFOLD C.M.D.
Mel. coll. by Lucy Broadwood
Arr. by Ralph Vaughan Williams (1872-1958)

Louis F. Benson, 1899 (1855-1930)

1. O sing a song of Beth-le-hem, Of shep-herds watch-ing there,
2. O sing a song of Naz-a-reth, Of sun-ny days of joy,
3. O sing a song of Cal-va-ry, Its glo-ry and dis-may;

And of the news that came to them From an-gels in the air:
O sing of fra-grant flow-ers breath, And of the sin-less Boy:
Of Him who hung up-on the tree, And took our sins a-way:

The light that shone on Beth-le-hem Fills all the world to-day;
For now the flowers of Naz-a-reth In ev-ery heart may grow;
For He who died on Cal-va-ry Is ris-en from the grave;

Of Je-sus' birth and peace on earth The an-gels sing al-way.
Now spreads the fame of His dear name On all the winds that blow.
And Christ, our Lord, by heaven a-dored, Is might-y now to save.

Music from *The English Hymnal* by permission of Oxford University Press.　　Alternate tune, FOREST GREEN, No. 90

LIFE AND MINISTRY

RILEY 7.7.7.7.D.

Christopher Wordsworth (1807-1885)

Martin Shaw (1875-1958)

1. Songs of thank - ful - ness and praise, Je - sus, Lord, to You we raise,
2. Man - i - fest at Jor - dan's stream, Proph-et, Priest, and King su - preme;
3. Man - i - fest in mak - ing whole Pal - sied limbs and faint - ing soul;
4. Grant us grace to see You, Lord, Mir - rored in Your ho - ly Word;

Man - i - fest - ed by the star To the sag - es from a - far;
And at Ca - na, wed - ding guest, In Your God-head man - i - fest;
Man - i - fest in val - iant fight, Quell - ing all the dev - il's might;
May we im - i - tate Your way, And be pure, as pure we may,

Branch of roy - al Da - vid's stem In Your birth at Beth - le - hem;
Man - i - fest in power di - vine, Chang-ing wa - ter in - to wine;
Man - i - fest in gra - cious will, Ev - er bring-ing good from ill;
That we like to You may be At Your great e - piph - a - ny;

1,2,3. An - thems be to You ad - dressed, God in man made man - i - fest.
4. Let us praise You, ev - er blest, God in man made man - i - fest.

Music copyright © J. Curwen & Sons. Used by permission of G. Schirmer, Inc., U. S. A. agents.

Alternate tune, ST. GEORGE'S WINDSOR, No. 557

LIFE AND MINISTRY

146 I Think When I Read That Sweet Story

Matt. 19:14,15
Jemima Luke (1813-1906)

EAST HORNDON Irregular
English traditional melody
Arr. by Ralph Vaughan Williams (1872-1958)

1. I think when I read that sweet sto - ry of old, When Je - sus was here a - mong men, How He called lit - tle chil - dren as lambs to His fold, I should like to have been with Him then.

2. I wish that His hands had been placed on my head, That His arm had been thrown a - round me, And that I might have seen His kind look when He said, "Let the lit - tle ones come un - to Me."

3. I long for the joy of that glo - ri - ous time, The sweet - est and bright - est and best, When the dear lit - tle chil - dren of ev - er - y clime Shall crowd to His arms and be blest.

Music from the *English Hymnal* by permission of Oxford University Press.

Christ Upon the Mountain Peak

Mark 9:2-7; Matt. 17:1-5
Brian Wren (1936-   )

FENITON 7.8.7.8.Alleluia
Sydney H. Nicholson (1875-1947)

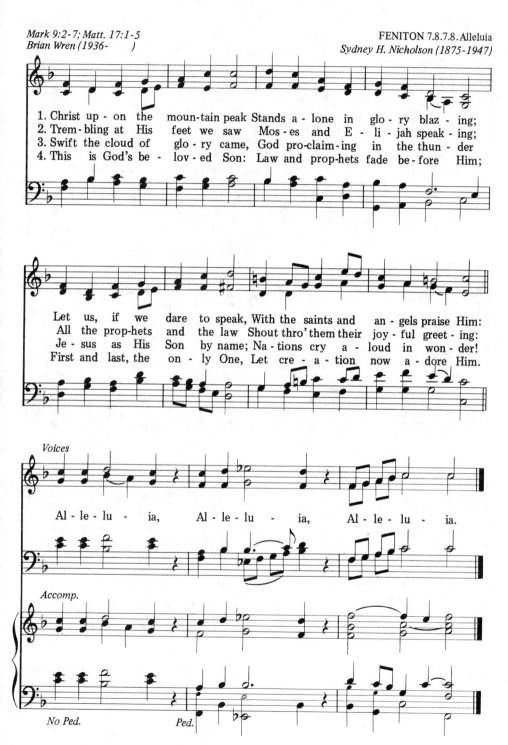

1. Christ up-on the moun-tain peak Stands a-lone in glo-ry blaz-ing;
2. Trem-bling at His feet we saw Mos-es and E-li-jah speak-ing;
3. Swift the cloud of glo-ry came, God pro-claim-ing in the thun-der
4. This is God's be-lov-ed Son: Law and proph-ets fade be-fore Him;

Let us, if we dare to speak, With the saints and an-gels praise Him:
All the proph-ets and the law Shout thro' them their joy-ful greet-ing:
Je-sus as His Son by name; Na-tions cry a-loud in won-der!
First and last, the on-ly One, Let cre-a-tion now a-dore Him.

Voices

Al-le-lu-ia, Al-le-lu-ia, Al-le-lu-ia.

Accomp.

No Ped.   *Ped.*

LIFE AND MINISTRY

148 O Love, How Deep, How Broad

Attr. to Thomas a Kempis (1380-1471)
Tr. by Benjamin Webb (1820-1885) alt.

INFINITE LOVE L.M.
James Bingham, 1984 (1945-   )

1. O love, how deep, how broad, how high, Be - yond all
2. For us bap - tized, for us He bore His ho - ly
3. For us by wick - ed - ness be - trayed, For us, in
4. For us He rose from death a - gain, For us He
5. All glo - ry to our Lord and God For love so

thought and fan - ta - sy, That God, the Son of
fast and hun - gered sore; For us temp - ta - tion
crown of thorns ar - rayed, He bore the shame - ful
went on high to reign; For us He sent His
deep, so high, so broad; The Trin - i - ty whom

God, should take Our mor - tal form for mor - tal's sake!
sharp He knew; For us the temp - ter o - ver - threw.
cross and death; For us He gave His dy - ing breath.
Spir - it here To guide, to strength - en, and to cheer.
we a - dore For - ev - er and for - ev - er - more.

Music copyright © 1984 by James Bingham.   Alternate tune, DEUS TUORUM MILITUM, No. 404

LIFE AND MINISTRY

Once in Royal David's City

149

IRBY 8.7.8.7.7.7.

Cecil Frances Alexander, 1848 (1818-1895)

Henry J. Gauntlett, 1849 (1805-1876)

1. Once in roy-al Da-vid's cit-y Stood a low-ly cat-tle shed, Where a moth-er laid her Ba-by In a man-ger for His bed; Ma-ry was that moth-er mild, Je-sus Christ her lit-tle Child.

2. He came down to earth from heav-en, Who is God and Lord of all, And His shel-ter was a sta-ble, And His cra-dle was a stall; With the poor, and mean, and low-ly, Lived on earth our Sav-ior ho-ly.

3. And through all His won-drous child-hood He would hon-or and o-bey, Love and watch the low-ly moth-er In whose gen-tle arms He lay. Chris-tian chil-dren all must be Mild, o-be-dient, good as He.

4. And our eyes at last shall see Him, Through His own re-deem-ing love; For that Child so dear and gen-tle Is our Lord in heaven a-bove; And He leads His chil-dren on To the place where He is gone.

LIFE AND MINISTRY

150 Who Is He in Yonder Stall?

RESONET IN LAUDIBUS 7.7.8.8.Ref.

Benjamin R. Hanby (1833-1867)

German carol melody, 14th cent.

Unison

1. Who is He in yon-der stall, At whose feet the shep-herds fall?
2. Who is He in deep dis-tress, Fast-ing in the wil-der-ness?
3. Who is He, the gath-ering throng Greet with loud tri-um-phant song?
4. Lo, at mid-night, who is He Prays in dark Geth-sem-a-ne?
5. Who is He on yon-der tree Dies in shame and a-go-ny?

'Tis the Lord, O won-drous sto-ry, 'Tis the Lord, the King of glo-ry!

Refrain

At His feet we hum-bly fall, Crown Him, crown Him Lord of all.

At His feet we hum-bly fall— the Lord of all. Crown Him,

crown Him, Je - sus, Je - sus, Crown Him Lord of all.

6. Who is He that from the grave
Comes to heal and help and save?
'Tis the Lord, O wondrous story,
'Tis the Lord, the King of glory!
(Refrain)

7. Who is He that from His throne
Rules through all the world alone?
'Tis the Lord, O wondrous story,
'Tis the Lord, the King of glory!
(Refrain)

Jesus Walked This Lonesome Valley 151

8.8.10.8.

American White Spiritual   *Arr. by Allen W. Foster, 1984 (1940-)*

1. Je - sus walked this lone - some val - ley; He had to
2. I must go and stand my tri - al. I have to
3. Je - sus walked this lone - some val - ley; He had to

walk it by Him - self. O no - bod - y else could walk it
stand it by my - self. O no - bod - y else could stand it
walk it by Him - self. O no - bod - y else could walk it

for Him. He had to walk it by Him - self.
for me. I have to stand it by my - self.
for Him. He had to walk it by Him - self.

LIFE AND MINISTRY

Tell Me the Story of Jesus

8.7.8.7.D.Ref.

Fanny J. Crosby (1820-1915)

John R. Sweney (1837-1899)

1. Tell me the sto-ry of Je-sus, Write on my heart ev-ery word,
2. Fast-ing, a-lone in the des-ert, Tell of the days that He passed,
3. Tell of the cross where they nailed Him, Writh-ing in an-guish and pain;

Tell me the sto-ry most pre-cious Sweet-est that ev-er was heard;
How for our sins He was tempt-ed, Yet was tri-um-phant at last;
Tell of the grave where they laid Him, Tell how He liv-eth a-gain;

Tell how the an-gels, in cho-rus, Sang as they wel-comed His birth,
Tell of the years of His la-bor, Tell of the sor-row He bore,
Love in that sto-ry so ten-der, Clear-er than ev-er I see;

Glo-ry to God in the high-est, Peace and good ti-dings to earth.
He was de-spised and af-flict-ed, Home-less, re-ject-ed, and poor.
Stay, let me weep while you whis-per, Love paid the ran-som for me.

LIFE AND MINISTRY

Refrain

Tell me the sto-ry of Je - sus, Write on my heart ev - ery word,

Tell me the sto - ry most pre-cious, Sweet-est that ev - er was heard.

Prince of Peace, Control My Will 153

TRYGGARE KAN INGEN VARA L.M.
Swedish folk melody
Arr. by Melvin West, 1984 (1930-   )

Anon.

Unison

1. Prince of Peace, con - trol my will, Bid this strug-gling heart be still;
2. Thou hast bought me with Thy blood, O-pened wide the gate to God;
3. May Thy will, not mine, be done, May Thy will and mine be one;

Bid my fears and doubt-ings cease, Hush my spir - it in - to peace.
Peace, I ask, but peace must be, Lord, in be - ing one with Thee.
Chase these doubt-ings from my heart, Now Thy per - fect peace im-part.

Harmony setting, No. 101

LIFE AND MINISTRY

154 When I Survey the Wondrous Cross

HAMBURG L.M.

Gal. 6:14
Isaac Watts, 1707 (1674-1748)

From a Gregorian Chant
Arr. by Lowell Mason (1792-1872)

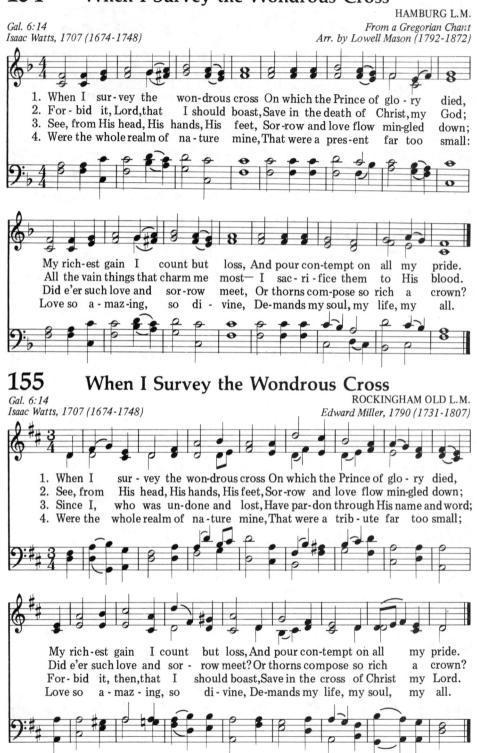

1. When I sur-vey the won-drous cross On which the Prince of glo-ry died,
2. For-bid it, Lord, that I should boast, Save in the death of Christ, my God;
3. See, from His head, His hands, His feet, Sor-row and love flow min-gled down;
4. Were the whole realm of na-ture mine, That were a pres-ent far too small:

My rich-est gain I count but loss, And pour con-tempt on all my pride.
All the vain things that charm me most— I sac-ri-fice them to His blood.
Did e'er such love and sor-row meet, Or thorns com-pose so rich a crown?
Love so a-maz-ing, so di-vine, De-mands my soul, my life, my all.

155 When I Survey the Wondrous Cross

ROCKINGHAM OLD L.M.

Gal. 6:14
Isaac Watts, 1707 (1674-1748)

Edward Miller, 1790 (1731-1807)

1. When I sur-vey the won-drous cross On which the Prince of glo-ry died,
2. See, from His head, His hands, His feet, Sor-row and love flow min-gled down;
3. Since I, who was un-done and lost, Have par-don through His name and word;
4. Were the whole realm of na-ture mine, That were a trib-ute far too small;

My rich-est gain I count but loss, And pour con-tempt on all my pride.
Did e'er such love and sor-row meet? Or thorns compose so rich a crown?
For-bid it, then, that I should boast, Save in the cross of Christ my Lord.
Love so a-maz-ing, so di-vine, De-mands my life, my soul, my all.

SUFFERINGS AND DEATH

Alternate tune, MCCABE, No. 401

O Sacred Head Now Wounded

156

Attr. to Bernard of Clairvaux, (1091-1153)
Tr. (German) by Paul Gerhardt, 1656 (1607-1676)
Tr. (English) by James W. Alexander, 1830 (1804-1859)

PASSION CHORALE 7.6.7.6.D.
Hans Leo Hassler, 1601 (1564-1612)
Arr. by J. S. Bach, 1729 (1685-1750)

1. O sa - cred head, now wound - ed, With grief and shame weighed down,
2. What Thou, my Lord, hast suf - fered Was all for sin - ners' gain;
3. What lan - guage shall I bor - row To thank Thee, dear - est friend,

Now scorn - ful - ly sur - round - ed With thorns, Thine on - ly crown:
Mine, mine was the trans - gres - sion, But Thine the dead - ly pain.
For this Thy dy - ing sor - row, Thy pit - y with - out end?

O sa - cred head, what glo - ry, What bliss till now was Thine!
Lo, here I fall, my Sav - ior! 'Tis I de - serve Thy place;
O make me Thine for - ev - er; And should I faint - ing be,

Yet, though de - spised and gor - y, I joy to call Thee mine.
Look on me with Thy fa - vor, Vouch - safe to me Thy grace.
Lord, let me nev - er, nev - er Out - live my love to Thee.

SUFFERINGS AND DEATH

TSDAH-6

Go to Dark Gethsemane

GETHSEMANE 7.7.7.7.7.7.

James Montgomery, 1820 (1771-1854)

Richard Redhead, 1853 (1820-1901)

1. Go to dark Geth-sem-a-ne, Ye that feel the tempt-er's power; Your Re-deem-er's con-flict see; Watch with Him one bit-ter hour; Turn not from His griefs a-way; Learn of Je-sus Christ to pray.

2. See Him at the judg-ment hall, Beat-en, bound, re-viled, ar-raigned; See Him meek-ly bear-ing all; Love to man His soul sus-tained; Shun not suf-fering, shame, or loss; Learn of Christ to bear the cross.

3. Cal-vary's mourn-ful moun-tain climb; There a-dor-ing at His feet, Mark that mir-a-cle of time, God's own sac-ri-fice com-plete; "It is fin-ished!" hear Him cry; Learn of Je-sus Christ to die.

SUFFERINGS AND DEATH

Were You There?

American Negro Spiritual

10.10.14.10.

1. Were you there when they cru-ci-fied my Lord? Were you
2. Were you there when they nailed Him to the tree? Were you
3. Were you there when they pierced Him in the side? Were you
4. Were you there when the sun re-fused to shine? Were you
5. Were you there when they laid Him in the tomb? Were you

there when they cru-ci-fied my Lord?
there when they nailed Him to the tree?
there when they pierced Him in the side? O!
there when the sun re-fused to shine?
there when they laid Him in the tomb?

Some-times it caus-es me to trem-ble, trem-ble, trem-ble.

Were you there when they cru-ci-fied my Lord?
Were you there when they nailed Him to the tree?
Were you there when they pierced Him in the side?
Were you there when the sun re-fused to shine?
Were you there when they laid Him in the tomb?

SUFFERINGS AND DEATH

159 The Old Rugged Cross

George Bennard, 1913 (1873-1958)

12.8.12.8.Ref.
George Bennard, 1913

1. On a hill far a-way stood an old rug-ged cross, The em-blem of suf-fering and shame, And I love that old cross where the dear-est and best For a world of lost sin-ners was slain.

2. Oh, that old rug-ged cross, so de-spised by the world, Has a won-drous at-trac-tion for me, For the dear Lamb of God left His glo-ry a-bove, To bear it to dark Cal-va-ry.

3. To the old rug-ged cross I will ev-er be true, Its shame and re-proach glad-ly bear; Then He'll call me some day to my home far a-way, Where His glo-ry for-ev-er I'll share.

Refrain

So I'll cher-ish the old rug-ged cross,
cross, the old rug-ged cross,
Till my

SUFFERINGS AND DEATH

tro - phies at last I lay down; I will cling to the

old rug - ged cross, And ex-change it some day for a crown.
cross, the old rug - ged cross,

Ride On in Majesty 160

CANNOCK L.M.

Henry H. Milman, 1827 (1791-1868)

Walter K. Stanton (1891-1978)

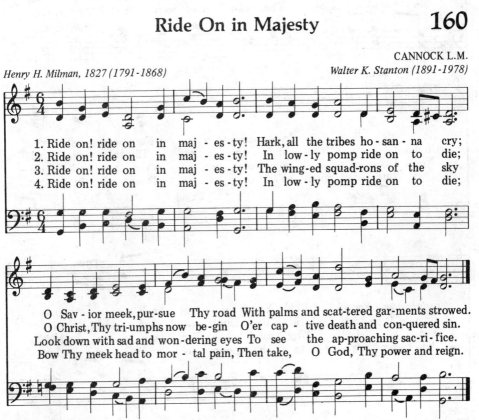

1. Ride on! ride on in maj - es - ty! Hark, all the tribes ho - san - na cry;
2. Ride on! ride on in maj - es - ty! In low - ly pomp ride on to die;
3. Ride on! ride on in maj - es - ty! The wing - ed squad-rons of the sky
4. Ride on! ride on in maj - es - ty! In low - ly pomp ride on to die;

O Sav - ior meek, pur-sue Thy road With palms and scat-tered gar-ments strowed.
O Christ, Thy tri-umphs now be-gin O'er cap - tive death and con-quered sin.
Look down with sad and won-dering eyes To see the ap-proaching sac-ri-fice.
Bow Thy meek head to mor - tal pain, Then take, O God, Thy power and reign.

Music from the *BBC Hymn Book* by permission of Oxford University Press.

SUFFERINGS AND DEATH

161 Throned Upon the Awful Tree

ARFON 7.7.7.7.7.7.
Matt. 27:45,46
John Ellerton, 1875 (1826-1893) alt.
Traditional melody, France and Wales
Adapt. by Hugh Davies, c. 1906 (1844-1907)

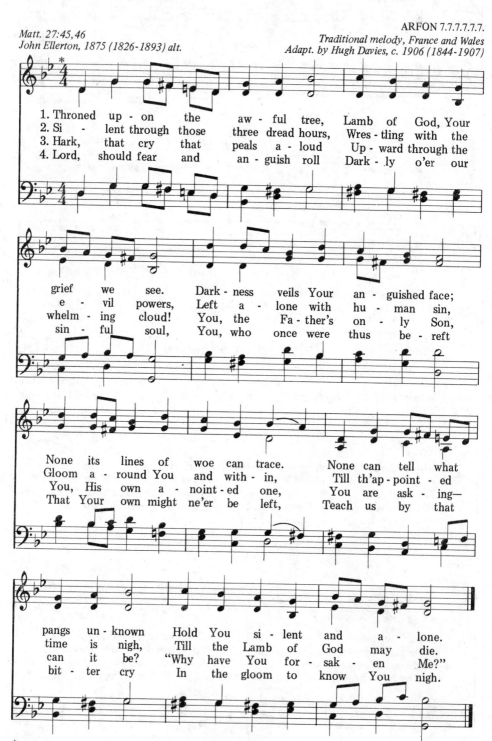

1. Throned up-on the aw-ful tree, Lamb of God, Your
2. Si - lent through those three dread hours, Wres-tling with the
3. Hark, that cry that peals a-loud Up-ward through the
4. Lord, should fear and an-guish roll Dark-ly o'er our

grief we see. Dark-ness veils Your an-guished face;
e - vil powers, Left a - lone with hu - man sin,
whelm-ing cloud! You, the Fa-ther's on - ly Son,
sin-ful soul, You, who once were thus be - reft

None its lines of woe can trace. None can tell what
Gloom a - round You and with-in, Till th'ap-point-ed
You, His own a - noint-ed one, You are ask - ing—
That Your own might ne'er be left, Teach us by that

pangs un-known Hold You si - lent and a - lone.
time is nigh, Till the Lamb of God may die.
can it be? "Why have You for-sak-en Me?"
bit - ter cry In the gloom to know You nigh.

*This hymn may also be played and sung in G major.

SUFFERINGS AND DEATH

Wondrous Love

WONDROUS LOVE 6.6.6.3.6.6.6.6.6.3.
Southern Harmony, *1835*
Harm. by Richard Proulx, 1975 (1937-   )

Attr. to Alexander Means

1. What won-drous love is this, O my soul, O my soul? What
2. To God and to the Lamb I will sing, I will sing; To
3. And when from death I'm free, I'll sing on, I'll sing on; And

won-drous love is this, O my soul? What won-drous love is
God and to the Lamb, I will sing; To God and to the
when from death I'm free, I'll sing on; And when from death I'm

this That caused the Lord of bliss To bear the dread-ful curse for my
Lamb Who is the great I am, While mil-lions join the theme, I will
free, I'll sing and joy-ful be, And through e - ter - ni - ty I'll sing

soul, for my soul; To bear the dread-ful curse for my soul?
sing, I will sing; While mil-lions join the theme, I will sing.
on, I'll sing on! And through e - ter - ni - ty, I'll sing on.

SUFFERINGS AND DEATH

163

At the Cross

Isaac Watts (1674-1748)
Ref. by Ralph E. Hudson

C.M.Ref.
Ralph E. Hudson (1843-1901)

1. A - las, and did my Sav - ior bleed? And did my Sov-ereign die?
2. Was it for crimes that I have done, He suf-fered on the tree?
3. But drops of grief can ne'er re - pay The debt of love I owe:

Would He de - vote that sa - cred head For some-one such as I?
A - maz - ing pit - y! grace un-known! And love be-yond de - gree!
Here, Lord, I give my - self a - way, 'Tis all that I can do!

Refrain

At the cross, at the cross where I first saw the light, And the

bur - den of my heart rolled a - way, It was there by faith

SUFFERINGS AND DEATH

Alternate tune without refrain, MARTYRDOM, No. 113

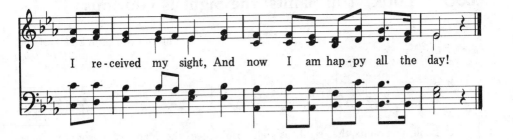

I re-ceived my sight, And now I am hap-py all the day!

There Is a Green Hill Far Away

164

Cecil Frances Alexander, 1848 (1818-1895)

HORSLEY C.M.

William Horsley, 1844 (1774-1858)

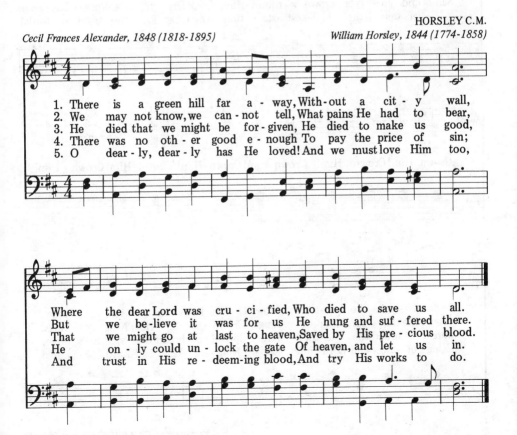

1. There is a green hill far a - way, With-out a cit - y wall,
2. We may not know, we can - not tell, What pains He had to bear,
3. He died that we might be for - given, He died to make us good,
4. There was no oth - er good e - nough To pay the price of sin;
5. O dear - ly, dear - ly has He loved! And we must love Him too,

Where the dear Lord was cru - ci - fied, Who died to save us all.
But we be - lieve it was for us He hung and suf - fered there.
That we might go at last to heaven, Saved by His pre - cious blood.
He on - ly could un - lock the gate Of heaven, and let us in.
And trust in His re - deem-ing blood, And try His works to do.

SUFFERINGS AND DEATH

165 Look, You Saints! the Sight Is Glorious

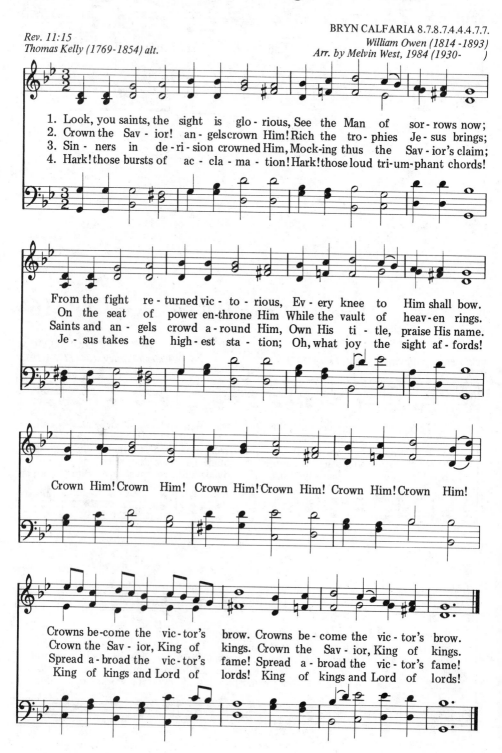

BRYN CALFARIA 8.7.8.7.4.4.4.7.7.
William Owen (1814 -1893)
Arr. by Melvin West, 1984 (1930-   )

Rev. 11:15
Thomas Kelly (1769-1854) alt.

1. Look, you saints, the sight is glo-rious, See the Man of sor-rows now;
2. Crown the Sav-ior! an-gels crown Him! Rich the tro-phies Je-sus brings;
3. Sin-ners in de-ri-sion crowned Him, Mock-ing thus the Sav-ior's claim;
4. Hark! those bursts of ac-cla-ma-tion! Hark! those loud tri-um-phant chords!

From the fight re-turned vic-to-rious, Ev-ery knee to Him shall bow.
On the seat of power en-throne Him While the vault of heav-en rings.
Saints and an-gels crowd a-round Him, Own His ti-tle, praise His name.
Je-sus takes the high-est sta-tion; Oh, what joy the sight af-fords!

Crown Him! Crown Him! Crown Him! Crown Him! Crown Him! Crown Him!

Crowns be-come the vic-tor's brow. Crowns be-come the vic-tor's brow.
Crown the Sav-ior, King of kings. Crown the Sav-ior, King of kings.
Spread a-broad the vic-tor's fame! Spread a-broad the vic-tor's fame!
King of kings and Lord of lords! King of kings and Lord of lords!

Alternate tune, CWM RHONDDA, Nos. 201, 538

RESURRECTION AND ASCENSION

Christ the Lord Is Risen Today

166

WORGAN 7.7.7.7. Alleluias
From Lyra Davidica, 1708

Charles Wesley, 1739, (1707-1788) and others

1. Christ the Lord is risen to-day, Al - le - lu - ia!
2. Lives a-gain our glo-rious King, Al - le - lu - ia!
3. Love's re-deem-ing work is done, Al - le - lu - ia!
4. Soar we then where Christ has led, Al - le - lu - ia!

Sons of men and an-gels say, Al - le - lu - ia!
Where, O death, is now thy sting? Al - le - lu - ia!
Fought the fight, the bat-tle won, Al - le - lu - ia!
Fol-lowing our ex-alt-ed Head, Al - le - lu - ia!

Raise your joys and tri-umphs high, Al - le - lu - ia!
Once He died, our souls to save, Al - le - lu - ia!
Death in vain for-bids Him rise, Al - le - lu - ia!
Made like Him, like Him we rise, Al - le - lu - ia!

Sing, ye heavens, and earth re-ply, Al - le - lu - ia!
Where's thy vic-tory, boast-ing grave? Al - le - lu - ia!
Christ hath o-pened Par-a-dise, Al - le - lu - ia!
Ours the cross, the grave, the skies, Al - le - lu - ia!

RESURRECTION AND ASCENSION

167

Alleluia! Sing to Jesus!

HYFRYDOL 8.7.8.7.D.
Rowland Hugh Pritchard, c. 1830 (1811-1887)
Arr. by Melvin West, 1984 (1930-   )

William C. Dix, 1866 (1837-1898)

1. Al - le - lu - ia! sing to Je - sus! His the scep - ter, His the throne;
2. Al - le - lu - ia! not as or - phans Are we left in sor - row now;
3. Al - le - lu - ia! Bread of heav - en, Thou on earth our food, our stay!

Al - le - lu - ia! His the tri - umph, His the vic - to - ry a - lone;
Al - le - lu - ia! He is near us, Faith be - lieves, nor ques - tions how:
Al - le - lu - ia! here the sin - ful Flee to Thee from day to day:

Hark! the songs of peace - ful Si - on Thun - der like a might - y flood;
Though the cloud from sight re - ceived Him, When the for - ty days were o'er,
In - ter - ces - sor, Friend of sin - ners, Earth's Re - deem - er plead for me,

Je - sus out of ev - ery na - tion Hath re - deemed us by His blood.
Shall our hearts for - get His prom - ise, "I am with you ev - er - more"?
Where the songs of all the sin - less Sweep a - cross the crys - tal sea.

Alternate harmony, No. 204

RESURRECTION AND ASCENSION

And Have the Bright Immensities

FOREST GREEN C.M.D.
Traditional English melody
Arr. by Ralph Vaughan Williams, 1906 (1872-1958)

Howard C. Robbins (1876-1952)

1. And have the bright im - men - si - ties Re-ceived our ris - en Lord,
2. The heav'n that hides Him from our sight Knows nei-ther near nor far;

Where light years frame the Ple - ia - des And point O - ri-on's sword?
A lit - tle can - dle sheds its light As sure-ly as a star.

Do flam-ing suns His foot-steps trace Thro' cor - ri-dors sub - lime,
And where His lov-ing peo - ple meet To share the gift di - vine,

The Lord of in - ter - stel - lar space And con-quer - or of time?
There stands He with un - hur-rying feet; There heav'n-ly splen-dors shine.

Words reprinted by permission of Morehouse-Barlow Co., Inc.
Music from *The English Hymnal* by permission of Oxford University Press.

RESURRECTION AND ASCENSION

169 Come, You Faithful

John of Damascus, 8th century
Tr. by John M. Neale, 1859 (1818-1866)

ST. KEVIN 7.6.7.6.D.
Arthur S. Sullivan, 1872 (1842-1900)

1. Come, you faith - ful, raise the strain   Of   tri - um-phant glad - ness;
2. 'Tis   the spring   of   souls to - day;   Christ has burst His   pris - on;
3. "Al - le - lu - ia!" now   we   cry   To   our King im - mor - tal,

God has brought His   peo - ple forth   In - to   joy from   sad - ness.
From the frost   and gloom of death   Light and life have   ris - en.
Who, tri - um - phant, burst the bars   Of   the tomb's dark   por - tal;

Now re - joice, Je - ru - sa - lem,   And with true af - fec - tion
All   the win - ter   of   our sins,   Long and dark, is   fly - ing
"Al - le - lu - ia!" with the Son,   God the Fa - ther prais - ing;

Wel - come in   un - wea - ried strains   Je - sus' res - ur - rec - tion.
From His light, to   whom we give   Thanks and praise un - dy - ing.
"Al - le - lu - ia!" yet a - gain   To   the Spir - it   rais - ing.

RESURRECTION AND ASCENSION

Come, You Faithful 170

John of Damascus, 8th century
Tr. by John M. Neale (1818-1866) alt.

AVE VIRGO VIRGINUM 7.6.7.6.D.
Leisentritt's Gesangbuch, 1584

1. Come, you faith-ful, raise the strain Of tri-um-phant glad-ness;
2. 'Tis the spring of souls to-day; Christ has burst His pris-on,
3. Now the queen of sea-sons, bright With the day of splen-dor,
4. For to-day a-mong the twelve Christ ap-peared, be-stow-ing
5. "Al-le-lu-ia!" now we cry To our King im-mor-tal,

God has brought His Is-ra-el In-to joy from sad-ness;
And from three days' sleep in death As a sun has ris-en;
With the roy-al feast of feasts, Comes its joy to ren-der;
His deep peace, which ev-er-more Pass-es hu-man know-ing.
Who, tri-um-phant, burst the bars Of the tomb's dark por-tal;

Loosed from Pharo-ah's bit-ter yoke Ja-cob's sons and daugh-ters;
All the win-ter of our sins, Long and dark, is fly-ing
Comes to glad-den faith-ful hearts Which with true af-fec-tion
Nei-ther could the gates of death, Nor the tomb's dark por-tal,
"Al-le-lu-ia" with the Son, God the Fa-ther prais-ing;

Led them with un-moist-ened foot Through the Red Sea wa-ters.
From His light, to whom is giv'n Laud and praise un-dy-ing.
Wel-come in un-wea-ried strain Je-sus' res-ur-rec-tion.
Nor the watch-ers, nor the seal, Hold Him as a mor-tal.
"Al-le-lu-ia!" yet a-gain To the Spir-it rais-ing.

RESURRECTION AND ASCENSION

Thine Is the Glory

171

Edmond Budry, 1884 (1854-1932)
Tr. by R. Birch Hoyle, 1923 (1875-1939)

JUDAS MACCABEUS 5.5.6.5.6.5.6.5.Ref.
George Frederick Handel, 1747 (1685-1759)

1. Thine is the glo - ry, Ris - en, con-quering Son; End - less is the
2. Lo! Je - sus meets us. Ris - en from the tomb, Lov - ing - ly He
3. No more we doubt Thee, Glo - rious Prince of life! Life is nought with-

vic - tory Thou o'er death hast won. An - gels in bright rai - ment
greets us, Scat - ters fear and gloom; Let His Church with glad - ness
out Thee; Aid us in our strife; Make us more than con-querors,

Rolled the stone a - way, Kept the fold - ed grave - clothes
Hymns of tri - umph sing, For her Lord now liv - eth;
Through Thy death - less love; Bring us safe through Jor - dan

Refrain

Where Thy bod - y lay.
Death hath lost its sting. Thine is the glo - ry, Ris - en, con-quering Son;
To Thy home a - bove.

RESURRECTION AND ASCENSION

Endless is the victory Thou o'er death hast won.

The Strife Is O'er

172

Latin Hymn, c. 1695
Tr. by Francis Pott (1832-1909)

VICTORY 8.8.8. Alleluias
Giovanni P. da Palestrina (1525-1594), adapt.

Alleluia, alleluia, alleluia!

1. The strife is o'er, the battle done; Now is the victor's
2. The pow'rs of death have done their worst, But Christ their legions
3. The three sad days have quickly sped, He rises glorious
4. Lord, by the stripes which wounded You, From death's sting free Your

tri-umph won! Now be the song of praise begun. Allelu-ia!
has dis-persed. Let shouts of holy joy outburst. Allelu-ia!
from the dead. All glory to our risen head! Allelu-ia!
ser-vants too, That we may live and sing to You. Allelu-ia!

* These Alleluias to be sung before stanza 1 and after stanza 4.   Alternate tune, GELOBT SEI GOTT, No. 173

RESURRECTION AND ASCENSION

173

Good Christian Friends, Rejoice!

Cyril A. Alington, 1931 (1872-1955)

GELOBT SEI GOTT 8.8.8.Alleluias
Melchior Vulpius, 1609 (c. 1560-1616)

1. Good Christian friends, re - joice and sing! Now is the tri - umph of our King! To all the world glad news we bring:
2. The Lord of life is risen for aye; Bring flowers of song to strew His way; Let all man - kind re - joice and say:
3. Praise we in songs of vic - to - ry That love, that life which can - not die, And sing with hearts up - lift - ed high:
4. Thy name we bless, O ris - en Lord, And sing to - day with one ac - cord The life laid down, the life re - stored:

Refrain

Al - le - lu - ia! Al - le - lu - ia! Al - le - lu - ia!

Words by permission of *Hymns Ancient and Modern.*

174

Star of Our Hope

1 Thess. 4:16,17
Anon.

WAREHAM L.M.
William Knapp, 1738 (1698-1768)

1. Star of our hope! He'll soon ap-pear, The last loud trum-pet speaks Him near;
2. From heaven angel - ic voi - ces sound: Be-hold the Lord of glo - ry crowned,
3. The grave yields up its pre-cious trust, Which long has slumbered in the dust,
4. De-scend - ing with His az - ure throne, He claims the king-dom for His own;

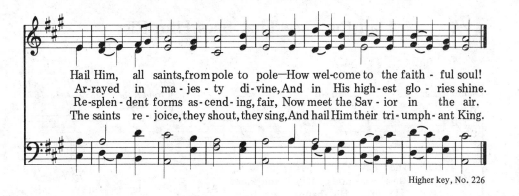

Hail Him, all saints, from pole to pole—How welcome to the faithful soul!
Arrayed in majesty divine, And in His highest glories shine.
Resplendent forms ascending, fair, Now meet the Savior in the air.
The saints rejoice, they shout, they sing, And hail Him their triumphant King.

Higher key, No. 226

Now the Green Blade Rises 175

NOËL NOUVELET 11.10.10.11.

French carol

John M. C. Crum (1872-1958)

Arr. by Martin Shaw (1875-1958)

1. Now the green blade rises from the buried grain, Wheat that in dark earth many days has lain; Love lives again, that with the dead has been; Love is come again like wheat arising green.

2. In the grave they laid Him, love by hatred slain, Thinking that He would never wake again, Laid in the earth like grain that sleeps unseen; Love is come again like wheat arising green.

3. Forth He came in triumph, like the risen grain, He that for three days in the grave had lain; Raised from the dead, my living Lord is seen; Love is come again like wheat arising green.

4. When our hearts are wintry, grieving, or in pain, Your touch can call us back to life again, Fields of our hearts that dead and bare have been; Love is come again like wheat arising green.

Words and arrangement from the *Oxford Book of Carols* by permission of Oxford University Press.

RESURRECTION AND ASCENSION

176   Hail the Day That Sees Him Rise

LLANFAIR 7.7.7.7.Alleluias
Robert Williams, 1817 (1781-1821)
Arr. by John Roberts, 1837 (1822-1877)

Charles Wesley, 1739 (1707-1788) alt.

1. Hail the day that sees Him rise,
2. There the glo-rious tri-umph waits;
3. See! He lifts His hands a-bove;
4. Lord be-yond our mor-tal sight,

Al - le - lu - ia!

Glo-rious to His na-tive skies;
Lift your heads, e-ter-nal gates!
See! He shows the prints of love:
Raise our hearts to reach Thy height,

Al - le - lu - ia!

Christ, a-while to mor-tals giv'n,
Wide un-fold the ra-diant scene;
Hark! His gra-cious lips be-stow,
There Thy face un-cloud-ed see,

Al - le - lu - ia!

Unison

En-ters now the high-est heav'n!
Take the King of glo-ry in!
Bless-ings on His Church be-low.
Find our heav'n of heav'ns in Thee.

Al - le - lu - ia!

RESURRECTION AND ASCENSION

Jesus, Your Blood and Righteousness 177

Nicolaus L. von Zinzendorf (1700-1760)
Tr. by John Wesley (1703-1791) alt.

GARDINER L.M.
Wm. Gardiner's Sacred Melodies, 1815

1. Je-sus, Your blood and righ-teous-ness My beau-ty are, my glo-rious dress; Mid flam-ing worlds, in these ar-rayed, With joy shall I lift up my head.
2. Bold shall I stand in that great day, Cleansed and re-deemed, no debt to pay; For by Your cross, ab-solved I am From sin and guilt, from fear and shame.
3. Lord, I be-lieve Your pre-cious blood, Which at the mer-cy seat of God Pleads for the cap-tives' lib-er-ty, Was al-so shed in love for me.
4. When from the dust of death I rise To claim my man-sion in the skies, This then shall be my on-ly plea: Christ Je-sus lived and died for me.

Higher key, No. 355

178 The Unveiled Christ

Mark 15:37,38
N. B. Herrell, 1916 (1879-1954)

8.7.8.7.Ref.
N. B. Herrell, 1916

1. Once our bless-ed Christ of beau-ty   Was veiled off from hu-man view;
2. Yes, He is with God, the Fa - ther, In - ter-ced-ing there for you;
3. Ho - ly an-gels bow be-fore Him, Men of earth give prais-es due;

But through suf-fering, death, and sor-row   He has rent the veil in two.
For He   is   the Well - be - lov - ed   Since He rent the veil in two.
For He   is   the might - y Con-queror Since He rent the veil in two.

Refrain

O   be-hold the Man of Sor - rows! O   be-hold Him in plain view!

Lo! He   is   the might-y Con-queror Since He rent the veil in two;

PRIESTHOOD

Lo! He is the might-y Con-queror Since He rent the veil in two.

The Wonders of Redeeming Love 179

Heb. 4:14-16
Roswell F. Cottrell (1814-1892)

LA SIERRA C.M.
Perry Beach, 1984 (1917-)

1. The won-ders of re-deem-ing love Our high-est thoughts ex-ceed;
2. He gives Him-self, His life, His all, A sin-less sac-ri-fice.
3. And now be-fore His Fa-ther's face His pre-cious blood He pleads;
4. He knows the frail-ties of our frame, For He has borne our grief;
5. His love will not be sat-is-fied, Till He in glo-ry sees

The Son of God comes from a-bove For sin-ful man to bleed.
For man He drains the cup of gall, For man the vic-tim dies.
For those who seek the throne of grace His love still in-ter-cedes.
Our great High Priest once felt the same, And He can send re-lief.
The faith-ful ones for whom He died From sin for-ev-er free.

180   O Listen to Our Wondrous Story

WHAT DID HE DO? 9.7.9.7.Ref.

James M. Gray (1851-1935)

William Owen (1813-1893)

1. O lis-ten to our won-drous sto-ry, Count-ed once a-mong the lost;
2. No an-gel could His place have tak-en, High-est of the high tho' he;
3. Will you sur-ren-der to this Sav-ior? To His scep-ter hum-bly bow?

Yet One came down from heaven's glo-ry, Sav-ing us at aw-ful cost!
The loved One on the cross for-sak-en Was One of the God-head three!
You, too, shall come to know His fa-vor, He will save you, save you now.

Refrain

Who saved us from e-ter-nal loss?   What did He do? He
Who but God's Son up-on the cross?

Where is He now? In heav-en in-ter-ced - ing!
died for you! Be - lieve it thou, In heav-en in-ter-ced - ing!

Does Jesus Care?

181

1 Peter 5:7
Frank E. Graeff (1860-1919)

9.8.10.8.Ref.
J. Lincoln Hall (1866-1930)

1. Does Je-sus care when my heart is pained Too deep-ly for
2. Does Je-sus care when my way is dark With a name-less
3. Does Je-sus care when I've said good-bye To the dear-est on

mirth and song; As the bur-dens press, and the cares dis-tress,
dread and fear? As the day-light fades in-to deep night shades,
earth to me, And my sad heart aches till it near-ly breaks—

Refrain

And the way grows wea-ry and long?
Does He care e-nough to be near? O yes, He cares— I
Is it aught to Him? does He see?

know He cares! His heart is touched with my grief; When the days are

wea-ry, the long nights drea-ry, I know my Sav-ior cares. (He cares.)

LOVE OF CHRIST FOR US

182 Christ Is Alive

TRURO L.M.

Brian Wren, 1968 (1936-)

Thomas Williams' Psalmodia Evangelica, *1789*

1. Christ is a - live! Let Chris - tians sing. His cross stands emp - ty
2. Christ is a - live! No lon - ger bound To dis - tant years in
3. In ev - ery in - sult, rift, and war Where col - or, scorn or
4. Christ is a - live! As - cend - ed Lord He rules the world His

to the sky. Let streets and homes with prais - es
Pal - es - tine, He comes to claim the here and
wealth di - vide, He suf - fers still, yet loves the
Fa - ther made, Till, in the end, His love a -

ring. His love in death shall nev - er die.
now And con - quer ev - ery place and time.
more, And lives, though ev - er cru - ci - fied.
dored Shall be to all on earth dis - played.

I Will Sing of Jesus' Love

7.7.7.7.Ref.

F. E. Belden, 1886 (1858-1945)

F. E. Belden, 1886

1. I will sing (I will sing) of Je - sus' love, Sing of
2. O the depths (O the depths) of love di - vine! Earth or
3. Noth - ing good (noth - ing good) for Him I've done; How could

Him (sing of Him) who first loved me; For He left (for He left) bright
heaven(earth or heaven)can nev - er know How that sins (how that sins) as
He (how could He) such love be - stow? Lord, I own (Lord, I own) my

Refrain

worlds a - bove, And died on Cal - va - ry.
dark as mine Can be made as white as snow. I will sing (I will sing) of
heart is won, Help me now my love to show.

Je - sus' love, End - less praise (end - less praise) my heart shall give; He has

died (He has died) that I might live— I will sing His love to me.

LOVE OF CHRIST FOR US

184 Jesus Paid It All

6.6.6.6.Ref.

Mrs. Elvina M. Hall, 1865 (1820-1889)

John T. Grape (1835-1915)

1. I hear the Sav - ior say, "Thy strength in - deed is small;
2. Lord, now in - deed I find Thy power, and Thine a - lone,
3. Since noth - ing good have I Where - by Thy grace to claim,
4. And when be - fore the throne I stand in Him com - plete,

Child of weak - ness, watch and pray, Find in Me thine all in all."
Can change the lep - er's spots, And melt the heart of stone.
I'll wash my gar - ment white In the blood of Cal - vary's Lamb.
I'll lay my tro - phies down, All down at Je - sus' feet.

Refrain

Je - sus paid it all, All to Him I owe;

Sin had left a crim - son stain; He washed it white as snow.

LOVE OF CHRIST FOR US

Will L. Thompson (1847-1909)

ELIZABETH Irregular
Will L. Thompson, 1904

1. Je - sus is all the world to me, My life, my joy, my all;
2. Je - sus is all the world to me, My Friend in tri - als sore;
3. Je - sus is all the world to me, And true to Him I'll be;
4. Je - sus is all the world to me, I want no bet - ter friend;

He is my strength from day to day, With-out Him I would fall.
I go to Him for bless - ings, and He gives them o'er and o'er.
O how could I this Friend de - ny, When He's so true to me?
I trust Him now, I'll trust Him when Life's fleet-ing days shall end.

When I am sad to Him I go, No oth - er one can
He sends the sun - shine and the rain, He sends the har - vest's
Fol - low - ing Him I know I'm right, He watch - es o'er me
Beau - ti - ful life with such a Friend; Beau - ti - ful life that

cheer me so; When I am sad He makes me glad, He's my Friend.
gold - en grain; Sun - shine and rain, har - vest of grain, He's my Friend.
day and night; Fol - low - ing Him by day and night, He's my Friend.
has no end; E - ter - nal life, e - ter - nal joy, He's my Friend.

LOVE OF CHRIST FOR US

186   I've Found a Friend

FRIEND 8.7.8.7.D.

J. G. Small, 1863 (1817-1888)

George C. Stebbins, 1878 (1846-1945)

1. I've found a Friend; oh, such a Friend! He loved me ere I knew Him;
2. I've found a Friend; oh, such a Friend! He bled, He died to save me;
3. I've found a Friend; oh, such a Friend! All power to Him is giv - en;
4. I've found a Friend; oh, such a Friend! So kind, and true, and ten - der,

He drew me with the cords of love, And thus He bound me to Him.
And not a - lone the gift of life, But His own self He gave me.
To guard me on my up - ward course, And bring me safe to heav - en.
So wise a coun - se - lor and guide, So might - y a de - fend - er.

And 'round my heart still close - ly twine Those ties which nought can sev - er,
Nought that I have my own I call, I hold it for the Giv - er;
The e - ter - nal glo - ries gleam a - far, To nerve my faint en - deav - or;
From Him, who lov - eth me so well, What power my soul can sev - er?

For I am His, and He is mine, For - ev - er and for - ev - er.
My heart, my strength, my life, my all, Are His, and His for - ev - er.
So now to watch, to work, to war, And then to rest for - ev - er.
Shall life or death, or earth, or hell? No; I am His for - ev - er.

LOVE OF CHRIST FOR US

Jesus, What a Friend for Sinners

HOLY MANNA 8.7.8.7. Ref.
From Wm. Moore's Columbian Harmony, *1825*
Arr. by Wayne Hooper, 1984 (1920-)
J. Wilbur Chapman, 1910 (1859-1918)

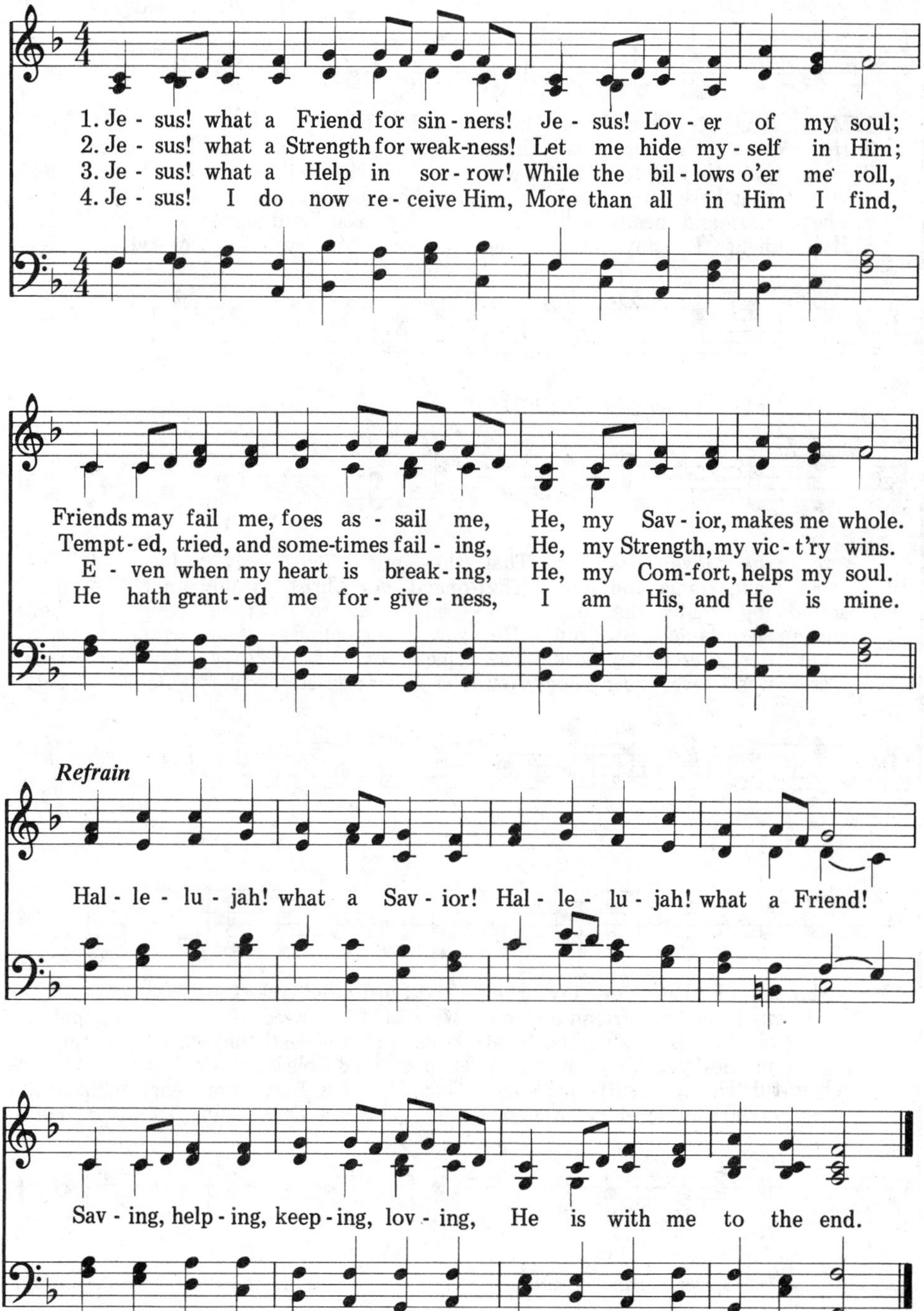
1. Je - sus! what a Friend for sin - ners! Je - sus! Lov - er of my soul;
2. Je - sus! what a Strength for weak-ness! Let me hide my - self in Him;
3. Je - sus! what a Help in sor - row! While the bil - lows o'er me roll,
4. Je - sus! I do now re - ceive Him, More than all in Him I find,
Friends may fail me, foes as - sail me, He, my Sav - ior, makes me whole.
Tempt - ed, tried, and some-times fail - ing, He, my Strength, my vic - t'ry wins.
E - ven when my heart is break - ing, He, my Com-fort, helps my soul.
He hath grant - ed me for - give - ness, I am His, and He is mine.
Refrain
Hal - le - lu - jah! what a Sav - ior! Hal - le - lu - jah! what a Friend!
Sav - ing, help - ing, keep - ing, lov - ing, He is with me to the end.

188 My Song Is Love Unknown

LOVE UNKNOWN 6.6.6.6.8.8.

Samuel Crossman (1624-1683)

John Ireland (1879-1962)

1. My song is love un - known, My Sav - ior's love to me, Love to the love - less shown, That they might love - ly be. O who am I that for my sake My Lord should take frail flesh and die?

2. He came from His blest throne, Sal - va - tion to be - stow, But men made strange, and none The longed - for Christ would know. But O my Friend, my Friend in - deed Who at my need His life did spend.

3. Some - times they strew His way, And His sweet prais - es sing, Re - sound - ing all the day, Ho - san - nas to their King. Then "Cru - ci - fy" is all their breath, And for His death they thirst and cry.

4. Why, what hath my Lord done? What makes this rage and spite? He made the lame to run, He gave the blind their sight. Sweet in - ju - ries! yet they at these Them - selves dis - please, and 'gainst Him rise.

5. They rise, and needs will have My dear Lord made a - way; A mur - der - er they save, The Prince of life they slay. Yet cheer - ful He to suff - 'ring goes, That He His foes from thence might free.

6. Here might I stay and sing, No sto - ry so di - vine: Nev - er was love, dear King, Nev - er was grief like Thine! This is my Friend, in whose sweet praise I all my days could glad - ly spend.

Alternate tune, RHOSYMEDRE, No. 650

LOVE OF CHRIST FOR US

All That Thrills My Soul

8.7.8.7.Ref.

Thoro Harris, 1931 (1873-1955)

Thoro Harris

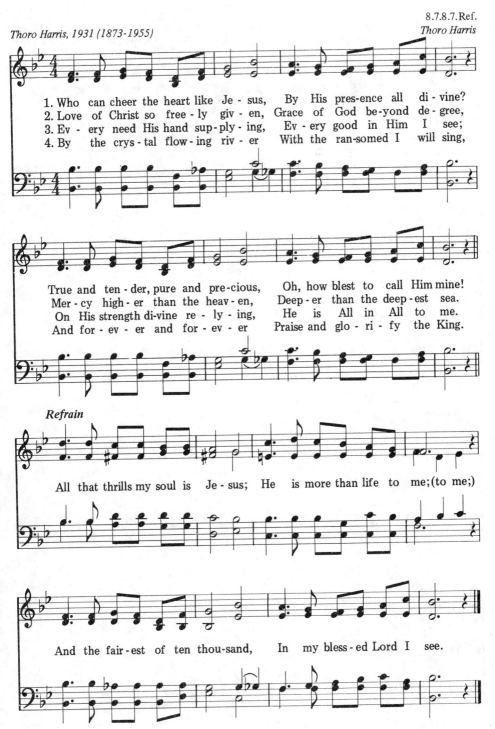

1. Who can cheer the heart like Je - sus, By His pres-ence all di - vine?
2. Love of Christ so free - ly giv - en, Grace of God be-yond de - gree,
3. Ev - ery need His hand sup-ply - ing, Ev - ery good in Him I see;
4. By the crys - tal flow - ing riv - er With the ran-somed I will sing,

True and ten - der, pure and pre-cious, Oh, how blest to call Him mine!
Mer - cy high - er than the heav - en, Deep - er than the deep - est sea.
On His strength di-vine re - ly - ing, He is All in All to me.
And for - ev - er and for - ev - er Praise and glo - ri - fy the King.

Refrain

All that thrills my soul is Je - sus; He is more than life to me;(to me;)

And the fair - est of ten thou-sand, In my bless - ed Lord I see.

LOVE OF CHRIST FOR US

190

Jesus Loves Me

Prov. 8:17
Anna B. Warner (1827-1915) alt.

BRADBURY 7.7.7.7.Ref.
William B. Bradbury, 1862 (1816-1868)

1. Je - sus loves me! this I know, For the Bi - ble tells me so;
2. Je - sus loves me! He who died Heav-en's gate to o - pen wide:
3. Je - sus, take this heart of mine, Make it pure and whol - ly Thine;

Lit - tle ones to Him be - long, They are weak, but He is strong.
He will wash a - way my sin, Let His lit - tle child come in.
On the cross You died for me, I will love and live for Thee.

Refrain

Yes, Je - sus loves me! Yes, Je - sus loves me!

Yes, Je - sus loves me! The Bi - ble tells me so.

LOVE OF CHRIST FOR US

Love Divine

Charles Wesley, 1747 (1707-1788)

BEECHER 8.7.8.7.D.
John Zundel, 1870 (1815-1882)

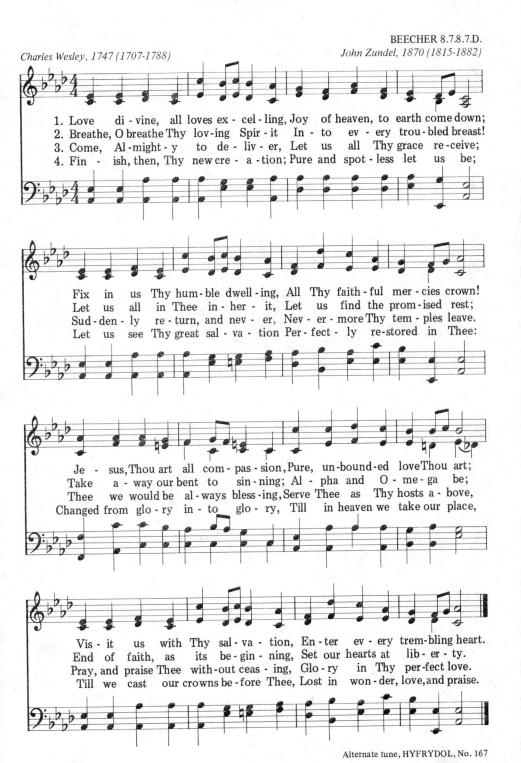

1. Love di - vine, all loves ex - cel - ling, Joy of heaven, to earth come down;
2. Breathe, O breathe Thy lov - ing Spir - it In - to ev - ery trou - bled breast!
3. Come, Al - might - y to de - liv - er, Let us all Thy grace re - ceive;
4. Fin - ish, then, Thy new cre - a - tion; Pure and spot - less let us be;

Fix in us Thy hum - ble dwell - ing, All Thy faith - ful mer - cies crown!
Let us all in Thee in - her - it, Let us find the prom - ised rest;
Sud - den - ly re - turn, and nev - er, Nev - er - more Thy tem - ples leave.
Let us see Thy great sal - va - tion Per - fect - ly re - stored in Thee:

Je - sus, Thou art all com - pas - sion, Pure, un - bound - ed love Thou art;
Take a - way our bent to sin - ning; Al - pha and O - me - ga be;
Thee we would be al - ways bless - ing, Serve Thee as Thy hosts a - bove,
Changed from glo - ry in - to glo - ry, Till in heaven we take our place,

Vis - it us with Thy sal - va - tion, En - ter ev - ery trem - bling heart.
End of faith, as its be - gin - ning, Set our hearts at lib - er - ty.
Pray, and praise Thee with - out ceas - ing, Glo - ry in Thy per - fect love.
Till we cast our crowns be - fore Thee, Lost in won - der, love, and praise.

Alternate tune, HYFRYDOL, No. 167

LOVE OF CHRIST FOR US

192

O Shepherd Divine

John 10:16
Herbert Work (1904-1982)

MY SHEPHERD Irregular
Herbert Work

1. O Shep-herd di-vine, I know Thou art mine; Thy search in the night was for me. This bleak world is cold, but warm is Thy fold; My Shep-herd, I fol-low Thee. Thy beau-ti-ful lamp shin-eth bright o'er my way, Thy glo-ri-ous light un-to Thy per-fect day. Thro'

2. O Shep-herd di-vine, I know Thou art mine; Thy great heart was bro-ken for me. Thy grace and Thy law I pic-ture in awe; They kissed up-on Cal-va-ry. Ah! life that was giv-en to ran-som my soul, Ah! heart that was bro-ken to make sin-ners whole, This

3. O Shep-herd di-vine, I know Thou art mine; I hear Thee say, "Fol-low thou Me." Thy mes-sage to-day il-lu-mines my way; The Spir-it of Proph-e-cy. I thrill at Thy mar-vel-ous love to Thy sheep, The way Thou dost lead to the still wa-ters deep, One

Duet

Four-Part

LOVE OF CHRIST FOR US

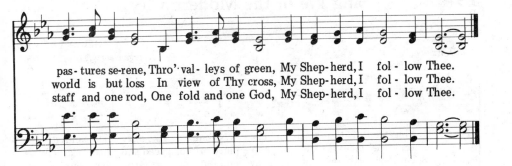

pas-tures se-rene, Thro' val-leys of green, My Shep-herd, I fol-low Thee.
world is but loss In view of Thy cross, My Shep-herd, I fol-low Thee.
staff and one rod, One fold and one God, My Shep-herd, I fol-low Thee.

Savior, Teach Me 193

7.7.7.7.

Jane Eliza Leeson (1807-1882)   A. L. Butler, 1969 (1933-   )

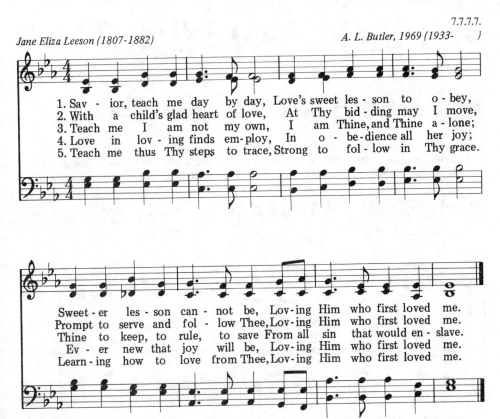

1. Sav - ior, teach me day by day, Love's sweet les - son to o - bey,
2. With a child's glad heart of love, At Thy bid - ding may I move,
3. Teach me I am not my own, I am Thine, and Thine a - lone;
4. Love in lov - ing finds em-ploy, In o - be-dience all her joy;
5. Teach me thus Thy steps to trace, Strong to fol-low in Thy grace.

Sweet-er les - son can - not be, Lov-ing Him who first loved me.
Prompt to serve and fol - low Thee, Lov-ing Him who first loved me.
Thine to keep, to rule, to save From all sin that would en - slave.
Ev - er new that joy will be, Lov-ing Him who first loved me.
Learn-ing how to love from Thee, Lov-ing Him who first loved me.

LOVE OF CHRIST FOR US

194 Sing We of the Modern City

Fred H. Kaan (1929-)
Unison

GENEVA 8.7.8.7.D.
George Henry Day (1883-1966)

1. Sing we of the mod-ern cit - y, Scene a - like of joy and stress;
2. In the cit - y full of peo - ple, World of speed and hec - tic days,
3. God is not re - mote in heav - en, But on earth to share our shame,

Sing we of its name-less peo - ple In their ur - ban wil - der - ness.
In the ev - er-chang-ing set - ting Of the lat - est trend and craze,
Chang-ing graph and mass and num - ber In - to per-sons with a name.

In - to end - less rows of hous-es Life is set a mil - lion -fold,
Christ is pres - ent, and a - mong us; In the crowd we see Him stand.
Christ has shown, be - yond sta - tis - tics, Hu - man life with glo - ry crowned,

Life ex - pressed in hu - man be - ings Dai - ly born and grow-ing old.
In the bus - tle of the cit - y Je - sus Christ is ev - ery man.
By His time-less pres-ence prov-ing Peo - ple mat - ter, peo - ple count!

LOVE OF CHRIST FOR US

Showers of Blessing

Eze. 34:26
Daniel W. Whittle (1840-1901)

8.7.8.7.Ref.
James McGranahan (1840-1915)

1. "There shall be show-ers of bless-ing;"This is the prom-ise of love;
2. "There shall be show-ers of bless-ing—"Pre-cious re-viv-ing a-gain;
3. "There shall be show-ers of bless-ing;"Send them up-on us, O Lord;
4. "There shall be show-ers of bless-ing;" O that to-day they might fall,

There shall be sea-sons re-fresh-ing, Sent from the Sav-ior a-bove.
O - ver the hills and the val-leys, Sound of a-bun-dance of rain.
Grant to us now a re-fresh-ing; Come, and now hon-or Thy word.
Now as to God we're con-fess-ing, Now as on Je-sus we call!

Refrain

Show - ers of bless-ing, Show-ers of bless-ing we need;
Show - ers, show-ers of bless-ing,

Mer - cy drops round us are fall-ing, But for the show-ers we plead.

LOVE OF CHRIST FOR US

196 Tell Me the Old, Old Story

Katherine Hankey, 1886 (1834-1911)

EVANGEL 7.6.7.6.D.Ref.
William H. Doane, 1867 (1832-1915)

1. Tell me the old, old sto - ry, Of un - seen things a - bove,
2. Tell me the sto - ry soft - ly, With ear - nest tones and grave;
3. Tell me the same old sto - ry, When you have cause to fear

Of Je - sus and His glo - ry, Of Je - sus and His love;
Re - mem - ber I'm the sin - ner Whom Je - sus came to save;
That this world's emp - ty glo - ry Is cost - ing me too dear;

Tell me the sto - ry sim - ply, As to a lit - tle child,
Tell me the sto - ry al - ways, If you would real - ly be,
Yes, and when that world's glo - ry Is dawn - ing on my soul,

For I am weak and wea - ry, And help-less and de - filed.
In an - y time of trou - ble, A com-fort - er to me.
Tell me the old, old sto - ry: "Christ Je - sus makes thee whole."

LOVE OF CHRIST FOR US

Refrain

Tell me the old, old sto-ry, Tell me the old, old sto-ry,

Tell me the old, old sto-ry, Of Je-sus and His love.

The King of Love My Shepherd Is 197

Psalm 23
H. W. Baker, 1868 (1821-1877)

DOMINUS REGIT ME 8.7.8.7.
John B. Dykes, 1868 (1823-1876)

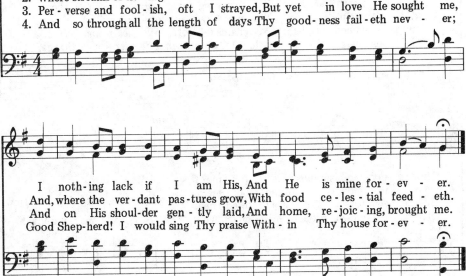

1. The King of love my Shep-herd is, Whose good-ness fail-eth nev - er;
2. Where streams of liv-ing wa-ter flow My ran-somed soul He lead - eth,
3. Per-verse and fool-ish, oft I strayed, But yet in love He sought me,
4. And so through all the length of days Thy good-ness fail-eth nev - er;

I noth-ing lack if I am His, And He is mine for-ev - er.
And, where the ver-dant pas-tures grow, With food ce-les-tial feed - eth.
And on His shoul-der gen-tly laid, And home, re-joic-ing, brought me.
Good Shep-herd! I would sing Thy praise With-in Thy house for-ev - er.

Alternate tune, ST. COLUMBA, No. 639

LOVE OF CHRIST FOR US

198

And Can It Be?

SAGINA 8.8.8.8.8.8.Ref.

Charles Wesley (1707-1788)

Thomas Campbell, 1812 (1777-1844)

1. And can it be that I should gain An in-t'rest in the
2. He left His Fa-ther's throne a - bove, So free, so in-fi-
3. Long my im-pris-oned spir-it lay Fast bound in sin and
4. No con-dem-na-tion now I dread; Je - sus, and all in

Sav-ior's blood? Died He for me, who caused His pain? For me, who
nite His grace; Emp-tied Him-self of all but love, And bled for
na-ture's night; Thine eye dif-fused a quick-'ning ray, I woke, the
Him, is mine! A - live in Him, my liv-ing Head, And clothed in

Him to death pur-sued? A - maz-ing love! how can it be That
Ad-am's help-less race; 'Tis mer-cy all, im-mense and free; For,
dun-geon flamed with light; My chains fell off, my heart was free; I
righ-teous-ness di - vine, Bold I ap-proach th'e-ter-nal throne, And

Refrain

Thou, my God, shouldst die for me?
O my God, it found out me.
rose, went forth and fol-lowed Thee. A - maz-ing love! How
claim the crown, through Christ my own. A - maz-ing love!

LOVE OF CHRIST FOR US

can it be   That Thou,   my   God, shouldst   die   for   me?
How can it be   That Thou, my God,

The Head That Once Was Crowned   199

ST. MAGNUS C.M.
Jeremiah Clark (1669-1707)
Arr. by Melvin West, 1984 (1930-   )

Thomas Kelly (1769-1855)

1. The head that once was crowned with thorns Is crowned with glo - ry   now;
2. The high- est place that heaven af - fords Is   His,   is   His   by   right;
3. The joy of   all who dwell a - bove, The joy   of   all   be - low,
4. To them the cross, with all   its shame, With all   its grace   is   given;

A roy - al   di - a - dem a - dorns The might - y vic - tor's   brow.
The King of   kings, and Lord of   lords, And heaven's e - ter - nal   light.
To whom He   man - i - fests His   love, And grants His name to   know.
Their name an   ev - er - last - ing name, Their joy the joy   of   heaven.

Alternate harmony, No. 19

LOVE OF CHRIST FOR US

200 The Lord Is Coming

1 Cor. 16:22
Anon. c. 1849
St. 4 by Mary A. Steward, c. 1886

THE SOLID ROCK L.M.Ref.
Wm. B. Bradbury, 1863 (1816-1868)
Arr. by Melvin West, 1984 (1930-   )

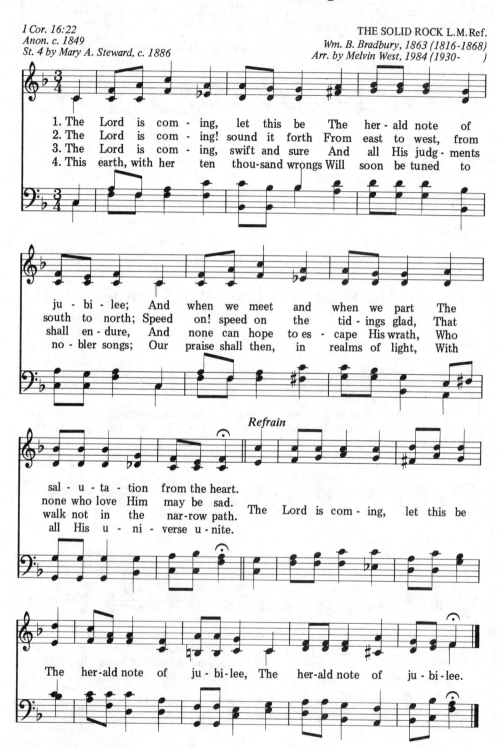

1. The Lord is com - ing, let this be The her - ald note of
2. The Lord is com - ing! sound it forth From east to west, from
3. The Lord is com - ing, swift and sure And all His judg - ments
4. This earth, with her ten thou-sand wrongs Will soon be tuned to

ju - bi - lee; And when we meet and when we part The
south to north; Speed on! speed on the tid - ings glad, That
shall en - dure, And none can hope to es - cape His wrath, Who
no - bler songs; Our praise shall then, in realms of light, With

Refrain

sal - u - ta - tion from the heart.
none who love Him may be sad.
walk not in the nar-row path.
all His u - ni - verse u - nite.
The Lord is com - ing, let this be

The her-ald note of ju - bi-lee, The her-ald note of ju - bi-lee.

Arrangement copyright © 1984 by Melvin West.

Alternate harmony, No. 522

SECOND ADVENT

Christ Is Coming

201

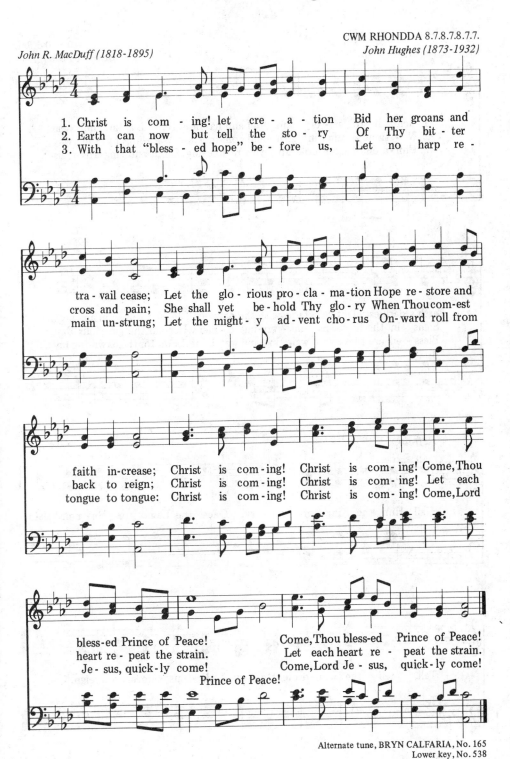

CWM RHONDDA 8.7.8.7.8.7.7.

John R. MacDuff (1818-1895)

John Hughes (1873-1932)

1. Christ is com - ing! let cre - a - tion Bid her groans and tra - vail cease; Let the glo - rious pro - cla - ma - tion Hope re - store and faith in - crease; Christ is com - ing! Christ is com - ing! Come, Thou bless-ed Prince of Peace! Come, Thou bless-ed Prince of Peace!

2. Earth can now but tell the sto - ry Of Thy bit - ter cross and pain; She shall yet be - hold Thy glo - ry When Thou com-est back to reign; Christ is com - ing! Christ is com - ing! Let each heart re - peat the strain. Let each heart re - peat the strain.

3. With that "bless - ed hope" be - fore us, Let no harp re - main un - strung; Let the might - y ad - vent cho - rus On - ward roll from tongue to tongue: Christ is com - ing! Christ is com - ing! Come, Lord Je - sus, quick - ly come! Come, Lord Je - sus, quick - ly come!

Prince of Peace!

Alternate tune, BRYN CALFARIA, No. 165
Lower key, No. 538

SECOND ADVENT

Hail Him the King of Glory

Henry de Fluiter, 1916 (1872-1970)

10.5.10 6. Ref.
Henry de Fluiter, 1916

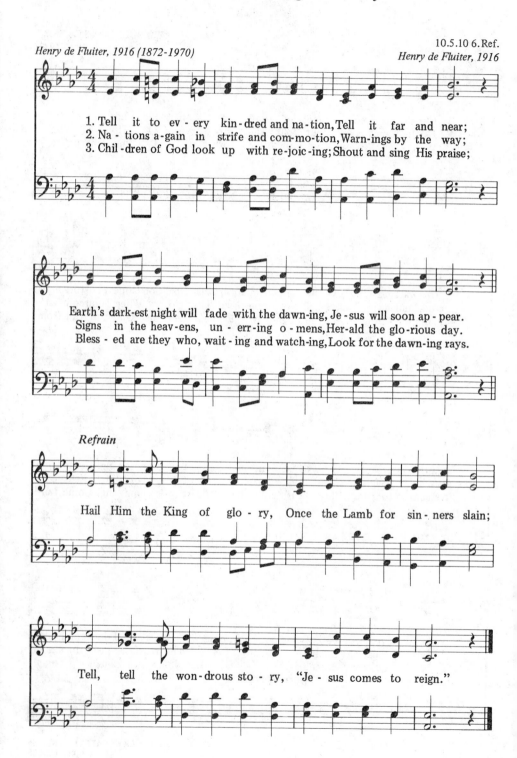

1. Tell it to ev - ery kin - dred and na - tion, Tell it far and near;
2. Na - tions a - gain in strife and com - mo - tion, Warn-ings by the way;
3. Chil - dren of God look up with re - joic - ing; Shout and sing His praise;

Earth's dark-est night will fade with the dawn-ing, Je - sus will soon ap - pear.
Signs in the heav-ens, un - err - ing o - mens, Her-ald the glo-rious day.
Bless - ed are they who, wait - ing and watch-ing, Look for the dawn-ing rays.

Refrain

Hail Him the King of glo - ry, Once the Lamb for sin - ners slain;

Tell, tell the won - drous sto - ry, "Je - sus comes to reign."

SECOND ADVENT

This Is the Threefold Truth

203

CHALLENGE 6.6.6.6.3.4.5.Ref.

Fred Pratt Green (1903-   )

Allen W. Foster, 1984 (1940-   )

1. This is the three-fold truth On which our faith de-pends;
2. By this we are up-held When doubt and grief as-sail
3. This is the three-fold truth Which, if we hold it fast,

And with this joy-ful cry Wor-ship be-gins and ends;
Our Chris-tian for-ti-tude, And on-ly grace a-vails.
Chang-es the world and us And brings us home at last.

Refrain

Christ has died! Christ is ris-en! Christ will come a-gain!

SECOND ADVENT

204   # Come, Thou Long Expected Jesus

HYFRYDOL 8.7.8.7.D.

Charles Wesley, 1744 (1707-1788) alt.

Rowland H. Prichard, c. 1830 (1811-1887)
Arr. by Ralph Vaughan Williams, 1951 (1872-1958)

1. Come, Thou long-ex-pect-ed Je-sus! Born to set Thy peo-ple free,
2. Born Thy peo-ple to de-liv-er, Born a child, and yet a King,

From our fears and sins re-lease us, Let us find our rest in Thee.
Born to reign in us for-ev-er, Now Thy gra-cious king-dom bring,

Is-rael's strength and con-so-la-tion, Hope of all the earth Thou art;
By Thy own e-ter-nal Spir-it, Rule in all our hearts a-lone;

Dear De-sire of ev-ery na-tion, Joy of ev-ery long-ing heart.
By Thy all-suf-fi-cient mer-it, Raise us to Thy glo-rious throne.

Music from the *English Hymnal* by permission of Oxford University Press.

SECOND ADVENT

Alternate tune, STUTTGART, No. 659
Alternate harmony, No. 167

Gleams of the Golden Morning

10.5.10.5.Ref.

S. J. Graham

S. J. Graham

1. The gold-en morn-ing is fast ap-proach-ing; Je-sus soon will come
2. The gos-pel sum-mons will soon be car-ried To the na-tions round;
3. At-tend-ed by all the shin-ing an-gels, Down the flam-ing sky
4. There those loved ones who have long been part-ed, Will all meet that day;

To take His faith-ful and hap-py chil-dren To their prom-ised home.
The Bride-groom then will cease to tar-ry And the trum-pet sound.
The Judge will come, and will take His peo-ple Where they will not die.
The tears of those who are bro-ken-heart-ed Will be wiped a-way.

Refrain

O, we see the gleams of the gold-en morn-ing

Pierc-ing through this night of gloom! O, we see the

gleams of the gold-en morn-ing That will burst the tomb.

SECOND ADVENT

206 Face to Face

8.7.8.7. Ref.

Mrs. Frank A. Breck, 1898 (1855-1934)　　　　　　　*Grant Colfax Tullar, 1898 (1869-1950)*

1. Face to face with Christ my Sav - ior, Face to face, what will it be,
2. On - ly faint - ly now I see Him, With the dark-ening veil be-tween,
3. What re - joic - ing in His pres-ence, When are ban-ished grief and pain;
4. Face to face! oh, bliss - ful mo-ment! Face to face—to see and know;

When with rap-ture I be-hold Him, Je - sus Christ, who died for me?
But a bless-ed day is com-ing, When His glo - ry shall be seen.
When the crook-ed ways are straight-ened, And the dark things shall be plain!
Face to face with my Re-deem - er, Je - sus Christ, who loves me so.

Refrain

Face to face shall I be-hold Him, Far be-yond the star-ry sky;

Face to face in all His glo - ry I shall see Him by and by!

SECOND ADVENT

It May Be at Morn

Mark 13:35
H. L. Turner, 19th century

12.12.12.7.Ref.
James McGranahan (1840-1907)

1. It may be at morn, when the day is a - wak - ing, When sun-light through dark - ness and shad - ow is break-ing, That Je - sus will come in the full - ness of glo - ry To re - ceive from the world His own.

2. It may be at mid - day, it may be at twi - light, It may be, per - chance, that the black - ness of mid-night Will burst in - to light in the blaze of His glo - ry, When Je - sus re - ceives His own.

3. O joy! O de - light! should we go with-out dy - ing, No sick - ness, no sad - ness, no dread, and no cry - ing, Caught up through the clouds with our Lord in - to glo - ry, When Je - sus re - ceives His own.

Refrain

O Lord Je - sus, how long, how long Ere we shout the glad song? Christ re - turn - eth, Hal - le - lu - jah! hal - le - lu - jah! A - men, Hal - le - lu - jah! A - men.

SECOND ADVENT

208 There'll Be No Dark Valley

10.10.10.7.Ref.

William O. Cushing (1823-1902)

Ira D. Sankey (1840-1908)

1. There'll be no dark val-ley when Je-sus comes, There'll be no dark
2. There'll be no more sor-row when Je-sus comes, There'll be no more
3. There'll be songs of greet-ing when Je-sus comes, There'll be songs of

val-ley when Je-sus comes; There'll be no dark val-ley when Je-sus
sor-row when Je-sus comes; But a glo-rious mor-row when Je-sus
greet-ing when Je-sus comes; And a joy-ful meet-ing when Je-sus

Refrain

comes To gath-er His loved ones home. To gath-er His loved ones

home, To gath-er His loved ones home; There'll be
safe home, safe home;

no dark val-ley when Je-sus comes To gath-er His loved ones home.

SECOND ADVENT

That Glorious Day Is Coming

CHEROKEE LANE 7.6.7.6.D.

Anon.

Melvin West, 1984 (1930-)

1. That glo-rious day is com-ing, The hour is has-tening on;
2. The saints, then all vic-to-rious Will go to meet their Lord;
3. O Chris-tian, keep from sleep-ing, And let your love a-bound;

Its ra-diant light is near-ing, Far bright-er than the sun;
An earth both bright and glo-rious, Will then be their re-ward;
Be watch-ful, prayer-ful, faith-ful, The trum-pet soon will sound!

In yon-der clouds of heav-en, The Sav-ior will ap-pear,
And God Him-self there reign-ing, Will wipe all tears a-way;
O sin-ner, hear the warn-ing! To Je-sus quick-ly fly!

And gath-er all His cho-sen, To meet Him in the air.
Nor clouds nor night re-main-ing, But one e-ter-nal day.
Then you, in that blest morn-ing, May meet Him in the sky!

Music copyright © 1984 by Melvin West.

SECOND ADVENT

210 Wake, Awake, for Night Is Flying

Matt. 25:6, 7
Philip Nicolai, 1599 (1556-1608)
Tr. Catherine Winkworth, 1858 (1827-1878)

WACHET AUF Irregular
Melody by Philip Nicolai, 1599
Harm. by J. S. Bach (1685-1750)

1. Wake, a-wake, for night is fly - ing, The watch-men on the heights are cry - ing, A - wake, Je - ru - sa - lem, a - rise! Rise up, with will-ing feet Go forth, the Bride-groom meet; Al - le - lu - ia! Bear through the night your well-trimmed light, Speed forth to join the mar - riage rite.

Mid-night's sol-emn hour is toll - ing, His char - iot wheels are near - er roll - ing, He comes; pre - pare, ye vir - gins wise.

2. Zi - on hears the watch-men sing - ing, Her heart with deep de - light is spring - ing, She wakes, she ris - es from her gloom; All hail, in-car-nate Lord, Our crown, and our re - ward! Al - le - lu - ia! We haste a - long, in pomp of song, And glad-some join the mar - riage throng.

Forth her Bride-groom comes, all - glo - rious, In grace ar-rayed, by truth vic - to - rious; Her Star is risen, her Light is come!

3. Lamb of God, the heavens a - dore Thee, And men and an - gels sing be - fore Thee, With harp and cym - bal's clear-est tone. No vi - sion ev - er brought, No ear hath ev - er caught, Such bliss and joy; We raise the song, we swell the throng, To praise Thee a - ges all a - long.

By the pearl - y gates in won - der We stand, and swell the voice of thun - der, That ech - oes round Thy daz - zling throne.

SECOND ADVENT

Lo! He Comes

Rev. 1:7
John Cennick, 1752 (1718-1755)
Charles Wesley, 1758 (1707-1788)
Alt. by Martin Madan, 1760 (1726-1790)

HOLYWOOD 8.7.8.7.8.7.
J. F. Wade's Cantus Diversi, *1751*

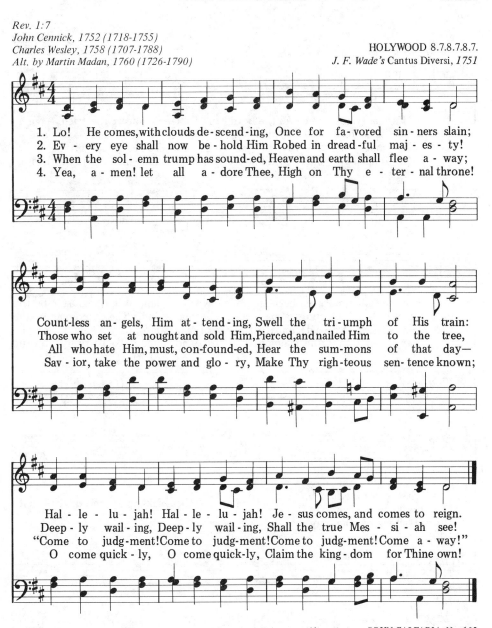

1. Lo! He comes, with clouds de-scend-ing, Once for fa-vored sin-ners slain;
2. Ev-ery eye shall now be-hold Him Robed in dread-ful maj-es-ty!
3. When the sol-emn trump has sound-ed, Heaven and earth shall flee a-way;
4. Yea, a-men! let all a-dore Thee, High on Thy e-ter-nal throne!

Count-less an-gels, Him at-tend-ing, Swell the tri-umph of His train:
Those who set at nought and sold Him, Pierced, and nailed Him to the tree,
All who hate Him, must, con-found-ed, Hear the sum-mons of that day—
Sav-ior, take the power and glo-ry, Make Thy righ-teous sen-tence known;

Hal-le-lu-jah! Hal-le-lu-jah! Je-sus comes, and comes to reign.
Deep-ly wail-ing, Deep-ly wail-ing, Shall the true Mes-si-ah see!
"Come to judg-ment! Come to judg-ment! Come to judg-ment! Come a-way!"
O come quick-ly, O come quick-ly, Claim the king-dom for Thine own!

Alternate tune, BRYN CALFARIA, No. 165

212   'Tis Almost Time for the Lord to Come

9.6.8.9.Ref.

G. W. Sederquist, c. 1902

G. W. Sederquist

1. 'Tis al - most time for the Lord to come, I hear the peo - ple
2. The signs fore - told in the sun and moon, In earth and sea and
3. It must be time for the wait - ing church To cast her pride a -
4. Go quick - ly out in the streets and lanes And in the broad high -

say; The stars of heav-en are grow - ing dim, It must be the
sky, A - loud pro-claim to all man - kind, The coming of the
way, With gird - ed loins and burn - ing lamps, To look for the
way, And call the maimed, the halt, and blind, To be ready for the

Refrain

break-ing of the day.
Mast - er draw-eth nigh.
break-ing of the day.
break-ing of the day.

O it must be the break-ing of the day! O it

must be the breaking of the day! The night is al-most gone, The

SECOND ADVENT

day is com-ing on; O it must be the break-ing of the day!

Jesus Is Coming Again
213

10.7.10.7.Ref.

Jessie E. Strout, 1872

George E. Lee, 1872

1. Lift up the trum-pet, and loud let it ring: Je-sus is com-ing a-gain!
2. Ech - o it, hill-tops; pro-claim it, ye plains: Je-sus is com-ing a-gain!
3. Heav-ings of earth, tell the vast, wondering throng: Je-sus is com-ing a-gain!
4. Na - tions are an-gry— by this we do know Je-sus is com-ing a-gain!

Cheer up, ye pil-grims, be joy - ful and sing; Je-sus is com-ing a-gain!
Com-ing in glo - ry, the Lamb that was slain; Je-sus is com-ing a-gain!
Tem-pests and whirlwinds, the an - them pro-long; Je-sus is com-ing a-gain!
Knowl-edge in-creas-es; men run to and fro; Je-sus is com-ing a-gain!

Refrain

Com - ing a-gain, com-ing a-gain, Je - sus is com-ing a-gain!

SECOND ADVENT

214   We Have This Hope

GENERAL CONFERENCE 10.8.10.8.7.7.7.7.10.8.

Wayne Hooper, 1962 (1920-)

Wayne Hooper

We have this hope that burns with-in our hearts,

Hope in the com-ing of the Lord.

We have this faith that Christ a - lone im - parts,

Faith in the prom-ise of His Word.

We be-lieve the time is here, When the na - tions far and near

SECOND ADVENT

*High notes optional.

The King Shall Come

215

MORNING SONG C.M.

Based on the Greek
John Brownlie, 1907 (1859-1925) alt.

From Kentucky Harmony, 1816
Arr. by Melvin West, 1984 (1930-   )

1. The King shall come when morn-ing dawns And light tri - um-phant breaks,
2. Not as of old a lit - tle child, To bear and fight and die,
3. O, bright-er than the ris - ing morn When Christ, vic-to - rious, rose
4. O, bright-er than that glo-rious morn Shall dawn up - on our race
5. The King shall come when morn-ing dawns And light and beau-ty brings.

When beau-ty gilds the east-ern hills And life to joy a-wakes.
But crowned with glo-ry like the sun That lights the morn-ing sky.
And left the lone-some place of death, De - spite the rage of foes.
The day when Christ in splen-dor comes, And we shall see His face.
Hail, Christ the Lord! Your peo-ple pray: Come quick-ly, King of kings.

Harmony setting, No. 576

SECOND ADVENT

216 When the Roll Is Called Up Yonder

15.11.15.11.Ref.
J. M. Black

J. M. Black (1856-1938)

1. When the trum-pet of the Lord shall sound, and time shall be no more,
2. On that bright and cloud-less morn-ing, when the dead in Christ shall rise,
3. Let us la-bor for the Mas-ter from the dawn till set-ting sun,

And the morn-ing breaks, e-ter-nal, bright and fair; When the saved of
And the glo-ry of His res-ur-rec-tion share; When His cho-sen
Let us talk of all His won-drous love and care, Then, when all of

earth shall gath-er o-ver on the oth-er shore, And the roll is
ones shall gath-er to their home be-yond the skies, And the roll is
life is o-ver, and our work on earth is done, And the roll is

Refrain

called up yon-der, I'll be there. When the roll...... is called up yon - der,
When the roll is called up yon-der, I'll be there,

SECOND ADVENT

When the roll.......... is called up yon - der, When the
When the roll is called up yon - der, I'll be there,

roll........ is called up yon-der, When the roll is called up yon-der, I'll be there.
When the roll

The Church Has Waited Long 217

GARDEN CITY S.M.

Horatius Bonar (1808-1889)

Horatio W. Parker, 1890 (1863-1919)

1. The church has wait - ed long   Her ab - sent Lord   to   see;
2. How long, O Lord our God,   Ho - ly and true and good,
3. We long to   hear Thy voice,   To see Thee face to face,
4. Come, Lord, and wipe a - way   The curse, the sin, the stain,

And still   in lone - li - ness she waits, A friend - less strang - er she.
Wilt Thou not judge Thy suffer-ing church, Her sighs and   tears and blood?
To share Thy crown and glo - ry   then, As now we   share Thy grace.
And make this blight - ed world of ours Thine own fair world a - gain.

SECOND ADVENT

218

When He Cometh

Mal. 3:17
W. O. Cushing, 1866 (1823-1903)

8.6.8.5.Ref.
George F. Root (1820-1895)

1. When He com-eth, when He com-eth To make up His jew-els,
2. He will gath-er, He will gath-er The gems for His king-dom,
3. Lit-tle chil-dren, lit-tle chil-dren Who love their Re-deem-er,

All His jew-els, pre-cious jew-els, His loved and His own.
All the pure ones, all the bright ones, His loved and His own.
Are the jew-els, pre-cious jew-els, His loved and His own.

Refrain

Like the stars of the morn-ing, His bright crown a-dorn-ing,

They shall shine in their beau-ty, Bright gems for His crown.

SECOND ADVENT

When Jesus Comes in Glory

NORWICK 7.6.7.6.D.

Samuel M. Miller, 1922 (1890-)
Unison

Bertram Ernest Woods (1900-1982)

1. When Je - sus comes in glo - ry, As Lord and King of kings,
2. His voice like rush - ing wa - ters Will reach with might-y sound
3. And we who are be - liev - ing And His ap - pear - ing love,
4. O   has - ten Thine ap - pear - ing, Thou bright and Morn - ing Star!

O what a won-drous sto - ry The bless - ed Bi - ble brings:
In - to the deep-est quar-ters Of all cre - a - tion round;
Shall know we are re - ceiv-ing His glo - ry from a - bove;
Lord, may we soon be hear-ing The trum-pet sound a - far;

His face will shine like sun-light, His head be white as snow,
And at this won-drous greet-ing The dead in Christ shall rise,
His res - ur - rec - tion pow-er Will raise us to the place
Thy peo - ple all are yearn-ing To be Thy rap-tured bride,

His eyes like flam-ing fire-light, His feet like brass a - glow.
Their Lord and Sav - ior meet-ing In glo - ry in the skies.
Where we that won-drous ho - ur Shall see Him face to face.
And at Thine own re - turn-ing Be caught up to Thy side.

*To simplify, right hand plays treble chords, left hand plays the lowest bass line.
Music copyright © 1933 by Methodist Conference.

Alternate tune, ST. THEODULPH, No. 230

SECOND ADVENT

220

When He Comes

1 Thess. 4:14-17
Timothy Dudley-Smith, 1967 (1926-   )

DAVID 3.3.11.8.8.11.Ref.
Wayne Hooper, 1984 (1920-   )

When He comes, (when He comes) When He comes, (when He comes) We shall

1. see the Lord in glo - ry when He comes!
2. hear the trum - pet sound - ed when He comes! (when He comes)
3. all rise up to meet Him when He comes!

As I read the gos - pel sto - ry, We shall see the Lord in glo - ry,
We shall hear the trum-pet sound-ed, See the Lord by saints sur-round-ed,
We shall all rise up to meet Him, When He calls His own to greet Him

We shall see the Lord in glo - ry when He comes! (when He comes)
We shall hear the trum - pet sound-ed when He comes! (when He comes)
We shall all rise up to meet Him when He comes! (when He comes)

SECOND ADVENT

Refrain

With the al - le - lu - ias ring-ing to the sky, (to the sky)

With the al - le - lu - ias ring-ing to the sky! (to the sky)

As I read the gos-pel sto - ry, We shall see the Lord in glo - ry,
We shall hear the trum-pet sound-ed, See the Lord by saints sur-round-ed,
We shall all rise up to meet Him, When He calls His own to greet Him,

With the al - le - lu - ias ring-ing to the sky! (to the sky)

SECOND ADVENT

221 Rejoice, the Lord Is King

Phil. 4:4
Charles Wesley (1707-1788)

DARWALL'S 148th 6.6.6.6.8.8.
John Darwall (1731-1789)

1. Re - joice, the Lord is King! Your Lord and King a - dore!
2. Je - sus, the Sav - ior, reigns, The God of truth and love;
3. His king-dom can - not fail, He rules o'er earth and heaven;
4. Re - joice, in glo - rious hope! Our Lord the judge shall come,

Re - joice, give thanks, and sing, And tri - umph
When He had purged our stains, He took His
The keys of death and grave Are to our
And take His ser - vants up To their e -

ev - er - more: Lift up your heart, lift up your voice!
seat a - bove: Lift up your heart, lift up your voice!
Je - sus given: Lift up your heart, lift up your voice!
ter - nal home: Lift up your heart, lift up your voice!

Re - joice, a - gain I say, re - joice!
Re - joice, a - gain I say, re - joice!
Re - joice, a - gain I say, re - joice!
Re - joice, a - gain I say, re - joice!

SECOND ADVENT

Hark! Ten Thousand Harps and Voices   222

HARWELL 8.7.8.7.7.7.8.6.

Thomas Kelly (1769-1854)

Lowell Mason (1792-1872)

1. Hark! ten thou-sand harps and voic-es Sound the note   of praise a-bove;
2. King of   glo-ry, reign for-ev-er, Thine an   ev-er-last-ing crown;
3. Sav-ior, has-ten Thine ap-pear-ing; Bring, O bring   the glo-rious day,

Je-sus reigns, and heaven re-joic-es,   Je-sus reigns, the God of   love:
Noth-ing from Thy love shall sev-er Those whom Thou hast made Thine own:
When, the aw-ful sum-mons hear-ing, Heaven and earth shall pass a-way:

See, He sits on yon-der throne;   Je-sus rules the world a-
See, He   sits   on yon-der throne; Je-sus rules   the world a-
Hap-py ob-jects of Thy grace,   Des-tined to be-hold Thy
Hap-py   ob-   jects of Thy grace,   Des-tined to   be-hold Thy
Then, with gold-en harps we'll sing,   "Glo-ry, glo-ry to our
Then, with gold-   en harps we'll sing, "Glo-ry, glo-   ry to our

lone.   Al-le-lu-ia! Al-le-lu-ia! Al-le-lu-ia! A-men.
face.   Al-le-lu-ia! Al-le-lu-ia! Al-le-lu-ia! A-men.
King!" Al-le-lu-ia! Al-le-lu-ia! Al-le-lu-ia! A-men.

KINGDOM AND REIC

223 Crown Him With Many Crowns

Rev. 19:12
Matthew Bridges, 1851, (1800-1894), and
Rev. by Godfrey Thring, 1874 (1823-1903)

DIADEMATA S.M.D.
George J. Elvey, 1868 (1816-1893)

1. Crown Him with man - y crowns, The Lamb up - on His throne;
2. Crown Him the Lord of love! Be - hold His hands and side,
3. Crown Him the Lord of peace! Whose hand a scep - ter sways
4. Crown Him the Lord of years, The Po - ten - tate of time,

Hark! how the heaven - ly an - them drowns All mu - sic but its own!
Those wounds, yet vis - i - ble a - bove, In beau - ty glo - ri - fied;
From pole to pole, that wars may cease, And all be prayer and praise;
Cre - a - tor of the roll - ing spheres, In - ef - fa - bly sub - lime!

A - wake, my soul, and sing Of Him who died for thee;
No an - gel in the sky Can ful - ly bear that sight,
His reign shall know no end, And round His pierc - ed feet
All hail! Re - deem - er, hail! For Thou hast died for me;

And hail Him as thy match - less King Through all e - ter - ni - ty.
But down - ward bends his won - dering eye At mys - ter - ies so great.
Fair flowers of Par - a - dise ex - tend, Their fra - grance ev - er sweet.
Thy praise shall nev - er, nev - er fail Through - out e - ter - ni - ty.

Alternate harmony, No. 616

M AND REIGN

Seek Ye First the Kingdom

224

Norman Elliott, 1951 (1893-1973)

CRANHAM 11.11.11.11.
Gustav Holst (1874-1934)

1. Seek ye first the king - dom, 'Tis your Fa - ther's will.
2. As for hid - den trea - sure, Or for match - less pearl,
3. As the si - lent leav - en works its se - cret way,
4. As the ten - der seed - ling grows up tall and strong,
5. Hum - blest shall be great - est, poor in spir - it reign;

So the voice of Je - sus bids us fol - low still.
When at last dis - cov - ered, some will sell their all:
Or as grows the seed grain through the night and day;
And the birds of heav - en to its branch - es throng;
Home shall come the child - like, born through Thee a - gain;

Sav - ior, we would hear Thee, Fol - low, find, and see;
So, when breaks the vi - sion of that king - dom fair,
Lord, so be the in - crease, peace - a - ble but sure,
So shall all God's chil - dren, from the east and west,
Ea - ger hearts ar - rive there on the pil - grim's road,

And in life's ad - ven - ture Thy dis - ci - ples be.
Ours shall be its rich - es And its beau - ty rare.
Of Thy word with - in us, And Thy king - dom's power.
Gath - er to His king - dom, In its shad - ow rest.
Hail! the king - dom glo - rious Of the liv - ing God!

Alternate tune, CUDDESON, No. 360

KINGDOM AND REIGN

225 God Is Working His Purpose Out

Hab. 2:14
Arthur C. Ainger, 1894 (1841-1919)

PURPOSE Irregular
Martin Shaw, 1931 (1875-1958)

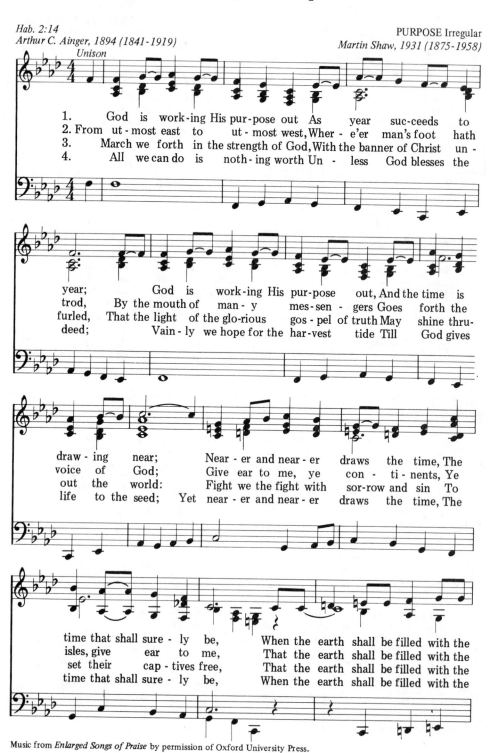

1. God is work-ing His pur-pose out As year suc-ceeds to year; God is work-ing His pur-pose out, And the time is draw-ing near; Near-er and near-er draws the time, The time that shall sure-ly be, When the earth shall be filled with the

2. From ut-most east to ut-most west, Wher-e'er man's foot hath trod, By the mouth of man-y mes-sen-gers Goes forth the voice of God; Give ear to me, ye con-ti-nents, Ye isles, give ear to me, That the earth shall be filled with the

3. March we forth in the strength of God, With the banner of Christ un-furled, That the light of the glo-rious gos-pel of truth May shine thru-out the world: Fight we the fight with sor-row and sin To set their cap-tives free, That the earth shall be filled with the

4. All we can do is noth-ing worth Un-less God blesses the deed; Vain-ly we hope for the har-vest tide Till God gives life to the seed; Yet near-er and near-er draws the time, The time that shall sure-ly be, When the earth shall be filled with the

Music from *Enlarged Songs of Praise* by permission of Oxford University Press.

KINGDOM AND REIGN

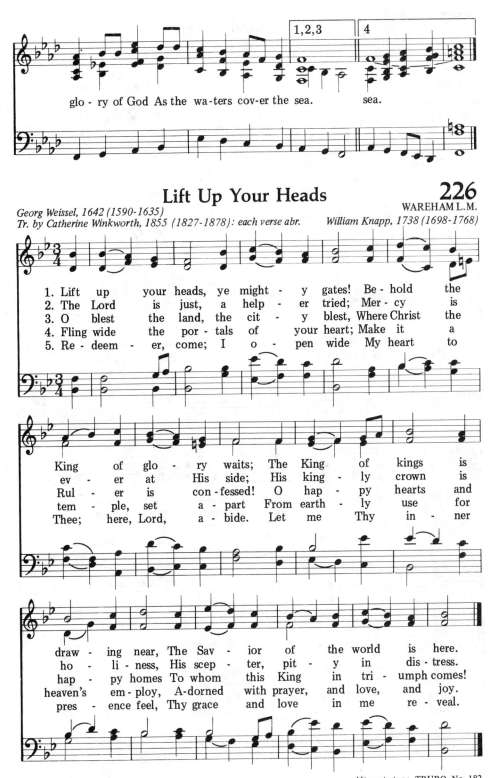

Lift Up Your Heads

226

WAREHAM L.M.

Georg Weissel, 1642 (1590-1635)
Tr. by Catherine Winkworth, 1855 (1827-1878): each verse abr.

William Knapp, 1738 (1698-1768)

glo - ry of God As the wa-ters cov-er the sea. sea.

1. Lift up your heads, ye might - y gates! Be - hold the
2. The Lord is just, a help - er tried; Mer - cy is
3. O blest the land, the cit - y blest, Where Christ the
4. Fling wide the por - tals of your heart; Make it a
5. Re - deem - er, come; I o - pen wide My heart to

King of glo - ry waits; The King of kings is
ev - er at His side; His king - ly crown is
Rul - er is con - fessed! O hap - py hearts and
tem - ple, set a - part From earth - ly use for
Thee; here, Lord, a - bide. Let me Thy in - ner

draw - ing near, The Sav - ior of the world is here.
ho - li - ness, His scep - ter, pit - y in dis - tress.
hap - py homes To whom this King in tri - umph comes!
heaven's em - ploy, A-dorned with prayer, and love, and joy.
pres - ence feel, Thy grace and love in me re - veal.

Alternate tune, TRURO, No. 182
Lower key, No. 174

KINGDOM AND REIGN

227

Jesus Shall Reign

Psalm 72:8-19
Isaac Watts (1674-1748)

DUKE STREET L.M.
John Hatton (1710-1793)
Arr. by Melvin West, 1984 (1930-   )

1. Je - sus shall reign wher - e'er the sun
2. Peo - ple and realms of ev - ery tongue
3. Bless - ings a - bound wher - e'er He reigns:
4. Let ev - ery crea - ture rise and bring

Does its suc - ces - sive jour - neys run;
Dwell on His love with sweet - est song;
The pris -'ners leap to lose their chains,
Hon - ors pe - cu - liar to our King;

His king - dom stretch from shore to shore,
And in - fant voic - es shall pro - claim
The wea - ry find e - ter - nal rest,
An - gels de - scend with songs a - gain,

Till moons shall wax and wane no more.
Their earth - ly bless - ings on His name.
And all who suf - fer want are blest.
And earth re - peat the loud a - men.

KINGDOM AND REIGN

Alternate harmony, No. 82

A Hymn of Glory Let Us Sing

228

LASST UNS ERFREUEN L.M. Alleluias
Geistliche Kirchengesänge, *Köln, 1623*
Arr. by Ralph Vaughan Williams, 1906 (1872-1958)

The Venerable Bede (673-735)
Tr. Lutheran Book of Worship, *1978*

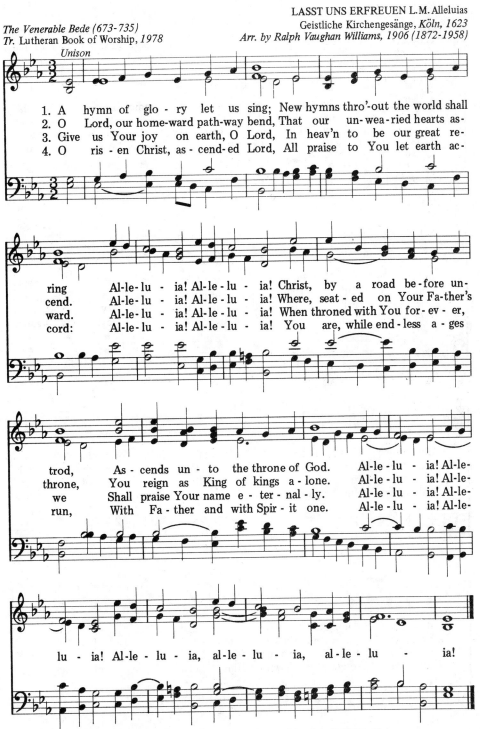

1. A hymn of glo-ry let us sing; New hymns thro'-out the world shall
2. O Lord, our home-ward path-way bend, That our un-wea-ried hearts as-
3. Give us Your joy on earth, O Lord, In heav'n to be our great re-
4. O ris-en Christ, as-cend-ed Lord, All praise to You let earth ac-

ring   Al-le-lu - ia! Al-le-lu - ia! Christ, by a road be-fore un-
cend.   Al-le-lu - ia! Al-le-lu - ia! Where, seat-ed on Your Fa-ther's
ward.   Al-le-lu - ia! Al-le-lu - ia! When throned with You for-ev-er,
cord: Al-le-lu - ia! Al-le-lu - ia! You are, while end-less a-ges

trod,   As-cends un-to the throne of God. Al-le-lu - ia! Al-le-
throne, You reign as King of kings a-lone. Al-le-lu - ia! Al-le-
we   Shall praise Your name e-ter-nal-ly. Al-le-lu - ia! Al-le-
run,   With Fa-ther and with Spir-it one. Al-le-lu - ia! Al-le-

lu - ia! Al-le-lu - ia, al-le-lu - ia, al-le-lu - ia!

Lower key, No. 2

GLORY AND PRAISE

229   All Hail the Power of Jesus' Name

Edward Perronet, 1779 (1726-1792)

CORONATION C.M.
Oliver Holden, 1793 (1765-1844)

1. All hail the power of Jesus' name! Let angels prostrate fall; Bring forth the royal diadem, And crown Him Lord of all! Bring forth the royal diadem, And crown Him Lord of all.

2. Ye seed of Israel's chosen race, Ye ransomed of the fall, Hail Him who saves you by His grace, And crown Him Lord of all! Hail Him who saves you by His grace, And crown Him Lord of all.

3. Let every kindred, every tribe, On this terrestrial ball, To Him all majesty ascribe, And crown Him Lord of all! To Him all majesty ascribe, And crown Him Lord of all.

4. Oh, that with yonder sacred throng We at His feet may fall, Join in the everlasting song, And crown Him Lord of all! Join in the everlasting song, And crown Him Lord of all.

GLORY AND PRAISE

All Glory, Laud, and Honor

Matt. 21:8,9
Theodulph of Orleans (750-821)
Tr. by John M. Neale (1818-1866)

ST. THEODULPH 7.6.7.6.D.
Melchior Teschner, 1613 (1584-1635)

230

1. All glo-ry, laud, and hon - or To Thee, Re-deem-er, King,
2. The com-pa-ny of an - gels Are prais-ing Thee on high,
3. To Thee, be-fore Thy pas - sion, They sang their hymns of praise;

To whom the lips of chil - dren Made sweet ho-san-nas ring.
And mor-tal men and all things Cre - at - ed make re - ply.
To Thee, now high ex - alt - ed, Our mel - o - dy we raise.

Thou art the King of Is - ra - el, Thou, Da-vid's roy - al Son,
The peo - ple of the He - brews With palms be - fore Thee went;
Thou didst ac - cept their prais - es; Ac-cept the praise we bring,

Who in the Lord's name com - est, The King and Bless-ed One.
Our praise and prayer and an - thems Be - fore Thee we pre - sent.
Who in all good de - light - est, Thou good and gra-cious King.

GLORY AND PRAISE

231
Blest Be the King

Mark 11:9,10
Frederico J. Pagura (1923-)
Tr. by Fred Pratt Green (1903-)

STOKESAY CASTLE 7.6.7.6.D.
Eric H. Thiman (1900-1975)

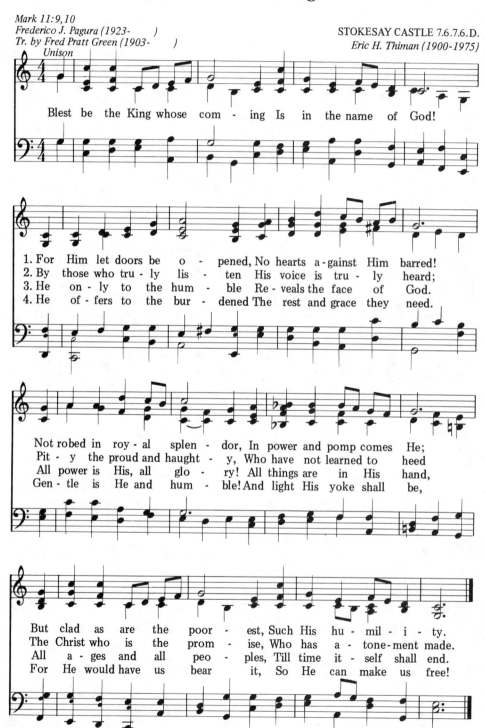

Blest be the King whose com - ing Is in the name of God!

1. For Him let doors be o - pened, No hearts a-gainst Him barred!
2. By those who tru - ly lis - ten His voice is tru - ly heard;
3. He on - ly to the hum - ble Re - veals the face of God.
4. He of - fers to the bur - dened The rest and grace they need.

Not robed in roy - al splen - dor, In power and pomp comes He;
Pit - y the proud and haught - y, Who have not learned to heed
All power is His, all glo - ry! All things are in His hand,
Gen - tle is He and hum - ble! And light His yoke shall be,

But clad as are the poor - est, Such His hu - mil - i - ty.
The Christ who is the prom - ise, Who has a - tone-ment made.
All a - ges and all peo - ples, Till time it - self shall end.
For He would have us bear it, So He can make us free!

Alternate tune, ST. THEODULPH, No. 230

GLORY AND PRAISE

At the Name of Jesus

232

Phil. 2:8-11
Caroline M. Noel, 1870 (1817-1977)

KING'S WESTON 6.5.6.5.D.
Ralph Vaughan Williams, 1925 (1872-1958)

Unison

1. At the name of Je - sus Ev - ery knee shall bow,
2. At His voice cre - a - tion Sprang at once to sight,
3. Hum - bled for a sea - son, To re - ceive a name
4. In your hearts en - throne Him: There let Him sub - due
5. Sure - ly, this Lord Je - sus Shall re - turn a - gain,

Ev - ery tongue con - fess Him King of glo - ry now;
All the an - gel fac - es, All the hosts of light,
From the lips of sin - ners, Un - to whom He came;
All that is not ho - ly, All that is not true;
With His Fa - ther's glo - ry, With His an - gel train;

'Tis the Fa - ther's plea - sure We should call Him Lord,
Thrones and dom - i - na - tions, Stars up - on their way,
He is God the Sav - ior, He is Christ the Lord,
Crown Him as your cap - tain In temp - ta - tion's hour,
For all wreaths of em - pire Meet up - on His brow,

Who from the be - gin - ning Was the might - y Word.
All the heaven - ly or - ders In their great ar - ray.
Ev - er to be wor - shiped, Trust - ed and a - dored.
Let His will en - fold you In its light and power.
And our hearts con - fess Him King of glo - ry now.

Harmony setting, No. 581

GLORY AND PRAISE

233   Christ, Whose Glory Fills the Skies

RATISBON 7.7.7.7.7.7.
J. G. Werner's Choralbuch, *1815*
Arr. by W. H. Monk (1823-1889)

Charles Wesley (1707-1788)

1. Christ, whose glo - ry fills the skies, Christ, the true, the only light, Sun of Righteousness, arise, Triumph o'er the shades of night; Day-spring from on high, be near; Day-star, in my heart appear.

2. Dark and cheer - less is the morn Un - ac - com - pa - nied by Thee; Joy - less is the day's return Till Thy mer - cy's beams I see; Till they in - ward light im - part, Cheer my eyes and warm my heart.

3. Vis - it, then, this soul of mine; Pierce the gloom of sin and grief; Fill me, Radian - cy di - vine; Scat - ter all my un - be - lief; More and more Thy - self dis - play, Shin - ing to the per - fect day.

Christ Is the World's Light

234

CHRISTE SANCTORUM 10.11.11.6.
Melody from Paris Antiphoner, *1746*

Fred Pratt Green, 1969 (1903-)

Unison

1. Christ is the world's Light, He and none oth-er; born in our dark-ness, He be-came our broth-er. If we have seen Him, we have seen the Fa-ther: Glo-ry to God on high!

2. Christ is the world's Peace, He and none oth-er; no one can serve Him and de-spise an-oth-er. Who else u-nites us one in God the Fa-ther? Glo-ry to God on high!

3. Christ is the world's Life, He and none oth-er; sold once for sil-ver, mur-dered here, our broth-er, He who re-deems us reigns with God the Fa-ther. Glo-ry to God on high!

4. Give God the glo-ry, God and none oth-er; give God the glo-ry, Spir-it, Son, and Fa-ther; give God the glo-ry, God in Man my broth-er; Glo-ry to God on high!

GLORY AND PRAISE

235 Christ Is Made the Sure Foundation

Eph. 2:20; 1 Pet. 2:6
Latin Hymn, c. 7th century
Tr. by John M. Neale (1818-1866) alt.

EDEN CHURCH 8.7.8.7.8.7.
Dale Wood (1934-   )

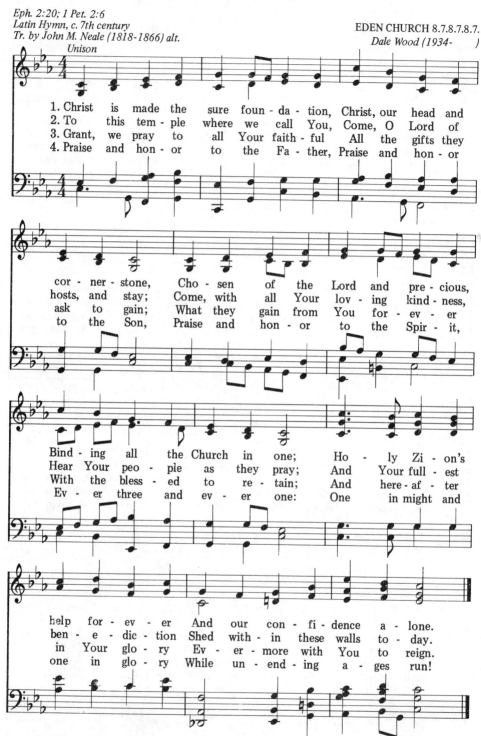

1. Christ is made the sure foun-da-tion, Christ, our head and cor-ner-stone, Cho-sen of the Lord and pre-cious, Bind-ing all the Church in one; Ho-ly Zi-on's help for-ev-er And our con-fi-dence a-lone.

2. To this tem-ple where we call You, Come, O Lord of hosts, and stay; Come, with all Your lov-ing kind-ness, Hear Your peo-ple as they pray; And Your full-est ben-e-dic-tion Shed with-in these walls to-day.

3. Grant, we pray to all Your faith-ful All the gifts they ask to gain; What they gain from You for-ev-er With the bless-ed to re-tain; And here-af-ter in Your glo-ry Ev-er-more with You to reign.

4. Praise and hon-or to the Fa-ther, Praise and hon-or to the Son, Praise and hon-or to the Spir-it, Ev-er three and ev-er one: One in might and one in glo-ry While un-end-ing a-ges run!

Alternate tune, WESTMINSTER ABBEY, No. 607

GLORY AND PRAISE

I Love Thee

I LOVE THEE 11.11.11.11.
Ingall's Christian Harmony, *1805*

Anon.

1. I love Thee, I love Thee, I love Thee, my Lord;
2. I'm hap-py, I'm hap-py, O, won-drous ac-count!
3. O Je-sus, my Sav-ior, with Thee I am blest,
4. O, who's like my Sav-ior? He's Sa-lem's bright King;

I love Thee, my Sav-ior, I love Thee, my God.
My joys are im-mor-tal, I stand on the mount!
My life and sal-va-tion, my joy and my rest:
He smiles, and He loves me, and helps me to sing.

I love Thee, I love Thee, and that Thou dost know;
I gaze on my trea-sure and long to be there,
Thy name be my theme, and Thy love be my song;
I'll praise Him, I'll praise Him, with notes loud and clear,

But how much I love Thee my ac-tions will show.
With Je-sus and an-gels, and kin-dred so dear.
Thy grace shall in-spire both my heart and my tongue.
While riv-ers of plea-sure my spir-it do cheer.

GLORY AND PRAISE

237   In the Cross of Christ I Glory

RATHBUN 8.7.8.7.

John Bowring, 1825 (1792-1872)

Ithamar Conkey, 1849 (1815-1867)

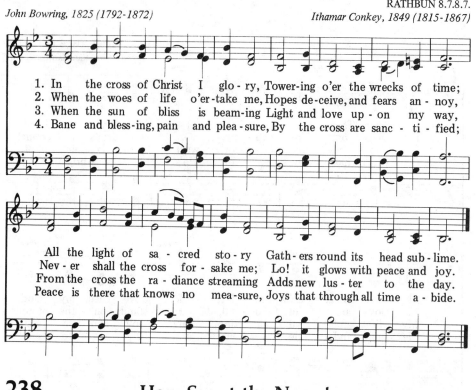

1. In the cross of Christ I glo-ry, Tower-ing o'er the wrecks of time;
2. When the woes of life o'er-take me, Hopes de-ceive, and fears an-noy,
3. When the sun of bliss is beam-ing Light and love up-on my way,
4. Bane and bless-ing, pain and plea-sure, By the cross are sanc-ti-fied;

All the light of sa-cred sto-ry Gath-ers round its head sub-lime.
Nev-er shall the cross for-sake me; Lo! it glows with peace and joy.
From the cross the ra-diance streaming Adds new lus-ter to the day.
Peace is there that knows no mea-sure, Joys that through all time a-bide.

238   How Sweet the Name!

Song of Sol. 1:3

ST. PETER C.M.

John Newton, 1779 (1725-1807)

Alexander R. Reinagle, 1836 (1799-1877)

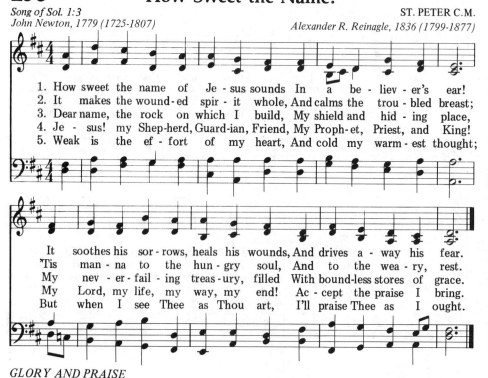

1. How sweet the name of Je-sus sounds In a be-liev-er's ear!
2. It makes the wound-ed spir-it whole, And calms the trou-bled breast;
3. Dear name, the rock on which I build, My shield and hid-ing place,
4. Je-sus! my Shep-herd, Guard-ian, Friend, My Proph-et, Priest, and King!
5. Weak is the ef-fort of my heart, And cold my warm-est thought;

It soothes his sor-rows, heals his wounds, And drives a-way his fear.
'Tis man-na to the hun-gry soul, And to the wea-ry, rest.
My nev-er-fail-ing treas-ury, filled With bound-less stores of grace.
My Lord, my life, my way, my end! Ac-cept the praise I bring.
But when I see Thee as Thou art, I'll praise Thee as I ought.

GLORY AND PRAISE

Jesus, Priceless Treasure

239

JESU, MEINE FREUDE 6.6.5.D.7.8.6.

Johann Franck (1618-1677)
Tr. by Catherine Winkworth (1827-1878)

Mel. by Johann Crüger (1598-1662)
Arr. by Johann S. Bach (1685-1750)

1. Je - sus, price - less trea - sure, Source of pur - est plea - sure,
2. In Thine arm I rest me; Foes who would mo - lest me
3. Hence all fears and sad - ness! For the Lord of glad - ness,

Tru - est Friend to me: Ah! how long I've pant - ed, And my heart has
Can - not reach me here; Though the earth be shak - ing, Ev - ery heart be
Je - sus en - ters in; Those who love the Fa - ther, Tho' the storms may

faint - ed, Thirst - ing, Lord, for Thee. Thine I am, O spot - less Lamb,
quak - ing, Je - sus calms my fear; Sin and hell in con - flict fell
gath - er, Still have peace with - in; Yea, what - e'er I here must bear,

I will suf - fer naught to hide Thee, Nought I ask be - side Thee.
With their bit - ter storms as - sail me: Je - sus will not fail me.
Still in Thee lies pur - est plea - sure, Je - sus, price - less trea - sure!

GLORY AND PRAISE

240   Fairest Lord Jesus

Gesangbuch, *Munster, 1672*
Tr. by *Joseph A. Seiss (1823-1904)*

CRUSADER'S HYMN 5.6.8.5.5.8.
From Schlesische Volkslieder, *1842*
Arr. by Richard S. Willis (1819-1900)

1. Fair - est Lord Je - sus, Rul - er of all na - ture,
2. Fair are the mead - ows, Fair - er still the wood - lands,
3. Fair is the sun - shine, Fair - er still the moon - light,
4. Beau - ti - ful Sav - ior, Lord of the na - tions,

O Thou of God and man the Son! Thee will I cher - ish,
Robed in the bloom - ing garb of spring; Je - sus is fair - er,
And all the twin - kling, star - ry host; Je - sus shines bright - er,
Son of God and Son of Man! Glo - ry and hon - or,

Thee will I hon - or, Thou art my glo - ry, joy, and crown.
Je - sus is pur - er, Who makes the woe - ful heart to sing.
Je - sus shines pur - er Than all the an - gels heaven can boast.
Praise, ad - o - ra - tion, Now and for - ev - er - more be Thine!

241   Jesus, the Very Thought of Thee

Attrib. to Bernard of Clairvaux (1091-1153)
Tr. by Edward Caswall, 1849 (1814-1878)

ST. AGNES C.M.
John B. Dykes, 1866 (1823-1876)

1. Je - sus, the ver - y thought of Thee, With sweet-ness fills my breast;
2. No voice can sing, no heart can frame, Nor can the mem - ory find
3. O hope of ev - ery con - trite heart! O joy of all the meek,
4. But what to those who find? Ah! this Nor tongue nor pen can show:
5. Je - sus, our on - ly joy be Thou, As Thou our prize wilt be;

GLORY AND PRAISE

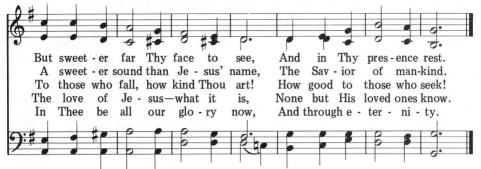

But sweet-er far Thy face to see, And in Thy pres-ence rest.
A sweet-er sound than Je-sus' name, The Sav-ior of man-kind.
To those who fall, how kind Thou art! How good to those who seek!
The love of Je-sus—what it is, None but His loved ones know.
In Thee be all our glo-ry now, And through e-ter-ni-ty.

Jesus, Thou Joy of Loving Hearts   242

Bernard of Clairvaux (1091-1153)
Tr. by Ray Palmer (1808-1887)

ABENDS L.M.

Herbert S. Oakley, 1874 (1830-1903)

1. Je - sus, Thou joy of lov - ing hearts! Thou fount of
2. Thy truth un-changed has ev - er stood; Thou sav - est
3. We taste Thee, O Thou liv - ing Bread, And long to
4. Our rest-less spir - its yearn for Thee, Where-e'er our
5. O Je - sus, ev - er with us stay; Make all our

life! Thou light of men! From the best bliss that
those that on Thee call; To them that seek Thee
feast up - on Thee still; We drink of Thee, the
change - ful lot is cast; Glad, when Thy gra - cious
mo - ments calm and bright; Chase the dark night of

earth im - parts, We turn un - filled to Thee a - gain.
Thou art good, To them that find Thee, all in all.
Foun - tain - head, And thirst our souls from Thee to fill!
smile we see, Blest, when our faith can hold Thee fast.
sin a - way, Shed o'er the world Thy ho - ly light!

GLORY AND PRAISE

243 King of Glory, King of Peace

GWALCHMAI 7.4.7.4.D.

George Herbert (1593-1633)

Joseph David Jones (1827-1870)

1. King of glo-ry, King of peace, I will love Thee;
2. Where-fore with my ut-most art I will sing Thee,
3. Seven whole days, not one in seven, I will praise Thee;

And that love may nev-er cease, I will move Thee.
And the cream of all my heart I will bring Thee.
In my heart, though not in heav'n, I can raise Thee.

Thou hast grant-ed my re-quest, Thou hast heard me;
Though my sins a-gainst me cried, Thou didst clear me;
Small it is, in this poor sort To en-roll Thee:

Thou didst note my work-ing breast, Thou hast spared me.
And a-lone, when they re-plied, Thou didst hear me.
Ev'n e-ter-ni-ty's too short To ex-tol Thee.

Alternate tune, LLANFAIR, No. 176

GLORY AND PRAISE

My Song Shall Be of Jesus

NYLAND 7.6.7.6.D.

Fanny J. Crosby, 1875 (1820-1915)
Adapt. by E. Margaret Clarkson, 1973 (1915-   )

Traditional Finnish Melody
Arr. by David Evans, 1928 (1874-1948)

1. My song shall be of Je - sus, His mer - cy crowns my days,
2. My song shall be of Je - sus, When sit - ting at His feet,
3. My song shall be of Je - sus, While press-ing on my way

He fills my cup with bless - ings, And tunes my heart to praise;
I call to mind His good - ness And know my joy's com - plete;
To where my home shines glo - rious In pure and per - fect day.

My song shall be of Je - sus, The pre - cious Lamb of God,
My song shall be of Je - sus, What - ev - er ills be - fall,
And when my soul shall en - ter The man - y man-sions fair,

Who gave Him - self my ran - som, And bought me with His blood.
I'll sing the grace that saves me, And tri - umphs o - ver all.
A song of praise to Je - sus I'll sing for - ev - er there.

GLORY AND PRAISE

245 More About Jesus

L.M.Ref.

Eliza E. Hewitt, 1887 (1851-1920)

John R. Sweney, 1887 (1837-1899)

1. More a-bout Je - sus I would know, More of His grace to oth - ers show;
2. More a-bout Je - sus let me learn, More of His ho - ly will dis - cern;
3. More a-bout Je - sus; in His word, Hold-ing com-mun-ion with my Lord,
4. More a-bout Je - sus; on His throne, Rich-es in glo - ry all His own;

1 More of His sav - ing full - ness see, More of His love who died for me.
2 Spir - it of God, my teach - er be, Show-ing the things of Christ to me.
3 Hear - ing His voice in ev - ery line, Mak-ing each faith-ful say - ing mine.
4 More of His king-dom's sure in-crease; More of His com - ing, Prince of Peace.

Refrain

More, more a-bout Je - sus, More, more a-bout Je - sus;

More of His sav - ing full - ness see, More of His love who died for me.

GLORY AND PRAISE

Worthy, Worthy Is the Lamb

246

Rev. 5:12
Anon.

WORTHY 7.7.7.3.Ref.
Arranged

1. Wor - thy, wor - thy is the Lamb, Wor - thy, wor - thy is the Lamb;
2. Sav - ior, let Thy king - dom come! Now the power of sin con - sume;
3. Thus may we each mo - ment feel, Love Him, serve Him, praise Him still,

Wor - thy, wor - thy is the Lamb That was slain.
Bring Thy blest mil - len - ni - um, Ho - ly Lamb.
Till we all on Zi - on's hill See the Lamb.

Refrain

Glo - ry, hal - le - lu - jah! Praise Him, hal - le - lu - jah!

Glo - ry, hal - le - lu - jah To the Lamb!

GLORY AND PRAISE

247   Come, My Way

COME, MY WAY 7.7.7.7.

George Herbert (1593-1633)   *Alexander Brent Smith (1889-1950)*

1. Come, my Way, my Truth, my Life: Such a Way, as gives us breath; Such a Truth, as ends all strife; Such a Life, as kill-eth death.

2. Come, my Light, my Feast, my Strength: Such a Light, as shows a feast; Such a Feast, as mends in length; Such a Strength, as makes His guest.

3. Come, my Joy, my Love, my Heart: Such a Joy, as none can move; Such a Love, as none can part; Such a Heart, as joys in love.

Alternate tune, TRYGGARE KAN INGEN VARA, No. 101

O, How I Love Jesus

C.M.Ref.

Frederick Whitfield, 1855 (1829-1904)

19th century American Melody

1. There is a name I love to hear, I love to sing its worth;
2. It tells me of a Sav-ior's love, Who died to set me free;
3. It tells of One whose lov-ing heart Can feel my deep-est woe,

It sounds like mu - sic in my ear, The sweet - est name on earth.
It tells me of His pre-cious blood, The sin - ner's per - fect plea.
Who in each sor - row bears a part That none can bear be - low.

Refrain

O, how I love Je - sus, O, how I love Je - sus,

O, how I love Je - sus— Be - cause He first loved me!

GLORY AND PRAISE

249 Praise Him! Praise Him!

12.10.12.10.11.10. Ref.

Fanny J. Crosby, 1869 (1820-1915)

Chester G. Allen (1812-1877)

1. Praise Him! praise Him! Je-sus, our bless-ed Re-deem-er! Sing, O earth—His won-der-ful love pro-claim! Hail Him! hail Him! high-est arch-an-gels in glo-ry; Strength and hon-or give to His ho-ly name! Like a shep-herd, Je-sus will guard His chil-dren, In His arms He

2. Praise Him! praise Him! Je-sus, our bless-ed Re-deem-er! For our sins He suf-fered, and bled and died; He—our Rock, our hope of e-ter-nal sal-va-tion, Hail Him! hail Him! Je-sus, the cru-ci-fied. Sound His prais-es! Je-sus who bore our sor-rows, Love un-bound-ed,

3. Praise Him! praise Him! Je-sus, our bless-ed Re-deem-er! Heaven-ly por-tals, loud with ho-san-nas ring! Je-sus, Sav-ior, reign-eth for-ev-er and ev-er; Crown Him! crown Him! Pro-phet, and Priest, and King! Christ is com-ing o-ver the world vic-to-rious, Power and glo-ry

GLORY AND PRAISE

Refrain

car - ries them all   day long;
won - der - ful, deep   and strong;   Praise Him! praise Him! tell   of His
un - to   the Lord   be - long;

ex - cel - lent great-ness; Praise Him! praise Him ev - er in joy - ful song!

O for a Thousand Tongues to Sing   **250**

AZMON C.M.

Carl G. Gläser (1784-1829)
Arr. by Lowell Mason (1792-1872)

Charles Wesley, 1739 (1707-1788)

1. O   for a   thou-sand tongues to sing My great Re - deem - er's praise,
2. My   gra - cious Mas - ter   and my God, As - sist me   to pro - claim,
3. Je - sus! the name that charms our fears, That bids our sor - rows cease,
4. He   breaks the power of   can - celed sin, He sets the pris - oner   free;
5. He   speaks, and listen-ing   to   His voice, New life the dead re - ceive;
6. Hear Him, ye deaf; His   praise, ye dumb, Your loos-ened tongues em - ploy;

The glo - ries of   my God and King, The   tri - umphs of His grace!
To   spread thro' all   the earth a - broad The   hon - ors of Thy name.
'Tis mu - sic in   the sin - ners' ears, 'Tis   life, and health, and peace.
His blood can make the foul - est clean; His   blood a - vailed for   me.
The mourn-ful, bro - ken hearts re - joice; The   hum - ble poor, be - lieve.
Ye   blind, be - hold your Sav - ior come; And   leap, ye lame, for   joy.

251 He Lives

7.6.7.6.7.6.7.4. Ref.

Alfred H. Ackley, 1933 (1887-1960)

Alfred H. Ackley, 1933

1. I serve a ris-en Sav-ior, He's in the world to-day; I know that He is liv-ing, what-ev-er men may say; I see His hand of mer-cy, I hear His voice of cheer, And just the time I need Him He's al-ways near.

2. In all the world a-round me I see His lov-ing care, And tho' my heart grows wea-ry I nev-er will de-spair; I know that He is lead-ing thru all the storm-y blast, The day of His ap-pear-ing will come at last.

3. Re-joice, re-joice, O Chris-tian, lift up your voice and sing E-ter-nal hal-le-lu-jahs to Je-sus Christ the King! The hope of all who seek Him, the help of all who find, None oth-er is so lov-ing, so good and kind.

Refrain

He lives, He lives, Christ Je-sus lives to-day! He walks with me and talks with me a-long life's nar-row way. He lives, He lives, sal-

(He lives, He lives, He lives, He lives, He lives, He lives,)

GLORY AND PRAISE

va-tion to im-part! You ask me how I know He lives? He lives with-in my heart.

Come, Let Us Sing

252

Rev. 5:9-13
James Montgomery, 1841 (1771-1854)

RUSSIA L.M.
Adapted from D. Bortnianski, 1825 (1752-1825)

1. Come, let us sing the song of songs— The an- gels
2. Slain to re- deem us by His blood, To cleanse from
3. To Him who suf- fered on the tree, Our souls, at
4. To Him, en- throned by fil- ial right All power in
5. Long as we live, and when we die, And while in

first be- gan the strain— The hom- age which to
ev- ery sin- ful stain, And make us kings and
His soul's price, to gain, Bless- ing, and praise, and
heaven and earth pro- claim, Hon- or, and maj- es-
heaven with Him we reign, This song our song of

Christ be- longs: "Wor-thy the Lamb, for He was slain!"
priests to God: "Wor-thy the Lamb, for He was slain!"
glo- ry be: "Wor-thy the Lamb, for He was slain!"
ty, and might: "Wor-thy the Lamb, for He was slain!"
songs shall be: "Wor-thy the Lamb, for He was slain!"

Alternate tune, WAREHAM, Nos. 174, 226

GLORY AND PRAISE

253   There's No Other Name Like Jesus

Acts 4:12
F. E. Belden, 1886 (1858-1945)

8.7.8.7.Ref.
F. E. Belden, 1886

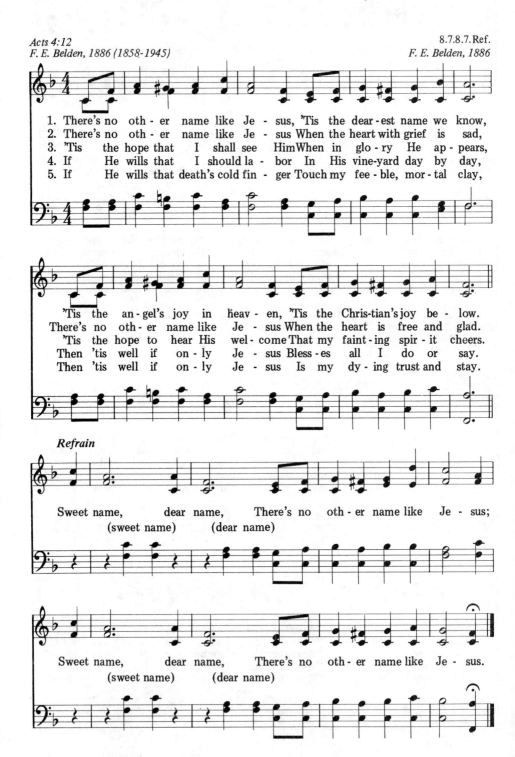

1. There's no oth - er name like Je - sus, 'Tis the dear - est name we know,
2. There's no oth - er name like Je - sus When the heart with grief is sad,
3. 'Tis the hope that I shall see Him When in glo - ry He ap - pears,
4. If He wills that I should la - bor In His vine-yard day by day,
5. If He wills that death's cold fin - ger Touch my fee - ble, mor - tal clay,

'Tis the an - gel's joy in heav - en, 'Tis the Chris-tian's joy be - low.
There's no oth - er name like Je - sus When the heart is free and glad.
'Tis the hope to hear His wel - come That my faint - ing spir - it cheers.
Then 'tis well if on - ly Je - sus Bless - es all I do or say.
Then 'tis well if on - ly Je - sus Is my dy - ing trust and stay.

Refrain

Sweet name, dear name, There's no oth - er name like Je - sus;
(sweet name) (dear name)

Sweet name, dear name, There's no oth - er name like Je - sus.
(sweet name) (dear name)

GLORY AND PRAISE

The Great Physician Now Is Near   254

8.7.8.7.Ref.

William Hunter, 1859 (1811-1877)   Arr. by J. H. Stockton (1813-1877)

1. The Great Phy-si-cian now is near, The sym-pa-thiz-ing Je - sus;
2. All glo-ry to the dy-ing Lamb! I now be-lieve in Je - sus;
3. His name dis-pels my guilt and fear; No oth-er name but Je - sus;
4. And when He comes to bring the crown—The crown of life and glo - ry—

He speaks, the droop-ing heart to cheer, O hear the voice of Je - sus!
I love the bless-ed Sav-ior's name, I love the name of Je - sus.
O how my soul de-lights to hear The pre-cious name of Je - sus!
Then by His side we will sit down, And tell re-demp-tion's sto - ry.

Refrain

Sweet-est note in ser-aph song, Sweet-est name on mor-tal tongue,

Sweet-est car-ol ev-er sung— Je - sus, bless-ed Je - sus!

GLORY AND PRAISE

TSDAH-9

255

I Cannot Tell Why

W. Y. Fullerton (1857-1932)

LONDONDERRY AIR 11.10.11.10.11.10.11.12.
Irish melody arr. by John Barnard (1948-   )

1. I can - not tell why He whom an - gels wor - ship
2. I can - not tell how si - lent - ly He suf - fered
3. I can - not tell how He will win the na - tions,
4. I can - not tell how all the lands shall wor - ship,

Should set His love up - on the souls of men,
As with His peace He graced this place of tears,
How He will claim His earth - ly her - i - tage,
When at His bid - ing ev - ery storm is stilled,

Or why as Shep - herd He should seek the wan - derers,
Nor how His heart up - on the cross was bro - ken,
How sat - is - fy the needs and as - pi - ra - tions
Or who can say how great the ju - bi - la - tion

To bring them back, they know not how nor when.
The crown of pain to three and thir - ty years.
Of east and west, of sin - ner and of sage.
When all our hearts with love for Him are filled.

GLORY AND PRAISE

But this I know that He was born of Ma - ry
But this I know He heals the bro - ken heart - ed
But this I know all flesh shall see His glo - ry,
But this I know the skies shall sound His prais - es,

When Beth-lehem's man - ger was His on - ly home,
And stays our sin and calms our lurk - ing fear,
And He shall reap the har - vest He has sown,
Ten thou - sand thou - sand hu - man voic - es sing,

And that He lived at Naz - a - reth and la - bored;
And lifts the bur - den from the heav - y la - den;
And some glad day His sun will shine in splen - dor
And earth to heaven, and heaven to earth will an - swer,

And so the Sav - ior, Sav - ior of the world, has come.
For still the Sav - ior, Sav - ior of the world, is here.
When He the Sav - ior, Sav - ior of the world, is known.
At last the Sav - ior, Sav - ior of the world, is King!

GLORY AND PRAISE

256   Ye Servants of God

Charles Wesley, 1744 (1707-1788)

HANOVER 10.10.11.11.
William Croft, 1708 (1678-1727)

1. Ye ser-vants of God, your Mas-ter pro-claim, And pub-lish a-broad His won-der-ful name; The name all vic-to-rious of Je-sus ex-tol; His king-dom is glo-rious, He rules o-ver all.
2. God rul-eth on high, al-might-y to save; And still He is nigh— His pres-ence we have; The great con-gre-ga-tion His tri-umph shall sing, A-scrib-ing sal-va-tion to Je-sus our King.
3. "Sal-va-tion to God, Who sits on the throne," Let all cry a-loud, and hon-or the Son; The prais-es of Je-sus the an-gels pro-claim, Fall down on their fac-es, and wor-ship the Lamb.
4. Then let us a-dore, and give Him His right, All glo-ry and power, all wis-dom and might, All hon-or and bless-ing, with an-gels a-bove, And thanks nev-er ceas-ing, for in-fi-nite love.

GLORY AND PRAISE

Come Down, O Love Divine

257

Bianco da Siena (?   -1434)
Tr. Richard F. Littledale, 1867 (1833-1890)

DOWN AMPNEY 6.6.11.6.6.11.
Ralph Vaughan Williams, 1906 (1872-1958)

1. Come down, O Love di - vine, Seek Thou this soul of mine,
2. O let it free - ly burn, Till earth - ly pas - sions turn
3. Let ho - ly char - i - ty Mine out - ward ves - ture be,
4. And so the yearn - ing strong, With which the soul will long,

And vis - it it with Thine own ar - dor glow - ing;
To dust and ash - es in its heat con - sum - ing;
And low - li - ness be - come my in - ner cloth - ing;
Shall far out - pass the power of hu - man tell - ing;

O Com - fort - er, draw near, With - in my heart ap - pear,
And let Thy glo - rious light Shine ev - er on my sight,
True low - li - ness of heart Which takes the hum - bler part,
For none can guess its grace, Till he be - come the place

And kin - dle it, Thy ho - ly flame be - stow - ing.
And clothe me round, the while my path il - lum - ing.
And o'er its own short - com - ings weeps with loath - ing.
Where in the Ho - ly Spir - it makes His dwell - ing.

HOLY SPIRIT

Baptize Us Anew

W. A. Ogden (1841-1897)

5.5.6.5.Ref.
W. A. Ogden

1. Bap - tize us a - new With power from on high,
2. Un - wor - thy we cry, Un - ho - ly, un - clean,
3. O heav - en - ly Dove, De - scend from on high!
4. O list the glad voice! From heav - en it came:

With love, O re - fresh us! Dear Sav - ior, draw nigh.
O wash us and cleanse us From sin's guilt - y stain.
We plead Thy rich bless - ing; In mer - cy draw nigh.
Thou art My be - lov - ed, Well pleas - ed I am.

Refrain

We hum - bly be - seech Thee, Lord Je - sus, we pray,
(Last vs.) We praise Thee, we bless Thee, dear Lamb that was slain,

With love and the Spir - it bap - tize us to - day.
We laud and a - dore Thee, A - men and A - men.

HOLY SPIRIT

Draw Us in the Spirit's Tether

259

UNION SEMINARY 8.7.8.7.4.4.7.
Harold Friedell (1905-1958)
Adapt. by Jet Turner (1928-   )

Percy Dearmer (1867-1936)

1. Draw us in the Spir-it's teth - er, For when hum - bly in Thy name, Two or three are met to-geth - er, Thou art in the midst of them; Al-le-lu - ia! Al-le-lu - ia! Touch we now Thy gar - ment's hem.

2. As the breth - ren used to gath - er In the name of Christ to sup, Then with thanks to God the Fa - ther Break the bread and bless the cup, Al-le-lu - ia! Al-le-lu - ia! So knit Thou our friend - ship up.

3. All our meals and all our liv - ing Make as sac - ra - ments of Thee, That by car - ing, help-ing, giv - ing, We may true dis - ci - ples be. Al-le-lu - ia! Al-le-lu - ia! We will serve Thee faith - ful - ly.

HOLY SPIRIT

Hover O'er Me, Holy Spirit

Ellwood H. Stokes, 1879 (1815-1895)

SWENEY 8.7.8.7.Ref.
John R. Sweney (1837-1899)

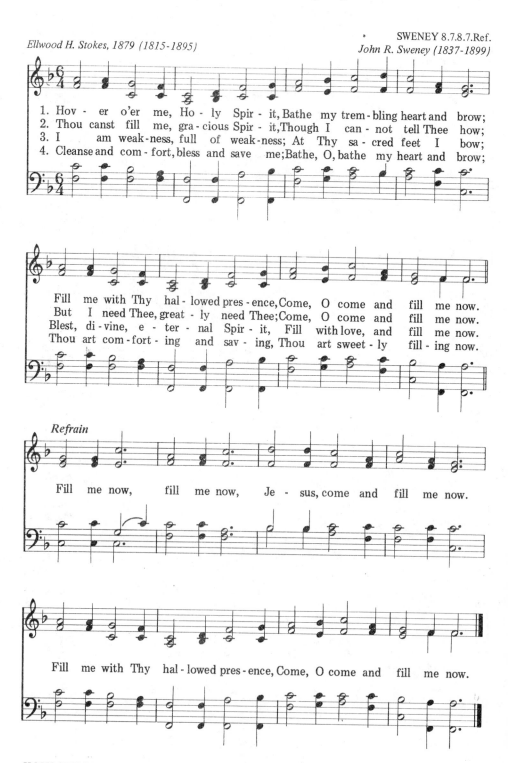

1. Hov - er o'er me, Ho - ly Spir - it, Bathe my trem-bling heart and brow;
2. Thou canst fill me, gra - cious Spir - it, Though I can - not tell Thee how;
3. I am weak-ness, full of weak-ness; At Thy sa - cred feet I bow;
4. Cleanse and com - fort, bless and save me; Bathe, O, bathe my heart and brow;

Fill me with Thy hal - lowed pres - ence, Come, O come and fill me now.
But I need Thee, great - ly need Thee; Come, O come and fill me now.
Blest, di - vine, e - ter - nal Spir - it, Fill with love, and fill me now.
Thou art com - fort - ing and sav - ing, Thou art sweet - ly fill - ing now.

Refrain

Fill me now, fill me now, Je - sus, come and fill me now.

Fill me with Thy hal - lowed pres - ence, Come, O come and fill me now.

HOLY SPIRIT

The Spirit of the Lord Revealed

261

SOLLS SEIN C.M.D.

Melody from Geistliche Nachtigal, *Vienna, 1658*
Edited by David Gregor Corner (1585-1648)

George W. Briggs (1875-1959)

1. The Spir-it of the Lord re-vealed His will to saints of old;
2. The proph-ets passed; at length there came To so-journ and a-bide,
3. E-ter-nal Spir-it, who dost speak To mind and con-science still,

Their heart and mind and lips un-sealed His glo-ry to un-fold.
The Word in-car-nate, to whose name The proph-ets tes-ti-fied;
That we in this our day, may seek To do our Fa-ther's will,

A-mid the gloom of an-cient night They hailed the dawn-ing Word,
And He, the twi-light o-ver-past, Him-self, the Light of light,
To us the word of life im-part, Of Christ, the liv-ing way;

And in the com-ing of the light Pro-claimed the com-ing Lord.
As man with man, re-vealed at last The Fa-ther to our sight.
Give us the qui-et, hum-ble heart To hear and to o-bey.

HOLY SPIRIT

262   Sweet, Sweet Spirit

Doris Akers, 1965 (1922-   )

9.11.Ref.
Doris Akers

1. There's a sweet, sweet spir-it in this place, And I
(2.) sweet ex-pres-sions on each face, And I

know that it's the spir-it of the Lord; 2. There are
know they feel the pres-ence of the Lord.

Refrain

Sweet Ho-ly Spir-it, Sweet Heav-en-ly Dove,

Stay right here with us Fill-ing us with Your love,

And for these bless-ings we lift our hearts in praise, With-out a

HOLY SPIRIT

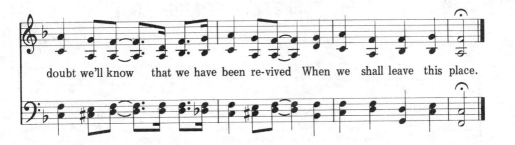

doubt we'll know that we have been re-vived When we shall leave this place.

Fire of God, Thou Sacred Flame 263

SONG 13 7.7.7.7.

Albert F. Bayly (1901-1984)

Adapt. from Orlando Gibbons (1583-1625)

1. Fire of God, Thou sa-cred flame, Spir-it who in splen-dor came,
2. Breath of God, that swept in power In the pen-te-cos-tal hour,
3. Strength of God, Thy might with-in Con-quers sor-row, pain, and sin:
4. Truth of God, Thy pierc-ing rays Pen-e-trate my se-cret ways.
5. Love of God, Thy grace pro-found Know-eth nei-ther age nor bound:

Let Thy heat my soul re-fine Till it glows with love di-vine.
Ho-ly Breath, be Thou in me Source of vi-tal en-er-gy.
For-ti-fy from e-vil's art All the gate-ways of my heart.
May the light that shames my sin Guide me ho-lier paths to win.
Come, my heart's own guest to be, Dwell for-ev-er-more in me.

HOLY SPIRIT

O for That Flame of Living Fire

MENDON L.M.
German Melody
Arr. by Samuel Dyer, 1825 (1785-1835)

William H. Bathurst, 1831 (1796-1877)

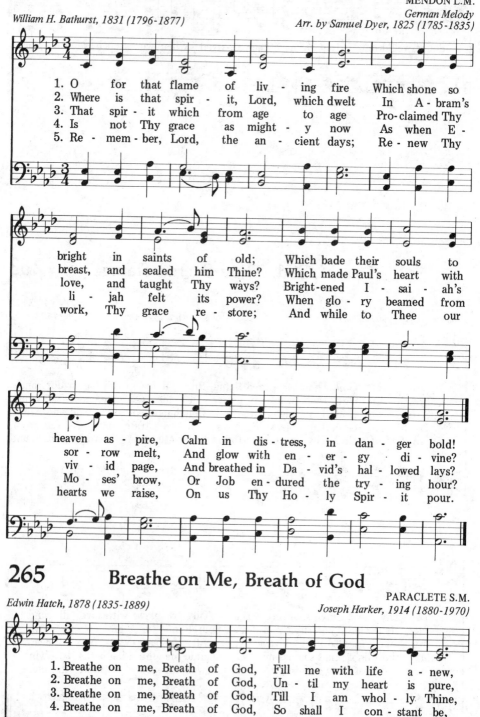

1. O for that flame of liv - ing fire Which shone so bright in saints of old; Which bade their souls to heaven as - pire, Calm in dis - tress, in dan - ger bold!
2. Where is that spir - it, Lord, which dwelt In A - bram's breast, and sealed him Thine? Which made Paul's heart with sor - row melt, And glow with en - er - gy di - vine?
3. That spir - it which from age to age Pro - claimed Thy love, and taught Thy ways? Bright-ened I - sai - ah's viv - id page, And breathed in Da - vid's hal - lowed lays?
4. Is not Thy grace as might - y now As when E - li - jah felt its power? When glo - ry beamed from Mo - ses' brow, Or Job en - dured the try - ing hour?
5. Re - mem - ber, Lord, the an - cient days; Re - new Thy work, Thy grace re - store; And while to Thee our hearts we raise, On us Thy Ho - ly Spir - it pour.

Breathe on Me, Breath of God

PARACLETE S.M.
Edwin Hatch, 1878 (1835-1889)
Joseph Harker, 1914 (1880-1970)

1. Breathe on me, Breath of God, Fill me with life a - new,
2. Breathe on me, Breath of God, Un - til my heart is pure,
3. Breathe on me, Breath of God, Till I am whol - ly Thine,
4. Breathe on me, Breath of God, So shall I con - stant be,

HOLY SPIRIT

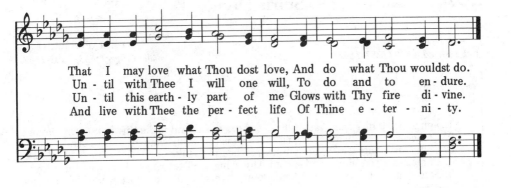

That I may love what Thou dost love, And do what Thou wouldst do.
Un - til with Thee I will one will, To do and to en - dure.
Un - til this earth - ly part of me Glows with Thy fire di - vine.
And live with Thee the per - fect life Of Thine e - ter - ni - ty.

Spirit of God
266

MORECAMBE 10.10.10.10.

George Croly, 1854 (1780-1860)

Frederick C. Atkinson 1870 (1841-1896)

1. Spir - it of God! de - scend up - on my heart; Wean it from
2. I ask no dream, no proph - et ec - sta - sies; No sud - den
3. Hast Thou not bid us love Thee, God and King? All, all Thine
4. Teach me to feel that Thou art al - ways nigh; Teach me the
5. Teach me to love Thee as Thine an - gels love, One ho - ly

earth; through all its puls - es move; Stoop to my weak - ness,
rend - ing of the veil of clay; No an - gel vis - i -
own, soul, heart, and strength, and mind; I see Thy cross, there
strug - gles of the soul to bear; To check the ris - ing
pas - sion fill - ing all my frame; The bap - tism of the

might - y as Thou art, And make me love Thee as I ought to love.
tant, no op - 'ning skies; But take the dim - ness of my soul a - way.
teach my heart to cling: O let me seek Thee, and O let me find!
doubt, the reb - el sigh; Teach me the pa - tience of un - an - swered prayer.
heav'n - de - scend - ed dove, My heart an al - tar, and Thy love the flame.

HOLY SPIRIT

Spirit Divine

Andrew Reed, 1829 (1787-1862)

GRÄFENBERG C.M.
Johann Crüger, 1653 (1598-1662)

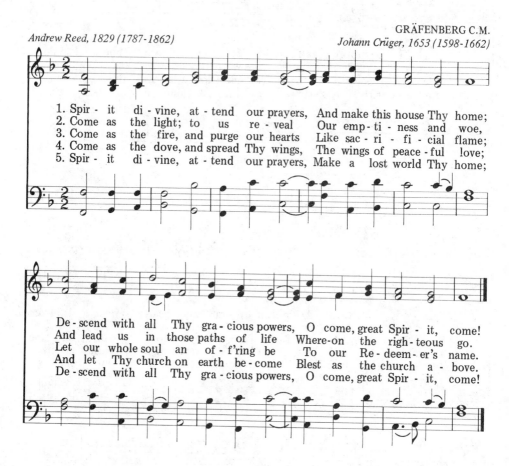

1. Spir - it   di - vine, at - tend   our prayers, And make this house Thy home;
2. Come as   the light; to   us   re - veal   Our emp - ti - ness and   woe,
3. Come as   the fire, and purge our hearts   Like sac - ri - fi - cial flame;
4. Come as   the dove, and spread Thy wings, The wings of peace - ful   love;
5. Spir - it   di - vine, at - tend   our prayers, Make a   lost world Thy home;

De - scend with all   Thy gra - cious powers,   O come, great Spir - it,   come!
And lead   us   in   those paths of life   Where - on   the righ - teous   go.
Let our whole soul   an   of - f'ring be   To our   Re - deem - er's   name.
And let   Thy church on earth be - come   Blest as   the church a - bove.
De - scend with all   Thy gra - cious powers,   O come, great Spir - it,   come!

Holy Spirit, Light Divine

MERCY 7.7.7.7.

Andrew Reed, 1817 (1787-1862), alt.

Louis M. Gottschalk, 1854   (1829-1869)
Arr. by Edwin P. Parker, c. 1888   (1836-1925)

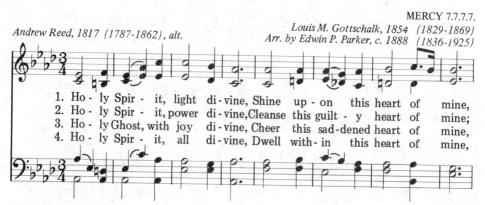

1. Ho - ly Spir - it, light di - vine, Shine up - on   this heart of   mine,
2. Ho - ly Spir - it, power di - vine, Cleanse this guilt - y   heart of   mine;
3. Ho - ly Ghost, with joy di - vine, Cheer this sad - dened heart of   mine,
4. Ho - ly Spir - it, all   di - vine, Dwell with - in   this heart of   mine,

HOLY SPIRIT

Chase the shades of night a - way, Turn my dark - ness in - to day.
Long has sin, with-out con - trol, Held do - min - ion o'er my soul.
Bid my man - y woes de - part, Heal my wound- ed, bleed-ing heart.
Cast down ev - ery i - dol throne, Reign su - preme, and reign a - lone.

Come, Holy Spirit

269

ST. AGNES C.M.

Isaac Watts (1674-1748)

John B. Dykes, 1866 (1823-1876)

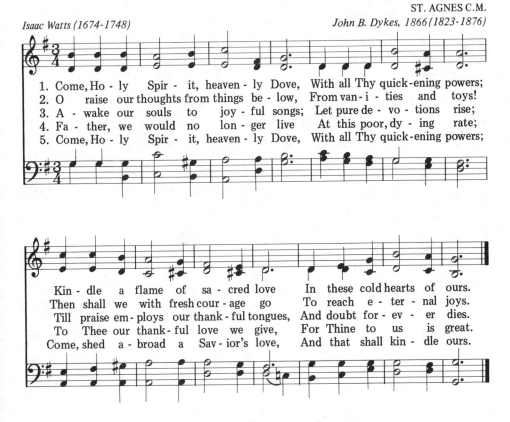

1. Come, Ho - ly Spir - it, heaven - ly Dove, With all Thy quick-ening powers;
2. O raise our thoughts from things be - low, From van - i - ties and toys!
3. A - wake our souls to joy - ful songs; Let pure de - vo - tions rise;
4. Fa - ther, we would no lon - ger live At this poor, dy - ing rate;
5. Come, Ho - ly Spir - it, heaven - ly Dove, With all Thy quick-ening powers;

Kin - dle a flame of sa - cred love In these cold hearts of ours.
Then shall we with fresh cour - age go To reach e - ter - nal joys.
Till praise em - ploys our thank - ful tongues, And doubt for - ev - er dies.
To Thee our thank - ful love we give, For Thine to us is great.
Come, shed a - broad a Sav - ior's love, And that shall kin - dle ours.

HOLY SPIRIT

O Holy Dove of God Descending

LOIS 9.9.9.6.

Bryan Jeffery Leech (1931-   )

Bryan Jeffery Leech

Unison

1. O ho-ly Dove of God de-scend - ing, You are the
2. O ho-ly Wind of God now blow - ing, You are the
3. O ho-ly Rain of God now fall - ing, You make the
4. O ho-ly Flame of God now burn - ing, You are the

love that knows no end - ing. All of our shat - tered
seed that God is sow - ing. You are the life that
Word of God en - thrall - ing, You are that in - ner
power of Christ re - turn - ing. You are the an - swer

dreams You're mend - ing: Spir - it, now live in me.
starts us grow - ing: Spir - it, now live in me.
voice now call - ing: Spir - it, now live in me.
to our yearn - ing: Spir - it, now live in me.

HOLY SPIRIT

Break Thou the Bread of Life

Matt. 14:19
Mary A. Lathbury (1842-1913)
Alexander Groves, stanza 3, (1842-1909)

BREAD OF LIFE 6.4.6.4.D.
William F. Sherwin, 1877 (1826-1888)

1. Break Thou the bread of life, Dear Lord, to me,
2. Bless Thou the truth, dear Lord, To me, to me,
3. Thou art the bread of life, O Lord, to me;
4. Spir - it and life are they, Words Thou dost speak;

As Thou didst break the loaves Be - side the sea;
As Thou didst bless the bread By Gal - i - lee;
Thy ho - ly Word the truth That sav - eth me;
I has - ten to o - bey, But I am weak;

Be - yond the sa - cred page I seek Thee, Lord;
Then shall all bond - age cease, All fet - ters fall;
Give me to eat and live With Thee a - bove;
Thou art my on - ly help, Thou art my life;

My spir - it pants for Thee, O liv - ing Word.
And I shall find my peace, My all in all.
Teach me to love Thy truth, For Thou art love.
Heed - ing Thy ho - ly Word I win the strife.

HOLY SCRIPTURES

272 Give Me the Bible

HOLY SCRIPTURES

Pre-cept and prom-ise, law and love com-bin-ing, 'Till night shall van-ish in e-ter-nal day.

Lord, I Have Made Thy Word My Choice 273

Psalm 119:111
Isaac Watts (1674-1748)

WETHERBY C.M.
Samuel S. Wesley (1810-1876)

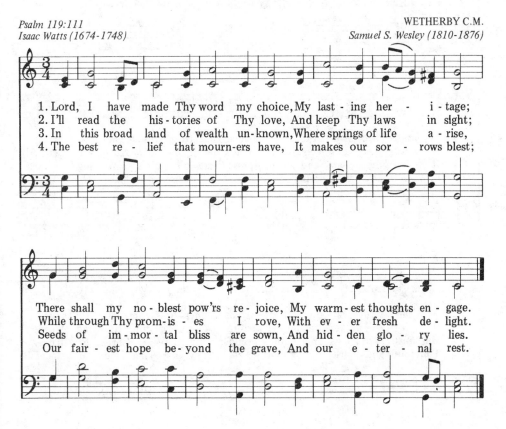

1. Lord, I have made Thy word my choice, My last-ing her-i-tage;
2. I'll read the his-tories of Thy love, And keep Thy laws in sight;
3. In this broad land of wealth un-known, Where springs of life a-rise,
4. The best re-lief that mourn-ers have, It makes our sor-rows blest;

There shall my no-blest pow'rs re-joice, My warm-est thoughts en-gage.
While through Thy prom-is-es I rove, With ev-er fresh de-light.
Seeds of im-mor-tal bliss are sown, And hid-den glo-ry lies.
Our fair-est hope be-yond the grave, And our e-ter-nal rest.

HOLY SCRIPTURES

O Word of God Incarnate

MUNICH 7.6.7.6.D.

Prov. 6:23
William Walsham How, 1867 (1823-1897)
Neuvermehrtes Meiningisches Gesangbuch, *1693*
Arr. by Felix Mendelssohn, (1809-1847)

1. O Word of God In-car-nate, O Wis-dom from on high,
2. The church from her dear Mas-ter Re-ceived the gift di - vine,
3. It float-eth like a ban - ner Be-fore God's host un - furled;
4. O make Thy church, dear Sav-ior, A lamp of pur-est gold,

O Truth un-changed, un - chang - ing, O Light of our dark sky,
And still that light she lift - eth O'er all the earth to shine.
It shin-eth like a bea - con A-bove the dark-ling world.
To bear be-fore the -na - tions Thy true light, as of old.

We praise Thee for the ra - diance That from the hal-lowed page,
It is the gold-en cas - ket, Where gems of truth are stored;
It is the chart and com - pass That o'er life's surg-ing sea,
O teach Thy wan-dering pil - grims By this their path to trace,

A lan-tern to our foot-steps, Shines on from age to age.
It is the heaven-drawn pic - ture Of Christ, the liv-ing Word.
'Mid mists and rocks and quick-sands, Still guides, O Christ, to Thee.
Till, clouds and dark-ness end - ed, They see Thee face to face.

HOLY SCRIPTURES

O God of Light

275

ATKINSON 11.10.11.10.

Sarah E. Taylor (1883-1954) alt.

H. Barrie Cabena (1933-   )

Unison

1. O God of light, Your Word, a lamp un - fail - ing,
2. From days of old, through blind and will - ful a - ges,
3. Un - dimmed by time, those words are still re - veal - ing
4. To all the world Your sum-mons You are send - ing,

Shall pierce the dark - ness of our earth-bound way
Though we re - belled, You gent - ly sought a - gain,
To sin - ful hearts Your jus - tice and Your grace;
Through all the earth, to ev - ery land and race,

And show your grace, Your plan for us un - veil - ing,
And spoke through saints, a - pos - tles, proph - ets, sa - ges,
And quest - ing mor - tals long - ing for Your heal - ing,
That myr - iad tongues, in one great an - them blend - ing,

And guide our foot-steps to the per - fect day.
Who wrote with ea - ger or re - luc - tant pen.
See Your com - pas - sion in the Sav - ior's face.
May praise and cel - e - brate Your gift of grace.

HOLY SCRIPTURES

276

Thanks to God

R. T. Brooks (1918-   )
Unison

WYLDE GREEN 8.7.8.7.4.7.
Peter Cutts, 1956 (1937-   )

1. Thanks to God whose Word was spo - ken In the deed that made the earth. His the voice that called a na - tion; His the fires that tried her worth. God has spo - ken; Praise Him for His o - pen Word.

2. Thanks to God whose Word in - car - nate Glo - ri - fied the flesh of man. Deeds and words and death and ris - ing Tell the grace in heav - en's plan. God has spo - ken; Praise Him for His o - pen Word.

3. Thanks to God whose Word is an - swered By the Spir - it's voice with - in. Here we drink of joy un - mea - sured, Life re - deemed from death and sin. God is speak - ing; Praise Him for His o - pen Word.

HOLY SCRIPTURES

For Your Holy Book We Thank You 277

HOLY BOOK 8.7.8.7.7.7.

Ruth Carter, 1932 (1900-1982)

Blythe Owen, 1984 (1898-)

1. For Your ho - ly book we thank You, And for all who
2. For Your ho - ly book we thank You, And for those who
3. For Your ho - ly book we thank You, May its mes - sage
4. For Your ho - ly book we thank You, May its mes - sage

served You well, Writ - ing, guard - ing, and trans - lat - ing,
work to - day, That the peo - ple of all na - tions,
be our guide, May we un - der - stand the wis - dom
in our hearts Lead us now to see in Je - sus

That its pag - es might forth tell Your strong love and
Read - ing it and fol - l'wing, may Know Your love and
Of the laws it will pro - vide: And Your love and
All the grace Your word im - parts: All Your love and

ten - der care For Your peo - ple ev - ery - where.
ten - der care For Your peo - ple ev - ery - where.
ten - der care For Your peo - ple ev - ery - where.
ten - der care For Your peo - ple ev - ery - where.

HOLY SCRIPTURES

278 Lord Jesus, Once You Spoke to Men

BLUEBONNET L.M.

John Read, 1984 (1933-   )
Arr. by Melvin West (1930-   )

H. C. A. Gaunt (1902-   )
Unison

1. Lord Je - sus, once You spoke to men Up - on the
2. We all have se - cret fears to face, Our minds and
3. The gos - pel speaks; and we re - ceive Your light, Your

moun - tain and the plain, O help us lis - ten
mo - tives to a - mend. We seek Your truth, we
love, Your own com - mand. O help us live what

now as then And won - der at Your words a - gain.
need Your grace, Our liv - ing Lord and pres - ent friend.
we be - lieve, In dai - ly word of heart and hand.

HOLY SCRIPTURES

Only Trust Him

279

INVITATION

280 Come, Ye Sinners

RESTORATION 8.7.8.7.Ref.
Traditional American Melody
Arr. by Melvin West, 1984 (1930-   )

Joseph Hart, 1759 (1712-1768)

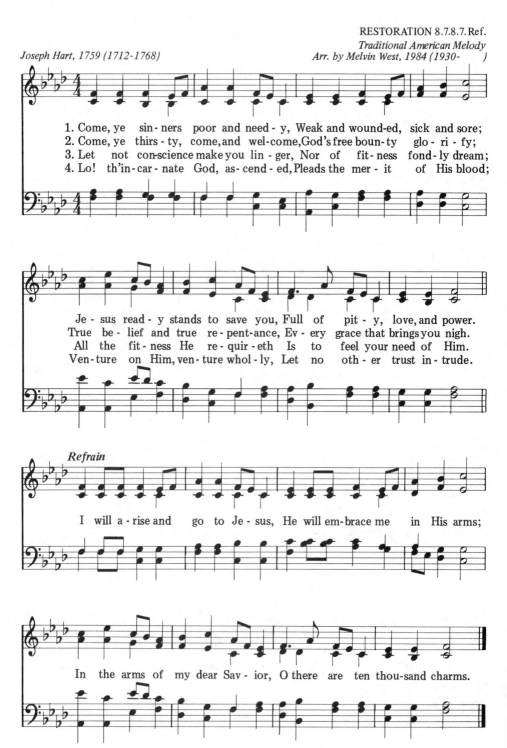

1. Come, ye sin-ners poor and need-y, Weak and wound-ed, sick and sore;
2. Come, ye thirs-ty, come, and wel-come, God's free boun-ty glo-ri-fy;
3. Let not con-science make you lin-ger, Nor of fit-ness fond-ly dream;
4. Lo! th'in-car-nate God, as-cend-ed, Pleads the mer-it of His blood;

Je-sus read-y stands to save you, Full of pit-y, love, and power.
True be-lief and true re-pent-ance, Ev-ery grace that brings you nigh.
All the fit-ness He re-quir-eth Is to feel your need of Him.
Ven-ture on Him, ven-ture whol-ly, Let no oth-er trust in-trude.

Refrain

I will a-rise and go to Je-sus, He will em-brace me in His arms;

In the arms of my dear Sav-ior, O there are ten thou-sand charms.

INVITATION

I Gave My Life for Thee

WHITE 6.6.6.6.6.6.

Frances Ridley Havergal, 1858 (1836-1879)

J. E. White (1849-1928)

281

1. I gave My life for thee, My pre-cious blood I shed,
2. My Fa-ther's house of light, My glo - ry cir - cled throne,
3. I suf-fered much for thee, More than thy tongue can tell,

That thou might'st ran - somed be, And quick-ened from the dead;
I left for earth - ly night, For wan-derings sad and lone;
Of bit - terest ag - o - ny, To res - cue thee from hell;

I gave, I gave My life for thee, What hast thou given for Me?
I left, I left it all for thee, Hast thou left aught for Me?
I've borne, I've borne it all for thee, What hast thou borne for Me?

I gave, I gave My life for thee, What hast thou given for Me?
I left, I left it all for thee, Hast thou left aught for Me?
I've borne, I've borne it all for thee, What hast thou borne for Me?

INVITATION

282   I Hear Thy Welcome Voice

S.M. Ref.

Lewis Hartsough, 1872 (1828-1919)

Lewis Hartsough, 1872

1. I hear Thy wel-come voice, That calls me, Lord, to Thee;
2. Though com - ing weak and vile, Thou dost my strength as - sure;
3. 'Tis Je - sus calls me on To per - fect faith and love,
4. All hail, a - ton - ing blood! All hail, re - deem - ing grace!

For cleans-ing in Thy pre - cious blood, That flowed on Cal - va - ry.
Thou dost my vile-ness ful - ly cleanse, Till spot - less all, and pure.
To per - fect hope, and peace, and trust, For earth and heaven a - bove.
All hail! the gift of Christ, our Lord, Our Strength and Righ-teous-ness.

Refrain

I am com-ing, Lord! Com - ing now to Thee!

Wash me, cleanse me, in the blood That flowed on Cal-va - ry.

INVITATION

O Jesus, Thou Art Standing

283

ST. HILDA 7.6.7.6.D.
Justin H. Knecht, 1799 (1752-1817)
Alt. by Edward Husband, 1871 (1843-1908)

Rev. 3:20
William Walsham How, 1867 (1823-1897)

1. O Je - sus, Thou art stand - ing Out - side the fast - closed door,
2. O Je - sus, Thou art knock - ing; And, lo, that hand is scarred,
3. O Je - sus, Thou art plead - ing In ac - cents meek and low,

In low - ly pa - tience wait - ing To pass the thresh - old o'er:
And thorns Thy brow en - cir - cle, And tears Thy face have marred.
"I died for you, My chil - dren, And will ye treat Me so?"

O shame, pro - fess - ing Chris - tian, His name and sign who bear,
O love that pass - eth knowl - edge, So pa - tient - ly to wait!
O Lord, with shame and sor - row We o - pen now the door;

O shame, thrice shame up - on us, To keep Him stand - ing there!
O sin that hath no e - qual, So fast to bar the gate!
Dear Sav - ior, en - ter, en - ter, And leave us nev - er - more.

INVITATION

284　For You I Am Praying

11.11.12.11.Ref.

Samuel O'Malley Cluff (1837-1910)　　　　　*Ira D. Sankey, 1874 (1840-1908)*

1. I have a Sav - ior, He's plead - ing in glo - ry, A dear, lov - ing
2. I have a Fa - ther; to me He has giv - en A hope for e -
3. I have a robe; 'tis re - splen-dent in white-ness, A - wait - ing in
4. When Je - sus has found you, tell oth-ers the sto - ry, That my lov - ing

Sav - ior, though earth friends be few; And now He is watch - ing in
ter - ni - ty, bless - ed and true; And soon He will call me to
glo - ry my won - der - ing view; Oh, when I re - ceive it, all
Sav - ior is your Sav - ior, too; Then pray that your Sav - ior will

ten - der - ness o'er me, But oh that my Sav - ior were
meet Him in heav - en, But oh that He'd let me bring
shin - ing in bright - ness, Dear friend, could I see you re -
bring them to glo - ry, And prayer will be an - swered—'twas

Refrain

your Sav - ior, too.
you with me, too!
ceiv - ing one, too!　　For you I am pray - ing, For you I am
an - swered for you!

INVITATION

pray - ing, For you I am pray - ing, I'm pray - ing for you.

Jesus Calls Us

285

GALILEE 8.7.8.7.

Mrs. Cecil Frances Alexander, 1852 (1818-1895)   *William H. Jude, 1874 (1851-1922)*

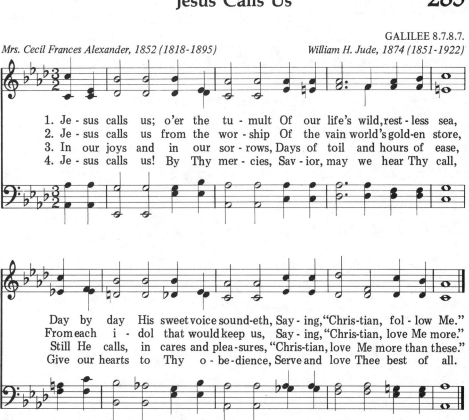

1. Je - sus calls us; o'er the tu - mult Of our life's wild, rest - less sea,
2. Je - sus calls us from the wor - ship Of the vain world's gold - en store,
3. In our joys and in our sor - rows, Days of toil and hours of ease,
4. Je - sus calls us! By Thy mer - cies, Sav - ior, may we hear Thy call,

Day by day His sweet voice sound - eth, Say - ing, "Chris - tian, fol - low Me."
From each i - dol that would keep us, Say - ing, "Chris - tian, love Me more."
Still He calls, in cares and plea - sures, "Chris - tian, love Me more than these."
Give our hearts to Thy o - be - dience, Serve and love Thee best of all.

INVITATION

286 Wonderful Words of Life

P. P. Bliss, 1874 (1838-1876)

8.6.8.6.6.6.Ref.
P. P. Bliss, 1874

1. Sing them o - ver a - gain to me, Won - der - ful words of life;
2. Christ, the bless - ed One, gives to all Won - der - ful words of life;
3. Sweet - ly ech - o the gos - pel call, Won - der - ful words of life;

Let me more of their beau - ty see, Won - der - ful words of life.
Sin - ner, list to the lov - ing call, Won - der - ful words of life.
Of - fer par - don and peace to all, Won - der - ful words of life.

Words of life and beau - ty, Teach me faith and du - ty;
All so free - ly giv - en, Woo - ing us to heav - en;
Je - sus, on - ly Sav - ior, Sanc - ti - fy for - ev - er;

Refrain

Beau - ti - ful words, won - der - ful words, Won - der - ful words of life,

Beau - ti - ful words, won - der - ful words, Won - der - ful words of life.

INVITATION

Softly and Tenderly

287

11.7.11.7.Ref.

Will L. Thompson (1847-1909)   *Will L. Thompson*

1. Soft - ly and ten-der - ly Je - sus is call - ing, Call - ing for you and for
2. Why should we tar - ry when Je - sus is plead-ing, Plead-ing for you and for
3. Think of the won-der - ful love He has prom-ised, Prom-ised for you and for

me;   At the heart's por - tal He's wait - ing and watch - ing,
me?   Why should we lin - ger and heed not His mer - cies,
me;   Though we have sinned, He has mer - cy and par - don,

Refrain

Watch-ing for you and for me. Come home, come home,
Mer-cies for you and for me? Come home, come home,
Par - don for you and for me.

Ye who are wea-ry, come home; Ear - nest-ly, ten-der - ly

Je - sus is call - ing, Call - ing, O sin-ner, come home!

TSDAH-10

INVITATION

288   I Am Going to Calvary

Brian Wren, 1971 (1936-   )

SEE SAW SACCARA DOWN 7.7.7.7.D.
Arr. by Charles Strange, 1972 (1902-   )

1. I am go-ing to Cal - va - ry. Would you like to come with Me
2. If I wear a thorn - y crown, If the sol - diers knock Me down
3. When I go a-long the road, I shall lift a heav - y load.
4. I am go-ing to stretch My hands, Reach-ing out to all the lands.

All the way and back a-gain? You must fol-low the Lead - er then.
Can I real - ly be a king? Love will an - swer ev - ery-thing
I will car-ry a cross for you. You will learn to car-ry it too
Can I real - ly be a king? Love's the lord of ev - ery-thing,

You must fol-low the Lead - er, You must fol-low the Lead - er,
If you fol-low the Lead - er, If you fol-low the Lead - er,
When you fol-low the Lead - er, When you fol-low the Lead - er,
When you fol-low the Lead - er, When you fol-low the Lead - er,

All the way and back a-gain, You must fol-low the Lead - er.
Love will an - swer ev - ery-thing If you fol-low the Lead - er.
You will learn to car-ry it too If you fol-low the Lead - er.
Love's the lord of ev - ery-thing When you fol-low the Lead - er.

INVITATION

The Savior Is Waiting

289

CARMICHAEL 11.7.11.7.Ref.

Ralph Carmichael (1927-   )

Ralph Carmichael

1. The Sav - ior is wait - ing to en - ter your heart, Why don't you
2. If you'll take one step toward the Sav - ior, my friend, You'll find His

let Him come in? There's noth - ing in this world to keep you a -
arms o - pen wide; Re - ceive Him, and all of your dark - ness will

Refrain

part, What is your an - swer to Him? Time af - ter time He has
end, With - in your heart He'll a - bide.

wait - ed be - fore, And now He is wait - ing a - gain To see

if you're will - ing to o - pen the door: O how He wants to come in.

INVITATION

290 Turn Your Eyes Upon Jesus

Helen H. Lemmel (1864-1961)

9.8.9.8.Ref.
Helen H. Lemmel

1. O soul, are you wea-ry and trou - bled? No light in the
2. Through death in - to life ev - er - last - ing He passed, and we
3. His word shall not fail you He prom - ised; Be - lieve Him and

dark-ness you see? There's light for a look at the Sav - ior,
fol - low Him there; O - ver us sin no more hath do - min - ion,
all will be well: Then go to a world that is dy - ing,

Refrain

And life more a - bun-dant and free!
For more than con-qu'rors we are! Turn your eyes up-on Je-
His per - fect sal - va - tion to tell!

sus, Look full in His won-der - ful face; And the things of

earth will grow strange-ly dim In the light of His glo-ry and grace.

INVITATION

We Have Not Known Thee

ST. CHRYSOSTOM 8.8.8.8.8.8.

Thomas B. Pollock, 1889 (1836-1896)

Joseph Barnby, 1871 (1838-1896)

1. We have not known Thee as we ought, Nor learned Thy wis - dom, grace, and power; The things of earth have filled our thought, And tri - fles of the pass - ing hour. Lord, give us light Thy truth to see, And make us wise in know - ing Thee.

2. We have not feared Thee as we ought, Nor bowed be - neath Thine aw - ful eye, Nor guard - ed deed, and word, and thought, Re - mem - ber - ing that God was nigh. Lord, give us faith to know Thee near, And grant the grace of ho - ly fear.

3. We have not loved Thee as we ought, Nor cared that we are loved by Thee; Thy pres - ence we have cold - ly sought, And fee - bly longed Thy face to see. Lord, give a pure and lov - ing heart To feel and own the love Thou art.

4. We have not served Thee as we ought; A - las! the du - ties left un - done, The work with lit - tle fer - vor wrought, The bat - tles lost, or scarce - ly won! Lord, give the zeal, and give the might, For Thee to toil, for Thee to fight.

5. When shall we know Thee as we ought, And fear, and love, and serve a - right! When shall we, out of tri - al brought, Be per - fect in the land of light! Lord, may we day by day pre - pare To see Thy face, and serve Thee there.

REPENTANCE

292

Jesus, I Come

W. T. Sleeper, 1887 (1819-1904)

Irregular
George C. Stebbins, 1887 (1846-1945)

1. Out of my bond - age, sor - row and night, Je - sus, I come,
2. Out of my shame - ful fail - ure and loss, Je - sus, I come,
3. Out of un - rest and ar - ro-gant pride, Je - sus, I come,
4. Out of the fear and dread of the tomb, Je - sus, I come,

Je - sus, I come; In - to Thy free - dom, glad - ness and light,
Je - sus, I come; In - to the glo - rious gain of Thy cross,
Je - sus, I come; In - to Thy bless - ed will to a - bide,
Je - sus, I come; In - to the joy and light of Thy home,

Je - sus, I come to Thee; Out of my sick - ness
Je - sus, I come to Thee; Out of earth's sor - rows
Je - sus, I come to Thee; Out of my - self to
Je - sus, I come to Thee; Out of the depths of

in - to Thy health, Out of my want and in - to Thy wealth,
in - to Thy balm, Out of life's storms and in - to Thy calm,
dwell in Thy love, Out of de - spair in - to rap - tures a - bove,
ru - in un - told, In - to the peace of Thy shel - ter - ing fold,

REPENTANCE

Out of my sin and in - to Thy-self, Je - sus, I come to Thee.
Out of dis - tress to ju - bi-lant psalm, Je - sus, I come to Thee.
Up - ward for aye on wings like a dove, Je - sus, I come to Thee.
Ev - er Thy glo-rious face to be - hold, Je - sus, I come to Thee.

Heavenly Father, Bless Us Now 293

AUS DER TIEFE 7.7.7.7.

Alexander Clark (1834-1879)

Attr. to Martin Herbst (1654-1681)

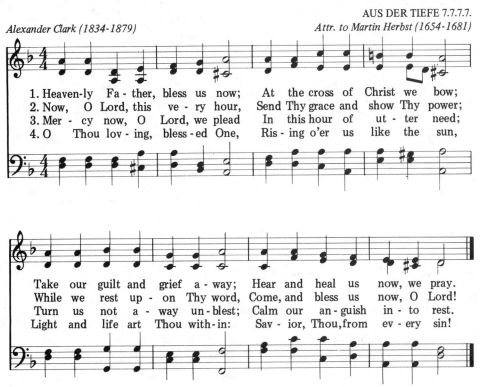

1. Heaven-ly Fa - ther, bless us now; At the cross of Christ we bow;
2. Now, O Lord, this ve - ry hour, Send Thy grace and show Thy power;
3. Mer - cy now, O Lord, we plead In this hour of ut - ter need;
4. O Thou lov - ing, bless - ed One, Ris - ing o'er us like the sun,

Take our guilt and grief a - way; Hear and heal us now, we pray.
While we rest up - on Thy word, Come, and bless us now, O Lord!
Turn us not a - way un - blest; Calm our an - guish in - to rest.
Light and life art Thou with-in: Sav - ior, Thou, from ev - ery sin!

Alternate tune, TRYGGARE KAN INGEN VARA, No. 101

REPENTANCE

294

Power in the Blood

Lewis E. Jones, 1899 (1865-1936)

10.9.10.8.Ref.
Lewis E. Jones, 1899

1. Would you be free from the bur-den of sin? There's pow'r in the blood,
2. Would you be free from your pas-sion and pride? There's pow'r in the blood,
3. Would you do ser-vice for Je-sus your King? There's pow'r in the blood,

pow'r in the blood; Would you o'er e - vil a vic-to-ry win? There's
pow'r in the blood; Come for a cleans-ing to Cal-va-ry's tide? There's
pow'r in the blood; Would you live dai-ly His prais-es to sing? There's

Refrain

won-der-ful pow'r in the blood. There is pow'r, pow'r, won-der-work-ing pow'r
There is

In the blood of the Lamb; There is pow'r, pow'r,
In the blood of the Lamb; There is

REPENTANCE

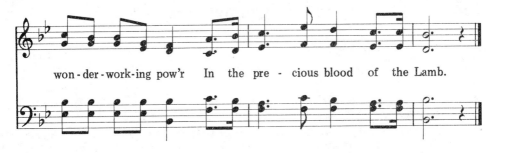

won - der - work-ing pow'r In the pre - cious blood of the Lamb.

Chief of Sinners 295

SPANISH HYMN 7.7.7.7.7.7.

William McComb (1738-18 ?)

Arr. by Benjamin Carr, 1826 (1769-1831)

1. Chief of sin - ners though I be, Je - sus shed His blood for me;
2. O the height of Je - sus' love! High - er than the heaven a - bove,
3. Chief of sin - ners though I be, Christ is all in all to me;

Died that I might live on high, Died that I might nev - er die;
Deep - er than the deep-est sea, Last - ing as e - ter - ni - ty;
All my wants to Him are known, All my sor-rows are His own;

As the branch is to the vine, I am His, and He is mine.
Love that found me— won-drous thought! Found me when I sought Him not!
Safe with Him from earth-ly strife, He sus-tains the hid - den life.

REPENTANCE

296 Lord, I'm Coming Home

Luke 15:18
William J. Kirkpatrick, 1902 (1838-1921)

8.5.8.5.Ref.
William J. Kirkpatrick, 1902

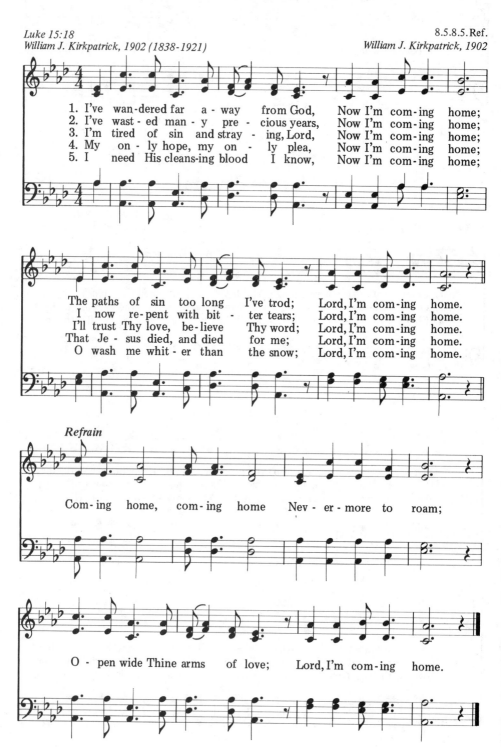

1. I've wan-dered far a - way from God, Now I'm com-ing home;
2. I've wast - ed man - y pre - cious years, Now I'm com-ing home;
3. I'm tired of sin and stray - ing, Lord, Now I'm com-ing home;
4. My on - ly hope, my on - ly plea, Now I'm com-ing home;
5. I need His cleans-ing blood I know, Now I'm com-ing home;

The paths of sin too long I've trod; Lord, I'm com-ing home.
I now re-pent with bit - ter tears; Lord, I'm com-ing home.
I'll trust Thy love, be-lieve Thy word; Lord, I'm com-ing home.
That Je - sus died, and died for me; Lord, I'm com-ing home.
O wash me whit - er than the snow; Lord, I'm com-ing home.

Refrain

Com-ing home, com-ing home Nev - er - more to roam;

O - pen wide Thine arms of love; Lord, I'm com-ing home.

REPENTANCE

God Be Merciful to Me

Psalm 51
Anon.

REFUGE 7.7.7.7.D.
Joseph P. Holbrook, 1862 (1822-1888)

1. God, be mer - ci - ful to me, On Thy grace I rest my plea;
2. I am e - vil, born in sin; Thou de - sir - est truth with - in.
3. Gra - cious God, my heart re - new, Make my spir - it right and true;
4. Sin - ners then shall learn from me And re - turn, O God, to Thee;

Plen - teous in com - pas - sion Thou, Blot out my trans - gres - sions now;
Thou a - lone my Sav - ior art, Teach Thy wis - dom to my heart;
Cast me not a - way from Thee, Let Thy Spir - it dwell in me;
Sav - ior, all my guilt re - move, And my tongue shall sing Thy love;

Wash me, make me pure with - in, Cleanse, O cleanse me from my sin,
Make me pure, Thy grace be - stow, Wash me whit - er than the snow,
Thy sal - va - tion's joy im - part, Stead - fast make my will - ing heart,
Touch my si - lent lips, O Lord, And my mouth shall praise ac - cord,

Wash me, make me pure with - in, Cleanse, O cleanse me from my sin.
Make me pure, Thy grace be - stow, Wash me whit - er than the snow.
Thy sal - va - tion's joy im - part, Stead - fast make my will - ing heart.
Touch my si - lent lips, O Lord, And my mouth shall praise ac - cord.

FORGIVENESS

I Lay My Sins on Jesus

BRADLEY 7.6.7.6.

Horatius Bonar, 1843 (1808-1889)

Allen W. Foster, 1964 (1940-   )

1. I lay my sins on Je - sus, The spot-less Lamb of God; He bears them all, and frees us From the ac-curs - ed load, From the ac-curs - ed load.
2. I bring my guilt to Je - sus, To wash my crim - son stains White in His blood most pre - cious, Till not a stain re - mains, Till not a stain re - mains.
3. I lay my wants on Je - sus, All full - ness dwells in Him; He heal - eth my dis - eas - es, He doth my soul re - deem, He doth my soul re - deem.
4. I long to be with Je - sus, Meek, lov - ing, low - ly, mild; I long to be like Je - sus, The Fa-ther's ho - ly child, The Fa-ther's ho - ly child.
5. I long to be with Jesus A - mid the heav - 'nly throng, To sing with them His prais - es, And learn the an - gels' song. And learn the an - gels' song.

Music copyright © 1965 by Allen W. Foster

Alternate tune, ST. HILDA, No. 283

Forgive Our Sins as We Forgive

Matt. 6:12

DETROIT C.M.

Rosamond E. Herklots (1905-   ) alt.

The Sacred Harp, Philadelphia, 1844

Unison

1. "For - give our sins as we for-give," You taught us, Lord, to pray;
2. How can Your par - don reach and bless The un - for - giv - ing heart
3. In blaz - ing light Your cross re - veals The truth we dim - ly knew:
4. Lord, cleanse the depths with - in our souls And bid re - sent - ment cease;

FORGIVENESS

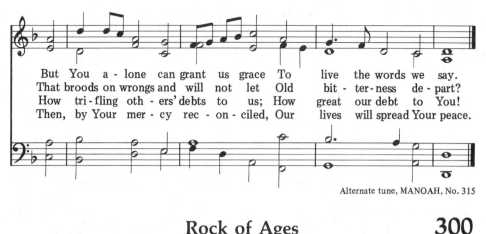

But You a - lone can grant us grace To live the words we say.
That broods on wrongs and will not let Old bit - ter - ness de - part?
How tri - fling oth - ers' debts to us; How great our debt to You!
Then, by Your mer - cy rec - on - ciled, Our lives will spread Your peace.

Alternate tune, MANOAH, No. 315

Rock of Ages 300

TOPLADY 7.7.7.7.7.7.

Augustus M. Toplady, 1776 (1740-1778) alt.   *Thomas Hastings, 1830 (1784-1872)*

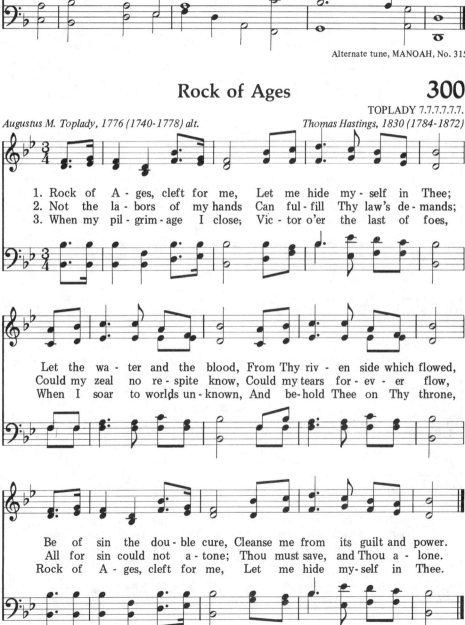

1. Rock of A - ges, cleft for me, Let me hide my - self in Thee;
2. Not the la - bors of my hands Can ful - fill Thy law's de - mands;
3. When my pil - grim - age I close; Vic - tor o'er the last of foes,

Let the wa - ter and the blood, From Thy riv - en side which flowed,
Could my zeal no re - spite know, Could my tears for - ev - er flow,
When I soar to worlds un - known, And be - hold Thee on Thy throne,

Be of sin the dou - ble cure, Cleanse me from its guilt and power.
All for sin could not a - tone; Thou must save, and Thou a - lone.
Rock of A - ges, cleft for me, Let me hide my - self in Thee.

Alternate tune, GETHSEMANE, No. 157

FORGIVENESS

Nearer, Still Nearer

Mrs. C. H. Morris (1862-1929)

MORRIS 9.10.9.10.10.
Mrs. C. H. Morris, 1898

1. Near - er, still near - er, close to Thy heart, Draw me, my Sav - ior, so pre - cious Thou art; Fold me, O fold me close to Thy breast, Shel - ter me safe in that ha - ven of rest, Shel - ter me safe in that ha - ven of rest.

2. Near - er, still near - er, noth - ing I bring, Nought as an of - fering to Je - sus my King— On - ly my sin - ful now con - trite heart; Grant me the cleans - ing Thy blood doth im - part, Grant me the cleans - ing Thy blood doth im - part.

3. Near - er, still near - er, Lord, to be Thine; Sin, with its fol - lies, I glad - ly re - sign, All of its pleas - ures, pomp and its pride; Give me but Je - sus, my Lord cru - ci - fied, Give me but Je - sus, my Lord cru - ci - fied.

4. Near - er, still near - er, while life shall last; Till safe in glo - ry my an - chor is cast; Through end - less a - ges, ev - er to be, Near - er, my Sav - ior, still near - er to Thee, Near - er, my Sav - ior, still near - er to Thee.

CONSECRATION

Deeper Yet

DEEPER YET 6.6.6.6.Ref.

Johnson Oatman, Jr. (1856-1930)

William J. Kirkpatrick (1838-1921)

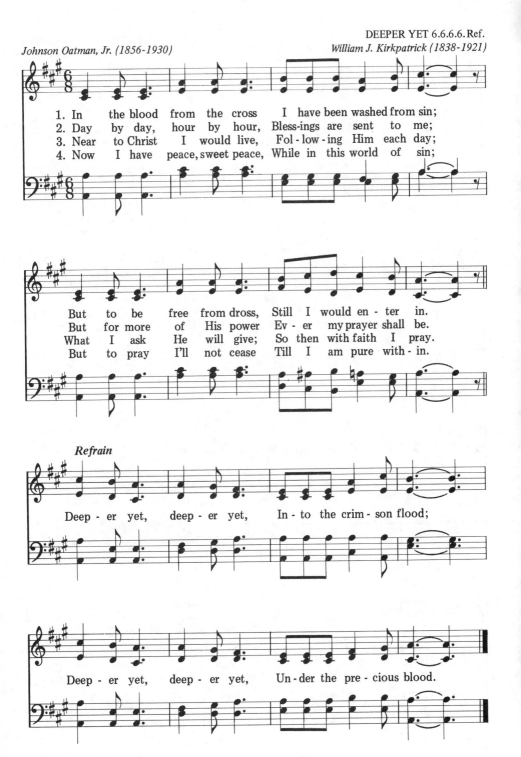

1. In the blood from the cross I have been washed from sin;
2. Day by day, hour by hour, Bless-ings are sent to me;
3. Near to Christ I would live, Fol-low-ing Him each day;
4. Now I have peace, sweet peace, While in this world of sin;

But to be free from dross, Still I would en-ter in.
But for more of His power Ev-er my prayer shall be.
What I ask He will give; So then with faith I pray.
But to pray I'll not cease Till I am pure with-in.

Refrain

Deep-er yet, deep-er yet, In-to the crim-son flood;

Deep-er yet, deep-er yet, Un-der the pre-cious blood.

CONSECRATION

303

Beneath the Cross of Jesus

Prov. 14:26
Elizabeth C. Clephane, 1872 (1830-1869)

ST. CHRISTOPHER 7.6.8.6.8.6.8.6.
Frederick C. Maker, 1881 (1844-1927)

1. Be - neath the cross of Je - sus I fain would take my stand,
2. Up - on that cross of Je - sus Mine eye at times can see
3. I take, O cross, thy shad - ow For my a - bid - ing place;

The shad - ow of a might - y rock With - in a wea - ry land;
The ver - y dy - ing form of One Who suf - fered there for me;
I ask no oth - er sun-shine than The sun - shine of His face;

A home with - in the wil - der - ness, A rest up - on the way,
And from my smit - ten heart with tears Two won - ders I con - fess:
Con - tent to let the world go by, To know no gain nor loss,

From the burn - ing of the noon-tide heat, And the bur - den of the day.
The won - ders of re - deem - ing love And my un - wor - thi - ness.
My sin - ful self my on - ly shame, My glo - ry all the cross.

Faith of Our Fathers

ST. CATHERINE 8.8.8.8.8.8.
Henri F. Hemy, 1864 (1818-1888)
Frederick W. Faber, 1849 (1814-1863)
Alt. by James G. Walton, 1874 (1821-1905)

1. Faith of our fa - thers! liv - ing still In spite of dun - geon,
2. Our fa - thers, chained in pris - ons dark, Were still in heart and
3. Faith of our fa - thers! we will love Both friend and foe in

fire, and sword, O how our hearts beat high with joy
con - science free; How sweet would be their chil - dren's fate,
all our strife, And preach thee, too, as love knows how,

When - e'er we hear that glo - rious word. Faith of our
If they, like them, could die for thee! Faith of our
By kind - ly words and vir - tuous life. Faith of our

fa - thers! ho - ly faith! We will be true to thee till death.
fa - thers! ho - ly faith! We will be true to thee till death.
fa - thers! ho - ly faith! We will be true to thee till death.

CONSECRATION

305

Give Me Jesus

7.7.7.4.Ref.

American Negro Spiritual

Arr. by Alma Blackmon, 1984 (1921-   )

1. In the morn-ing when I rise, In the morn-ing when I rise, In the morn-ing when I rise, Give me Je - sus.
2. Dark mid-night was my cry, Dark mid-night was my cry, Dark mid-night was my cry, Give me Je - sus.
3. Just a - bout the break of day, Just a - bout the break of day, Just a - bout the break of day, Give me Je - sus.
4. Oh, when I come to die, Oh, when I come to die, Oh, when I come to die, Give me Je - sus.

Refrain

Give me Je - sus, Give me Je - sus,

You may have all this world, Give me Je - sus.

CONSECRATION

Draw Me Nearer

306

10.7.10.7.Ref.

Fanny J. Crosby, 1875 (1820-1915)

William H. Doane (1832-1915)

1. I am Thine, O Lord, I have heard Thy voice, And it told Thy
2. Con - se - crate me now to Thy ser - vice, Lord, By the power of
3. O the pure de - light of a sin - gle hour That be - fore Thy

love to me; But I long to rise in the arms of faith,
grace di - vine; May my soul look up with a stead-fast hope
throne I spend, When I kneel in prayer, and with Thee, my God,

Refrain

And be clos - er drawn to Thee. Draw me near - er,
And my will be lost in Thine. near - er, near - er,
I com-mune as friend with friend!

near - er, bless-ed Lord, To the cross where Thou hast died; Draw me

near - er, near - er, near - er, bless-ed Lord, To Thy pre - cious, bleed - ing side.

CONSECRATION

307 I Am Coming to the Cross

7.7.7.7.Ref.

William McDonald, 1870 (1820-1901)

William G. Fischer (1835-1912)

1. I am com-ing to the cross; I am poor, and weak, and blind;
2. Long my heart has sighed for Thee; Long has e-vil reigned with-in;
3. Here I give my all to Thee—Friends, and time, and earth-ly store;
4. Je-sus comes! He fills my soul! Per-fect-ed in Him I am;

I am count-ing all but dross; I shall full sal-va-tion find.
Je-sus sweet-ly speaks to me, "I will cleanse you from all sin."
Soul and bod-y Thine to be, Whol-ly Thine for-ev-er-more.
I am ev-ery whit made whole—Glo-ry, glo-ry to the Lamb!

Refrain

I am trust-ing, Lord, in Thee, O Thou Lamb of Cal-va-ry;

Hum-bly at Thy cross I bow; Save me, Je-sus, save me now.

CONSECRATION

Wholly Thine

9.6.9.5. Ref.

F. E. Belden, 1886 (1858-1945)

F. E. Belden, 1886

1. I would be, dear Sav-ior, whol-ly Thine; Teach me how, teach me how;
2. What is world-ly plea-sure, wealth, or fame, With-out Thee, with-out Thee?
3. As I cast earth's tran-sient joys be-hind, Come Thou near, come Thou near;

I would do Thy will, O Lord, not mine; Help me, help me now.
I will leave them all for Thy dear name, This my wealth shall be.
In Thy pres-ence all in all I find, 'Tis my com-fort here.

Refrain

Whol-ly Thine, whol-ly Thine, Whol-ly Thine, this is my vow;
O Lord, O Lord,

Whol-ly Thine, whol-ly Thine, Whol-ly Thine, O Lord, just now.
O Lord, O Lord,

CONSECRATION

309

I Surrender All

J. W. VanDeVenter, 1896 (1855-1939)

8.7.8.7.Ref.
W. S. Weeden (1847-1908)

1. All to Jesus I surrender, All to Him I freely give;
2. All to Jesus I surrender; Humbly at His feet I bow,
3. All to Jesus I surrender; Make me, Savior, wholly Thine;
4. All to Jesus I surrender; Now I feel the sacred flame.

I will ever love and trust Him, In His presence daily live;
Worldly pleasures all forsaken; Take me, Jesus, take me now;
Let me feel the Holy Spirit, Truly know that Thou art mine;
O the joy of full salvation! Glory, glory to His name!

Refrain

I surrender all, I surrender all;
I surrender all, I surrender all,

All to Thee, my blessed Savior, I surrender all.

CONSECRATION

I Would Draw Nearer to Jesus

8.7.8.7.Ref.
Robert Harkness

Robert Harkness (1880-1961)

1. I would draw near-er to Je - sus, In His sweet pres-ence a - bide,
2. I would draw near-er to Je - sus, Noth-ing with-hold-ing from Him,
3. I would draw near-er to Je - sus, Seek-ing His strength to be true,

Con-stant-ly try-ing to serve Him, Safe and se-cure at His side.
Know-ing He loves to be gra-cious, I would draw near-er to Him.
Will-ing to tell of His good-ness, Glad-ly His blest will to do.

Refrain

I would draw near-er to Je - sus, I would draw near-er to Him;

Ful - ly sur-ren-dered each mo-ment, I would draw near-er to Him.

CONSECRATION

311 I Would Be Like Jesus

C.M.Ref.

James Rowe (1865-1933)

B. D. Ackley (1872-1958)

1. Earth - ly plea - sures vain - ly call me; I would be like Je - sus;
2. He has bro - ken ev - ery fet - ter, I would be like Je - sus;
3. All the way from earth to glo - ry, I would be like Je - sus;
4. That in heav - en He may meet me, I would be like Je - sus;
   would be like Je - sus;

Noth - ing world - ly shall en - thrall me; I would be like Je - sus.
That my soul may serve Him bet - ter, I would be like Je - sus.
Tell - ing o'er and o'er the sto - ry, I would be like Je - sus.
That His words "Well done" may greet me, I would be like Je - sus.
would be like Je - sus.

Refrain

Be like Je - sus, this my song, In the home and in the throng;

Be like Je - sus, all day long! I would be like Je - sus.

CONSECRATION

Near the Cross

7.6.7.6. Ref.

Fanny J. Crosby, 1869 (1820-1915)

William H. Doane, 1869 (1832-1915)

1. Je - sus, keep me near the cross; There a pre-cious foun - tain
2. Near the cross, a trem-bling soul, Love and mer - cy found me;
3. Near the cross! O Lamb of God, Bring its scenes be - fore me;
4. Near the cross I'll watch and wait, Hop - ing, trust - ing ev - er,

Free to all, a heal - ing stream, Flows from Cal - vary's moun - tain.
There the bright and Morn - ing Star Sheds its beams a - round me.
Help me walk from day to day, With its shad - ows o'er me.
Till I reach the gold - en strand, Just be - yond the riv - er.

Refrain

In the cross, in the cross, Be my glo - ry ev - er,

Till my rap - tured soul shall find Rest be - yond the riv - er.

CONSECRATION

313

Just as I Am

Charlotte Elliott, 1834 (1789-1871)

SAFFRON WALDEN 8.8.8.6.
Arthur H. Brown (1830-1926)

1. Just as I am, with-out one plea, But that Thy blood was shed for me, And that Thou bid'st me come to Thee,
2. Just as I am, and wait-ing not To rid my soul of one dark blot, To Thee whose blood can cleanse each spot,
3. Just as I am, though tossed a-bout With man-y a con-flict, man-y a doubt; "Fight-ings with-in, and fears with-out,"
4. Just as I am, poor, wretch-ed, blind; Sight, rich-es, heal-ing of the mind, Yea, all I need, in Thee I find,
5. Just as I am, Thou wilt re-ceive, Wilt wel-come, par-don, cleanse, re-lieve; Be-cause Thy prom-ise I be-lieve,
6. Just as I am, Thy love I own Has bro-ken ev-ery bar-rier down; Now to be Thine, and Thine a-lone,

O Lamb of God, I come.

Music by permission of Oxford University Press.

Alternate tune, WOODWORTH, No. 314

CONSECRATION

Just as I Am 314

WOODWORTH L.M.

Charlotte Elliott, 1836 (1789-1871)

William B. Bradbury, 1849 (1816-1868)

1. Just as I am, with-out one plea But that Thy blood was shed for me

And that Thou bid'st me come to Thee, O Lamb of God, I come, I come.

Alternate tune, SAFFRON WALDEN, and other stanzas, No. 313

O for a Closer Walk! 315

MANOAH C.M.

William Cowper, 1769 (1731-1800)

Henry W. Greatorex's Collection, Boston, 1851

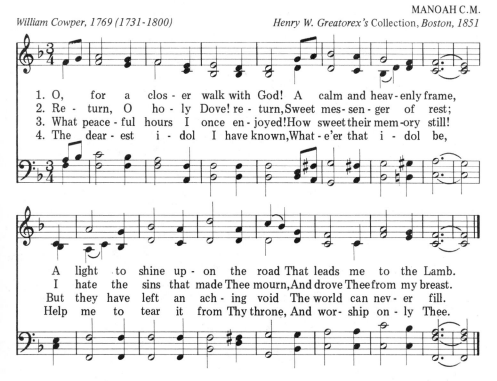

1. O, for a clos-er walk with God! A calm and heav-enly frame,
2. Re-turn, O ho-ly Dove! re-turn, Sweet mes-sen-ger of rest;
3. What peace-ful hours I once en-joyed! How sweet their mem-ory still!
4. The dear-est i-dol I have known, What-e'er that i-dol be,

A light to shine up-on the road That leads me to the Lamb.
I hate the sins that made Thee mourn, And drove Thee from my breast.
But they have left an ach-ing void The world can nev-er fill.
Help me to tear it from Thy throne, And wor-ship on-ly Thee.

CONSECRATION

316 Live Out Thy Life Within Me

AURELIA 7.6.7.6.D.

Frances Ridley Havergal (1836-1879)

Samuel Wesley, 1864 (1810-1876)

1. Live out Thy life with-in me, O Je-sus, King of kings!
2. The tem-ple has been yield-ed, And pu-ri-fied of sin;
3. Its mem-bers ev-ery mo-ment Held sub-ject to Thy call,
4. But rest-ful, calm, and pli-ant, From bend and bi-as free,

Be Thou Thy-self the an-swer To all my ques-tion-ings;
Let Thy She-ki-nah glo-ry Now shine forth from with-in,
Read-y to have Thee use them, Or not be used at all;
A-wait-ing Thy de-ci-sion, When Thou hast need of me.

Live out Thy life with-in me, In all things have Thy way!
And all the earth keep si-lence, The bod-y hence-forth be
Held with-out rest-less long-ing, Or strain, or stress, or fret,
Live out Thy life with-in me, O Je-sus, King of kings!

I, the trans-par-ent med-ium Thy glo-ry to dis-play.
Thy si-lent, gen-tle ser-vant, Moved on-ly as by Thee.
Or chaf-ings at Thy deal-ings, Or thoughts of vain re-gret.
Be Thou the glo-rious an-swer To all my ques-tion-ings.

Alternate tune, EWING, No. 429

CONSECRATION

Lead Me to Calvary

C.M.Ref.

Jennie E. Hussey, 1921 (1874-1958)

William J. Kirkpatrick, 1921 (1838-1921)

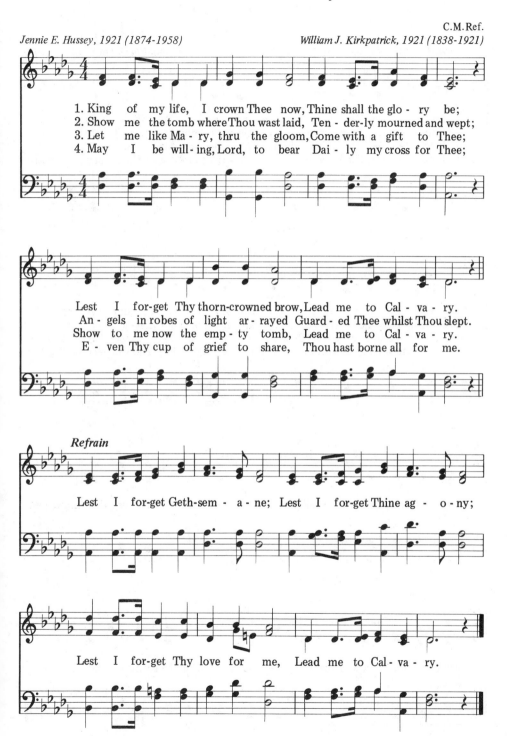

1. King of my life, I crown Thee now, Thine shall the glo - ry be;
2. Show me the tomb where Thou wast laid, Ten - der-ly mourned and wept;
3. Let me like Ma - ry, thru the gloom, Come with a gift to Thee;
4. May I be will - ing, Lord, to bear Dai - ly my cross for Thee;

Lest I for-get Thy thorn-crowned brow, Lead me to Cal - va - ry.
An - gels in robes of light ar - rayed Guard - ed Thee whilst Thou slept.
Show to me now the emp - ty tomb, Lead me to Cal - va - ry.
E - ven Thy cup of grief to share, Thou hast borne all for me.

Refrain

Lest I for-get Geth-sem - a - ne; Lest I for-get Thine ag - o - ny;

Lest I for-get Thy love for me, Lead me to Cal - va - ry.

CONSECRATION

318 Whiter Than Snow

11.11.11.11.Ref.

James Nicholson, 1872 (1828-1876)

William G. Fischer (1835-1912)

1. Lord Je - sus, I long to be per - fect - ly whole; I want Thee for -
2. Lord Je - sus, look down from Thy throne in the skies, And help me to
3. Lord Je - sus, for this I most hum - bly en - treat; I wait, bless - ed
4. Lord Je - sus, Thou seest I pa - tient - ly wait; Come now, and with -

ev - er to live in my soul; Break down ev - ery i - dol, cast out ev - ery foe;
make a com-plete sac - ri - fice; I give up my-self, and what-ev - er I know;
Lord, at Thy cru - ci - fied feet, By faith, for my cleans-ing; I see Thy blood flow;
in me a new heart create; To those who have sought Thee, Thou nev-er said'st No;

Refrain

Now wash me, and I shall be whit - er than snow. Whit - er than snow, yes,

whit - er than snow; Now wash me, and I shall be whit - er than snow.

CONSECRATION

Lord, I Want to Be a Christian 319

American Negro Spiritual

8.6.8.3.3.3.8.3.

1. Lord, I want to be a Chris-tian In my heart, in my heart;
2. Lord, I want to be more lov-ing In my heart, in my heart;
3. Lord, I want to be more ho-ly In my heart, in my heart;
4. Lord, I want to be like Je-sus In my heart, in my heart;

Lord, I want to be a Chris-tian In my heart.
Lord, I want to be more lov-ing In my heart.
Lord, I want to be more ho-ly In my heart.
Lord, I want to be like Je-sus In my heart.

In my heart, In my heart,
In my heart, In my heart,

Lord, I want to be a Chris-tian In my heart.
Lord, I want to be more lov-ing In my heart.
Lord, I want to be more ho-ly In my heart.
Lord, I want to be like Je-sus In my heart.

CONSECRATION

320

Lord of Creation

SLANE 10.11.10.11.
Irish Melody
Jack Copley Winslow (1882-1974) alt.
Arr. by Melvin West, 1984 (1930-   )

1. Lord of cre - a - tion, to You be all praise! Most
2. Lord of all pow - er, I give You my will, In
3. Lord of all wis - dom, I give You my mind, Rich
4. Lord of all be - ing, I give You my all; If I

might - y Your work - ing, most won - drous Your ways! Your
joy - ful o - be - dience Your tasks to ful - fill. Your
truth that sur - pass - es man's knowl-edge to find; What
ev - er dis - own You, I stum - ble and fall; But

glo - ry and might are be - yond us to tell, And
bond - age is free - dom; Your ser - vice is song; And
eye has not seen and what ear has not heard Is
led in Your ser - vice Your word to o - bey, I'll

yet in the heart of the hum - ble You dwell.
held in Your keep - ing, my weak - ness is strong.
taught by Your Spir - it and shines from Your Word.
walk in Your free - dom to the end of the way.

Unison setting, No. 547

CONSECRATION

My Jesus, I Love Thee

321

GORDON 11.11.11.11.

William Ralf Featherstone (1846-1873)

Adoniram J. Gordon (1836-1895)

1. My Je - sus, I love Thee, I know Thou art mine;
2. I love Thee be - cause Thou hast first lov - ed me,
3. I'll love Thee in life, I will love Thee 'til death,
4. In man - sions of glo - ry and end - less de - light,

For Thee all the fol - lies of sin I re - sign;
And pur - chased my par - don on Cal - va - ry's tree;
And praise Thee as long as Thou lend - est me breath;
I'll ev - er a - dore Thee in heav - en so bright;

My gra - cious Re - deem - er, my Sav - ior art Thou;
I love Thee for wear - ing the thorns on Thy brow;
And say when the death dew lies cold on my brow,
I'll sing with the glit - ter - ing crown on my brow,

If ev - er I loved Thee, my Je - sus, 'tis now.

CONSECRATION

TSDAH-11

322 Nothing Between

10.9.10.9.Ref.

Charles A. Tindley (1851-1933)

Charles A. Tindley
Arr. by Wayne Hooper, 1984 (1920-   )

1. Noth-ing be-tween my soul and the Sav-ior, Naught of this world's de-
2. Noth-ing be-tween, like world-ly plea-sure: Hab-its of life, though
3. Noth-ing be-tween, e'en man-y hard tri-als, Though the whole world a-

lu - sive dream: I have re-nounced all sin - ful plea-sure—
harm-less they seem, Must not my heart from Him ev - er sev-er—
gainst me con-vene; Watch-ing with prayer and much self-de-ni-al—

Je - sus is mine! There's noth-ing be-tween.
He is my all! There's noth-ing be-tween. Noth-ing be-tween my
Tri-umph at last, With noth-ing be-tween!

Refrain

soul and the Sav-ior, So that His bless-ed face may be seen; Noth-ing pre-

vent-ing the least of His fa-vor: Keep the way clear! Let noth-ing be-tween.

Arrangement copyright © 1984 by Wayne Hooper

CONSECRATION

O for a Heart to Praise My God! 323

BEATITUDO C.M.

Charles Wesley, 1742 (1707-1788)

John B. Dykes, 1875 (1823-1876)

1. O for a heart to praise my God! A heart from sin set free,
2. A heart re-signed, sub-mis-sive, meek, My dear Re-deem-er's throne,
3. A heart in ev-ery thought re-newed, And full of love di-vine,
4. Thy na-ture, gra-cious Lord, im-part; Come quick-ly from a-bove;

A heart that al-ways feels Thy blood, So free-ly shed for me.
Where on-ly Christ is heard to speak, Where Je-sus reigns a-lone.
Per-fect, and right, and pure, and good, A cop-y, Lord, of Thine.
Write Thy new name up-on my heart, Thy new, best name of Love.

Just as I Am, Thine Own to Be 324

JUST AS I AM 8.8.8.6.

Marianne Hearn, 1887 (1834-1909)

Joseph Barnby, 1893 (1838-1896)

1. Just as I am, Thine own to be, Friend of the young, who lov-est
2. In the glad morn-ing of my day, My life to give, my vows to
3. I would live ev-er in the light; I would work ev-er for the
4. Just as I am, young, strong, and free, To be the best that I can

me, To con-se-crate my-self to Thee, O Je-sus Christ, I come.
pay, With no re-serve and no de-lay, With all my heart I come.
right; I would serve Thee with all my might; There-fore, to Thee I come.
be For truth, and righ-teous-ness, and Thee, Lord of my life, I come.

CONSECRATION

325

Jesus, I My Cross Have Taken

Henry F. Lyte, 1824 (1793-1847)

ELLESDIE 8.7.8.7.D.
Arr. from Mozart by Hubert P. Main, 1873 (1839-1926)

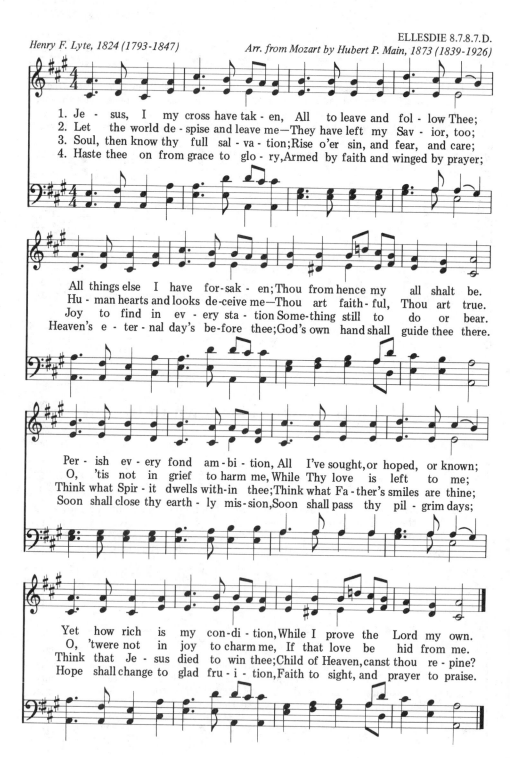

1. Je - sus, I my cross have tak - en, All to leave and fol - low Thee;
2. Let the world de - spise and leave me—They have left my Sav - ior, too;
3. Soul, then know thy full sal - va - tion; Rise o'er sin, and fear, and care;
4. Haste thee on from grace to glo - ry, Armed by faith and winged by prayer;

All things else I have for - sak - en; Thou from hence my all shalt be.
Hu - man hearts and looks de-ceive me—Thou art faith - ful, Thou art true.
Joy to find in ev - ery sta - tion Some-thing still to do or bear.
Heaven's e - ter - nal day's be-fore thee; God's own hand shall guide thee there.

Per - ish ev - ery fond am - bi - tion, All I've sought, or hoped, or known;
O, 'tis not in grief to harm me, While Thy love is left to me;
Think what Spir - it dwells with - in thee; Think what Fa - ther's smiles are thine;
Soon shall close thy earth - ly mis-sion, Soon shall pass thy pil - grim days;

Yet how rich is my con-di - tion, While I prove the Lord my own.
O, 'twere not in joy to charm me, If that love be hid from me.
Think that Je - sus died to win thee; Child of Heaven, canst thou re - pine?
Hope shall change to glad fru - i - tion, Faith to sight, and prayer to praise.

CONSECRATION

Open My Eyes That I May See

Irregular
Clara H. Scott, 1895

Clara H. Scott, 1895 (1841-1897)

1. O - pen my eyes, that I may see Glimps-es of truth Thou hast for me;
2. O - pen my ears, that I may hear Voic - es of truth Thou send-est clear;
3. O - pen my mouth, and let me bear Glad - ly the warm truth ev - ery-where;

Place in my hands the won-der-ful key That shall un-clasp and set me free.
And while the wave-notes fall on my ear, Ev - ery-thing false will dis - ap-pear.
O - pen my heart, and let me pre-pare Love with Thy chil-dren thus to share.

Refrain

Si - lent-ly now I wait for Thee, Read-y, my God, Thy will to see;

O - pen my eyes, il - lu - mine me, Spir - it di - vine!
O - pen my ears, il - lu - mine me, Spir - it di - vine!
O - pen my heart, il - lu - mine me, Spir - it di - vine!

CONSECRATION

I'd Rather Have Jesus

11.11.11.10.Ref.

Rhea F. Miller, 1922 (1894-1966)

George Beverly Shea, 1939 (1909-   )

1. I'd rath - er have Je - sus than sil - ver or gold, I'd rath - er be
2. I'd rath - er have Je - sus than men's ap - plause, I'd rath - er be
3. He's fair - er than lil - ies of rar - est bloom, He's sweet - er than

His than have rich - es un - told; I'd rath - er have Je - sus than
faith - ful to His dear cause; I'd rath - er have Je - sus than
hon - ey from out the comb; He's all that my hun - ger - ing

hous - es or lands, I'd rath - er be led by His nail - pierced hand.
world - wide fame, I'd rath - er be true to His ho - ly name.
spir - it needs, I'd rath - er have Je - sus and let Him lead.

Refrain

Than to be the king of a vast do - main Or be held in sin's dread sway;

CONSECRATION

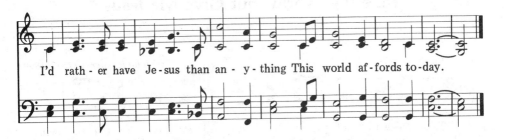

I'd rath-er have Je-sus than an - y-thing This world af-fords to-day.

Must Jesus Bear the Cross Alone 328

MAITLAND C.M.

Thomas Shepherd, 1693 (1665-1739) and others   *George N. Allen, 1846 (1812-1877)*

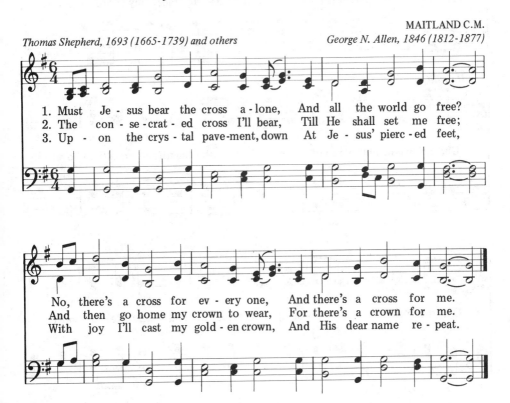

1. Must Je - sus bear the cross a - lone, And all the world go free?
2. The con - se -crat - ed cross I'll bear, Till He shall set me free;
3. Up - on the crys - tal pave-ment, down At Je - sus' pierc - ed feet,

No, there's a cross for ev - ery one, And there's a cross for me.
And then go home my crown to wear, For there's a crown for me.
With joy I'll cast my gold - en crown, And His dear name re - peat.

329

Take the World, but Give Me Jesus

Fanny J. Crosby (1820-1915)

8.7.8.7.Ref.

John R. Sweney (1837-1899)

1. Take the world, but give me Jesus; All its joys are but a name,
2. Take the world, but give me Jesus, Sweet-est comfort of my soul;
3. Take the world, but give me Jesus; Let me view His con-stant smile;
4. Take the world, but give me Jesus; In His cross my trust shall be,

But His love a-bid-eth ev-er, Through e-ter-nal years the same.
With my Sav-ior watch-ing o'er me, I can sing, though bil-lows roll.
Then through-out my pil-grim jour-ney Light will cheer me all the while.
Till, with clear-er, bright-er vi-sion, Face to face my Lord I see.

Refrain

Oh, the height and depth of mer-cy! Oh, the length and breadth of love!

Oh, the full-ness of re-demp-tion, Pledge of end-less life a-bove.

CONSECRATION

Take My Life and Let It Be

HENDON 7.7.7.7.

Frances Ridley Havergal, 1874 (1836-1879)

H. A. César Malan, 1827 (1787-1864)

1. Take my life, and let it be Con - se - crat - ed, Lord, to Thee; Take my hands, and let them move At the im - pulse of Thy love, At the im - pulse of Thy love.
2. Take my feet, and let them be Swift and beau - ti - ful for Thee; Take my voice, and let me sing Al - ways, on - ly, for my King, Al - ways, on - ly, for my King.
3. Take my lips, and let them be Filled with mes - sag - es from Thee; Take my sil - ver and my gold, Not a mite would I with - hold, Not a mite would I with - hold.
4. Take my will and make it Thine; It shall be no lon - ger mine; Take my heart, it is Thine own! It shall be Thy roy - al throne, It shall be Thy roy - al throne.
5. Take my love; my Lord, I pour At Thy feet its trea - sure store; Take my - self, and I will be, Ev - er, on - ly, all for Thee, Ev - er, on - ly, all for Thee.

O Jesus, I Have Promised

John E. Bode, 1866 (1816-1874)

ANGEL'S STORY 7.6.7.6.D.
Arthur H. Mann, 1881 (1850-1929)

1. O Je-sus, I have prom-ised To serve Thee to the end;
2. O let me feel Thee near me; The world is ev-er near!
3. O Je-sus, Thou hast prom-ised To all who fol-low Thee

Be Thou for-ev-er near me, My Mas-ter and my Friend;
I see the sights that daz-zle, The tempt-ing sounds I hear;
That where Thou art in glo-ry There shall Thy serv-ant be;

I shall not fear the bat-tle If Thou art by my side,
My foes are ev-er near me, A-round me and with-in;
And, Je-sus, I have prom-ised To serve Thee to the end;

Nor wan-der from the path-way If Thou wilt be my Guide.
But, Je-sus, draw Thou near-er, And shield my soul from sin.
O give me grace to fol-low My Mas-ter and my Friend.

CONSECRATION

The Cleansing Wave

332

C.M.Ref.

Mrs. Phoebe Palmer (1807-1874)   *Mrs. Joseph F. Knapp (1839-1908)*

1. O now I see the crim-son wave, The foun-tain deep and wide;
2. I see the new cre-a-tion rise, I hear the speak-ing blood;
3. I rise to walk in heaven's own light, A-bove the world and sin;
4. A-maz-ing grace! 'tis heaven be-low To feel the blood ap-plied,

Je-sus, my Lord, might-y to save, Points to His wound-ed side.
It speaks—pol-lut-ed na-ture dies, Sinks 'neath the cleans-ing flood.
With heart made pure and gar-ments white, And Christ en-throned with-in.
And Je-sus, on-ly Je-sus, know, My Je-sus cru-ci-fied.

Refrain

The cleans-ing stream I see, I see, I plunge, and O, it cleans-eth me!

O praise the Lord! it cleans-eth me, It cleans-eth me, yes, cleans-eth me.

BAPTISM

333 On Jordan's Banks the Baptist's Cry

Luke 3:2-4
Charles Coffin (1676-1749) Tr. composite

PUER NOBIS L.M.
Adapt. from Michael Praetorius (1571-1621)

1. On Jordan's banks the Baptist's cry Announces that the Lord is nigh; Awake and hearken, for he brings Glad tidings of the King of kings!

2. Then cleansed be every life from sin; Make straight the way for God within, And let us all our hearts prepare For Christ to come and enter there.

3. We hail You as our Savior, Lord, Our refuge and our great reward; Without Your grace we waste away Like flow'rs that wither and decay.

4. Stretch forth Your hand, our health restore, And make us rise to fall no more; Oh, let Your face upon us shine And fill the world with love divine.

Come, Thou Fount of Every Blessing 334

Robert Robinson, 1758 (1735-1790)

NETTLETON 8.7.8.7.D.
John Wyeth's Respository, 1813

1. Come, Thou Fount of ev-ery bless-ing, Tune my heart to sing Thy grace;
2. Here I raise my Eb-en - e - zer, Hith-er by Thy help I've come,
3. O, to grace how great a debt - or Dai - ly I'm con-strained to be!

Streams of mer - cy, nev - er ceas - ing, Call for songs of loud-est praise.
And I hope by Thy good plea - sure Safe - ly to ar - rive at home.
Let Thy good-ness, like a fet - ter, Bind me clos - er still to Thee.

Teach me ev - er to a - dore Thee, May I still Thy good-ness prove,
Je - sus sought me when a strang - er, Wan-dering from the fold of God;
Prone to wan - der, Lord, I feel it, Prone to leave the God I love;

While the hope of end-less glo - ry Fills my heart with joy and love.
He to res - cue me from dan - ger In - ter-posed His pre-cious blood.
Here's my heart— O, take and seal it; Seal it for Thy courts a - bove.

SALVATION AND REDEMPTION

What a Wonderful Savior

8.7.8.7.Ref.

Elisha A. Hoffman, 1891 (1839-1929)

Elisha A. Hoffman

1. Christ has for sin a-tone-ment made, What a won-der-ful Sav-ior!
2. I praise Him for the cleans-ing blood, What a won-der-ful Sav-ior!
3. He walks be-side me all the way, What a won-der-ful Sav-ior!
4. He gives me o-ver-com-ing power, What a won-der-ful Sav-ior!

We are re-deemed! the price is paid! What a won-der-ful Sav-ior!
That rec-on-ciled my soul to God; What a won-der-ful Sav-ior!
And keeps me faith-ful day by day; What a won-der-ful Sav-ior!
And tri-umph in each try-ing hour; What a won-der-ful Sav-ior!

Refrain

What a won-der-ful Sav-ior is Je-sus, my Je-sus!

What a won-der-ful Sav-ior is Je-sus, my Lord!

SALVATION AND REDEMPTION

There Is a Fountain

336

CLEANSING FOUNTAIN C.M.D.
Early American Melody

William Cowper, 1770 (1731-1800)

1. There is a foun-tain filled with blood, Drawn from Im-man-uel's veins;
2. The dy-ing theif re-joiced to see That foun-tain in his day;
3. Thou dy-ing Lamb! Thy pre-cious blood Shall nev-er lose its power,
4. E'er since by faith I saw the stream Thy flow-ing wounds sup-ply,
5. Lord, I be-lieve Thou hast pre-pared, Un-wor-thy though I be,
6. There in a no-bler, sweet-er song, I'll sing Thy power to save,

And sin-ners plunged be-neath that flood, Lose all their guilt-y stains,
And there may I, though vile as he, Wash all my sins a-way,
Till all the ran-somed church of God Are saved, to sin no more,
Re-deem-ing love has been my theme, And shall be till I die,
For me a blood-bought, free re-ward, A gold-en harp for me!
When this poor lisp-ing, stam-mering tongue Is ran-somed from the grave,

Lose all their guilt-y stains, Lose all their guilt-y stains;
Wash all my sins a-way, Wash all my sins a-way;
Are saved, to sin no more, Are saved, to sin no more;
And shall be till I die, And shall be till I die;
A gold-en harp for me! A gold-en harp for me!
Is ran-somed from the grave, Is ran-somed from the grave;

And sin-ners plunged be-neath that flood, Lose all their guilt-y stains.
And there may I, though vile as he, Wash all my sins a-way.
Till all the ran-somed church of God Are saved, to sin no more.
Re-deem-ing love has been my theme, And shall be till I die.
For me a blood-bought, free re-ward, A gold-en harp for me!
When this poor lisp-ing, stammering tongue Is ran-somed from the grave.

SALVATION AND REDEMPTION

337   Redeemed!

Lam. 3:58   9.8.9.8.Ref.
Fanny J. Crosby, 1882 (1820-1915)   William J. Kirkpatrick, 1882 (1838-1921)

1. Redeemed! how I love to pro-claim it! Redeemed by the blood of the Lamb;
2. Redeemed! and so hap-py in Je - sus! No lan-guage my rap-ture can tell;
3. I   know there's a crown that is wait-ing In yon-der bright mansion for me;

Redeemed through His in - fi-nite mer-cy, His child, and for-ev - er, I am.
I know that the light of His pres-ence With me doth con-tin - ual - ly dwell.
And soon, with the saints   made per-fect, At home with the Lord I shall be.

Refrain

Re-deemed,   re-deemed,   Redeemed by the blood of the Lamb;
Redeemed,   redeemed,

Re-deemed,   re-deemed,   His child, and for-ev- er, I am.
Redeemed,   redeemed,

SALVATION AND REDEMPTION

Redeemed!

338

Lam. 3:58
Fanny J. Crosby, 1882 (1820-1915)

ADA 9.8.9.8.Ref.
A. L. Butler, 1967 (1933-   )

1. Re-deemed, how I love to pro-claim it! Re-deemed by the
2. I think of my bless - ed Re-deem-er, I think of Him
3. I know I shall see in His beau-ty The King in whose

blood of the Lamb; Re-deemed thro' His in - fi-nite mer - cy, His
all the day long; I sing, for I can - not be si - lent; His
law I de-light, Who lov - ing - ly guard - eth my foot-steps, And

Refrain
Harmony

child, and for - ev - er, I am.
love is the theme of my song. Re - deemed, re-deemed, Re-
giv - eth me songs in the night.

Unison

deemed by the blood of the Lamb; Re - deemed, how I

love to pro-claim it! His child and for - ev - er I am.

SALVATION AND REDEMPTION

339 God Is My Strong Salvation

Psalm 27:1-3,14
James Montgomery (1771-1854)

WIE LIEBLICH IST DER MAIEN 7.6.7.6.D.
J. Steurlein, 1575 (1547-1613)

1. God is my strong sal - va - tion, What foe have I to fear?
2. Place on the Lord re - li - ance; My soul with cour-age wait;

In dark-ness and temp - ta - tion, My Light, my Help, is near:
His truth be thine af - fi - ance, When faint and des - o - late.

Though hosts en - camp a - round me, Firm in the fight I stand;
His might thy heart shall strength - en, His love thy joy in - crease;

What ter - ror can con - found me, With God at my right hand?
Mer - cy thy days shall length - en; The Lord will give thee peace.

SALVATION AND REDEMPTION

7.6.7.6.7.7.7.6.

Priscilla J. Owens (1829-1899)

William J. Kirkpatrick, 1882 (1838-1921)

1. We have heard a joy-ful sound, Je-sus saves, Je-sus saves;
2. Waft it on the roll-ing tide, Je-sus saves, Je-sus saves;
3. Sing a-bove the bat-tle's strife, Je-sus saves, Je-sus saves;
4. Give the winds a might-y voice, Je-sus saves, Je-sus saves;

1 Spread the glad-ness all a-round, Je-sus saves, Je-sus saves;
2 Tell to sin-ners, far and wide, Je-sus saves, Je-sus saves;
3 By His death and end-less life, Je-sus saves, Je-sus saves;
4 Let the na-tions now re-joice, Je-sus saves, Je-sus saves;

1 Bear the news to ev-er-y land, Climb the steeps and cross the waves,
2 Sing, ye is-lands of the sea. Ech-o back, ye o-cean caves,
3 Sing it soft-ly through the gloom, When the heart for mer-cy craves,
4 Shout sal-va-tion full and free, High-est hills and deep-est caves,

1 On-ward, 'tis our Lord's com-mand, Je-sus saves, Je-sus saves.
2 Earth shall keep her ju-bi-lee, Je-sus saves, Je-sus saves.
3 Sing in tri-umph o'er the tomb, Je-sus saves, Je-sus saves.
4 This our song of vic-to-ry, Je-sus saves, Je-sus saves.

341 To God Be the Glory

11.11.11.11.Ref.

Fanny J. Crosby, 1875 (1820-1915)

William H. Doane (1832-1915)

1. To God be the glo - ry, great things He hath done; So loved He the
2. O per - fect re - demp-tion, the pur -chase of blood, To ev - ery be -
3. Great things He hath taught us, great things He hath done, And great our re -

world that He gave us His Son, Who yield - ed His life an a -
liev - er the prom - ise of God; The vil - est of-fend - er who
joic - ing through Je - sus the Son; But pur - er, and high - er, and

tone-ment for sin, And o - pened the life gate that all may go in.
tru - ly be - lieves, That mo-ment from Je - sus a par-don re - ceives.
great - er will be Our won-der, our trans-port, when Je - sus we see.

Refrain

Praise the Lord, praise the Lord, Let the earth hear His voice; Praise the

Lord, praise the Lord, Let the peo-ple re - joice; O come to the Fa-ther, through

SALVATION AND REDEMPTION

Je - sus the Son, And give Him the glo - ry, great things He hath done.

Is This a Day of New Beginnings? 342

DRONFIELD 9.8.9.8.
Melody by Brian Wren
Arr. by Peter Cutts (1937-   )

Brian Wren, 1978 (1936-   )
Unison

1. Is this a day of new be - gin - nings,
2. How can the sea - sons of a plan - et
3. Yet thro' the life and death of Je - sus
4. Then let us, with the Spir - it's dar - ing,
5. Christ is a - live, and goes be - fore us

Time to re-
Mind-less - ly
Love's might - y
Step from the
To show and

mem - ber and move on, Time to be - lieve what
spin - ning round its sun With just a hu - man
Spir - it, now as then, Can make for us a
past and leave be - hind Its dis - ap - point - ment,
share what love can do. This is a day of

love is bring - ing, Lay - ing to rest the pain that's gone?
name and num - ber Say that some new thing has be - gun?
world of dif - ference As faith and hope are born a - gain.
guilt, and griev - ing, Seek - ing new paths, and sure to find.
new be - gin - nings; Our God is mak - ing all things new.

SALVATION AND REDEMPTION

343   I Will Sing of My Redeemer

8.7.8.7.Ref.

Philip P. Bliss, 1876 (1838-1876)   *James McGranahan, 1877 (1840-1907)*

1. I will sing of my Re-deem-er, And His won-drous love to me;
2. I will tell the won-drous sto-ry, How my lost es-tate to save,
3. I will sing of my Re-deem-er, And His heav-'nly love to me;

On the cru-el cross He suf-fered From the curse to set me free.
In His bound-less love and mer-cy, He the ran-som free-ly gave.
He from death to life hath brought me, Son of God, with Him to be.

Refrain

Sing, Oh, sing of my Re-deem-er, With His
Sing, Oh, sing

blood He pur-chased me; On the cross He sealed my
With His blood On the cross

par - don, Paid the debt and made me free.
Paid the debt made me free.

Alternate tune, HYFRYDOL, Nos. 167, 204

I Love Your Kingdom, Lord 344

ST. THOMAS S.M.

Timothy Dwight (1752-1817)   *Aaron Williams*, The New Universal Psalmodist, *1770*

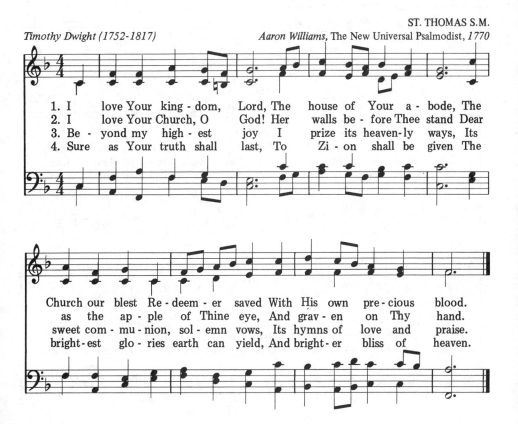

1. I love Your king - dom, Lord, The house of Your a - bode, The
2. I love Your Church, O God! Her walls be - fore Thee stand Dear
3. Be - yond my high - est joy I prize its heaven-ly ways, Its
4. Sure as Your truth shall last, To Zi - on shall be given The

Church our blest Re - deem - er saved With His own pre - cious blood.
as the ap - ple of Thine eye, And grav - en on Thy hand.
sweet com - mu - nion, sol - emn vows, Its hymns of love and praise.
bright-est glo - ries earth can yield, And bright - er bliss of heaven.

COMMUNITY IN CHRIST

345 Christ Is the World's True Light

DARMSTADT 6.7.6.7.6.6.6.6.
Ahasuerus Fritsch, 1679 (1629-1701)
Arr. by J. S. Bach (1685-1750)

George W. Briggs, 1931 (1875-1959)

1. Christ is the world's true light, Its cap-tain of sal-va-tion,
The day-star clear and bright Of ev-ery man and na-tion;
New life, new hope a-wakes Wher-e'er men own His sway:
Free-dom her bond-age breaks, And night is turned to day.

2. In Christ all rac-es meet, Their an-cient feuds for-get-ting,
The whole round world com-plete, From sun-rise to its set-ting:
When Christ is throned as Lord, Men shall for-sake their fear,
To plow-share beat the sword, To prun-ing-hook the spear.

3. One Lord, in one great name U-nite us all who own Thee,
Cast out our pride and shame That hin-der to en-throne Thee;
The world has wait-ed long, Has tra-vailed long in pain,
To heal its an-cient wrong, Come, Prince of Peace, and reign.

COMMUNITY IN CHRIST

Lord, Who Dost Give to Thy Church 346

SEVENTH AND JAMES 11.10.11.10.

Ernest A. Payne, 1966 (1902-   )

Charles F. Brown, 1974 (1942-   )

Unison

1. Lord, who dost give to Thy church for its heal - ing
2. Clear be the voice - es of preach - ers and proph - ets
3. Ten - der and wise be the hearts of the pas - tors,
4. May those who teach grow in knowl - edge and pa - tience,
5. Lord, ev - er give to us gifts in due mea - sure,

Gifts, and the grace to sus - tain and re - new,
Fear - less - ly speak - ing the word of the Lord,
Guid - ing and guard - ing the souls in their care,
Guid - ing to wis - dom the young and the old,
Each need - ing oth - er, and all hav - ing worth;

Hear as we pray that to - day and each mor - row
Word of re - demp - tion thro' God's Son in - car - nate,
Firm with the way - ward, a strength to the doubt - ing,
Train - ing for wor - ship and wit - ness and ser - vice,
So to the Fa - ther, the Son, and the Spir - it,

We to Thy pur - pose may show our - selves true.
Bless - ing for curs - ing, and peace for the sword.
Help - ing the need - y their bur - dens to bear.
Foes to all false - hood, in truth - ful - ness bold.
Glo - ry be shown by the church here on earth.

COMMUNITY IN CHRIST

347 Built on the Rock

Nikolai F. S. Grundvig (1783-1872)
Tr. by Carl Doving (1867-1937) adapt.

KIRKEN DEN ER ET 8.8.8.8.8.8.
Ludvig M. Lindeman (1812-1887)

1. Built on the Rock the Church shall stand, E - ven when stee - ples are
2. Not in our tem - ples made with hands God, the Al - might - y, is
3. We are God's house of liv - ing stones, Built for His own hab - i -
4. Yet in this house, an earth - ly frame, Je - sus His chil - dren is
5. Thro' all the pass - ing years, O Lord, Grant that, when church bells are

fall - ing; Crum-bled have spires in ev - ery land, Bells still are
dwell - ing; High in the heav'ns His tem - ple stands, All earth - ly
ta - tion; He fills our hearts, His hum - ble thrones, Grant-ing us
bless - ing; Hith - er we come to praise His name, Faith in our
ring - ing, Man - y may come to hear God's Word Where He this

chim-ing and call - ing—Call - ing the young and old to rest, Call - ing the
tem-ples ex - cel - ling. Yet He who dwells in heav'n a - bove Deigns to a -
life and sal - va - tion. Were two or three to seek His face, He in their
Sav - ior con - fess - ing. Je - sus to us His Spir - it sent, Mak - ing with
prom-ise is bring - ing: I know My own, My own know Me: You, not the

souls of those dis-tressed, Long-ing for life ev - er - last - ing.
bide with us in love, Mak-ing our bod - ies His tem - ple.
midst would show His grace, Bless-ings up - on them be-stow - ing.
us His cov - e - nant, Grant-ing His chil-dren the king - dom.
world, My face shall see; My peace I leave with you. A - men.

COMMUNITY IN CHRIST

The Church Has One Foundation 348

AURELIA 7.6.7.6.D.
Samuel J. Stone, 1866 (1839-1900)
Samuel S. Wesley, 1864 (1810-1876)

1. The church has one foun-da-tion, 'Tis Je-sus Christ her Lord;
2. E-lect from ev-ery na-tion, Yet one o'er all the earth,
3. Though with a scorn-ful won-der, Men see her sore op-pressed,
4. 'Mid toil and trib-u-la-tion, And tu-mult of her war,

She is His new cre-a-tion, By wa-ter and the word;
Her char-ter of sal-va-tion, One Lord, one faith, one birth;
Though foes would rend a-sun-der The Rock where she doth rest,
She waits the con-sum-ma-tion Of peace for-ev-er-more;

From heaven He came and sought her To be His ho-ly bride;
One ho-ly name she bless-es, Par-takes one ho-ly food,
Yet saints their faith are keep-ing; Their cry goes up, "How long?"
Till with the vi-sion glo-rious Her long-ing eyes are blest,

With His own blood He bought her, And for her life He died.
And to one hope she press-es, With ev-ery grace en-dued.
And soon the night of weep-ing Shall be the morn of song.
And the great church vic-to-rious Shall be the church at rest.

COMMUNITY IN CHRIST

349 God Is Love

1 John 4:7, 8
Tr. James Quinn (1919-   )

UBI CARITAS 13.12.12.12.12.
A. Gregory Murray, 1939 (1905-   )

Refrain

God is love, and where true love is God Him-self is there.

1. Here in Christ we gath - er, love of Christ our call - ing.
2. When we Chris-tians gath - er, mem - bers of one bod - y,
3. Grant us love's ful - fill - ment, joy with all the bless - ed,

Christ, our love, is with us, glad-ness be His greet - ing.
Let there be in us no dis - cord but one spir - it.
When we see Your face, O Sav - ior, in its glo - ry.

Let us fear Him, yes, and love Him, God e - ter - nal.
Ban - ished now be an - ger, strife, and ev - ery quar - rel.
Shine on us, O pur - est Light of all cre - a - tion,

COMMUNITY IN CHRIST

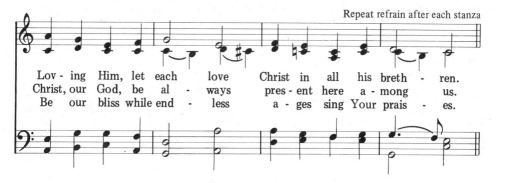

Lov - ing Him, let each love Christ in all his breth - ren.
Christ, our God, be al - ways pres - ent here a - mong us.
Be our bliss while end - less a - ges sing Your prais - es.

Blest Be the Tie That Binds 350

DENNIS S.M.
From Johann G. Naegeli (1768-1836)
Arr. by Lowell Mason, 1845 (1792-1872)

John Fawcett, 1772 (1740-1817)

1. Blest be the tie that binds Our hearts in Chris - tian love!
2. Be - fore our Fa - ther's throne We pour our ar - dent prayers;
3. We share our mu - tual woes, Our mu - tual bur - dens bear,
4. When we a - sun - der part, It gives us in - ward pain;

The fel - low-ship of kin - dred minds Is like to that a - bove.
Our fears, our hopes, our aims are one, Our com - forts, and our cares.
And of - ten for each oth - er flows The sym - pa - thiz - ing tear.
But we shall still be joined in heart, And hope to meet a - gain.

COMMUNITY IN CHRIST

351   Thy Hand, O God Has Guided

Eph. 4:5

Edward Hayes Plumptre, 1889 (1821-1891)

THORNBURY 7.6.7.6.D.

Basil Harwood, 1898 (1859-1949)

1. Thy hand, O God, has guid - ed Thy flock from age to age;
2. Thy her - alds brought glad tid - ings To great - est as to least;
3. When shad - ows thick were fall - ing, And all seemed sunk in night,
4. Thy mer - cy will not fail us, Nor leave Thy work un - done;

The won-drous tale is writ - ten Full clear on ev - ery page;
They bade men rise and has - ten To share the great King's feast:
Thou, Lord, did send Thy ser - vants, Thy cho - sen sons of light.
With Thy right hand to help us, The vic - t'ry shall be won;

Our fa - thers owned Thy good - ness, And we their deeds re - cord;
And this was all their teach - ing, In ev - ery deed and word,
On them and on Thy peo - ple Thy plen-teous grace was poured,
And then by men and an - gels Thy name shall be a - dored,

And both of this bear wit - ness,
To all a - like pro-claim-ing
And this was still their mes-sage:
And this shall be their an - them:

One church, one faith, one Lord.

Music used by permission of the Executors of the late Basil Harwood.

COMMUNITY IN CHRIST

This Is My Will

John 15:12-17
James Quinn, 1969 (1919-   )

SUANTRAI L.M.
Irish Melody, arr. by T. H. Weaving

1. This is My will, My one com-mand, That love should
2. No great-er love a man can have Than that he
3. You chose not Me, but I chose you That you should
4. All that I ask My Fa-ther, dear, For My name's

dwell a-mong you all. This is My will that you should
die to save his friends. You are My friends if you o-
go and bear much fruit. I chose you out that you in
sake you shall re-ceive. This is My will, My one com-

love As I have shown that I love you.
bey What I com-mand that you should do.
Me Should bear much fruit that will a-bide.
mand, That love should dwell in each, in all.

COMMUNITY IN CHRIST

353 Father, Help Your People

WHITWORTH 11.11.11.11.

Fred Kaan, 1966 (1929-)

Walter MacNutt, 1973 (1910-)

Unison

1. Fa - ther, help Your peo - ple in this world to build
2. Lord of desk and al - tar, bind our lives in one,
3. Ho - ly is the set - ting of each room and yard,
4. Strength - en, Lord, for ser - vice hand and heart and brain;

Some - thing of Your king - dom and to do Your will,
That in work and wor - ship love may set the tone.
Lec - ture-hall and kitch - en, of - fice, shop, and ward.
Help us good re - la - tions dai - ly to main - tain.

Lead us to dis - cov - er part - ner-ship in love;
Give us grace to lis - ten, clar - i - ty of speech;
Ho - ly is the rhy - thm of our work-ing hours;
Let the liv - ing pres - ence of the ser - vant Christ

Bless our ways of shar - ing and our pride re - move.
Make us tru - ly thank - ful for the gifts of each.
Hal - low then our pur - pose, en - er - gy, and pow'rs.
Height - en our de - vo - tion, make our life a feast.

COMMUNITY IN CHRIST

Thy Love, O God

354

NORTHBROOK 11.10.11.10.

Albert F. Bayly, 1947 (1901-1984)

Reginald S. Thatcher (1888-1957)

1. Thy love, O God, has all man-kind cre-at-ed,
And led Thy peo-ple to this pres-ent hour;
In Christ we see life's glo-ry con-sum-mat-ed;
Thy Spir-it man-i-fests His liv-ing power.

2. From out the dark-ness of our hope's frus-tra-tion,
From all the bro-ken i-dols of our pride,
We turn to seek Thy truth's il-lu-mi-na-tion,
And find Thy mer-cy wait-ing at our side.

3. In pit-y look up-on Thy chil-dren's striv-ing
For life and free-dom, peace and broth-er-hood,
Till at the full-ness of Thy truth ar-riv-ing,
We find in Christ the crown of ev-ery good.

4. In-spire Thy church, mid earth's dis-cor-dant voic-es,
To preach the gos-pel of her Lord a-bove,
Un-til the day this war-ring world re-joic-es
To hear the might-y har-mo-nies of love.

Words by permission of Oxford University Press.
Music from the *Clarendon Hymn Book* by permission of Oxford University Press.

COMMUNITY IN CHRIST

TSDAH-12

355 Where Cross the Crowded Ways of Life

GARDINER L.M.

Frank M. North (1850-1935) alt.

Wm. Gardiner's Sacred Melodies, *1815*

1. Where cross the crowd-ed ways of life, Where sound the
2. From ten-der child-hood's help-less-ness, From hu-man
3. The cup of wa-ter giv'n for You Still holds the
4. O Mas-ter, from the moun-tain-side Make haste to
5. Till all the world shall learn Your love, And fol-low

cries of race and clan, A-bove the noise of
grief and bur-dened toil, From fam-ished souls, from
fresh-ness of Your grace; Yet long these mul-ti-
heal these hearts of pain; A-mong these rest-less
where Your feet have trod; Till glo-rious from Your

self-ish strife, We hear Your voice, O Son of Man.
sor-row's stress, Your heart has nev-er known re-coil.
tudes to view The strong com-pas-sion in Your face.
throngs a-bide; O tread the cit-y's streets a-gain;
heav'n a-bove, Shall come the cit-y of our God.

Lower key, No. 177

MISSION OF THE CHURCH

All Who Love and Serve Your City 356

BIRABUS 8.7.8.7.

Erik Routley (1917-1982)

Peter Cutts 1962 (1937-   )

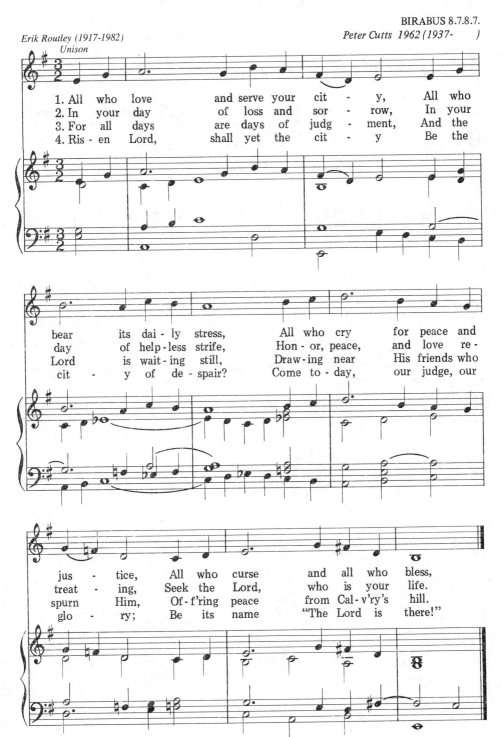

1. All who love and serve your cit - y, All who
2. In your day of loss and sor - row, In your
3. For all days are days of judg - ment, And the
4. Ris - en Lord, shall yet the cit - y Be the

bear its dai - ly stress, All who cry for peace and
day of help - less strife, Hon - or, peace, and love re -
Lord is wait - ing still, Draw - ing near His friends who
cit - y of de - spair? Come to - day, our judge, our

jus - tice, All who curse and all who bless,
treat - ing, Seek the Lord, who is your life.
spurn Him, Of - f'ring peace from Cal - v'ry's hill.
glo - ry; Be its name "The Lord is there!"

MISSION OF THE CHURCH

357

Come, Labor On

Jane L. Borthwick, 1863 (1813-1897) alt.

ORA LABORA 4.10.10.10.4.
T. Tertius Noble, 1916 (1867-1953)

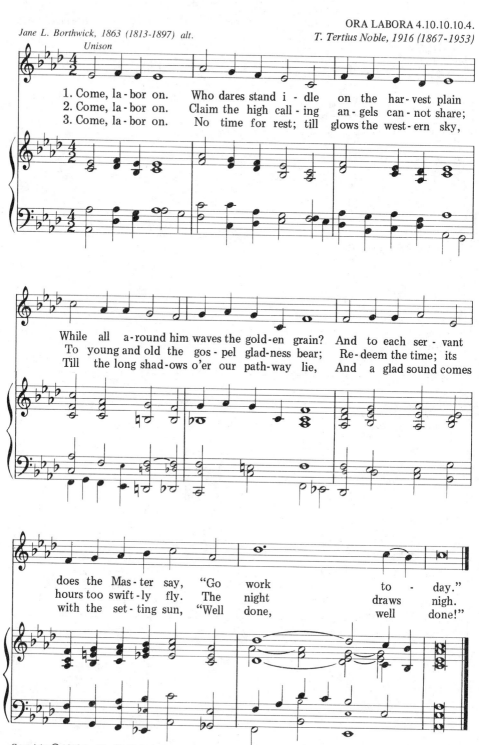

1. Come, la-bor on. Who dares stand i - dle on the har-vest plain
2. Come, la-bor on. Claim the high call-ing an-gels can-not share;
3. Come, la-bor on. No time for rest; till glows the west-ern sky,

While all a-round him waves the gold-en grain? And to each ser - vant
To young and old the gos-pel glad-ness bear; Re-deem the time; its
Till the long shad-ows o'er our path-way lie, And a glad sound comes

does the Mas-ter say, "Go work to - day."
hours too swift-ly fly. The night draws nigh.
with the set-ting sun, "Well done, well done!"

MISSION OF THE CHURCH

Far and Near the Fields Are Teeming 358

HARVEST 8.7.8.7.Ref.

J. O. Thompson, 1885

J. B. O. Clemm, 1895

1. Far and near the fields are teem-ing With the sheaves of rip-ened grain;
2. Send them forth with morn's first beam-ing, Send them in the noon-tide's glare;
3. O thou, whom thy Lord is send-ing, Gath-er now the sheaves of gold;

Far and near their gold is gleam-ing O'er the sun-ny slope and plain.
When the sun's last rays are stream-ing, Bid them gath-er ev-ery-where.
Heaven-ward then at eve-ning wend-ing Thou shalt come with joy un-told.

Refrain

Lord of har-vest, send forth reap-ers! Hear us, Lord, to Thee we cry;

Send them now the sheaves to gath-er, Ere the har-vest-time pass by.

MISSION OF THE CHURCH

359 Hark! the Voice of Jesus Calling

Isa. 6:8
Daniel March, 1868 (1816-1909)

FILLMORE 8.7.8.7.D.
F. E. Belden, 1886 (1858-1945)

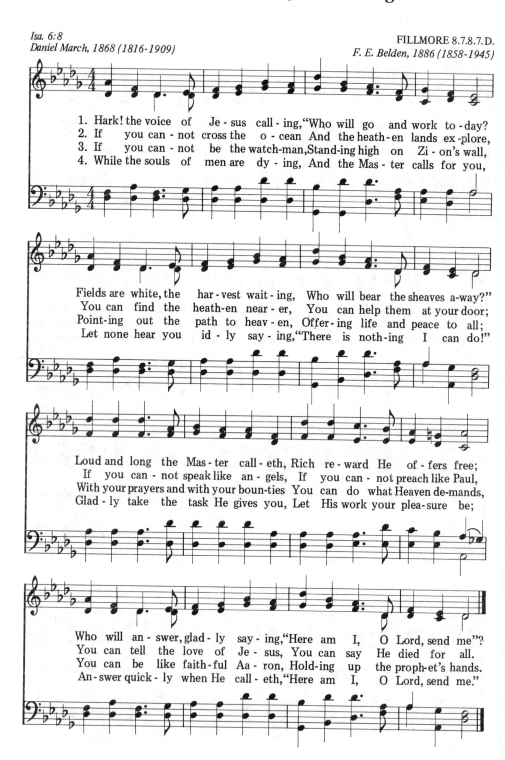

1. Hark! the voice of Jesus call-ing, "Who will go and work to-day?
2. If you can-not cross the o-cean And the heath-en lands ex-plore,
3. If you can-not be the watch-man, Stand-ing high on Zi-on's wall,
4. While the souls of men are dy-ing, And the Mas-ter calls for you,

Fields are white, the har-vest wait-ing, Who will bear the sheaves a-way?"
You can find the heath-en near-er, You can help them at your door;
Point-ing out the path to heav-en, Offer-ing life and peace to all;
Let none hear you id-ly say-ing, "There is noth-ing I can do!"

Loud and long the Mas-ter call-eth, Rich re-ward He of-fers free;
If you can-not speak like an-gels, If you can-not preach like Paul,
With your prayers and with your boun-ties You can do what Heaven de-mands,
Glad-ly take the task He gives you, Let His work your plea-sure be;

Who will an-swer, glad-ly say-ing, "Here am I, O Lord, send me"?
You can tell the love of Je-sus, You can say He died for all.
You can be like faith-ful Aa-ron, Hold-ing up the proph-et's hands.
An-swer quick-ly when He call-eth, "Here am I, O Lord, send me."

MISSION OF THE CHURCH

From the Eastern Mountains

360

Matt. 2:1,2
Godfrey Thring, 1873 (1823-1903)

CUDDESON 6.5.6.5.D.
William H. Ferguson (1874-1950)

Unison

1. From the east-ern moun-tains Press-ing on they come,
2. There their Lord and Sav-ior Meek and low-ly lay,
3. Gath-er in the out-casts All who've gone a-stray,
4. Un-til ev-ery na-tion, Wheth-er bond or free,

Wise men in their wis-dom, To His hum-ble home;
Won-drous light that led them On-ward on their way,
Throw Thy ra-diance o'er them, Guide them on their way;
'Neath Thy star-lit ban-ner, Je-sus fol-lows thee.

Stirred by deep de-vo-tion, Hast-ing from a-far,
Ev-er now to light-en Na-tions from a-far,
Those who nev-er knew Thee, Those who've wan-dered far,
O'er the dis-tant moun-tains To that heav-enly home,

Ev-er jour-neying on-ward, Guid-ed by a star.
As they jour-ney home-ward By that guid-ing star.
Guide them by the bright-ness Of Thy guid-ing star.
Where no sin nor sor-row Ev-er-more shall come.

Music by permission of Oxford University Press.

Alternate tune, RUTH No. 110

MISSION OF THE CHURCH

361 Hark! 'Tis the Shepherd's Voice I Hear

L.M.Ref.

Alexcenah Thomas, 19th century

W. A. Ogden (1841-1897)

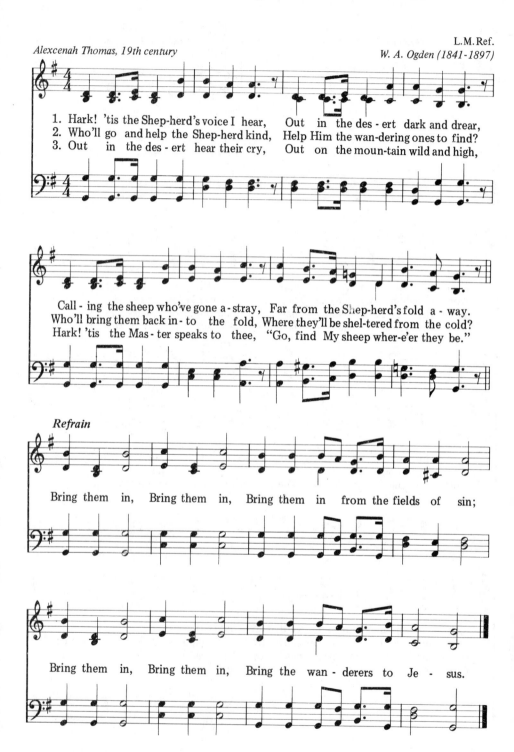

1. Hark! 'tis the Shep-herd's voice I hear, Out in the des-ert dark and drear,
2. Who'll go and help the Shep-herd kind, Help Him the wan-dering ones to find?
3. Out in the des-ert hear their cry, Out on the moun-tain wild and high,

Call-ing the sheep who've gone a-stray, Far from the Shep-herd's fold a-way.
Who'll bring them back in-to the fold, Where they'll be shel-tered from the cold?
Hark! 'tis the Mas-ter speaks to thee, "Go, find My sheep wher-e'er they be."

Refrain

Bring them in, Bring them in, Bring them in from the fields of sin;

Bring them in, Bring them in, Bring the wan-derers to Je - sus.

MISSION OF THE CHURCH

Lift High the Cross

362

John 12:32
George W. Kitchin (1827-1912)
Michael R. Newbolt (1874-1956)

CRUCIFER 10.10.10.10.
Sydney H. Nicholson (1875-1947)

Refrain *Unison*

Lift high the cross, the love of Christ pro-claim Till
all the world a-dore His sa-cred name.

Harmony

1. Come, Chris - tians, fol - low where our Cap - tain trod,
2. Led on their way by this tri - um-phant sign,
3. All new - born sol - diers of the Cru - ci - fied
4. O Lord, once lift - ed on the glo - rious tree,
5. So shall our song of tri - umph ev - er be:

D.C.

Our King vic - to - rious, Christ, the Son of God.
The hosts of God in con-qu'ring ranks com-bine.
Bear on their brows the seal of Him who died.
As Thou hast prom - ised, draw us all to Thee.
Praise to the Cru - ci - fied for vic - to - ry!

MISSION OF THE CHURCH

363 Lord, Whose Love in Humble Service

Isa. 58:6, 7
Albert F. Bayly (1901-1984)

BEACH SPRING 8.7.8.7.D.
The Sacred Harp, 1844

Unison

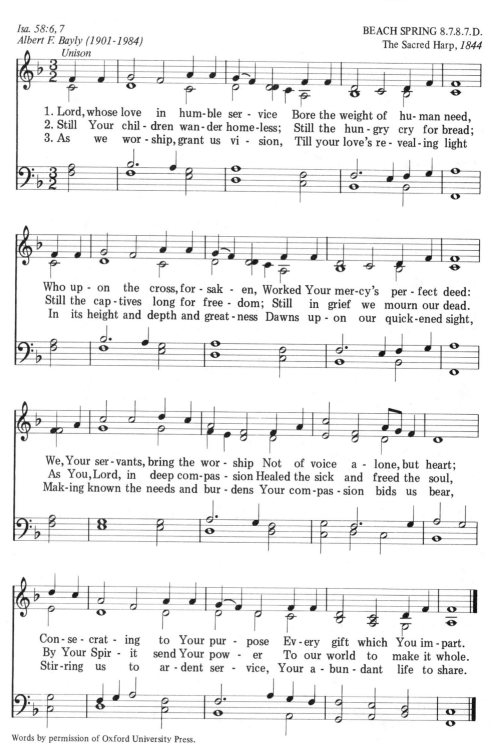

1. Lord, whose love in hum-ble ser-vice Bore the weight of hu-man need,
2. Still Your chil-dren wan-der home-less; Still the hun-gry cry for bread;
3. As we wor-ship, grant us vi-sion, Till your love's re-veal-ing light

Who up-on the cross, for-sak-en, Worked Your mer-cy's per-fect deed:
Still the cap-tives long for free-dom; Still in grief we mourn our dead.
In its height and depth and great-ness Dawns up-on our quick-ened sight,

We, Your ser-vants, bring the wor-ship Not of voice a-lone, but heart;
As You, Lord, in deep com-pas-sion Healed the sick and freed the soul,
Mak-ing known the needs and bur-dens Your com-pas-sion bids us bear,

Con-se-crat-ing to Your pur-pose Ev-ery gift which You im-part.
By Your Spir-it send Your pow-er To our world to make it whole.
Stir-ring us to ar-dent ser-vice, Your a-bun-dant life to share.

MISSION OF THE CHURCH

Harmony setting, No. 634
Alternate tune, ABBOT'S LEIGH, No. 61

O Jesus Christ, to You

364

Luke 19:41
Bradford G. Webster, 1954 (1898-   )

HIGHWOOD 11.10.11.10.
Richard R. Terry (1865-1938)

1. O Jesus Christ, to You may hymns be rising
In every city for Your love and care;
Inspire our worship, grant the glad surprising
That Your blest Spirit brings men everywhere.

2. Grant us new courage, sacrificial, humble,
Strong in Your strength to venture and to dare,
To lift the fallen, guide the feet that stumble,
Seek out the lonely and God's mercy share.

3. Show us Your Spirit, brooding o'er each city,
As You did weep above Jerusalem,
Seeking to gather all in love and pity,
And healing those who touch Your garment's hem.

Words copyright © 1954. Renewal 1982 by The Hymn Society of America, Texas Christian University, Fort Worth, TX 76129.
Used by permission.
Music by permission of Oxford University Press.

MISSION OF THE CHURCH

O Zion, Haste

Mary A. Thomson, 1871 (1834-1923)

TIDINGS 11.10.11.10.Ref.
James Walch, 1875 (1837-1901)

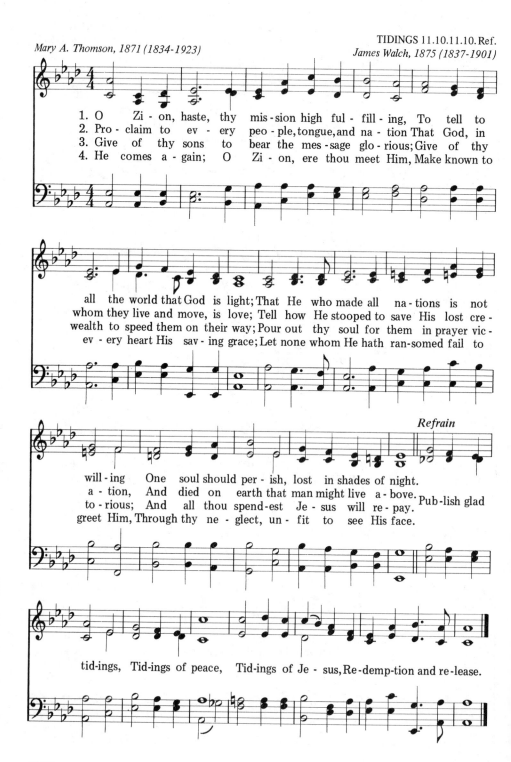

1. O Zi-on, haste, thy mis-sion high ful-fill-ing, To tell to all the world that God is light; That He who made all na-tions is not will-ing One soul should per-ish, lost in shades of night.

2. Pro-claim to ev-ery peo-ple, tongue, and na-tion That God, in whom they live and move, is love; Tell how He stooped to save His lost cre-a-tion, And died on earth that man might live a-bove.

3. Give of thy sons to bear the mes-sage glo-rious; Give of thy wealth to speed them on their way; Pour out thy soul for them in prayer vic-to-rious; And all thou spend-est Je-sus will re-pay.

4. He comes a-gain; O Zi-on, ere thou meet Him, Make known to ev-ery heart His sav-ing grace; Let none whom He hath ran-somed fail to greet Him, Through thy ne-glect, un-fit to see His face.

Refrain

Pub-lish glad tid-ings, Tid-ings of peace, Tid-ings of Je-sus, Re-demp-tion and re-lease.

MISSION OF THE CHURCH

O Where Are the Reapers?

366

Eben E. Rexford (1848-1916)

George F. Root (1820-1895)

10.10.10.10.Ref.

1. O where are the reap-ers that gar-ner in The sheaves of the good from the fields of sin? With sick-les of truth must the work be done, And no one may rest till the "har-vest home."
2. The fields all are rip-ening, and far and wide The world now is wait-ing the har-vest tide: But reap-ers are few, and the work is great, And much will be lost should the har-vest wait.
3. So come with your sick-les, ye sons of men, And gath-er to-geth-er the gold-en grain; Toil on till the Lord of the har-vest come, Then share ye His joy in the "har-vest home."

Refrain

Where are the reap-ers? O who will come And share in the glo-ry of the "har-vest home"? O who will help us to gar-ner in The sheaves of good from the fields of sin?

MISSION OF THE CHURCH

367 Rescue the Perishing

Fanny J. Crosby, 1869 (1820-1915)

6.5.10.6.5.10.Ref.

W. H. Doane, 1869 (1832-1915)

1. Res - cue the per - ish - ing, Care for the dy - ing; Snatch them in
2. Though they are slight-ing Him, Still He is wait - ing, Wait - ing the
3. Res - cue the per - ish - ing, Du - ty de-mands it; Strength for thy

pit - y from sin and the grave; Weep o'er the err - ing one,
pen - i - tent child to re - ceive. Plead with them ear - nest - ly,
la - bor the Lord will pro - vide; Back to the nar - row way

Lift up the fall - en, Tell them of Je - sus, the might - y to save.
Plead with them gent - ly; He will for - give if they on - ly be - lieve.
Pa - tient - ly win them; Tell the poor wan - derer a Sav - ior has died.

Refrain

Res - cue the per - ish - ing, Care for the dy - ing;

Je - sus is mer - ci - ful, Je - sus will save.

MISSION OF THE CHURCH

Watchman, Blow the Gospel Trumpet 368

8.7.8.7. Ref.

H. L. Gilmour, 1894

William J. Kirkpatrick (1838-1921)

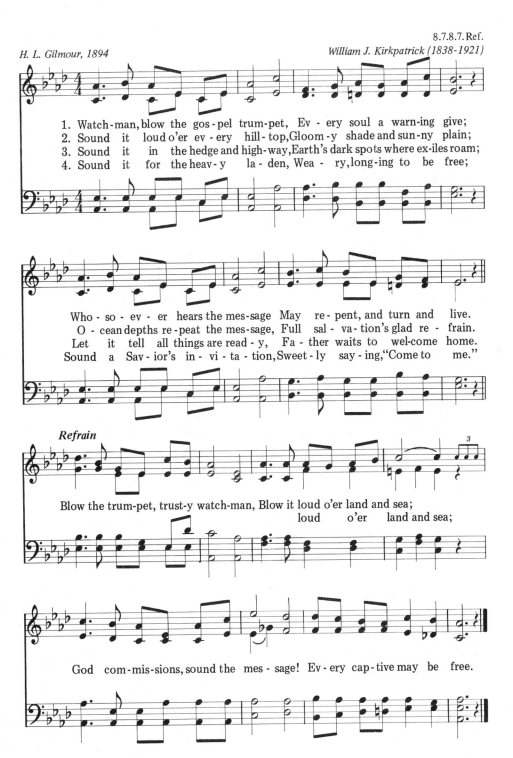

1. Watch-man, blow the gos-pel trum-pet, Ev-ery soul a warn-ing give;
2. Sound it loud o'er ev-ery hill-top, Gloom-y shade and sun-ny plain;
3. Sound it in the hedge and high-way, Earth's dark spots where ex-iles roam;
4. Sound it for the heav-y la-den, Wea-ry, long-ing to be free;

Who-so-ev-er hears the mes-sage May re-pent, and turn and live.
O-cean depths re-peat the mes-sage, Full sal-va-tion's glad re-frain.
Let it tell all things are read-y, Fa-ther waits to wel-come home.
Sound a Sav-ior's in-vi-ta-tion, Sweet-ly say-ing, "Come to me."

Refrain

Blow the trum-pet, trust-y watch-man, Blow it loud o'er land and sea;
loud o'er land and sea;

God com-mis-sions, sound the mes-sage! Ev-ery cap-tive may be free.

MISSION OF THE CHURCH

369 Bringing in the Sheaves

12.11.12.11.Ref.

Knowles Shaw (1834-1878)

George A. Minor (1845-1904)

1. Sow-ing in the morn-ing, sow-ing seeds of kind-ness, Sow-ing in the
2. Sow-ing in the sun-shine, sow-ing in the shad-ows, Fear-ing nei - ther
3. Go - ing forth with weep-ing, sow-ing for the Mas - ter, Though the loss sus-

noon - tide and the dew- y eve; Wait-ing for the har - vest,
clouds nor win-ter's chill- ing breeze; By and by the har - vest,
stained our spir - it oft - en grieves; When our weep-ing's o - ver,

and the time of reap - ing, We shall come re - joic - ing,
and the la - bor end - ed, We shall come re - joic - ing,
He will bid us wel - come, We shall come re - joic - ing,

Refrain

bring-ing in the sheaves. Bring-ing in the sheaves, Bring-ing in the sheaves,

We shall come re-joic - ing, Bring-ing in the sheaves; Bring-ing in the sheaves,

MISSION OF THE CHURCH

Bring-ing in the sheaves, We shall come re - joic - ing, Bring-ing in the sheaves.

Christ for the World 370

ITALIAN HYMN 6.6.4.6.6.6.4.

Samuel Wolcott, 1869 (1813-1886)

Felice de Giardini, 1769 (1716-1796)

1. Christ for the world we sing; The world to Christ we bring
2. Christ for the world we sing; The world to Christ we bring
3. Christ for the world we sing; The world to Christ we bring

With lov - ing zeal; The poor and them that mourn, The faint and
With fer - vent prayer; The way - ward and the lost, By rest - less
With joy - ful song; The new - born souls, whose days, Re - claimed from

o - ver - borne, Sin - sick and sor - row - worn, Whom Christ doth heal.
pas - sions tossed, Re - deemed at count - less cost From dark de - spair.
er - ror's ways, In - spired with hope and praise, To Christ be - long.

Alternate harmony, No. 71

MISSION OF THE CHURCH

371 Lift Him Up

May E. Warren

8.7.8.7.D.Ref.
D. S. Hakes

1. Lift Him up, 'tis He that bids you, Let the dy - ing look and live;
2. Lift Him up, this pre-cious Sav - ior, Let the mul - ti - tude be - hold;
3. Lift Him up in all His glo - ry, 'Tis the Son of God on high;
4. O then lift Him up in sing - ing, Lift the Sav - ior up in prayer;

To all wea - ry, thirst-ing sin - ners, Liv - ing wa - ters will He give;
They with will - ing hearts shall seek Him, He will draw them to His fold;
Lift Him up, His love shall draw them, E'en the care - less shall draw nigh;
He, the glo - ri - ous Re - deem - er, All the sins of men did bear;

And though once so meek and low - ly, Yet the Prince of heaven was He;
They shall gath - er from the way - side, Has-tening on with joy - ous feet,
Let them hear a - gain the sto - ry Of the cross, the death of shame;
Yes, the young shall bow be - fore Him, And the old their voic - es raise;

And the blind, who grope in dark - ness, Through the blood of Christ shall see.
They shall bear the cross of Je - sus, And shall find sal - va - tion sweet.
And from tongue to tongue re - peat it; Might - y throngs shall bless His name.
All the deaf shall hear ho - san - nah; And the dumb shall shout His praise.

MISSION OF THE CHURCH

Refrain

Lift Him up, the ris-en Sav-ior, High a-mid the wait-ing throng;

Lift Him up, 'tis He that speak-eth, Now He bids you flee from wrong.

How Beauteous Are Their Feet 372

Isa. 52:7-9
Isaac Watts, 1719 (1674-1748)

ST. THOMAS S.M.
From Williams' Psalmody, *1770*

1. How beau-teous are their feet Who stand on Zi-on's hill;
2. How charm-ing is their voice, So sweet the ti-dings are:
3. How hap-py are our ears, That hear the joy-ful sound
4. How bless-ed are our eyes, That see this heaven-ly light;
5. The watch-men join their voice, And tune-ful notes em-ploy;

Who bring sal-va-tion on their tongues, And words of peace re-veal!
"Zi-on, be-hold thy Sav-ior King; He reigns and tri-umphs here!"
Which kings and proph-ets wait-ed for, And sought, but nev-er found!
Proph-ets and kings de-sired it long, But died with-out the sight!
Je-ru-sa-lem breaks forth in songs, And des-erts learn the joy.

Seeking the Lost

William A. Ogden (1841-1897)

10.9.10.9.Ref.
William A. Ogden

1. Seek-ing the lost—yes, kind-ly en-treat-ing Wan-der-ers on the
2. Seek-ing the lost—and point-ing to Je-sus Souls that are weak and
3. Thus I would go on mis-sions of mer-cy, Fol-low-ing Christ from

moun-tain a-stray; "Come un-to Me," His mes-sage re-peat-ing,
hearts that are sore, Lead-ing them forth in ways of sal-va-tion,
day un-to day, Cheer-ing the faint and rais-ing the fall-en,

Words of the Mas-ter speak-ing to-day.
Show-ing the path to life ev-er-more.
Point-ing the lost to Je-sus, the Way.

Refrain

{ Go-ing a-far up-on the moun-tain,
{ In-to the fold of my Re-deem-er,

{ Go-ing a-far up-on the moun-tain, Bring-ing the
{ In-to the fold of my Re-deem-er, Je-sus, the

MISSION OF THE CHURCH

Bring-ing the wan-d'rer back a - gain, back a-gain,
Je - sus, the Lamb for sin - ners

slain, for sin-ners slain.

wan - d'rer back a - gain,
Lamb for sin - ners

slain.

Jesus, With Thy Church Abide   374

SONG 13 7.7.7.6.

Thomas B. Pollock (1836-1896)   *Adapt. from Orlando Gibbons (1583-1625)*

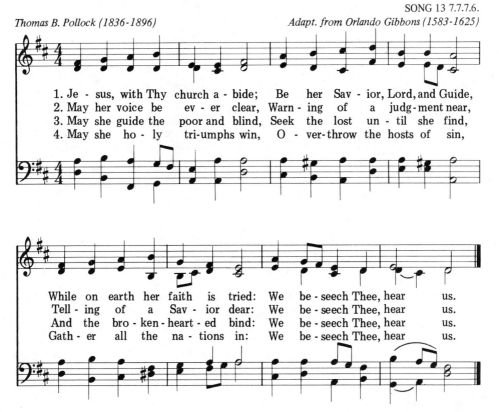

1. Je - sus, with Thy church a - bide; Be her Sav - ior, Lord, and Guide,
2. May her voice be ev - er clear, Warn - ing of a judg-ment near,
3. May she guide the poor and blind, Seek the lost un - til she find,
4. May she ho - ly tri-umphs win, O - ver-throw the hosts of sin,

While on earth her faith is tried: We be - seech Thee, hear us.
Tell - ing of a Sav - ior dear: We be - seech Thee, hear us.
And the bro - ken - heart - ed bind: We be - seech Thee, hear us.
Gath - er all the na - tions in: We be - seech Thee, hear us.

MISSION OF THE CHURCH

375 Work, for the Night Is Coming

John 9:4
Mrs. Anna L. Coghill, 1854 (1836-1907) alt.

WORK SONG 7.6.7.5.D.
Lowell Mason, 1864 (1792-1872)
Arr. by Melvin West, 1984 (1930-   )

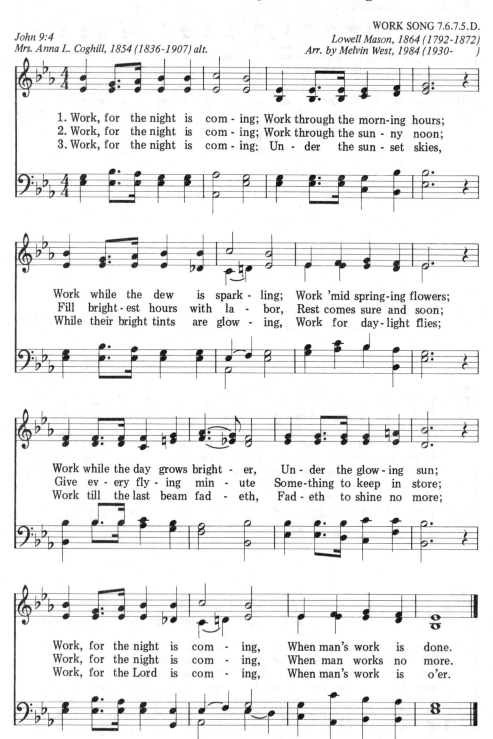

1. Work, for the night is com - ing; Work through the morn-ing hours;
2. Work, for the night is com - ing; Work through the sun - ny noon;
3. Work, for the night is com - ing: Un - der the sun - set skies,

Work while the dew is spark - ling; Work 'mid spring-ing flowers;
Fill bright - est hours with la - bor, Rest comes sure and soon;
While their bright tints are glow - ing, Work for day - light flies;

Work while the day grows bright - er, Un - der the glow - ing sun;
Give ev - ery fly - ing min - ute Some-thing to keep in store;
Work till the last beam fad - eth, Fad - eth to shine no more;

Work, for the night is com - ing, When man's work is done.
Work, for the night is com - ing, When man works no more.
Work, for the Lord is com - ing, When man's work is o'er.

MISSION OF THE CHURCH

All Things Are Thine

GARDINER L.M.

John Greenleaf Whittier, 1872 (1807-1892)   *Wm. Gardiner's* Sacred Melodies, *1815*

1. All things are Thine; no gift have we, Lord of all gifts, to of - fer Thee; And hence with grate - ful hearts to - day, Thine own be - fore Thy feet we lay.
2. Thy will was in the build - er's thought; Thy hand un - seen a - midst us wrought; Thro' mor - tal mo - tive, scheme and plan, Thy wise, e - ter - nal pur - pose ran.
3. No lack Thy per - fect full - ness knew; For hu - man needs and long - ings grew This house of prayer— this home of rest. Here may Thy saints be of - ten blessed.
4. In weak-ness and in want we call On Thee, for whom the heav'ns are small; Thy glo - ry is Thy chil - dren's good, Thy joy Thy ten - der Fa - ther - hood.
5. O Fa - ther! deign these walls to bless; Make this the a - bode of righ - teous - ness, And let these doors a gate - way be To lead us from our - selves to Thee!

Lower key, No. 177

CHURCH DEDICATION

377 Go Forth, Go Forth With Christ

G. B. Timms (1910-), alt.

DARWALL'S 148th 6.6.6.6.8.8.
John Darwall (1731-1789)

1. Go forth, go forth with Christ, Who called you to this day, He who has led, will lead And keep you in His way: His word is fast, His prom-ise sure To all who serve Him and en - dure.

2. Go forth, go forth with Christ, With pur-pose not your own, Each vic - t'ry you shall gain Through Him your Lord a - lone: To guard you in fi - del - i - ty His Spir - it shall your strength-'ner be.

3. Go forth, go forth with Christ, His Priest-hood you shall share, Who bought us by His blood To be His ser - vants here: Walk in the way your Sav - ior trod, Go forth with Him, go forth with God.

From *English Praise* by permission of Oxford University Press.

ORDINATION

Go, Preach My Gospel

Mark 16:15-17
Isaac Watts, 1709 (1674-1748)

TRURO L.M.
T. Williams' Psalmodia Evangelica, 1789

1. "Go, preach My gos - pel," saith the Lord; "Bid the whole world My grace re - ceive; He shall be saved who trusts My word, And they con - demned who dis - be - lieve.

2. "I'll make your great com - mis - sion known, And ye shall prove My gos - pel true By all the works that I have done, By all the won - ders ye shall do.

3. "Teach all the na - tions My com - mands; I'm with you till the world shall end; All power is vest - ed in My hands; I can de - stroy, and I de - fend."

4. He spake, and light shone round His head; On a bright cloud to heaven He rode; They to the far - thest na - tions spread The grace of their as - cend - ed Lord.

379 We Give This Child to You

CASCADEL C.M.

Mrs. Carol Mayes, 1984 (1924-)   *Wayne Hooper, 1984 (1920-)*

1. We give this child to You, Our pre-cious gift of love.
2. O bless each child of Yours, And grant when they are grown,
3. We give our-selves to You, And may Your Spir-it fill

Help us to lead each step a-right With guid-ance from a-bove.
They will have learned to love Your way, And choose it for their own.
Our hearts and home, that all we do Be sub-ject to Your will.

Words copyright © 1985 by Carol Mayes.
Music copyright © 1984 by Wayne Hooper.

CHILD DEDICATION

380 Welcome, Day of Sweet Repose

EVANS 7.7.7.7.

I. H. Evans (1862-1945)   *I. A. Steinel, 1939 (1884-1945)*

1. Wel-come, day of sweet re-pose! Bless-ed be thy sa-cred hours!
2. Wel-come, day in E-den born! Ho-ly rest for sin-less man!
3. Wel-come, day blessed by our Lord! Toil shall cease and anx-ious care.
4. Wel-come, day our Sav-ior kept! Keep-ing, wrought our righ-teous-ness,

We would trust the One who knows All our weak and fail-ing powers.
Like the dawn-ing of fair morn Come thy hours to us a-gain.
Day com-mand-ed by His word, Day for song and praise and prayer.
Day God bids us ne'er for-get, Day of days His name to bless.

SABBATH

Alternate tune, MERCY, No. 268

Holy Sabbath Day of Rest

381

7.7.7.7.Ref.

L. E. C. Joers, 1921 (1900-   )

John F. Anderson, 1924 (1893-1974)

1. Ho - ly Sab-bath day of rest, By our Mas-ter rich-ly blest,
2. Seek not pleasures of this earth, With its fol - ly, noise, and mirth,
3. As the Sab-bath draw-eth on Fri - day eve at set of sun,
4. Ask - ing Him for sav - ing grace, Al - so vic-t'ry in the race,

God - cre - a - ted and di - vine, Set a - side for ho - ly time.
There are bet - ter things in store, O - ver on the oth - er shore.
Chris - tian house-hold then should meet, Sing and pray at Je - sus' feet,
And to help us by His pow'r, To keep ho - ly ev - ery hour.

Refrain

Yes, the ho - ly Sab-bath rest, By our God di-vine-ly blest,

It to us a sign shall be Through-out all e - ter - ni - ty.

SABBATH

382   O Day of Rest and Gladness

ELLACOMBE 7.6.7.6.D.

Christopher Wordsworth (1807-1885) alt.

Gesangbuch der Herzogl, *Hofkapelle, 1784*

1. O day of rest and glad - ness, O day of joy and light,
2. Thou art a port pro - tect - ed From storms that round us rise,
3. A day of sweet re - flec - tion Thou art, a day of love;

O balm of care and sad - ness, Most beau - ti - ful, most bright;
A gar - den in - ter - sect - ed With streams of par - a - dise;
A day to raise af - fec - tion From earth to things a - bove.

On thee, the high and low - ly, Who bend be - fore the throne,
Thou art a cool - ing foun - tain In life's dry, drear - y sand;
New grac - es ev - er gain - ing From this our day of rest

Sing, ho - ly, ho - ly, ho - ly, To the E - ter - nal One.
From thee, like Pis - gah's moun - tain, We view our prom - ised land.
We seek the rest re - main - ing In man - sions of the blest.

SABBATH

O Day of Rest and Gladness

383

MENDEBRAS 7.6.7.6.D.
German Melody
Christopher Wordsworth, 1862; alt. (1807-1885)   *Arr. by Lowell Mason, 1839 (1792-1872)*

1. O day of rest and glad-ness, O day of joy and light,
2. Thou art a port pro-tect-ed From storms that round us rise,
3. A day of sweet re-flec-tion Thou art, a day of love;

O balm of care and sad-ness, Most beau-ti-ful, most bright;
A gar-den in-ter-sect-ed With streams of Par-a-dise;
A day to raise af-fec-tion From earth to things a-bove.

On thee, the high and low-ly, Who bend be-fore the throne,
Thou art a cool-ing foun-tain In life's dry, drear-y sand;
New grac-es ev-er gain-ing From this our day of rest,

Sing, Ho-ly, ho-ly, ho-ly, To the E-ter-nal One.
From thee, like Pis-gah's moun-tain, We view our prom-ised land.
We seek the rest re-main-ing In man-sions of the blest.

SABBATH

Safely Through Another Week

SABBATH 7.7.7.7.7.7.

John Newton, 1774; alt. (1725-1807)   *Lowell Mason, 1824 (1792-1872)*

1. Safe - ly through an - oth - er week God has brought us on our way;
2. While we seek sup-plies of grace Through the dear Re-deem-er's name,
3. When the morn shall bid us rise, May we feel Thy pres-ence near,
4. May the gos - pel's joy-ful sound Con-quer sin - ners, com-fort saints;

Let us now a bless-ing seek, Wait - ing in His courts to - day;
Show Thy rec - on - cil - ing face, Take a - way our sin and shame;
May Thy glo - ry meet our eyes When we in Thy house ap - pear;
Make the fruits of grace a - bound, Bring re - lief to all com - plaints;

Day of all the week the best, Em - blem of e - ter - nal rest;
From our world - ly cares set free May we rest this day in Thee.
Here af - ford us, Lord, a taste Of our ev - er - last - ing feast.
Thus may all our Sab-baths be Till we rise to reign with Thee.

Day of all the week the best, Em - blem of e - ter - nal rest.
From our world - ly cares set free May we rest this day in Thee.
Here af - ford us, Lord, a taste Of our ev - er - last - ing feast.
Thus may all our Sab-baths be Till we rise to reign with Thee.

Crowning Jewel of Creation

JEWEL 8.7.8.7.7.7.

Gem Fitch, 1982 (1934-   )

Wayne Hooper, 1984 (1920-   )

1. Crown - ing jew - el of cre - a - tion, Blest and hal - lowed,
2. Sin and sick - ness, prayer and weep - ing Cease at close of
3. Teach us, Lord, in storm or sun - shine How to tru - ly

sanc - ti - fied; Time and chang - es all tran - scend - ing,
earth - ly days; But Thy Sab - bath is e - ter - nal,
rest in Thee, May Thy Sab - bath peace en - fold us

Refrain

Shared for - ev - er, glo - ri - fied. Bless - ed Sab - bath
Joy - ful thanks to Thee we raise!
And our shel - ter ev - er be.

made for man, Gift from the Cre - a - tor's hand.

Alternate tune, IRBY, No. 149

SABBATH

386 The Sacred Anthem

WALLOWA 8.6.8.6.5.8.6.8.6.

Ottilie Stafford, 1984 (1921-   )

Melvin West, 1984 (1930-   )

1. The sa-cred an-them slow-ly rang A-cross the fields of praise,
2. But now in our di-min-ished lives We sing a blem-ished song;
3. And arch-ing o-ver time and space The Lord of Sab-baths wills

When earth's first Sab-bath made com-plete All crea-tures and all days.
The earth is worn and dis - ar-rayed And all our work goes wrong.
Re - new - al for the wea - ry earth And heal-ing for our ills.

Walk - ing with God, there, Wom - an and man to -
Still in our wor - ship, Join - ing in praise and
Hearts will re - joice then; There will be no more

geth - er share The bless - ed Sab - bath mood; And
fel - low-ship, By Sab - bath ra - diance blessed, We
weep - ing, when We know. and shall be known. With

Words copyright © 1984 by Ottilie Stafford.
Music copyright © 1984 by Melvin West.

SABBATH

in that green and gold - en world Know all God's works are good.
put our doubt and fear a - way And rest with - in God's rest.
hosts of the re - deemed we'll sing A - round God's shin - ing throne.

Come, O Sabbath Day
387

SABBATH 7.7.7.7.3.3.

Gustav Gottheil (1827-1903)

A. W. Binder (1895-1966)

1. Come, O Sab - bath day, and bring Peace and heal - ing
2. Earth - ly long - ings bid re - tire, Quench the pas - sions'
3. Wipe from ev - ery cheek the tear, Ban - ish care and

on thy wing; And to ev - ery trou-bled breast Speak of the di -
hurt - ful fire; To the way - ward, sin op-pressed, Bring thou thy di -
si - lence fear; All things work-ing for the best, Teach us the di -

Unison

vine be - hest: Thou shalt rest, Thou shalt rest!
vine be - hest: Thou shalt rest, Thou shalt rest!
vine be - hest: Thou shalt rest, Thou shalt rest!

From *Union Hymnal* © 1932, Central Conference of American Rabbis.

SABBATH

388 Don't Forget the Sabbath

Fanny J. Crosby (1820-1915)

12.13.13.13.Ref.
William B. Bradbury (1816-1868)

1. Don't for-get the Sab-bath, The Lord our God hath blest, Of all the
2. Keep the Sab-bath ho - ly, And wor-ship Him to - day, Who said to
3. Day of sa - cred plea-sure! Its gold - en hours we'll spend In thank-ful

week the bright-est, Of all the week the best; It brings re - pose from
His dis - ci - ples, "I am the liv-ing way;" And if we meek-ly
hymns to Je - sus, The chil-dren's dear - est Friend; O gen - tle lov-ing,

la - bor, It tells of joy di - vine, Its beams of light de - scend-ing,
fol - low Our Sav - ior here be - low, He'll give us of the foun-tain
Sav - ior, How good and kind Thou art, How pre - cious is Thy prom-ise

Refrain

With heaven-ly beau - ty shine.
Whose streams e - ter - nal flow.   Wel-come, wel-come, ev - er wel-come,
To dwell in ev - ery heart!

SABBATH

Bless-ed Sab-bath day. Wel-come, wel-come, ev-er wel-come, Bless-ed Sab-bath day.

Light of Light, Enlighten Me   389

Benjamin Schmolck, 1714 (1672-1737)
Tr. by Catherine Winkworth, 1858 (1827-1878)

HINCHMAN 7.8.7.8.7.7.
Uzziah C. Burnap, 1869 (1834-1900)

1. Light of light, en-light-en me, Now a-new the day is dawn-ing;
2. Let me with my heart to-day, Ho-ly, ho-ly, ho-ly, sing-ing,
3. Hence all care, all van-i-ty! For the day to God is ho-ly;

Sun of grace, the shad-ows flee; Bright-en Thou my Sab-bath morn-ing;
Rapt a-while from earth a-way, All my soul to Thee up spring-ing,
Come, Thou glo-rious Maj-es-ty, Deign to fill this tem-ple low-ly;

With Thy joy-ous sun-shine blest, Hap-py is my day of rest.
Have a fore-taste in-ward given How they wor-ship Thee in heaven.
Nought to-day my soul shall move, Sim-ply rest-ing in Thy love.

SABBATH

390 We Love Thy Sabbath, Lord

Myrtle H. Dorland (1920-   )

TRENTHAM S.M.
Robert Jackson (1842-1914)

1. We love Thy Sab - bath, Lord, And wor - ship at Thy will;
2. Thine an - gels sang for joy Cre - a - tion's work to see;
3. Praise for Thy won - drous love, That sealed this sa - cred day,
4. O great Cre - a - tor King, Through Thy re - deem - ing grace,
5. And with the white - robed throng, Up - on Mount Si - on be,

Oh may these hours sweet peace af - ford And deep - er faith in - still.
We too, this day, would raise our hearts In grate - ful praise to Thee.
A sign that all may un - der-stand We own Thy sov - ereign sway.
Re - new and sanc - ti - fy our hearts That we may see Thy face.
And joy - ful sing our Sab - bath song Through all e - ter - ni - ty.

Alternate tune, PARACLETE, No. 265

391 Welcome, Welcome, Day of Rest

Anon.

PLEYEL'S HYMN 7.7.7.7.
Arr. from Ignace Pleyel, 1791 (1757-1831)

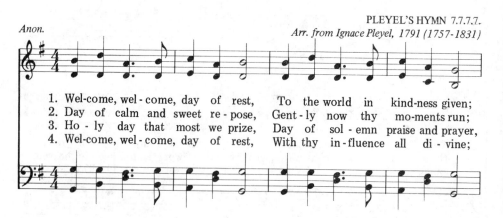

1. Wel-come, wel - come, day of rest, To the world in kind-ness given;
2. Day of calm and sweet re - pose, Gent - ly now thy mo-ments run;
3. Ho - ly day that most we prize, Day of sol - emn praise and prayer,
4. Wel-come, wel - come, day of rest, With thy in - fluence all di - vine;

SABBATH

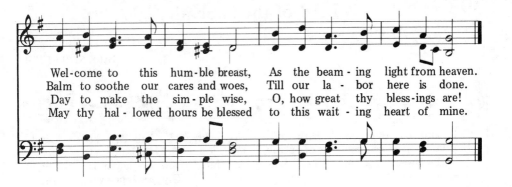

Wel-come to this hum-ble breast, As the beam-ing light from heaven.
Balm to soothe our cares and woes, Till our la-bor here is done.
Day to make the sim-ple wise, O, how great thy bless-ings are!
May thy hal-lowed hours be blessed to this wait-ing heart of mine.

Dear Lord, We Come at Set of Sun 392

STRACATHRO C.M.
Charles Hutcheson (1792-1860)
Arr. by David Evans (1874-1948)

Mary Speidel, 1984 (1915-   )

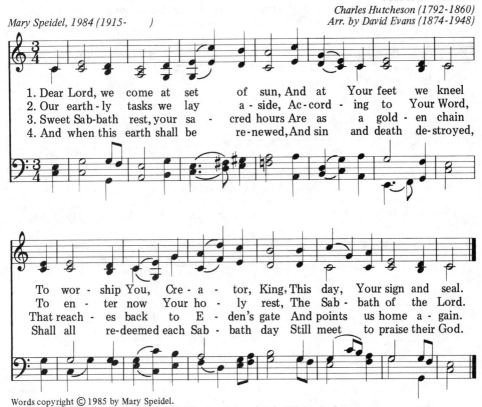

1. Dear Lord, we come at set of sun, And at Your feet we kneel
2. Our earth-ly tasks we lay a-side, Ac-cord-ing to Your Word,
3. Sweet Sab-bath rest, your sa-cred hours Are as a gold-en chain
4. And when this earth shall be re-newed, And sin and death de-stroyed,

To wor-ship You, Cre-a-tor, King, This day, Your sign and seal.
To en-ter now Your ho-ly rest, The Sab-bath of the Lord.
That reach-es back to E-den's gate And points us home a-gain.
Shall all re-deemed each Sab-bath day Still meet to praise their God.

Alternate tune, SERENITY, No. 455

SABBATH

393
Lord of the Sabbath

Anon.

PARK STREET L.M.
Arr. from Frederick M. A. Venua, c. 1810 (1788-1872)

1. Lord of the Sab - bath and its light, I hail Thy hal - lowed
2. O sa - cred day of peace and joy, Thy hours are ev - er
3. How sweet - ly now they glide a - long! How hal-lowed is the
4. O Je - sus, let me ev - er hail Thy pres-ence with the

day of rest; It is my wea - ry soul's de - light, The sol - ace
dear to me; Ne'er may a sin - ful thought de -stroy The ho - ly
calm they yield! Transport - ing is their rap - turous song, And heaven-ly
day of rest; Then will Thy ser - vant nev - er fail To deem Thy

of my care - worn breast, The sol - ace of my care - worn breast.
calm I find in thee, The ho - ly calm I find in thee.
vi - sions seem re - vealed, And heavenly vi - sions seem re - vealed.
Sab - bath dou - bly blest, To deem Thy Sab - bath dou - bly blest.

SABBATH

Far From All Care

PEVENSEY 11.10.11.10.
D. A. R. Aufranc, 1940

D. A. R. Aufranc (1892-1980)

1. Far from all care we hail the Sab-bath morn - ing;
2. Though man a - lone, Lord, of Thy great cre - a - tion
3. Lord of the Sab - bath, Sav - ior and Cre - a - tor,
4. Strong in Thy might and qui - et in Thy meek - ness,

O'er wav - ing fields and from the dis - tant sea
Fails now to laud Thee for Thy love and power,
Calm now the throb - bings of each trou - bled breast.
May we Thine im - age bear from day to day.

Swell notes of praise in har - mo - ny re - sound - ing
Yet still a rem - nant love Thee and re - mem - ber
Speak to our hearts the peace of Thy com - mand - ments,
Then may we en - ter pearl - y gates e - ter - nal

As all cre - a - tion turns her heart to Thee.
Thy ho - ly law and each sweet Sab - bath hour.
Breathe on each soul fair E - den's hal - lowed rest.
And sing re - demp-tion's song each Sab - bath day.

SABBATH

395 As Birds Unto the Genial Homeland

David Levy (1854-   )

Irregular
Max Grauman

1. As birds un-to the gen - ial home-land fly, The
2. Here at Thy shrine we leave all vex - ing care, For -
3. Bless all who spend this night in pain and woe, The
4. Come, Sab - bath joy, each trust - ing heart now fill, And

win - ter's cold and low'r-ing skies to flee, So
get the dis-ap-point - ment, grief and tear, And
bur - dened heart, the faint-ing, and dis-tressed, Thy
bliss - ful peace with - in our homes a - bide, May

seeks my soul Thy gra - cious presence here And
on the wings of hope - ful song and prayer We
com - fort send to dark - ened homes be - reaved, Thy
thank - ful praise each grate - ful heart now thrill, And

finds, O God, its rest and peace in Thee.
rise, and ris - ing feel Thy Spir - it here.
sav - ing help to those by want op - pressed.
to God's lov-ing care their lives con - fide.

SABBATH

Lord God, Your Love Has Called Us Here 396

RYBURN 8.8.8.8.8.8.

Brian A. Wren (1936-)

Norman Cocker (1889-1953)

1. Lord God, Your love has called us here, As we, by love, for love were made. Your living likeness still we bear Tho' marred, dishonored, disobeyed. We come, with all our heart and mind Your call to hear, Your love to find.

2. We come with self-inflicted pains Of broken trust and chosen wrong, Half-free, half-bound by inner chains, By social forces swept along, By powers and systems close confined, Yet seeking hope for human kind.

3. Lord God, in Christ You call our name, And then receive us as Your own, Not thro' some merit, right, or claim, But by Your gracious love alone. We strain to glimpse Your mercy-seat, And find You kneeling at our feet.

4. Then take the towel, and break the bread, And humble us, and call us friends. Suffer and serve till all are fed, And show how grandly love intends To work till all creation sings, To fill all worlds, to crown all things.

5. Lord God, in Christ You set us free Your life to live, Your joy to share. Give us Your Spirit's liberty To turn from guilt and dull despair And offer all that faith can do, While love is making all things new.

COMMUNION

397

An Upper Room

O WALY WALY 9.8.9.8.
English Traditional Melody
Arr. by John Wilson (1905-)

Fred Pratt Green, 1973 (1903-)

1. An up-per room did our Lord pre-pare For those He loved un-til the end: And His dis-ci-ples still gath-er there, To cel-e-brate their ris-en Friend.
2. And af-ter sup-per He washed their feet, For ser-vice, too, is sac-ra-ment. In Him our joy shall be made com-plete Sent out to serve, as He was sent.
3. A last-ing gift Je-sus gave His own: To share His bread, His lov-ing cup. What-ev-er bur-dens may bow us down, He by His cross shall lift us up.
4. No end there is! we de-part in peace. He loves be-yond our ut-ter-most: In ev-ery room in our Fa-ther's house, He will be there, as Lord and host.

398

Bread of the World

COMMUNION 9.8.9.8.
Stanley Ledington, 1939 (1889-1974)

Reginald Heber, (1783-1826)

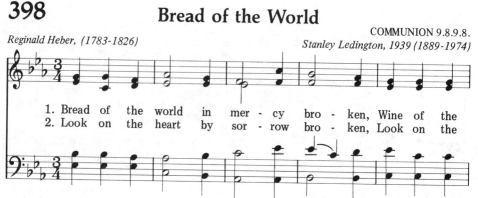

1. Bread of the world in mer-cy bro-ken, Wine of the
2. Look on the heart by sor-row bro-ken, Look on the

COMMUNION

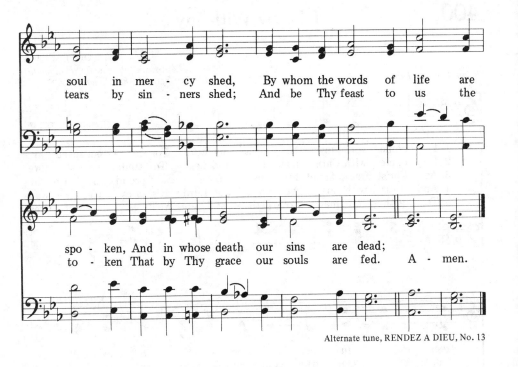

soul in mer - cy shed, By whom the words of life are
tears by sin - ners shed; And be Thy feast to us the

spo - ken, And in whose death our sins are dead;
to - ken That by Thy grace our souls are fed. A - men.

Alternate tune, RENDEZ A DIEU, No. 13

Beneath the Forms of Outward Rite 399

Mark 14:15, 22, 23
James A. Blaisdell, 1928 (1867-1957)

PERRY C.M.
Leo Sowerby, 1962 (1895-1968)

1. Be - neath the forms of out-ward rite Thy sup - per, Lord, is spread
2. The bread is al - ways con - se - crate Which men di - vide with men;
3. The bless - ed cup is on - ly passed True mem - o - ry of Thee,
4. O Mas - ter, through these sym-bols shared, Thine own dear self im - part,

In ev - ery qui - et up - per room Where faint-ing souls are fed.
And ev - ery act of broth-er - hood Re - peats Thy feast a - gain.
When life a - new pours out its wine With rich suf - fi - cien - cy.
That in our dai - ly life may flame The pas - sion of Thy heart.

COMMUNION

400

I Come With Joy

DOVE OF PEACE C.M.
American folk melody, 19th century
Arr. by Charles G. Frischmann (1938-   )

Brian A. Wren (1936-   )

1. I come with joy to meet my Lord, For - giv - en, loved and
2. I come with Chris - tians far and near To find, as all are
3. As Christ breaks bread for us to share Each proud di - vi - sion
4. And thus with joy we meet our Lord. His pres - ence al - ways
5. To - geth - er met, to - geth - er bound, We'll go our dif - f'rent

free,   In awe and won - der to re - call His
fed,   Our true com - mu - ni - ty of love In
ends.   That love that made us makes us one, And
near,   Is in such friend - ship bet - ter known: We
ways,   And as His peo - ple in the world, We'll

life laid down   for me,   His life laid down   for me.
Christ's com - mu - nion bread, In Christ's com - mu - nion bread.
strang - ers now are friends,   And strang - ers now are friends.
see and praise   Him here,   We see and praise   Him here.
live and speak   His praise,   We'll live and speak His praise.

COMMUNION

In Imitation, Lord of Thee

401

John 13:14
William Brickey, c. 1886

MCCABE L.M.
E. S. Widdemer

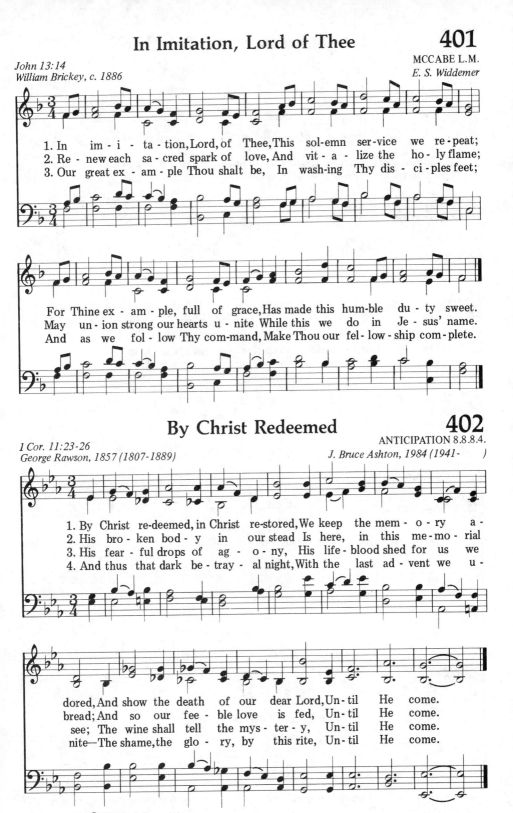

1. In im - i - ta - tion, Lord, of Thee, This sol-emn ser-vice we re-peat;
2. Re - new each sa - cred spark of love, And vit - a - lize the ho - ly flame;
3. Our great ex - am - ple Thou shalt be, In wash-ing Thy dis - ci - ples feet;

For Thine ex - am - ple, full of grace, Has made this hum-ble du - ty sweet.
May un - ion strong our hearts u - nite While this we do in Je - sus' name.
And as we fol - low Thy com-mand, Make Thou our fel - low - ship com-plete.

By Christ Redeemed

402

1 Cor. 11:23-26
George Rawson, 1857 (1807-1889)

ANTICIPATION 8.8.8.4.
J. Bruce Ashton, 1984 (1941-   )

1. By Christ re-deemed, in Christ re-stored, We keep the mem - o - ry a -
2. His bro - ken bod - y in our stead Is here, in this me - mo - rial
3. His fear - ful drops of ag - o - ny, His life-blood shed for us we
4. And thus that dark be - tray - al night, With the last ad - vent we u -

dored, And show the death of our dear Lord, Un - til He come.
bread; And so our fee - ble love is fed, Un - til He come.
see; The wine shall tell the mys - ter - y, Un - til He come.
nite—The shame, the glo - ry, by this rite, Un - til He come.

Music copyright © 1984 by J. Bruce Ashton.

COMMUNION

403 Let Us Break Bread Together

Mal. 4:2
American Negro Spiritual

10.10.4.Ref.
From Contemporary Worship 4

1. Let us break bread to-geth-er on our knees;
2. Let us drink wine to-geth-er on our knees;

Let us break bread to-geth-er on our knees.
Let us drink wine to-geth-er on our knees.

Refrain

When I fall on my knees, With my face to the ris-ing

sun, O Lord, have mer-cy on me.

COMMUNION

3. Let us praise God to-geth-er on our knees;

Let us praise God to-geth-er on our knees.

Refrain

When I fall on my knees, With my face to the ris - ing

sun, O Lord, have mer-cy on me.

404 Now Let Us From This Table Rise

DEUS TUORUM MILITUM L.M.

Grenoble Antiphoner, 1753

Fred H. Kaan (1929-)

Arr. by Melvin West, 1984 (1930-)

1. Now let us from this ta - ble rise Re - newed in
2. With minds a - lert, up - held by grace, To spread the
3. To fill each hu - man house with love, It is the
4. Then grant us cour - age, Fa - ther God, To choose a -

bod - y, mind, and soul; With Christ we die and
word in speech and deed, We fol - low in the
sac - ra - ment of care; The work that Christ be -
gain the pil - grim way And help us to ac -

live a - gain, His self - less love has made us whole.
steps of Christ, At one with all in hope and need.
gan to do We hum - bly pledge our-selves to share.
cept with joy The chal - lenge of to - mor - row's day.

405 O God, Unseen, Yet Ever Near

MEDITATION C.M.

Edward Osler, 1836 (1798-1863) alt.

John H. Gower, 1890 (1855-1922)

1. O God, un - seen, yet ev - er near, Re - veal Thy pres-ence now
2. Here may Thy faith-ful peo - ple know The bless-ings of Thy love,
3. We come, o - bed-ient to Thy Word To feast on heav'n-ly food,
4. Thus may we all Thy words o - bey, For we, O God, are Thine,

COMMUNION

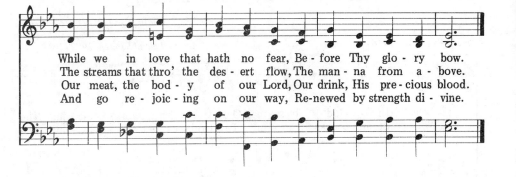

While we in love that hath no fear, Be - fore Thy glo - ry bow.
The streams that thro' the des - ert flow, The man - na from a - bove.
Our meat, the bod - y of our Lord, Our drink, His pre - cious blood.
And go re - joic - ing on our way, Re - newed by strength di - vine.

Love Consecrates the Humblest Act 406

John 13:14
S. B. McManus, c. 1902 (1845-1917) alt.

TWENTY-FOURTH C.M.
Attr. to Lucius Chapin (1760-1842)

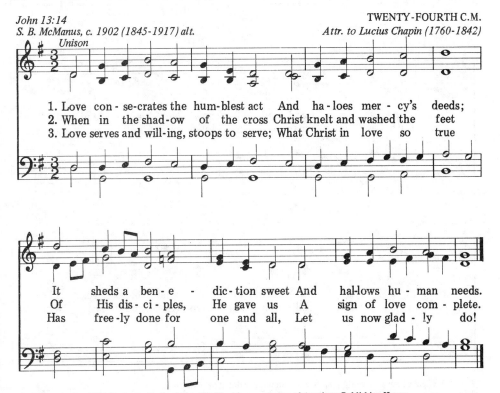

Unison

1. Love con - se-crates the hum-blest act And ha - loes mer - cy's deeds;
2. When in the shad - ow of the cross Christ knelt and washed the feet
3. Love serves and will - ing, stoops to serve; What Christ in love so true

It sheds a ben - e - dic - tion sweet And hal - lows hu - man needs.
Of His dis - ci - ples, He gave us A sign of love com - plete.
Has free - ly done for one and all, Let us now glad - ly do!

Harmony setting, No. 681

COMMUNION

407 Sent Forth by God's Blessing

THE ASH GROVE 6.6.11 6.6.11.
Welsh folk melody
Omer Westendorf (1916-) alt.
Arr. by Leland Sateren, 1972 (1913-)

1. Sent forth by God's bless-ing, Our true faith con-fess-ing, The
2. With praise and thanks-giv-ing To God ev-er-liv-ing, The

peo-ple of God from His dwell-ing take leave.
tasks of our ev-ery-day life we will face.

The sup-per is end-ed. Oh, now be ex-tend-ed The
Our faith ev-er shar-ing, In love ev-er car-ing, Em-

fruits of this ser-vice in all who be-lieve. The
brac-ing His chil-dren of each tribe and race. With

COMMUNION

seed of His teach - ing, Re - cep - tive souls reach - ing, Shall
Your feast You feed us, With Your light now lead us; U -

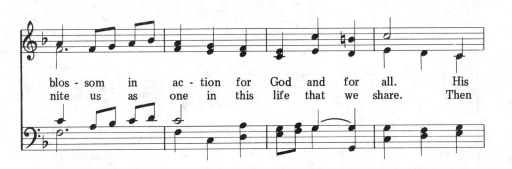

blos - som in ac - tion for God and for all. His
nite us as one in this life that we share. Then

grace did in - vite us, His love shall u - nite us To
may all the liv - ing With praise and thanks - giv - ing Give

work for God's king - dom and an - swer His call.
hon - or to Christ and His name that we bear.

Harmony setting, No. 560
COMMUNION

408 Lord, Enthroned in Heavenly Splendor

KINGLEY VALE 8.7.8.7.4.7.

George Hugh Bourne (1840-1927)

Hugh Percy Allen (1869-1946)

Unison

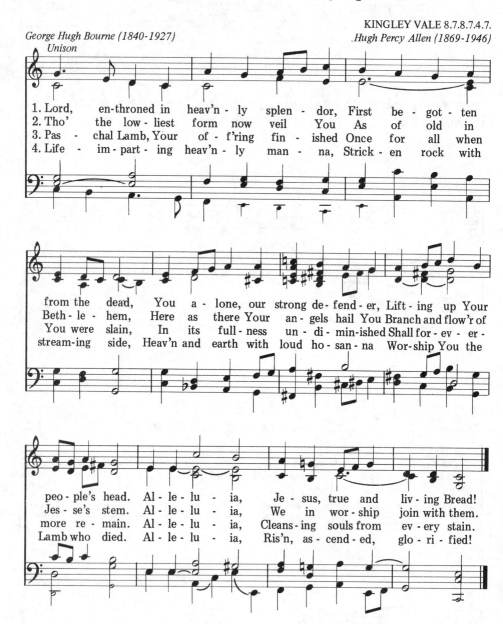

1. Lord, en-throned in heav'n-ly splen-dor, First be-got-ten from the dead, You a-lone, our strong de-fend-er, Lift-ing up Your peo-ple's head. Al-le-lu-ia, Je-sus, true and liv-ing Bread!

2. Tho' the low-liest form now veil You As of old in Beth-le-hem, Here as there Your an-gels hail You Branch and flow'r of Jes-se's stem. Al-le-lu-ia, We in wor-ship join with them.

3. Pas-chal Lamb, Your of-f'ring fin-ished Once for all when You were slain, In its full-ness un-di-min-ished Shall for-ev-er-more re-main. Al-le-lu-ia, Cleans-ing souls from ev-ery stain.

4. Life-im-part-ing heav'n-ly man-na, Strick-en rock with stream-ing side, Heav'n and earth with loud ho-san-na Wor-ship You the Lamb who died. Al-le-lu-ia, Ris'n, as-cend-ed, glo-ri-fied!

Jesus Invites His Saints

409

SCHUMANN S.M.

Isaac Watts, 1719 (1674-1748)

Mason and Webb's Cantica Laudis, *Boston, 1850*

1. Je - sus in - vites His saints To meet a - round His board,
2. We take the bread and wine As em - blems of Thy death;
3. Faith eats the bread of life, And drinks the liv - ing wine;
4. Soon shall the night be gone, Our Lord will come a - gain;

And sup in mem - ory of the death And suf - ferings of their Lord.
Lord, raise our souls a - bove the sign, To feast on Thee by faith.
It looks be - yond this scene of strife—U - nites us to the Vine.
The mar - riage sup - per of the Lamb Will ush - er in His reign.

Thy Broken Body, Gracious Lord

410

JANICE L.M.

Anon. from Hymns and Tunes, *1886*

Wayne Hooper, 1966 (1920-)

1. Thy bro - ken bod - y, gra - cious Lord, Is shad - owed by this bro - ken bread;
2. And while we meet to - geth - er thus, We show that we are one in Thee;
3. We have one hope that Thou wilt come, Thee in the air we wait to see;

The wine which in this cup is poured, Points to the blood which Thou hast shed.
Thy pre - cious blood was shed for us, Thy death, O Lord, hast set us free!
When Thou wilt give Thy saints a home, And we shall ev - er reign with Thee.

COMMUNION

411

The Son of God Proclaim

DAY OF PRAISE C.M.
Charles Steggall (1826-1905)

Basil E. Bridge (1927-   )

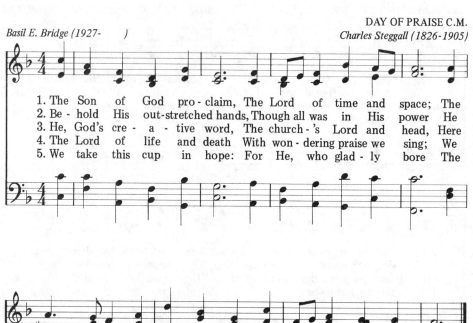

1. The Son of God pro-claim, The Lord of time and space; The
2. Be-hold His out-stretched hands, Though all was in His power He
3. He, God's cre-a-tive word, The church-'s Lord and head, Here
4. The Lord of life and death With won-dering praise we sing; We
5. We take this cup in hope: For He, who glad-ly bore The

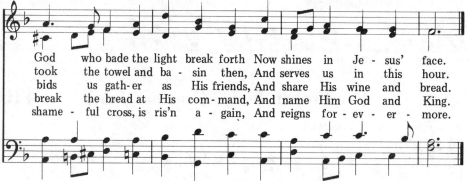

God who bade the light break forth Now shines in Je-sus' face.
took the towel and ba-sin then, And serves us in this hour.
bids us gath-er as His friends, And share His wine and bread.
break the bread at His com-mand, And name Him God and King.
shame-ful cross, is ris'n a-gain, And reigns for-ev-er-more.

Words used by permission of Basil E. Bridge.

Cover With His Life

9.9.9.9.Ref.

412

F. E. Belden, 1899 (1858-1945)

F. E. Belden, 1899

1. Look up-on Je - sus, sin-less is He;   Fa-ther, im-pute His
2. Deep are the wounds trans-gres-sion has made;   Red are the stains; my
3. Long-ing the joy of par-don to know;   Je - sus holds out a
4. Rec - on-ciled by His death for my sin,   Jus - ti - fied by His

life un - to me.   My life of scar - let, my sin and woe,
soul is a - fraid.   O to be cov - ered, Je - sus, with Thee,
robe white as snow;   "Lord, I ac - cept it! leav - ing my own,
life pure and clean,   Sanc - ti - fied by o - bey - ing His word,

Refrain

Cov - er with His life, whit - er than snow.
Safe from the law that now judg-eth me!
Glad - ly I wear Thy pure life a - lone."   Cov - er with His life,
Glo - ri - fied when re - turn-eth my Lord.

whit - er than snow;   Full-ness of His life then shall I know;

My life of scar-let, my sin and woe,   Cov-er with His life, whit-er than snow.

LAW AND GRACE

413 God Has Spoken by His Prophets

Heb. 1:1,2
George Wallace Briggs, 1952 (1875-1959) alt. 1972

TON-Y-BOTEL 8.7.8.7.D.
Thomas John Williams, 1890 (1869-1944)

1. God has spo-ken by His proph-ets, Spo-ken His un-chang-ing Word, Each from age to age pro-claim-ing God, the one, the righ-teous Lord. Mid the world's de-spair and tur-moil, One firm an-chor hold-ing fast; God is King, His

2. God has spo-ken by Christ Je-sus, Christ, the ev-er-last-ing Son, Bright-ness of the Fa-ther's glo-ry, With the Fa-ther ev-er one; Spo-ken by the Word in-car-nate, God of God, ere time be-gan, Light of light, to

3. God yet speaks by His own Spir-it Speak-ing to the hearts of men, In the age-long Word ex-pound-ing God's own mes-sage, now as then; Through the rise and fall of na-tions One sure faith yet stand-ing fast, God is King, His

SPIRITUAL GIFTS

throne e - ter - nal, God the first, and God the last.
earth de - scend - ing, Man, re - veal - ing God to man.
Word un - chang - ing, God the first, and God the last.

Fruitful Trees, the Spirit's Sowing 414

Gal. 5:22,23
Timothy Dudley-Smith, 1981 (1926-   )

ALL FOR JESUS 8.7.8.7.
John Stainer (1840-1901)

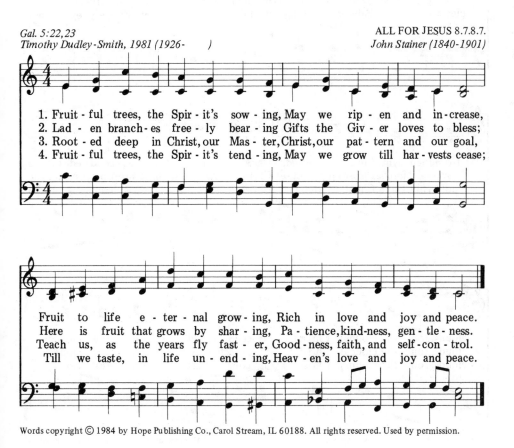

1. Fruit - ful trees, the Spir - it's sow - ing, May we rip - en and in - crease,
2. Lad - en branch - es free - ly bear - ing Gifts the Giv - er loves to bless;
3. Root - ed deep in Christ, our Mas - ter, Christ, our pat - tern and our goal,
4. Fruit - ful trees, the Spir - it's tend - ing, May we grow till har - vests cease;

Fruit to life e - ter - nal grow - ing, Rich in love and joy and peace.
Here is fruit that grows by shar - ing, Pa - tience, kind - ness, gen - tle - ness.
Teach us, as the years fly fast - er, Good - ness, faith, and self - con - trol.
Till we taste, in life un - end - ing, Heav - en's love and joy and peace.

SPIRITUAL GIFTS

415 Christ the Lord, All Power Possessing

Matt. 28:18-20; Dan. 7:9-14; Rev. 1:7
C. Mervyn Maxwell, 1984 (1925-   )

CWM RHONDDA 8.7.8.7.8.7.7.
John Hughes (1873-1932)

1. Christ, the Lord, all power pos - sess - ing, Part - ing, mount - ed
2. Dan - iel views earth's judg - ment hour, An - gels gath - ering,
3. Rev - e - la - tion's word ful - fill - ing, Trum - pet, voic - es

heav - en's height, Gra - cious hands out-stretched in bless-ing, Clouds re-ceived Him
o - pen books. God en-throned in flam - ing pow - er For His Son's ar -
pierce the air. Saint and sin - ner faint - ing, thrill-ing, Ev - ery eye be -

from their sight. Christ as-cend-ed, Christ as-cend-ed, Christ as - cend - ed on the
riv - al looks. Christ ap-proach-es, Christ ap-proach-es, Christ ap-proach-es on the
hold Him there. Christ is com-ing, Christ is com-ing, Christ is com - ing on the

clouds. (on the clouds) Christ as-cend - ed on the clouds.
clouds. (on the clouds) Christ ap-proach - es on the clouds.
clouds. (on the clouds) Christ is com - ing on the clouds.

Words copyright © 1984 by C. Mervyn Maxwell.

Alternate tune, UNSER HERRSCHER, No. 45
Higher key, No. 201

JUDGMENT

The Judgment Has Set

416

F. E. Belden, 1886 (1858-1945)

11.8.9.7.Ref.

F. E. Belden, 1886

1. The judg-ment has set, the books have been o - pened; How shall we
2. The work is be - gun with those who are sleep-ing, Soon will the
3. O, how shall we stand that mo - ment of search-ing, When all our

stand in that great day When ev - ery thought, and word, and ac - tion,
liv - ing here be tried, Out of the books of God's re-mem-brance,
sins those books re - veal? When from that court, each case de - cid - ed,

Refrain

God, the righ - teous Judge, shall weigh?
His de - ci - sion to a - bide. How shall we stand in
Shall be grant - ed no ap - peal?

that great day? How shall we stand in that great day? Shall we be

found be - fore Him want-ing? Or with our sins all washed a - way?

JUDGMENT

417
O Solemn Thought

Roswell F. Cottrell, 1886 (1814-1892)

FINALLY L.M.D.
Allen W. Foster, 1984 (1940-   )

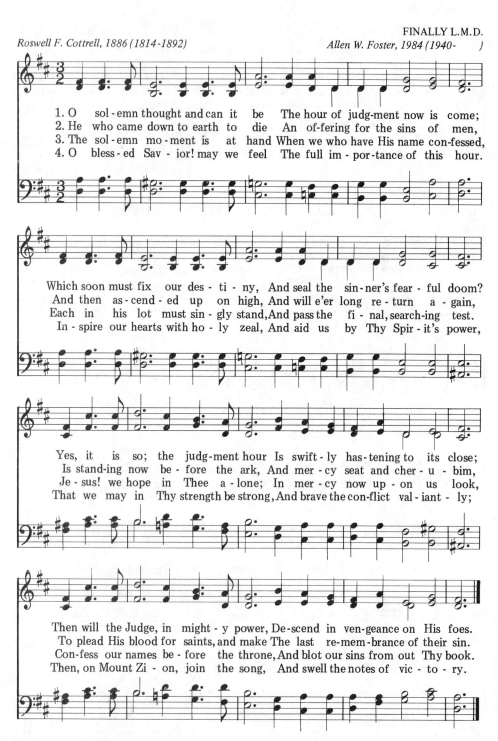

1. O sol-emn thought and can it be The hour of judg-ment now is come;
2. He who came down to earth to die An of-fering for the sins of men,
3. The sol-emn mo-ment is at hand When we who have His name con-fessed,
4. O bless-ed Sav-ior! may we feel The full im-por-tance of this hour.

Which soon must fix our des-ti-ny, And seal the sin-ner's fear-ful doom?
And then as-cend-ed up on high, And will e'er long re-turn a-gain,
Each in his lot must sin-gly stand, And pass the fi-nal, search-ing test.
In-spire our hearts with ho-ly zeal, And aid us by Thy Spir-it's power,

Yes, it is so; the judg-ment hour Is swift-ly has-tening to its close;
Is stand-ing now be-fore the ark, And mer-cy seat and cher-u-bim,
Je-sus! we hope in Thee a-lone; In mer-cy now up-on us look,
That we may in Thy strength be strong, And brave the con-flict val-iant-ly;

Then will the Judge, in might-y power, De-scend in ven-geance on His foes.
To plead His blood for saints, and make The last re-mem-brance of their sin.
Con-fess our names be-fore the throne, And blot our sins from out Thy book.
Then, on Mount Zi-on, join the song, And swell the notes of vic-to-ry.

Alternate tune, DUANE STREET, No. 441

JUDGMENT

Day of Judgment, Day of Wonders! 418

UNSER HERRSCHER 8.7.8.7.8.7.

John Newton (1725-1807)

Joachim Neander, 1680 (1650-1680)

1. Day of judg - ment, day of won - ders! Hark the trum- pet's
2. See the Lord in glo - ry near - ing, Clothed in maj - es -
3. At His call the dead a - wak - en, Rise to life from
4. But to those who have con - fessed Loved and served the

aw - ful sound, Loud - er than a thou - sand thun - ders,
ty di - vine. You who long for His ap - pear - ing,
earth and sea! All the powers of na - ture shak - en
Lord be - low, He will say, "Come near, ye bless - ed,

Shakes the vast cre - a - tion round! How the sum - mons,
Then shall say, "This God is mine!" Gra - cious Sav - ior,
By His looks pre - pare to flee. Care - less sin - ner,
See the king - dom I be - stow; You for - ev - er,

How the sum - mons Will the sin - ner's heart con - found!
Gra - cious Sav - ior, Own me in that day as Thine.
Care - less sin - ner, What will then be - come of thee?
You for - ev - er Shall My love and glo - ry know."

Alternate tune, CWM RHONDDA, No. 415
Alternate harmony, No. 45

RESURRECTION OF THE SAINTS

419   Soon Shall the Trump of God

UNITED MAN S.M.

Anon.

Norman L. Warren (1934-   )

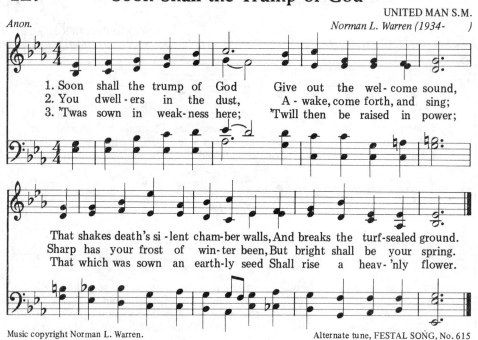

1. Soon shall the trump of God   Give out the wel-come sound,
2. You dwell-ers in the dust,   A-wake, come forth, and sing;
3. 'Twas sown in weak-ness here;   'Twill then be raised in power;

That shakes death's si-lent cham-ber walls, And breaks the turf-sealed ground.
Sharp has your frost of win-ter been, But bright shall be your spring.
That which was sown an earth-ly seed Shall rise a heav-'nly flower.

Music copyright Norman L. Warren.

Alternate tune, FESTAL SONG, No. 615

RESURRECTION OF THE SAINTS

420   Jerusalem, My Happy Home

LAND OF REST C.M.

Traditional American melody

Anon., c. 1585

Coll. and Arr. by Annabel M. Buchanan (1888-   )

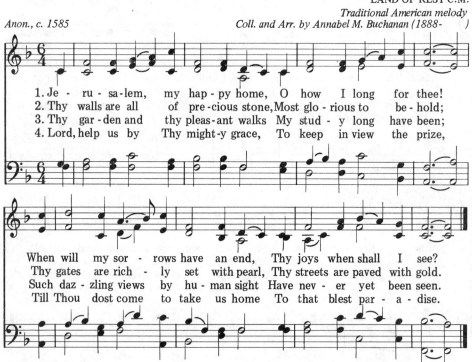

1. Je-ru-sa-lem, my hap-py home, O how I long for thee!
2. Thy walls are all of pre-cious stone, Most glo-rious to be-hold;
3. Thy gar-den and thy pleas-ant walks My stud-y long have been;
4. Lord, help us by Thy might-y grace, To keep in view the prize,

When will my sor-rows have an end, Thy joys when shall I see?
Thy gates are rich-ly set with pearl, Thy streets are paved with gold.
Such daz-zling views by hu-man sight Have nev-er yet been seen.
Till Thou dost come to take us home To that blest par-a-dise.

ETERNAL LIFE

For All the Saints

421

SINE NOMINE 10.10.10. Alleluias

William W. How (1823-1897)

Ralph Vaughan Williams (1872-1958)

Unison

1. For all the saints who from their la - bors rest, Who Thee by faith be -
2. Thou wast their Rock, their For - tress and their Might; Thou, Lord, their captain
3. O may Thy sol - diers, faith-ful, true, and bold, Fight as the saints who
4. And when the strife is fierce, the war - fare long, Steals on the ear the
5. From earth's wide bounds, from ocean's farthest coast, Thro' gates of pearl streams

fore the world confessed, Thy name, O Je - sus, be for - ev - er blest.
in the well-fought fight; Thou, in the dark - ness drear, their one true light.
no - bly fought of old, And win with them the vic - tor's crown of gold.
dis - tant tri - umph song, And hearts are brave a - gain, and arms are strong.
in the count-less host, Sing-ing to Fa - ther, Son, and Ho - ly Ghost,

Al - le - lu - ia! Al - le - lu - ia!

Music from *The English Hymnal* by permission of Oxford University Press.

Alternate tune, ENGELBERG, No. 32

ETERNAL LIFE

422   Marching to Zion

S.M.Ref.

Isaac Watts, 1707 (1674-1748)   *Robert Lowry, 1867 (1826-1899)*

1. Come, we that love the Lord, And let our joys be known; Join
2. Let those re - fuse to sing Who nev - er knew our God; But
3. The hill of Zi - on yields A thou-sand sa - cred sweets, Be -
4. Then let our songs a-bound, And ev - ery tear be dry; We're

in a song with sweet ac - cord, Join in a song with sweet ac - cord,
chil-dren of the heaven-ly King, But chil - dren of the heaven-ly King,
fore we reach the heaven-ly fields, Be - fore we reach the heaven-ly fields,
march-ing through Im-man-uel's ground, We're march-ing through Im-man-uel's ground,

And thus sur - round the throne, And thus sur-round the throne.
May speak their joys a - broad, May speak their joys a - broad.
Or walk the gold - en streets, Or walk the gold - en streets.
To fair - er worlds on high, To fair - er worlds on high.

And thus sur-round the throne, And thus sur -round the throne.

Refrain

We're march - ing to Zi - on, Beau - ti-ful, beau - ti-ful Zi - on;
We're march-ing on to Zi - on,

We're march-ing up-ward to Zi - on, The beau-ti-ful cit-y of God.
heaven-ly Zi - on,

ETERNAL LIFE

Glorious Things of Thee Are Spoken 423

AUSTRIA 8.7.8.7.D.

John Newton, 1779 (1725-1807)

F. Joseph Haydn, 1797 (1732-1809)

1. Glo - rious things of thee are spo - ken, Zi - on, cit - y of our God;
2. See the streams of liv - ing wa - ters Spring-ing from e - ter - nal love,
3. Round each hab - i - ta - tion hover-ing, See the cloud and fire ap - pear
4. Sav - ior, if of Zi - on's cit - y I, through grace, a mem - ber am,

He whose word can - not be bro - ken Formed thee for His own a - bode;
Well sup - ply thy sons and daugh-ters, And all fear and want re - move;
For a glo - ry and a cover-ing, Show-ing that the Lord is near;
Let the world de - ride or pit - y, I will glo - ry in Thy name;

On the Rock of A - ges found - ed, What can shake thy sure re - pose?
Who can faint when such a riv - er Ever flows their thirst to as - suage?
Blest in - hab - it - ants of Zi - on, Washed in the Re-deem-er's blood;
Fad - ing is the world-ling's plea - sure, All his boast - ed pomp and show;

With sal - va -tion's wall sur-round-ed, Thou mayst smile at all thy foes.
Grace, which, like the Lord, the Giv - er, Nev - er fails from age to age.
Je - sus, whom their souls re - ly on, Makes them kings and priests to God.
Sol - id joys and last - ing trea-sure None but Zi - on's chil-dren know.

Alternate tune, ABBOT'S LEIGH, No. 61

ETERNAL LIFE

TSDAH-14

424   For Thee, O Dear, Dear Country

Rev. 21
Bernard of Cluny, c. 1145
Tr. by John Mason Neale, 1858 (1818-1866) alt.

ELY CATHEDRAL 7.6.7.6.D.
T. Tertius Noble, 1895 (1867-1953)

1. For thee, O dear, dear coun - try, Mine eyes their vig - ils keep;
2. O one, O on - ly man - sion! O Par - a - dise of joy!
3. With jas - per glow thy bul - warks, Thy streets with em - eralds blaze;
4. The cross is all thy splen - dor, The Cru - ci - fied thy praise;
5. O sweet and bless - ed coun - try, The home of God's e - lect!

Accomp.

For ve - ry love be - hold - ing Thy ho - ly name, they weep.
Where tears are ev - er ban - ish'd And smiles have no al - loy;
The sar - dius and the to - paz U - nite in thee their rays;
His laud and ben - e - dic - tion Thy ran - som'd saints shall raise;
O sweet and bless - ed coun - try That ea - ger hearts ex - pect!

ETERNAL LIFE

The men - tion of thy glo - ry Is unc - tion to the breast,
Thy love - li - ness op - press - es All hu - man thought and heart,
Thine age - less walls are bond - ed With am - e - thyst un - priced;
Up - on the Rock of A - ges They build thy ho - ly tower;
Je - sus, in mer - cy bring us To that dear land of rest,

And med - i - cine in sick - ness, And love, and life, and rest.
And none, O Peace, O Si - on, Can sing thee as thou art.
The saints shall build thy fab - ric, And the cor - ner - stone is Christ.
Thine is the vic - tor's lau - rel, And thine the gold - en dower.
Who art, with God the Fa - ther, And Spir - it, ev - er blest.

ETERNAL LIFE

425   Holy, Holy, Is What the Angels Sing

Johnson Oatman, Jr., 1894 (1856-1922)

8.7.8.7.D.Ref.

John R. Sweney (1837-1899)

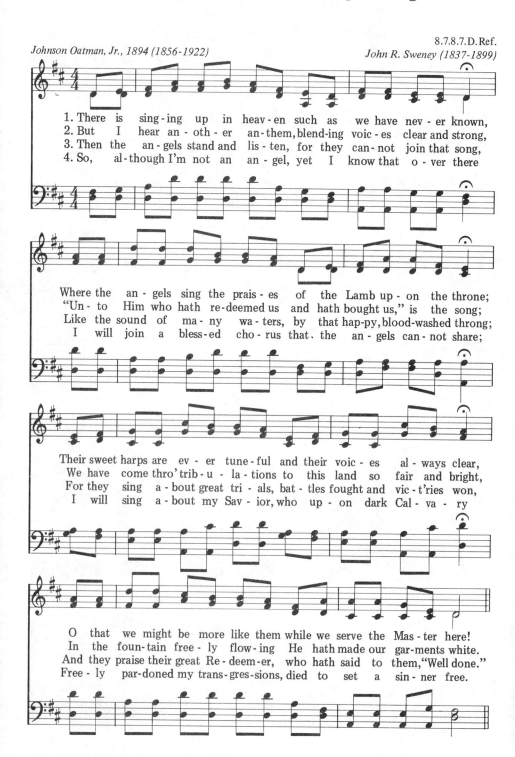

1. There is sing-ing up in heav-en such as we have nev-er known,
2. But I hear an-oth-er an-them, blend-ing voic-es clear and strong,
3. Then the an-gels stand and lis-ten, for they can-not join that song,
4. So, al-though I'm not an an-gel, yet I know that o-ver there

Where the an-gels sing the prais-es of the Lamb up-on the throne;
"Un-to Him who hath re-deemed us and hath bought us," is the song;
Like the sound of ma-ny wa-ters, by that hap-py, blood-washed throng;
I will join a bless-ed cho-rus that the an-gels can-not share;

Their sweet harps are ev-er tune-ful and their voic-es al-ways clear,
We have come thro' trib-u-la-tions to this land so fair and bright,
For they sing a-bout great tri-als, bat-tles fought and vic-t'ries won,
I will sing a-bout my Sav-ior, who up-on dark Cal-va-ry

O that we might be more like them while we serve the Mas-ter here!
In the foun-tain free-ly flow-ing He hath made our gar-ments white.
And they praise their great Re-deem-er, who hath said to them, "Well done."
Free-ly par-doned my trans-gres-sions, died to set a sin-ner free.

ETERNAL LIFE

Refrain

Ho - ly, ho - ly, is what the an - gels sing, And I ex - pect to

help them make the courts of heav-en ring; But when I sing re-demp-tion's sto- ry,

they will fold their wings, For an -gels nev-er felt the joys that our sal- va -tion brings.

426

I Shall See the King

10.7.10.7.Ref.

W. C. Poole (1875-1949)

B. D. Ackley (1872-1958)

1. I shall see the King Where the an-gels sing, I shall see the King some day, In the bet-ter land, On the gold-en strand, And with Him shall ev-er stay.

2. In the land of song, In the glo-ry throng, Where there nev-er comes a night, With my Lord once slain I shall ev-er reign In the glo-ry land of light.

3. I shall see the King, All my trib-utes bring, And shall look up-on His face; Then my song shall be How He ran-somed me And has kept me by His grace.

Refrain

In His glo-ry, I shall see the King, And for-ev-er end-less prais-es sing; 'Twas on Cal-va-ry Je-sus died for me; I shall see the King some day.

ETERNAL LIFE

No Night There

John R. Clements

7.6.7.6.Ref.
H. P. Danks (1834-1903)

1. In the land of fade-less day Lies "the cit-y four-square;" It shall
2. All the gates of pearl are made, In "the cit-y four-square;" All the
3. And the gates shall nev-er close To "the cit-y four-square;" There life's
4. There they need no sun-shine bright, In "that cit-y four-square," For the

Refrain

nev-er pass a-way, And there is "no night there." God shall "wipe
streets with gold are laid, And there is "no night there." God shall "wipe
crys-tal riv-er flows, And there is "no night there." God shall
Lamb is all the light, And there is "no night there."

a-way all tears;" There's no death, no pain, nor fears;
"wipe a-way all tears;" There's no death, no pain, nor fears;

And they count not time by years, For there is "no night there."
And they count not time by years, by years, For there is "no night there."

ETERNAL LIFE

428 Sweet By and By

S. F. Bennett, 1867 (1836-1898)

J. P. Webster, 1867 (1819-1875)

9.9.9.9.Ref.

1. There's a land that is fair-er than day, And by faith we can see it a-far; For the Fa-ther waits o-ver the way, To pre-pare us a dwell-ing place there.

2. We shall sing on that beau-ti-ful shore The me-lo-di-ous songs of the blest, And our spir-its shall sor-row no more, Not a sigh for the bless-ing of rest.

3. To our boun-ti-ful Fa-ther a-bove, We will of-fer a trib-ute of praise, For the glo-ri-ous gift of His love, And the bless-ings that hal-low our days.

Refrain

In the sweet by and by, We shall meet on that beau-ti-ful shore; In the sweet by and by, We shall meet on that beau-ti-ful shore.

In the sweet by and by, by and by, In the sweet by and by,

ETERNAL LIFE

Jerusalem the Golden

429

Bernard of Cluny, 12th century
Tr. by John M. Neale, 1851 (1818-1866)

EWING 7.6.7.6.D.
Alexander Ewing, 1853 (1830-1895)

1. Je - ru - sa - lem the gold - en, With milk and hon - ey blest,
2. They stand, those halls of Zi - on, All ju - bi - lant with song,
3. There is the throne of Da - vid, And there, from care re - leased,
4. O sweet and bless - ed coun - try, The home of God's e - lect!

Be - neath thy con - tem - pla - tion Sink heart and voice op - pressed.
And bright with man - y an an - gel, And all the mar - tyr throng.
The shout of them that tri - umph, The song of them that feast;
O sweet and bless - ed coun - try, That ea - ger hearts ex - pect!

I know not, O I know not What ho - ly joys are there;
The Prince is ev - er in them, The day - light is se - rene;
And they who, with their Lead - er, Have con - quered in the fight,
Je - sus, in mer - cy bring us To that dear land of rest;

What ra - di - ancy of glo - ry, What bliss be - yond com - pare.
The pas - tures of the bless - ed Are decked in glo - rious sheen.
For - ev - er and for - ev - er Are clad in robes of white.
Who art, with God the Fa - ther, And Spir - it, ev - er blest.

ETERNAL LIFE

430

Joy By and By

F. E. Belden (1858-1945)

Irregular
F. E. Belden, 1886

1. O there'll be joy when the work is done, Joy when the reap - ers
2. Sweet are the songs that we hope to sing, Grate - ful the thanks our
3. Pure are the joys that a - wait us there, Man - y the gold - en

gath - er home, Bring - ing the sheaves at set of sun To the
hearts shall bring, Prais - ing for - ev - er Christ our King In the
man - sions fair; Je - sus Him - self doth them pre - pare, In the

Refrain

New Je - ru - sa - lem. Joy, joy, there'll be joy by and by,
Joy, joy, joy, joy by and by,

Joy, joy, where the joys nev - er die; Joy, joy;
Joy, joy, joy, joys nev - er die; Joy, joy, joy,

for the day draw - eth nigh When the work - ers gath - er home.

ETERNAL LIFE

Over Yonder

431

7.6.7.7.Ref.

Henry de Fluiter, 1918 (1872-1970)

Henry de Fluiter, 1918

1. Come, let us sing of home-land, Down by the crys-tal sea;
2. Wa - ter of life there flow - eth, Fruit in a - bun - dant store;
3. Come go with me to home-land, Je - sus in-vites you there;

Won - der - ful land where Je - sus Build-eth a man-sion for me.
Cit - i - zens of that coun-try Hun - ger and thirst nev - er - more.
Help spread the in - vi - ta - tion, Tell it to men ev - ery-where.

Refrain

O - ver yon-der, down by the crys - tal sea,
down by the crys-tal sea,

O - ver yon-der,

There's where I long to be,
There's where I long to be,

No more sor - row, toil, grief, nor

care, In the home-land bright and fair, O - ver, o - ver there.

o - ver there.

ETERNAL LIFE

432 Shall We Gather at the River

Robert Lowry, 1864 (1826-1899)

8.7.8.7.Ref.
Robert Lowry, 1864

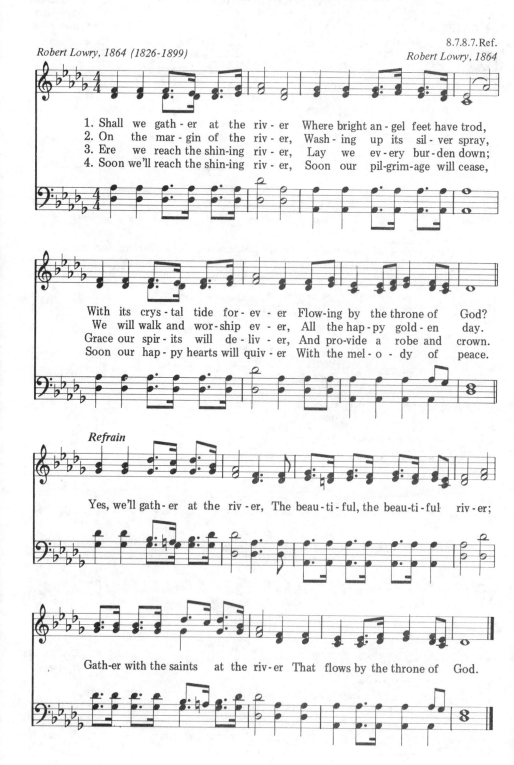

1. Shall we gath-er at the riv-er Where bright an-gel feet have trod,
2. On the mar-gin of the riv-er, Wash-ing up its sil-ver spray,
3. Ere we reach the shin-ing riv-er, Lay we ev-ery bur-den down;
4. Soon we'll reach the shin-ing riv-er, Soon our pil-grim-age will cease,

With its crys-tal tide for-ev-er Flow-ing by the throne of God?
We will walk and wor-ship ev-er, All the hap-py gold-en day.
Grace our spir-its will de-liv-er, And pro-vide a robe and crown.
Soon our hap-py hearts will quiv-er With the mel-o-dy of peace.

Refrain

Yes, we'll gath-er at the riv-er, The beau-ti-ful, the beau-ti-ful riv-er;

Gath-er with the saints at the riv-er That flows by the throne of God.

ETERNAL LIFE

Ten Thousand Times Ten Thousand 433

ALFORD 7.6.8.6.D.

H. Alford, 1867 (1810-1871)

John B. Dykes, 1866 (1823-1876)

1. Ten thou-sand times ten thou-sand, In spar-kling rai-ment bright,
The ar-mies of the ran-somed saints Throng up the steeps of light.
'Tis fin-ished, all is fin-ished, Their fight with death and sin.
Fling o-pen wide the gold-en gates, And let the vic-tors in.

2. What rush of hal-le-lu-jahs Fills all the earth and sky!
The ring-ing of a thou-sand harps Pro-claims the tri-umph high.
O day for which cre-a-tion And all its tribes were made!
O joy, for all its form-er woes A thou-sand-fold re-paid!

3. O then what rap-tured greet-ings On Ca-naan's hap-py shore!
What knit-ting sev-ered friend-ship where Death part-ings are no more!
Then eyes with joy shall spar-kle, That brimmed with tears of late;
Or-phans no lon-ger fa-ther-less, Nor wid-ows des-o-late.

4. Bring near Thy great sal-va-tion, Thou Lamb for sin-ners slain,
Fill up the roll of Thine e-lect, Then take Thy power and reign!
Ap-pear, De-sire of na-tions, Thine ex-iles long for home;
Show in the heavens Thy prom-ised sign; Thou Prince and Sav-ior, come!

ETERNAL LIFE

434   We Speak of the Realms

Elizabeth Mills (1805-1829)

CONTRAST L.M.D.
Early American Melody
Lewis Edson (1784-1820)

1. We speak of the realms of the blest, That coun-try so bright and so fair,
2. We speak of its free-dom from sin, From sor-row, temp-ta-tion and care,
3. Our mourn-ing is all at an end, When, raised by the life-giv-ing word,
4. Do Thou, midst temp-ta-tion and woe, For heav-en my spir-it pre-pare;

And oft are its glo-ries con-fessed— But what must it be to be there!
From tri-als with-out and with-in— But what must it be to be there!
We see the new cit-y de-scend, A-dorned as a bride for her Lord;
And short-ly I al-so shall know And feel what it is to be there.

We speak of its path-way of gold— Its walls decked with jew-els so rare,
We speak of its ser-vice of love, Of the robes which the glo-ri-fied wear,
The cit-y so ho-ly and clean, No sor-row can breathe in the air;
Then o'er the bright fields we shall roam, In glo-ry ce-les-tial and fair,

Its won-ders and plea-sures un-told— But what must it be to be there!
Of the church of the First-born above— But what must it be to be there!
No gloom of af-flic-tion or sin, No shad-ow of e-vil, is there.
With saints and with an-gels at home, And Je-sus Him-self will be there.

ETERNAL LIFE

The Glory Song

435

10.10.10.10.Ref.

Charles H. Gabriel, 1900 (1856-1932)

Charles H. Gabriel, 1900

1. When all my la-bors and tri-als are o'er, And I am safe on that
2. When, by the gift of His in-fi-nite grace, I am ac-cord-ed in
3. Friends will be there I have loved long a-go; Joy like a riv-er a-

beau-ti-ful shore, Just to be near the dear Lord I a-dore,
heav-en a place, Just to be there and to look on His face,
round me will flow, Yet, just a smile from my Sav-ior, I know,

Refrain

Will through the a-ges be glo-ry for me. O that will be

O that will

glo-ry for me, Glo-ry for me, glo-ry for me; When by His grace
be glo-ry for me, Glo-ry for me, glo-ry for me;

I shall look on His face, That will be glo-ry, be glo-ry for me.

ETERNAL LIFE

436

The Homeland

Rev. 21:1,4
Hugh R. Haweis, 1855 (1838-1901)

7.6.7.6.D.
George C. Stebbins, 1903 (1846-1945)

1. The home-land! O the home-land! The land of the free-born! There's no night in the home-land, But aye the fade-less morn; I'm sigh-ing for the home-land, My heart is ach-ing here; There is no pain in the home-land To which I'm draw-ing near;

2. My Lord is in the home-land, With an-gels bright and fair; There's no sin in the home-land, And no temp-ta-tion there; The mu-sic of the home-land Is ring-ing in my ears; And when I think of the home-land My eyes are filled with tears;

3. The dwell-ers in the home-land Are beckon-ing me to come, Where nei-ther death nor sor-row In-vades their ho-ly home; O dear, dear na-tive coun-try! O rest and peace a-bove! Christ bring us all to the home-land Of Thy re-deem-ing love;

ETERNAL LIFE

There is no pain in the home - land To which I'm draw - ing near.
And when I think of the home - land My eyes are filled with tears.
Christ bring us all to the home - land Of Thy re - deem - ing love.

I'm Going Home

437

L.M.Ref.

Rev. 21:4
William Hunter (1811-1877)

William Miller, 19th century
Arr. by William McDonald (1820-1901)

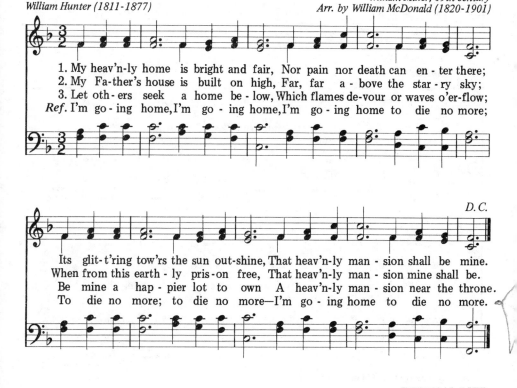

1. My heav'n-ly home is bright and fair, Nor pain nor death can en - ter there;
2. My Fa-ther's house is built on high, Far, far a - bove the star - ry sky;
3. Let oth - ers seek a home be - low, Which flames de-vour or waves o'er-flow;
Ref. I'm go - ing home, I'm go - ing home, I'm go - ing home to die no more;

D.C.

Its glit-t'ring tow'rs the sun out-shine, That heav'n-ly man - sion shall be mine.
When from this earth - ly pris-on free, That heav'n-ly man - sion mine shall be.
Be mine a hap - pier lot to own A heav'n-ly man - sion near the throne.
To die no more; to die no more—I'm go - ing home to die no more.

ETERNAL LIFE

438 You Will See Your Lord A-Coming

8.8.8.5.Ref.

Early Advent hymn sung by James White
Arr. by Wayne Hooper, 1984 (1920-   )

From Millennial Harp, 1843

1. You will see your Lord a - com - ing, You will see your Lord a -
2. Ga - briel sounds his might - y trum - pet, Ga - briel sounds his might - y
3. You will see the saints a - ris - ing, You will see the saints a -
4. An - gels bear them to the Sav - ior, An - gels bear them to the
5. Then we'll shout, our suf - f'rings o - ver, Then we'll shout our suf - f'rings

com - ing, You will see your Lord a - com - ing In a few more days.
trum - pet, Ga - briel sounds his might - y trum - pet In a few more days.
ris - ing, You will see the saints a - ris - ing In a few more days.
Sav - ior, An - gels bear them to the Sav - ior In a few more days.
o - ver, Then we'll shout, our suf - f'rings o - ver In a few more days.

Refrain

Hear the band of mu - sic, Hear the band of mu - sic,
(heav'n - ly band) (heav'n - ly band)

Hear the band of mu - sic which is sound - ing thro' the air.
(heav'n - ly band)

Arrangement copyright © 1984 by Wayne Hooper.

EARLY ADVENT

How Far From Home?

TIS MIDNIGHT HOUR 8.8.8.6.D.

Annie R. Smith, 1853 (1828-1855)

Arranged

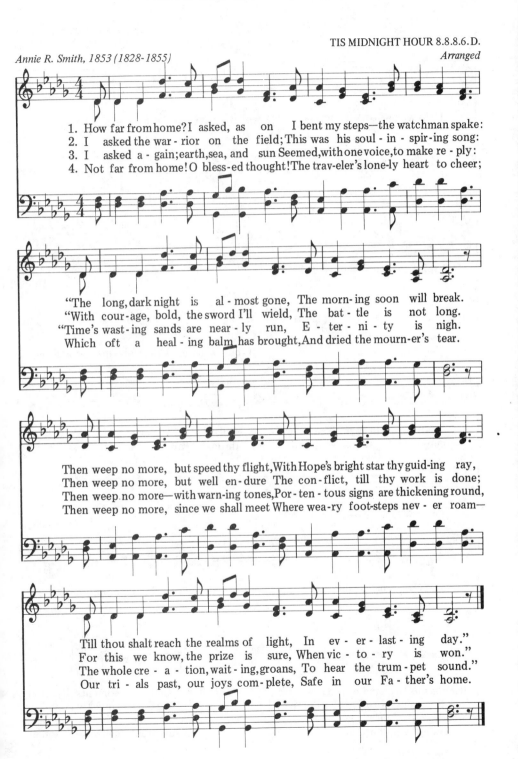

1. How far from home? I asked, as on I bent my steps—the watchman spake:
2. I asked the war-rior on the field; This was his soul-in-spir-ing song:
3. I asked a-gain; earth, sea, and sun Seemed, with one voice, to make re-ply:
4. Not far from home! O bless-ed thought! The trav-eler's lone-ly heart to cheer;

"The long, dark night is al-most gone, The morn-ing soon will break.
"With cour-age, bold, the sword I'll wield, The bat-tle is not long.
"Time's wast-ing sands are near-ly run, E-ter-ni-ty is nigh.
Which oft a heal-ing balm has brought, And dried the mourn-er's tear.

Then weep no more, but speed thy flight, With Hope's bright star thy guid-ing ray,
Then weep no more, but well en-dure The con-flict, till thy work is done;
Then weep no more—with warn-ing tones, Por-ten-tous signs are thickening round,
Then weep no more, since we shall meet Where wea-ry foot-steps nev-er roam—

Till thou shalt reach the realms of light, In ev-er-last-ing day."
For this we know, the prize is sure, When vic-to-ry is won."
The whole cre-a-tion, wait-ing, groans, To hear the trum-pet sound."
Our tri-als past, our joys com-plete, Safe in our Fa-ther's home.

EARLY ADVENT

440 How Cheering Is the Christian's Hope

EXHORTATION C.M.
S. Hibbard, 1869

Anon.

1. How cheer - ing is the Chris - tian's hope, While toil - ing here be - low! It buoys us up while passing through This wil - der - ness of woe, It buoys us up while pass - ing through This wil - der - ness of woe, buoys us up while pass - ing through This wil - der - ness of woe.

2. It points us to a land of rest,
    Where saints with Christ will reign;
    Where we shall meet the loved of earth,
    And never part again.

3. Fly, lingering moments, fly, O, fly,
    Dear Savior, quickly come!
    We long to see Thee as Thou art,
    And reach that blissful home.

EARLY ADVENT

I Saw One Weary

441

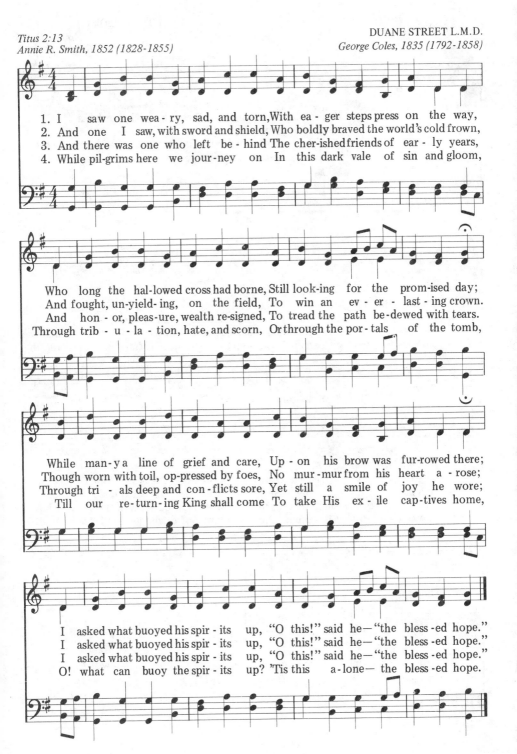

EARLY ADVENT

442 How Sweet Are the Tidings

BONNIE ELOISE 12.8.12.8. Ref.
Arranged from
John R. Thomas, 1858

Anon.

1. How sweet are the tid-ings that greet the pil-grim's ear, As he
2. The moss-y old graves where the pil - grims sleep Shall be
3. There we'll meet ne'er to part in our hap-py E - den home, Sweet
4. Hal - le - lu - jah, A - men! hal - le - lu - jah a - gain! Soon, if

wan - ders in ex - ile from home! Soon, soon will the Sav - ior in
o - pen as wide as be - fore, And the mil - lions that sleep in the
songs of re - demp - tion we'll sing; From the north, from the south, all the
faith - ful, we all shall be there; O, be watch - ful, be hope - ful, be

glo - ry ap - pear, And soon will the king-dom come.
might - y deep Shall live on this earth once more.
ran - somed shall come, And wor - ship our heaven - ly King.
joy - ful till then, And a crown of bright glo - ry we'll wear.

Refrain

He's com - ing, com - ing, com - ing soon I know, Com - ing

EARLY ADVENT

back to this earth a-gain; And the wea-ry pil-grims will to glo-ry go, When the Sav-ior comes to reign.

There'll Be No Sorrow There 443

Rev. 21:4
Frederick D. Huntington (1819-1904)

NO SORROW THERE S.M.
E. W. Dunbar, c. 1850s

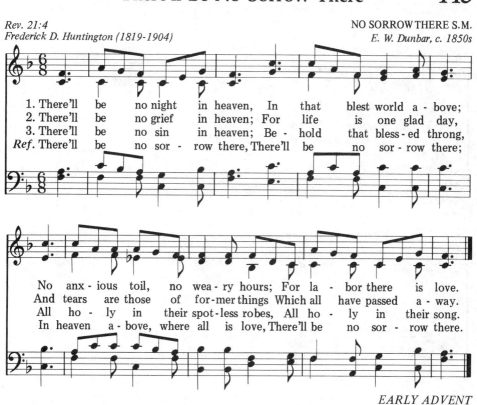

1. There'll be no night in heaven, In that blest world a-bove;
2. There'll be no grief in heaven; For life is one glad day,
3. There'll be no sin in heaven; Be-hold that bless-ed throng,
Ref. There'll be no sor-row there, There'll be no sor-row there;

No anx-ious toil, no wea-ry hours; For la-bor there is love.
And tears are those of for-mer things Which all have passed a-way.
All ho-ly in their spot-less robes, All ho-ly in their song.
In heaven a-bove, where all is love, There'll be no sor-row there.

EARLY ADVENT

I'm a Pilgrim

Mary S. B. Dana, 1841 (1810-1883)

9.11.10.10.Ref.
Arr. from an Italian air

1. I'm a pil - grim, and I'm a stran - ger; I can tar - ry, I can
2. There the glo - ry is ev - er shin - ing! O, my long - ing heart, my
3. There's the cit - y to which I jour - ney; My Re - deem - er, my Re -

tar - ry but a night; Do not de - tain me, for I am go - ing
long - ing heart is there; Here in this coun - try so dark and drear - y,
deem - er is its light! There is no sor - row, nor an - y sigh - ing,

Refrain

To where the foun - tains are ev - er flow - ing.
I long have wan - dered for - lorn and wea - ry.   I'm a pil - grim, and
Nor an - y tears there, or an - y dy - ing.

I'm a stran - ger; I can tar - ry, I can tar - ry but a night.

EARLY ADVENT

I'm But a Stranger Here

OAK 6.4.6.4.6.6.6.4.

445

Thomas R. Taylor, 1835

Lowell Mason, 1854 (1792-1872)

1. I'm but a stran - ger here, Heaven is my home;
2. What though the tem - pest rage, Heaven is my home;
3. There at my Sav - ior's side, Heaven is my home;

Earth is a des - ert drear, Heaven is my home;
Short is my pil - grim - age, Heaven is my home.
I shall be glo - ri - fied, Heaven is my home.

Dan - ger and sor - row stand Round me on ev - ery hand;
Time's cold and win - try blast Soon will be o - ver - past;
There'll be the good and blest, Those I love most and best,

Heaven is my Fa - ther - land, Heaven is my home.
I shall reach home at last; Heaven is my home.
There, too, I soon shall rest; Heaven is my home.

EARLY ADVENT

446 Lo, What a Glorious Sight Appears

Rev. 21:1-4
Isaac Watts, 1707 (1674-1748)

NEW JERUSALEM C.M.Ref.
Attr. to Abraham D. Merrill (1796-1878)

1. Lo, what a glo-rious sight ap-pears To our be-liev-ing eyes! The earth and seas are passed a-way, And the old roll-ing skies. And the old roll-ing skies, And the old roll-ing skies; The earth and seas are

2. At-tend-ing an-gels shout for joy And the bright ar-mies sing— Mor-tals! be-hold the sa-cred seat Of your de-scend-ing King. Of your de-scend-ing King, Of your de-scend-ing King; Mor-tals! be-hold the

3. His own soft hand shall wipe the tears From ev-ery weep-ing eye; And pains, and groans, and griefs, and fears, And death it-self shall die! And death it-self shall die, And death it-self shall die; And pains, and groans, and

4. How long, dear Sav-ior! oh, how long Shall this bright hour de-lay? Fly swift-er round, ye wheels of time! And bring the wel-come day. And bring the wel-come day, And bring the wel-come day; Fly swift-er round, ye

passed a way, And the old roll - ing skies.
sa - cred seat Of your de - scend - ing King.
griefs, and fears, And death it - self shall die.
wheels of time! And bring the wel - come day.

Refrain

O that will be joy - ful, joy - ful, joy - ful!

O that will be joy - ful When we meet to part no more!

When we meet to part no more on Ca-naan's hap - py shore; 'Tis

there we'll meet at Je - sus' feet, When we meet to part no more!

EARLY ADVENT

447 Long Upon the Mountains

Eze. 34:12
Annie R. Smith, 1851 (1828-1855)

GREENVILLE 8.7.8.7.D.
Jean J. Rousseau, 1752 (1712-1778)

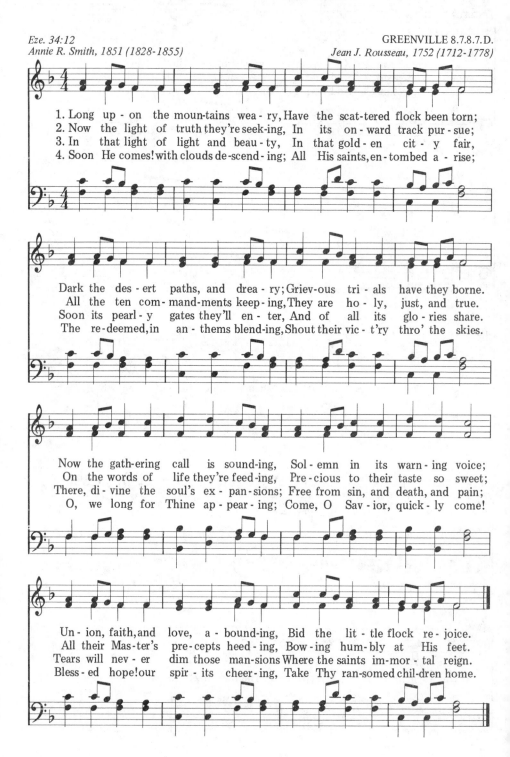

1. Long up-on the moun-tains wea-ry, Have the scat-tered flock been torn;
2. Now the light of truth they're seek-ing, In its on-ward track pur-sue;
3. In that light of light and beau-ty, In that gold-en cit-y fair,
4. Soon He comes! with clouds de-scend-ing; All His saints, en-tombed a-rise;

Dark the des-ert paths, and drea-ry; Griev-ous tri-als have they borne.
All the ten com-mand-ments keep-ing, They are ho-ly, just, and true.
Soon its pearl-y gates they'll en-ter, And of all its glo-ries share.
The re-deemed, in an-thems blend-ing, Shout their vic-t'ry thro' the skies.

Now the gath-ering call is sound-ing, Sol-emn in its warn-ing voice;
On the words of life they're feed-ing, Pre-cious to their taste so sweet;
There, di-vine the soul's ex-pan-sions; Free from sin, and death, and pain;
O, we long for Thine ap-pear-ing; Come, O Sav-ior, quick-ly come!

Un-ion, faith, and love, a-bound-ing, Bid the lit-tle flock re-joice.
All their Mas-ter's pre-cepts heed-ing, Bow-ing hum-bly at His feet.
Tears will nev-er dim those man-sions Where the saints im-mor-tal reign.
Bless-ed hope! our spir-its cheer-ing, Take Thy ran-somed chil-dren home.

EARLY ADVENT

O, When Shall I See Jesus 448

THE MORNING TRUMPET 13.11.13.11.

From The Sacred Harp, *1844*

John Leland, Early 19th century

Arr. by Melvin West, 1984 (1930-   )

1. O, when shall I see Je - sus and reign with Him a - bove, And shall
2. Gird on the gos - pel ar - mor of faith and hope and love, And you'll
3. Our ears shall hear with trans - port the host of heav - en sing, And shall

hear the trum-pet sound in that morn - ing? And from the flow - ing
hear the trum-pet sound in that morn - ing. And when the com-bat's
hear the trum-pet sound in that morn - ing. Our tongues shall chant the

foun - tain drink ev - er - last - ing love, And shall hear the trum-pet
end - ed He'll car - ry you a - bove, And you'll hear the trum-pet
glo - ries of our im - mor - tal King, And shall hear the trum-pet

Refrain

sound in that morn - ing. O, shout, glo - ry! For I shall mount a-bove the

skies, When I hear the trum-pet sound in that morn - ing.

Arrangement copyright © 1984 by Melvin West.

EARLY ADVENT

449   Never Part Again

C.M.Ref.

From Timbrel of Zion, *1853*
Arr. by Donald F. Haynes (1907-1975)

Isaac Watts (1674-1748)

1. There is a land of pure de-light, Where bliss e-ter-nal reigns,
2. There ev-er-last-ing spring a-bides, And nev-er with-'ring flowers,
3. Could we but stand where Mos-es stood, And view the land-scape o'er,

In-fi-nite day ex-cludes the night And plea-sures ban-ish pain.
And but a lit-tle space di-vides This heav-'nly land from ours.
Not all this world's pre-tend-ed good Could ev-er charm us more.

Refrain

We're trav-'ling to Im-man-uel's land, We soon shall hear the trum-pet sound,

And soon we shall with Je-sus reign, And nev-er, nev-er part a-gain.

What! Nev-er part a-gain? No, nev-er part a-gain, What!

Arrangement used by permission of Dona Haynes Schultz.

EARLY ADVENT

Nev-er part a-gain? No, nev-er part a-gain, And soon we shall with Je-sus reign, And, nev-er, nev-er part a-gain.

Beautiful Zion

450

L.M.

From Hymns and Tunes..., *1869*
Arr. by Wayne Hooper, 1984 (1920-   )

Anon.

1. Beau-ti-ful Zi - on, built a - bove, Beau-ti-ful cit - y that I love,
2. Beau-ti-ful trees for-ev - er there, Beau-ti-ful fruit they al - ways bear,
3. Beau-ti-ful crowns on ev - ery brow, Beau-ti-ful palms the con-querors show,

Beau-ti-ful gates of pearl-y white, Beau-ti-ful tem - ple, God its light.
Beau-ti-ful riv - ers glid - ing by, Beau-ti-ful foun-tains nev-er dry.
Beau-ti-ful robes the ran-somed wear, Beau-ti-ful all who en - ter there.

EARLY ADVENT

451 Together Let Us Sweetly Live

CANAAN 8.9.8.9.Ref.
Early Advent Hymn

Millennial Harp, *1843*

Arr. by Melvin West 1984 (1930-   )

1. To - geth - er let us sweet - ly live, I am bound for the land of Ca - naan.
2. To - geth - er let us watch and pray; I am bound for the land of Ca - naan.
3. Our songs of praise shall fill the skies; I am bound for the land of Ca - naan.
4. Then come with me, be - lov - ed friend; I am bound for the land of Ca - naan.

To - geth - er love to Je - sus give; I am bound for the land of Ca - naan.
And wait re - demp - tion's joy - ous day; I am bound for the land of Ca - naan.
While high - er still our joys shall rise; I am bound for the land of Ca - naan.
The joys to come shall nev - er end; I am bound for the land of Ca - naan.

Refrain

O Ca - naan, bright Ca - naan, I am bound for the land of Ca - naan. O

Ca - naan, it is my hap - py home, I am bound for the land of Ca - naan.

EARLY ADVENT

What Heavenly Music

452

EARLY ADVENT

TSDAH-15

453

We Have Heard

W. H. Hyde, 1850

WE HAVE HEARD P.M.
Unknown

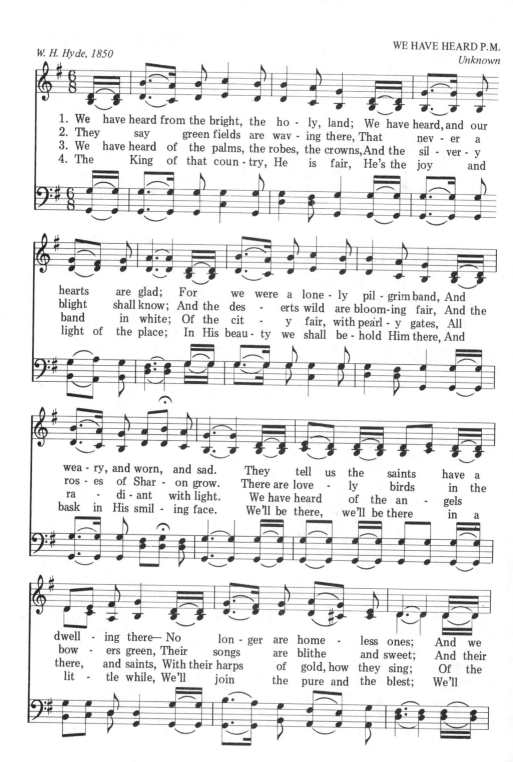

1. We have heard from the bright, the ho - ly, land; We have heard, and our
2. They say green fields are wav - ing there, That nev - er a
3. We have heard of the palms, the robes, the crowns, And the sil - ver - y
4. The King of that coun - try, He is fair, He's the joy and

hearts are glad; For we were a lone - ly pil - grim band, And
blight shall know; And the des - erts wild are bloom-ing fair, And the
band in white; Of the cit - y fair, with pearl - y gates, All
light of the place; In His beau - ty we shall be - hold Him there, And

wea - ry, and worn, and sad. They tell us the saints have a
ros - es of Shar - on grow. There are love - ly birds in the
ra - di - ant with light. We have heard of the an - gels
bask in His smil - ing face. We'll be there, we'll be there in a

dwell - ing there— No lon - ger are home - less ones; And we
bow - ers green, Their songs are blithe and sweet; And their
there, and saints, With their harps of gold, how they sing; Of the
lit - tle while, We'll join the pure and the blest; We'll

EARLY ADVENT

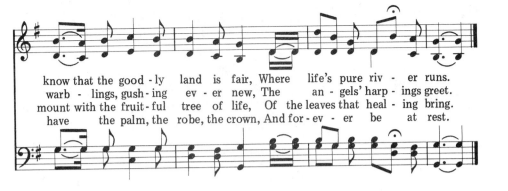

know that the good - ly land is fair, Where life's pure riv - er runs.
warb - lings, gush - ing ev - er new, The an - gels' harp - ings greet.
mount with the fruit - ful tree of life, Of the leaves that heal - ing bring.
have the palm, the robe, the crown, And for - ev - er be at rest.

Don't You See My Jesus Coming? 454

WARRENTON 8.7.8.7.Ref.

Hymns and Spiritual Songs . . ., 1812
Millennial Harp, 1843

C. C. Abbott's Pocket Companion, 1822
Arr. by Wayne Hooper, 1984 (1920-)

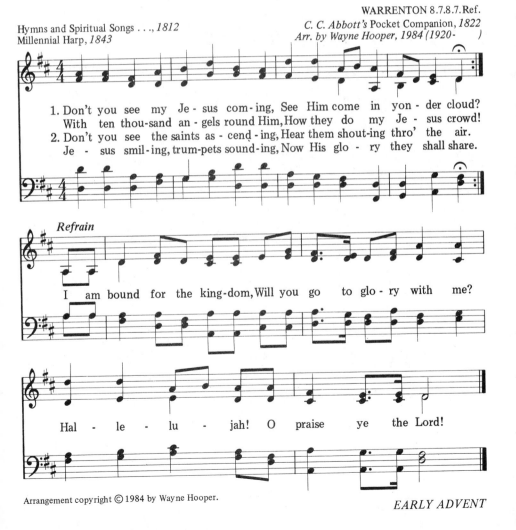

1. Don't you see my Je - sus com - ing, See Him come in yon - der cloud?
With ten thou-sand an - gels round Him, How they do my Je - sus crowd!
2. Don't you see the saints as - cend - ing, Hear them shout-ing thro' the air.
Je - sus smil - ing, trum-pets sound - ing, Now His glo - ry they shall share.

Refrain

I am bound for the king-dom, Will you go to glo - ry with me?

Hal - le - lu - jah! O praise ye the Lord!

EARLY ADVENT

455 Immortal Love, Forever Full

John Greenleaf Whittier (1807-1892)

SERENITY C.M.
Arr. from William V. Wallace (1814-1865)

1. Im - mor - tal Love, for - ev - er full, For-ev - er flow-ing free, For-ev - er shared, for-ev - er whole, A nev - er ebb-ing sea!
2. We may not climb the heaven-ly steeps To bring the Lord Christ down; In vain we search the low - est deeps, For Him no depths can drown.
3. But warm, sweet, ten - der, e - ven yet A pres - ent help is He; And faith has still its Ol - i - vet, And love its Gal - i - lee.
4. The heal - ing of His seam - less dress Is by our beds of pain; We touch Him in life's throng and press, And we are whole a - gain.
5. Through Him the first fond prayers are said, Our lips of child-hood frame; The last low whis - pers of our dead Are bur - dened with His name.
6. O Lord and Mas - ter of us all: What-e'er our name or sign, We own Thy sway, we hear Thy call, We test our lives by Thine!

My Lord and I

456

6.8.6.8.6.7.4.

Mary Ann Shorey, 1890 (1851- ?)

Hubert P. Main (1839-1925)

1. I have a Friend so pre-cious, So ver-y dear to me,
2. Some-times I'm faint and wea-ry, He knows that I am weak,
3. I tell Him all my sor-rows, I tell Him all my joys,
4. He knows that I am long-ing Some wea-ry soul to win,

He loves me with such ten-der love, He loves so faith-ful-ly;
And as He bids me lean on Him, His help I glad-ly seek;
I tell Him all that pleas-es me, I tell Him what an-noys,
And so He bids me go and speak The lov-ing word for Him;

I could not live a-part from Him, I love to feel Him nigh,
He leads me in the paths of light, Be-neath a sun-ny sky,
He tells me what I ought to do, He tells me how to try,
He bids me tell His won-drous love, And why He came to die,

And so we dwell to-geth-er, My Lord and I.
And so we walk to-geth-er, My Lord and I.
And so we talk to-geth-er, My Lord and I.
And so we work to-geth-er, My Lord and I.

OUR LOVE FOR GOD

457 I Love to Tell the Story

Katherine Hankey, 1866 (1834-1911)

7.6.7.6.D.Ref.
William G. Fischer, 1869 (1835-1912)

1. I love to tell the sto - ry Of un - seen things a - bove,
2. I love to tell the sto - ry; More won - der - ful it seems
3. I love to tell the sto - ry; 'Tis pleas - ant to re - peat
4. I love to tell the sto - ry; For those who know it best

Of Je - sus and His glo - ry, Of Je - sus and His love;
Than all the gold - en fan - cies Of all our gold - en dreams;
What seems each time I tell it, More won - der - ful ly sweet;
Seem hun - ger - ing and thirst - ing To hear it like the rest;

I love to tell the sto - ry, Be - cause I know 'tis true;
I love to tell the sto - ry, It did so much for me,
I love to tell the sto - ry, For some have nev - er heard
And when in scenes of glo - ry I sing the new, new song,

1 It sat - is - fies my long - ing As noth - ing else can do.
2 And that is just the rea - son I tell it now to thee.
3 The mes - sage of sal - va - tion From God's own ho - ly word.
4 'Twill be the old, old sto - ry That I have loved so long.

Refrain

I love to tell the sto - ry; 'Twill be my theme in glo - ry

To tell the old, old sto - ry Of Je - sus and His love.

458

More Love to Thee

Mrs. E. Prentiss, 1856 (1818-1878)

6.4.6.4.6.6.6.4.
William H. Doane, 1868 (1832-1915)

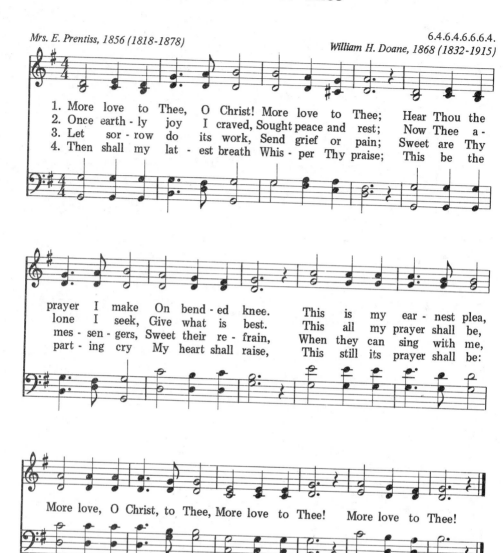

1. More love to Thee, O Christ! More love to Thee; Hear Thou the
2. Once earth-ly joy I craved, Sought peace and rest; Now Thee a-
3. Let sor-row do its work, Send grief or pain; Sweet are Thy
4. Then shall my lat-est breath Whis-per Thy praise; This be the

prayer I make On bend-ed knee. This is my ear-nest plea,
lone I seek, Give what is best. This all my prayer shall be,
mes-sen-gers, Sweet their re-frain, When they can sing with me,
part-ing cry My heart shall raise, This still its prayer shall be:

More love, O Christ, to Thee, More love to Thee! More love to Thee!

OUR LOVE FOR GOD

As the Bridegroom to His Chosen 459

From John Tauler (1300-1361)
Tr. Emma F. Bevan, 1858

BRIDEGROOM 8.7.8.7.6.
Peter Cutts, 1969 (1937-   )

Unison

1. As the bride-groom to his cho - sen, as the king un - to his
2. As the foun - tain in the gar - den, as the can - dle in the
3. As the ru - by in the set - ting, as the hon - ey in the
4. As the sun - shine in the heav - ens, as the im-age in the

realm, As the keep un - to the cas - tle, as the
dark, As the trea - sure in the cof - fer, as the
comb, As the light with - in the lan - tern, as the
glass, As the fruits up - on the fig tree, as the

pi - lot to the helm, So, Lord, art Thou to me.
man-na in the ark, So, Lord, art Thou to me.
fa-ther in the home, So, Lord, art Thou to me.
dew up-on the grass, So, Lord, art Thou to me.

OUR LOVE FOR GOD

460 As Water to the Thirsty

Timothy Dudley-Smith (1926-   )

OASIS 7.6.7.6.6.6.4.4.6.

T. Brian Coleman (1920-   )

Unison

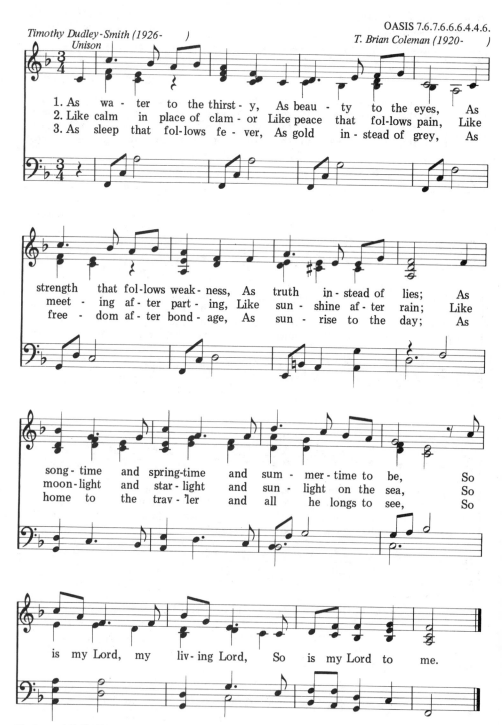

1. As wa - ter to the thirst - y, As beau - ty to the eyes, As
2. Like calm in place of clam - or Like peace that fol-lows pain, Like
3. As sleep that fol-lows fe - ver, As gold in - stead of grey, As

strength that fol-lows weak - ness, As truth in - stead of lies; As
meet - ing af - ter part - ing, Like sun - shine af - ter rain; Like
free - dom af - ter bond - age, As sun - rise to the day; As

song - time and spring-time and sum - mer - time to be, So
moon - light and star - light and sun - light on the sea, So
home to the trav - 'ler and all he longs to see, So

is my Lord, my liv - ing Lord, So is my Lord to me.

OUR LOVE FOR GOD

Be Still, My Soul

461

Psalm 46:10; 1 Thess. 4:17
Katharina von Schlegel, 1752 (1697-?   )
Tr. by Jane Borthwick, 1855 (1813-1897)

FINLANDIA 10.10.10.10.10.10.
Jean Sibelius, 1899 (1865-1957)

1. Be still, my soul: the Lord is on thy side; Bear pa-tient-ly the
2. Be still, my soul: thy God doth un-der-take To guide the fu-ture
3. Be still, my soul: the hour is has-tening on When we shall be for-

cross of grief or pain; Leave to thy God to or-der and pro-vide;
as He has the past. Thy hope, thy con-fi-dence let noth-ing shake;
ev-er with the Lord, When dis-ap-point-ment, grief, and fear are gone,

In ev-ery change He faith-ful will re-main. Be still, my soul: thy
All now mys-te-rious shall be bright at last. Be still, my soul: the
Sor-row for-got, love's pur-est joys re-stored. Be still, my soul: when

best, thy heaven-ly friend Through thorn-y ways leads to a joy-ful end.
waves and winds still know His voice who ruled them while He dwelt be-low.
change and tears are past, All safe and bless-ed we shall meet at last.

Melody used by permission of Breitkopf & Härtel, Wiesbaden. Arrangement copyright 1933 by the Presbyterian Board of
Christian Education; renewed 1961; from *The Hymnal*. Used by permission of Westminster Press, Philadelphia, PA.

JOY AND PEACE

462   Blessed Assurance, Jesus Is Mine!

Fanny J. Crosby, 1873 (1820-1915)

9.10.9.9.Ref.

Mrs. Joseph F. Knapp, 1873 (1839-1908)

1. Bless-ed as-sur-ance, Je-sus is mine!   O, what a fore-taste
2. Per-fect sub-mis-sion, per-fect de-light,   Vi-sions of rap-ture
3. Per-fect sub-mis-sion, all is at rest,   I in my Sav-ior

of glo-ry di-vine!   Heir of sal-va-tion, pur-chase of God,
now burst on my sight.   An-gels de-scend-ing bring from a-bove
am hap-py and blest,   Watch-ing and wait-ing, look-ing a-bove,

Refrain

Born of His Spir-it, washed in His blood.
Ech-oes of mer-cy, whis-pers of love.   This is my sto-ry,
Filled with His good-ness, lost in His love.

this is my song,   Prais-ing my Sav-ior all the day long;   This is my

JOY AND PEACE

sto - ry, this is my song, Prais-ing my Sav - ior all the day long.

Peace, Perfect Peace

463

PAX TECUM 10.10.
George T. Caldbeck (1852-1918)
Arr. by Charles J. Vincent, 1877(1852 -1934)

Isa. 26:3
Edward H. Bickersteth, 1875 (1825-1906)

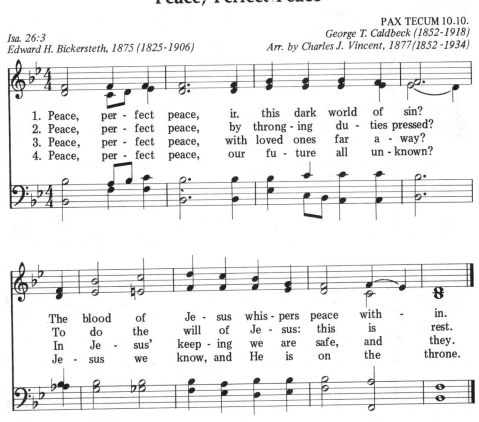

1. Peace, per - fect peace, in this dark world of sin?
2. Peace, per - fect peace, by throng - ing du - ties pressed?
3. Peace, per - fect peace, with loved ones far a - way?
4. Peace, per - fect peace, our fu - ture all un - known?

The blood of Je - sus whis - pers peace with - in.
To do the will of Je - sus: this is rest.
In Je - sus' keep - ing we are safe, and they.
Je - sus we know, and He is on the throne.

JOY AND PEACE

464 When I Can Read My Title Clear

PISGAH 8.6.8.6.6.6.8.6.

Isaac Watts, 1707 (1674-1748)

Traditional American melody
Arr. by Wayne Hooper, 1984 (1920-   )

1. When I can read my ti-tle clear To man-sions in the skies
2. Should earth a-gainst my soul en-gage, And fi-ery darts be hurled,
3. Let cares like a wild del-uge come, And storms of sor-row fall!

I'll bid fare-well to ev-ery fear, And wipe my weep-ing eyes;
Then I can smile at Sa-tan's rage, And face a frown-ing world;
May I but safe-ly reach my home, My God, my heav'n, my all;

And wipe my weep-ing eyes, And wipe my weep-ing eyes,
And face a frown-ing world, And face a frown-ing world,
My God, my heav'n, my all, My God, my heav'n, my all,

I'll bid fare-well to ev-ery fear, And wipe my weep-ing eyes.
Then I can smile at Sa-tan's rage, And face a frown-ing world.
May I but safe-ly reach my home, My God, my heav'n, my all.

Arrangement copyright © 1984 by Wayne Hooper.

JOY AND PEACE

I Heard the Voice of Jesus

KINGSFOLD C.M.D.
Mel. coll. by Lucy Broadwood
Arr. by Ralph Vaughan Williams (1872-1958)

Horatius Bonar (1808-1889)

1. I heard the voice of Je-sus say, "Come un-to Me and rest;
2. I heard the voice of Je-sus say, "Be - hold, I free-ly give
3. I heard the voice of Je-sus say, "I am this dark world's light;

Lay down, thou wea-ry one, lay down Thy head up-on My breast."
The liv-ing wa-ter; thirst-y one, Stoop down and drink and live."
Look un-to Me, thy morn shall rise, And all thy day be bright."

I came to Je-sus as I was, Wea-ry and worn and sad,
I came to Je-sus, and I drank Of that life-giv-ing stream;
I looked to Je-sus, and I found In Him my star, my sun;

I found in Him a rest-ing place, And He has made me glad.
My thirst was quench'd, my soul re-vived, And now I. live in Him.
And in that light of life I'll walk, Till trav-'ling days are done.

Music from *The English Hymnal* by permission of Oxford University Press.

JOY AND PEACE

466 Wonderful Peace

W. D. Cornell; alt. 1889

12.9.12.9.Ref.
W. G. Cooper (1840-1927)

1. Far a - way in the depths of my spir - it to - night, Rolls a
2. What a trea - sure I have in this won - der - ful peace, Bur - ied
3. I be - lieve when I rise to that cit - y of peace, Where the
4. Wea - ry soul, with-out glad - ness or com - fort or rest, Pass - ing

mel - o - dy sweet - er than psalm; In ce - les - tial - like strains it un -
deep in my in - ner - most soul, So se - cure that no pow - er can
Au - thor of peace I shall see, That one strain of the song which the
down the rough path-way of time! Make the Sav - ior your friend ere the

ceas - ing - ly falls O'er my soul like an in - fi - nite calm.
mine it a - way, While the years of e - ter - ni - ty roll!
ran-somed will sing, In that heav - en - ly king - dom will be—
shad - ows grow dark; O ac - cept of this peace so sub - lime.

Refrain

Peace! peace! won-der-ful peace, Com-ing down from the Fa-ther a-bove; Sweep

o - ver my spir-it for - ev-er, I pray, In fath-om-less bil-lows of love.

JOY AND PEACE

Life Is Great! So Sing About It

467

LITHEROP 8.7.8.7.8.7.

Brian Wren (1936-   )

Peter Cutts, 1970 (1937-   )

1. Life is great! so sing a-bout it, As we can and as we should— Shops and bus - es, towns and peo - ple, Vil - lage, farm - land, field and wood. Life is great and life is giv - en; Life is love - ly, free and good.
2. Life is great!—what ev - er hap - pens, Snow or sun - shine, joy or pain, Hard - ship, grief or dis - il - lu - sion, Suf - fering that I can't ex - plain— Life is great if some-one loves me, Holds my hand and calls my name.
3. Love is great!—the love of lov - ers, Whis-pered words and long - ing eyes; Love that gaz - es at the cra - dle Where a child of lov - ing lies; Love that lasts when youth has fad - ed, Bends with age, but nev - er dies.
4. Love is giv - ing and re-ceiv - ing— Boy and girl, or friend with friend; Love is bear - ing and for-giv - ing Love that suf - fered, hoped and trust - ed way of liv - ing, Hop - ing, trust - ing to the end.
5. God is great! in Christ He loved us, As we should, but nev - er can— Love that suf - fered, hoped and trust - ed When dis - ci - ples turned and ran, Love that broke through death for - ev - er. Praise that lov - ing, liv - ing Man!

Alternate tune, LAUDA ANIMA, No. 4

JOY AND PEACE

468

A Child of the King

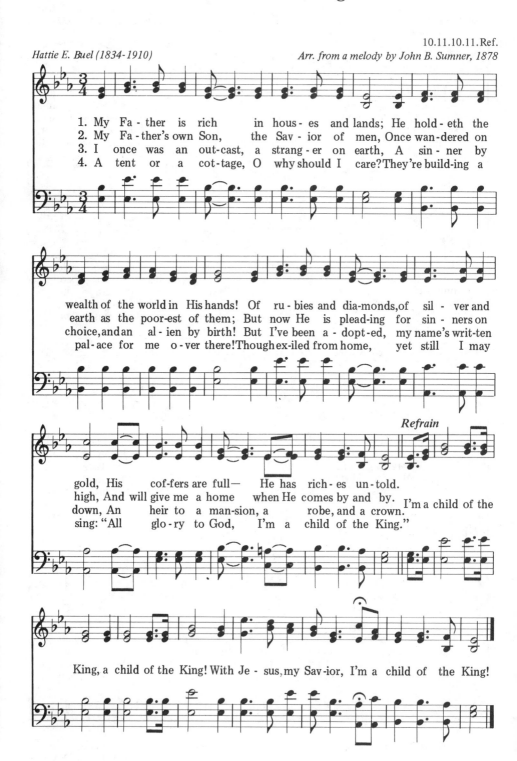

JOY AND PEACE

Leaning on the Everlasting Arms

469

Deut. 33:27
E. A. Hoffman, 1887 (1839-1929)

10.9.10.9.Ref.
A. J. Showalter (1858-1924)

1. What a fel-low-ship, what a joy di-vine, Lean-ing on the
2. O how sweet to walk in this pil-grim way, Lean-ing on the
3. What have I to dread, what have I to fear, Lean-ing on the

ev-er-last-ing arms; What a bless-ed-ness, what a peace is mine,
ev-er-last-ing arms; O how bright the path grows from day to day,
ev-er-last-ing arms? I have bless-ed peace with my Lord so near,

Refrain

Lean-ing on the ev-er-last-ing arms. Lean - ing,
Lean-ing on the ev-er-last-ing arms.
Lean-ing on the ev-er-last-ing arms. Lean-ing on Je - sus,

lean - ing, Safe and se-cure from all a-larms; Lean -
lean-ing on Je - sus, Lean-ing on

ing, lean - ing, Lean-ing on the ev-er-last-ing arms.
Je - sus, lean-ing on Je - sus,

JOY AND PEACE

470   There's Sunshine in My Soul Today

C.M.Ref.

E. E. Hewitt (1851-1920)

John R. Sweney (1837-1899)

1. There's sun-shine in my soul to-day, More glo-ri-ous and bright
2. There's mu-sic in my soul to-day, A car-ol to my King,
3. There's spring-time in my soul to-day, For when the Lord is near,
4. There's glad-ness in my soul to-day, And hope, and praise, and love,

Than glows in an-y earth-ly sky, For Je-sus is my light.
And Je-sus, lis-ten-ing, can hear The songs I can-not sing.
The dove of peace sings in my heart, The flowers of grace ap-pear.
For bless-ings which He gives me now, For joys "laid up" a-bove.

Refrain

O there's sun - shine, bless - ed sun - shine,
sun-shine in the soul, bless - ed sun-shine in the soul,

When the peace - ful, hap-py mo-ments roll;
hap-py mo-ments roll,

When Je-sus shows His smil-ing face There is sun-shine in the soul.

JOY AND PEACE

Grant Us Your Peace

Latin source unknown
English, Ottilie Stafford; French, Marcel Pichot
Spanish, Espi Wasmer

Attr. to Palestrina (1525-1594)
Accomp. by Melvin West, 1984 (1930-   )

1. Do - na   no - bis   pa - cem, pa - cem;   Do - na
2. Fa - ther,   grant   us,   grant us Your peace;   Oh, lov - ing
3. Ac - cor - de - nous   ta   paix, ta paix;   Ac - cor -
4. Pa - dre,   da - nos   tu   paz, tu paz;   Pa - dre,

no - bis   pa - cem.   Do - na   no - bis   pa - cem;
Fa - ther, grant   us Your peace.   Grant   us,   grant   us peace;
de - nous   ta   paix.   Ac - cor - de - nous ta paix;
da - nos, da - nos tu paz.   Pa - dre,   da - nos tu paz;

Do - na   no - bis   pa - cem.   Do - na
Grant us,   grant us,   grant   us Your peace.   Grant   us,
Ac - cor - de - nous   ta   paix.   Ac - cor -
Pa - dre,   da - nos,   da - nos tu   paz.   Pa - dre,

no - bis   pa - cem;   Do - na   no - bis   pa - cem.
grant   us   peace;   Lov - ing   Fa - ther,   grant   us Your peace.
de - nous   ta paix;   Ac - cor - de - nous   ta   paix.
da - nos   tu paz;   Pa - dre,   da - nos,   da - nos tu   paz.

*Accomp.

*Accompaniment may repeat either or both of these scores for the duration of the canon.
Arrangement copyright © 1984 by Melvin West.

JOY AND PEACE

472 A Song of Heaven and Homeland

7.6.7.6.D.Ref.
E. E. Rexford (1848-1916)
Ira D. Sankey (1840-1908)

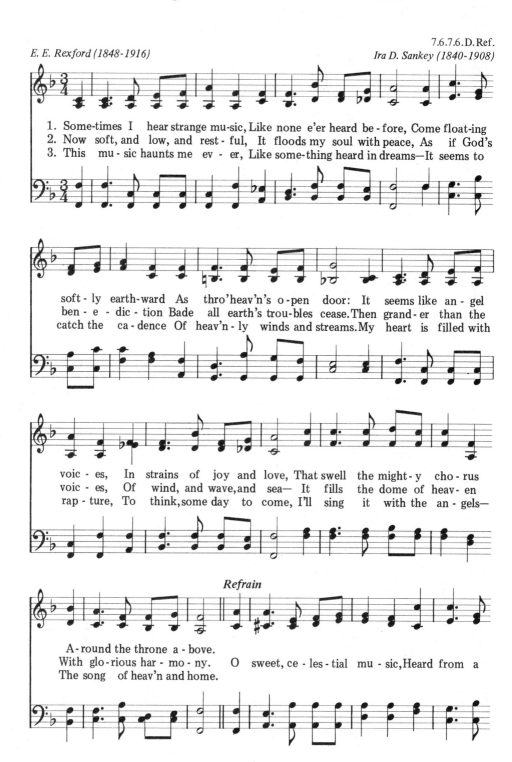

1. Some-times I hear strange mu-sic, Like none e'er heard be-fore, Come float-ing
2. Now soft, and low, and rest-ful, It floods my soul with peace, As if God's
3. This mu-sic haunts me ev-er, Like some-thing heard in dreams—It seems to

soft-ly earth-ward As thro' heav'n's o-pen door: It seems like an-gel
ben-e-dic-tion Bade all earth's trou-bles cease. Then grand-er than the
catch the ca-dence Of heav'n-ly winds and streams. My heart is filled with

voic-es, In strains of joy and love, That swell the might-y cho-rus
voic-es, Of wind, and wave, and sea— It fills the dome of heav-en
rap-ture, To think, some day to come, I'll sing it with the an-gels—

Refrain

A-round the throne a-bove.
With glo-rious har-mo-ny. O sweet, ce-les-tial mu-sic, Heard from a
The song of heav'n and home.

HOPE AND COMFORT

land a - far—The song of Heav'n and Home-land, Thro' doors God leaves a - jar!

Nearer My God, to Thee

473

Gen. 28:10-19
Sarah F. Adams, 1841 (1805-1848)

BETHANY 6.4.6.4.6.6.6.4.
Lowell Mason, 1856 (1792-1872)

1. Near - er, my God, to Thee, Near - er to Thee! E'en though it be a cross That rais-eth me! Still all my song shall be, Near - er, my God, to Thee, Near - er, my God, to Thee, Near - er to Thee.

2. Though like a wan - der - er, Day - light all gone, Dark - ness be o - ver me, My rest a stone; Yet in my dreams I'd be Near - er, my God, to Thee, Near - er, my God, to Thee, Near - er to Thee.

3. There let the way ap - pear, Steps up to heaven; All that Thou send-est me, In mer-cy given; An - gels to beck - on me Near - er, my God, to Thee, Near - er, my God, to Thee, Near - er to Thee.

4. Then, with my wak - ing thoughts Bright with Thy praise, Out of my ston - y griefs Beth - el I'll raise; So by my woes to be Near - er, my God, to Thee, Near - er, my God, to Thee, Near - er to Thee.

5. Or if, on joy - ful wing Cleav - ing the sky, Sun, moon, and stars for - got, Up - ward I fly, Still all my song shall be, Near - er, my God, to Thee, Near - er, my God, to Thee, Near - er to Thee.

HOPE AND COMFORT

474 Take the Name of Jesus With You

8.7.8.7.Ref.

Lillian Baxter, 1870 (1809-1874)

William H. Doane, 1871 (1832-1915)

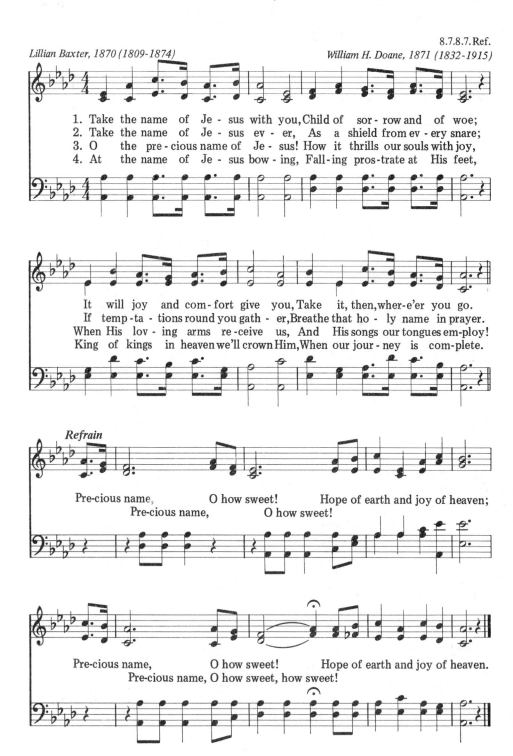

1. Take the name of Je-sus with you, Child of sor-row and of woe;
2. Take the name of Je-sus ev-er, As a shield from ev-ery snare;
3. O the pre-cious name of Je-sus! How it thrills our souls with joy,
4. At the name of Je-sus bow-ing, Fall-ing pros-trate at His feet,

It will joy and com-fort give you, Take it, then, wher-e'er you go.
If temp-ta-tions round you gath-er, Breathe that ho-ly name in prayer.
When His lov-ing arms re-ceive us, And His songs our tongues em-ploy!
King of kings in heaven we'll crown Him, When our jour-ney is com-plete.

Refrain

Pre-cious name, O how sweet! Hope of earth and joy of heaven;
Pre-cious name, O how sweet!

Pre-cious name, O how sweet! Hope of earth and joy of heaven.
Pre-cious name, O how sweet, how sweet!

HOPE AND COMFORT

Balm in Gilead

Jeremiah 8:22
American Negro Spiritual

C.M.D.

There is a balm in Gil-e-ad to make the wound-ed whole;

Fine

There is a balm in Gil-e-ad to heal the sin-sick soul.

1. Some - times I feel dis - cour -aged, And   think my work's in   vain,
2. If   you can - not preach like Pe - ter, If you can - not pray like Paul,

D. C. Fine

But   then the Ho - ly Spir - it Re-vives my soul a - gain.
You can tell the love of Je - sus, And say He died for   all.

HOPE AND COMFORT

Burdens Are Lifted at Calvary

8.6.9.6.Ref.

John M. Moore (1925-   )

John M. Moore

1. Days are filled with sor-row and care, Hearts are lone-ly and drear;
2. Cast your care on Je-sus to-day, Leave your wor-ry and fear;
3. Trou-bled soul, the Sav-ior can see Ev-ery heart-ache and tear;

Bur-dens are lift-ed at Cal-va-ry, Je-sus is ver-y near.
Bur-dens are lift-ed at Cal-va-ry, Je-sus is ver-y near.
Bur-dens are lift-ed at Cal-va-ry, Je-sus is ver-y near.

Refrain

Bur-dens are lift-ed at Cal-va-ry, Cal-va-ry, Cal-va-ry;

Bur-dens are lift-ed at Cal-va-ry, Je-sus is ver-y near.

HOPE AND COMFORT

Come, Ye Disconsolate

477

Thomas Moore, 1816 (1779-1852)
St. 3, Thomas Hastings, 1831 (1784-1872)

CONSOLATOR 11.10.11.10.
German Melody
Arr. by Samuel Webbe, 1792 (1740-1816)

1. Come, ye dis-con-so-late, wher-e'er ye lan-guish;
2. Joy of the com-fort-less, light of the stray-ing,
3. Here see the Bread of Life; see wa-ters flow-ing

Come to the mer-cy seat, fer-vent-ly kneel;
Hope of the pen-i-tent, fade-less and pure!
Forth from the throne of God, pure from a-bove;

Here bring your wound-ed hearts, here tell your an-guish;
Here speaks the Com-fort-er, ten-der-ly say-ing,
Come to the feast of love— come, ev-er know-ing

Earth has no sor-row that heaven can-not heal.
"Earth has no sor-row that heaven can-not cure."
Earth has no sor-row but heaven can re-move.

HOPE AND COMFORT

478 Sweet Hour of Prayer

SWEET HOUR L.M.D.

William W. Walford, c. 1842 (1772-1850)

William B. Bradbury, 1859 (1816-1868)

1. Sweet hour of prayer, sweet hour of prayer, That calls me from a world of care,
2. Sweet hour of prayer! sweet hour of prayer! Thy wings shall my pe - ti - tion bear
3. Sweet hour of prayer! sweet hour of prayer! May I thy con - so - la - tion share

And bids me, at my Fa - ther's throne, Make all my wants and wish - es known!
To Him whose truth and faith - ful - ness En - gage the wait - ing soul to bless.
Till from Mount Pis-gah's loft - y height I view my home and take my flight.

In sea - sons of dis - tress and grief, My soul has oft - en found re - lief,
And since He bids me seek His face, Be - lieve His word, and trust His grace,
In my im - mor - tal flesh I'll rise To seize the ev - er - last - ing prize.

And oft es - caped the tempt-ers snare, By thy re - turn, sweet hour of prayer.
I'll cast on Him my ev - ery care, And wait for thee, sweet hour of prayer.
And shout while pass - ing through the air, "Fare-well, fare-well, sweet hour of prayer!"

MEDITATION AND PRAYER

Tread Softly

6.5.6.5.Ref.

Fanny J. Crosby (1820-1915)

William H. Doane (1832-1915)

1. Be si - lent, be si - lent, A whis - per is heard;
2. Be si - lent, be si - lent, For ho - ly this place,
3. Be si - lent, be si - lent, Breathe hum - bly our prayer;
4. Be si - lent, be si - lent, His mer - cy re - cord;

Be si - lent, and lis - ten, Oh, trea - sure each word.
This al - tar that ech - oes The mes - sage of grace.
A fore - taste of E - den This mo - ment we share.
Be si - lent, be si - lent, And wait on the Lord.

Refrain

Tread soft - ly, tread soft - ly, The Mas - ter is here;
Tread soft - ly here, tread soft - ly here,

Tread soft - ly, tread soft - ly, He bids us draw near.
Tread soft - ly here, tread soft - ly here,

MEDITATION AND PRAYER

480 Dear Lord and Father

REPTON 8.6.8.8.6.

John Greenleaf Whittier, 1872 (1807-1892)

Charles H. H. Parry (1848-1918)

1. Dear Lord and Fa-ther of man-kind, For-give our fool-ish
2. In sim-ple trust like theirs who heard, Be-side the Sy-rian
3. O Sab-bath rest by Gal-i-lee, O calm of hills a-
4. Drop Thy still dews of qui-et-ness, Till all our striv-ings
5. Breathe thro' the heats of our de-sire, Thy cool-ness and Thy

ways; Re-clothe us in our right-ful mind, In pur-er lives Thy
sea, The gra-cious call-ing of the Lord, Let us, like them, with-
bove, Where Je-sus knelt to share with Thee The si-lence of e-
cease; Take from our souls the strain and stress, And let our or-dered
balm; Let sense be dumb, let flesh re-tire; Speak thro' the earth-quake,

ser-vice find, In deep-er rev-erence praise, In deep-er rev-erence, praise.
out a word, Rise up and fol-low Thee, Rise up and fol-low Thee.
ter-ni-ty, In-ter-pret-ed by love, In-ter-pret-ed by love.
lives con-fess The beau-ty of Thy peace, The beau-ty of Thy peace.
wind, and fire, O still small voice of calm, O still small voice of calm.

481 Dear Lord and Father

REST 8.6.8.8.6.

John Greenleaf Whittier, 1872 (1807-1892)

F. C. Maker, 1887 (1844-1927)

Dear Lord and Fa-ther of man-kind, For-give our fever-ish

MEDITATION AND PRAYER

ways; Re - clothe us in our right - ful mind In pur - er lives Thy ser - vice find, In deep - er rev - erence praise.

Alternate tune and additional stanzas, REPTON, No. 480

Father, Lead Me Day by Day 482

POSEN 7.7.7.7.

John P. Hopps, 1876 (1834-1912)

George C. Strattner, 1691 (1650-1704)

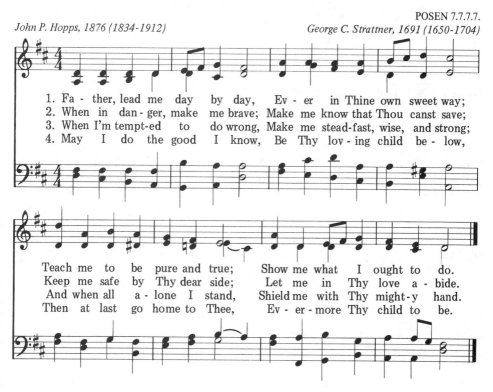

1. Fa - ther, lead me day by day, Ev - er in Thine own sweet way;
2. When in dan - ger, make me brave; Make me know that Thou canst save;
3. When I'm tempt - ed to do wrong, Make me stead-fast, wise, and strong;
4. May I do the good I know, Be Thy lov - ing child be - low,

Teach me to be pure and true; Show me what I ought to do.
Keep me safe by Thy dear side; Let me in Thy love a - bide.
And when all a - lone I stand, Shield me with Thy might-y hand.
Then at last go home to Thee, Ev - er - more Thy child to be.

MEDITATION AND PRAYER

483   I Need Thee Every Hour

6.4.6.4.Ref.

Annie S. Hawks, 1872 (1835-1918)   Robert Lowry, 1872 (1826-1899)

1. I need Thee ev-ery hour, Most gra - cious Lord;
2. I need Thee ev-ery hour, Stay Thou near by;
3. I need Thee ev-ery hour, In joy or pain;
4. I need Thee ev-ery hour, Teach me Thy will,

No ten - der voice like Thine Can peace af - ford.
Temp - ta - tions lose their power When Thou art nigh.
Come quick - ly, and a - bide, Or life is vain.
And Thy rich prom - is - es In me ful - fill.

Refrain

I need Thee, O I need Thee; Ev - ery hour I need Thee!

O bless me now, my Sav - ior— I come to Thee.

MEDITATION AND PRAYER

I Need Thee, Precious Jesus

RUTHERFORD 7.6.7.6.D.
Chretien D'Urhan, 1834 (1788-1845)
Arr. by Edward F. Rimbault, 1867 (1816-1876)

Frederick Whitefield, 1855 (1829-1904)

1. I need Thee, pre - cious Je - sus, For I am ver - y poor;
2. I need the heart of Je - sus To feel each anx - ious care,
3. I need Thee, pre - cious Je - sus, I hope to see Thee soon,

A stran - ger and a pil - grim, I have no earth - ly store.
To tell my ev - ery tri - al, And all my sor - rows share.
En - cir - cled with the rain - bow, And seat - ed on Thy throne.

I need the love of Je - sus To cheer me on my way,
I need the Ho - ly Spir - it. To teach me what I am,
There, with Thy blood-bought chil - dren, My joy shall ev - er be

To guide my doubt - ing foot - steps, To be my strength and stay.
To show me more of Je - sus, To point me to the Lamb.
To sing Thy cease - less prais - es, To gaze, my Lord, on Thee!

MEDITATION AND PRAYER

485   I Must Tell Jesus

Elisha A. Hoffman (1839-1929)

10.9.10.9.Ref.
Elisha A. Hoffman

1. I must tell Je - sus all of my tri - als; I can - not bear these
2. I must tell Je - sus all of my trou - bles, He is a kind, com -
3. O how the world to e - vil al - lures me! O how my heart is

bur - dens a - lone, In my dis - tress He kind - ly will help me,
pas - sion - ate Friend; If I but ask Him, He will de - liv - er,
tempt - ed to sin! I must tell Je - sus, and He will help me

Refrain

He ev - er loves and cares for His own.
Makes of my trou - bles quick - ly an end.   I must tell Je - sus! I must tell
O - ver the world the vic - t'ry to win.

Je - sus! I can - not bear my bur - dens a - lone; I must tell

MEDITATION AND PRAYER

Je - sus! I must tell Je - sus! Je - sus can help me, Je - sus a - lone.

I Do Believe 486

I DO BELIEVE C.M.

Charles Wesley, 1741 (1707-1788)

Arranged

1. Fa - ther, I stretch my hands to Thee; No oth - er help I know;
2. On Thy dear Son I now be - lieve, O let me feel Thy power;
3. Au - thor of faith! to Thee I lift My wea - ry, long - ing eyes;
4. Sure - ly Thou canst not let me die; O speak, and I shall live;
5. How would my faint - ing soul re - joice Could I but see Thy face!
6. I do be - lieve, I now be - lieve That Je - sus died for me,

If Thou with-draw Thy - self from me, Ah, whith - er shall I go?
And all my var - ied wants re - lieve, In this ac - cept - ed hour.
O let me now re - ceive that gift; My soul with-out it dies.
And here I will un - wea - ried lie, Till Thou Thy Spir - it give.
Now let me hear Thy quick-ening voice, And taste Thy par - doning grace.
And that He shed His pre-cious blood From sin to set me free.

MEDITATION AND PRAYER

487   In the Garden

John 20:15-17
C. Austin Miles, 1912 (1868-1946)

Irregular
C. Austin Miles, 1912

1. I come to the gar-den a-lone, While the dew is still on the ros - es; And the voice I hear, fall-ing on my ear, The Son of God dis-clos - es.

2. He speaks, and the sound of His voice Is so sweet the birds hush their sing - ing, And the mel - o - dy that He gave to me With-in my heart is ring - ing.

3. I'd stay in the gar-den with Him Though the night a-round me be fall - ing, But He bids me go; through the voice of woe, His voice to me is call - ing.

Refrain

And He walks with me, and He talks with me, And He tells me I am His own; And the

MEDITATION AND PRAYER

joy we share as we tar - ry there, None oth-er has ev-er known.

At First I Prayed for Light

488

WOOLWICH S.M.

Mrs. E. D. Cheney (1824-1904)

C. E. Kettle (1833-1927)

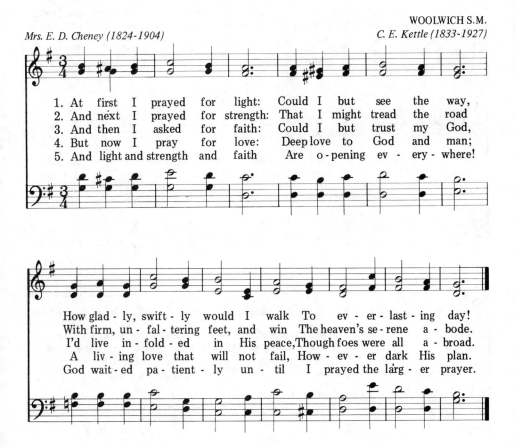

1. At first I prayed for light: Could I but see the way,
2. And next I prayed for strength: That I might tread the road
3. And then I asked for faith: Could I but trust my God,
4. But now I pray for love: Deep love to God and man;
5. And light and strength and faith Are o - pening ev - ery - where!

How glad - ly, swift - ly would I walk To ev - er - last - ing day!
With firm, un - fal - tering feet, and win The heaven's se - rene a - bode.
I'd live in - fold - ed in His peace, Though foes were all a - broad.
A liv - ing love that will not fail, How - ev - er dark His plan.
God wait - ed pa - tient - ly un - til I prayed the larg - er prayer.

MEDITATION AND PRAYER

Jesus, Lover of My Soul

MARTYN 7.7.7.7.D.

Charles Wesley, 1740 (1707-1788)

Simeon B. Marsh, 1834 (1798-1875) alt.

1. Je - sus, lov - er of my soul, Let me to Thy bos - om fly,
2. Oth - er ref - uge have I none, Hangs my help - less soul on Thee;
3. Thou, O Christ, art all I want, More than all in Thee I find;
4. Plen - teous grace with Thee is found— Grace to par - don all my sin;

While the bil - lows near me roll, While the tem - pest still is high;
Leave, O leave me not a - lone! Still sup - port and com - fort me;
Raise the fall - en, cheer the faint, Heal the sick, and lead the blind.
Let the heal - ing streams a - bound, Make and keep me pure with - in;

Hide me, O my Sav - ior, hide! Till the storm of life is past;
All my trust on Thee is stayed, All my help from Thee I bring;
Just and ho - ly is Thy name, I am all un right-teous-ness;
Thou of life the Foun - tain art, Free - ly let me take of Thee;

Safe in - to the ha - ven guide, O re - ceive my soul at last!
Cov - er my de-fense - less head With the shad - ow of Thy wing.
Vile and full of sin I am, Thou art full of truth and grace.
Spring Thou up with - in my heart, Rise to all e - ter - ni - ty.

Alternate tune, REFUGE, No. 297

MEDITATION AND PRAYER

Jesus, Lover of My Soul

HOLLINGSIDE 7.7.7.7.D.

Charles Wesley, 1740 (1707-1788)

John B. Dykes, 1861 (1823-1876)

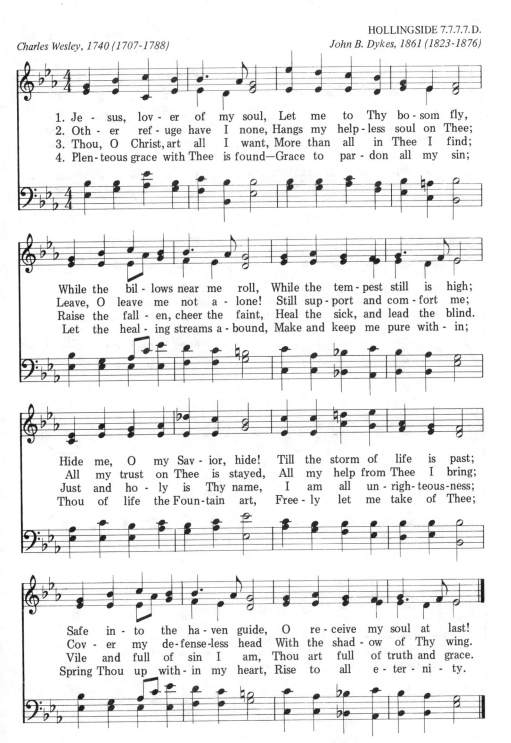

1. Je - sus, lov - er of my soul, Let me to Thy bo - som fly,
2. Oth - er ref - uge have I none, Hangs my help - less soul on Thee;
3. Thou, O Christ, art all I want, More than all in Thee I find;
4. Plen - teous grace with Thee is found—Grace to par - don all my sin;

While the bil - lows near me roll, While the tem - pest still is high;
Leave, O leave me not a - lone! Still sup - port and com - fort me;
Raise the fall - en, cheer the faint, Heal the sick, and lead the blind.
Let the heal - ing streams a - bound, Make and keep me pure with - in;

Hide me, O my Sav - ior, hide! Till the storm of life is past;
All my trust on Thee is stayed, All my help from Thee I bring;
Just and ho - ly is Thy name, I am all un - righ - teous - ness;
Thou of life the Foun - tain art, Free - ly let me take of Thee;

Safe in - to the ha - ven guide, O re - ceive my soul at last!
Cov - er my de - fense - less head With the shad - ow of Thy wing.
Vile and full of sin I am, Thou art full of truth and grace.
Spring Thou up with - in my heart, Rise to all e - ter - ni - ty.

Alternate tune, ABERYSTWYTH, No. 592

MEDITATION AND PRAYER

491

In the Hour of Trial

James Montgomery, 1834 (1771-1854)

PENITENCE 6.5.6.5.D.
Spencer Lane, 1879 (1843-1903)

1. In the hour of tri - al, Je - sus, plead for me,
2. With for - bid - den plea - sures, Would this vain world charm;
3. Should Thy mer - cy send me Sor - row, toil, and woe,

Lest by base de - ni - al I de - part from Thee;
Or its sor - did trea - sures Spread to work me harm;
Or should pain at - tend me On my path be - low,

When Thou see'st me wa - ver, With a look re - call,
Bring to my re - mem - brance Sad Geth - sem - a - ne,
Grant that I may nev - er Fail Thy hand to see;

Nor, for fear or fa - vor, Suf - fer me to fall.
Or, in dark - er sem - blance, Cross-crowned Cal - va - ry.
Grant that I may ev - er Cast my care on Thee.

MEDITATION AND PRAYER

Like Jesus

7.7.7.6.Ref.

A. D. Ellington
Ref. by Harold A. Miller

Harold A. Miller, 1931 (1891-1966)
Arr. by Wayne Hooper, 1984, (1920-   )

1. Teach, me, Fa - ther, what to say; Teach me, Fa - ther, how to pray;
2. Teach me as the days go by, Teach me not to rea - son why,
3. Teach me that the time is short, Teach me how to live and work,
4. Teach me how we may be one, Like the Fa - ther and the Son;

Teach me all a - long the way How to be like Je - sus.
Teach me that to do and die, Is to be like Je - sus.
Teach me that to nev - er shirk Is to be like Je - sus.
And when all is o - ver-come, I will be like Je - sus.

Refrain

I would be like Je - sus, I would be like Je - sus!

Help me, Lord, to dai - ly grow More and more like Je - sus!

MEDITATION AND PRAYER

493 Fill My Cup, Lord

Richard Blanchard (1925-)

Irregular
Richard Blanchard

1. Like the wom-an at the well I was seek-ing For things that
2. There are mil-lions in this world who are crav-ing The plea - sure
3. So, my chil-dren, if the things this world gave you Leave hun - gers

could not sat - is - fy; And then I heard my Sav - ior speak-ing: "Draw
earth - ly things af - ford; But none can match the won-drous trea-sure
that won't pass a - way, My bless - ed Lord will come and save you,

Refrain

from My well that nev - er shall run dry."
That I find in Je - sus Christ my Lord. Fill my cup, Lord, I lift it
If you kneel to Him and hum - bly pray:

up, Lord! Come and quench this thirst-ing of my soul; Bread of heav-en,

feed me till I want no more—Fill my cup, fill it up and make me whole!

MEDITATION AND PRAYER

We Would See Jesus

494

John 12:21
Anna B. Warner (1820-1915)

11.10.11.10.
F. E. Belden (1858-1945)

1. "We would see Je - sus;" for the shad - ows length - en
2. "We would see Je - sus," Rock of our sal - va - tion,
3. "We would see Je - sus;" oth - er lights are pal - ing,
4. "We would see Je - sus;" this is all we're need - ing—

A - cross the lit - tle land - scape of our life;
Where - on our feet were set with sov - ereign grace;
Which for long years we did re - joice to see;
Strength, joy, and will - ing - ness come with the sight;

We would see Je - sus, our weak faith to strength - en
Not life, nor death, with all their ag - i - ta - tion,
The bless - ings of this sin - ful world are fail - ing;
We would see Je - sus, dy - ing, ris - en, plead - ing,

For the last con - flict, in this mor - tal strife.
Can thence re - move us, gaz - ing on His face.
We would not mourn them, in ex - change for Thee.
Soon to re - turn and end this mor - tal night!

MEDITATION AND PRAYER

Near to the Heart of God

C.M.Ref.

Cleland B. McAfee (1866-1944)

Cleland B. McAfee, 1901

1. There is a place of qui - et rest, Near to the heart of God,
2. There is a place of com - fort sweet, Near to the heart of God,
3. There is a place of full re - lease, Near to the heart of God,

A place where sin can - not mo - lest, Near to the heart of God.
A place where we our Sav - ior meet, Near to the heart of God.
A place where all is joy and peace, Near to the heart of God.

Refrain

O Je - sus, blest Re - deem - er, Sent from the heart of God,

Hold us, who wait be - fore Thee, Near to the heart of God.

MEDITATION AND PRAYER

Eternal Love, We Have No Good

496

Rev. 8:3
Amy Carmichael (1867-1951)

ETERNAL LOVE 11.10.11.10.
Kenneth S. Proctor, 1960 (1895-   )

Unison

1. E - ter - nal Love,   we have no good to bring   Thee,
2. And yet we come;   and when our faith would fal - ter

No sin - gle good of all our hands   have wrought,
Show us, O Love, the qui - et place   of prayer,

No wor - thy mu - sic have we found to sing   Thee,
The gold - en cen - ser and the gold - en al - tar,

No jew - elled word, no quick up - soar - ing thought.
And the great an - gel wait - ing for us there.

From *Wings* by Amy Carmichael. Copyright by Dohnavur Fellowship.

MEDITATION AND PRAYER

497   O Gracious Father of Mankind

HALIFAX C.M.D.

George Frederick Handel, 1748 (1685-1759)
Arr. by Winfred Douglas, 1941 (1867-1944)

Henry H. Tweedy, 1926 (1868-1953)

1. O gra-cious Fa-ther of man-kind, Our spir-its' un-seen
2. Thou hear-est these, the good and ill, Deep bur-ied in each
3. Our best is but Thy-self in us, Our high-est thought Thy
4. Thou seek-est us in love and truth More than our minds seek

friend, High heav-en's Lord, our hearts' dear guest, To
breast; The se-cret thought, the hid-den plan, Wrought
will; To hear Thy voice we need but love, And
Thee; Through o-pen gates Thy power flows in Like

Thee our prayers as-cend. Thou dost not wait till
out or un-ex-pressed. O cleanse our prayers from
lis-ten, and be still. We would not bend Thy
flood tides from the sea. No more we seek Thee

hu-man speech Thy gifts di-vine im-plore; Our
hu-man dross, At-tune our lives to Thee, Un-
will to ours, But blend our wills with Thine; Not
from a-far, Nor ask Thee for a sign, Con-

MEDITATION AND PRAYER

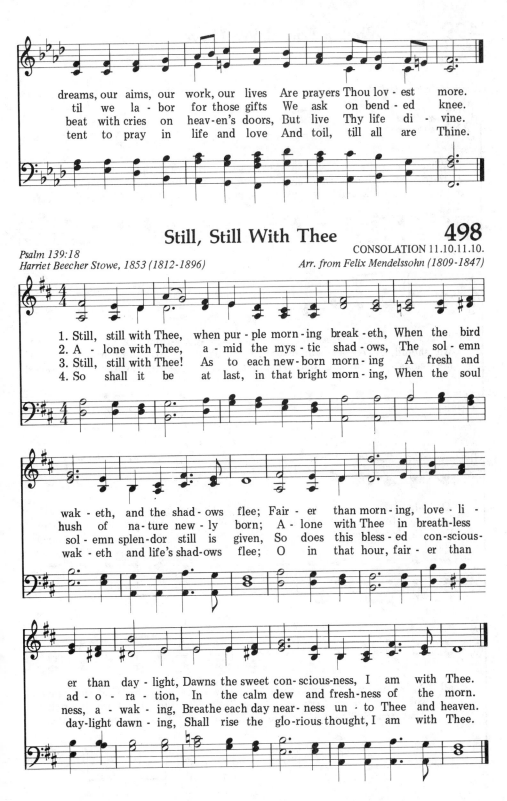

dreams, our aims, our work, our lives Are prayers Thou lov - est more.
til we la - bor for those gifts We ask on bend - ed knee.
beat with cries on heav-en's doors, But live Thy life di - vine.
tent to pray in life and love And toil, till all are Thine.

Still, Still With Thee

498

CONSOLATION 11.10.11.10.

Psalm 139:18
Harriet Beecher Stowe, 1853 (1812-1896)

Arr. from Felix Mendelssohn (1809-1847)

1. Still, still with Thee, when pur - ple morn - ing break - eth, When the bird
2. A - lone with Thee, a - mid the mys - tic shad - ows, The sol - emn
3. Still, still with Thee! As to each new-born morn - ing A fresh and
4. So shall it be at last, in that bright morn - ing, When the soul

wak - eth, and the shad - ows flee; Fair - er than morn - ing, love - li -
hush of na - ture new - ly born; A - lone with Thee in breath-less
sol - emn splen-dor still is given, So does this bless - ed con-scious-
wak - eth and life's shad-ows flee; O in that hour, fair - er than

er than day - light, Dawns the sweet con - scious-ness, I am with Thee.
ad - o - ra - tion, In the calm dew and fresh-ness of the morn.
ness, a - wak - ing, Breathe each day near - ness un - to Thee and heaven.
day-light dawn - ing, Shall rise the glo-rious thought, I am with Thee.

MEDITATION AND PRAYER

499   What a Friend We Have in Jesus

Joseph M. Scriven, 1855 (1820-1886)

CONVERSE 8.7.8.7.D.
Charles C. Converse, 1868 (1832-1918)

1. What a friend we have in Je - sus, All our sins and griefs to bear;
2. Have we tri - als and temp-ta - tions? Is there trou-ble an - y-where?
3. Are we weak and heav - y lad - en, Cum-bered with a load of care?

What a priv - i - lege to car - ry Ev - ery-thing to God in prayer!
We should nev - er be dis-cour - aged; Take it to the Lord in prayer!
Pre - cious Sav - ior, still our ref - uge, Take it to the Lord in prayer!

O what peace we of - ten for - feit, O what need-less pain we bear,
Can we find a friend so faith - ful, Who will all our sor-rows share?
Do thy friends de-spise, for-sake thee? Take it to the Lord in prayer!

All be-cause we do not car - ry Ev - ery-thing to God in prayer.
Je - sus knows our ev - ery weak - ness; Take it to the Lord in prayer!
In His arms He'll take and shield thee, Thou wilt find a sol - ace there.

MEDITATION AND PRAYER

Take Time to Be Holy

500

1 Peter 1:16
W. D. Longstaff, 1882 (1822-1894)

HOLINESS 6.5.6.5.D.
George C. Stebbins, 1890 (1846-1945)

1. Take time to be ho - ly, Speak oft with thy Lord;
2. Take time to be ho - ly, The world rush - es on;
3. Take time to be ho - ly, Let Him be thy Guide,
4. Take time to be ho - ly, Be calm in thy soul,

A - bide in Him al - ways, And feed on His word;
Spend much time in se - cret With Je - sus a - lone;
And run not be - fore Him, What - ev - er be - tide;
Each thought and each mo - tive Be - neath His con - trol;

Make friends of God's chil - dren, Help those who are weak,
By look - ing to Je - sus, Like Him thou shalt be;
In joy or in sor - row, Still fol - low thy Lord,
Thus led by His Spir - it To foun - tains of love,

For - get - ting in noth - ing His bless - ing to seek.
Thy friends in thy con - duct His like - ness shall see.
And, look - ing to Je - sus, Still trust in His word.
Thou soon shalt be fit - ted For ser - vice a - bove.

MEDITATION AND PRAYER

501 'Tis the Blessed Hour of Prayer

13.12.13.7.6.Ref.

Fanny J. Crosby, 1880 (1820-1915)

William H. Doane (1832-1915)

1. 'Tis the bless-ed hour of prayer, when our hearts low-ly bend,
2. 'Tis the bless-ed hour of prayer, when the Sav-ior draws near,
3. 'Tis the bless-ed hour of prayer, when the tempt-ed and tried
4. At the bless-ed hour of prayer, trust-ing Him we be-lieve,

And we gath-er to Je-sus, our Sav-ior and Friend;
With a ten-der com-pas-sion His chil-dren to hear;
To the Sav-ior who loves them their sor-rows con-fide;
That the bless-ings we're need-ing we'll sure-ly re-ceive;

If we come to Him in faith, His pro-tec-tion to share,
When He tells us we may cast at His feet ev-ery care,
With a sym-pa-thiz-ing heart He re-moves ev-ery care;
In the full-ness of this trust we shall lose ev-ery care;

What a balm for the wea-ry! O how sweet to be there!

MEDITATION AND PRAYER

Refrain

Bless-ed hour of prayer, Bless-ed hour of prayer,

What a balm for the wea-ry! O how sweet to be there!

Sun of My Soul

502

HURSLEY L.M.

John Keble, 1820 (1792-1866)

Adapted from Katholisches Gesangbuch, *c. 1774*

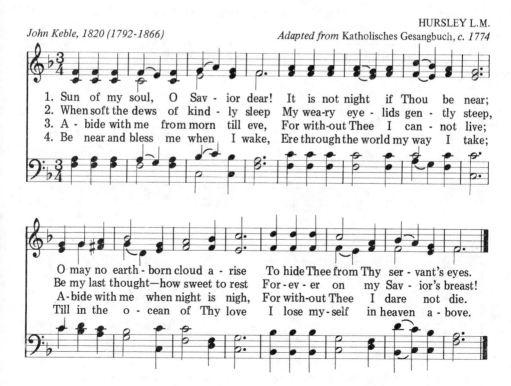

1. Sun of my soul, O Sav - ior dear! It is not night if Thou be near;
2. When soft the dews of kind - ly sleep My wea-ry eye - lids gen - tly steep,
3. A - bide with me from morn till eve, For with-out Thee I can - not live;
4. Be near and bless me when I wake, Ere through the world my way I take;

O may no earth - born cloud a - rise   To hide Thee from Thy ser - vant's eyes.
Be my last thought—how sweet to rest   For - ev - er on   my Sav - ior's breast!
A - bide with me   when night is nigh,   For with-out Thee   I dare   not die.
Till in the   o - cean of Thy love   I lose my - self   in heaven a - bove.

MEDITATION AND PRAYER

503 A Quiet Place

6.6.8.6.8.6.D.
Ralph Carmichael

Ralph Carmichael (1927-)

There is a qui - et place, Far from the rap - id pace where

God can soothe my trou - bled mind. Shel - tered by

tree and flow'r, There in my qui - et hour with Him my

cares are left be - hind. Wheth - er a gar - den small,

Or on a moun - tain tall, New strength and cour - age

MEDITATION AND PRAYER

there I find; Then from this qui - et place I go pre-

pared to face a new day With love for all man - kind.

Lord Jesus, Think on Me 504

Synesius of Cyrene (c. 375-430)
Tr. by Allen W. Chatfield (1808-1896)

SOUTHWELL S.M.
Adapt. from Damon's Psalmes, 1579

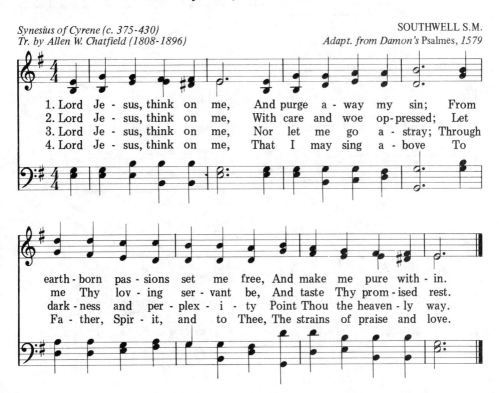

1. Lord Je - sus, think on me, And purge a - way my sin; From
2. Lord Je - sus, think on me, With care and woe op-pressed; Let
3. Lord Je - sus, think on me, Nor let me go a - stray; Through
4. Lord Je - sus, think on me, That I may sing a - bove To

earth-born pas - sions set me free, And make me pure with - in.
me Thy lov - ing ser - vant be, And taste Thy prom - ised rest.
dark - ness and per - plex - i - ty Point Thou the heaven - ly way.
Fa - ther, Spir - it, and to Thee, The strains of praise and love.

MEDITATION AND PRAYER

505   I Need the Prayers

James D. Vaughan (1864-1941)

L.M.Ref.
James D. Vaughan, 1908

1. I need the prayers of those I love, While trav-'ling o'er life's rug-ged way,
2. I need the prayers of those I love, To help me in each try-ing hour,
3. I want my friends to pray for me, To hold me up on wings of faith,

That I may true and faith-ful be, And live for Je-sus ev-ery day.
To bear my tempt-ed soul to Him, That He may keep me by His pow'r.
That I may walk the nar-row way, Kept by our Fa-ther's glo-rious grace.

Refrain

I want my friends to pray for me, To bear my tempt-ed soul a-bove,

And in-ter-cede with God for me; I need the prayers of those I love.

MEDITATION AND PRAYER

A Mighty Fortress

506

Psalm 46:1
Martin Luther, 1529 (1483-1546)
Tr. by Frederick H. Hedge, 1852 (1805-1890)

EIN' FESTE BURG 8.7.8.7.6.6.6.6.7.
Martin Luther, 1529

1. A might-y for-tress is our God, A bul-wark nev-er fail-ing;
2. Did we in our own strength con-fide, Our striv-ing would be los-ing,
3. And though this world, with dev-ils filled, Should threaten to un-do us,
4. That word a-bove all earth-ly powers, No thanks to them, a-bid-eth;

Our help-er He, a-mid the flood Of mor-tal ills pre-vail-ing.
Were not the right man on our side, The man of God's own choos-ing.
We will not fear, for God hath willed His truth to tri-umph through us.
The Spir-it and the gifts are ours Through Him who with us sid-eth;

For still our an-cient foe Doth seek to work us woe; His craft and
Dost ask who that may be? Christ Je-sus, it is He, Lord Sab-a-
The prince of dark-ness grim, We trem-ble not for him; His rage we
Let goods and kin-dred go, This mor-tal life al-so; The bod-y

power are great; And armed with cru-el hate, On earth is not his e-qual.
oth His name, From age to age the same, And He must win the bat-tle.
can en-dure, For lo! his doom is sure, One lit-tle word shall fell him.
they may kill; God's truth a-bid-eth still, His king-dom is for-ev-er.

FAITH AND TRUST

507 Moment by Moment

Daniel W. Whittle, 1893 (1840-1901)

10.10.10.10.Ref.
Mary Whittle, 1893

1. Dy-ing with Je-sus, by death reck-oned mine, Liv-ing with Je-sus, a
2. Nev-er a tri-al that He is not there, Nev-er a bur-den that
3. Nev-er a heart-ache, and nev-er a groan, Nev-er a tear-drop and
4. Nev-er a weak-ness that He doth not feel, Nev-er a sick-ness that

new life di-vine, Look-ing to Je-sus till glo-ry doth shine,
He doth not bear, Nev-er a sor-row that He doth not share,
nev-er a moan; Nev-er a dan-ger but there on the throne,
He can-not heal; Mo-ment by mo-ment, in woe or in weal,

Refrain

Mo-ment by mo-ment, O Lord, I am Thine.
Mo-ment by mo-ment I'm un-der His care.
Mo-ment by mo-ment He thinks of His own. Mo-ment by mo-ment I'm
Je-sus, my Sav-ior, a-bides with me still.

kept in His love; Mo-ment by mo-ment I've life from a-bove; Look-ing to

Je-sus till glo-ry doth shine; Mo-ment by mo-ment, O Lord, I am Thine.

FAITH AND TRUST

Anywhere With Jesus

11.11.11.11.Ref.

Jessie H. Brown, 1886 (1861-1921)   *Daniel B. Towner, 1887 (1850-1909)*

1. An - y-where with Je - sus I can safe - ly go, An - y-where He
2. An - y-where with Je - sus I am not a - lone; Oth - er friends may
3. An - y-where with Je - sus I can go to sleep, When the gloom - y

leads me in this world be - low; An - y-where with-out Him, dear - est
fail me, He is still my own; Though His hand may lead me o - ver
shad - ows round a - bout me creep, Know-ing I shall wak - en nev - er -

joys would fade; An - y-where with Je - sus I am not a - fraid.
drear - y ways, An - y-where with Je - sus is a house of praise.
more to roam; An - y-where with Je - sus will be home sweet home.

Refrain

An - y-where! an - y-where! Fear I can - not know;

An - y-where with Je - sus I can safe - ly go.

FAITH AND TRUST

509 How Firm a Foundation

FOUNDATION 11.11.11.11.

Rippon's A Selection of Hymns, *1787*

Funk's . . . Genuine Church Music, *1832*
Arr. by Melvin West, 1984 (1930-   )

1. How firm a foun - da - tion, ye saints of the Lord,
2. "Fear not, I am with thee, O be not dis - mayed;
3. "When thro' the deep wa - ters I call thee to go,
4. "When thro' fi - ery tri - als thy path - way shall lie,
5. "The soul that on Je - sus hath leaned for re - pose,

Is laid for your faith in His ex - cel - lent Word!
For I am thy God, and will still give thee aid;
The riv - ers of sor - row shall not o - ver - flow;
My grace, all suf - fi - cient, shall be thy sup - ply;
I will not, I will not de - sert to His foes;

What more can He say than to you He hath said,
I'll strength - en thee, help thee, and cause thee to stand,
For I will be with thee, thy trou - bles to bless,
The flame shall not hurt thee; I on - ly de - sign
That soul, though all hell should en - deav - or to shake,

To you who for ref - uge to Je - sus hath fled?
Up - held by My righ - teous, om - nip - o - tent hand."
And sanc - ti - fy to thee thy deep - est dis - tress."
Thy dross to con - sume, and thy gold to re - fine."
I'll nev - er, no nev - er, no nev - er for - sake!"

Alternate tune, ADESTE FIDELIS, No. 132

FAITH AND TRUST

If You But Trust in God to Guide You 510

Psalm 55:22
George Neumark (1621-1681) alt.

WER NUR DEN LIEBEN GOTT 9.8.9.8.8.8.
George Neumark

1. If you but trust in God to guide you And place your con - fi - dence in Him, You'll find Him al - ways there be - side you, To give you hope and strength with - in. For those who trust God's change-less love Build on the rock that will not move.

2. What gain is there in fu - tile weep - ing, In help - less an - ger and dis - tress? If you are in His care and keep - ing, In sor - row will He love you less? For He who took for you a cross Will bring you safe through ev - ery loss.

3. In pa - tient trust a - wait His lei - sure In cheer - ful hope, with heart con - tent To take what - e'er your Fa - ther's plea - sure And all - dis - cern - ing love have sent; Doubt not your in - most wants are known To Him who chose you for His own.

4. Sing, pray, and keep His ways un - swerv - ing, Of - fer your ser - vice faith - ful - ly, And trust His word; though un - de - serv - ing, You'll find His prom - ise true to be. God nev - er will for - sake in need The soul that trusts in Him in - deed.

FAITH AND TRUST

511   I Know Whom I Have Believed

2 Timothy 1:12
Daniel W. Whittle, 1883 (1840-1901)

C.M.Ref.
James McGranahan, 1883 (1840-1907)

1. I know not why God's won-drous grace To me He hath made known,
2. I know not how this sav-ing faith To me He did im-part,
3. I know not how the Spir-it moves, Con-vinc-ing men of sin,
4. I know not when my Lord may come, At night or noon-day fair,

Nor why, un-wor-thy, Christ in love Re-deemed me for His own.
Nor how be-liev-ing in His word Wrought peace with-in my heart.
Re-veal-ing Je-sus through the word, Cre-at-ing faith in Him.
Nor if I walk the vale with Him, Or meet Him in the air.

Refrain

But "I know whom I have be-liev-ed, and am per-suad-ed that He is

a-ble To keep that which I've com-mit-ted Un-to Him a-gainst that day."

FAITH AND TRUST

Just When I Need Him Most

512

9.9.9.6.Ref.

William Poole, 1907 (1875-1949)

Charles H. Gabriel, 1907 (1856-1932)

1. Just when I need Him, Je-sus is near, Just when I fal - ter, just when I fear; Read-y to help me, read-y to cheer, Just when I need Him most.
2. Just when I need Him, Je-sus is true, Nev-er for-sak-ing, all the way through; Giv-ing for bur-dens plea-sures a-new,
3. Just when I need Him, Je-sus is strong, Bear-ing my bur-dens all the day long; For all my sor-row giv-ing a song,
4. Just when I need Him, He is my all, An-swer-ing when up-on Him I call; Ten-der-ly watch-ing lest I should fall,

Refrain

Just when I need Him most, Just when I need Him most; Je-sus is near to com-fort and cheer, Just when I need Him most.

FAITH AND TRUST

513   In Heavenly Love Abiding

Psalm 23
Anna Waring, 1850 (1820-1910)

NYLAND 7.6.7.6.D.
Finnish Hymn Arr. by David Evans, 1927 (1874-1948)

1. In heaven-ly love a-bid-ing, No change my heart shall fear;
2. Wher-ev-er He may guide me, No want shall turn me back;
3. Green pas-tures are be-fore me, Which yet I have not seen;

And safe is such con-fid-ing, For noth-ing chang-es here.
My Shep-herd is be-side me, And noth-ing can I lack.
Bright skies will soon be o'er me, Where dark-est clouds have been.

The storm may roar with-out me, My heart may low be laid;
His wis-dom ev-er wak-eth, His sight is nev-er dim;
My hope I can-not mea-sure, My path to life is free;

But God is round a-bout me, And can I be dis-mayed?
He knows the way He tak-eth, And I will walk with Him.
My Sav-ior has my trea-sure, And He will walk with me.

Music from the *Revised Church Hymnary 1927* by permission of Oxford University Press.

FAITH AND TRUST

Lord of Our Life

514

M. A. Von Lowenstern, 1644 (1594-1648)
Tr. Philip Pusey, 1834 (1799-1855)

CLOISTERS 11.11.11.5.
Joseph Barnby, 1868 (1838-1896)

1. Lord of our life, and God of our sal-
va-tion, Star of our night, and hope of
ev-ery na-tion, Hear and re-ceive Thy
church's sup-pli-ca-tion, Lord God Al-might-y.

2. Lord, Thou canst help when earth-ly ar-mor
fail-eth; Lord, Thou canst save when dead-ly
sin as-sail-eth; Lord, o'er Thy rock nor
death nor hell pre-vail-eth; Grant us Thy peace, Lord.

3. Peace in our hearts our e-vil thoughts as-
suag-ing; Peace in Thy church, where broth-ers
are en-gag-ing; Peace, when the world its
bus-y war is wag-ing; Send us, O Sav-ior.

4. Grant us Thy help till foes are back-ward
driv-en; Grant them Thy truth that they may
be for-giv-en; Grant peace on earth, and,
aft-er we have striv-en, Peace in Thy heav-en.

FAITH AND TRUST

515

The Lord Is My Light

10.10.11.11.Ref.

James Nicholson (1828-1876)

Dr. J. W. Bischoff (1849-1909)

1. The Lord is my light; then why should I fear? By day and by night His pres-ence is near; He is my sal-va-tion from sor-row and sin; This bless-ed per-sua-sion the Spir-it brings in.

2. The Lord is my light; though clouds may a-rise, Faith, strong-er than sight, looks up to the skies Where Je-sus for-ev-er in glo-ry doth reign: Then how can I ev-er in dark-ness re-main?

3. The Lord is my light, the Lord is my strength; I know in His might I'll con-quer at length; My weak-ness in mer-cy He cov-ers with power, And, walk-ing by faith, He up-holds me each hour.

4. The Lord is my light, my all and in all; There is in His sight no dark-ness at all; He is my Re-deem-er, my Sav-ior and King; With saints and with an-gels His prais-es I sing.

FAITH AND TRUST

The Lord is my light, my joy, and my song; By day and by

night He leads me a-long; The Lord is my light, my

joy, and my song; By day and by night He leads me a-long.

FAITH AND TRUST

516

All the Way

Fanny J. Crosby, 1875; alt. (1820-1915)

LOWRY 8.7.8.7.D.
Robert Lowry, 1874 (1826-1899)

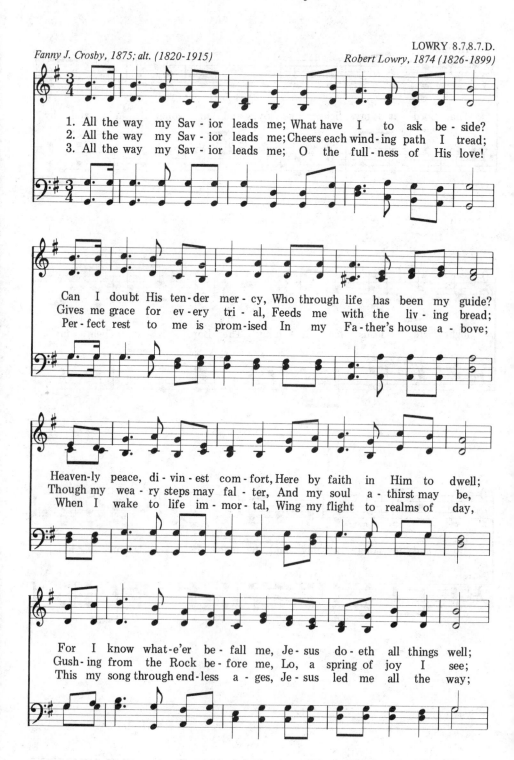

1. All the way my Sav - ior leads me; What have I to ask be - side?
2. All the way my Sav - ior leads me; Cheers each wind - ing path I tread;
3. All the way my Sav - ior leads me; O the full - ness of His love!

Can I doubt His ten - der mer - cy, Who through life has been my guide?
Gives me grace for ev - ery tri - al, Feeds me with the liv - ing bread;
Per - fect rest to me is prom - ised In my Fa - ther's house a - bove;

Heaven-ly peace, di - vin - est com - fort, Here by faith in Him to dwell;
Though my wea - ry steps may fal - ter, And my soul a - thirst may be,
When I wake to life im - mor - tal, Wing my flight to realms of day,

For I know what-e'er be - fall me, Je - sus do - eth all things well;
Gush-ing from the Rock be - fore me, Lo, a spring of joy I see;
This my song through end - less a - ges, Je - sus led me all the way;

FAITH AND TRUST

For I know what-e'er be-fall me, Je-sus do-eth all things well.
Gush-ing from the Rock be-fore me, Lo, a spring of joy I see.
This my song through end-less a-ges, Je-sus led me all the way.

My Faith Looks Up to Thee 517

OLIVET 6.6.4.6.6.6.4.

Ray Palmer, 1830 (1808-1887)

Lowell Mason, 1832 (1792-1872)

1. My faith looks up to Thee, Thou Lamb of Cal - va - ry,
2. May Thy rich grace im - part Strength to my faint - ing heart,
3. While life's dark maze I tread, And griefs a - round me spread,

Sav - ior di - vine; Now hear me while I pray, Take all my
My zeal in - spire; As Thou hast died for me, O may my
Be Thou my Guide; Bid dark-ness turn to day, Wipe sor-row's

guilt a - way, O let me from this day Be whol - ly Thine.
love to Thee Pure, warm, and change - less be, A liv - ing fire.
tears a - way. Nor let me ev - er stray From Thee a - side.

FAITH AND TRUST

Standing on the Promises

2 Peter 1:4
R. Kelso Carter (1849-1928)

11.11.11.9.Ref.
R. Kelso Carter, 1886

1. Stand-ing on the prom-is-es of Christ my King, Thru e-ter-nal
2. Stand-ing on the prom-is-es that can-not fail, When the howl-ing
3. Stand-ing on the prom-is-es of Christ the Lord, Bound to Him e-

a-ges let His prais-es ring; Glo-ry in the high-est I will
storms of doubt and fear as-sail, By the liv-ing word of God I
ter-nal-ly by love's strong cord, O-ver-com-ing dai-ly with the

Refrain

shout and sing, Stand-ing on the prom-is-es of God.
shall pre-vail, Stand-ing on the prom-is-es of God. Stand-
Spir-it's sword, Stand-ing on the prom-is-es of God. Stand-ing on the

ing, stand - ing, Stand-ing on the
prom-is-es, stand-ing on the prom-is-es, Stand-ing on the

FAITH AND TRUST

prom-is-es of God my Sav-ior; Stand - ing,
Stand-ing on the prom-is-es,

stand - ing, I'm stand-ing on the prom-is-es of God.
stand-ing on the prom-is-es,

Give to the Winds Your Fears

519

Psalm 37:5
Paul Gerhardt, 1653 (1607-1676)
Tr. by John Wesley, 1739 (1703-1791) alt.

ST. BRIDE S.M.
Samuel Howard, 1762 (1710-1781)

1. Give to the winds your fears; In hope be un - dis - mayed: God
2. To Him com - mit your griefs; Your ways put in His hands— To
3. O put your trust in God; In du - ty's path go on. Walk
4. Leave to His sov - ereign sway To choose and to com - mand; So

hears your sighs and counts your tears, God shall lift up your head.
His sure truth and ten - der care Who earth and heaven com - mands.
in His strength with faith and hope, So shall your work be done.
you shall, faith - ful, seek His way— How wise, how strong His hand!

FAITH AND TRUST

520 He Hideth My Soul

Fanny J. Crosby (1820-1915)

11.8.11.8.Ref.
William J. Kirkpatrick (1838-1921)

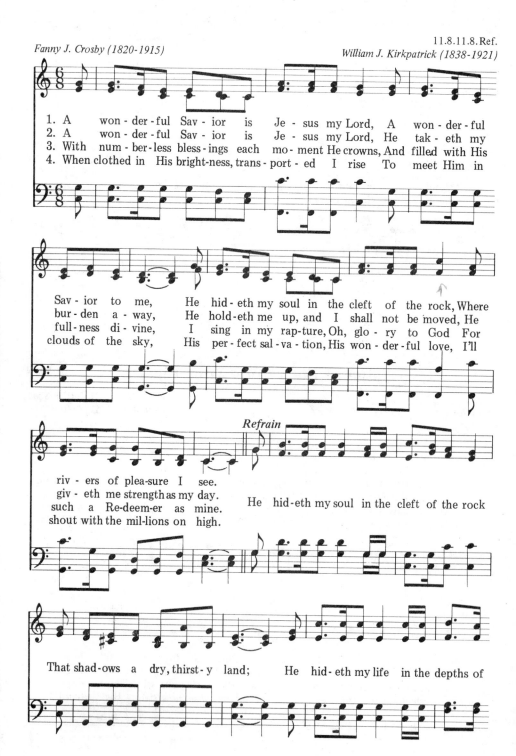

1. A won-der-ful Sav-ior is Je-sus my Lord, A won-der-ful
2. A won-der-ful Sav-ior is Je-sus my Lord, He tak-eth my
3. With num-ber-less bless-ings each mo-ment He crowns, And filled with His
4. When clothed in His bright-ness, trans-port-ed I rise To meet Him in

Sav-ior to me, He hid-eth my soul in the cleft of the rock, Where
bur-den a-way, He hold-eth me up, and I shall not be moved, He
full-ness di-vine, I sing in my rap-ture, Oh, glo-ry to God For
clouds of the sky, His per-fect sal-va-tion, His won-der-ful love, I'll

Refrain

riv-ers of plea-sure I see.
giv-eth me strength as my day.
such a Re-deem-er as mine.   He hid-eth my soul in the cleft of the rock
shout with the mil-lions on high.

That shad-ows a dry, thirst-y land; He hid-eth my life in the depths of

FAITH AND TRUST

His love, And cov-ers me there with His hand, And cov-ers me there with His hand.

Depth of Mercy

1 Tim. 1:15
Charles Wesley, 1740 (1707-1788)

ALETTA 7.7.7.7.
William B. Bradbury, 1857 (1816-1868)

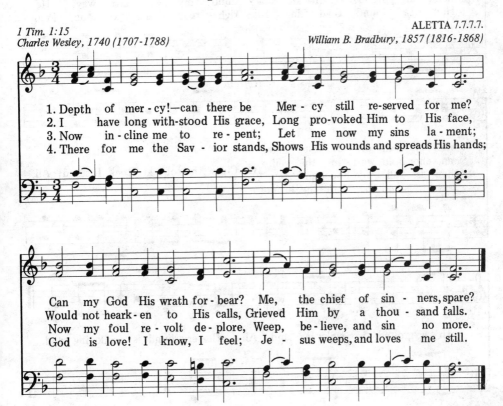

1. Depth of mer-cy!—can there be   Mer-cy still re-served for me?
2. I   have long with-stood His grace, Long pro-voked Him to   His face,
3. Now   in-cline me to   re-pent;   Let me now my sins   la-ment;
4. There for me the Sav-ior stands, Shows His wounds and spreads His hands;

Can   my God His wrath for-bear? Me,   the chief of sin-ners, spare?
Would not heark-en to   His calls, Grieved Him by   a thou-sand falls.
Now   my foul re-volt de-plore, Weep,   be-lieve, and sin   no more.
God   is love! I know, I feel; Je-sus weeps, and loves   me still.

FAITH AND TRUST

522   My Hope Is Built on Nothing Less

Edward Mote, 1834 (1797-1874)

THE SOLID ROCK L.M.Ref.
Wm. B. Bradbury, 1863 (1816-1868)

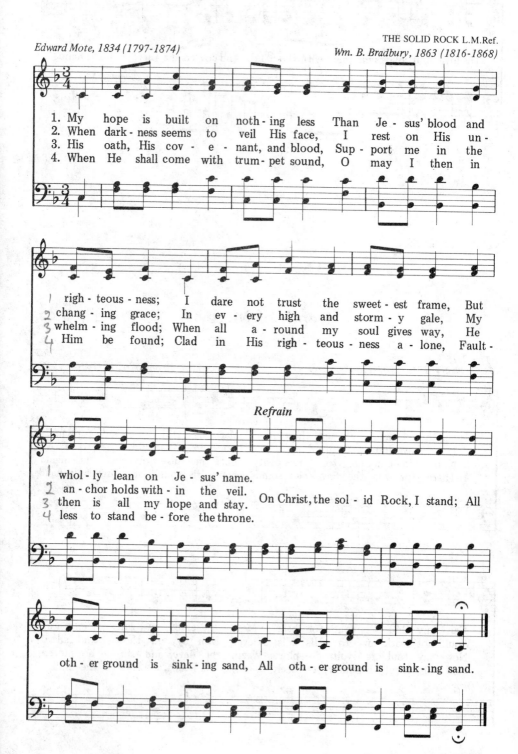

1. My hope is built on noth-ing less Than Je-sus' blood and
2. When dark-ness seems to veil His face, I rest on His un-
3. His oath, His cov-e-nant, and blood, Sup-port me in the
4. When He shall come with trum-pet sound, O may I then in

1. right-teous-ness; I dare not trust the sweet-est frame, But
2. chang-ing grace; In ev-ery high and storm-y gale, My
3. whelm-ing flood; When all a-round my soul gives way, He
4. Him be found; Clad in His righ-teous-ness a-lone, Fault-

Refrain

1. whol-ly lean on Je-sus' name.
2. an-chor holds with-in the veil.
3. then is all my hope and stay.   On Christ, the sol-id Rock, I stand; All
4. less to stand be-fore the throne.

oth-er ground is sink-ing sand, All oth-er ground is sink-ing sand.

FAITH AND TRUST

Alternate tune, MELITA, No. 85
Alternate harmony, No. 200

My Faith Has Found a Resting Place 523

NO OTHER PLEA C.M.Ref.
Norwegian Melody

Lidie H. Edmunds, c.1891

1. My faith has found a rest-ing place, Not in a man-made creed;
2. E-nough for me that Je-sus saves, This ends my fear and doubt;
3. My soul is rest-ing on the Word, The liv-ing Word of God:
4. The great Phy-si-cian heals the sick, The lost He came to save;

I trust the ev-er liv-ing One, That He for me will plead.
A sin-ful soul I come to Him, He will not cast me out.
Sal-va-tion in my Sav-ior's name, Sal-va-tion through His blood.
For me His pre-cious blood He shed, For me His life He gave.

Refrain

I need no oth-er ev-i-dence, I need no oth-er plea;

It is e-nough that Je-sus died And rose a-gain for me.

FAITH AND TRUST

524   'Tis So Sweet to Trust in Jesus

8.7.8.7.Ref.

Louisa M. R. Stead (1871-1917)   *William J. Kirkpatrick, 1882 (1838-1921)*

1. 'Tis so sweet to trust in Je - sus, Just to take Him at His word;
2. O how sweet to trust in Je - sus, Just to trust His cleans-ing blood;
3. Yes, 'tis sweet to trust in Je - sus, Just from sin and self to cease;
4. I'm so glad I learned to trust Thee, Pre - cious Je - sus, Sav - ior, Friend;

Just to rest up - on His prom-ise, Just to know, "Thus saith the Lord."
Just in sim - ple faith to plunge me 'Neath the heal - ing, cleans-ing flood.
Just from Je - sus sim - ply tak - ing Life, and rest, and joy, and peace.
And I know that Thou art with me, Wilt be with me till the end.

Refrain

Je - sus, Je - sus, how I trust Him; How I've proved Him o'er and o'er!

Je - sus, Je - sus, pre - cious Je - sus! O for grace to trust Him more!

FAITH AND TRUST

Hiding in Thee

Ps. 61:1, 2
William O. Cushing, 1876 (1823-1902)

11.11.11.11.Ref.
Ira D. Sankey, 1876 (1840-1908)

1. O safe to the Rock that is high - er than I, My
2. In the calm of the noon - tide, in sor - row's lone hour, In
3. How oft in the con - flict, when pressed by the foe, I have

soul in its con - flicts and sor - rows would fly; So
times when temp - ta - tion casts o'er me its power; In the
fled to my Ref - uge and breathed out my woe; How

sin - ful, so wea - ry, Thine, Thine would I be; Thou
tem - pests of life, on its wide, heav - ing sea, Thou
of - ten, when tri - als like sea bil - lows roll, Have I

Refrain

blest "Rock of A - ges," I'm hid - ing in Thee.
blest "Rock of A - ges," I'm hid - ing in Thee. Hid - ing in Thee,
hid - den in Thee, O Thou Rock of my soul.

Hid - ing in Thee, Thou blest "Rock of A - ges," I'm hid - ing in Thee.

FAITH AND TRUST

526

Because He Lives

Gloria Gaither, 1971 (1942-   )
William J. Gaither, 1971

RESURRECTION 9.8.9.12.Ref.
William J. Gaither, 1971 (1936-   )

1. God sent His Son, they called Him Je - sus, He came to love,
   heal, and for - give; He lived and died to buy my
   par - don, An emp - ty grave is there to prove my Sav - ior lives.

2. How sweet to hold a new-born ba - by, And feel the pride,
   and joy He gives; But great - er still the calm as -
   sur - ance, This child can face un-cer - tain days be-cause He lives.

Refrain

Be-cause He lives I can face to-mor - row, Be-cause He lives

FAITH AND TRUST

all fear is gone; Be-cause I know He holds the

fu - ture. And life is worth the liv-ing just be-cause He lives.

From Every Stormy Wind 527

Exodus 25:22
Hugh Stowell, 1828 (1799-1865)

RETREAT L.M.
Thomas Hastings, 1842 (1784-1872)

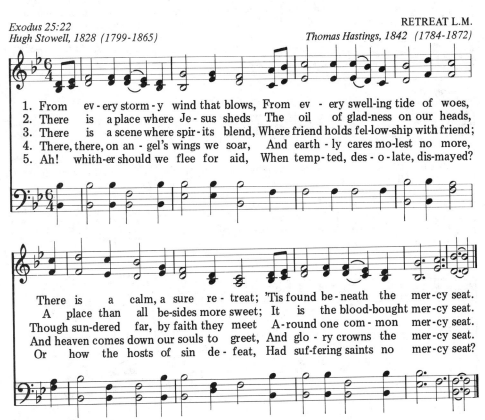

1. From ev - ery storm - y wind that blows, From ev - ery swell-ing tide of woes,
2. There is a place where Je - sus sheds The oil of glad-ness on our heads,
3. There is a scene where spir - its blend, Where friend holds fel-low-ship with friend;
4. There, there, on an - gel's wings we soar, And earth - ly cares mo-lest no more,
5. Ah! whith-er should we flee for aid, When temp-ted, des - o-late, dis-mayed?

There is a calm, a sure re - treat; 'Tis found be - neath the mer-cy seat.
A place than all be-sides more sweet; It is the blood-bought mer-cy seat.
Though sun-dered far, by faith they meet A-round one com - mon mer-cy seat.
And heaven comes down our souls to greet, And glo - ry crowns the mer-cy seat.
Or how the hosts of sin de - feat, Had suf-fering saints no mer-cy seat?

FAITH AND TRUST

528   A Shelter in the Time of Storm

L.M.Ref.

Vernon J. Charlesworth, 1880 (1839-1915) refrain added   *F. E. Belden, 1899 (1858-1945)*

1. The Lord's our Rock, in Him we hide, A shel-ter in the time of storm;
2. A shade by day, de-fense by night, A shel-ter in the time of storm;
3. The rag-ing floods may round us beat, A shel-ter in the time of storm;
4. O Rock di-vine, O Ref-uge dear, A shel-ter in the time of storm;

Se-cure what-ev-er may be-tide, A shel-ter in the time of storm.
No fears a-larm, no foes af-fright, A shel-ter in the time of storm.
We find in God a safe re-treat, A shel-ter in the time of storm.
Be Thou our help-er, ev-er near, A shel-ter in the time of storm.

Refrain

Might-y Rock in a wea-ry land, Cool-ing shade on the burn-ing sand,
Might-y Rock   Cool-ing shade

Faith-ful guide for the pil-grim band— A shel-ter in the time of storm.
Faith-ful guide

FAITH AND TRUST

Under His Wings

529

11.10.11.10.Ref.

W. O. Cushing (1823-1902)

Ira. D. Sankey, 1899 (1840-1908)

1. Un - der His wings I am safe - ly a - bid - ing; Though the night
2. Un - der His wings, what a ref - uge in sor - row! How the heart
3. Un - der His wings, O what pre - cious en - joy - ment! There will I

deep - ens and tem - pests are wild, Still I can trust Him; I
yearn - ing - ly turns to its rest! Of - ten when earth has no
hide till life's tri - als are o'er; Shel - tered, pro - tect - ed, no

know He will keep me; He has re-deemed me, and I am His child.
balm for my heal - ing, There I find com - fort, and there I am blest.
e - vil can harm me; Rest - ing in Je - sus I'm safe ev - er - more.

Refrain

Un - der His wings, un - der His wings, Who from His love can sev - er?

Un - der His wings my soul shall a - bide, Safe - ly a - bide for - ev - er.

FAITH AND TRUST

530   It Is Well With My Soul

Horatio G. Spafford, 1876 (1829-1888)

VILLE DU HAVRE 11.8.11.9. Ref.
Philip P. Bliss (1838-1876)

1. When peace, like a riv-er, at-tend-eth my way, When sor-rows like
2. My sin— O the joy of this glo-ri-ous thought—My sin, not in
3. And, Lord, haste the day when my faith shall be sight, The clouds be rolled

sea bil-lows roll— What-ev-er my lot, Thou hast taught me to say,
part, but the whole, Is nailed to the cross, and I bear it no more:
back as a scroll: The trump shall re-sound and the Lord shall de-scend,

Refrain

It is well, it is well with my soul. It is well
Praise the Lord, praise the Lord, O my soul!
"E-ven so" it is well with my soul. It is well

with my soul, It is well, it is well with my soul.
with my soul,

FAITH AND TRUST

We'll Build on the Rock

Matt. 7:24-26
F. E. Belden, 1886 (1858-1945)

9.8.9.7.Ref.
F. E. Belden, 1886

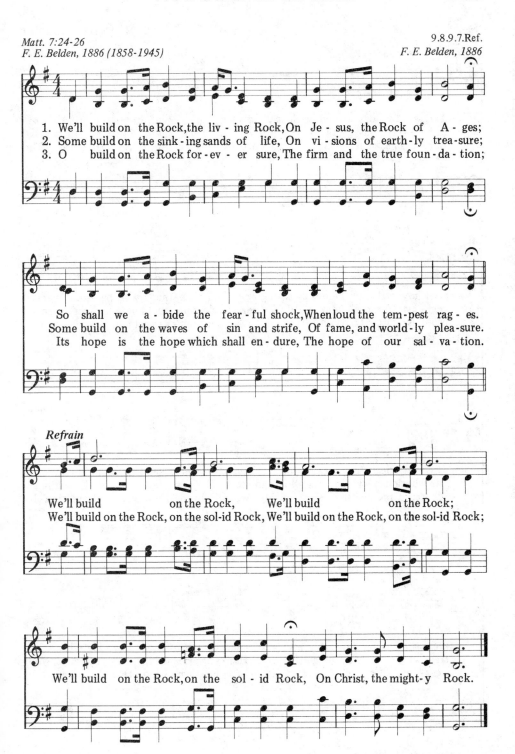

1. We'll build on the Rock, the liv - ing Rock, On Je - sus, the Rock of A - ges;
2. Some build on the sink - ing sands of life, On vi - sions of earth - ly trea - sure;
3. O build on the Rock for - ev - er sure, The firm and the true foun - da - tion;

So shall we a - bide the fear - ful shock, When loud the tem - pest rag - es.
Some build on the waves of sin and strife, Of fame, and world - ly plea - sure.
Its hope is the hope which shall en - dure, The hope of our sal - va - tion.

Refrain

We'll build on the Rock, We'll build on the Rock;
We'll build on the Rock, on the sol-id Rock, We'll build on the Rock, on the sol-id Rock;

We'll build on the Rock, on the sol - id Rock, On Christ, the might - y Rock.

FAITH AND TRUST

532   Day by Day

Deut. 33:25
Carolina Sandell Berg, 1865 (1832-1903)
Tr. by A. L. Skoog (1856-1934)

BLOTT EN DAG 10.9.10.9.D.
Oscar Ahnfelt (1813-1882)
Arr. by Melvin West, 1984 (1930-   )

1. Day by day and with each pass-ing mo-ment, Strength I find to
2. Ev - ery day the Lord Him-self is near me With a spe - cial
3. Help me then in ev-ery trib - u - la - tion So to trust Thy

meet my tri - als here; Trust-ing in my Fa-ther's wise be - stow-ment,
mer - cy for each hour; All my cares He fain would bear, and cheer me,
prom-is - es, O Lord, That I lose not faith's sweet con-so - la - tion

I've no cause for wor - ry or for fear. He whose heart is kind be - yond all
He whose name is Coun-sel - lor and power. The pro - tec - tion of His child and
Of-fered me with-in Thy ho - ly Word. Help me, Lord, when toil and trou - ble

mea - sure Gives un - to each day what He deems best. Lov - ing - ly, its
trea - sure Is a charge that on Him-self He laid; As your days, your
meet - ing, E'er to take, as from a Fa-ther's hand, One by one, the

FAITH AND TRUST

part of pain and plea-sure, Min-gling toil with peace and rest.
strength shall be in mea-sure, This the pledge to me He made.
days, the mo-ments fleet-ing, Till I reach the prom-ised land.

O for a Faith

533

NORTHFIELD C.M.

William H. Bathurst, 1830 (1796-1877)

Jeremiah Ingalls (1764-1828)

1. O for a faith that will not shrink, Though pressed by man-y a foe;
2. That will not mur-mur or com-plain Be-neath the chas-tening rod,
3. A faith that shines more bright and clear When tem-pests rage with-out;
4. That bears un-moved the world's dread frown, Nor heeds its scorn-ful smile;
5. Lord, give me such a faith as this, And then, what-e'er may come

That will not trem-ble on the brink of pov-er-ty,
But in the hour of grief or pain, of grief or pain,
That when in dan-ger knows no fear, knows of no fear,
That sin's wild o-cean can-not drown, no, can-not drown,
I'll taste e'en here the hal-lowed bliss, the hal-lowed bliss

Of pov-er-ty or woe; Of pov-er-ty or woe;
Can lean up-on its God; Can lean up-on its God.
In dark-ness feels no doubt; In dark-ness feels no doubt.
Nor its soft arts be-guile; Nor its soft arts be-guile.
Of an e-ter-nal home; Of an e-ter-nal home.

FAITH AND TRUST

534   Will Your Anchor Hold?

10.9.10.9.Ref.

Priscilla J. Owens (1829-1899)   *William J. Kirkpatrick (1850-1919)*

1. Will your an - chor hold in the storm of life, When the
2. If 'tis safe - ly moored, 'twill the storm with - stand, For 'tis
3. It will firm - ly hold in the straits of Fear, When the
4. It will sure - ly hold in the floods of death, When the
5. When our eyes be - hold, in the dawn - ing light, Shin - ing

clouds un - fold their wings of strife? When the strong tides lift,
well se - cured by the Sav - ior's hand; And the ca - bles, passed
break - ers tell that the reef is near; Though the tem - pest rave
wa - ters cold chill our lat - est breath; On the ris - ing tide
gates of pearl, our har - bor bright, We shall an - chor fast

and the ca - bles strain, Will your an - chor drift, or firm re - main?
from His heart to thine, Can de - fy the blast, through strength di - vine.
and the wild winds blow, Not an an - gry wave shall our bark o'erflow.
it can nev - er fail, While our hopes a - bide with - in the veil.
to the heaven - ly shore, With the storms all past for - ev - er - more.

Refrain

We have an an - chor that keeps the soul Stead - fast and

FAITH AND TRUST

sure while the bil - lows roll; Fas - tened to the Rock which

can - not move, Ground-ed firm and deep in the Sav - ior's love.

I Am Trusting Thee, Lord Jesus 535

Psalm 71:1
Frances R. Havergal, 1874 (1836-1879)

BULLINGER 8.5.8.3.
Ethelbert W. Bullinger, 1874 (1837-1913)

1. I am trust - ing Thee, Lord Je - sus, Trust-ing on - ly Thee;
2. I am trust - ing Thee for par - don; At Thy feet I bow;
3. I am trust - ing Thee to guide me; Thou a - lone shalt lead,
4. I am trust - ing Thee, Lord Je - sus; Nev - er let me fall;

Trust - ing Thee for full sal - va - tion, Great and free.
For Thy grace and ten - der mer - cy, Trust - ing now.
Ev - ery day and hour sup - ply - ing All my need.
I am trust - ing Thee for - ev - er, And for all.

FAITH AND TRUST

536 God, Who Stretched the Spangled Heavens

HENISEE 8.7.8.7.D.

Catherine Cameron (1927-   ) alt.

Eurydice V. Osterman, 1984 (1950-   )

1. God, who stretched the span-gled heav-ens In - fi - nite in time and place,
2. We have ven-tured worlds un-dreamed of Since the child-hood of our race;
3. As each far hor - i - zon beck - ons, May it chal-lenge us a - new:

Flung the suns in burn-ing radi-ance Through the si - lent fields of space:
Known the ec - sta - cy of wing-ing Through un-trav-eled realms of space,
Chil-dren of cre - a - tive pur-pose, Serv - ing oth - ers, honor-ing You.

We, Your chil-dren in Your like-ness, Share in - ven-tive powers with You;
Probed the se - crets of the at - om, Yield-ing un - im - ag - ined power,
May our dreams prove rich with prom-ise; Each en-deav-or well be - gun;

Great Cre - a - tor, still cre - at - ing, Show us what we yet may do.
Fac - ing us with life's de - struc-tion Or our most tri - um-phant hour.
Great Cre - a - tor, give us guid-ance Till our goals and Yours are one.

Alternate tune, HYMN TO JOY, No. 12

GUIDANCE

He Leadeth Me

537

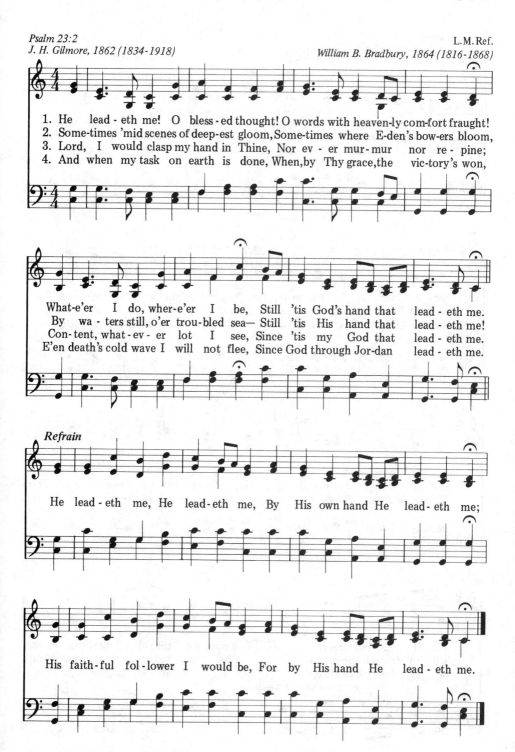

Psalm 23:2
J. H. Gilmore, 1862 (1834-1918)

L.M.Ref.
William B. Bradbury, 1864 (1816-1868)

1. He lead-eth me! O bless-ed thought! O words with heaven-ly com-fort fraught!
2. Some-times 'mid scenes of deep-est gloom, Some-times where E-den's bow-ers bloom,
3. Lord, I would clasp my hand in Thine, Nor ev-er mur-mur nor re-pine;
4. And when my task on earth is done, When, by Thy grace, the vic-tory's won,

What-e'er I do, wher-e'er I be, Still 'tis God's hand that lead-eth me.
By wa-ters still, o'er trou-bled sea— Still 'tis His hand that lead-eth me!
Con-tent, what-ev-er lot I see, Since 'tis my God that lead-eth me.
E'en death's cold wave I will not flee, Since God through Jor-dan lead-eth me.

Refrain

He lead-eth me, He lead-eth me, By His own hand He lead-eth me;

His faith-ful fol-lower I would be, For by His hand He lead-eth me.

GUIDANCE

538 Guide Me, O Thou Great Jehovah

William Williams, 1745 (1717-1791)
Stanza 1, tr. by Peter Williams (1722-1796)
Stanzas 2,3, tr. by the author

CWM RHONDDA 8.7.8.7.8.7.7.
John Hughes (1873-1932)

1. Guide me, O Thou great Je-ho-vah, Pil-grim through this bar-ren land; I am weak, but Thou art might-y; Hold me with Thy power-ful hand; Bread of heav-en, Bread of heav-en, Feed me till I want no more, Feed me till I want no more.

2. O-pen now the crys-tal foun-tain, Whence the heal-ing stream doth flow; Let the fire and cloud-y pil-lar Lead me all my jour-ney through; Strong de-liv-erer, strong de-liv-erer. Be Thou still my strength and shield, Be Thou still my strength and shield.

3. When I tread the verge of Jor-dan, Bid my anx-ious fears sub-side; Death of death and hell's de-struc-tion, Land me safe on Ca-naan's side; Songs of prais-es, songs of prais-es I will ev-er give to Thee, I will ev-er give to Thee.

want no more

Alternate tune, BRYN CALFARIA, No. 165
Higher key, No. 201

GUIDANCE

I Will Early Seek the Savior

8.7.8.7.Ref.

Mrs. L. M. B. Bateman

Fred A. Fillmore (1856-?)

1. I will ear - ly seek the Sav - ior, I will learn of Him each day;
2. I will has - ten where He bids me, I am not too young to go
3. He is stand - ing at the door - way Of es - cape from ev - ery sin;

I will fol - low in His foot - steps, I will walk the nar - row way.
In the path - way where He lead - eth, Not too young His will to know.
I will knock, for He has prom - ised, He will hear and let me in.

Refrain

For He loves me, yes, He loves me, Je - sus loves me, this I know.

Je - sus loves me, died to save me, This is why I love Him so.

GUIDANCE

540 Gentle Jesus, Meek and Mild

Charles Wesley, 1763 (1707-1788)

GENTLE JESUS 7.7.7.7.
Martin Shaw, 1915 (1875-1958)

1. Gen - tle Je - sus, meek and mild, Look up - on a lit - tle child;
2. Lamb of God, I look to Thee, Thou shalt my ex - am - ple be;
3. Fain I would be as Thou art; Give me Thy o - be - dient heart;
4. I shall then show forth Thy praise, Serve Thee all my hap - py days;

Pit - y my sim - plic - i - ty, Suf - fer me to come to Thee.
Thou art gen - tle, meek, and mild, Thou wast once a lit - tle child.
Thou art pit - i - ful and kind, Let me have Thy lov - ing mind.
Then the world shall al - ways see Christ, the Ho - ly Child, in me.

Music copyright © J. Curwen & Sons. Used by permission of G. Schirmer, Inc. U. S. A. agents.

Alternate tune, ORIENTUS PARTIBUS, No. 549

541 Lord, Speak to Me

Rom. 14:7
Frances Ridley Havergal, 1872 (1836-1879)

CANONBURY L.M.
Arr. from Robert A. Schumann, 1839 (1810-1856)

1. Lord, speak to me, that I may speak In liv - ing ech - oes of Thy tone;
2. O lead me, Lord, that I may lead The wan - dering and the wa - vering feet;
3. O strength - en me, that while I stand Firm on the Rock, and strong in Thee,

As Thou hast sought, so let me seek Thy err - ing chil - dren lost and lone.
O feed me, Lord, that I may feed Thy hun - gering ones with man - na sweet.
I may stretch out a lov - ing hand To wres - tlers with the trou - bled sea.

GUIDANCE

Jesus, Friend So Kind

542

TENDER SONG 8.7.8.7.8.7.

Philip E. Gregory (1886-1974)

Wayne Hooper, 1984 (1920-   )

1. Je - sus, Friend, so kind and gen - tle, Lit - tle ones we bring to Thee: Grant to them Thy dear - est bless - ing, Let Thine arms a - round them be; Now en - fold them in Thy good - ness, From all dan - ger keep them free.

2. Thou who did re - ceive the chil - dren To Thy - self so ten - der - ly, Give to all who teach and guide them Wis - dom and hu - mil - i - ty. Vi - sion true to keep them no - ble, Love to serve them faith - ful - ly.

GUIDANCE

543   Jesus, Friend of Little Children

SIMONSIDE 8.5.8.3.

W. J. Mathams, 1882 (1853-1931)

Joseph Harker (1880-1970)

1. Je - sus, Friend of lit - tle chil - dren, Be a Friend to me;
2. Teach me how to grow in good - ness, Dai - ly as I grow;
3. Step by step, O, lead me on - ward, Up - ward in - to youth;
4. Nev - er leave me, nor for - sake me, Ev - er be my Friend;

Take my hand and ev - er keep me Close to Thee.
Thou hast been a child, and sure - ly Thou dost know.
Wis - er, strong - er, still be - com - ing In Thy truth.
For I need Thee from life's dawn - ing To its end.

544   Jesus, Son of Blessed Mary

SHIPSTON 8.7.8.7.

English traditional melody
Arr. by Ralph Vaughan Williams (1872-1958)

Charles E. Riley (1884-1972)

1. Je - sus, Son of bless - ed Ma - ry, Once on earth a lit - tle child,
2. Though Thy ea - ger heart was yearn - ing Heav - y la - den souls to free,
3. Grant that we, like lit - tle chil - dren, Free from pride and guile may be;

Pat - tern fair of ho - ly liv - ing, Gra - cious, lov - ing, un - de - filed:
Yet Thou call - edst lit - tle chil - dren In their hap - pi - ness to Thee.
Cheer - ful, trust - ing, safe, pro - tect - ed By the bless - ed Trin - i - ty.

Music from the *English Hymnal* by permission of Oxford University Press.

Higher key, No. 55

GUIDANCE

Savior, Like a Shepherd

SHEPHERD 8.7.8.7.D.

Anonymous, in Hymns for the Young, *1836; alt.*

William B. Bradbury, 1859 (1816-1868)

1. Sav - ior, like a Shep-herd lead us, Much we need Thy ten-derest care;
2. We are Thine; do Thou be-friend us, Be the Guard-ian of our way;
3. Thou hast prom-ised to re-ceive us, Poor and sin-ful though we be;

In Thy pleas-ant pas-tures feed us, For our use Thy folds pre-pare.
Keep Thy flock, from sin de-fend us, Seek us when we go a-stray.
Thou hast mer-cy to re-lieve us, Grace to cleanse, and power to free.

Bless-ed Je - sus, bless-ed Je - sus, Thou hast bought us, Thine we are;
Bless-ed Je - sus, bless-ed Je - sus, Hear, O hear us, when we pray!
Bless-ed Je - sus, bless-ed Je - sus, We will ear - ly turn to Thee;

Bless-ed Je - sus, bless-ed Je - sus, Thou hast bought us, Thine we are.
Bless-ed Je - sus, bless-ed Je - sus, Hear, O hear us, when we pray!
Bless-ed Je - sus, bless-ed Je - sus, We will ear - ly turn to Thee.

GUIDANCE

546   The Lord's My Shepherd

Psalm 23
Scottish Psalter, 1650

BROTHER JAMES' AIR 8.6.8.6.8.6.
J. L. Macbeth Bain (c. 1840-1925) adapt.

1. The Lord's my Shep-herd; I'll not want. He makes me down to lie
2. My soul He doth re - store a - gain, And me to walk doth make
3. Yea, though I walk in death's dark vale, Yet will I fear no ill;
4. My ta - ble Thou hast fur - nish - ed In pres-ence of my foes;
5. Good-ness and mer - cy all my life Shall sure - ly fol - low me,

In pas-tures green; He lead-eth me The qui - et wa - ters by.
With - in the paths of right-teous-ness, E'en for His own name's sake;
For Thou art with me, and Thy rod And staff me com - fort still;
My head Thou dost with oil a - noint, And my cup o - ver - flows.
And in God's house for - ev - er-more My dwell-ing-place shall be.

He lead-eth me, He lead-eth me The qui - et wa - ters by.
With - in the paths of right-teous-ness, E'en for His own name's sake.
For Thou art with me, and Thy rod And staff me com - fort still.
My head Thou dost with oil a - noint, And my cup o - ver - flows.
And in God's house for - ev - er - more My dwell-ing place shall be.

Arrangement by permission of Oxford University Press.

Alternate tune, CRIMOND, No. 552

GUIDANCE

Be Thou My Vision

547

8th century Irish, Tr. by Mary Byrne, 1905 (1880-1931)
Versified by Eleanor Hull, 1912 (1860-1935)

SLANE 10.10.9.10.
Arr. by David Evans (1874-1948)

1. Be Thou my vi - sion, O Lord of my heart;
2. Be Thou my wis - dom, Be Thou my true word;
3. Rich - es I heed not, Nor man's emp - ty praise;
4. High King of heav - en, When vic - t'ry is won

Naught be all else to me Save that Thou art,
I ev - er with Thee, Thou with me, Lord;
Thou my in - her - it - ance, Now and al - ways:
May I reach heav - en's joys, O bright heaven's Sun!

Thou my best thought, By day or by night,
Thou my great Fa - ther, I Thy true son;
Thou and Thou on - ly, first in my heart,
Heart of my own heart, what - ev - er be - fall,

Wak - ing or sleep - ing, Thy pres - ence my light.
Thou in me dwell - ing, and I with Thee one.
High King of heav - en, my trea - sure Thou art.
Still be my vi - sion, O rul - er of all.

Words from *The Poem Book of the Gael*, edited by Eleanor Hull, by permission of the Editor's Estate and Chatto & Windus.
Arrangement from the *Revised Church Hymnary 1927* by permission of Oxford University Press.

Harmony setting, No. 320

GUIDANCE

548 **Now Praise the Hidden God of Love**

CANONBURY L.M.

Fred Pratt Green, 1975 (1903-)

Robert Schumann (1810-1856)

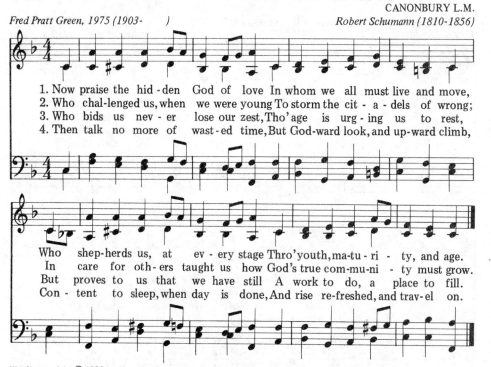

1. Now praise the hid - den God of love In whom we all must live and move,
2. Who chal - lenged us, when we were young To storm the cit - a - dels of wrong;
3. Who bids us nev - er lose our zest, Tho' age is urg - ing us to rest,
4. Then talk no more of wast - ed time, But God-ward look, and up-ward climb,

Who shep-herds us, at ev - ery stage Thro' youth, ma-tu - ri - ty, and age.
In care for oth - ers taught us how God's true com-mu-ni - ty must grow.
But proves to us that we have still A work to do, a place to fill.
Con - tent to sleep, when day is done, And rise re-freshed, and trav-el on.

549 **Loving Shepherd of Thy Sheep**

ORIENTIS PARTIBUS 7.7.7.7.

John 10:27, 28
Jane E. Leeson (1807-1882) alt.

French Melody, c. 1200
Arr. by Richard Redhead, 1835 (1820-1901)

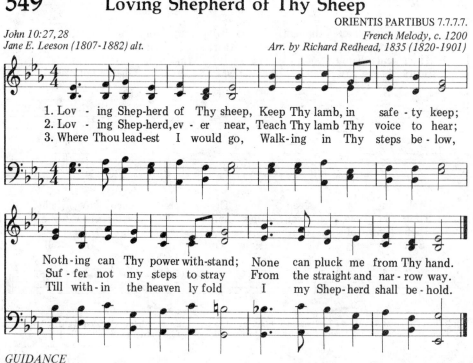

1. Lov - ing Shep-herd of Thy sheep, Keep Thy lamb, in safe - ty keep;
2. Lov - ing Shep-herd, ev - er near, Teach Thy lamb Thy voice to hear;
3. Where Thou lead-est I would go, Walk-ing in Thy steps be - low,

Noth-ing can Thy power with-stand; None can pluck me from Thy hand.
Suf - fer not my steps to stray From the straight and nar - row way.
Till with-in the heaven ly fold I my Shep-herd shall be - hold.

GUIDANCE

LAUREL Irregular

Fern Lazicki, 1966 (1916-)

Dale Wood (1934-)

1. Ev - ery flow'r that grows, Ev - ery brook that flows, Tell of
2. Gra-cious Lord a - bove, Look-ing down in love, Guide my
3. All my earth - ly days, I shall sing and praise God the

beau - ty God has giv'n for me: Through -
thoughts, my life, in my walk with Thee, That
Fa - ther, Spir - it, and Christ the Son. Grant

out my life may beau - ty be Deep with -
day by day the world may see Christ, the
faith when life on earth is done, I shall

in a heart from sin set free.
Lord and Sav - ior, lives in me.
sing with those whose rest is won.

*When sung as a canon, the second part enters at the asterisk, where the melody is also in the tenor.

GUIDANCE

TSDAH-18

551 Jesus, Savior, Pilot Me

PILOT 7.7.7.7.7.7.

Edward Hopper, 1871 (1818-1888)

John E. Gould, 1871 (1822-1875)

1. Je - sus, Sav - ior, pi - lot me   O - ver life's tem-pes-tuous sea;
2. As   a   moth - er stills   her child, Thou canst hush the o-cean wild;
3. When at   last   I near   the shore, And the fear - ful break-ers roar

Un-known waves be-fore me roll,   Hid - ing rock and treach-erous shoal;
Bois-terous waves o - bey Thy will   When Thou sayest to them, "Be still."
'Twixt me   and   the peace-ful rest,   Then, while lean - ing on Thy breast,

Chart and com - pass come from Thee; Je - sus, Sav - ior, pi - lot   me.
Won-drous Sov-ereign of   the   sea,   Je - sus, Sav - ior, pi - lot   me.
May I   hear Thee say   to   me, "Fear not, I   will pi - lot   thee."

552 The Lord's My Shepherd

Psalm 23
Scottish Psalter, 1650

CRIMOND C.M.
Jessie S. Irvine (1836-1887)

1. The Lord's my   Shep - herd, I'll   not want; He   makes   me down   to   lie
2. My soul He   doth   re - store   a - gain. And   me   to   walk doth make
3. Yea, though I   walk   in death's dark vale, Yet   will   I   fear   no   ill,
4. My   ta - ble Thou hast fur - nish - ed   In   pres - ence of   my foes;
5. Good-ness and   mer - cy   all   my life Shall   sure - ly fol - low me;

GUIDANCE

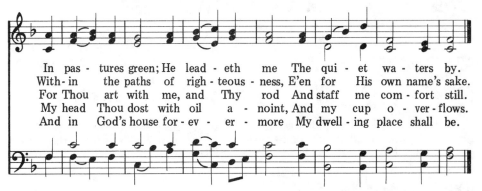

In pas - tures green; He lead - eth me The qui - et wa - ters by.
With - in the paths of righ - teous - ness, E'en for His own name's sake.
For Thou art with me, and Thy rod And staff me com - fort still.
My head Thou dost with oil a - noint, And my cup o - ver - flows.
And in God's house for - ev - er - more My dwell - ing place shall be.

Alternate tune, BROTHER JAMES' AIR, No. 546

Jesus, Guide Our Way 553

SEELENBRAUTIGAM 5.5.8.8.5.5.

Nicolaus Zinzendorf (1700-1760)
Tr. by Arthur T. Russell (1806-1874) and others

Adam Dreese (1620-1701)
Harm. by Samuel S. Wesley (1810-1876)

1. Je - sus, guide our way To e - ter - nal day: So shall
2. When we dan - ger meet Stead - fast make our feet; Lord, pre -
3. Or - der all our way Through the mor - tal day: In our

we, no more de - lay - ing, Fol - low Thee, Thy voice o -
serve us un - com - plain - ing Mid the dark - ness round us
toil, with aid be near us: In our need, with suc - cour

bey - ing: Lead us by the hand To our Fa - ther's land.
reign - ing: Through ad - ver - si - ty lies our way to Thee.
cheer us: Till we safe - ly stand In our Fa - ther's land.

GUIDANCE

554

O Let Me Walk With Thee

MORTON 8.8.8.8.8.8.

Mrs. L. D. Avery Stuttle (1855-1933)

Edwin Barnes, 1886 (1864-1930)

1. O let me walk with Thee, my God, As E-noch walked in days of old;
2. I can-not, dare not, walk a-lone; The tem-pest rag-es in the sky,
3. If I may rest my hand in Thine, I'll count the joys of earth but loss,

Place Thou my trem-bling hand in Thine, And sweet com-mun-ion with me hold;
A thou-sand snares be-set my feet, A thou-sand foes are lurk-ing nigh.
And firm-ly, brave-ly jour-ney on; I'll bear the ban-ner of the cross

E'en though the path I may not see, Yet, Je-sus, let me walk with Thee.
Still Thou the rag-ing of the sea, O Mas-ter! let me walk with Thee.
Till Zi-on's glo-rious gates I see; Yet, Sav-ior, let me walk with Thee.

GUIDANCE

Shepherd of Tender Youth

555

Deut. 32:7
Clement of Alexandria, c. 200
Tr. by Henry M. Dexter, 1846 (1821-1890)

KIRBY BEDON 6.6.4.6.6.6.4.
Edward Bunnett, 1887 (1834-1923)

1. Shep - herd of ten - der youth, Guid - ing in love and truth,
2. Thou art our ho - ly Lord, The all - sub - du - ing Word,
3. Thou art the great High Priest; Thou hast pre-pared the feast
4. Ev - er be Thou our Guide, Our Shep-herd and our pride,

Through de - vious ways; Christ our tri - um-phant King, We come Thy
Heal - er of strife; Thou didst Thy - self a - base, That from sin's
Of heaven - ly love; While in our mor - tal pain None calls on
Our staff and song; Je - sus, Thou Christ of God, By Thy per -

name to sing, Hith - er our chil - dren bring To shout Thy praise.
deep dis - grace Thou might-est save our race, And give us life.
Thee in vain; Help Thou dost not dis - dain, Help from a - bove.
en - nial word, Lead us where Thou hast trod, Make our faith strong.

The earliest Christian hymn extant.

556

As Saints of Old

REGWALL C.M.D.

Frank von Christierson (1900-   ) alt.

Leland B. Sateren (1913-   )

1. As saints of old their first-fruits brought Of or-chard, flock, and
2. A world in need now sum-mons us To la-bor, love, and
3. In grat-i-tude and hum-ble trust We bring our best to -

field To God, the giv-er of all good, The source of boun-teous
give; To make our life an of-fer-ing To God, that all may
day To serve Your cause and share Your love With all a-long life's

yield; So we to-day first-fruits would bring, The wealth of this good
live. The church of Christ is call-ing us To make the dream come
way. O God, who gave Your-self to us In Je-sus Christ Your

land, Of farm and mar-ket, shop and home, Of mind and heart and hand.
true: A world re-deemed by Christ-like love; All life in Christ made new.
Son, Teach us to give our-selves each day Un-til life's work is done.

THANKFULNESS

Come, Ye Thankful People

Henry Alford, 1844 (1810-1871)

ST. GEORGE'S, WINDSOR 7.7.7.7.D.
George J. Elvey, 1858 (1816-1893)

557

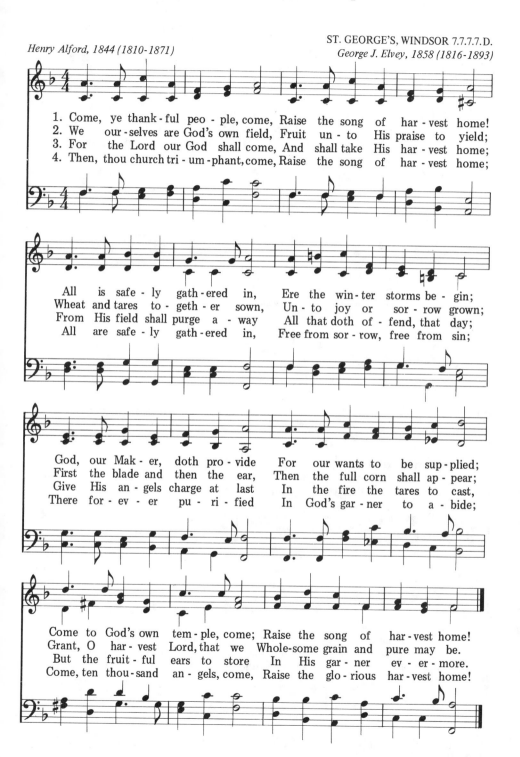

1. Come, ye thank-ful peo-ple, come, Raise the song of har-vest home! All is safe-ly gath-ered in, Ere the win-ter storms be-gin; God, our Mak-er, doth pro-vide For our wants to be sup-plied; Come to God's own tem-ple, come; Raise the song of har-vest home!

2. We our-selves are God's own field, Fruit un-to His praise to yield; Wheat and tares to-geth-er sown, Un-to joy or sor-row grown; First the blade and then the ear, Then the full corn shall ap-pear; Grant, O har-vest Lord, that we Whole-some grain and pure may be.

3. For the Lord our God shall come, And shall take His har-vest home; From His field shall purge a-way All that doth of-fend, that day; Give His an-gels charge at last In the fire the tares to cast, But the fruit-ful ears to store In His gar-ner ev-er-more.

4. Then, thou church tri-um-phant, come, Raise the song of har-vest home; All are safe-ly gath-ered in, Free from sor-row, free from sin; There for-ev-er pu-ri-fied In God's gar-ner to a-bide; Come, ten thou-sand an-gels, come, Raise the glo-rious har-vest home!

THANKFULNESS

558 For the Fruits of His Creation

EAST ACKLAM 8.4.8.4.8.8.8.4.

Fred Pratt Green (1903-   )

Francis Jackson (1917-   )

1. For the fruits of His cre-a-tion, thanks be to God;
2. In the just re-ward of la-bor, God's will is done;
3. For the har-vests of His Spir-it, thanks be to God;

For the gifts to ev-ery na-tion, thanks be to God;
In the help we give our neigh-bor, God's will is done;
For the good all men in-her-it, thanks be to God;

For the plow-ing, sow-ing, reap-ing, Si-lent growth while men are sleep-ing,
In our world-wide task of car-ing For the hun-gry and de-spair-ing,
For the won-ders that as-tound us, For the truths that still con-found us,

Fu-ture needs in earth's safe keep-ing, thanks be to God!
In the har-vests men are shar-ing, God's will is done.
Most of all, that love has found us, thanks be to God!

THANKFULNESS

Now Thank We All Our God

559

Martin Rinkart, 1636 (1586-1649)
Tr. Catherine Winkworth, 1858 (1827-1878)

NUN DANKET 6.7.6.7.6.6.6.6.
Johann Crüger, 1647 (1598-1662)

1. Now thank we all our God With heart and hands and voic - es,
2. O may this boun-teous God Through all our life be near us,
3. All praise and thanks to God, The Fa - ther, now be giv - en,

Who won-drous things hath done, In whom His world re - joic - es;
With ev - er joy - ful hearts And bless - ed peace to cheer us;
The Son, and Him who reigns With them in high-est heav - en,

Who, from our moth - ers' arms Hath blessed us on our way
And keep us in His grace, And guide us when per - plexed,
The one e - ter - nal God, Whom earth and heaven a - dore;

With count - less gifts of love, And still is ours to - day.
And free us from all ills In this world and the next.
For thus it was, is now, And shall be ev - er - more.

THANKFULNESS

560

Let All Things Now Living

THE ASH GROVE 12.11.12.11.D.

1 Chron. 16:23
Katherine K. Davis (1892-1980)

Traditional Welsh Melody
Arr. by Wayne Hooper, 1984 (1920-   )

1. Let all things now living a song of thanks-giv-ing To
2. His law He en-forc-es: the stars in their cours-es, The

God the Cre-a-tor tri-um-phant-ly raise, Who fash-ioned and
sun in His or-bit, o-be-dient-ly shine; The hills and the

made us, pro-tect-ed and stayed us, Who guid-eth us
moun-tains, the riv-ers and foun-tains, The deeps of the

on to the end of our days. His ban-ners are o'er us, His
o-cean pro-claim Him di-vine, We too should be voic-ing our

THANKFULNESS

light goes be - fore us, A pil - lar of fire shin - ing forth in the
love and re - joic - ing, With glad ad - o - ra - tion a song let us

night, 'Til shad - ows have van - ished and dark - ness is
raise, 'Til all things now liv - ing u - nite in thanks -

ban - ished, As for - ward we trav - el from light in - to light.
giv - ing To God in the high - est, ho - san - na and praise.

Unison setting, No. 407

THANKFULNESS

561 We Plow the Fields

Matthias Claudius (1740-1815)
Tr. by Jane M. Campbell (1817-1878)

WIR PFLÜGEN 7.6.7.6.D.Ref.
Johann A. P. Schulz (1747-1800)

1. We plow the fields and scat-ter The good seed on the land,
2. He on-ly is the Mak-er Of all things near and far;
3. We thank Thee then, O Fa-ther, For all things bright and good:

But it is fed and wa-tered By God's al-might-y hand.
He paints the way-side flow-er, He lights the eve-ning star.
The seed-time and the har-vest, Our life, our health, our food.

He sends the snow in win-ter, The warmth to swell the grain,
The winds and waves o-bey Him, By Him the birds are fed;
Ac-cept the gifts we of-fer For all Thy love im-parts,

The breez-es and the sun-shine, And soft, re-fresh-ing rain.
Much more, to us His chil-dren, He gives our dai-ly bread.
And, what Thou most de-sir-est, Our hum-ble, thank-ful hearts.

THANKFULNESS

All good gifts a-round us Are sent from heaven a-bove;

Then thank the Lord, O thank the Lord For all His love.

Come, Sing a Song of Harvest 562

LEBENDIGE GEMEINDE 7.6.7.6.

Fred Pratt Green, 1976 (1903-   )   *Horst Gehann, 1958 (1928-   )*

1. Come, sing a song of har - vest, Of thanks for dai - ly food!
2. Long, long a - go, the reap - ers, Be - fore they kept the feast,
3. Shall we, some-times for - get - ful Of where cre - a - tion starts,
4. May God, the great Cre - a - tor, To whom all life be - longs,
5. And lest the world go hun - gry While we our-selves are fed,

To of - fer God the first - fruits Is old as grat - i - tude.
Put first-fruits in a bas - ket, And took it to the priest.
With sci - ence in our pock - ets Lose won - der from our hearts?
Ac - cept these gifts we of - fer, Our ser - vice and our songs.
Make each of us more read - y To share our dai - ly bread.

THANKFULNESS

563   Praise and Thanksgiving

LOBET UND PREISET 10.10.8.
Alsatian canon

Edith Lovell Thomas, 1950

Accomp. by Melvin West, 1984 (1930-   )

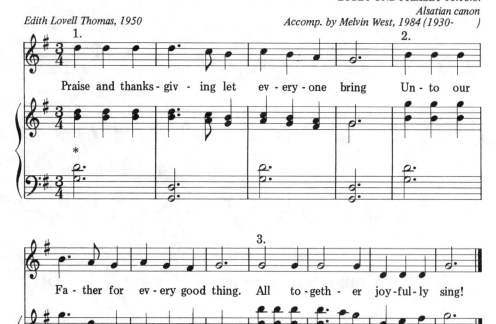

Praise and thanks-giv - ing let ev-ery-one bring Un-to our Fa - ther for ev-ery good thing. All to-geth - er joy-ful-ly sing!

*Accompaniment may repeat any 4-bar phrase for duration of the canon.
Used by permission of Friendship Press.

THANKFULNESS

For Sunrise Hope and Sunset Calm 564

HYMN OF PRAISE C.M.D.

Amy Carmichael (1867-1951)

Kenneth S. Proctor (1895-   )

1. For sun - rise hope and sun - set calm, And all that lies be - tween,
2. But O, we press far, far a - bove These gifts of pure de - light,

For all the sweet - ness and the balm That is and that has been,
And find in Thee, and in Thy love Con - tent-ment in - fi - nite.

For com - rade-ship for peace in strife, And light on dark-ened days;
O Lord, be - loved, in whom are found All joys of time and place,

For work to do and strength for life We sing our hymn of praise.
What will it be when joy is crowned By vi - sion of Thy face?

From *Wings* by Amy Carmichael. Copyright 1960 by Dohnavur Fellowship.

THANKFULNESS

565 For the Beauty of the Earth

DIX 7.7.7.7.7.7.

Folliott S. Pierpoint, 1864 (1835-1917)

Conrad Kocher, 1838 (1786-1872)
Arr. by William Monk, 1861 (1823-1889)

1. For the beau-ty of the earth, For the glo-ry of the skies,
2. For the joy of hu-man love, Broth-er, sis-ter, par-ent, child,
3. For the gift of Thy dear Son, For the hope of heaven at last,

For the love which from our birth O-ver and a-round us lies,
Friends on earth and Friend a-bove, Pleas-ures pure and un-de-filed,
For the Spir-it's vic-tory won, For the crown when life is past,

Lord of all, to Thee we raise This our grate-ful song of praise.
Lord of all, to Thee we raise This our grate-ful song of praise.
Lord of all, to Thee we raise Songs of grat-i-tude and praise.

Unison setting, No. 123

THANKFULNESS

Father, We Thank You

ALL KINDS OF LIGHT 5.8.8.5.5.
Caryl Micklem

Caryl Micklem (1925-)
Unison

1. Fa - ther, we thank You For the light that shines all the
2. Fa - ther, we thank You For the lamps that light - en the
3. Fa - ther, we thank You For the friends who bright - en our
4. Fa - ther, we thank You For Your love in Je - sus to -

day; For the bright sky You have giv - en
way; For hu - man skill's ex - plo - ra - tion
play; For Your com - mand to call oth - ers
day, Giv - ing us hope for to - mor - row

Most like Your heav - en; Fa - ther, we thank You.
Of Your cre - a - tion; Fa - ther, we thank You.
Sis - ters and broth - ers; Fa - ther, we thank You.
Through joy and sor - row; Fa - ther, we thank You.

THANKFULNESS

567 Have Thine Own Way, Lord

Adelaide Pollard (1862-1934)

ADELAIDE 9.9.9.9.
George C. Stebbins, 1907 (1846-1945)

1. Have Thine own way, Lord! Have Thine own way! Thou art the Pot- ter; I am the clay. Mold me and make me Af- ter Thy will, While I am wait- ing, Yield-ed and still.

2. Have Thine own way, Lord! Have Thine own way! Search me and try me, Mas- ter, to- day! Whit- er than snow, Lord, Wash me just now, As in Thy pres- ence Hum-bly I bow.

3. Have Thine own way, Lord! Have Thine own way! Wound-ed and wea- ry Help me, I pray! Pow- er— all pow- er— Sure- ly is Thine! Touch me and heal me, Sav- ior di- vine!

4. Have Thine own way, Lord! Have Thine own way! Hold o'er my be- ing Ab- so- lute sway! Fill with Thy Spir- it Till all shall see Christ on- ly, al- ways, Liv- ing in me!

HUMILITY

Make Me a Captive, Lord

LEOMINSTER S.M.D.
George W. Martin, 1862 (1828-1881)
Arr. by Arthur S. Sullivan, 1874 (1842-1900)

George Matheson, 1890 (1842-1906)

1. Make me a cap-tive, Lord, And then I shall be free;
2. My heart is weak and poor Till it a mas-ter find;
3. My will is not my own Till Thou hast made it Thine;

Force me to ren-der up my sword, And I shall con-queror be.
It has no spring of ac-tion sure— It var-ies with the wind.
If it would reach a mon-arch's throne It must its crown re-sign;

I sink in life's a-larms When by my-self I stand;
It can-not free-ly move Till Thou hast wrought its chain;
It on-ly stands un-bent, A-mid the clash-ing strife,

Im-pris-on me with-in Thine arms, And strong shall be my hand.
En-slave it with Thy match-less love, And death-less it shall reign.
When on Thy bos-om it has leant And found in Thee its life.

HUMILITY

569 Pass Me Not, O Gentle Savior

Fanny J. Crosby, 1868 (1820-1915)

8.5.8.5.Ref.
William H. Doane, 1870 (1832-1915)

1. Pass me not, O gentle Savior, Hear my humble cry;
2. Let me at Thy throne of mercy Find a sweet relief;
3. Trusting only in Thy merit, Would I seek Thy face;
4. Thou the spring of all my comfort, More than life for me;

While on others Thou art calling, Do not pass me by.
Kneeling there in deep contrition, Help my unbelief.
Heal my wounded, broken spirit, Save me by Thy grace.
Whom have I on earth beside Thee? Whom in heaven but Thee?

Refrain

Savior, Savior, hear my humble cry,

While on others Thou art calling, Do not pass me by.

HUMILITY

Not I, but Christ

570

A. A. F.
Arr. Fannie E. Bolton, 1900

BOLTON 11.10.11.10.
Fannie E. Bolton, Alt., 1900 (18?-1926)

1. Not I, but Christ, be hon-ored, loved, ex - alt - ed;
2. Not I, but Christ, to gen - tly soothe in sor - row,
3. Christ, on - ly Christ! no i - dle words e'er fall - ing,
4. Not I, but Christ, my ev - ery need sup - ply - ing,

Not I, but Christ, be seen, be known, be heard;
Not I, but Christ, to wipe the fall - ing tear;
Christ, on - ly Christ; no need - less bus - tling sound;
Not I, but Christ, my strength and health to be;

Not I, but Christ, in ev - ery look and ac - tion,
Not I, but Christ, to lift the wea - ry bur - den,
Christ, on - ly Christ; no self im - por - tant bear - ing;
Christ, on - ly Christ, for bod - y, soul, and spir - it,

Not I, but Christ, in ev - ery thought and word.
Not I, but Christ, to hush a - way all fear.
Christ, on - ly Christ; no trace of "I" be found.
Christ, on - ly Christ, here and e - ter - nal - ly.

HUMILITY

571 What Does the Lord Require?

Micah 6:8
Albert F. Bayly (1901-1984)

SHARPTHORNE 6.6.6.6.3.3.6.
Erik Routley (1917-1982)

Unison

1. What does the Lord re-quire for praise and of-fer-ing?
2. Rul-ers of men, give ear! should you not jus-tice show?
3. How shall our life ful-fill God's law so hard and high?

What sac-ri-fice, de-sire or trib-ute bid you
Will God your plead-ing hear, while crime and cruel-ty
Let Christ en-due our will with grace to for-ti-

bring? Do just-ly; Love mer-cy; Walk
grow? Do just-ly; Love mer-cy; Walk
fy. Then just-ly, in mer-cy we'll

[1,2]
hum-bly with your God.
hum-bly with your God.

[3]
hum-bly walk with God.

LOVING SERVICE

Give of Your Best to the Master

572

BARNARD 8.7.8.7.D.Ref.
Charlotte A. Barnard (1830-1869)

Howard B. Grose (1851-1939)

1. Give of your best to the Mas-ter, Give of the strength of your youth;
2. Give of your best to the Mas-ter, Give Him first place in your heart;
3. Give of your best to the Mas-ter, Naught else is wor-thy His love;
Ref. Give of your best to the Mas-ter, Give of the strength of your youth;

Throw your soul's fresh, glow-ing ar-dor In-to the bat-tle for truth.
Give Him first place in your ser-vice, Con-se-crate ev-ery part.
He gave Him-self for your ran-som, Gave up His glo-ry a-bove;
Clad in sal-va-tion's full ar-mor, Join in the bat-tle for truth.

Je-sus has set the ex-am-ple—Daunt-less was He, young and brave;
Give, and to you shall be giv-en—God His be-lov-ed Son gave;
Laid down His life with-out mur-mur, You from sin's ru-in to save;

Give Him your loy-al de-vo-tion, Give Him the best that you have.
Grate-ful-ly seek-ing to serve Him, Give Him the best that you have.
Give Him your heart's ad-o-ra-tion, Give Him the best that you have.

LOVING SERVICE

573   I'll Go Where You Want Me to Go

Mary Brown, 19th century

9.7.9.7.D.Ref.
Carrie E. Rounsefell (1861-1930)

1. It may not be on the moun-tain's height, Or o - ver the storm-y sea;
2. Per - haps to-day there are lov - ing words Which Je-sus would have me speak;
3. There's sure - ly somewhere a low - ly place In earth's harvest-fields so wide,

It may not be at the bat - tle's front My Lord will have need of me;
There may be now, in the paths of sin, Some wand'rer whom I should seek.
Where I may la - bor thro'life's short day For Je - sus, the Cru - ci - fied.

But if by a still, small voice He calls To paths I do not know,
O Sav - ior, if Thou wilt be my Guide, Tho' dark and rug-ged the way,
So, trust-ing my all un - to Thy care, I know Thou lov - est me!

I'll an-swer, dear Lord, with my hand in Thine, I'll go where You want me to go.
My voice shall ech- o the mes-sage sweet, I'll say what You want me to say.
I'll do Thy will with a heart sin-cere, I'll be what You want me to be.

LOVING SERVICE

I'll go where You want me to go, dear Lord, O'er moun-tain, or plain, or sea;

I'll say what You want me to say, dear Lord, I'll be what You want me to be.

O Master, Let Me Walk With Thee 574

Washington Gladden, 1879 (1836-1918)

MARYTON L.M.
H. Percy Smith, 1874 (1825-1898)

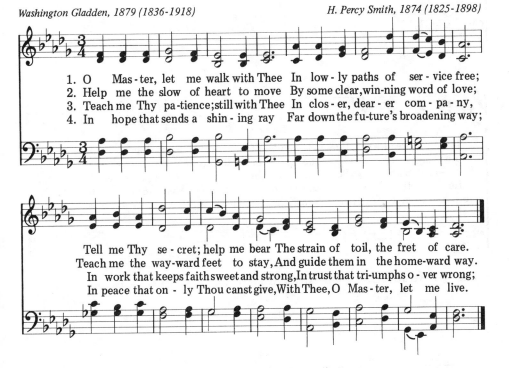

1. O Mas-ter, let me walk with Thee In low-ly paths of ser-vice free;
2. Help me the slow of heart to move By some clear, win-ning word of love;
3. Teach me Thy pa-tience; still with Thee In clos-er, dear-er com-pa-ny,
4. In hope that sends a shin-ing ray Far down the fu-ture's broadening way;

Tell me Thy se-cret; help me bear The strain of toil, the fret of care.
Teach me the way-ward feet to stay, And guide them in the home-ward way.
In work that keeps faith sweet and strong, In trust that tri-umphs o-ver wrong;
In peace that on-ly Thou canst give, With Thee, O Mas-ter, let me live.

LOVING SERVICE

575 Let Your Heart Be Broken

BJORKLUND 6.5.6.5.D.

Bryan Jeffery Leech, 1975 (1931-   )

Bryan Jeffery Leech

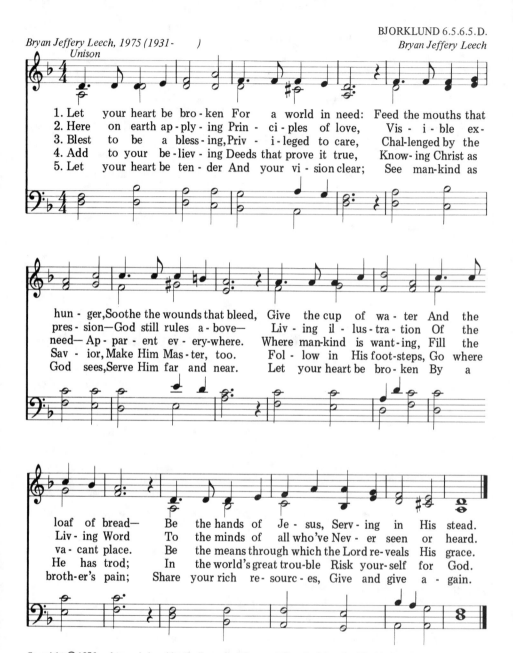

1. Let your heart be bro-ken For a world in need: Feed the mouths that hun-ger, Soothe the wounds that bleed, Give the cup of wa-ter And the loaf of bread— Be the hands of Je - sus, Serv-ing in His stead.
2. Here on earth ap-ply-ing Prin - ci-ples of love, Vis - i-ble ex-pres-sion—God still rules a-bove— Liv - ing il - lus-tra-tion Of the Liv - ing Word To the minds of all who've Nev - er seen or heard.
3. Blest to be a bless-ing, Priv - i-leged to care, Chal-lenged by the need—Ap - par - ent ev - ery-where. Where man-kind is want-ing, Fill the va - cant place. Be the means through which the Lord re-veals His grace.
4. Add to your be - liev - ing Deeds that prove it true, Know-ing Christ as Sav - ior, Make Him Mas-ter, too. Fol - low in His foot-steps, Go where He has trod; In the world's great trou-ble Risk your-self for God.
5. Let your heart be ten - der And your vi - sion clear; See man-kind as God sees, Serve Him far and near. Let your heart be bro-ken By a broth-er's pain; Share your rich re - sourc - es, Give and give a - gain.

LOVING SERVICE

Awake, Awake to Love and Work

MORNING SONG 8.6.8.6.8.6.

Melody, Kentucky Harmony, *1816*

Geoffrey A. Studdert-Kennedy, 1921 (1883-1929)   Harm. by C. Winfred Douglas, 1940 (1867-1944)

1. A - wake, a - wake to love and work! The lark is in the sky;
2. Come, let thy voice be one with theirs, Shout with their shout of praise;
3. To give and give, and give a - gain, What God hath giv - en thee;

The fields are wet with dia - mond dew; The worlds a - wake to cry
See how the gi - ant sun soars up, Great lord of years and days!
To spend thy - self nor count the cost; To serve right glo - rious - ly

Their bless - ings on the Lord of life, As He goes meek - ly by.
So let the love of Je - sus come And set thy soul a - blaze.
The God who gave all worlds that are, And all that are to be.

Unison setting, No. 215

LOVING SERVICE

577

In the Heart of Jesus

Alice Pugh

HEART OF JESUS 6.5.6.5.D.
C. H. Forrest, c. 1897

1. In the heart of Je - sus There is love for you,
2. In the mind of Je - sus There is thought for you,
3. In the field of Je - sus There is work for you;
4. In the home of Je - sus There's a place for you;

Love most pure and ten - der, Love most deep and true;
Warm as sum - mer sun - shine, Sweet as morn - ing dew;
Such as e - ven an - gels Might re - joice to do;
Glo - rious, bright, and joy - ous, Calm and peace - ful, too;

Why should you be lone - ly, Why for friend - ship sigh,
Why should you be fear - ful, Why take anx - ious thought,
Why stand i - dly sigh - ing For some life - work grand,
Why then, like a wan - derer, Roam with wea - ry pace,

When the heart of Je - sus Has a full sup - ply?
Since the mind of Je - sus Cares for those He bought?
While the field of Je - sus Seeks your reap - ing hand?
If the home of Je - sus Holds for you a place?

LOVING SERVICE

So Send I You

578

John 20:21
E. Margaret Clarkson, 1937 (1915-   )

TORONTO 11.10.11.10.Ref.
John W. Peterson, 1954 (1927-   )

1. So send I you— by grace made strong to tri-umph O'er hosts of hell, o'er dark-ness, death, and sin, My name to bear, and in that name to con-quer— So send I you, My vic-to-ry to win.

2. So send I you— to take to souls in bond-age The word of truth that sets the cap-tive free, To break the bonds of sin, to loose death's fet-ters— So send I you, to bring the lost to Me.

3. So send I you— My strength to know in weak-ness, My joy in grief, My per-fect peace in pain, To prove My power, My grace, My prom-ised pres-ence— So send I you, e-ter-nal fruit to gain.

4. So send I you— to bear My cross with pa-tience, And then one day with joy to lay it down, To hear My voice, "Well done, My faith-ful ser-vant— Come, share My throne, My king-dom, and My crown!" "As the Fa-ther hath sent Me, So send I you."

LOVING SERVICE

579 'Tis Love That Makes Us Happy

F. E. Belden, 1892

7.6.8.6.Ref.

F. E. Belden (1858-1945)

1. 'Tis love that makes us hap - py, 'Tis love that smooths the way;
2. This world is full of sor - row, Of sick - ness, death, and sin;
3. And when this life is o - ver, And we are called a - bove

It helps us mind, it makes us kind To oth - ers ev - ery day.
With lov - ing heart we'll do our part, And try some soul to win.
Our song shall be, e - ter - nal - ly, Of Je - sus and His love.

Refrain

God is love; we're His lit - tle chil - dren. God is love; we would be like

Him. 'Tis love that makes us hap - py, 'Tis love that smooths the way;

It helps us "mind," it makes us kind To oth - ers ev - ery day.

LOVING SERVICE

This Little Light of Mine

580

Irregular
Arr. by Alma Blackmon, 1984 (1921-   )
Adapt. from John W. Work (1901-1967)

American Negro Spiritual

1. This lit - tle light of mine,
2. Ev - ery - where I go,
3. All through the night,

I'm going to let it shine, (shine)

This lit - tle light of mine,
Ev - ery - where I go,
All through the night,

I'm going to let it shine, (shine)

of mine,

This lit - tle light of mine,
Ev - ery - where I go,
All through the night,

I'm going to let it shine,

Let it shine, let it shine, let it shine.

LOVING SERVICE

581 When the Church of Jesus

KING'S WESTON 6.5.6.5.D.
Fred Pratt Green (1903-   )
Ralph Vaughan Williams (1872-1958)

1. When the church of Je - sus Shuts its out - er door,
2. If our hearts are lift - ed Where de - vo - tion soars
3. Lest the gifts we of - fer, Mon - ey, tal - ents, time,

Lest the roar of traf - fic Drown the voice of prayer:
High a - bove this hun - gry Suf-fering world of ours:
Serve to salve our con - science To our se - cret shame:

May our prayers, Lord, make us Ten times more a - ware
Lest our hymns should drug us To for - get its needs,
Lord, re - prove, in - spire us By the way You give;

That the world we ban - ish Is our Chris - tian care.
Forge our Chris-tian wor - ship In - to Chris - tian deeds.
Teach us, dy - ing Sav - ior, How true Chris - tians live.

LOVING SERVICE

Working, O Christ, With Thee

582

ST. EDMUND 6.4.6.4.6.6.6.4.

W. A. Ogden (1841-1897)

Arthur S. Sullivan, 1872 (1842-1900)

1. Work - ing, O Christ, with Thee, Work - ing with Thee,
2. A - long the cit - y's waste, Work - ing with Thee,
3. Sav - ior, we wea - ry not, Work - ing with Thee,
4. So let us la - bor on, Work - ing with Thee,

Un - wor - thy, sin - ful, weak, Though we may be;
Our ea - ger foot-steps haste, Like Thee to be;
As hard as Thine our lot Can nev - er be;
Till earth to Thee is won, From sin set free;

Our all to Thee we give, For Thee a - lone we live,
The poor we gath - er in, The out - casts raise from sin,
Our joy and com - fort this, "Thy grace suf - fi - cient is;"
Till men, from shore to shore, Re - ceive Thee, and a - dore,

And by Thy grace a - chieve, Work - ing with Thee.
And la - bor souls to win, Work - ing with Thee.
This chang - es toil to bliss, Work - ing with Thee.
And join us ev - er - more, Work - ing with Thee.

LOVING SERVICE

583 You That Know the Lord

1 Peter 2:4-10
C. A. Alington, 1950 (1872-1955)

ABBOT'S LEIGH 8.7.8.7.D.
Cyril V. Taylor, 1941 (1907-   )

1. You that know the Lord is gra-cious, You for whom a
2. Liv - ing stones by God ap - point-ed Each to his al -
3. Tell the praise of Him who called you Out of dark - ness

cor - ner-stone Stands, of God, e - lect and pre - cious,
lot - ted place, Kings and priests, by God a - noint - ed,
in - to light, Broke the fet - ters that en - thralled you,

Laid that you may build there - on, See that on that
Shall you not de - clare His grace? You, a roy - al
Gave you free - dom, peace, and sight: Tell the tale of

sure foun - da - tion You a liv - ing tem - ple raise.
gen - er - a - tion, Tell the tid - ings of your birth,
sins for - giv - en, Strength re - newed and hope re - stored,

LOVING SERVICE

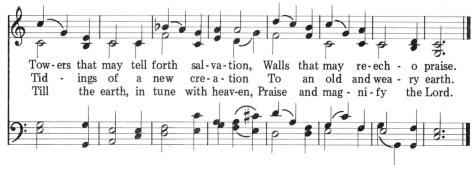

Tow-ers that may tell forth sal-va-tion, Walls that may re-ech - o praise.
Tid - ings of a new cre-a-tion To an old and wea - ry earth.
Till the earth, in tune with heav-en, Praise and mag - ni-fy the Lord.

Alternate tune, AUSTRIA, No. 423
Higher key, No. 61

There's a Spirit in the Air 584

LAUDS 7.7.7.7.

Brian Wren, 1974 (1936-   )   *John Wilson, 1969 (1905-   )*

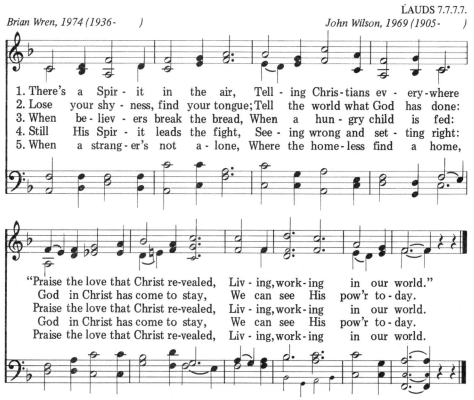

1. There's a Spir - it in the air, Tell - ing Chris-tians ev - ery-where
2. Lose your shy - ness, find your tongue; Tell the world what God has done:
3. When be - liev - ers break the bread, When a hun - gry child is fed:
4. Still His Spir - it leads the fight, See - ing wrong and set - ting right:
5. When a strang - er's not a - lone, Where the home-less find a home,

"Praise the love that Christ re-vealed, Liv - ing, work-ing in our world."
God in Christ has come to stay, We can see His pow'r to - day.
Praise the love that Christ re-vealed, Liv - ing, work-ing in our world.
God in Christ has come to stay, We can see His pow'r to - day.
Praise the love that Christ re-vealed, Liv - ing, work-ing in our world.

6. May His Spirit fill our praise,
   Guide our thoughts and change our ways.
   God in Christ has come to stay,
   We can see His power today.

7. There's a Spirit in the air,
   Calling people everywhere;
   Praise the love that Christ revealed:
   Living, working in our world.

LOVING SERVICE

585 When Christ Was Lifted From the Earth

ST. BOTOLPH C.M.

Brian Wren, 1970 (1936-   )

Gordon Slater (1896-1979)

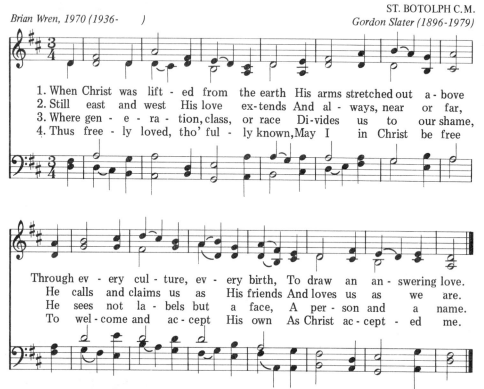

1. When Christ was lift - ed from the earth His arms stretched out a - bove
2. Still east and west His love ex - tends And al - ways, near or far,
3. Where gen - e - ra - tion, class, or race Di - vides us to our shame,
4. Thus free - ly loved, tho' ful - ly known, May I in Christ be free

Through ev - ery cul - ture, ev - ery birth, To draw an an - swering love.
He calls and claims us as His friends And loves us as we are.
He sees not la - bels but a face, A per - son and a name.
To wel - come and ac - cept His own As Christ ac - cept - ed me.

586 What Joy It Is to Worship Here

JEG ER SAA GLAD C.M.

Fred Pratt Green, 1980 (1903-   )

Peter Knudsen (1819-1863)

1. What joy it is to wor - ship here, And find our - selves at home,
2. Yet are no two of us a - like Of all the hu - man race,

LOVE FOR ONE ANOTHER

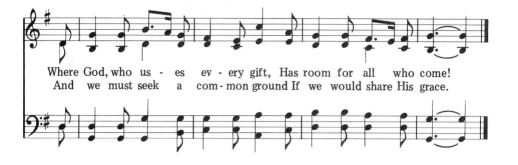

Where God, who us - es ev - ery gift, Has room for all who come!
And we must seek a com - mon ground If we would share His grace.

In Christ There Is No East nor West 587

ST. PETER C.M.

John Oxenham, 1908 (1852-1941)

Alexander R. Reinagle, 1836 (1799-1877)

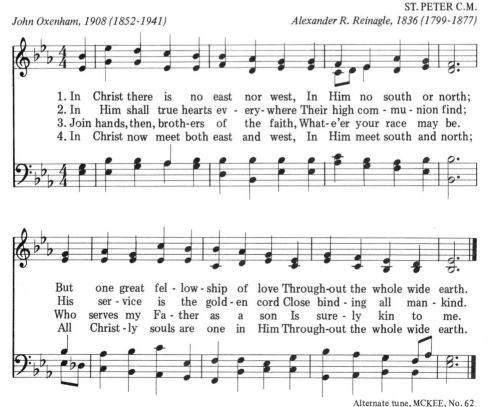

1. In Christ there is no east nor west, In Him no south or north;
2. In Him shall true hearts ev - ery-where Their high com - mu - nion find;
3. Join hands, then, broth-ers of the faith, What-e'er your race may be.
4. In Christ now meet both east and west, In Him meet south and north;

But one great fel - low - ship of love Through-out the whole wide earth.
His ser - vice is the gold - en cord Close bind - ing all man - kind.
Who serves my Fa - ther as a son Is sure - ly kin to me.
All Christ - ly souls are one in Him Through-out the whole wide earth.

Alternate tune, MCKEE, No. 62

LOVE FOR ONE ANOTHER

588 Lord of All Nations

Acts 10:34, 35
Olive Wise Spannaus (1916-   )

MELROSE L.M.
Frederick C. Maker (1844-1927)

1. Lord of all nations, grant me grace To love all peo - ple, ev - ery race, And in each per - son may I see My kin - dred loved, re - deemed by Thee.
2. Break down the wall that would di - vide Thy chil - dren, Lord, on ev - ery side. My neigh-bor's good let me pur - sue; Let Chris - tian love bind warm and true.
3. For - give me, Lord, where I have erred By love - less act and thought - less word. Make me to see the wrong I do Will cru - ci - fy my Lord a - new.
4. Give me Thy cour - age, Lord, to speak When-ev - er strong op - press the weak. Should I my - self the vic - tim be, Help me for - give, re - mem - b'ring Thee.
5. With Thine own love may I be filled And by Thy Ho - ly Spir - it willed, That all I touch, wher - e'er I be, May be di - vine - ly touched by Thee.

Words from *The Worship Supplement* copyright © 1969 by Concordia Publishing House. Used by permission.

LOVE FOR ONE ANOTHER

Holy Spirit, Gracious Guest

1 Cor. 13
Christopher Wordsworth (1807-1885)

GUILDFORD CATHEDRAL 7.7.7.5.
Grayston Ives (1948-   )

1. Ho - ly Spir - it, gra - cious guest, Hear and
2. Faith that moun - tains could re - move, Tongues of
3. Though I as a mar - tyr bleed, Give my
4. Love is kind and suf - fers long, Love is
5. Proph - e - cy will fade a - way, Melt - ing
6. Faith and hope and love we see Join - ing

*Ho - ly Spir - it, gra - cious guest,

grant our heart's re - quest For that gift su -
earth or heaven a - bove, Knowl-edge, all things,
goods the poor to feed, All is vain if
pure and thinks no wrong, Love than death it -
in the light of day; Love will ev - er
hand in hand a - gree— But the great - est

Hear and grant our heart's re - quest For that gift

preme and best: Ho - ly heav - 'nly love.
emp - ty prove If I have no love.
love I need: There-fore give me love.
self more strong: There-fore give us love.
with us stay: There-fore give us love.
of the three, And the best is love.

su - preme and best: Ho - ly heav - 'nly love.

*When sung as a canon, second part begins here.

Music printed by permission of Basil Ramsey Publisher of Music Ltd.

LOVE FOR ONE ANOTHER

590   Trust and Obey

6.6.9.6.6.9.Ref.

J. H. Sammis (1846-1919)

Daniel B. Towner (1850-1919)

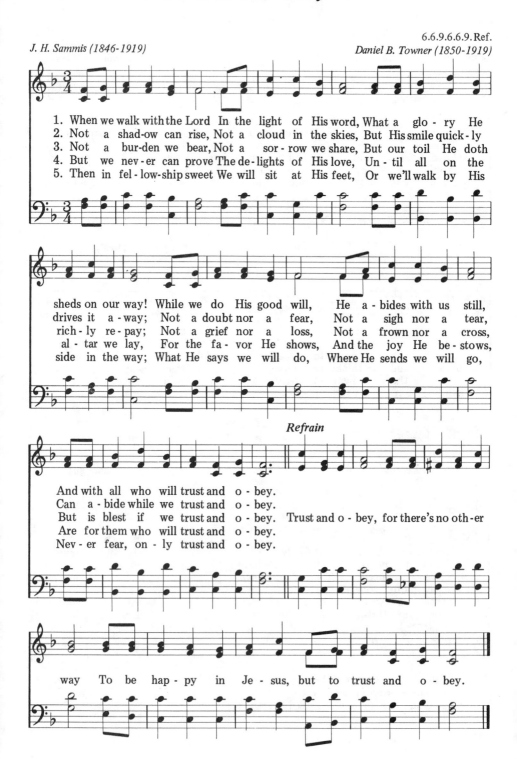

1. When we walk with the Lord In the light of His word, What a glo-ry He
2. Not a shad-ow can rise, Not a cloud in the skies, But His smile quick-ly
3. Not a bur-den we bear, Not a sor-row we share, But our toil He doth
4. But we nev-er can prove The de-lights of His love, Un-til all on the
5. Then in fel-low-ship sweet We will sit at His feet, Or we'll walk by His

sheds on our way! While we do His good will, He a-bides with us still,
drives it a-way; Not a doubt nor a fear, Not a sigh nor a tear,
rich-ly re-pay; Not a grief nor a loss, Not a frown nor a cross,
al-tar we lay, For the fa-vor He shows, And the joy He be-stows,
side in the way; What He says we will do, Where He sends we will go,

Refrain

And with all who will trust and o-bey.
Can a-bide while we trust and o-bey.
But is blest if we trust and o-bey.   Trust and o-bey, for there's no oth-er
Are for them who will trust and o-bey.
Nev-er fear, on-ly trust and o-bey.

way To be hap-py in Je-sus, but to trust and o-bey.

OBEDIENCE

In Our Work and in Our Play 591

ROSSLYN 7.7.7.7.7.7.

Whitfield G. Wills (1841-1891)

English Melody

OBEDIENCE

592 Watchman, Tell Us of the Night

Isa. 21:11,12
John Bowring, 1825 (1792-1872) alt. 1972

ABERYSTWYTH 7.7.7.7.D.
Joseph Parry, 1879 (1841-1903)

1. Watch-man, tell us of the night, What its signs of prom-ise are.
2. Watch-man, tell us of the night, High-er yet that star as-cends.
3. Watch-man, tell us of the night, For the morn-ing seems to dawn.

Trav-eler, o'er yon moun-tain's height, See that glo-ry-beam-ing star.
Trav-eler, bless-ed-ness and light, Peace and truth its course por-tends.
Trav-eler, dark-ness takes its flight, Doubt and ter-ror are with-drawn.

Watch-man, does its beau-teous ray Aught of joy or hope fore-tell?
Watch-man, will its beams a-lone Gild the spot that gave them birth?
Watch-man, let your wan-derings cease; Has-ten to your qui-et home.

Trav-eler, yes; it brings the day, Prom-ised day of Is-ra-el.
Trav-eler, a-ges are its own; See, it bursts o'er all the earth.
Trav-eler, lo, the Prince of Peace, Lo, the Son of God is come!

WATCHFULNESS

In Times Like These

593

9.9.8.10.Ref.

Ruth Caye Jones (1902-1972)

Ruth Caye Jones, 1944

1. In times like these you need a Sav-ior, In times like these you need an
2. In times like these you need the Bi-ble, In times like these O be not
3. In times like these I have a Sav-ior, In times like these I have an

an-chor; Be ver-y sure, be ver-y sure Your an-chor holds
i-dle; Be ver-y sure, be ver-y sure Your an-chor holds
an-chor; I'm ver-y sure, I'm ver-y sure My an-chor holds

Refrain

and grips the sol-id Rock! This Rock is Je-sus, Yes, He's the

One; This Rock is Je-sus, The on-ly One! 1, 2. Be ver-y sure,
3. I'm ver-y sure,

be ver-y sure Your an-chor holds and grips the sol-id Rock!
I'm ver-y sure My an-chor holds and grips the sol-id Rock!

WATCHFULNESS

594

Heir of the Kingdom

RODMAN 11.10.11.10.

Lowell Mason (1792-1872)

Anon.

1. Heir of the king - dom, O why dost thou slum - ber?
2. Heir of the king - dom, say, why dost thou lin - ger?
3. Earth's might - y na - tions, in strife and com - mo - tion,
4. Stay not, O stay not for earth's vain al - lure - ments!
5. Keep the eye sin - gle, the head up - ward lift - ed;

Why art thou sleep - ing so near thy blest home?
How canst thou tar - ry in sight of the prize?
Trem - ble with ter - ror, and sink in dis - may;
See how its glo - ry is pass - ing a - way;
Watch for the glo - ry of earth's com - ing King;

Wake thee, a - rouse thee, and gird on thine ar - mor,
Up, and a - dorn thee, the Sav - ior is com - ing;
Lis - ten, 'tis nought but the char - iot's loud rum - bling;
Break the strong fet - ters the foe hath bound o'er thee;
Lo! o'er the moun - tain-tops light is now break - ing;

Speed, for the mo - ments are hur - ry - ing on.
Haste to re - ceive Him de - scend - ing the skies.
Heir of the king - dom, no lon - ger de - lay.
Heir of the king - dom, turn, turn thee a - way.
Heirs of the king - dom, re - joice ye and sing.

WATCHFULNESS

Let Every Lamp Be Burning

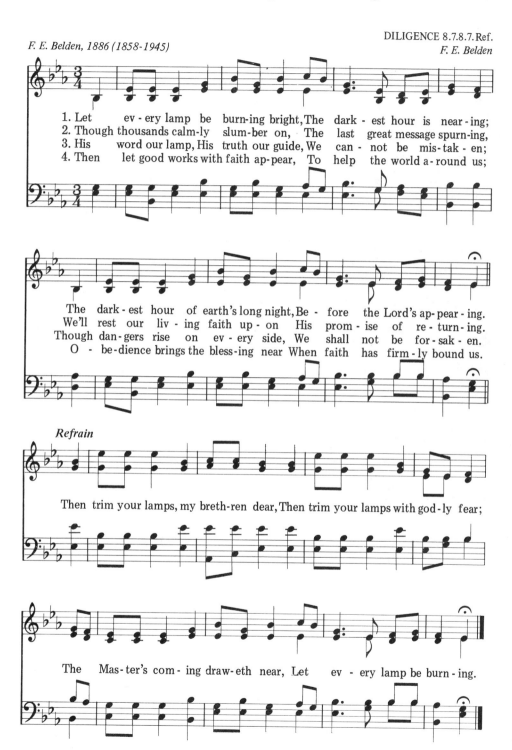

595

DILIGENCE 8.7.8.7.Ref.
F. E. Belden

F. E. Belden, 1886 (1858-1945)

1. Let ev - ery lamp be burn - ing bright, The dark - est hour is near - ing;
2. Though thousands calm - ly slum - ber on, The last great message spurn - ing,
3. His word our lamp, His truth our guide, We can - not be mis - tak - en;
4. Then let good works with faith ap - pear, To help the world a - round us;

The dark - est hour of earth's long night, Be - fore the Lord's ap - pear - ing.
We'll rest our liv - ing faith up - on His prom - ise of re - turn - ing.
Though dan - gers rise on ev - ery side, We shall not be for - sak - en.
O - be - dience brings the bless - ing near When faith has firm - ly bound us.

Refrain

Then trim your lamps, my breth - ren dear, Then trim your lamps with god - ly fear;

The Mas - ter's com - ing draw - eth near, Let ev - ery lamp be burn - ing.

WATCHFULNESS

596 Look for the Waymarks

Dan. 2:31-44
F. E. Belden, 1886 (1858-1945)

10.10.10.10.Ref.
F. E. Belden, 1886

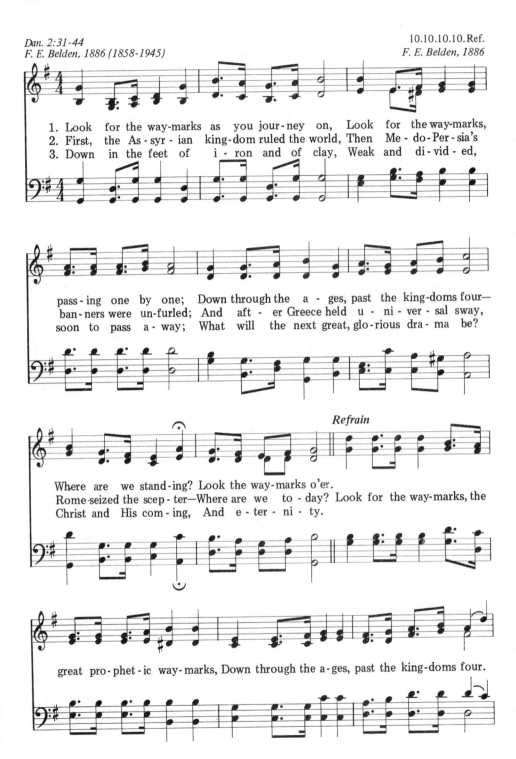

1. Look for the way-marks as you jour-ney on, Look for the way-marks,
2. First, the As-syr-ian king-dom ruled the world, Then Me-do-Per-sia's
3. Down in the feet of i-ron and of clay, Weak and di-vid-ed,

pass-ing one by one; Down through the a-ges, past the king-doms four—
ban-ners were un-furled; And aft-er Greece held u-ni-ver-sal sway,
soon to pass a-way; What will the next great, glo-rious dra-ma be?

Refrain

Where are we stand-ing? Look the way-marks o'er.
Rome seized the scep-ter—Where are we to-day? Look for the way-marks, the
Christ and His com-ing, And e-ter-ni-ty.

great pro-phet-ic way-marks, Down through the a-ges, past the king-doms four.

WATCHFULNESS

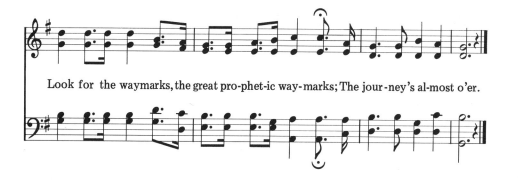

Look for the waymarks, the great pro-phet-ic way-marks; The jour-ney's al-most o'er.

Ye Servants of the Lord

597

Luke 12:35-37
Philip Doddridge (1702-1751)

GARELOCHSIDE S.M.
Kenneth G. Finlay, 1957 (1882-1974)

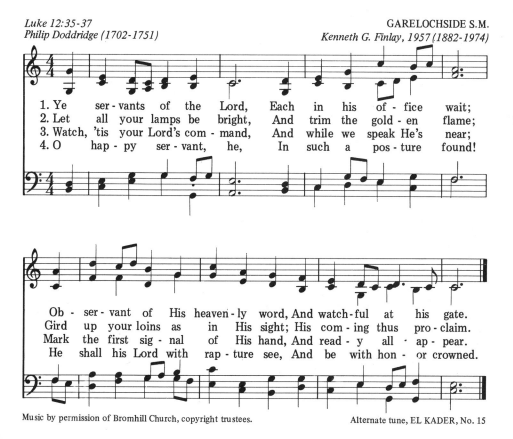

1. Ye ser-vants of the Lord, Each in his of-fice wait;
2. Let all your lamps be bright, And trim the gold-en flame;
3. Watch, 'tis your Lord's com-mand, And while we speak He's near;
4. O hap-py ser-vant, he, In such a pos-ture found!

Ob-ser-vant of His heaven-ly word, And watch-ful at his gate.
Gird up your loins as in His sight; His com-ing thus pro-claim.
Mark the first sig-nal of His hand, And read-y all ap-pear.
He shall his Lord with rap-ture see, And be with hon-or crowned.

Alternate tune, EL KADER, No. 15

WATCHFULNESS

598

Watch, Ye Saints

L.M.Ref.

Mrs. Phoebe Palmer, 1844 (1807-1874)

William J. Kirkpatrick (1838-1921)

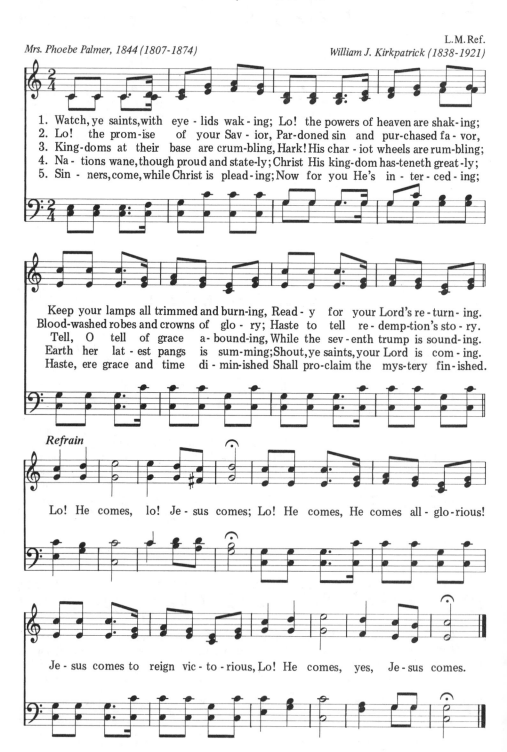

1. Watch, ye saints, with eye-lids wak-ing; Lo! the powers of heaven are shak-ing;
2. Lo! the prom-ise of your Sav-ior, Par-doned sin and pur-chased fa-vor,
3. King-doms at their base are crum-bling, Hark! His char-iot wheels are rum-bling;
4. Na-tions wane, though proud and state-ly; Christ His king-dom has-teneth great-ly;
5. Sin-ners, come, while Christ is plead-ing; Now for you He's in-ter-ced-ing;

Keep your lamps all trimmed and burn-ing, Read-y for your Lord's re-turn-ing.
Blood-washed robes and crowns of glo-ry; Haste to tell re-demp-tion's sto-ry.
Tell, O tell of grace a-bound-ing, While the sev-enth trump is sound-ing.
Earth her lat-est pangs is sum-ming; Shout, ye saints, your Lord is com-ing.
Haste, ere grace and time di-min-ished Shall pro-claim the mys-tery fin-ished.

Refrain

Lo! He comes, lo! Je-sus comes; Lo! He comes, He comes all-glo-rious!

Je-sus comes to reign vic-to-rious, Lo! He comes, yes, Je-sus comes.

WATCHFULNESS

Rejoice, Rejoice, Believers

Matt. 25:1-7
Laurentius Laurenti (1660-1772)
Tr. Sarah L. Findlater, 1854 (1823-1907) alt.

GREENLAND 7.6.7.6.D.
Johann Michael Haydn, 1806 (1737-1806)

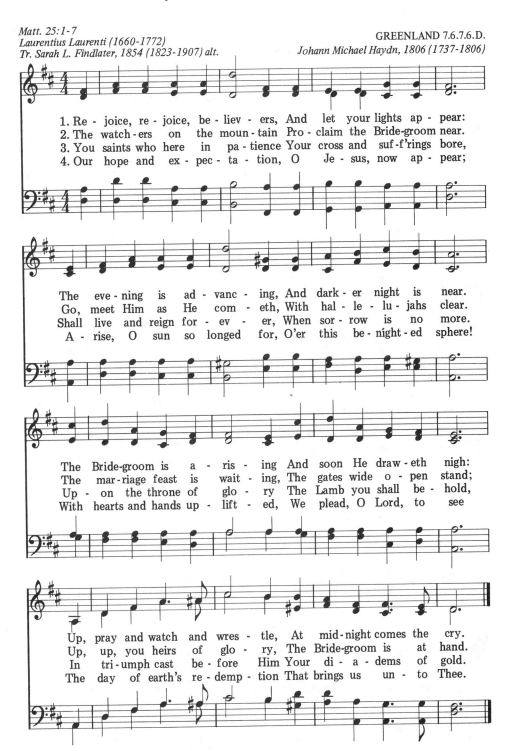

1. Re - joice, re - joice, be - liev - ers, And let your lights ap - pear:
2. The watch - ers on the moun - tain Pro - claim the Bride-groom near.
3. You saints who here in pa - tience Your cross and suf - f'rings bore,
4. Our hope and ex - pec - ta - tion, O Je - sus, now ap - pear;

The eve - ning is ad - vanc - ing, And dark - er night is near.
Go, meet Him as He com - eth, With hal - le - lu - jahs clear.
Shall live and reign for - ev - er, When sor - row is no more.
A - rise, O sun so longed for, O'er this be - night - ed sphere!

The Bride-groom is a - ris - ing And soon He draw - eth nigh:
The mar - riage feast is wait - ing, The gates wide o - pen stand;
Up - on the throne of glo - ry The Lamb you shall be - hold,
With hearts and hands up - lift - ed, We plead, O Lord, to see

Up, pray and watch and wres - tle, At mid-night comes the cry.
Up, up, you heirs of glo - ry, The Bride-groom is at hand.
In tri - umph cast be - fore Him Your di - a - dems of gold.
The day of earth's re - demp - tion That brings us un - to Thee.

WATCHFULNESS

600 Hold Fast Till I Come

F. E. Belden, 1886 (1858-1945)

10.11.10.11.Ref.
F. E. Belden, 1886

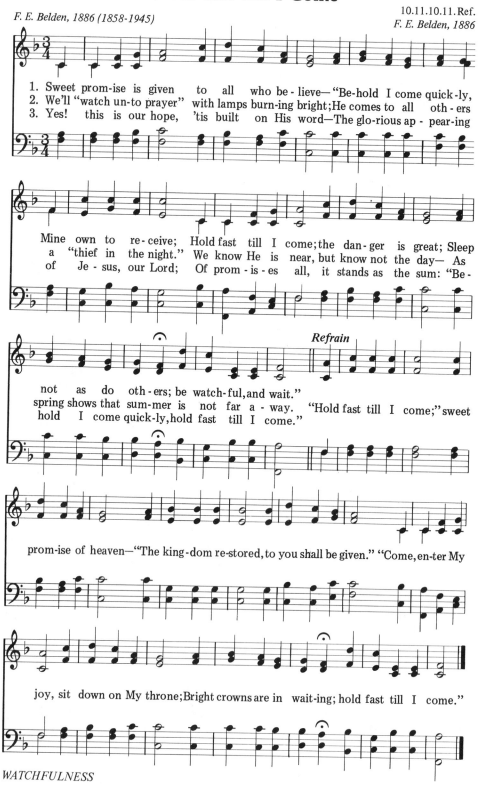

1. Sweet prom-ise is given to all who be-lieve—"Be-hold I come quick-ly,
2. We'll "watch un-to prayer" with lamps burn-ing bright; He comes to all oth-ers
3. Yes! this is our hope, 'tis built on His word—The glo-rious ap-pear-ing

Mine own to re-ceive; Hold fast till I come; the dan-ger is great; Sleep
a "thief in the night." We know He is near, but know not the day— As
of Je-sus, our Lord; Of prom-is-es all, it stands as the sum: "Be-

Refrain

not as do oth-ers; be watch-ful, and wait."
spring shows that sum-mer is not far a-way. "Hold fast till I come;" sweet
hold I come quick-ly, hold fast till I come."

prom-ise of heaven—"The king-dom re-stored, to you shall be given." "Come, en-ter My

joy, sit down on My throne; Bright crowns are in wait-ing; hold fast till I come."

WATCHFULNESS

Watchmen, on the Walls of Zion

ZION 8.7.8.7.4.7.
Thomas Hastings, 1830 (1784-1872)

Anon.

1. Watch-men, on the walls of Zi - on, What, O tell us, of the night?
2. Tell, O tell us, are the land-marks On our voy-age all passed by?
3. Light is beam-ing, day is com-ing! Let us sound a-loud the cry;
4. We have found the chart and com-pass, And are sure the land is near;

Is the day - star now a - ris - ing? Will the morn soon greet our sight?
Are we near-ing now the ha - ven? Can we e'en the land de - scry?
We be-hold the day-star ris - ing Pure and bright in yon - der sky!
On-ward, on - ward we are hast - ing, Soon the ha - ven will ap - pear;

O'er your vi - sion Shine there now some rays of light?
Do we tru - ly See the heaven - ly king - dom nigh?
Saints, be joy - ful; Your re - demp - tion draw - eth nigh;
Let your voic - es Sound a - loud your ho - ly cheer;

O'er your vi - sion Shine there now some rays of light?
Do we tru - ly See the heaven - ly king - dom nigh?
Saints, be joy - ful; Your re - demp - tion draw - eth nigh.
Let your voic - es Sound a - loud your ho - ly cheer.

WATCHFULNESS

602

O Brother, Be Faithful

Uriah Smith, 1853 (1832-1903)

FAITHFUL 11.8.11.8.D.
Isaac Woodbury, 1847 (1819-1858)

1. O brother, be faithful! soon Jesus will come,
For whom we have waited so long; O, soon we shall enter our
glorious home, And join in the conqueror's song.
O brother, be faithful! for why should we prove

2. O brother, be faithful! the city of gold,
Prepared for the good and the blest, Is waiting its portals of
pearl to unfold, And welcome thee into thy rest.
Then, brother, prove faithful! not long shall we stay

3. O brother, be faithful! He soon will descend,
Creation's omnipotent King, While legions of angels His
chariot attend, And palm wreaths, of victory bring.
O brother, be faithful! and soon shalt thou hear

4. O brother, be faithful! eternity's years
Shall tell for thy faithfulness now, When bright smiles of gladness shall
scatter thy tears, A coronet gleam on thy brow.
O brother, be faithful! the promise is sure,

WATCHFULNESS

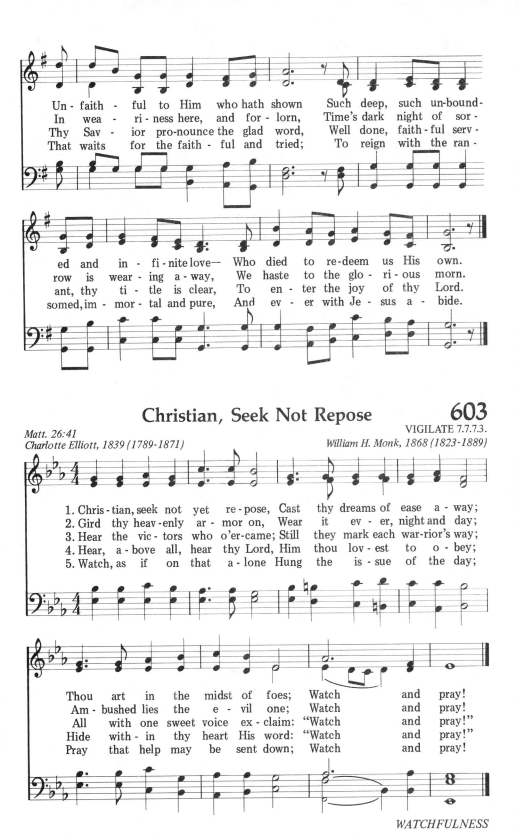

Un - faith - ful to Him who hath shown Such deep, such un-bound-
In wea - ri - ness here, and for - lorn, Time's dark night of sor-
Thy Sav - ior pro-nounce the glad word, Well done, faith - ful serv-
That waits for the faith - ful and tried; To reign with the ran-

ed and in - fi - nite love— Who died to re-deem us His own.
row is wear - ing a - way, We haste to the glo - ri - ous morn.
ant, thy ti - tle is clear, To en - ter the joy of thy Lord.
somed, im - mor - tal and pure, And ev - er with Je - sus a - bide.

Christian, Seek Not Repose 603

Matt. 26:41
Charlotte Elliott, 1839 (1789-1871)

VIGILATE 7.7.7.3.
William H. Monk, 1868 (1823-1889)

1. Chris - tian, seek not yet re-pose, Cast thy dreams of ease a - way;
2. Gird thy heav-enly ar - mor on, Wear it ev - er, night and day;
3. Hear the vic - tors who o'er-came; Still they mark each war-rior's way;
4. Hear, a - bove all, hear thy Lord, Him thou lov - est to o - bey;
5. Watch, as if on that a - lone Hung the is - sue of the day;

Thou art in the midst of foes; Watch and pray!
Am - bushed lies the e - vil one; Watch and pray!
All with one sweet voice ex - claim: "Watch and pray!"
Hide with - in thy heart His word: "Watch and pray!"
Pray that help may be sent down; Watch and pray!

WATCHFULNESS

604

We Know Not the Hour

Matt. 24:36-42
F. E. Belden, 1886 (1858-1945)

12.12.12.6.Ref.
F. E. Belden, 1886

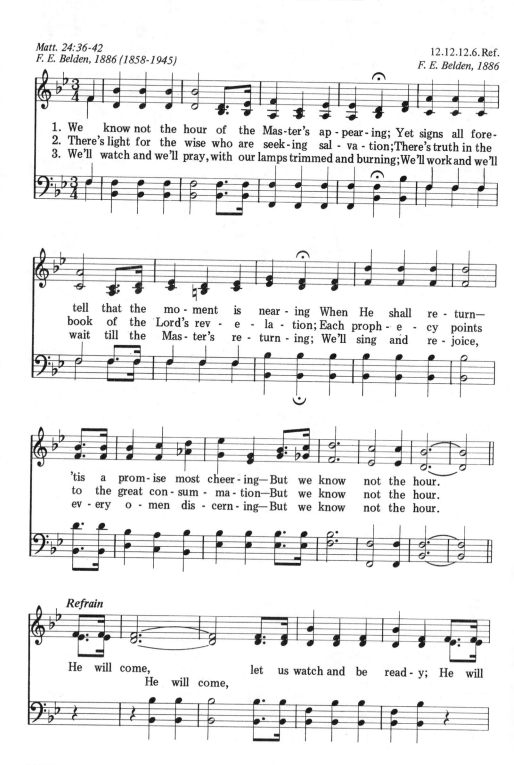

1. We know not the hour of the Mas-ter's ap - pear-ing; Yet signs all fore-
2. There's light for the wise who are seek-ing sal - va - tion; There's truth in the
3. We'll watch and we'll pray, with our lamps trimmed and burning; We'll work and we'll

tell that the mo - ment is near-ing When He shall re - turn—
book of the Lord's rev - e - la - tion; Each proph - e - cy points
wait till the Mas - ter's re - turn - ing; We'll sing and re - joice,

'tis a prom - ise most cheer - ing—But we know not the hour.
to the great con - sum - ma - tion—But we know not the hour.
ev - ery o - men dis - cern - ing—But we know not the hour.

Refrain

He will come, let us watch and be read - y; He will
He will come,

WATCHFULNESS

come, hal - le - lu - jah! hal - le - lu - jah! He will come in the
He will come,

clouds of His Fa-ther's bright glo - ry—But we know not the hour.

My Soul, Be on Thy Guard 605

LABAN S.M.

George Heath, 1781 (1745-1822)

Lowell Mason, 1830 (1792-1872)

1. My soul, be on thy guard! Ten thou-sand foes a - rise;
2. O watch, and fight, and pray! The bat - tle ne'er give o'er;
3. Ne'er think the vic - tory won, Nor lay thine ar - mor down;

The hosts of sin are press-ing hard To draw thee from the skies.
Re - new it bold-ly ev - ery day, And help di - vine im-plore.
Thy ar - duous task will not be done Till thou ob-tain the crown.

WATCHFULNESS

606 Once to Every Man and Nation

James Russell Lowell, 1845 (1819-1891) alt.

TON-Y-BOTEL 8.7.8.7.D.
T. J. Williams, 1890 (1869-1944)

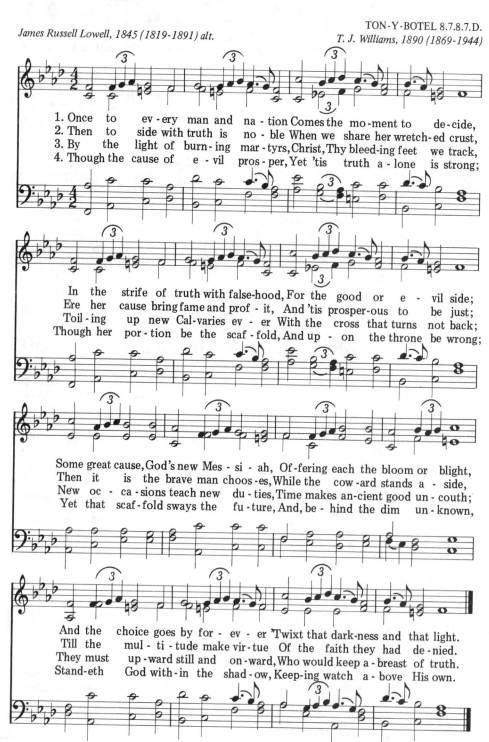

1. Once to ev-ery man and na-tion Comes the mo-ment to de-cide,
2. Then to side with truth is no-ble When we share her wretch-ed crust,
3. By the light of burn-ing mar-tyrs, Christ, Thy bleed-ing feet we track,
4. Though the cause of e-vil pros-per, Yet 'tis truth a-lone is strong;

In the strife of truth with false-hood, For the good or e-vil side;
Ere her cause bring fame and prof-it, And 'tis prosper-ous to be just;
Toil-ing up new Cal-varies ev-er With the cross that turns not back;
Though her por-tion be the scaf-fold, And up-on the throne be wrong;

Some great cause, God's new Mes-si-ah, Of-fering each the bloom or blight,
Then it is the brave man choos-es, While the cow-ard stands a-side,
New oc-ca-sions teach new du-ties, Time makes an-cient good un-couth;
Yet that scaf-fold sways the fu-ture, And, be-hind the dim un-known,

And the choice goes by for-ev-er 'Twixt that dark-ness and that light.
Till the mul-ti-tude make vir-tue Of the faith they had de-nied.
They must up-ward still and on-ward, Who would keep a-breast of truth.
Stand-eth God with-in the shad-ow, Keep-ing watch a-bove His own.

Music used by permission of Eluned Jones and Dilys Evans, representatives of the late Gwenlyn Evans.

CHRISTIAN WARFARE

God of Grace and God of Glory

WESTMINSTER ABBEY 8.7.8.7.8.7.

Harry Emmerson Fosdick (1878-1969)

Henry Purcell (1659-1695) alt.

1. God of grace and God of glo - ry, On Thy peo - ple pour Thy power; Now ful - fill Thy church - 's sto - ry, Bring her bud to glo - rious flower. Grant us wis - dom, grant us cour - age, For the fac - ing of this hour.

2. Lo, the hosts of e - vil round us Scorn Thy Christ, as - sail His ways; From the fears that long have bound us Free our hearts to faith and praise. Grant us wis - dom, grant us cour - age, For the fac - ing of this hour.

3. Cure Thy chil - dren's war - ring mad - ness, Bend our pride to Thy con - trol; Shame our wan - ton, self - ish glad - ness Rich in goods and poor in soul. Grant us wis - dom, grant us cour - age, Lest we miss Thy king - dom's goal.

4. Set our feet on loft - y plac - es, Gird our lives that they may be Ar - mored with all Christ - like grac - es In the fight to set all free. Grant us wis - dom, grant us cour - age, That we fail not man nor Thee.

Words copyright by Elinor Fosdick Downs.

Alternate tune, CWM RHONDDA, No. 201

CHRISTIAN WARFARE

608

Faith Is the Victory

John H. Yates, 1891 (1837-1900)

C.M.D.Ref.
Ira D. Sankey, 1891 (1840-1908)

1. En-camped a-long the hills of light, Ye Chris-tian sol-diers, rise,
2. On ev-ery hand the foe we find Drawn up in dread ar-ray;
3. To him that o-ver-comes the foe, White rai-ment shall be giv'n;

And press the bat-tle ere the night Shall veil the glow-ing skies.
Let tents of ease be left be-hind, And on-ward to the fray;
Be-fore the an-gels he shall know His name con-fessed in heav'n.

A-gainst the foe in vales be-low Let all our strength be hurled;
Sal-va-tion's hel-met on each head, With truth all girt a-bout,
Then on-ward from the hills of light, Our hearts with love a-flame,

Faith is the vic-to-ry, we know, That o-ver-comes the world.
The earth shall trem-ble 'neath our tread, And ech-o with our shout.
We'll van-quish all the hosts of night, In Je-sus' con-quering name.

CHRISTIAN WARFARE

Faith is the vic-to-ry! Faith is the vic-to-ry!

O, glo-ri-ous vic-to-ry, That o-ver-comes the world.

Am I a Soldier of the Cross? **609**

ARLINGTON C.M.

Isaac Watts, 1724 (1674-1748)

Thomas A. Arne, 1762 (1710-1778)

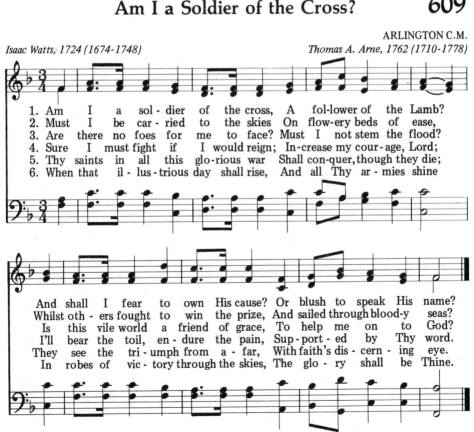

1. Am I a sol-dier of the cross, A fol-lower of the Lamb?
2. Must I be car-ried to the skies On flow-ery beds of ease,
3. Are there no foes for me to face? Must I not stem the flood?
4. Sure I must fight if I would reign; In-crease my cour-age, Lord;
5. Thy saints in all this glo-rious war Shall con-quer, though they die;
6. When that il-lus-trious day shall rise, And all Thy ar-mies shine

And shall I fear to own His cause? Or blush to speak His name?
Whilst oth-ers fought to win the prize, And sailed through blood-y seas?
Is this vile world a friend of grace, To help me on to God?
I'll bear the toil, en-dure the pain, Sup-port-ed by Thy word.
They see the tri-umph from a-far, With faith's dis-cern-ing eye.
In robes of vic-tory through the skies, The glo-ry shall be Thine.

CHRISTIAN WARFARE

610

Stand Like the Brave

Fanny J. Crosby (1820-1915)

W. B. Bradbury (1816-1868) and Philip Philipps (1834-1895)

11.11.11.11.Ref.

1. O Chris - tian, a - wake! 'tis the Mas - ter's com - mand;
2. The cause of thy Mas - ter with vig - or de - fend;
3. Press on, nev - er doubt - ing, thy Cap - tain is near,

With hel - met and shield, and a sword in thy hand,
Be watch - ful, be zeal - ous, and fight to the end;
With grace to sup - ply, and with com - fort to cheer;

To meet the bold tempt - er, go, fear - less - ly go,
Wher - ev - er He leads thee, go, val - iant - ly go,
His love, like a stream in the des - ert will flow;

Refrain

Then stand like the brave, with thy face to the foe. Stand like the

CHRISTIAN WARFARE

brave, stand like the brave, Stand like the brave, with thy face to the foe.

Awake, My Soul! 611

Phil. 3:14
Philip Doddridge (1702-1751)

CHESTERFIELD C.M.
Attr. to Thomas Haweis (1734-1820)

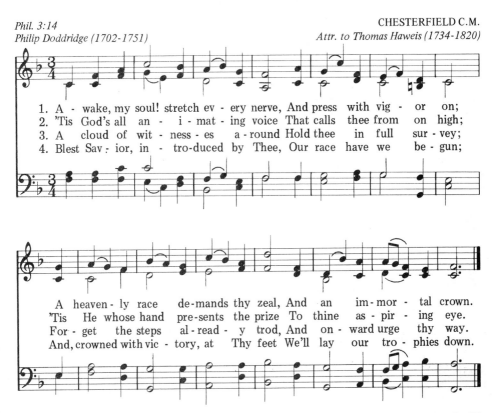

1. A - wake, my soul! stretch ev - ery nerve, And press with vig - or on;
2. 'Tis God's all an - i - mat - ing voice That calls thee from on high;
3. A cloud of wit - ness - es a - round Hold thee in full sur - vey;
4. Blest Sav - ior, in - tro-duced by Thee, Our race have we be - gun;

A heaven - ly race de-mands thy zeal, And an im - mor - tal crown.
'Tis He whose hand pre-sents the prize To thine as - pir - ing eye.
For - get the steps al - read - y trod, And on - ward urge thy way.
And, crowned with vic - tory, at Thy feet We'll lay our tro - phies down.

Alternate tune, ARLINGTON, No. 609

CHRISTIAN WARFARE

612 Onward, Christian Soldiers!

Sabine Baring-Gould, 1864 (1834-1924)

ST. GERTRUDE 6.5.6.5.D.Ref.
Arthur S. Sullivan, 1871 (1842-1899)

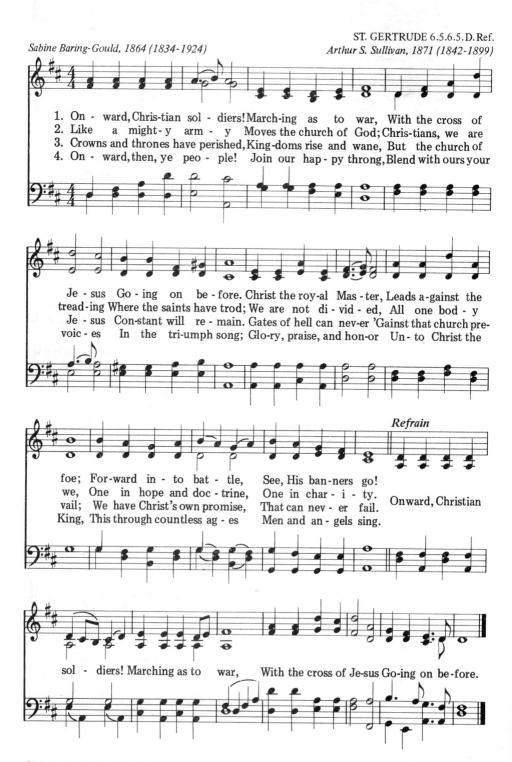

1. On - ward, Chris-tian sol - diers! March-ing as to war, With the cross of
2. Like a might-y arm - y Moves the church of God; Chris-tians, we are
3. Crowns and thrones have perished, King-doms rise and wane, But the church of
4. On - ward, then, ye peo - ple! Join our hap - py throng, Blend with ours your

Je - sus Go - ing on be - fore. Christ the roy-al Mas - ter, Leads a-gainst the
tread-ing Where the saints have trod; We are not di - vid - ed, All one bod - y
Je - sus Con-stant will re - main. Gates of hell can nev-er 'Gainst that church pre-
voic - es In the tri-umph song; Glo-ry, praise, and hon-or Un - to Christ the

Refrain

foe; For-ward in - to bat - tle, See, His ban-ners go!
we, One in hope and doc - trine, One in char - i - ty.
vail; We have Christ's own promise, That can nev - er fail.
King, This through countless ag - es Men and an - gels sing.

Onward, Christian

sol - diers! Marching as to war, With the cross of Je-sus Go-ing on be-fore.

CHRISTIAN WARFARE

Fight the Good Fight

1 Tim. 6:12
John S. B. Monsell (1811-1875)

PENTECOST L.M.
William Boyd (1847-1928)

1. Fight the good fight with all thy might, Christ is thy
2. Run the straight race through God's good grace; Lift up thine
3. Cast care a - side, lean on thy guide; His bound-less
4. Faint not, nor fear, His arms are near; He chang - eth

strength and Christ thy right; Lay hold on life and
eyes, and seek His face. Life with its path be -
mer - cy will pro - vide; Trust, and the trust - ing
not and thou art dear. On - ly be - lieve, and

it shall be Thy joy and crown e - ter - nal - ly.
fore us lies; Christ is the way, and Christ the prize.
soul shall prove Christ is its life, and Christ its love.
thou shalt see That Christ is all in all to thee.

Alternate tune, DUKE STREET, Nos. 82, 227

CHRISTIAN WARFARE

Sound the Battle Cry

10.8.10.9.Ref.

William F. Sherwin, 1869 (1826-1888)

William F. Sherwin

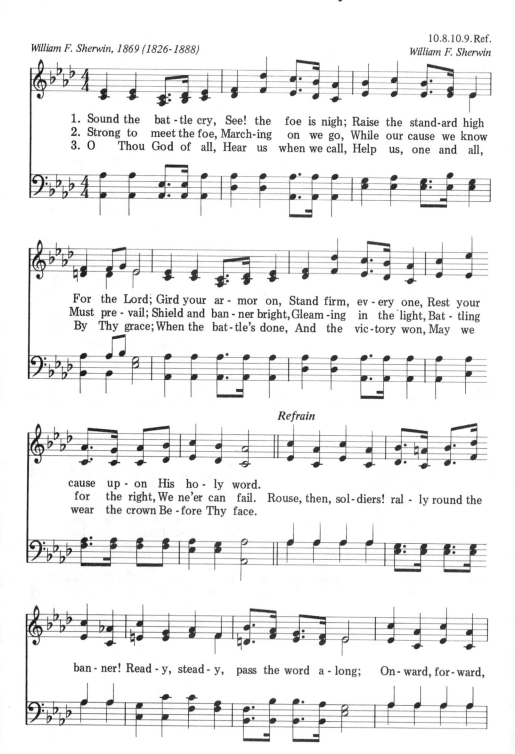

1. Sound the bat-tle cry, See! the foe is nigh; Raise the stand-ard high
2. Strong to meet the foe, March-ing on we go, While our cause we know
3. O Thou God of all, Hear us when we call, Help us, one and all,

For the Lord; Gird your ar-mor on, Stand firm, ev-ery one, Rest your
Must pre-vail; Shield and ban-ner bright, Gleam-ing in the light, Bat-tling
By Thy grace; When the bat-tle's done, And the vic-tory won, May we

Refrain

cause up-on His ho-ly word.
for the right, We ne'er can fail. Rouse, then, sol-diers! ral-ly round the
wear the crown Be-fore Thy face.

ban-ner! Read-y, stead-y, pass the word a-long; On-ward, for-ward,

CHRISTIAN WARFARE

shout a-loud ho-san - na! Christ is Cap-tain of the might-y throng.

Rise Up, O Church of God **615**

William P. Merrill, 1911 (1867-1954)
Adapt. by Ottilie Stafford, 1984 (1921-   )

FESTAL SONG S.M.
William H. Walter (1825-1893)

1. Rise up, O men of God! His king-dom tar-ries long.
2. Let wom-en all rise up! Have done with less - er things.
3. Rise up, cou-rag-eous youth! The church for you doth wait,
4. Lift high the cross of Christ! Tread where His feet have trod.

Bring in the day of broth-er-hood, And end the night of wrong.
Give heart and soul and mind and strength To serve the King of kings.
Her strength un-e-qual to her task. Rise up, and make her great!
Dis-ci-ples of the Son of man, Rise up, O church of God!

Lower key, No. 117

CHRISTIAN WARFARE

616   Soldiers of Christ, Arise

Eph. 6:13
Charles Wesley (1707-1788)

DIADEMATA S.M.D.
George J. Elvey. 1868 (1816-1893)
Arr. by Melvin West, 1984 (1930-   )

1. Sol - diers of Christ, a - rise, And put your ar - mor on,
2. Stand, then, in His great might, With all His strength en-dued;
3. From strength to strength go on; Wres-tle, and fight, and pray;

Strong in the strength which God sup - plies Through His e - ter - nal Son;
But take, to arm you for the fight, The pan - o - ply of God;
Tread all the powers of dark-ness down, And win the well-fought day;

Strong in the Lord of hosts, And in His might - y power,
That, hav - ing all things done, And all your con - flicts passed,
Still let the Spir - it cry, In all His sol - diers, "Come!"

Who in the strength of Je - sus trusts Is more than con-quer - or.
You may o'er-come thro' Christ a - lone, And stand en - tire at last.
Till Christ the Lord who reigns on high Shall take the con-querors home.

Alternate harmony, No. 223

CHRISTIAN WARFARE

We Are Living, We Are Dwelling

617

THE ALARM 8.7.8.7.D.

Arthur C. Coxe, 1840 (1818-1896)

Unknown

1. We are liv - ing, we are dwell-ing, In a grand and aw - ful time,
2. Chris - tian, rouse and arm for con - flict, Nerve thee for the bat - tle - field;
3. And the prince of e - vil spir - its, Great de - ceiv - er of the world!
4. Chris - tian, rouse! fight in this war - fare, Cease not till the vic - tory's won;

In an age on a - ges tell - ing— To be liv - ing is sub - lime.
Bear the hel - met of sal - va - tion, And the might - y gos - pel shield;
He who at the bless - ed Je - sus Once his dead - ly weap - ons hurled,
Till your Cap - tain loud pro - claim - eth, "Serv - ant of the Lord, well done!"

Hark! the wak - ing up of na - tions, Gog and Ma - gog to the fray;
Let the breast-plate, peace, be on thee, Take the Spir - it's sword in hand;
Com - eth with un - wont - ed pow - er, Know - ing that his reign will cease
He, a - lone, who thus is faith - ful, Who a - bid - eth to the end,

Hark! what sound - eth? Is cre - a - tion Groan - ing for her lat - ter day?
Bold - ly, fear - less - ly, go forth then, In Je - ho - vah's strength to stand.
When the king - dom shall be giv - en To the might - y Prince of Peace.
Hath the prom - ise, in the king - dom An e - ter - ni - ty to spend.

CHRISTIAN WARFARE

618   Stand Up! Stand Up for Jesus!

Eph. 6:14
George Duffield, 1858 (1818-1888)

WEBB 7.6.7.6.D.
George J. Webb, 1837 (1803-1887)

1. Stand up! stand up for Je - sus! Ye sol - diers of the cross;
2. Stand up! stand up for Je - sus! The trum - pet call o - bey;
3. Stand up! stand up for Je - sus! Stand in His strength a - lone;
4. Stand up! stand up for Je - sus! The strife will not be long;

Lift high His roy - al ban - ner, It must not suf - fer loss;
Forth to the might - y con - flict, In this His glo - rious day.
The arm of flesh will fail you; Ye dare not trust your own.
This day the noise of bat - tle, The next the vic - tor's song.

From vic - tory un - to vic - tory, His 'ar - my shall He lead,
Ye that are His now serve Him A - gainst un - num-bered foes;
Put on the gos - pel ar - mor, And, watch - ing un - to prayer,
To him that o - ver - com - eth, A crown of life shall be;

Till ev - ery foe is van-quished, And Christ is Lord in - deed.
Let cour - age rise with dan - ger, And strength to strength op-pose.
Where du - ty calls, or dan - ger, Be nev - er want-ing there.
He with the King of glo - ry Shall reign e - ter - nal - ly.

Alternate tune, ELLACOMBE, No. 382

CHRISTIAN WARFARE

Lead On, O King Eternal

619

LANCASHIRE 7.6.7.6.D.

Ernest W. Shurtleff, 1888 (1862-1917)

Henry Smart, 1835 (1813-1879)

1. Lead on, O King E-ter-nal, The day of march has come;
2. Lead on, O King E-ter-nal, Till sin's fierce war shall cease,
3. Lead on, O King E-ter-nal, We fol-low, not with fears,

Hence-forth in fields of con-quest Thy tents shall be our home;
And ho-li-ness shall whis-per The sweet A-men of peace;
For glad-ness breaks like morn-ing Wher-e'er Thy face ap-pears;

Through days of prep-a-ra-tion Thy grace has made us strong,
For not with swords, loud clash-ing, Nor roll of stir-ring drums,
Thy cross is lift-ed o'er us; We jour-ney in its light;

And now, O King E-ter-nal, We lift our bat-tle song.
With deeds of love and mer-cy, The heaven-ly king-dom comes.
The crown a-waits the con-quest; Lead on, O God of might.

CHRISTIAN WARFARE

620

On Jordan's Stormy Banks

PROMISED LAND C.M.Ref.

William Walker's Southern Harmony, *1835*

Samuel Stennett, 1787 (1727-1795)

Arr. by Melvin West, 1984 (1930-   )

1. On Jor-dan's storm-y banks I stand, And cast a wish-ful eye
2. O'er all those wide ex-tend-ed plains Shines one e-ter-nal day;
3. When shall I reach that hap-py place, And be for-ev-er blest?
4. Filled with de-light, my rap-tured soul Would here no lon-ger stay;

To Ca-naan's fair and hap-py land, Where my pos-ses-sions lie.
There, Christ, the Sun, for-ev-er reigns, And scat-ters night a-way.
When shall I see my Fa-ther's face, And in His king-dom rest?
Though Jor-dan's waves a-round me roll, Fear-less I'd launch a-way.

Refrain

I am bound for the prom-ised land, I am bound for the prom-ised land;

O who will come and go with me? I am bound for the prom-ised land.

PILGRIMAGE

Gracious Father, Guard Thy Children 621

ELLESDIE 8.7.8.7.D.
Arr. from Mozart
by Hubert P. Main, 1873 (1839-1926)

Anon.

1. Gra - cious Fa - ther, guard Thy chil - dren From the foe's de - struc - tive power;
2. We are in the time of wait - ing; Soon we shall be - hold our Lord,
3. With what joy - ful ex - ul - ta - tion Shall the saints Thy ban - ner see,

Save, O save them, Lord, from fall - ing In this dark and try - ing hour.
Waft - ed far a - way from sor - row, To re - ceive our rich re - ward.
When the Lord for whom we've wait - ed Shall pro - claim the ju - bi - lee!

Thou wilt sure - ly prove Thy peo - ple, All our grac - es must be tried;
Keep us, Lord, till Thine ap - pear - ing, Pure, un - spot - ted from the world;
Free - dom from this world's pol - lu - tions; Free - dom from all sin and pain;

But Thy word il - lumes our path - way, And in God we still con - fide.
Let Thy Ho - ly Spir - it cheer us Till Thy ban - ner is un - furled.
Free - dom from the wiles of Sa - tan, And from death's de - struc - tive reign.

PILGRIMAGE

622   Come, Come, Ye Saints

William Clayton, 1846 (1814-1879)
Alt. by Joseph F. Green, 1960 (1924-)

ALL IS WELL Irregular
American folk hymn
Adapt. from The Sacred Harp, 1844

1. Come, come, ye saints, no toil nor la-bor fear; But with joy wend your way.
2. We'll find the rest which God for us pre-pared, When at last He will call;

Though hard to you the jour-ney may ap-pear, Grace shall be as your day.
Where none will come to hurt or make a-fraid, He will reign o-ver all.

We have a liv-ing Lord to guide, And we can trust Him
We will make the air with mu-sic ring, Shout praise to God our

to pro-vide; Do this, and joy your hearts will swell: All is well! All is well!
Lord and King: O how we'll make the cho-rus swell: All is well! All is well!

Words copyright © 1960 by Broadman Press. All rights reserved. Used by permission.

PILGRIMAGE

I Will Follow Thee

623

LAWSON 8.7.8.7. Ref.

James Lawson Elginburg, 1886

James Lawson Elginburg, 1886

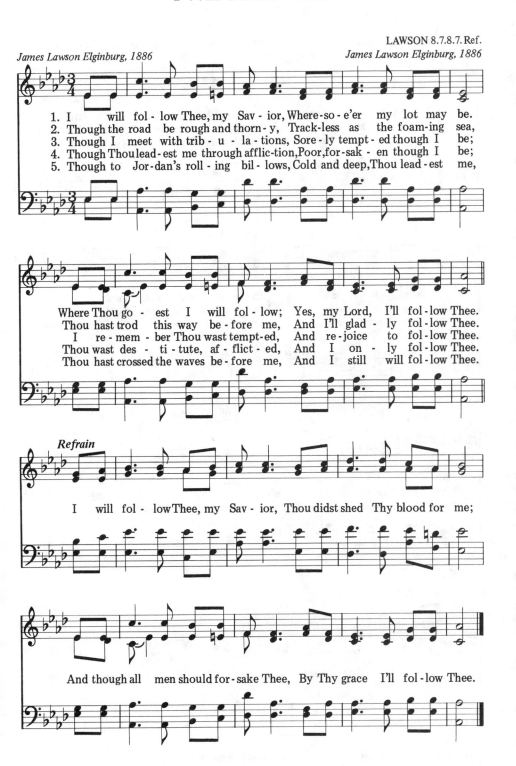

1. I will fol-low Thee, my Sav-ior, Where-so-e'er my lot may be.
2. Though the road be rough and thorn-y, Track-less as the foam-ing sea,
3. Though I meet with trib-u-la-tions, Sore-ly tempt-ed though I be;
4. Though Thou lead-est me through afflic-tion, Poor, for-sak-en though I be;
5. Though to Jor-dan's roll-ing bil-lows, Cold and deep, Thou lead-est me,

Where Thou go - est I will fol-low; Yes, my Lord, I'll fol-low Thee.
Thou hast trod this way be-fore me, And I'll glad-ly fol-low Thee.
I re-mem-ber Thou wast tempt-ed, And re-joice to fol-low Thee.
Thou wast des-ti-tute, af-flict-ed, And I on-ly fol-low Thee.
Thou hast crossed the waves be-fore me, And I still will fol-low Thee.

Refrain

I will fol-low Thee, my Sav-ior, Thou didst shed Thy blood for me;

And though all men should for-sake Thee, By Thy grace I'll fol-low Thee.

PILGRIMAGE

624   I Want Jesus to Walk With Me

L.M.

American Negro Spiritual

Arr. by Eurydice Osterman, 1984 (1950-   )

1. I want Je - sus to walk with me. (walk with me)
2. In my tri - als, Lord, walk with me. (walk with me)
3. In my sor - rows, Lord, walk with me. (walk with me)

I want Je - sus to walk with me. (walk with me)
In my tri - als, Lord, walk with me. (walk with me)
In my sor - rows, Lord, walk with me. (walk with me)

pil - grim

All a - long my pil - grim jour - ney,
When the shades of life are fall - ing,
When my heart with - in is ach - ing,

I want Je - sus to walk with me. (walk with me.)

PILGRIMAGE

Higher Ground

L.M.Ref.

Johnson Oatman, Jr. (1856-1922) *Charles H. Gabriel (1856-1932)*

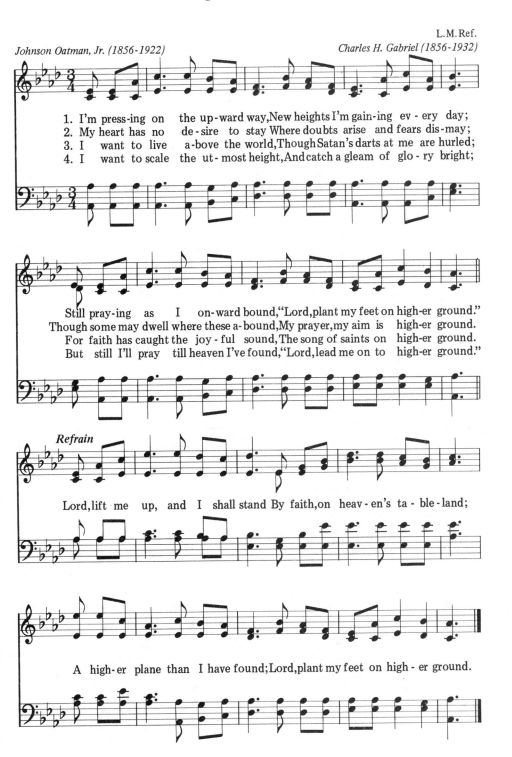

1. I'm press-ing on the up-ward way, New heights I'm gain-ing ev-ery day;
2. My heart has no de-sire to stay Where doubts arise and fears dis-may;
3. I want to live a-bove the world, Though Satan's darts at me are hurled;
4. I want to scale the ut-most height, And catch a gleam of glo-ry bright;

Still pray-ing as I on-ward bound, "Lord, plant my feet on high-er ground."
Though some may dwell where these a-bound, My prayer, my aim is high-er ground.
For faith has caught the joy-ful sound, The song of saints on high-er ground.
But still I'll pray till heaven I've found, "Lord, lead me on to high-er ground."

Refrain

Lord, lift me up, and I shall stand By faith, on heav-en's ta-ble-land;

A high-er plane than I have found; Lord, plant my feet on high-er ground.

PILGRIMAGE

626 In a Little While We're Going Home

Eliza E. Hewitt (1851-1920)

12.9.12.9.Ref.
Eliza E. Hewitt

1. Let us sing a song that will cheer us by the way, In a
2. We will do the work that our hands may find to do, In a
3. We will smooth the path for some wea - ry, way-worn feet, In a
4. There's a rest be - yond, there's re - lief from ev - ery care, In a

lit - tle while we're go - ing home; For the night will end in the
lit - tle while we're go - ing home; And the grace of God will our
lit - tle while we're go - ing home; And may lov - ing hearts spread a -
lit - tle while we're go - ing home; And no tears shall fall in that

ev - er - last - ing day,
dai - ly strength re - new,
round an in - fluence sweet! In a lit - tle while we're go - ing home.
cit - y bright and fair,

Refrain

In a lit - tle while, In a lit - tle while,
In a lit - tle while, In a lit - tle while,

PILGRIMAGE

We shall cross the bil-low's foam; We shall meet at last, When the
storm-y winds are past, In a lit-tle while we're go-ing home.

Jacob's Ladder

627

8.8.8.5.

American Negro Spiritual

Arr. by Melvin West, 1984 (1930-   )

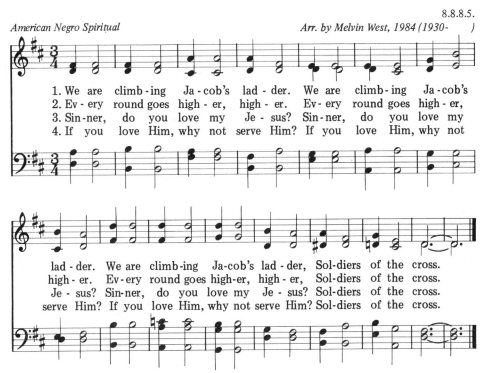

1. We are climb-ing Ja-cob's lad-der. We are climb-ing Ja-cob's
2. Ev-ery round goes high-er, high-er. Ev-ery round goes high-er,
3. Sin-ner, do you love my Je-sus? Sin-ner, do you love my
4. If you love Him, why not serve Him? If you love Him, why not

lad-der. We are climb-ing Ja-cob's lad-der, Sol-diers of the cross.
high-er. Ev-ery round goes high-er, high-er, Sol-diers of the cross.
Je-sus? Sin-ner, do you love my Je-sus? Sol-diers of the cross.
serve Him? If you love Him, why not serve Him? Sol-diers of the cross.

PILGRIMAGE

628   As Jacob With Travel Was Weary

Gen. 28:12
18th century

JACOB'S LADDER 11.11.11 11.Ref.
18th century English carol melody
Arr. by G. H. Knight (1908-   )

1. As Jacob with travel was weary one day, At night on a stone for a pillow he lay; He saw in a vision a ladder so high That its foot was on earth and its top in the sky.

2. Come let us ascend! all may climb it who will; For the angels of Jacob are guarding it still: And remember each step that by faith we pass o'er, Some prophet or martyr has trod it before.

3. And when we arrive at the haven of rest We shall hear the glad words, "Come up hither, ye blest, Here are regions of light, here are mansions of bliss." O who would not climb such a ladder as this?

Refrain

Alleluia to Jesus who died on the tree,

PILGRIMAGE

And has raised up a lad - der of mer - cy for me,

And has raised up a lad - der of mer - cy for me.

O Happy Band of Pilgrims

1 Pet. 1:6,7
From Joseph the Hymnographer, c. 840 (c. 800-883)
Tr. by John M. Neale, 1862 (1818-1866)

VULPIUS 7.6.7.6.
Arr. from Melchior Vulpius (1560-1616)

1. O hap - py band of pil - grims, If on - ward ye will tread
2. O hap - py if ye la - bor As Je - sus did for men;
3. The tri - als that be - set you, The sor - rows ye en - dure,
4. What are they but His jew - els Of right ce - les - tial worth?
5. O hap - py band of pil - grims, Look up - ward to the skies,

With Je - sus as your fel - low, To Je - sus as your Head!
O hap - py if ye hun - ger As Je - sus hun-gered then!
The man - i - fold temp - ta - tions That death a - lone can cure,
What are they but the lad - der Set up to heaven on earth?
Where such a light af - flic - tion Shall win you such a prize!

PILGRIMAGE

630 Rise, My Soul, and Stretch Thy Wings

AMSTERDAM 7.6.7.6.7.7.7.6.
James Nares (1715-1783)
From The Foundery Collection, 1742

Robert Seagrave, 1742 (1693-1759)

1. Rise, my soul, and stretch thy wings, Thy bet - ter por - tion trace;
2. Riv - ers to the o - cean run, Nor stay in all their course;
3. Cease, ye pil - grims, cease to mourn; Press on - ward to the prize;

Rise from tran - si - to - ry things Toward heaven, thy na - tive place:
Fire as - cend - ing seeks the sun; Both speed them to their source;
Soon our Sav - ior will re - turn, Tri - um - phant in the skies;

Sun, and moon, and stars de - cay; Time shall soon this earth re - move;
So a soul that's born of God, Longs to view His glo - rious face,
Yet a sea - son, and you know Hap - py en - trance will be given,

Rise, my soul, and haste a - way To seats pre - pared a - bove.
For - ward tends to His a - bode To rest in His em - brace.
All our sor - rows left be - low, And earth ex - changed for heaven.

PILGRIMAGE

When on Life a Darkness Falls

631

Brian Wren, 1983 (1936-   )

EMERALD GATES 7.6.7.6.D.
Anon. *from* Hymns and Tunes, *1886*

1. When on life a dark-ness falls, When the mist flows chill-ing,
2. When the dreams and vows of youth Pain-ful-ly ac-cuse us,
3. Come and meet Him, Friend and Lord, Thro' the gos-pel sto-ry:

Paths and sign-posts lost in doubt, Love-less, un-ful-fill-ing,
Stab our con-science, steal our worth, Christ will not re-fuse us:
O-pen door to life and peace, Win-dow in-to glo-ry.

Reach us, Je-sus, from Your cross, Though we feel for-sak-en;
Peace the world can-not pro-vide, Dai-ly res-ur-rec-tion,
All who seek Him, soon are found, Made His close re-la-tion:

Keep us through the ach-ing night Till new dawns a-wak-en.
Strong com-pan-ion at our side For each new di-rec-tion.
Christ our path-way, Christ our home, Christ our sure foun-da-tion.

PILGRIMAGE

632 Until Then

Stuart Hamblen (1908-   )

11.10.11.10.Ref.
Stuart Hamblen

1. My heart can sing when I pause to re-mem-ber
2. The things of earth will dim and lose their val-ue

A heart-ache here is but a step-ping stone
If we re-call they're bor-rowed for a while;

A-long a trail that's wind-ing al-ways up-ward,
And things of earth that cause the heart to trem-ble,

This trou-bled world is not my fi-nal home.
Re-mem-bered there will on-ly bring a smile.

PILGRIMAGE

PILGRIMAGE

633 When We All Get to Heaven

Eliza E. Hewitt (1851-1920)

Emily D. Wilson (1865-1942)

8.7.8.7.Ref.

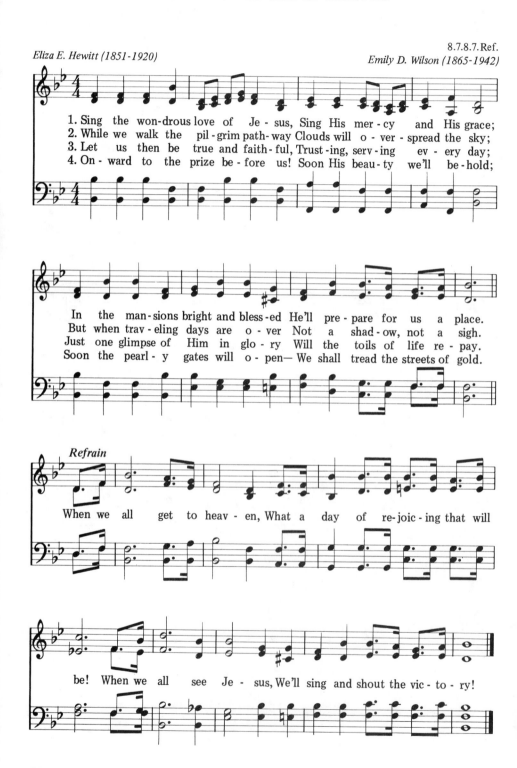

1. Sing the won-drous love of Je - sus, Sing His mer - cy and His grace;
2. While we walk the pil - grim path-way Clouds will o - ver-spread the sky;
3. Let us then be true and faith-ful, Trust-ing, serv-ing ev - ery day;
4. On - ward to the prize be - fore us! Soon His beau - ty we'll be-hold;

In the man-sions bright and bless-ed He'll pre - pare for us a place.
But when trav - eling days are o - ver Not a shad - ow, not a sigh.
Just one glimpse of Him in glo - ry Will the toils of life re - pay.
Soon the pearl - y gates will o - pen— We shall tread the streets of gold.

Refrain

When we all get to heav - en, What a day of re-joic - ing that will be! When we all see Je - sus, We'll sing and shout the vic - to - ry!

PILGRIMAGE

Come, All Christians, Be Committed 634

BEACH SPRING 8.7.8.7.D.
From The Sacred Harp, 1844
Arr. by Melvin West, 1984 (1930-   )

Eva B. Lloyd, alt. (1912-   )

1. Come, all Chris-tians, be com-mit-ted To the ser-vice of the Lord;
2. Of your time and tal-ents give ye, They are gifts from God a-bove;
3. God's com-mand to love each oth-er Is re-quired of ev-ery one;
4. Come in praise and ad-o-ra-tion, All who on Christ's name be-lieve;

Make your lives for Him more fit-ted, Tune your hearts with one ac-cord.
To be used by Chris-tians free-ly To pro-claim His won-drous love.
Show-ing mer-cy to an-oth-er Mir-rors His re-demp-tive plan.
Wor-ship Him with con-se-cra-tion, Grace and love you will re-ceive.

Come in-to His courts with glad-ness, Each his sa-cred vows re-new,
Come a-gain to serve the Sav-ior, Tithes and of-f'rings with you bring.
In com-pas-sion He has giv-en Of His love that is di-vine;
For His grace give Him the glo-ry, For the Spir-it and the Word,

Turn a-way from sin and sad-ness, Be trans-formed with life a-new.
In your work, with Him find fa-vor, And with joy His prais-es sing.
On the cross sins were for-giv-en; Joy and peace are ful-ly thine.
And re-peat the gos-pel sto-ry Till man-kind His name has heard.

Unison setting, No. 363

STEWARDSHIP

635 Lord of All Good

Albert F. Bayly (1901-1984)

MORESTEAD 10.10.10.10.
Sydney Watson (1903-   )

Unison

1. Lord of all good, our gifts we bring You now;
2. We give our minds to un-der-stand Your ways;
3. Fa - ther, whose boun - ty all cre - a - tion shows;

Use them Your ho - ly pur-pose to ful - fill.
Hands, voic - es, eyes to serve Your great de - sign;
Christ, by whose will - ing sac - ri - fice we live;

To - kens of love and pledg - es they shall be That
Hearts with the flame of Your own love a - blaze: Thus
Spir - it, from whom all life in full - ness flows: To

our whole life is of - fered to Your will.
for Your glo - ry all our pow'rs com - bine.
You with grate - ful hearts our - selves we give.

STEWARDSHIP

God, Whose Giving Knows No Ending　636

RUSTINGTON 8.7.8.7.D.

Robert L. Edwards (1915-　　)　　　　　　　*Charles H. H. Parry (1848-1918)*

1. God, whose giv - ing knows no end - ing, From Your rich and end - less store:
2. Skills and time are ours for press-ing Toward the goals of Christ, Your Son:
3. Trea - sure, too, You have en-trust-ed, Gain through pow'rs Your grace con-ferred:

Na - ture's won - der, Je - sus' wis-dom, Cost - ly cross, grave's shat-tered door.
All at peace in health and free-dom, Rac - es joined, the church made one.
Ours to use for home and kin-dred, And to spread the Gos - pel Word.

Gift - ed by You, we turn to You, Of-f'ring up Your-selves in praise:
Now di - rect our dai - ly la - bor, Lest we strive for self a - lone:
O - pen wide our hands in shar-ing, As we heed Christ's age-less call.

Thank-ful song shall rise for - ev - er, Gra-cious do - nor of our days.
Born with tal - ents, make us ser-vants Fit to an - swer at Your throne.
Heal-ing, teach-ing, and re - claim-ing, Serv - ing You by lov - ing all.

Alternate tune, NETTLETON, No. 334

STEWARDSHIP

637

Son of God, Eternal Savior

IN BABILONE 8.7.8.7.D.
Somerset C. Lowry (1855-1932)
Dutch folk tune, 18th century

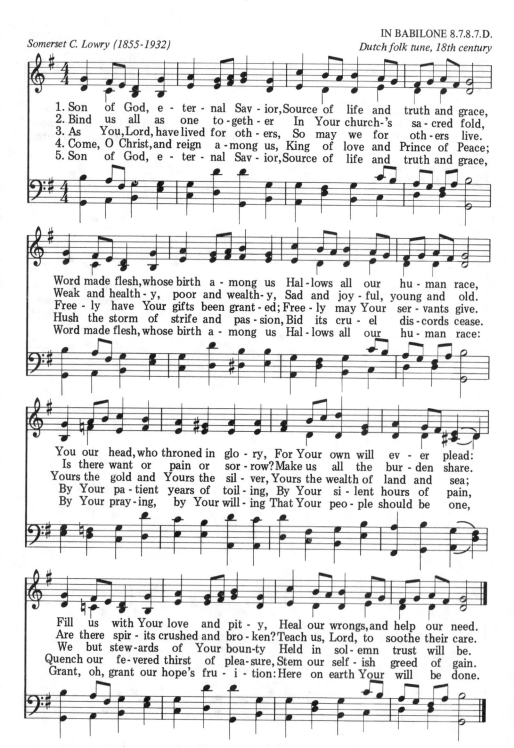

1. Son of God, e-ter-nal Sav-ior, Source of life and truth and grace,
2. Bind us all as one to-geth-er In Your church-'s sa-cred fold,
3. As You, Lord, have lived for oth-ers, So may we for oth-ers live.
4. Come, O Christ, and reign a-mong us, King of love and Prince of Peace;
5. Son of God, e-ter-nal Sav-ior, Source of life and truth and grace,

Word made flesh, whose birth a-mong us Hal-lows all our hu-man race,
Weak and health-y, poor and wealth-y, Sad and joy-ful, young and old.
Free-ly have Your gifts been grant-ed; Free-ly may Your ser-vants give.
Hush the storm of strife and pas-sion, Bid its cru-el dis-cords cease.
Word made flesh, whose birth a-mong us Hal-lows all our hu-man race:

You our head, who throned in glo-ry, For Your own will ev-er plead:
Is there want or pain or sor-row? Make us all the bur-den share.
Yours the gold and Yours the sil-ver, Yours the wealth of land and sea;
By Your pa-tient years of toil-ing, By Your si-lent hours of pain,
By Your pray-ing, by Your will-ing That Your peo-ple should be one,

Fill us with Your love and pit-y, Heal our wrongs, and help our need.
Are there spir-its crushed and bro-ken? Teach us, Lord, to soothe their care.
We but stew-ards of Your boun-ty Held in sol-emn trust will be.
Quench our fe-vered thirst of plea-sure, Stem our self-ish greed of gain.
Grant, oh, grant our hope's fru-i-tion: Here on earth Your will be done.

Music used by permission of Johanna Röntgen Schwartz.

STEWARDSHIP

The Wise May Bring Their Learning 638

TYROLESE 7.6.7.6.D.
Tyrolese Carol
Book of Praise for Children, *1881*
Arr. by Melvin West, 1984 (1930-   )

1. The wise may bring their learn - ing, The rich may bring their wealth,
2. We'll bring Him hearts that love Him, We'll bring Him thank - ful praise,
3. We'll bring the lit - tle du - ties We have to do each day;

And some may bring their great - ness, And some their strength and health:
And young souls meek - ly striv - ing To fol - low in His ways:
We'll try our best to please Him At home, at school, at play:

We too would bring our trea - sures To of - fer to the King,
And these shall be the trea - sures We of - fer to the King,
And bet - ter are these trea - sures To of - fer to the King

We have no wealth or learn - ing—What shall we chil - dren bring?
And these are gifts that ev - er The poor - est child may bring.
Than rich - est gifts with - out them: Yet these a child may bring.

STEWARDSHIP

639

A Diligent and Grateful Heart

ST. COLUMBA C.M.
Raymond Gunn (1925-)
Ancient Irish Melody

1. A diligent and grateful heart Prompts me to sing Thy praise. Thy love and mercies from the start Have blessed me all my days.

2. I thank Thee for the means to serve With talents and with tithes, For sharing brings the utmost joy When lifting other lives.

3. My thanks I give for stewardship To minister through deeds, To serve and share with patient care Thy people in their needs.

4. O Lord, I dedicate my all In this response to Thee. Help me to magnify this call In deep humility.

STEWARDSHIP

For Beauty of Meadows

640

ANNIVERSARY SONG 11.11.11.11.

Walter H. Farquharson (1936-   )

Jane Marshall, 1980 (1924-   )

Unison

1. For beau - ty of mead - ows, for gran - deur of trees,
2. As stew - ards of beau - ty re - ceived at Your hand,
3. Teach us once a - gain to be gar - deners in peace;

For flow - ers of wood-lands, for crea - tures' of seas,
As crea - tures who hear Your most ur - gent com - mand,
All na - ture a - round us is ours but on lease;

For all You cre - at - ed and gave us to share,
We turn from our waste - ful de - struc - tion of life,
Your name we would hal - low in all that we do,

We praise You, Cre - a - tor, ex - tol - ling Your care.
Con - fess - ing our fail - ures, con - fess - ing our strife.
Ful - fill - ing our call - ing, cre - at - ing with You.

STEWARDSHIP

641
God in His Love for Us

WALLOG 11.10.11.10.

Fred Pratt Green (1903-)

H. Walford Davies (1869-1941)

1. God in His love for us lent us this plan - et,
   Gave it a pur - pose in time and in space:
   Small as a spark from the fire of cre - a - tion,
   Cra - dle of life and the home of our race.

2. Thanks be to God for its boun - ty and beau - ty,
   Life that sus - tains us in bod - y and mind:
   Plen - ty for all, if we learn how to share it,
   Rich - es un - dreamed of to fath - om and find.

3. Long have our hu - man wars ru - ined its har - vest;
   Long has earth bowed to the ter - ror of force;
   Long have we wast - ed what oth - ers have need of,
   Poi - soned the foun - tain of life at its source.

4. Earth is the Lord's: it is ours to en - joy it,
   Ours, as His stew - ards, to farm and de - fend.
   From its pol - lu - tion, mis - use, and de - struc - tion,
   Good Lord, de - liv - er us, world with - out end!

Alternate tune, ETERNAL LOVE, No. 496

STEWARDSHIP

We Praise Thee With Our Minds 642

CLONMEL C.M.D.
Irish Melody

Hugh T. McElrath, 1964 (1932-   )   *Arr. by William J. Reynolds, 1952 (1920-   )*

Unison

1. We praise Thee with our minds, O Lord, Kept sharp to think Thy thought;
2. We praise Thee thro' our bod-ies, Lord, Kept strong to do Thy will;
3. We praise Thee in our hearts, O King, Kept pure to know Thy ways;

Come, Ho-ly Ghost with grace out-poured, To teach what Christ hath taught.
Thy Spir-it's tem-ples, which af-ford A means to praise Thee still.
And raise to Thee a hymn to sing E-ter-nal-ly Thy praise.

In all our learn-ing may we seek That wis-dom from a-bove
We give our-selves, a sac-ri-fice, To live as un-to Thee;
Al-tho a-dor-ing hearts will bow As age on a-ges roll;

Which comes to all: the brave, the meek, Who ask in faith and love.
For Thou a-lone hast paid the price To bring sal-va-tion free.
We praise Thee in our be-ings now, Mind, bod-y, heart, and soul.

HEALTH AND WHOLENESS

643

Father, Who on Us Do Shower

Percy Dearmer, 1906 (1867-1936) alt.

CHARING 8.8.8.7.
Studley L. Russell, 1931 (1901-1978)

Unison

1. Fa - ther, who on us do show - er Gifts of plen - ty from Your dow - er, To Your peo - ple give the pow - er All Your gifts to use a - right.

2. Give pure hap - pi - ness in lei - sure Tem - per - ance in ev - ery plea - sure, Whole-some use of earth - ly trea - sure Bod - ies clean and spir - its bright.

3. Lift from this and ev - ery na - tion All that brings us deg - ra - da - tion; Quell the for - ces of temp - ta - tion; Put Your en - e - mies to flight.

4. Fa - ther, You who sought and found us, Son of God, whose love has bound us, Ho - ly Spir - it, in us, round us, Hear us, God - head in - fi - nite.

Words from the *English Hymnal* by permission of Oxford University Press.
Music from *Enlarged Songs of Praise* by permission of Oxford University Press.

HEALTH AND WHOLENESS

O God, Whose Will Is Life and Good

BISHOPTHORPE C.M.

Hardwicke D. Rawnsley (1851-1920) alt.

Jeremiah Clark, 1700 (1669-1707)

644

1. O God, whose will is life and good
   For all of mor - tal breath:
   U - nite in bonds of ser - vant - hood
   All those who strive with death.

2. Make strong their hands and hearts and wills
   To drive dis - ease a - far,
   To strive a - gainst the bod - y's ills
   And wage Your heal - ing war.

3. By heal - ing of the sick and blind, Christ's
   mer - cy they pro - claim,
   Make known the great phy - si - cian's mind, Af -
   firm the Sav - ior's name.

4. Be - fore them set Your gra - cious will, That
   they, with heart and soul,
   To You may con - se - crate their skill
   And make the suf - ferer whole.

645

God of Our Fathers

NATIONAL HYMN 10.10.10.10.

Daniel C. Roberts, 1876 (1841-1907)

George W. Warren, 1892 (1828-1902)

Trumpets, before each stanza

1. God of our fa - thers, whose al - might - y hand
2. Thy love di - vine hath led us in the past,
3. From war's a - larms, from dead - ly pes - ti - lence,
4. Re - fresh Thy peo - ple on their toil - some way,

Leads forth in beau - ty all the star - ry band
In this free land by Thee our lot is cast;
Be Thy strong arm our ev - er sure de - fense;
Lead us from night to nev - er - end - ing day;

Of shin - ing worlds in splen - dor through the skies,
Be Thou our rul - er, guard - ian, guide, and stay,
Thy true re - li - gion in our hearts in - crease,
Fill all our lives with love and grace di - vine,

Our grate - ful songs be - fore Thy throne a - rise.
Thy word our law, Thy paths our cho - sen way.
Thy boun - teous good - ness nour - ish us in peace.
And glo - ry, laud, and praise be ev - er Thine.

LOVE OF COUNTRY

To the Name That Brings Salvation 646

Late 15th century
Tr. by John Mason Neale (1818-1866)
and Robert F. Neill

ST. LEONARD 8.7.8.7.7.7.
Johann Christoph Bach (1642-1703)

1. To the name that brings salvation Let the nations
2. He through ev-ery gen-er-a-tion Rules in end-less
3. Lord, we pray for up-right ru-lers: Guard them sure-ly

bow the head; Let them kneel in ad-o-ra-tion
maj-es-ty; May the kings of ev-ery na-tion
in their need From the van-i-ty of pow-er

When this name of names is said; Let them pray for
Now fore-swear their en-mi-ty, And with hum-ble
And the emp-ti-ness of greed; Let them see the

res-to-ra-tion Of all things in Christ the head.
ven-er-a-tion In the love of God a-gree.
truth of low-ness, And on jus-tice let them feed.

LOVE OF COUNTRY

647 Mine Eyes Have Seen the Glory

Julia Ward Howe, 1861 (1819-1910) alt.

BATTLE HYMN 15.15.15.6.Ref.
Arr. from camp meeting song

1. Mine eyes have seen the glo - ry of the com - ing of the Lord;
2. He has sound - ed forth the trum - pet that shall nev - er call re - treat;
3. In the beau - ty of the lil - ies Christ was born a - cross the sea,

He is tram - pling out the vin - tage where the grapes of wrath are stored;
He is sift - ing out the hearts of men be - fore His judg - ment seat;
With a glo - ry in His bos - om that trans - fig - ures you and me;

He has loosed the fate - ful light - ning of His ter - ri - ble swift sword;
O be swift, my soul, to an - swer Him; be ju - bi - lant, my feet!
As He died to make men ho - ly, let us live to make men free!

His truth is march-ing on.
Our God is march-ing on.
While God is march-ing on. Glo - ry! glo - ry! Hal - le -

lu - jah! Glo - ry! glo - ry! Hal - le - lu - jah!

Glo - ry! glo - ry! Hal - le - lu - jah! His truth is march-ing on.

648   I Vow to Thee, My Country

THAXTED 13.13.13.13.13.13.
From The Planets, *1918*
Gustav Holst (1874-1934)

Sir Cecil Spring-Rice, 1918 (1859-1918) alt.

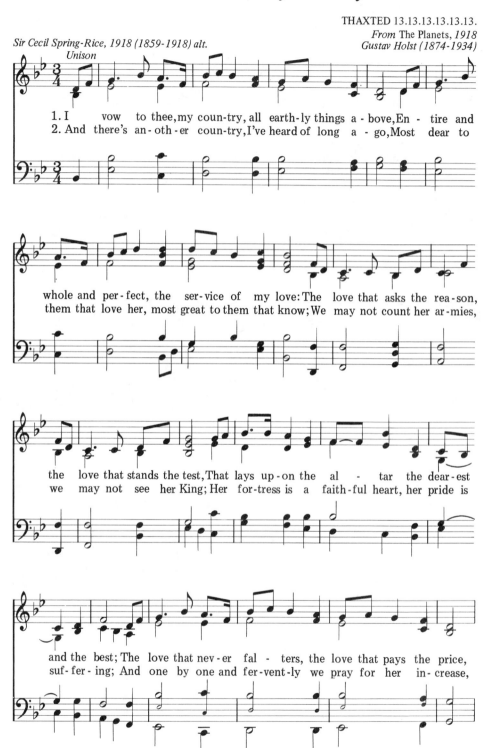

1. I vow to thee, my coun-try, all earth-ly things a-bove, En-tire and whole and per-fect, the ser-vice of my love: The love that asks the rea-son, the love that stands the test, That lays up-on the al - tar the dear-est and the best; The love that nev-er fal - ters, the love that pays the price,

2. And there's an-oth-er coun-try, I've heard of long a - go, Most dear to them that love her, most great to them that know; We may not count her ar-mies, we may not see her King; Her for-tress is a faith-ful heart, her pride is suf-fer - ing; And one by one and fer-vent-ly we pray for her in - crease,

LOVE OF COUNTRY

The love that makes un-daunt-ed the fi-nal sac-ri-fice.
And her ways are ways of gen-tle-ness and all her paths are peace.

Lord, While for All Mankind 649

DUNFERMLINE C.M.

John R. Wreford, 1837 (1800-1881)

Scottish Psalter, 1615

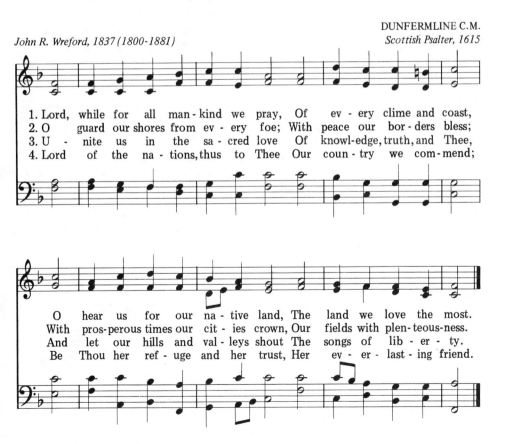

1. Lord, while for all man-kind we pray, Of ev-ery clime and coast,
2. O guard our shores from ev-ery foe; With peace our bor-ders bless;
3. U-nite us in the sa-cred love Of knowl-edge, truth, and Thee,
4. Lord of the na-tions, thus to Thee Our coun-try we com-mend;

O hear us for our na-tive land, The land we love the most.
With pros-perous times our cit-ies crown, Our fields with plen-teous-ness.
And let our hills and val-leys shout The songs of lib-er-ty.
Be Thou her ref-uge and her trust, Her ev-er-last-ing friend.

LOVE OF COUNTRY

650

Our Father, by Whose Name

F. Bland Tucker (1895-1984)

RHOSYMEDRE 6.6.6.6.8.8.8.
John D. Edwards (1806-1885)

1. Our Father, by whose name, All fa-ther-hood is known,
2. O Christ, Thy-self a child With-in an earth-ly home,
3. O Spir-it, who dost bind Our hearts in u-ni-ty,

Who dost in love pro-claim Each fam-i-ly Thine own,
With heart still un-de-filed, Thou didst to man-hood come;
Who teach-est us to find The love from self set free,

Bless Thou all par-ents, guard-ing well, With con-stant love as
Our chil-dren bless, in ev-ery place, That they may all be-
In all our hearts such love in-crease, That ev-ery home, by

sen-ti-nel, The homes in which Thy peo-ple dwell.
hold Thy face, And know-ing Thee may grow in grace.
this re-lease, May be the dwell-ing place of peace.

LOVE IN THE HOME

Happy the Home That Welcomes You 651

Karl J. P. Spitta (1801-1859)
Tr. by Honor Mary Thwaites (1914-   )

WELWYN 11.10.11.10.
Alfred Scott-Gatty (1847-1918)

1. Hap - py the home that wel-comes You, Lord Je - sus,
2. Hap - py the home where man and wife to - geth - er
3. Hap - py the home, O lov - ing Friend of chil - dren,

Tru - est of friends, most hon - ored guest of all,
Are of one mind be - liev - ing in Your love:
Where they are giv'n to You with hands of prayer,

Where hearts and eyes are bright with joy to greet You,
Through love and pain, pros - per - i - ty and hard - ship,
Where at Your feet they ear - ly learn to lis - ten

Your light - est wish - es ea - ger to ful - fill.
Through good and e - vil days Your care they prove.
To Your own words, and thank You for Your care.

LOVE IN THE HOME

652 Love at Home

7.5.7.5.7.7.7.5. Ref.

John H. McNaughton (1829-1891)

John H. McNaughton

1. There is beau-ty all a-round, When there's love at home; There is joy in
2. Kind-ly heav-en smiles a-bove, When there's love at home; All the earth is
3. Je - sus, make me whol-ly Thine, Then there's love at home; May Thy sac - ri -

ev - ery sound, When there's love at home. Peace and plen-ty here a-bide,
fill'd with love, When there's love at home. Sweet-er sings the brook-let by,
fice be mine, Then there's love at home. Safe-ly from all harm I'll rest,

Smil-ing fair on ev - ery side; Time doth soft-ly, sweet-ly glide,
Bright-er beams the az - ure sky; O, there's One who smiles on high
With no sin-ful care dis-tress'd, Thro' Thy ten-der mer-cy blessed,

Refrain

When there's love at home. Love at home, love at

home; Time doth soft-ly, sweet-ly glide, When there's love at home.

LOVE IN THE HOME

Lead Them, My God, to Thee

653

ROBINSON 6.4.6.4.6.6.6.4.

F. E. Belden, 1886 (1858-1945)

Words arranged

1. Lead them, my God, to Thee, Lead them to Thee, These chil-dren dear of
2. When earth looks bright and fair, Fes - tive and gay, Let no de - lu - sive
3. E'en for such lit - tle ones, Christ came a child, And in this world of
4. Yea, though my faith be dim, I would be-lieve That Thou this pre-cious

mine, Thou gav-est me; O, by Thy love di - vine, Lead them, my
snare Lure them a-stray; But from temp-ta-tion's power, Lead them, my
sin Lived un - de-filed. O, for His sake, I pray, Lead them, my
gift Wilt now re-ceive; O, take their young hearts now, Lead them, my

God, to Thee; Lead them, my God, to Thee, Lead them to Thee.

LOVE IN THE HOME

Lord, Bless Our Homes

Frank von Christierson, 1957 (1900-   )

CHARTERHOUSE 11.10.11.10.
David Evans, 1927 (1874-1948)

Unison

1. Lord, bless our homes with peace and love and laugh - ter,
2. May ev - ery heart re - ceive His lov - ing spir - it
3. For - give the hurts our self - ish - ness in - flict - ed
4. Fa - ther, in grat - i - tude for homes and loved ones,

With un - der - stand - ing and with loy - al - ty.
And know the truth that makes life tru - ly free;
On those we love and those who love us best.
We o - pen now our hearts to all man - kind.

May we to - geth - er fol - low Christ the Mas - ter
Then, in that spir - it may we live u - nit - ed,
Christ, heal the scars, and draw us all to - geth - er
Grant us Your spir - it— love for one an - oth - er—

LOVE IN THE HOME

And know the bless - ing of His sov - 'reign - ty.
And find in God our deep se - cur - i - ty.
In Him whose will is peace and joy and rest.
So in Your peace may we our con - cord find.

Happy the Home

655

Henry Ware, the younger, (1794-1843)

ST. AGNES C.M.
John B. Dykes, 1866 (1823-1876)

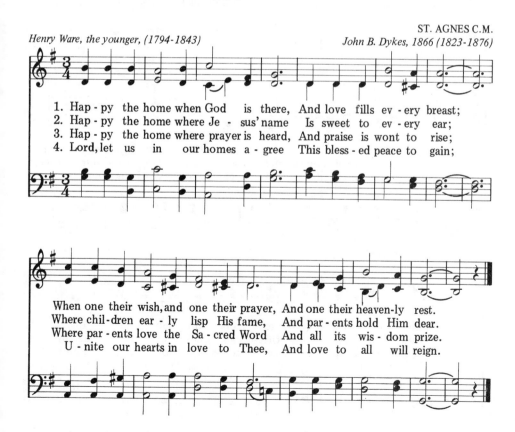

1. Hap - py the home when God is there, And love fills ev - ery breast;
2. Hap - py the home where Je - sus' name Is sweet to ev - ery ear;
3. Hap - py the home where prayer is heard, And praise is wont to rise;
4. Lord, let us in our homes a - gree This bless - ed peace to gain;

When one their wish, and one their prayer, And one their heaven-ly rest.
Where chil - dren ear - ly lisp His fame, And par - ents hold Him dear.
Where par - ents love the Sa - cred Word And all its wis - dom prize.
U - nite our hearts in love to Thee, And love to all will reign.

LOVE IN THE HOME

656

O Perfect Love

Dorothy Blomfield Gurney, 1883 (1858-1932)

O PERFECT LOVE 11.10.11.10.
Joseph Barnby, 1889 (1838-1896)

1. O per - fect Love, all hu - man thought tran - scend - ing,
2. O per - fect Life, be Thou their full as - sur - ance,
3. Grant them the joy which bright - ens earth - ly sor - row;

Low - ly we kneel in prayer be - fore Thy throne,
Of ten - der char - i - ty and stead - fast faith,
Grant them the peace which calms all earth - ly strife,

That theirs may be the love that has no end - ing,
Of pa - tient hope, and qui - et, brave en - dur - ance,
Add to life's day the glo - rious un - known mor - row

Whom Thou for - ev - er - more dost join in one.
With child - like trust that fears nor pain nor death.
That dawns up - on e - ter - nal love and life.

MARRIAGE

O God, From Whom Mankind

657

SLY PARK 10.10.10.10.

Fred H. Kaan (1929-)

Melvin West, 1984 (1930-)

1. O God from whom mankind derives its name;
2. May through their union other lives be blessed;
3. Preserve their days from inwardness of heart;
4. From stage to stage on life's unfolding way

Whose covenant of grace remains the same,
Their door be wide to stranger and to guest,
To each the gift of truthful speech impart.
Bring to their mind the vows they make this day,

Be with these two who now before You wait;
Give them the understanding that is kind,
Their bond be strong against all strain and strife
Your Spirit be their Guide in every move,

Enlarge the love they come to consecrate.
Grant them the blessing of an open mind.
Amid the changes of this earthly life.
Their faith in Christ the basis of their love.

Alternate tune, MORECAMBE, No. 266

MARRIAGE

658   Heavenly Father, Hear Our Prayer

NAME OF JESUS 7.6.7.6.8.8.7.7.

Barbara E. Adam (1939-   )

Ralph A. Strom (1901-1977)

1. Heav'n-ly Fa-ther, hear our prayer As we bow be-fore You:
2. As they pledge their love this day Here be-fore Your al - tar,
3. Blest Cre - a - tor, Lord of life, Hear our glad thanks-giv - ing.

Bless them in the life they share, Hum-bly we im-plore You.
May their hearts, up - on You stayed, Nev - er fail or fal - ter.
Hus-band You have joined to wife For their earth - ly liv - ing.

Be their guide in all en-deav-ors, Be their hope that noth-ing sev - ers;
Be their com-fort in all sor-row; Be their rea-son for to-mor-row.
Jus - ti - fied by Je - sus' mer - it, Life e - ter - nal they in-her - it.

Con-stant source of love di - vine, Let Your love with-in them shine!
Grant them strength to live each hour Trust-ing sole - ly in Your pow'r.
When their days on earth have passed, Take them to Your home at last!

MARRIAGE

May the Grace of Christ Our Savior 659

STUTTGART 8.7.8.7.

2 Cor. 13:14
John Newton (1725-1807)

Psalmodia Sacra, *Gotha, 1715*
Adapt. by Henry J. Gauntlett (1805-1876)

1. May the grace of Christ our Sav - ior And the Fa-ther's bound-less love,
2. Thus may they a - bide in un - ion With each oth - er and the Lord,

With the Ho - ly Spir-it's fa - vor, Rest up - on them from a - bove.
And pos - sess, in sweet com-mu - nion, Joys which earth can - not af - ford.

MARRIAGE

Glory Be to the Father 660

GLORIA PATRI

Anonymous, second century

H. W. Greatorex, 1851 (1811-1858)

Glo - ry be to the Fa - ther, and to the Son, and to the

Ho - ly Ghost; As it was in the be - gin - ning, is

now, and ev - er shall be, world with-out end. A - men, A - men.

SENTENCES AND RESPONSES

Holy, Holy, Holy

John Philipp Neumann
Tr. by Charles H. Davis

6.5.6.5.D.
Franz Schubert, 1827 (1797-1828)

1. Ho - ly, ho - ly, ho - ly, Ho - ly is the Lord!
2. Ho - ly, ho - ly, ho - ly, Ho - ly is the Lord!

Ho - ly, ho - ly, ho - ly, Ho - ly is our God!
Ho - ly, ho - ly, ho - ly, Ho - ly is our God!

He who al - ways liv - eth, Ev - er - more the same
Glo - rious and be - lov - ed Is the One a - dored!

Heav'n and earth He rul - eth, Come and praise His name!
Ho - ly, ho - ly, ho - ly, Ho - ly is the Lord.

SENTENCES AND RESPONSES

Let All Mortal Flesh Keep Silence

662

Liturgy of St. James
Tr. by Gerard Moultrie, 1864 (1829-1885)

PICARDY 8.7.8.7.8.7.
17th century French carol

Unison

Let all mor-tal flesh keep si-lence, And with fear and trem-bling stand; Pon-der noth-ing earth-ly mind-ed, For with bless-ing in His hand, Christ our God to earth de-scend - eth, Our full hom-age to de - mand. A - men.

SENTENCES AND RESPONSES

663   Amens

A.   **Dresden Amen**

Traditional

A - men,   A - men.

B.

Robert Ramsay (c. 1600-c. 1650)

A - men.

C.   *Melvin West, 1984 (1930-   )*

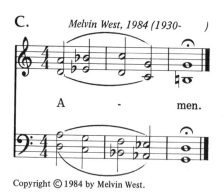

A - men.

Copyright © 1984 by Melvin West.

D.

Melvin West, 1984 (1930-   )

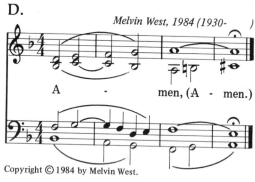

A - men, (A - men.)

Copyright © 1984 by Melvin West.

E.   *Melvin West, 1984 (1930-   )*

A - men.

Copyright © 1984 by Melvin West.

F.

Danish

A-men, A-men, A - men.

SENTENCES AND RESPONSES

Sevenfold Amen

664

John Stainer (1840-1901)

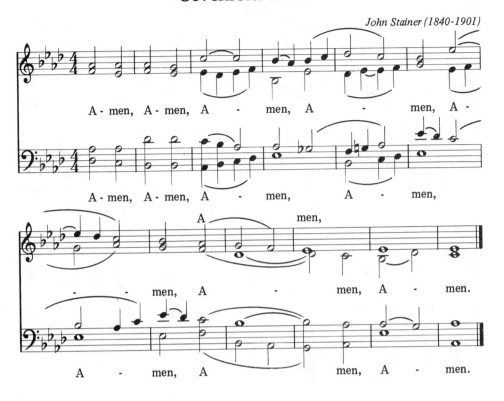

A-men, A-men, A - men, A - men, A - men, A - men, A - men,

A - men, A - men, A - men.

A - men, A - men, A - men.

All Things Come of Thee

665

1 Chron. 29:14
From Christ in Song, *1908*

Anon.

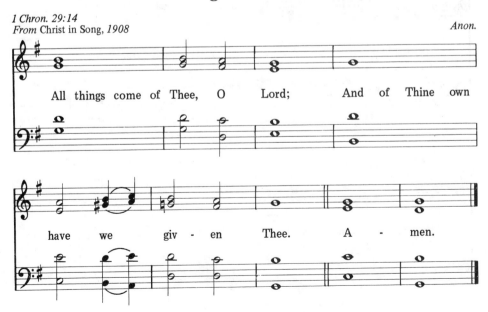

All things come of Thee, O Lord; And of Thine own

have we giv - en Thee. A - men.

666 Cast Thy Burden Upon the Lord

Psalms 55:22; 16:8

BIRMINGHAM Irregular
Felix Mendelssohn, 1846 (1809-1847)

Cast thy bur-den up-on the Lord, And He shall sus-tain thee; He

nev - er will suf - fer the righ-teous to fall; He is at thy

right hand. Thy mer - cy, Lord, is great, and far a - bove the

heavens; Let none be made a - sham-ed, that wait up-on Thee.

SENTENCES AND RESPONSES

Lord, Bless Thy Word to Every Heart 667

BENEDICTION C.M.

Pearl Waggoner Howard (1885-1969)

Stanley Ledington, 1939 (1889-1974)

Lord, bless Thy word to ev - ery heart In this Thy house to-day, And help us
each as now we part, Its pre-cepts to o - bey. A - men A - men.

O Thou Who Hearest 668

MORECAMBE 10.10.10.10.

Frederick A. Jackson (1867-1942)

Frederick Atkinson, 1870 (1841-1896)

O Thou who hear - est ev - ery heart-felt prayer, With Thy rich
grace, Lord, all our hearts pre-pare; Thou art our life, Thou art our
love and light, O let this Sab-bath hour with Thee be bright. A - men.

669   The Lord Bless You and Keep You

Num. 6:24-26

CHORAL BLESSING Irregular
Peter C. Lutkin, 1900 (1858-1931)

Music used by permission of Summy-Birchard Music division of Birch Tree Group Ltd.

SENTENCES AND RESPONSES

2, alternate ending

A - men, A

A - men, A - men, A - men,

A - men, A - men, A - men, A - men,

A - men, A - men, A - men, A -

men, A - men, A - men, A - men.

A - men, A - men, A - men.

A - men, A - men, A - men.

men, A - men, A - men, A - men.

We Give Thee But Thine Own   670

SCHUMANN S.M.
Mason and Webb's
Cantica Laudis, *Boston, 1850*

William Walsham How, 1858 (1823-1897)

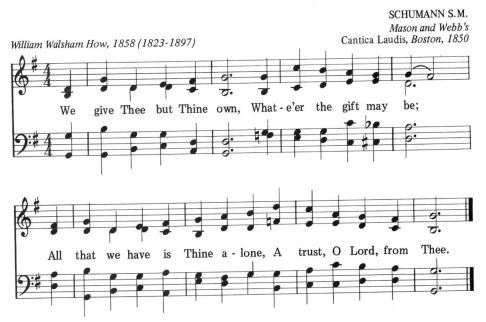

We give Thee but Thine own, What-e'er the gift may be;

All that we have is Thine a - lone, A trust, O Lord, from Thee.

SENTENCES AND RESPONSES

671 As We Come to You in Prayer

Ralph Carmichael (1927-   ) alt.

Irregular
Ralph Carmichael

Now, Dear Lord, as we pray, take our hearts and minds far a - way

From the press of the world all a - round To Your throne where grace

does a - bound. May our lives be trans-form'd by Your love, May our

souls be re-freshed from a - bove. At this mo - ment, let peo - ple

ev - ery-where Join us now as we come to You in prayer.

SENTENCES AND RESPONSES

Spirit of the Living God

672

Daniel Iverson, 1926 (1890-   )

Daniel Iverson, 1926
Arr. by Melvin West, 1984 (1930-   )

Spir-it of the liv-ing God, Fall a-fresh on me! Spir-it of the liv-ing God, Fall a-fresh on me! Break me, melt me, mold me, fill me! Spir-it of the liv-ing God, Fall a-fresh on me!

673 May God Be With You

Gen. 31:49
Anon.

MIZPAH 10.10.10.9.5.
Wayne Hooper, 1969 (1920-)

1. May God be with you Till we meet a-gain, May God be with you, Keep you safe till then; And may His bless-ings Be with-in your heart, May God be with you While we're a-part, May God be with you.

2. May God be with you, Watch you from a-bove, May God pro-tect you In His ten-der love; And with the dawn-ing Of each bright, new day, May God be with you, To guide your way, May God be with you.

SENTENCES AND RESPONSES

Shalom

Ancient Hebrew benediction
English text by Wayne Hooper, 1974 (1920-   )

Irregular

Accomp. by Melvin West, 1984 (1930-   )

1.*Sha - lom, my friends, sha - lom, my friends, Sha - lom, sha - lom.
2. May bless - ings at-tend you, an - gels de-fend, Sha - lom, sha - lom.
3. Till we meet a-gain, till we meet a-gain, Sha - lom, sha - lom.

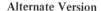

May peace be with you, God's peace be with you. Sha - lom, sha - lom.
God's mer - cies be-friend you un - to the end. Sha - lom, sha - lom.
May God be with you, His peace be with you. Sha - lom, sha - lom.

Accompaniment may repeat these two measures for the duration of the canon.

Words copyright © 1974 by Wayne Hooper.
Arrangement copyright © 1984 by Melvin West.

Alternate Version

Ancient Hebrew benediction

Irregular

Sha - lom, good friends, sha - lom, good friends, Sha - lom, sha - lom. Till

we meet a-gain, till we meet a-gain, Sha - lom, sha - lom.

From *Chansons de Notre Chalet,* copyright 1957 by Cooperative Recreation Service, Inc., Delaware, Ohio.
*The word "Shalom" has a triple meaning: hello, farewell, and peace - with special
overtones of loving concern and sincere caring for each other.
At the beginning of a meeting or as an expression of fellowship during a meeting, change text to "As we meet again."

SENTENCES AND RESPONSES

675   May the Lord Bless and Keep You

Melvin West (1930-)

Melvin West

Unison

May the Lord bless and keep you both now and ev-er-more. A-men, A-men.

676   Thy Word Is a Lantern

Psalm 119:105

Wihla Hutson (1901-)

Unison

Thy Word is a lan-tern un-to my feet, And a light un-to my path.

SENTENCES AND RESPONSES

Heavenly Father, to Thee We Pray

677

John Read, 1983 (1933-)

John Read

Heav-en-ly Fa-ther, to Thee we pray, On this ho-ly Sab-bath day; Through Thy Word Thy will make known; May each heart be-come Thy throne, Let Thy liv-ing wa-ter flow That we Thy bound-less love may know. A-men.

SENTENCES AND RESPONSES

God Be in My Head

Sarum Primer, *1558*

GOD BE IN MY HEAD Irregular
H. Walford Davies (1869-1941)

God be in my head, and in my un - der - stand - ing;

God be in mine eyes, and in my look - ing; God be in my

mouth, and in my speak - ing; God be in my heart, and in my

think - ing; God be at mine end, and at my de - part - ing.

Music used by permission of Oxford University Press.

SENTENCES AND RESPONSES

Sarum Primer, *1558*

Lorayne Coombs, *1958 (1919-   )*

God be in my head, And in my think - ing.

God be in my eyes, And in my look - ing.

God be in my mouth, And in my speak - ing. Oh,

God be in my heart, And in my un - der - stand - ing.

Music copyright © 1984 by Lorayne Coombs.

SENTENCES AND RESPONSES

680 Holy Spirit, Hear Us

William H. Parker (1845-1929)

ERNSTEIN 6.5.6.5.
James F. Swift (1847-1931)

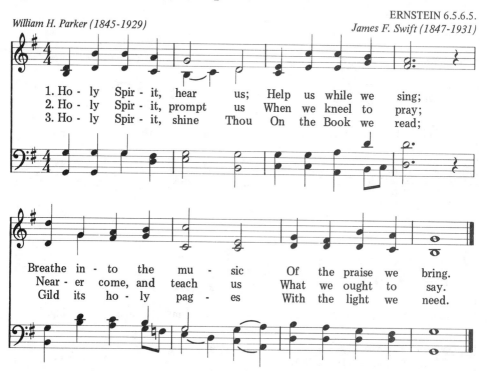

1. Ho - ly Spir - it, hear us; Help us while we sing;
2. Ho - ly Spir - it, prompt us When we kneel to pray;
3. Ho - ly Spir - it, shine Thou On the Book we read;

Breathe in - to the mu - sic Of the praise we bring.
Near - er come, and teach us What we ought to say.
Gild its ho - ly pag - es With the light we need.

681 This Is the Day the Lord Hath Made

Psalm 118:24
Isaac Watts, 1719 (1674-1748)

TWENTY FOURTH C.M.
Attr. to Lucius Chapin (1760-1842)

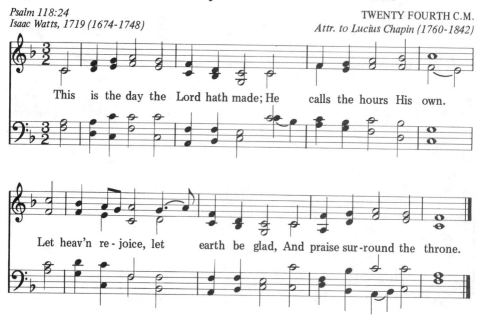

This is the day the Lord hath made; He calls the hours His own.

Let heav'n re - joice, let earth be glad, And praise sur - round the throne.

Unison setting, No. 406

SENTENCES AND RESPONSES

As You Have Promised, Lord

Luke 2:29-32
Adapt. by F. L. Battles, 1971

NUNC DIMITTIS Irregular
Ronald A. Nelson, 1971 (1927-   )

As You have prom-ised, Lord, to-day, You are let - ting Your ser - vant go a - way in peace. My eyes have seen You in broad day - light be - fore all na - tions, plan - ning sal - va - tion. Light of rev - e - la - tion for the na - tions, and glo - ry of Your peo - ple Is - ra - el.

TSDAH-22

SENTENCES AND RESPONSES

683

Jesus, Stand Among Us

John 20:19, 22
William Pennefather, 1873 (1816-1873)

BEMERTON 6.5.6.5.
Friedrich Filitz, 1847 (1804-1876)

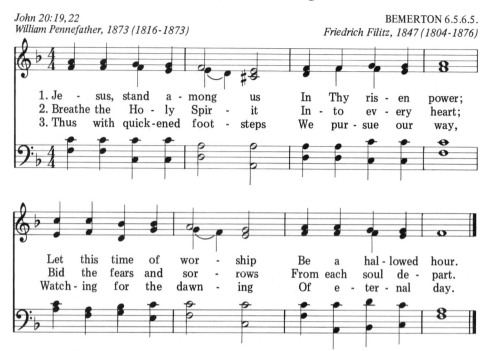

1. Je - sus, stand a - mong us In Thy ris - en power;
2. Breathe the Ho - ly Spir - it In - to ev - ery heart;
3. Thus with quick-ened foot - steps We pur - sue our way,

Let this time of wor - ship Be a hal - lowed hour.
Bid the fears and sor - rows From each soul de - part.
Watch - ing for the dawn - ing Of e - ter - nal day.

684

Hear Our Prayer, O Lord

George Whelpton, 1903 (1847-1930)

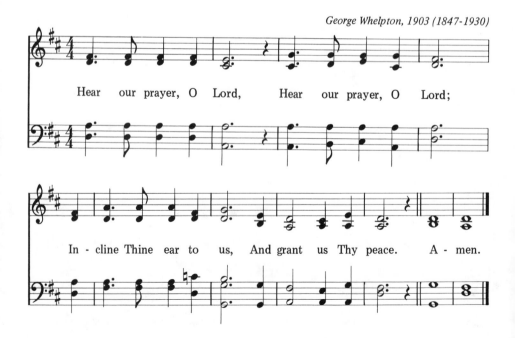

Hear our prayer, O Lord, Hear our prayer, O Lord;

In - cline Thine ear to us, And grant us Thy peace. A - men.

SENTENCES AND RESPONSES

Cause Me to Hear

685

Psalm 143:8, 9

Irregular
Melvin West, 1984 (1930-   )

Intro. Cause me to hear Thy lov-ing-kind-ness in the morn-ing, for in Thee do I trust. Cause me to know the way where-in I shall walk for I lift up my soul to Thee. A - - - men.

SENTENCES AND RESPONSES

686 Bless Thou the Gifts

CANONBURY L.M.

Samuel Longfellow, 1886 (1819-1892)

Arr. from Robert A. Schumann, 1839 (1810-1856)

Bless Thou the gifts our hands have brought; Bless
Thou the work our hearts have planned; Ours is the faith, the
will, the thought; The rest, O God, is in Thy hand. A-men.

687 The Lord Is in His Holy Temple

Hab. 2:20

Oliver S. Beltz (1887-1978)

The Lord is in His ho - ly tem - ple, The Lord is
in His ho - ly tem - ple, Let all the earth be

SENTENCES AND RESPONSES

be si - lent
si - lent, be si - lent be - fore Him.

Surely, Surely

688

9.8.8.9.

Eleanor Wright, 1978

Eleanor Wright (1926-   )

Sure - ly, sure - ly the Lord has been here, Sure - ly

an - gels still lin - ger near; I hear mu - sic

soft on my ear, I feel His Spir - it, I have no fear.

Day by Day, Dear Lord

Richard of Chichester (1197-1253)

11.11.9.
Harold W. Friedell (1905-1958)

Day by day, Dear Lord, of Thee three things I pray:

To see Thee more clear - ly, Love Thee more dear - ly,

To see Thee, Love Thee.

Fol - low Thee more near - ly, Day by day.

690 # Dismiss Us, Lord, With Blessing

L. E. Froom (1890-1974)

BENEDICTION 9.9.9.9.
L. E. Froom, 1934

Dis - miss us, Lord, with bless-ing, we pray;   As from Thy wor - ship

we go our ways; Guide in life's con - flicts, all through the day;

Save in Thy king - dom, Thine be the praise. A - men.

Lead Me, Lord

691

Psalms 5:8; 4:8

Samuel S. Wesley (1810-1876)

Lead me, Lord, lead me in Thy righ - teous - ness;

Make Thy way plain be - fore my face. For it is Thou, Lord,

Thou, Lord, on - ly That mak - est me dwell in safe - ty.

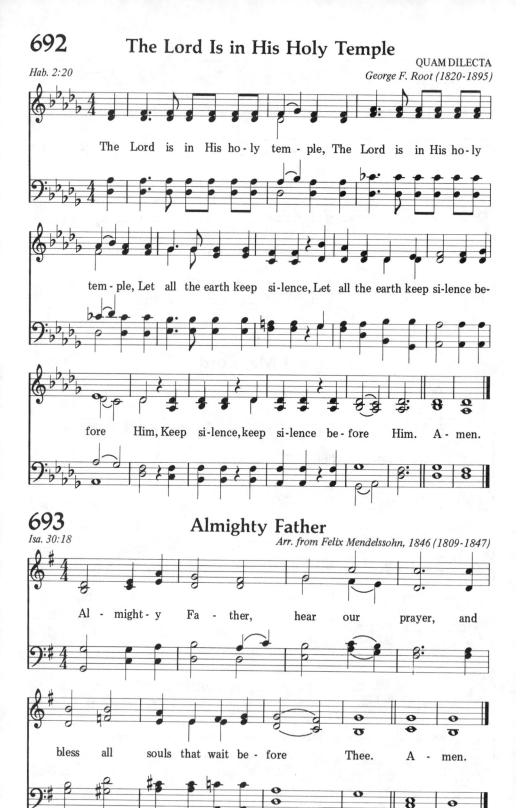

692 The Lord Is in His Holy Temple

Hab. 2:20

QUAM DILECTA
George F. Root (1820-1895)

The Lord is in His ho-ly tem-ple, The Lord is in His ho-ly tem-ple, Let all the earth keep si-lence, Let all the earth keep si-lence be-fore Him, Keep si-lence, keep si-lence be-fore Him. A-men.

693 Almighty Father

Isa. 30:18

Arr. from Felix Mendelssohn, 1846 (1809-1847)

Al - might-y Fa - ther, hear our prayer, and bless all souls that wait be - fore Thee. A - men.

SENTENCES AND RESPONSES

Praise God, From Whom All Blessings 694

Psalm 148:1,2
Thomas Ken, 1695 (1637-1710)

OLD HUNDREDTH L.M.
Louis Bourgeois, 1551 (1510-1561)

Praise God, from whom all bless-ings flow; Praise Him, all crea-tures here be - low;

Praise Him a - bove, ye heaven-ly host; Praise Fa - ther, Son, and Ho - ly Ghost.

Praise God, From Whom All Blessings 695

Psalm 148:1,2
Thomas Ken, 1695 (1637-1710)

OLD HUNDREDTH L.M.
Louis Bourgeois, 1551 (c.1510-1561)

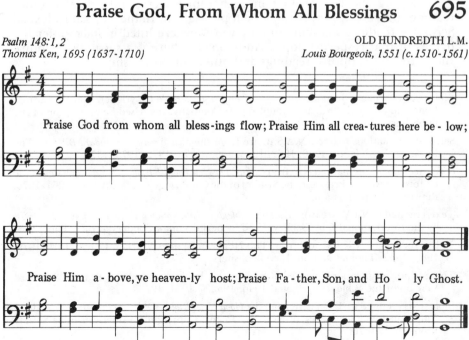

Praise God from whom all bless-ings flow; Praise Him all crea-tures here be - low;

Praise Him a - bove, ye heaven-ly host; Praise Fa - ther, Son, and Ho - ly Ghost.

SCRIPTURE READINGS

The use of Scripture should be central to the worship experience, and should involve each worshiper. Corporate reading of the Bible in a worship service includes several of the senses: sight, speech, and hearing. We see the words before us, we vocalize the words, and we hear a multitude of voices reinforcing our own. All this increases the impact of God's Word, impressing its message on our mind.

A congregation and its leaders should not feel bound by the responsive form in which these readings are presented. A variety of other forms will add to the significance of Scripture in worship: Any of the readings may be read in unison. Several readers, reflecting the sense of voices in the passage, may be used. Antiphonal reading, with the congregation suitably divided (e.g., choir and congregation, two sections of the church, men and women, youth and adults), can be a highly effective method of communicating the Word.

It may be further helpful if the reader introduces the passage by stating (1) the writer, (2) the audience to whom it was addressed, and (3) the circumstances under which it was written, all in just two or three sentences. This will help to re-create the mental environment of the Scripture passage and take the worshiper's attention from the reader to the passage itself.

These readings are arranged topically, using the same terminology and order as the hymns, thus facilitating the coordination of song and Word. A special category entitled "Canticles and Prayers" concludes the Scripture readings. These are literary gems from the New Testament, similar to psalms, that can be used in the same way as the other readings.

Following the last reading in each topic, a cross-reference to other readings that are appropriate to the topic is given. In the Topical Index, all Scripture readings pertaining to a given topic are listed in italics after the hymns of that respective topic. Additionally, there is a separate Scripture Index for the Scripture readings and other aids to worship.

696
I WILL EXTOL THE LORD

I will extol the Lord at all times;
his praise will always be on my lips.
My soul will boast in the Lord;
let the afflicted hear and rejoice.
Glorify the Lord with me;
let us exalt his name together.

*I sought the Lord, and he
answered me;
he delivered me from all my fears.
Those who look to him are radiant;
their faces are never covered
with shame.*

This poor man called,
and the Lord heard him;
he saved him out of all his troubles
The angel of the Lord encamps
around those who fear him,
and he delivers them.

*Taste and see that the Lord is good;
blessed is the man who takes
refuge in him.
Fear the Lord, you his saints,
for those who fear him lack nothing.*

The righteous cry out,
and the Lord hears them;
he delivers them from all
their troubles.
The Lord is close to the broken-
hearted
and saves those who are crushed
in spirit.

*Evil will slay the wicked;
the foes of the righteous will be
condemned.
The Lord Redeems his servants;
no one who takes refuge in him
will be condemned.*

—*From Psalm 34, N.I.V.*

697
SHOUT WITH JOY TO GOD, ALL THE EARTH!

Shout with joy to God, all the earth!
Sing to the glory of his name;
offer him glory and praise!

*Praise our God, O peoples,
let the sound of his praise be heard;
he has preserved our lives
and kept our feet from slipping.*

For you, O God, tested us;
you refined us like silver.
You brought us into prison
and laid burdens on our backs.

*You let men ride over our heads;
we went through fire and water,
but you brought us to a place of
abundance.*

I will come to your temple with
burnt offerings
and fulfill my vows to you—
vows my lips promised and my
mouth spoke when I was
in trouble.

*Come and listen, all you who
fear God;
let me tell you what he has done
for me.
I cried out to him with my mouth;
his praise was on my tongue.*

If I had cherished sin in my heart,
the Lord would not have listened;
but God has surely listened
and heard my voice in prayer.

*Praise be to God,
who has not rejected my prayer
or withheld his love from me!*

—*From Psalm 66, N.I.V*

698
HOW LOVELY IS THY DWELLING PLACE

How lovely is thy dwelling place,
O Lord of hosts!

My soul longs, yea, faints
for the courts of the Lord;
my heart and flesh sing for joy
to the living God.

Even the sparrow finds a home,
and the swallow a nest for herself,
where she may lay her young,
at thy altars, O Lord of hosts,
my King and my God.
Blessed are those who dwell in
thy house,
ever singing thy praise!

For a day in thy courts is better
than a thousand elsewhere.
I would rather be a doorkeeper
in the house of my God
than dwell in the tents of
wickedness.

For the Lord God is a sun and shield;
he bestows favor and honor.
No good thing does the Lord
withhold
from those who walk uprightly.

O Lord of hosts,
blessed is the man who trusts
in thee!
—*From Psalm 84, R.S.V.*

699
O COME, LET US SING UNTO THE LORD

O come, let us sing unto the Lord:
let us make a joyful noise
to the rock of our salvation.

Let us come before his presence
with thanksgiving,

and make a joyful noise unto him
with psalms.

For the Lord is a great God,
and a great King above all gods.

In his hand are the deep places
of the earth:
the strength of the hills is his also.
The sea is his, and he made it:
and his hands formed the dry land.

O come, let us worship and
bow down:
let us kneel before the Lord
our maker.

For he is our God;
and we are the people of his pasture,
and the sheep of his hand.
—*From Psalm 95, K.J.V.*

700
OH, SING TO THE LORD A NEW SONG!

Oh, sing to the Lord a new song!
Sing to the Lord, all the earth.
Sing to the Lord, bless His name;

Proclaim the good news of His
salvation from day to day.
Declare His glory among
the nations,
His wonders among all peoples.

For the Lord is great
and greatly to be praised;
He is to be feared above all gods.
For all the gods of the peoples are
idols,
But the Lord made the heavens.

Honor and majesty are before Him;
Strength and beauty are in His
sanctuary.

Give to the Lord,
O kindreds of the peoples,
Give to the Lord glory and strength.

Give to the Lord the glory due His
  name;
Bring an offering, and come into
  His courts.
Oh, worship the Lord in the beauty
  of holiness!
Tremble before Him, all the earth.

Say among the nations,
  "The Lord reigns;
The world also is firmly established,
It shall not be moved;
He shall judge the peoples
  righteously."

Let the heavens rejoice,
  and let the earth be glad;
Let the sea roar, and all its fullness;
Let the field be joyful,
  and all that is in it.
Then all the trees of the woods
  will rejoice before the Lord.

For He is coming, for He is coming
  to judge the earth.
He shall judge the world with
  righteousness,
And the peoples with His truth.
—From Psalm 96, N.K.J.V.

701
SHOUT JOYFULLY
TO THE LORD

Shout joyfully to the Lord,
  all the earth.
Serve the Lord with gladness;
Come before Him with joyful
  singing.

Know that the Lord Himself is God;
It is He who has made us, and not
  we ourselves;
We are His people and the sheep of
  His pasture.

Enter His gates with thanksgiving,
And His courts with praise.
Give thanks to Him; bless His name.

For the Lord is good;
His lovingkindness is everlasting,
And His faithfulness to all
  generations.
—From Psalm 100, N.A.S.B.

702
GIVE THANKS TO THE
LORD

Oh give thanks to the Lord, call upon
  His name;
Make known His deeds among
  the peoples.

Sing to Him, sing praises to Him;
Speak of all His wonders.

Glory in His holy name;
Let the heart of those who seek the
  Lord be glad.
Seek the Lord and His strength;
Seek His face continually.

Remember His wonders which He
  has done,
His marvels, and the judgments
  uttered by His mouth,
O seed of Abraham, His servant,
O sons of Jacob, His chosen ones!

He is the Lord our God;
His judgments are in all the earth.

He has remembered His covenant
  forever,
The word which He commanded
  to a thousand generations.
—From Psalm 105, N.A.S.B.

703
PRAISE THE LORD, YOU
THAT ARE HIS SERVANTS

O praise the Lord.
Praise the Lord, you that are his
  servants,
praise the name of the Lord.

Blessed be the name of the Lord
now and evermore.
From the rising of the sun to
its setting
may the Lord's name be praised.

High is the Lord above all nations,
his glory above the heavens.
There is none like the Lord our God
in heaven or on earth,
who sets his throne so high
but deigns to look down so low;

who lifts the weak out of the dust
and raises the poor from the
dunghill,
giving them a place among princes,
among the princes of
his people;
who makes the woman in a childless
house a happy mother of
children.

O praise the Lord.
—*From Psalms 113 and 114, N.E.B.*

704
IF I LIFT UP MY
EYES TO THE HILLS

If I lift up my eyes to the hills,
where shall I find help?

Help comes only from the Lord,
maker of heaven and earth.

How could he let your foot stumble?
How could he, your guardian, sleep?

The guardian of Israel
never slumbers, never sleeps.

The Lord is your guardian,
your defence at your
right hand;
the sun will not strike you by day
nor the moon by night.

The Lord will guard you against
all evil;
he will guard you, body
and soul.

The Lord will guard your going and
your coming, now and for
evermore.
—*From Psalm 121, N.E.B.*

705
I WILL EXALT YOU,
MY GOD THE KING

I will exalt you, my God the King;
I will praise your name for ever
and ever.
Every day I will praise you
and extol your name for ever
and ever.

Great is the Lord and most worthy
of praise;
his greatness no one can fathom.
One generation will commend your
works to another;
they will tell of your mighty acts.

They will celebrate your abundant
goodness
and joyfully sing of your
righteousness.
The Lord is gracious and
compassionate,
slow to anger and rich in love.

The Lord is faithful to all his
promises
and loving toward all he has made.
The Lord upholds all those who fall
and lifts up all who are
bowed down.

The eyes of all look to you,
and you give them their food at the
proper time.
You open your hand
and satisfy the desires
of every living thing.

The Lord is righteous in all his ways
and loving toward all he has made.
The Lord is near to all who
    call on him,
to all who call on him in truth.

He fulfills the desires of those who
    fear him;
he hears their cry and saves them.
The Lord watches over all
    who love him,
but all the wicked he will destroy.

My mouth will speak in praise
of the Lord.
Let every creature praise his holy
    name for ever and ever.
    —From Psalm 145, N.I.V.

706
LET HEAVEN PRAISE
THE LORD

Alleluia!
Let heaven praise Yahweh:
praise him, heavenly heights,
praise him, all his angels,
praise him, all his armies!

Praise him, sun and moon,
praise him, shining stars,
praise him, highest heavens,
and waters above the heavens!

Let them all praise the name
    of Yahweh,
at whose command they were
    created;
he has fixed them in their place
    for ever,
by an unalterable statute.

Let earth praise Yahweh:
sea-monsters and all the deeps,
fire and hail, snow and mist,
gales that obey his decree,

mountains and hills,
orchards and forests,

wild animals and farm animals,
snakes and birds,

all kings on earth and nations,
princes, all rulers in the world,
young men and girls,
old people, and children too!

Let them all praise the name
    of Yahweh,
for his name and no other is sublime,
transcending earth and heaven
    in majesty,
raising the fortunes of his people,
to the praises of the devout,
of Israel, the people dear to him.
    —From Psalm 148, Jerusalem.

707
O PRAISE GOD IN
HIS HOLY PLACE

O praise the Lord.
O praise God in his holy place,
praise him in the vault of heaven,
    the vault of his power;

praise him for his mighty works,
praise him for his immeasurable
    greatness.

Praise him with fanfares on the
    trumpet,
praise him upon lute and harp;

praise him with tambourines and
    dancing,
praise him with flute and strings;

praise him with the clash of cymbals,
praise him with triumphant
    cymbals;

let everything that has breath praise
    the Lord!
O praise the Lord.
    —From Psalm 150, N.E.B.

708
PRAISE AT GOD'S THRONE

"Holy, holy, holy is the Lord God
    Almighty,
who was, and is, and is to come."

*"You are worthy, our Lord
    and God,
to receive glory and honor and
    power,
for you created all things,
and by your will they were created
and have their being."*

*"Great and marvelous are your
    deeds,
Lord God Almighty.
Just and true are your ways,
King of the ages.

*"Who will not fear you, O Lord,
and bring glory to your name?
For you alone are holy.
All nations will come
    and worship before you,
for your righteous acts have been
    revealed."* *

"Hallelujah!
Salvation and glory and power
    belong to our God,
for true and just are his judgments."

*"Amen!
Praise and glory and wisdom
    and thanks and honor
    and power and strength
be to our God for ever and ever.
Amen!"*

        —From Revelation 4, 15, 19,
              and 7, N.I.V.

---

* Song of Moses and the Lamb.

WORSHIP: See also No. 780.

ADORATION AND PRAISE: See also
    Nos. 718, 728, 742, 785, 841, 859.

709
TRINITY

Blessed be the God and Father of
    our Lord Jesus Christ,
who has blessed us in Christ
with every spiritual blessing in the
    heavenly places.

*In him we have redemption
    through his blood,
the forgiveness of our trespasses,
according to the riches of his grace
which he lavished upon us.*

In him you also, who have heard the
    word of truth,
the gospel of your salvation,
and have believed in him,
were sealed with the promised
    Holy Spirit,
which is the guarantee of our
    inheritance
until we acquire possession of it,
to the praise of his glory.

*But now in Christ Jesus you who
    once were far off
have been brought near in the blood
    of Christ.*

He came and preached peace to you
who were far off and peace to
    those who were near;
for through him we both have access
    in one Spirit to the Father.

*There is one body and one Spirit,
just as you were called to the
    one hope
that belongs to your call,
one Lord, one faith, one baptism,
one God and Father of us all,
who is above all and through all and
    in all.*

      —From Ephesians 1, 2, and 4, R.S.V.

710
BOW DOWN YOUR EAR, O LORD, HEAR ME

Bow down Your ear, O Lord,
    hear me;
For I am poor and needy. . . .
For You, Lord, are good, and ready
    to forgive,
And abundant in mercy to all those
    who call upon You.

Give ear, O Lord, to my prayer;
And attend to the voice of my
    supplications.
In the day of my trouble
    I will call upon You,
For You will answer me. . . .
For You are great,
    and do wondrous things;
You alone are God.

Teach me Your way, O Lord;
I will walk in Your truth;
Unite my heart to fear Your name.

I will praise You, O Lord my God,
    with all my heart,
And I will glorify Your name
    forevermore.
For great is Your mercy toward me,
And You have delivered my soul
    from the depths of sheol.

O God, the proud have risen
    against me,
And a mob of violent men
    have sought my life,
And have not set You before them.

But You, O Lord, are a God full
    of compassion, and gracious,
Longsuffering and abundant in
    mercy and truth.

Oh, turn to me, and have mercy
    on me!
Give Your strength to Your servant,
And save the son of Your
    maidservant.

Show me a sign for good,
That those who hate me
    may see it and be ashamed,
Because You, Lord, have helped me
    and comforted me.
        —From Psalm 86, N.K.J.V.

711
PRAISE THE LORD, O MY SOUL

Praise the Lord, O my soul;
all my inmost being, praise his
    holy name.
Praise the Lord, O my soul,
and forget not all his benefits.

He forgives all my sins
and heals all my diseases;
he redeems my life from the pit
and crowns me with love and
    compassion.
He satisfies my desires with
    good things,
so that my youth is renewed
    like the eagle's.

The Lord is compassionate and
    gracious,
slow to anger, abounding in love. . . .
He does not treat us as our sins
    deserve
or repay us according to our
    iniquities.

For as high as the heavens are above
    the earth,
so great is his love for those who
    fear him;
as far as the east is from the west,
so far has he removed our
    transgressions from us.

Praise the Lord, O my soul.
        —From Psalm 103, N.I.V.

712
HIS LOVE ENDURES

It is good to give thanks to the Lord,
for his love endures for ever.*

*Give thanks to the God of gods;
his love endures for ever.*

Give thanks to the Lord of lords;
his love endures for ever.

*Alone he works great marvels;
his love endures for ever.*

In wisdom he made the heavens;
his love endures for ever.

*He laid the earth upon the waters;
his love endures for ever.*

He made the great lights,
his love endures for ever,

*The sun to rule by day,
his love endures for ever,*

The moon and the stars to rule
by night;
his love endures for ever.

*He remembered us when we were
cast down,
his love endures for ever,*

and rescued us from our enemies;
his love endures for ever.

*He gives food to all his creatures;
his love endures for ever.*

Give thanks to the God of heaven,
for his love endures for ever.
　　　　　　　—From Psalm 136, N.E.B.

───────

*Alternately, the congregation may
　respond by reading this phrase in
　each couplet.

713
LOVE OF GOD

In this the love of God was mani-
　　fested toward us,
that God has sent His only begotten
　　Son into the world,
that we might live through Him.

*"For God did not send His Son into
　　the world
to condemn the world,
but that the world through Him
might be saved."*

In this is love,
not that we loved God,
but that He loved us and sent His
　　Son to be the propitiation for
　　our sins.

*God is love,
and he who abides in love abides
　　in God,
and God in him.*

Beloved, if God so loved us,
we also ought to love one another.

*If someone says,
"I love God," and hates his brother,
　　he is a liar;
for he who does not love his brother
　　whom he has seen,
how can he love God whom he has
　　not seen?*

And this commandment we have
　　from Him:
that he who loves God
must love his brother also.
　　　—From 1 John 4 and John 3, N.K.J.V.
───────

LOVE: See also Nos. 703, 704.

714
O LORD, HOW MAJESTIC IS YOUR NAME

O Lord, our Lord,
how majestic is your name in
all the earth!
You have set your glory above the
heavens.

From the lips of children
and infants
you have ordained praise
because of your enemies,
to silence the foe and the avenger.

When I consider your heavens,
the work of your fingers,
the moon and the stars,
which you have set in place,

what is man that you are mindful
of him,
the son of man that you
care for him?

You made him a little lower
than the heavenly beings
and crowned him with glory
and honor.

You made him ruler over the works
of your hands:
you put everything under his feet:
all flocks and herds,
and the beasts of the field,
the birds of the air,
and the fish of the sea,
all that swim the paths of the seas.

O Lord, our Lord,
how majestic is your name in all
the earth!
—*From Psalm 8, N.I.V.*

715
I WILL EXTOL THE LORD WITH ALL MY HEART

Praise the Lord.
I will extol the Lord with all my heart
in the council of the upright
and in the assembly.

Great are the works of the Lord;
they are pondered by all who
delight in them.
Glorious and majestic are his deeds,
and his righteousness endures
forever.

He has caused his wonders
to be remembered;
the Lord is gracious and
compassionate.
He provides food for those who
fear him;
he remembers his covenant forever.

He has shown his people the power
of his works,
giving them the lands of other
nations.
The works of his hands are
faithful and just;
all his precepts are trustworthy.

They are steadfast for ever and ever,
done in faithfulness and
uprightness.
He provided redemption for
his people;
he ordained his covenant forever—
holy and awesome is his name.

The fear of the Lord
is the beginning of wisdom;
all who follow his precepts
have good understanding.
To him belongs eternal praise.
—*From Psalm 111, N.I.V.*

716
THE LIBERATING CREATOR

Thus speaks the Lord who is God,
he who created the skies and
   stretched them out,
who fashioned the earth and all
   that grows in it,
who gave breath to its people, the
   breath of life to all who walk
   upon it:

*I, the Lord, have called you with
   righteous purpose and taken
   you by the hand;*
I have formed you,
*and appointed you to be a light to all
   peoples, a beacon for
   the nations,*
to open eyes that are blind,
*to bring captives out of prison, out
   of the dungeons where they lie
   in darkness.*

I am the Lord; the Lord is my name;
I will not give my glory to
   another god,
   nor my praise to any idol.

*See how the first prophecies have
   come to pass,*
and now I declare new things;
*before they break from the bud
   I announce them to you.*

Sing a new song to the Lord,
sing his praise throughout the earth,
you that sail the sea, and all sea-
   creatures, and you that inhabit
   the coasts and islands.

*Let the wilderness and its towns
   rejoice,*
*and the villages of the tribe of
   Kedar.*
*Let those who live in Sela shout
   for joy*
and cry out from the hill-tops.

You coasts and islands, all uplift his
   praises;
let all ascribe glory to the Lord.
                    —From Isaiah 42, N.E.B.

———

*MAJESTY AND POWER: See also No.
838.*

717
THE HEAVENS DECLARE THE GLORY OF GOD

The heavens declare the
   glory of God;
the skies proclaim the work of
   his hands.
Day after day they pour
   forth speech;
night after night they display
   knowledge.

*There is no speech or language
where their voice is not heard.
Their voice goes out into
   all the earth,
their words to the ends of the world.*

In the heavens he has pitched a tent
   for the sun,
which is like a bridegroom
   coming forth from his pavilion,
like a champion rejoicing
   to run his course.

*It rises at one end of the heavens
and makes its circuit to the other;
nothing is hidden from its heat.*

The heavens declare the glory
   of God;
the skies proclaim the work of
   his hands.
                    —From Psalm 19, N.I.V.

718
REJOICE IN THE LORD

Rejoice in the Lord, O you
    righteous!
For praise from the upright is
    beautiful.

Praise the Lord with the harp;
Make melody to Him with an
    instrument of ten strings.

Sing to Him a new song;
Play skillfully with a shout of joy.

For the word of the Lord is right,
And all His work is done in truth.
He loves righteousness and justice;
The earth is full of the goodness
    of the Lord.

By the word of the Lord
    the heavens were made,
And all the host of them
    by the breath of His mouth.
He gathers the waters of the sea
    together as a heap;
He lays up the deep in storehouses.

Let all the earth fear the Lord;
Let all the inhabitants of the world
    stand in awe of Him.
For He spoke, and it was done;
He commanded, and it stood fast.
    —*From Psalm 33, N.K.J.V.*

719
OUR LORD THE CREATOR

This is what God the Lord says—
he who created the heavens and
    stretched them out,
who spread out the earth,
    and all that comes out of it,
who gives breath to its people,
and life to those who walk on it.

"I am the Lord, and there is no
    other;
apart from me there is no God.
I will strengthen you, though you
    have not acknowledged me,
so that from the rising of the sun
    to the place of its setting
men may know there is none
    besides me.
I am the Lord, and there is
    no other."

"You heavens above,
    rain down righteousness;
let the clouds shower it down.
Let the earth open wide,
let salvation spring up,
let righteousness grow with it;
I, the Lord, have created it."

For this is what the Lord says—
he who created the heavens,
    he is God;
he who fashioned and made the
    earth, he founded it;
he did not create it to be empty,
    but formed it to be inhabited—
he says:

"I am the Lord,
and there is no other. . . .
Turn to me and be saved,
all you ends of the earth;
for I am God, and there is no other."
    —*From Isaiah 42 and 45, N.I.V.*

POWER IN NATURE: See also Nos.
706, 712, 714, 760, 769, 785, 803.

720
GOD IS OUR REFUGE AND STRENGTH

God is our refuge and strength,
A very present help in trouble.

Therefore we will not fear,
Though the earth be removed,
And though the mountains be

carried into the midst of the sea;
Though its waters roar and be
troubled,
Though the mountains shake
with its swelling.

There is a river whose streams
shall make glad the city of God,
The holy place of the tabernacle
of the Most High.
God is in the midst of her,
she shall not be moved;
God shall help her,
just at the break of dawn.

The nations raged,
the kingdoms were moved;
He uttered His voice,
the earth melted.

The Lord of hosts is with us;
The God of Jacob is our refuge.

Come, behold the works of
the Lord,
Who has made desolations
in the earth.
He makes wars cease to the end of
the earth;
He breaks the bow
and cuts the spear in two;
He burns the chariot in the fire.

Be still, and know that I am God;
I will be exalted among the nations,
I will be exalted in the earth!

The Lord of hosts is with us;
The God of Jacob is our refuge.
                    —*From Psalm 46, N.K.J.V.*

721
LORD, YOU HAVE BEEN OUR REFUGE

Lord, you have been
our refuge age after age.

Before the mountains were born,
before the earth or the world
came to birth,
you were God from all eternity and
for ever.

You can turn man back into dust
by saying, "Back to what you
were, you sons of men!"
To you, a thousand years are a
single day,
a yesterday now over, an hour of
the night.

You brush men away like
waking dreams,
they are like grass
sprouting and flowering in the
morning,
withered and dry before dusk.

We too are burnt up by your anger
and terrified by your fury;
having summoned up our sins
you inspect our secrets by
your own light.

Our days dwindle under
your wrath,
our lives are over in a breath
—our life lasts for seventy years,
eighty with good health,

but they all add up to anxiety
and trouble—
over in a trice, and then we are gone.
Who yet has felt the full force of
your fury,
or learnt to fear the violence of
your rage?

Teach us to count how few days
we have
and so gain wisdom of heart.
                    —*From Psalm 90, Jerusalem.*

722
HE THAT DWELLETH IN THE SECRET PLACE

He that dwelleth in the secret place
    of the most High
shall abide under the shadow
    of the Almighty.

I will say of the Lord,
He is my refuge and my fortress:
my God; in him will I trust.

Surely he shall deliver thee
    from the snare of the fowler,
and from the noisome pestilence.

He shall cover thee with
*   his feathers,*
and under his wings shalt
*   thou trust:*
his truth shall be thy shield
*   and buckler.*

Thou shalt not be afraid
    for the terror by night;
nor for the arrow that flieth by day;
nor for the pestilence that walketh
    in darkness;
nor for the destruction
    that wasteth at noonday.

A thousand shall fall at thy side,
and ten thousand at thy right hand;
but it shall not come nigh thee.

Only with thine eyes shalt thou
    behold and see
the reward of the wicked.

Because thou hast made the Lord,
which is my refuge,
even the most High, thy habitation;
there shall no evil befall thee,
neither shall any plague
*   come nigh thy dwelling.*

For he shall give his angels charge
    over thee,
to keep thee in all thy ways.
        —*From Psalm 91, K.J.V.*

723
O GIVE THANKS TO THE LORD, FOR HE IS GOOD

O give thanks to the Lord, for
    he is good;
for his steadfast love endures
    for ever!

Let the redeemed of the Lord say so,
whom he has redeemed from
*   trouble*
and gathered in from the lands,
from the east and from the west,
from the north and from the south.

Some wandered in desert wastes,
finding no way to a city to dwell in;
hungry and thirsty,
their soul fainted within them.

Then they cried to the Lord in
*   their trouble,*
and he delivered them from
*   their distress;*
he led them by a straight way,
till they reached a city to dwell in.

Let them thank the Lord for his
    steadfast love,
for his wonderful works to the sons
    of men!
For he satisfies him who is thirsty,
and the hungry he fills with
    good things.

Some sat in darkness and in gloom,
prisoners in affliction and in irons,
for they had rebelled against the
*   words of God,*
and spurned the counsel of the
*   Most High.*

Their hearts were bowed down with
    hard labor;
they fell down, with none to help.

Then they cried to the Lord in
*   their trouble,*

and he delivered them from
    their distress;
he brought them out of darkness
    and gloom,
and broke their bonds asunder.

Let them thank the Lord for his
    steadfast love,
for his wonderful works to the sons
    of men!
            —From Psalm 107, R.S.V.

724
O LORD, YOU HAVE SEARCHED ME

O Lord, You have searched me and
    known me.
You know my sitting down and my
    rising up;
You understand my thought
    afar off.

You comprehend my path
    and my lying down,
And are acquainted with all
    my ways.
For there is not a word
    on my tongue,
But behold, O Lord,
    You know it altogether.

You have hedged me behind
    and before,
And laid Your hand upon me.
Such knowledge is too wonderful
    for me;
It is high, I cannot attain it.

Where can I go from Your Spirit?
Or where can I flee from
    Your presence?
If I ascend into heaven, You
    are there;
If I make my bed in hell,
    behold, You are there.

If I take the wings of the morning,

And dwell in the uttermost parts
    of the sea,
Even there Your hand shall lead me,
And Your right hand shall hold me.

If I say, "Surely the darkness
    shall fall on me,"
Even the night shall be light
    about me;
Indeed, the darkness
    shall not hide from You,
But the night shines as the day;
The darkness and the light are both
    alike to You.

For You have formed my
    inward parts;
You have covered me in my
    mother's womb.
I will praise You, for I am fearfully
    and wonderfully made;
Marvelous are Your works,
And that my soul knows very well.

Search me, O God, and know
    my heart;
Try me, and know my anxieties;
And see if there is any wicked way
    in me,
And lead me in the way everlasting.
          —From Psalm 139, N.K.J.V.

725
GOD WORKS FOR GOOD

I consider that our present
    sufferings
are not worth comparing
    with the glory that will be
    revealed in us.

The creation waits in eager
    expectation
for the sons of God to be revealed.

For the creation was subjected
to frustration, not by its own choice,
but by the will of the one
    who subjected it,

in hope that the creation itself
will be liberated from its bondage
    to decay
and brought into the glorious
    freedom
of the children of God.

And we know that in all things
God works for the good
    of those who love him,
who have been called
    according to his purpose.

What, then, shall we say in response
    to this?
If God is for us, who can be
    against us?

He who did not spare his own Son,
but gave him up for us all—
how will he not also, along
    with him,
graciously give us all things?
        —From Romans 8, N.I.V.

———

FAITHFULNESS: See also Nos. 696,
    701, 704, 715, 726, 727, 740, 751,
    801.

726
THE LORD IS
MY SHEPHERD

The Lord is my shepherd;
I shall not want.

He maketh me to lie down in green
    pastures:
he leadeth me beside
    the still waters.

He restoreth my soul:
he leadeth me in the paths of
    righteousness for his
    name's sake.

Yea, though I walk through the
    valley of the shadow of death,

I will fear no evil:
for thou art with me;
thy rod and thy staff they
    comfort me.

Thou preparest a table before me
in the presence of mine enemies:
thou anointest my head with oil;
my cup runneth over.

Surely goodness and mercy shall
    follow me
all the days of my life:
and I will dwell in the house of the
    Lord for ever.
        —Psalm 23, K.J.V.

727
THE LORD IS MY LIGHT

The Lord is my light and my
    salvation;
Whom shall I fear?
The Lord is the strength of my life;
Of whom shall I be afraid?

When the wicked came against me
    To eat up my flesh,
My enemies and foes,
They stumbled and fell.

Though an army should encamp
    against me,
My heart shall not fear;
Though war should rise against me,
    In this I will be confident.

One thing I have desired of
    the Lord,
That will I seek:
That I may dwell in the house
    of the Lord
All the days of my life,
To behold the beauty of the Lord,
And to inquire in His temple.

For in the time of trouble
He shall hide me in His pavilion;

In the secret place of His tabernacle
    He shall hide me;
He shall set me high upon a rock.

And now my head shall be lifted up
    above my enemies all
    around me;
Therefore I will offer sacrifices of
    joy in His tabernacle;
I will sing, yes, I will sing praises to
    the Lord.

When my father and my mother
    forsake me,
Then the Lord will take care of me.

Teach me Your way, O Lord,
And lead me in a smooth path,
    because of my enemies.

Wait on the Lord;
Be of good courage,
And He shall strengthen your heart;
Wait, I say, on the Lord!
          —From Psalm 27, N.K.J.V.

728
LET THE REDEEMED THANK THE LORD

Let [the redeemed] thank the Lord
    for his steadfast love,
for his wonderful works to the sons
    of men! . . .
And let them offer sacrifices of
    thanksgiving,
and tell of his deeds in songs of joy!

Some went down to the sea in ships,
doing business on the great waters;
they saw the deeds of the Lord,
his wondrous works in the deep.

For he commanded,
    and raised the stormy wind,
which lifted up the waves of the sea.

They mounted up to heaven,
    they went down to the depths;

their courage melted away in their
    evil plight;
they reeled and staggered like
    drunken men,
and were at their wits' end.

Then they cried to the Lord in
    their trouble,
and he delivered them from
    their distress;
he made the storm be still,
and the waves of the sea
    were hushed.

Then they were glad
    because they had quiet,
and he brought them to their
    desired haven.
Let them thank the Lord for his
    steadfast love,
for his wonderful works to the
    sons of men!

Let them extol him in the congrega-
    tion of the people,
and praise him in the assembly
    of the elders.

He turns rivers into a desert,
springs of water into thirsty
    ground,
a fruitful land into a salty waste,
because of the wickedness
    of its inhabitants.

He turns a desert into pools of water,
a parched land into springs of water.
And there he lets the hungry dwell,
and they establish a city to live in;
they sow fields, and plant vineyards,
and get a fruitful yield.

Whoever is wise, let him give heed
    to these things;
let men consider the steadfast love
    of the Lord.
          —From Psalm 107, R.S.V.

———

GRACE AND MERCY: *See also Nos.*
710, 722, 725, 765.

729
THE SAVIOUR IS COMING

"Comfort, yes, comfort My people!"
Says your God.
"Speak comfort to Jerusalem,
    and cry out to her,
That her warfare is ended,
That her iniquity is pardoned;
For she has received from the
    Lord's hand
Double for all her sins."

The voice of one crying in the
    wilderness:
"Prepare the way of the Lord;
Make straight in the desert
A highway for our God.

"Every valley shall be exalted,
And every mountain and hill
    shall be made low;
The crooked places
    shall be made straight,
And the rough places smooth;

"The glory of the Lord shall
    be revealed,
And all flesh shall see it together;
For the mouth of the Lord has
    spoken."

O Zion,
You who bring good tidings,
Get up into the high mountain;
O Jerusalem,
You who bring good tidings,
Lift up your voice with strength,
Lift it up, be not afraid;
Say to the cities of Judah,
    "Behold your God!"

Behold, the Lord God shall come
    with a strong hand,
And His arm shall rule for Him;
Behold, His reward is with Him,
And His work before Him.

He will feed His flock like a
    shepherd;
He will gather the lambs with
    His arm,
And carry them in His bosom,
And gently lead those who are
    with young.
                —*From Isaiah 40, N.K.J.V.*

———

FIRST ADVENT: See also Nos. 835, 836.

730
THE BIRTH OF CHRIST

This is how the birth of Jesus Christ
    came about.

His mother Mary was pledged to be
    married to Joseph,
but before they came together,
she was found to be with child
    through the Holy Spirit.

An angel of the Lord appeared to
    him in a dream and said,
"Joseph son of David,
do not be afraid to take Mary home
    as your wife,
because what is conceived in her
is from the Holy Spirit.

"She will give birth to a son,
and you are to give him the name
    Jesus,
because he will save his people
    from their sins."

And there were shepherds living
    out in the fields nearby,
keeping watch over their flocks
    at night.
An angel of the Lord appeared
    to them,
and the glory of the Lord shone
    around them, and they were
    terrified.

But the angel said to them,
"Do not be afraid.

I bring you good news of great joy
that will be for all the people.

"Today in the town of David a Savior
has been born to you;
he is Christ the Lord.
This will be a sign to you:
You will find a baby wrapped in
    strips of cloth and lying
    in a manger."

Suddenly a great company of the
    heavenly host appeared with
    the angel, praising God
    and saying,
"Glory to God in the highest,
and on earth peace to men
    on whom his favor rests."
    —*From Matthew 1 and Luke 2, N.I.V.*

731
THE VISIT OF
THE WISE MEN

Now when Jesus was born in
    Bethlehem of Judea
in the days of Herod the king,
    behold,
wise men from the East came
    to Jerusalem, saying,

"Where is he who has been born
    king of the Jews?
For we have seen his star in the East,
and have come to worship him."

When Herod the king heard this,
he was troubled, and all Jerusalem
    with him;
and assembling all the chief priests
    and scribes of the people,
he inquired of them where the
    Christ was to be born.

They told him, "In Bethlehem
    of Judea;
for so it is written by the prophet:
'And you, O Bethlehem, in the
    land of Judah,

are by no means least among the
    rulers of Judah;
for from you shall come a ruler
who will govern my
    people Israel.'"

Then Herod summoned the wise
    men secretly
and ascertained from them
what time the star appeared;
and he sent them to Bethlehem,
    saying,
"Go and search diligently for
    the child,
and when you have found him bring
    me word,
that I too may come and
    worship him."

When they had heard the king
they went their way;
and lo, the star which they had seen
    in the East
went before them,
till it came to rest over the place
    where the child was.

When they saw the star, they rejoiced
    exceedingly with great joy;
and going into the house they saw
    the child with Mary his mother,
and they fell down and
    worshiped him.

Then, opening their treasures,
they offered him gifts,
gold and frankincense and myrrh.
    —*From Matthew 2, R.S.V.*

———

BIRTH: See also Nos. 837, 842, 844.

732
JESUS' PRAYER FOR HIS
DISCIPLES

"Father, the time has come.
Glorify your Son,
that your Son may glorify you."

"Now this is eternal life:
that they may know you, the only
*   true God,*
and Jesus Christ, whom you
*   have sent."*

"I have revealed you to those
whom you gave me out of the world.
They were yours;
you gave them to me
and they have obeyed your word."

"I pray for them.
I am not praying for the world,
but for those you have given me,
for they are yours. . . .
Glory has come to me through
*   them."*

"Holy Father, protect them
    by the power of your name—
    the name you gave me—so that
    they may be one as we are one."

"I am coming to you now,
but I say these things
while I am still in the world,
so that they may have the full
measure of my joy within them."

"My prayer is not that you take them
        out of the world
but that you protect them
        from the evil one.
They are not of the world,
even as I am not of it.

"Sanctify them by the truth;
your word is truth.
As you sent me into the world,
I have sent them into the world.
For them I sanctify myself,
that they too may be truly
*   sanctified.*

"My prayer is not for them alone.
I pray also for those who will believe
        in me through their message,
that all of them may be one, Father,
just as you are in me and I am in
        you."

"May they be brought to
*   complete unity*
to let the world know that you
*   sent me*
and have loved them even as you
*   have loved me.*

"Father, I want those you have
        given me
to be with me where I am,
and to see my glory,
the glory you have given me
because you loved me
before the creation of the world."
                        —*From John 17, N.I.V.*

———

LIFE AND MINISTRY: See also No.
842.

733
CHRIST'S SUFFERINGS
AND DEATH—I

Who has believed our message,
and to whom has the arm of the Lord
        been revealed?

He grew up before him like a
*   tender shoot,*
and like a root out of dry ground.
He had no beauty or majesty
*   to attract us to him,*
nothing in his appearance
*   that we should desire him.*

He was despised and rejected
        by men,
a man of sorrows, and familiar with
        suffering.
Like one from whom men hide
        their faces
he was despised, and we esteemed
        him not.

Surely he took up our infirmities
*   and carried our sorrows,*
yet we considered him stricken by
*   God, smitten by him,*
*   and afflicted.*

But he was pierced for our transgressions,
he was crushed for our iniquities;
the punishment that brought us
peace was upon him,
and by his wounds we are healed.

We all, like sheep, have gone astray,
each of us has turned to his
own way;
and the Lord has laid on him
the iniquity of us all.

He was oppressed and afflicted,
yet he did not open his mouth;
he was led like a lamb to the
slaughter,
and as a sheep before her shearers
is silent,
so he did not open his mouth.

By oppression and judgment, he
was taken away.
And who can speak of his
descendants?
For he was cut off from the land of
the living;
for the transgression of my people
he was stricken.

He was assigned a grave with
the wicked,
and with the rich in his death,
though he had done no violence,
nor was any deceit in his mouth.

Yet it was the Lord's will to crush
him and cause him to suffer,
and though the Lord makes his life a
guilt offering,
he will see his offspring and
prolong his days,
and the will of the Lord will prosper
in his hand.

After the suffering of his soul,
he will see the light of life and
be satisfied;
by his knowledge my righteous ser-
vant will justify many,
and he will bear their iniquities.

Therefore I will give him a portion
among the great,
and he will divide the spoils with
the strong,
because he poured out his life
unto death,
and was numbered with the
transgressors.
For he bore the sin of many,
and made intercession for the
transgressors.
—*From Isaiah 53, N.I.V.*

734
CHRIST'S SUFFERINGS
AND DEATH—II

Early in the morning, all the chief
priests and the elders of the people
came to the decision to put Jesus
to death.
They bound him, led him away
and handed him over to Pilate,
the governor.

"What shall I do, then, with Jesus
who is called Christ?" Pilate asked.
They all answered, "Crucify him!"
"Why? What crime has he commit-
ted?" asked Pilate.
But they shouted all the louder,
"Crucify him!"

Then he released Barabbas to them.
But he had Jesus flogged,
and handed him over to be crucified.
Then the governor's soldiers took
Jesus into the Praetorium
and gathered the whole company of
soldiers around him.

They stripped him and put a scarlet
robe on him,
and then wove a crown of thorns
and set it on his head.
They put a staff in his right hand
and knelt in front of him and
mocked him.
"Hail, King of the Jews!" they said.

They spit on him,
and took the staff and struck him
    on the head again and again.
After they had mocked him,
they took off the robe and
    put his own clothes on him.
Then they led him away to
    crucify him.

*And when Jesus had cried out again
    in a loud voice,
he gave up his spirit.*

At that moment the curtain of the
    temple was torn in two from top
    to bottom.
The earth shook and the rocks split.

*When the centurion and those with
    him who were guarding Jesus
saw the earthquake and all that had
    happened,
they were terrified, and exclaimed,
"Surely he was the Son of God!"*
    —*From Matthew 27, N.I.V.*

---

*SUFFERINGS AND DEATH: See also
    No. 842.*

735
THE RESURRECTION OF JESUS

After the Sabbath, at dawn on the
    first day of the week,
Mary Magdalene and the other Mary
    went to look at the tomb.

*There was a violent earthquake,
for an angel of the Lord came down
    from heaven and, going to
    the tomb,
rolled back the stone and sat on it.*

His appearance was like lightning,
and his clothes were white as snow.
The guards were so afraid of him
that they shook and became like
    dead men.

*The angel said to the women,
"Do not be afraid,
for I know that you are looking
    for Jesus,
who was crucified.*

"He is not here; he has risen, just
    as he said. . . .
Go quickly and tell his disciples:
'He has risen from the dead.'"

*So the women hurried away from
    the tomb,
afraid yet filled with joy,
and ran to tell his disciples.*

Suddenly Jesus met them.
"Greetings," he said.

*They came to him, clasped his feet
and worshiped him.**
    —*From Matthew 28, N.I.V.*

---

* This reading and the following can be
    combined as one reading.

736
THE GLORIFIED CHRIST

After the Lord Jesus had spoken
    to them,
he was taken up into heaven
and he sat at the right hand of God.

*If Christ has not been raised,
our preaching is useless and so is
    your faith. . . .
But Christ has indeed been raised
    from the dead,
the firstfruits of those who have
    fallen asleep.*

Among the lampstands was
    someone "like a son of man,"
dressed in a robe reaching down to
    his feet
and with a golden sash around his
    chest.

His head and hair were white like
  wool, as white as snow,
and his eyes were like blazing fire.
His feet were like bronze glowing in
  a furnace,
and his voice was like the sound of
  rushing waters.

In his right hand he held
  seven stars,
and out of his mouth came a sharp
  double-edged sword.
His face was like the sun shining in
  all its brilliance.

When I saw him,
I fell at his feet as though dead.
Then he placed his right hand on me
  and said:

"Do not be afraid. I am the First and
  the Last.
I am the Living One; I was dead,
and behold I am alive for ever
  and ever!
And I hold the keys of death
  and Hades."
  —*From Mark 16, 1 Corinthians 15,*
    and Revelation 1, N.I.V.

737
THE ASCENSION

[Jesus] showed himself to these men
  after his death,
and gave ample proof that he
  was alive:
over a period of forty days he
  appeared to them and taught
  them about the kingdom
  of God.

While he was in their company
  he told them not to leave
  Jerusalem.
"You must wait," he said,
"for the promise made by my
  Father,
about which you have heard
  me speak:

"John, as you know, baptized
  with water,
but you will be baptized with the
  Holy Spirit,
and within the next few days."

So, when they were all together,
  they asked him,
"Lord, is this the time
when you are to establish once
  again the sovereignty
  of Israel?"

He answered,
"It is not for you to know about
  dates or times,
which the Father has set within
  his own control.
But you will receive power when the
  Holy Spirit comes upon you;
and you will bear witness for me in
  Jerusalem, and all over Judaea
  and Samaria,
and away to the ends of the earth."

When he had said this, as
  they watched,
he was lifted up,
and a cloud removed him from
  their sight.
As he was going,
and as they were gazing intently
  into the sky,
all at once there stood beside them
  two men in white who said,

"Men of Galilee,
why stand there looking up into
  the sky?
This Jesus, who has been taken away
  from you up to heaven,
will come in the same way as you
  have seen him go."
  —*From Acts 1, N.E.B.*

———

RESURRECTION AND ASCEN-
SION: See also No. 785.

738

OUR UNDERSTANDING PRIEST

We see Jesus,
who was made a little lower than
   the angels,
now crowned with glory and honor
because he suffered death,
so that by the grace of God
he might taste death for everyone.

*For this reason he had to be made
   like his brothers in every way,
in order that he might become
   a merciful and faithful high
   priest in service to God,
and that he might make atonement
   for the sins of the people.*

Because he himself suffered
   when he was tempted,
he is able to help those
   who are being tempted.

*Therefore, since we have a great
   high priest
who has gone through the heavens,
   Jesus the Son of God,
let us hold firmly to the faith
   we profess. . . .
Let us then approach the throne of
   grace with confidence,
so that we may receive mercy and
   find grace to help us in our
   time of need.*

We have this hope as an anchor for
   the soul, firm and secure.
      —From Hebrews 2, 4, and 6, N.I.V.

739

CHRIST'S PRIESTHOOD

Now the point in what we are saying
   is this:
we have such a high priest,
one who is seated at the right hand
of the throne of the Majesty
   in heaven,

a minister in the sanctuary
and the true tent
which is set up not by man
   but by the Lord.

*For every high priest is appointed
to offer gifts and sacrifices;
hence it is necessary for this
   priest also
to have something to offer.*

Now if he were on earth,
he would not be a priest at all,
since there are priests
who offer gifts according to the law.

*But when Christ appeared as a
   high priest
of the good things that have come,
then through the greater and more
   perfect tent
(not made with hands, that is, not
   of this creation)
he entered once for all into the
   Holy Place,
taking not the blood of goats and
   calves but his own blood,
thus securing an eternal
   redemption.*

For Christ has entered,
not into a sanctuary made with
   hands, a copy of the true one,
but into heaven itself,
now to appear in the presence of
   God on our behalf.

*Nor was it to offer himself
   repeatedly,
as the high priest enters the
   Holy Place
yearly with blood not his own;
for then he would have had to suffer
repeatedly since the foundation of
   the world.*

But as it is, he has appeared
   once for all at the end of the age
to put away sin by the sacrifice
   of himself.

*And just as it is appointed for men
   to die once,
and after that comes judgment,
   so Christ,
having been offered once to bear the
   sins of many,
will appear a second time,
not to deal with sin but to save those
who are eagerly waiting for him.*
   —*From Hebrews 8 and 9, R.S.V.*

———

PRIESTHOOD: *See also No. 778.*

740
CHRIST THE DELIVERER

This is what the Lord says—
   he who created you, O Jacob,
   he who formed you, O Israel:
"Fear not, for I have redeemed you;
I have called you by name; you
   are mine.

*"When you pass through the
   waters,
I will be with you;
and when you pass through
   the rivers,
they will not sweep over you.
When you walk through the fire,
   you will not be burned; the
   flames will not set you ablaze.*

"For I am the Lord, your God,
   the Holy One of Israel,
   your Savior. . . .
Since you are precious and honored
   in my sight, and because
   I love you,
I will give men in exchange for you,
and people in exchange
   for your life.

*"Do not be afraid, for I am with you;
I will bring your children from
   the east and gather you from
   the west.
I will say to the north, 'Give
   them up!'*

and to the south, 'Do not hold
   them back.'

"Bring my sons from afar
and my daughters from the ends of
   the earth—
everyone who is called by my name,
   whom I created for my glory,
   whom I formed and made."
   —*From Isaiah 43, N.I.V.*

741
THE SHEPHERD CARES
FOR HIS PEOPLE

These are the words of the
   Lord God:
Now I myself will ask after my sheep
   and go in search of them.

*As a shepherd goes in search of
   his sheep
when his flock is dispersed all
   around him,
so I will go in search of my sheep
   and rescue them,
no matter where they were scattered
   in dark and cloudy days.*

I will bring them out from
   every nation,
gather them in from other lands,
and lead them home to their
   own soil.

*I will graze them on the mountains
   of Israel, by her streams and in
   all her green fields.
I will feed them on good
   grazing-ground,
and their pasture shall be the high
   mountains of Israel.*

There they will rest, there in
   good pasture,
and find rich grazing on the moun-
   tains of Israel.

I myself will tend my flock,
I myself pen them in their fold, says
   the Lord God.

I will search for the lost,
recover the straggler, bandage
   the hurt,
strengthen the sick,
leave the healthy and strong to play,
and give them their proper food.
   —*From Ezekiel 34, N.E.B.*

742
THE LORD WORKS JUSTICE

The Lord works vindication
   and justice
for all who are oppressed.

He made known his ways to Moses,
his acts to the people of Israel.

As far as the east is from the west,
so far does he remove our transgressions from us.

As a father pities his children,
so the Lord pities those who
   fear him.
For he knows our frame;
he remembers that we are dust.

As for man, his days are like grass;
he flourishes like a flower
   of the field;
for the wind passes over it,
   and it is gone,
and its place knows it no more.

But the steadfast love of the Lord
   is from everlasting to
   everlasting
upon those who fear him,
and his righteousness
   to children's children,
to those who keep his covenant
and remember to do his
   commandments.

The Lord has established his throne
   in the heavens,
and his kingdom rules over all.

Bless the Lord, O you his angels,
you mighty ones who do his word,
hearkening to the voice of his word!

Bless the Lord, all his hosts,
his ministers that do his will!

Bless the Lord, all his works,
in all places of his dominion.
Bless the Lord, O my soul!
   —*From Psalm 103, R.S.V.*

743
SEEKING THE LOST

"What man among you,
if he has a hundred sheep
   and has lost one of them,
does not leave the ninety-nine
   in the open pasture,
and go after the one which is lost,
until he finds it?"

"And when he comes home,
he calls together his friends
   and his neighbors, saying
   to them,
'Rejoice with me,
for I have found my sheep which
   was lost!'

"I tell you that in the same way,
there will be more joy in heaven
over one sinner who repents,
than over ninety-nine
   righteous persons
who need no repentance.

"Or what woman,
if she has ten silver coins
   and loses one coin,
does not light a lamp and sweep
   the house
and search carefully until
   she finds it?

LOVE OF CHRIST FOR US

"And when she has found it,
she calls together her friends
    and neighbors, saying,
'Rejoice with me,
for I have found the coin which I had
    lost!'

"In the same way, I tell you,
there is joy in the presence
*   of the angels of God*
over one sinner who repents."
          —From Luke 15, N.A.S.B.

744
THE GOOD SHEPHERD

"I tell you most solemnly,
anyone who does not enter the
    sheepfold through the gate,
but gets in some other way
is a thief and a brigand.

"The one who enters through
*   the gate*
is the shepherd of the flock;
the gatekeeper lets him in,
the sheep hear his voice,
one by one he calls his own sheep
and leads them out.

"When he has brought out his flock,
he goes ahead of them,
and the sheep follow because they
    know his voice.

"They never follow a stranger
*   but run away from him:*
they do not recognise the voice
*   of strangers."*

"I tell you most solemnly,
I am the gate of the sheepfold.
All others who have come
    are thieves and brigands;
but the sheep took no notice of them.

"I am the gate.
Anyone who enters through me
*   will be safe:*

he will go freely in and out
and be sure of finding pasture.

"The thief comes only to steal and
    kill and destroy.
I have come so that they may
    have life
and have it to the full.

"I am the good shepherd:
the good shepherd is one who lays
*   down his life for his sheep.*

"The hired man, since he is not
    the shepherd
and the sheep do not belong to him,
abandons the sheep and runs away
as soon as he sees a wolf coming,
and then the wolf attacks and
    scatters the sheep;
this is because he is only a hired man
and has no concern for the sheep.

"I am the good shepherd;
I know my own and my own
*   know me,*
just as the Father knows me
*   and I know the Father;*
and I lay down my life for my sheep.

"And there are other sheep I have
that are not of this fold,
and these I have to lead as well.
They too will listen to my voice,
and there will be only one flock,
and one shepherd."
          —From John 10, Jerusalem.

745
THE CHRISTIAN'S
ASSURANCE

This is the assurance we have
    in approaching God:
that if we ask anything according
    to his will, he hears us.

For he has rescued us
*   from the dominion of darkness*

and brought us into the kingdom
  of the Son he loves,
in whom we have redemption,
  the forgiveness of sins.

Because you are sons,
God sent the Spirit of his Son into
  our hearts,
the Spirit who calls out,
  "*Abba*, Father."
So you are no longer a slave,
but a son; and since you are a son,
God has made you also an heir.

*What, then, shall we say in response
  to this?*
*If God is for us, who can be
  against us?*

Christ Jesus, who died—
more than that, who was raised
  to life—
is at the right hand of God
and is also interceding for us.

** Who shall separate us from the
  love of Christ?*
*Shall trouble or hardship or
  persecution*
or famine or nakedness
or danger or sword?

As it is written:
"For your sake we face death
  all day long;
we are considered as sheep
  to be slaughtered."
No, in all these things
we are more than conquerors
  through him who loved us.

*For I am convinced that neither
  death nor life,*
neither angels nor demons,
neither the present nor the future,
nor any powers,
neither height nor depth,
nor anything else in all creation,
will be able to separate us

from the love of God
that is in Christ Jesus our Lord.*
—*From 1 John 5, Colossians 1, Galatians 4,
  and Romans 8, N.I.V.*

———

* This section, Paul's Song of Assurance,
  is one of the New Testament
  canticles.

———

LOVE OF CHRIST FOR US: *See also
  Nos. 713, 772, 782, 800, 807.*

746
SIGNS OF CHRIST'S COMING

When [Jesus] was sitting on the
  Mount of Olives
the disciples came and asked
  him privately,
"Tell us, when is this going
  to happen,
and what will be the sign
  of your coming
and of the end of the world?"

*And Jesus answered them, "Take
  care that no one*
*deceives you; because many will
  come using my name*
and saying, 'I am the Christ,'
and they will deceive many.

"You will hear of wars and rumours
  of wars;
do not be alarmed, for this is
  something
that must happen, but the end
  will not be yet.
For nation will fight against nation,
and kingdom against kingdom.
There will be famines and
  earthquakes here and there. . . .
Then they will hand you over to be
  tortured and put to death;
and you will be hated by all
  the nations
on account of my name."

"This Good News of the kingdom
will be proclaimed to
the whole world as a witness to all
the nations.
And then the end will come."

"There will be great distress such as,
    until now,
since the world began, there never
    has been,
nor ever will be again. . . .
False Christs and false prophets
    will arise
and produce great signs
    and portents,
enough to deceive even the chosen,
if that were possible.
There, I have forewarned you."

"Immediately after the distress of
those days
the sun will be darkened,
the moon will lose its brightness,
the stars will fall from the sky
and the powers of heaven
will be shaken.

"And then the sign of the Son of Man
    will appear in heaven;
then too all the peoples of the earth
    will beat their breasts;
and they will see the Son of Man
    coming
on the clouds of heaven with power
    and great glory.

"And he will send his angels with a
loud trumpet
to gather his chosen from the
four winds,
from one end of heaven
to the other."
                —*From Matthew 24, Jerusalem.*

747
CHRIST'S SECOND COMING

Let not your heart be troubled:
ye believe in God, believe also in me.

In my Father's house are many
mansions:
if it were not so, I would have
told you.

I go to prepare a place for you.
And if I go and prepare a place
    for you,
I will come again,
and receive you unto myself;
that where I am, there ye may
    be also.

While they looked stedfastly
toward heaven as he went up,
behold,
two men stood by them in
white apparel;
which also said,

Ye men of Galilee,
Why stand ye gazing up into heaven?
this same Jesus, which is taken up
    from you into heaven,
shall so come in like manner
as ye have seen him go into heaven.

Watch therefore:
for ye know not what hour
your Lord doth come.

But know this, that if the goodman
of the house had known
in what watch the thief would come,
he would have watched,
and would not have suffered
    his house
to be broken up.

Therefore be ye also ready:
for in such an hour as ye think not
the Son of man cometh.

Who then is a faithful and
  wise servant,
whom his Lord hath made ruler over
  his household,
to give them meat in due season?

**Blessed is that servant,
whom his Lord when he cometh
shall find so doing.**

—*From John 14, Acts 1,
  and Matthew 24, K.J.V.*

SECOND ADVENT: *See also Nos. 729,
  737, 751, 781, 816.*

748
REWARD OF THE SAINTS

The desert and the parched land
  will be glad;
the wilderness will rejoice
  and blossom.
Like the crocus, it will burst
  into bloom;
it will rejoice greatly and
  shout for joy.

**The glory of Lebanon will be
  given to it,
the splendor of Carmel and Sharon;
they will see the glory of the Lord,
  the splendor of our God.**

Strengthen the feeble hands,
steady the knees that give way;
say to those with fearful hearts,
"Be strong, do not fear;
your God will come,
he will come with vengeance;
with divine retribution
he will come to save you."

**Then will the eyes of the blind
  be opened
and the ears of the deaf unstopped.
Then will the lame leap like a deer,
and the tongue of the dumb
  shout for joy.**

Water will gush forth in the
  wilderness
and streams in the desert.
The burning sand will become
  a pool,
the thirsty ground bubbling springs.
In the haunts where jackals once lay,
grass and reeds and papyrus
  will grow.

**And a highway will be there;
it will be called the Way of
  Holiness.
The unclean will not journey on it;
it will be for those who walk
  in that Way;
wicked fools will not go about on it.**

No lion will be there,
nor will any ferocious beast
  get up on it;
they will not be found there.
But only the redeemed will
  walk there,
and the ransomed of the Lord
  will return.

**They will enter Zion with singing;
everlasting joy will crown
  their heads.
Gladness and joy will
  overtake them,
and sorrow and sighing will
  flee away.**

—*From Isaiah 35, N.I.V.*

749
A SONG OF TRIUMPH

I looked and there before me was a
  great multitude that no one
  could count,
from every nation, tribe, people
  and language,
standing before the throne and in
  front of the Lamb.
They were wearing white robes
and were holding palm branches in
  their hands.

And they cried out in a loud voice:
"Salvation belongs to our God,
who sits on the throne, and to
the Lamb."

All the angels were standing around
the throne
and around the elders and the four
living creatures.
They fell down on their faces before
the throne
and worshiped God, saying:

"Amen! Praise and glory and
wisdom and thanks and honor
and power and strength
be to our God for ever and ever.
Amen!"

Then one of the elders asked me,
"These in white robes—
who are they,
and where did they come from?"
I answered, "Sir, you know."
And he said, "These are they who
have come out of the great
tribulation;
they have washed their robes and
made them white
in the blood of the Lamb. Therefore,

"they are before the throne of God
and serve him day and night in
his temple;
and he who sits on the throne
will spread his tent over them.

"Never again will they hunger;
never again will they thirst.
The sun will not beat upon them,
nor any scorching heat.

"For the Lamb at the center of
the throne
will be their shepherd;
he will lead them to springs of
living water.
And God will wipe away every tear
from their eyes."
—From *Revelation 7, N.I.V.*

750
REIGNING FOREVER
WITH GOD

"I am the Alpha and the Omega,
the Beginning and the End.
I will give of the fountain
of the water of life freely
to him who thirsts.

"He who overcomes shall inherit
all things,
and I will be his God and he shall be
My son."

And he showed me
a pure river of water of life,
clear as crystal,
proceeding from the throne of God
and of the Lamb.

In the middle of its street,
and on either side of the river,
was the tree of life,
which bore twelve fruits,
each tree yielding its fruit
every month.
And the leaves of the tree were for
the healing of the nations.

And there shall be no more curse,
but the throne of God and of the
Lamb shall be in it,
and His servants shall serve Him.
They shall see His face,
and His name shall be on their
foreheads.

And there shall be no night there:
They need no lamp nor light
of the sun,
for the Lord God gives them light.
And they shall reign forever
*and ever.**
—From *Revelation 21 and 22, N.K.J.V.*

* May be effectively combined with
No. 783.

KINGDOM AND REIGN: See also No.
783.

751
O LORD, THOU ART MY GOD

O Lord, thou art my God;
I will exalt thee, I will praise
    thy name;
for thou hast done
    wonderful things;
thy counsels of old
    are faithfulness and truth.

Thou hast been a strength
    to the poor,
a strength to the needy
    in his distress,
a refuge from the storm,
a shadow from the heat,
when the blast of the terrible ones is
    as a storm against the wall.

He will swallow up death in victory;
and the Lord God will wipe away
    tears from off all faces;
and the rebuke of his people
shall he take away from all the earth:
for the Lord hath spoken it.

And it shall be said in that day,
Lo, this is our God;
we have waited for him,
and he will save us:
this is the Lord;
we have waited for him,
we will be glad and rejoice
    in his salvation.
        —*From Isaiah 25, K.J.V.*

GLORY AND PRAISE: See also Nos.
735, 736, 841, 842, 843.

752
THE HOLY SPIRIT

"I will pray the Father,
and he will give you another
    Counselor,
to be with you for ever,

"even the Spirit of truth,
whom the world cannot receive,
because it neither sees him nor
    knows him;
you know him, for he dwells
    with you,
and will be in you.

"I will not leave you desolate;
I will come to you."

"Nevertheless I tell you the truth:
it is to your advantage that
    I go away,
for if I do not go away,
the Counselor will not come to you;
but if I go, I will send him to you.

"And when he comes, he will
    convince
the world concerning sin and
    righteousness and judgment:

"concerning sin, because they do
    not believe in me;
concerning righteousness,
because I go to the Father,
    and you will see me no more;
concerning judgment,
    because the ruler of this world
    is judged."

"When the Spirit of truth comes,
he will guide you into all the truth;
for he will not speak on his
    own authority,
but whatever he hears he will speak,
and he will declare to you
the things that are to come.

"He will glorify me,
for he will take what is mine
and declare it to you."

"But when the Counselor comes,
whom I shall send to you from
    the Father, . . .
he will bear witness to me."

"But the Counselor, the Holy Spirit,

whom the Father will send
    in my name,
he will teach you all things,
and bring to your remembrance
all that I have said to you."
    —*From John 14, 15, and 16, R.S.V.*

———

HOLY SPIRIT: See also Nos. 737, 776,
    839.

753
GOD'S WORD

How can a youth remain pure?
By behaving as your word
    prescribes.

I have sought you with all my heart,
do not let me stray from your
    commandments.

I have treasured your promises in
    my heart,
since I have no wish to sin
    against you.

How blessed are you, Yahweh!
Teach me your statutes!

With my lips I have repeated them,
all these rulings from your
    own mouth.

In the way of your decrees lies my
    joy,
a joy beyond all wealth.

I mean to meditate on your precepts
and to concentrate on your paths.

I find my delight in your statutes,
I do not forget your word.

Open my eyes: I shall concentrate
on the marvels of your Law.

Now your word is a lamp to my feet,
a light to my path.

As your word unfolds, it gives light,
and the simple understand.

Faithfulness is the essence of
    your word,
your righteous rulings hold good
    for ever.

Universal peace for those who love
    your Law,
no stumbling-blocks for them!
    —*From Psalm 119, Jerusalem.*

754
THE HOLY SCRIPTURES

The secret things belong to the
    Lord our God,
but those things which are revealed
belong to us and to our
    children forever,
that we may do all the words
    of this law.

We also have the prophetic word
made more sure,
which you do well to heed
as a light that shines in a dark place,
until the day dawns
and the morning star rises in
    your hearts;

knowing this first,
that no prophecy of Scripture
is of any private interpretation,
for prophecy never came
    by the will of man,
but holy men of God spoke
as they were moved by the
    Holy Spirit.

From childhood you have known
    the Holy Scriptures,
which are able to make you wise
    for salvation through faith
    which is in Christ Jesus.

All Scripture is given by inspiration
    of God,

and is profitable for doctrine,
for reproof, for correction,
for instruction in righteousness,
that the man of God may
    be complete,
thoroughly equipped for every
    good work.

"You search the Scriptures,
for in them you think you have
    eternal life;
and these are they which testify of
    Me."

The word of God is living
    and powerful,
and sharper than any
    two-edged sword,
piercing even to the division
    of soul and spirit,
    and of joints and marrow,
and is a discerner of the thoughts
    and intents of the heart.

Your words were found, and
    I ate them,
And Your word was to me
the joy and rejoicing of my heart.
    —From Deuteronomy 29, 2 Peter 1,
    2 Timothy 3, John 5, Hebrews 4,
    and Jeremiah 15, N.K.J.V.

755
THE CALL

Oh, come to the water all you who
    are thirsty;
though you have no money, come!
Buy corn without money, and eat,
and, at no cost, wine and milk.
Why spend money on what
    is not bread,
your wages on what fails to satisfy?

Listen, listen to me,
and you will have good things to eat
and rich food to enjoy.
Pay attention, come to me;
listen, and your soul will live.

With you I will make an everlasting
    covenant
out of the favours promised
    to David.
See, I have made of you a witness to
    the peoples,
a leader and a master of the nations.

See, you will summon a nation you
    never knew,
those unknown will come hurrying
    to you,
for the sake of Yahweh your God,
of the Holy One of Israel
    who will glorify you.

Seek Yahweh while he is still
    to be found,
call to him while he is still near.
Let the wicked man abandon
    his way,
the evil man his thoughts.

Let him turn back to Yahweh
    who will take pity on him,
to our God who is rich in forgiving;
for my thoughts are not your
    thoughts,
my ways not your ways—
    it is Yahweh who speaks.

Yes, the heavens are as high
    above earth
as my ways are above your ways,
my thoughts above your thoughts.
    —From Isaiah 55, Jerusalem.

———

INVITATION: See also No. 744.

756
HAVE MERCY ON ME,
O GOD

Have mercy on me, O God,
according to your unfailing love;
according to your great compassion
    blot out my transgressions.
Wash away all my iniquity
    and cleanse me from my sin.

INVITATION, REPENTANCE

For I know my transgressions,
and my sin is always before me.
Against you, you only,
     have I sinned
and done what is evil in your sight,
so that you are proved right when
     you speak
and justified when you judge.

Surely I have been a sinner
     from birth,
 sinful from the time my mother
     conceived me.
Surely you desire truth in the
     inner parts;
you teach me wisdom in the
     inmost place.

Cleanse me with hyssop, and I will
     be clean;
wash me, and I will be whiter
     than snow.

Let me hear joy and gladness;
let the bones you have
     crushed rejoice.
Hide your face from my sins
and blot out all my iniquity.

Create in me a pure heart, O God,
and renew a steadfast spirit
     within me.
Do not cast me from your presence
or take your Holy Spirit from me.
Restore to me the joy of
     your salvation
and grant me a willing spirit,
     to sustain me.

Then I will teach transgressors
     your ways,
and sinners will turn back to you.
Save me from bloodguilt, O God,
the God who saves me;
and my tongue will sing of your
     righteousness.

O Lord, open my lips,
and my mouth will declare
     your praise.

You do not delight in sacrifice,
     or I would bring it;
you do not take pleasure in burnt
     offerings.

The sacrifices of God are a
     broken spirit;
a broken and contrite heart,
O God, you will not despise.
                    —*From Psalm 51, N.I.V.*

757
RETURNING TO GOD

[Jesus] said:
"There was once a man who had
     two sons;
and the younger said to his father,
'Father, give me my share of the
     property.'
So he divided his estate
     between them.

"A few days later the younger son
turned the whole of his share
     into cash
and left home for a distant country,
where he squandered it in
     reckless living.

"He had spent it all,
when a severe famine fell upon
     that country
and he began to feel the pinch.
So he went and attached himself
     to one of the local landowners,
who sent him on to his farm to mind
     the pigs.

"He would have been glad to
     fill his belly
with the pods that the pigs
     were eating;
and no one gave him anything.

"Then he came to his senses
     and said,
'How many of my father's
     paid servants

have more food than they can eat, and here am I, starving to death!

"'I will set off and go to my father, and say to him,
"Father, I have sinned, against God and against you;
I am no longer fit to be called your son;
treat me as one of your paid servants."'
So he set out for his father's house.

"But while he was still a long way off his father saw him, and his heart went out to him.
He ran to meet him,
flung his arms round him,
and kissed him.

"The son said, 'Father, I have sinned, against God and against you;
I am no longer fit to be called your son.'

"But the father said to his servants, 'Quick! fetch a robe, my best one, and put it on him;
put a ring on his finger and shoes on his feet.
Bring the fatted calf and kill it,
and let us have a feast to celebrate the day.
For this son of mine was dead and has come back to life;
he was lost and is found.'

"And the festivities began."
—*From Luke 15, N.E.B.*

———

REPENTANCE: See also Nos. 743, 755.

758
BLESSED IS HE WHOSE TRANSGRESSIONS ARE FORGIVEN

Blessed is he whose transgressions are forgiven, whose sins are covered.
Blessed is the man whose sin the Lord does not count against him and in whose spirit is no deceit.

When I kept silent, my bones wasted away through my groaning all day long.
For day and night your hand was heavy upon me;
my strength was sapped as in the heat of summer.

Then I acknowledged my sin to you and did not cover up my iniquity.
I said, "I will confess my transgressions to the Lord"—
and you forgave the guilt of my sin.

Therefore let everyone who is godly pray to you while you may be found;
surely when the mighty waters rise, they will not reach him.
You are my hiding place; you will protect me from trouble and surround me with songs of deliverance.

I will instruct you and teach you in the way you should go; I will counsel you and watch over you.
—*From Psalm 32, N.I.V.*

———

FORGIVENESS: See also Nos. 711, 742, 761, 762, 798, 814.

———

CONSECRATION: See also No. 786.

759
BAPTISM

Jesus answered, "Truly, truly, I say
to you,
unless one is born of water
and the Spirit,
he cannot enter the kingdom
of God."

By one spirit we were all baptized
into one body—
Jews or Greeks, slaves or free—
and all were made to drink
of one Spirit.

Do you not know that all of us
who have been baptized into
Christ Jesus
were baptized into his death?

We were buried therefore with him
by baptism into death,
so that as Christ was raised from the
dead by the glory of the Father,
we too might walk in newness
of life.

For if we have been united with him
in a death like his,
we shall certainly be united with him
in a resurrection like his.

We know that our old self was
crucified with him
so that the sinful body might
be destroyed,
and we might no longer be enslaved
to sin.
For he who has died is freed
from sin.

"Go therefore and make disciples of
all nations,
baptizing them in the name of the
Father and of the Son and of the
Holy Spirit,
teaching them to observe all
that I have commanded you;

"and lo, I am with you always,
to the close of the age."
—From John 3, 1 Corinthians 12, Romans 6,
and Matthew 28, R.S.V.

760
TIMES OF BEGINNING

In the beginning God created the
heavens and the earth. . . .
God saw all that he had made,
and it was very good.

In the beginning was the Word,
and the Word was with God,
and the Word was God.

In him was life,
and that life was the light of men.
The Word became flesh
and lived for a while among us.

We have seen his glory,
the glory of the one and only Son,
who came from the Father,
full of grace and truth.

All have sinned and fall short of the
glory of God,
and are justified freely by his grace
through the redemption
that came by Christ Jesus.

Therefore, if anyone is in Christ,
he is a new creation;
the old has gone, the new has come!

"Behold, I will create
new heavens and a new earth.
Be glad and rejoice forever
in what I will create."
—From Genesis 1, John 1, Romans 3,
2 Corinthians 5, and Isaiah 65, N.I.V.

761
RIGHTEOUSNESS BY FAITH

Righteousness from God comes
through faith
in Jesus Christ to all who believe.
There is no difference,
for all have sinned and fall short of
the glory of God,
and are justified freely by his grace
through the redemption that came
by Christ Jesus.

*God presented him as a sacrifice of
atonement,*
through faith in his blood.
*He did this to demonstrate
his justice,*
*because in his forbearance
he had left the sins committed
beforehand unpunished—*

he did it to demonstrate his justice at
the present time,
so as to be just
and the one who justifies the man
who has faith in Jesus.

*Therefore, there is now no
condemnation*
for those who are in Christ Jesus,
because through Christ Jesus
*the law of the Spirit of life set me
free from the law of
sin and death.*

What, then, shall we say in response
to this?
If God is for us,
who can be against us?

He who did not spare his own Son,
but gave him up for us all—
*how will he not also, along
with him,*
graciously give us all things?

Who will bring any charge
against those

whom God has chosen?
It is God who justifies.

It is because of him
that you are in Christ Jesus,
*who has become for us wisdom
from God—*
*that is, our righteousness,
holiness and redemption.*

*—From Romans 3, 8,
and 1 Corinthians 1, N.I.V.*

762
JUSTIFICATION

[Jesus] was delivered over to death
for our sins
and was raised to life for our
justification.

*Therefore, since we have been
justified through faith,*
*we have peace with God through
our Lord Jesus Christ,*
*through whom we have gained
access by faith*
*into this grace in which we
now stand.*

And we rejoice in the hope of the
glory of God.
Not only so,
but we also rejoice in our sufferings,
because we know that suffering
produces perseverance;
perseverance, character; and
character, hope.

And hope does not disappoint us,
*because God has poured
out his love*
*into our hearts by the Holy Spirit,
whom he has given us.*

You see, at just the right time,
when we were still powerless,
Christ died for the ungodly.
Very rarely will anyone die for a
righteous man,

though for a good man someone
might possibly dare to die.

*But God demonstrates his own love
for us in this:
While we were still sinners,
Christ died for us.
Since we have now been justified by
his blood,
how much more shall we be saved
from God's wrath through him!*

For if, when we were God's enemies,
we were reconciled to him through
the death of his Son,
how much more, having been
reconciled,
shall we be saved through his life!

*Not only is this so,
but we also rejoice in God through
our Lord Jesus Christ,
through whom we have now
received reconciliation.*
—*From Romans 4 and 5, N.I.V.*

763
SANCTIFICATION

Do you not know
that the wicked will not inherit
the kingdom of God?
Do not be deceived:

*Neither the sexually immoral nor
idolaters
nor adulterers nor male prostitutes
nor homosexual offenders
nor thieves
nor the greedy nor drunkards
nor slanderers nor swindlers
will inherit the kingdom of God.*

And that is what some of you were.
But you were washed, you
were sanctified,
You were justified in the name
of the Lord Jesus Christ
and by the Spirit of our God.

*Both the one who makes men holy
and those who are made holy
are of the same family.
So Jesus is not ashamed
to call them brothers.*

Remind the people to be subject
to rulers and authorities,
to be obedient, to be ready to do
whatever is good,
to slander no one,
to be peaceable and considerate,
and to show true humility toward
all men.

*At one time we too were foolish,
disobedient, deceived and enslaved
by all kinds of passions
and pleasures.
We lived in malice and envy,
being hated and hating one another.*

But when the kindness and love
of God our Savior appeared,
he saved us,
not because of righteous things we
had done,
but because of his mercy.

*He saved us through the washing of
rebirth and renewal by
the Holy Spirit,
whom he poured out on us
generously through Jesus
Christ our Savior, so that,
having been justified by his grace,
we might become heirs
having the hope of eternal life.*
—*From 1 Corinthians 6, Hebrews 2,
and Titus 3, N.I.V.*

764
RECONCILIATION

We are ruled by the love of Christ,
now that we recognize that one man
died for everyone,
which means that they all share in his
death.

He died for all, so that those who
live should no longer live for
themselves,
but only for him who died
and was raised to life for their sake.

No longer, then, do we judge anyone
by human standards.
Even if at one time we judged Christ
according to human standards,
we no longer do so.

When anyone is joined to Christ,
he is a new being;
the old is gone,
the new has come.

All this is done by God,
who through Christ changed us
from enemies into his friends
and gave us the task of making
others his friends also.

Our message is that God was
making all mankind his
friends through Christ.
God did not keep an account of
their sins,
and he has given us the message
which tells how he makes them
his friends.

Here we are, then, speaking for
Christ,
as though God himself were making
his appeal through us.
We plead on Christ's behalf:
let God change you from enemies
into his friends!

Christ was without sin,
but for our sake God made him
share our sin in order that in
union with him
we might share the righteousness of
God.
—*From 2 Corinthians 5, T.E.V.*

765
CONVERSION

Time was when you were dead in
your sins and wickedness,
when you followed the evil ways
of this present age,
when you obeyed the commander of
the spiritual powers of the air,
the spirit now at work
among God's rebel subjects.

We too were once of their number:
we all lived our lives in sensuality,
and obeyed the promptings of our
own instincts and notions.

In our natural condition we,
like the rest,
lay under the dreadful judgement
of God.
But God, rich in mercy,
for the great love he bore us,
brought us to life with Christ
even when we were dead in our sins;
it is by his grace you are saved.

And in union with Christ Jesus
he raised us up
and enthroned us with him
in the heavenly realms,
so that he might display in the ages
to come
how immense are the resources of
his grace,
and how great his kindness to us
in Christ Jesus.

For it is by his grace you are saved,
through trusting him;
it is not your own doing.
It is God's gift,
not a reward for work done.

There is nothing for anyone
to boast of.
For we are God's handiwork,
created in Christ Jesus
to devote ourselves to the
good deeds
for which God has designed us.
—*From Ephesians 2, N.E.B.*

SALVATION AND REDEMPTION

766
THE GREAT CONTROVERSY

Now war arose in heaven,
Michael and his angels fighting
  against the dragon;
and the dragon and his
  angels fought,
but they were defeated and there
  was no longer any place for
  them in heaven.

*And the great dragon was
  thrown down,
that ancient serpent, who is called
  the Devil and Satan,
the deceiver of the whole world—
he was thrown down to the earth,
and his angels were thrown down
  with him.*

And I heard a loud voice in heaven,
  saying,
"Now the salvation and the power
  and the kingdom
of our God and the authority of his
  Christ have come,
for the accuser of our brethren has
  been thrown down,
who accuses them day and night
  before our God.

*"And they have conquered him
  by the blood
of the Lamb and by the word of their
  testimony,
for they loved not their lives even
  unto death.*

"Rejoice then, O heaven and you
that dwell therein!
But woe to you, O earth and sea,
for the devil has come down to you in
  great wrath,
because he knows that his
  time is short!"

*And there were loud voices in
  heaven, saying,*

*"The kingdom of the world
  has become
the kingdom of our Lord and of
  his Christ,
and he shall reign for ever
  and ever."*
  —*From Revelation 12 and 11, R.S.V.*

SALVATION AND REDEMPTION:
See also Nos. 696, 715, 716, 739, 745,
749, 778, 782, 789, 806, 807,
808, 843, 859.

767
THE BODY OF CHRIST

Just as each of us has one body with
  many members,
and these members do not all
  have the same function,
So in Christ we who are many form
  one body,
and each member belongs to
  all the others.

*We were all baptized by one Spirit
  into one body—
whether Jews or Greeks, slave or
  free—
and we were all given the one Spirit
  to drink.*

Now the body is not made up of one
  part but of many. . . .
In fact God has arranged the parts in
  the body,
every one of them, just as he wanted
  them to be.
If they were all one part,
where would the body be?
As it is, there are many parts,
  but one body.

*The eye cannot say to the hand, "I
  don't need you!"
And the head cannot say to the feet,
  "I don't need you!"
On the contrary, those parts of the
  body that seem to be weaker are
  indispensable.*

There should be no division
in the body,
but . . . its parts should have equal
concern for each other.
If one part suffers,
every part suffers with it;
if one part is honored,
every part rejoices with it.

**Now you are the body of Christ,
and each one of you is a part of it.**
*—From Romans 12
and 1 Corinthians 12, N.I.V.*

*COMMUNITY IN CHRIST: See also
No. 777.*

zealous for good works.

"Go therefore and make disciples of
all the nations,
baptizing them in the name
of the Father and of the Son and of
the Holy Spirit,
teaching them to observe all things
that I have commanded you;

**"and lo, I am with you always,
even to the end of the age." Amen.**
*—From 1 Peter 2, Titus 2,
and Matthew 28, N.K.J.V.*

*MISSION OF THE CHURCH: See also
Nos. 729, 737, 759, 776, 800, 806.*

768
MISSION OF THE CHURCH

You are a chosen generation, a royal
priesthood,
a holy nation, His own
special people,
that you may proclaim the praises
of Him
who called you out of darkness
into His marvelous light.

**For the grace of God that brings
salvation
has appeared to all men, teaching
us that,
denying ungodliness and
worldly lusts,
we should live soberly, righteously,
and godly in the present age,**

looking for the blessed hope
and glorious
appearing of our great God and
Savior Jesus Christ,

**who gave Himself for us,
that He might redeem us from every
lawless deed
and purify for Himself His own
special people,**

769
THE SABBATH—1

Thus the heavens and the earth,
and all the host of them,
were finished.

**And on the seventh day
God ended His work
which He had done,
and He rested on the seventh day
from all His work which
He had done.**

Then God blessed the seventh day
and sanctified it,
because in it He rested from
all His work
which God had created and made.

**By [Christ] all things were created
that are in heaven and that are on
earth, visible and invisible,
whether thrones or dominions
or principalities or powers.
All things were created through
Him and for Him.**

You alone are the Lord;
You have made heaven,
The heaven of heavens,
with all their host,

The earth and all things on it,
The seas and all that is in them,
And You preserve them all.
The host of heaven worships You. . . .
You made known to them
Your holy Sabbath.

**"Remember the Sabbath day, to
keep it holy.
Six days you shall labor
and do all your work,
but the seventh day is the Sabbath
of the Lord your God.**

"In it you shall do no work:
you, nor your son, nor your daughter,
nor your manservant, nor your
maidservant,
nor your cattle, nor your stranger
who is within your gates.

**"For in six days the Lord made the
heavens and the earth, the sea,
and all that is in them,
and rested the seventh day.
Therefore the Lord blessed the
Sabbath day and hallowed it."**

[Jesus] said to them,
"The Sabbath was made for man,
and not man for the Sabbath.
Therefore the Son of Man is also
Lord of the Sabbath."
—*From Genesis 2, Colossians 1,
Nehemiah 9, Exodus 20,
and Mark 2, N.K.J.V.*

770
THE SABBATH—2

"Keep my Sabbaths holy,
that they may be a sign between us.
Then you will know
that I am the Lord your God."

**" '[The Sabbath] will be a sign
between me and the Israelites
forever,**

**for in six days the Lord made the
heavens and the earth,
and on the seventh day
he abstained from work
and rested.' "**

"As the new heavens and the
new earth
that I make will endure before me,"
declares the Lord,
"so will your name and descendants
endure.

**"From one New Moon to another
and from one Sabbath to another,
all mankind will come and bow
down before me," says
the Lord.**

"If you keep your feet
from breaking the Sabbath
and from doing as you please on my
holy day,
if you call the Sabbath a delight
and the Lord's holy day honorable,
and if you honor it by not going your
own way
and not doing as you please or
speaking idle words,

**"then you will find your joy
in the Lord,
and I will cause you to ride on the
heights of the land
and to feast on the inheritance of
your father Jacob."
The mouth of the Lord has spoken.**

[Jesus] went to Nazareth,
where he had been brought up,
and on the Sabbath day
he went into the synagogue,
as was his custom.

He said to them,*
**"If any of you has a sheep
and it falls into a pit on the Sabbath,
will you not take hold of it and
lift it out?**

*How much more valuable is a man
than a sheep!
Therefore it is lawful to do good on
the Sabbath!"*

—From Ezekiel 20, Exodus 31,
Isaiah 66, 58, Luke 4,
and Matthew 12, N.I.V.

_____

*This is a different occasion from that
described in the previous verse.

771
LIVING BREAD

Jesus said to them, "I am the bread
of life.
Whoever comes to me shall
never be hungry,
and whoever believes in me shall
never be thirsty.
But you, as I said, do not believe
although you have seen.

*"All that the Father gives me will
come to me,
and the man who comes to me I will
never turn away.
I have come down from heaven,
not to do my own will,
but the will of him who sent me.
It is his will that I should not lose
even one of all that he has given
me,
but raise them all up on the last day.*

"For it is my Father's will
that everyone
who looks upon the Son and puts his
faith in him
shall possess eternal life;
and I will raise him up on
the last day."

*"In truth, in very truth I tell you,
the believer possesses eternal life.
I am the bread of life.
Your forefathers ate the manna in
the desert and they are dead.
I am speaking of the bread that*

*comes down from heaven,
which a man may eat, and never die.*

"I am that living bread which has
come down from heaven;
if anyone eats this bread he shall live
for ever.
Moreover, the bread which I will
give is my own flesh;
I give it for the life of the world."

*This led to a fierce dispute among
the Jews.
"How can this man give us his
flesh to eat?" they said.*

Jesus replied, "In truth, in very truth
I tell you,
unless you eat the flesh of the Son
of Man and
drink his blood you can have
no life in you.
Whoever eats my flesh and drinks
my blood
possesses eternal life,
and I will raise him up on
the last day.
My flesh is real food; my blood is
real drink.

*"Whoever eats my flesh and drinks
my blood
dwells continually in me and I
dwell in him.
As the living Father sent me,
and I live because of the Father,
so he who eats me shall live because
of me.
This is the bread which came down
from heaven;
and it is not like the bread which our
fathers ate:
they are dead,
but whoever eats this bread shall
live for ever."*

—From John 6, N.E.B.

772
MEMORIAL OF HUMILITY

Jesus knew that the time had come
    for him to leave this world and
    go to the Father.
Having loved his own
    who were in the world,
he now showed them the full extent
    of his love.

He got up from the meal,
took off his outer clothing,
and wrapped a towel around
    his waist.
After that,
he poured water into a basin
and began to wash his
    disciples' feet,
drying them with the towel
that was wrapped around him.

He came to Simon Peter, who said
    to him,
"Lord, are you going to wash
    my feet?"
Jesus replied, "You do not realize
    now what I am doing,
but later you will understand."
"No," said Peter, "you shall never
    wash my feet."

Jesus answered,
"Unless I wash you,
you have no part with me."

"Then, Lord," Simon Peter replied,
"not just my feet but my hands and
    my head as well!"

Jesus answered,
"A person who has had a bath
needs only to wash his feet;
his whole body is clean."

When he had finished washing
    their feet,
he put on his clothes and returned to
    his place.

"Do you understand what I have
    done for you?" he asked them.

"You call me 'Teacher' and 'Lord,'
and rightly so, for that is what I am.

"Now that I, your Lord
    and Teacher,
have washed your feet,
you also should wash one
    another's feet.
I have set you an example that you
    should do as I have done
    for you."

"Now that you know these things,
you will be blessed if you do them."
    —From John 13, N.I.V.

773
THE LORD'S SUPPER

I received from the Lord
that which I also delivered to you:

that the Lord Jesus on the same
    night
in which He was betrayed
    took bread:
and when He had given thanks,
He broke it and said,

"Take, eat; this is My body
which is broken for you;
do this in remembrance of Me."

In the same manner He also took the
    cup after supper, saying,

"This cup is the new covenant in
    My blood.
This do, as often as you drink it,
in remembrance of Me."

For as often as you eat this bread
    and drink this cup,
you proclaim the Lord's death
    till He comes.

Therefore whoever eats this bread
or drinks this cup of the Lord
in an unworthy manner
will be guilty of the body and blood
of the Lord.

**But let a man examine himself,
and so let him eat of that bread
and drink of that cup.**
—From 1 Corinthians 11, N.K.J.V.

COMMUNION: *See also Nos. 733, 734.*

774
THE LAW OF THE LORD IS PERFECT

The law of the Lord is perfect,
concerting the soul;
The testimony of the Lord is sure,
making wise the simple;

**The statutes of the Lord are right,
rejoicing the heart;
The commandment of the Lord is
pure, enlightening the eyes.**

The fear of the Lord is clean,
enduring forever;
The judgments of the Lord are true
and righteous altogether.

**More to be desired are they than
gold,
Yea, than much fine gold;
Sweeter also than honey and the
honeycomb.
Moreover by them Your servant
is warned,
And in keeping them there is
great reward.**

Who can understand his errors?
Cleanse me from secret faults.
Keep back Your servant also
from presumptuous sins;
Let them not have dominion over me.
Then I shall be blameless,
And I shall be innocent of great
transgression.

**Let the words of my mouth
and the meditation of my heart
Be acceptable in Your sight,
O Lord, my strength and
my redeemer.**
—From Psalm 19, N.K.J.V.

775
THE TEN COMMANDMENTS

God spake all these words, saying,
I am the Lord thy God,
which have brought thee out of the
land of Egypt,
out of the house of bondage.

**Thou shalt have no other gods
before me.**

Thou shalt not make unto thee any
graven image,
or any likeness of any thing
that is in heaven above,
or that is in the earth beneath,
or that is in the water under
the earth:

**Thou shalt not bow down thyself to
them, nor serve them:
for I the Lord thy God am a
jealous God,
visiting the iniquity of the fathers
upon the children
unto the third and fourth
generation
of them that hate me;**

And shewing mercy unto thousands
of them that love me,
and keep my commandments.

**Thou shalt not take the name
of the Lord thy God in vain:
for the Lord will not hold
him guiltless
that taketh his name in vain.**

Remember the sabbath day, to keep
   it holy,
Six days shalt thou labour, and
   do all thy work:

but the seventh day is the sabbath of
   the Lord thy God:
in it thou shalt not do any work,
thou, nor thy son, nor thy daughter,
thy manservant, nor thy
   maidservant, nor thy cattle,
nor thy stranger that is within
   thy gates:

for in six days the Lord made heaven
   and earth,
the sea, and all that in them is,
and rested the seventh day:

wherefore the Lord blessed the
   sabbath day,
and hallowed it.

Honour thy father and thy mother,
that thy days may be long
upon the land which the Lord thy
   God giveth thee.

Thou shalt not kill.

Thou shalt not commit adultery.

Thou shalt not steal.

Thou shalt not bear false witness
   against thy neighbour.

Thou shalt not covet thy
   neighbour's house,
thou shalt not covet thy neighbour's
   wife,
nor his manservant, nor his
   maidservant,
nor his ox, nor his ass,
nor any thing that is thy
   neighbour's.
   —*From Exodus 20, K.J.V.*

LAW AND GRACE: *See also Nos. 753,*
797.

776
GIFTS OF THE SPIRIT

Now about spiritual gifts, brothers,
I do not want you to be ignorant.

There are different kinds of gifts,
but the same Spirit.
There are different kinds
   of service,
but the same Lord.
There are different kinds
   of working,
but the same God works all of them
   in all men.

Now to each one the manifestation
   of the Spirit
is given for the common good.
To one there is given through the
   Spirit the message of wisdom,
to another the message of knowledge by means of the
   same Spirit;

to another faith by the same Spirit,
to another gifts of healing
   by that one Spirit,
to another miraculous powers,

to another prophecy,
to another the ability to distinguish
   between spirits,
to another the ability to speak
   in different kinds of tongues,
and to still another
   the interpretation of tongues.

All these are the work of one
   and the same Spirit,
and he gives them to each man,
just as he determines.

The body is a unit,
though it is made up of many parts;
and though all its parts are many,
they form one body.

So it is with Christ.
   —*From 1 Corinthians 12, N.I.V.*

777
CHRISTIAN UNITY

As a prisoner for the Lord, then,
I urge you to live a life
worthy of the calling you
    have received.

Be completely humble and gentle;
be patient, bearing with one another
    in love.
Make every effort to keep
the unity of the Spirit through the
    bond of peace.

There is one body and one Spirit—
just as you were called to one hope
    when you were called—
one Lord, one faith, one baptism;
one God and Father of all,
who is over all and through all
    and in all.

But to each one of us grace has been
    given as Christ apportioned it.
This is why it says:
    "When he ascended on high,
    he led captives in his train
    and gave gifts to men."

It was he who gave some
    to be apostles,
some to be prophets, some to be
    evangelists,
and some to be pastors and teachers,

To prepare God's people
    for works of service,
so that the body of Christ may
    be built up
until we all reach unity in the faith
and in the knowledge of the
    Son of God
and become mature,
attaining to the whole measure
    of the fullness of Christ.

Then we will no longer be infants,
tossed back and forth by the waves,
and blown here and there
by every wind of teaching
and by the cunning and craftiness of
    men in their deceitful
    scheming.

Instead, speaking the truth in love,
we will in all things grow up into
    him who is the Head, that is,
    Christ.
From him the whole body,
joined and held together
    by every supporting ligament,
grows and builds itself up in love,
as each part does its work.
>   —*From Ephesians 4, N.I.V.*

———

SPIRITUAL GIFTS: See also Nos. 716, 839.

778
OUR ATONING JUDGE

Why do you judge your brother?
Or why do you look down on your
    brother?
For we will all stand before God's
    judgment seat.

It is written:
" 'As surely as I live,' says the Lord,
'Every knee will bow before me;
every tongue will confess to God.' "

So then, each of us will give an
    account of himself to God.

My dear children, I write this to you
so that you will not sin.

But if anybody does sin, we have one
    who speaks to the Father in our
    defense—Jesus Christ,
    the Righteous One.

He is the atoning sacrifice
    for our sins,
and not only for ours but also
for the sins of the whole world.
>   —*From Romans 14 and 1 John 2, N.I.V.*

SPIRITUAL GIFTS, JUDGMENT

779
DAY OF JUDGMENT

"Thrones were set in place
and one of great age took his seat.
His robe was white as snow,
the hair of his head as pure as wool.
His throne was a blaze of flames,
its wheels were a burning fire.

"A stream of fire poured out,
issuing from his presence.
A thousand thousand waited
    on him,
ten thousand times ten thousand
    stood before him.
A court was held
and the books were opened."

I saw the dead, both great and small,
standing in front of his throne,
while the book of life was opened,
and other books opened
which were the record of what they
    had done in their lives,
by which the dead were judged.

Then I saw a new heaven and
    a new earth;
the first heaven and the first earth
    had disappeared now,
and there was no longer any sea.

I saw the holy city, and the
    new Jerusalem,
coming down from God out
    of heaven
as beautiful as a bride all dressed for
    her husband.

"Here God lives among men.
He will make his home
    among them;
they shall be his people,
and he will be their God;
his name is God-with-them."

"Very soon now, I shall be with
    you again,
bringing the reward to be given
to every man according to what he
    deserves."

—*From Daniel 7 and*
Revelation 20 through 22, Jerusalem.

780
THE THREE ANGELS'
MESSAGES

I saw another angel fly in the midst
    of heaven,
having the everlasting gospel
to preach unto them that dwell on
    the earth,
and to every nation, and kindred,
    and tongue, and people,
saying with a loud voice,

Fear God, and give glory to him;
for the hour of his judgment
    is come:
and worship him
that made heaven, and earth, and
    the sea,
and the fountains of waters.

And there followed another angel,
    saying,
Babylon is fallen, is fallen,
that great city,
because she made all nations
drink of the wine of the wrath
    of her fornication.

And the third angel followed them,
saying with a loud voice,
If any man worship the beast and
    his image,
and receive his mark in his
    forehead, or in his hand,

the same shall drink of the wine
    of the wrath of God,
which is poured out without mixture
into the cup of his indignation;
and he shall be tormented
    with fire and brimstone
in the presence of the holy angels,
and in the presence of the Lamb:

and the smoke of their torment
 ascendeth up for ever and ever:
and they have no rest day nor night,
who worship the beast and
 his image,
and whosoever receiveth the mark
 of his name.

Here is the patience of the saints:
here are they that keep the commandments of God,
and the faith of Jesus.
 —*From Revelation 14, K.J.V.*

___

*JUDGMENT: See also Nos. 700, 810,
 859.*

781
THE RESURRECTION OF GOD'S PEOPLE

To this end Christ died and
 lived again,
that he might be Lord
both of the dead and of the living.

*If for this life only
we have hoped in Christ,
we are of all men most to be pitied.
But in fact Christ has been raised
 from the dead,
the first fruits of those
 who have fallen asleep.*

For as by a man came death,
by a man has come also the resurrection of the dead.
For as in Adam all die,
so also in Christ shall all be
 made alive.

*For this we declare to you by the
 word of the Lord,
that we who are alive,
who are left until the coming
 of the Lord,
shall not precede those who have
 fallen asleep.*

For the Lord himself will descend
from heaven with a cry of command,
with the archangel's call,
and with the sound of the trumpet
 of God.
And the dead in Christ will rise first;

*then we who are alive, who are left,
shall be caught up together
 with them in the clouds
to meet the Lord in the air;
and so we shall always be
 with the Lord.
Therefore comfort one another
 with these words.*

Lo! I tell you a mystery.
We shall not all sleep,
but we shall all be changed,
in a moment, in the twinkling
 of an eye,
at the last trumpet.
For the trumpet will sound,
and the dead will be raised
 imperishable,
and we shall be changed.

*Thanks be to God,
who gives us the victory
 through our Lord Jesus Christ.*
 —*From Romans 14, 1 Corinthians 15,
 and 1 Thessalonians 4, R.S.V.*

___

*RESURRECTION OF THE SAINTS:
See also No. 771.*

782
ASSURANCE OF ETERNAL LIFE

"Yes, God loved the world so much
that he gave his only Son,
so that everyone who believes in him
 may not be lost
but may have eternal life.

*"For God sent his Son
 into the world
not to condemn the world,*

but so that through him
the world might be saved."

"The sheep that belong to me
    listen to my voice;
I know them and they follow me.
I give them eternal life;
they will never be lost
and no one will steal them from me.

"The Father who gave them to me
    is greater than anyone,
and no one can steal from
    the Father.
The Father and I are one."

This is the testimony:
God has given us eternal life
and this life is in his Son;
anyone who has the Son has life,
anyone who does not have the Son
    does not have life.

I have written all this to you
so that you who believe
    in the name of the Son of God
may be sure that you have
    eternal life.
—From John 3, 10, and 1 John 5, Jerusalem.

783
A NEW HEAVEN
AND A NEW EARTH

I saw a new heaven and a new earth,
for the first heaven and the first
    earth had passed away.
Also there was no more sea.

Then I, John, saw the holy city,
    New Jerusalem,
coming down out of heaven
    from God,
prepared as a bride adorned
    for her husband.

And I heard a loud voice
    from heaven saying,

"Behold, the tabernacle of God
    is with men,
and He will dwell with them,
and they shall be His people,
and God Himself will be with them
    and be their God.

"And God will wipe away every tear
    from their eyes;
there shall be no more death,
nor sorrow, nor crying;
and there shall be no more pain,
for the former things have
    passed away."

Then He who sat on the throne said,
"Behold, I make all things new."
And He said to me,
"Write, for these words
    are true and faithful." *
            —From Revelation 21, N.K.J.V.

___

*May be combined with No. 750.

___

ETERNAL LIFE: See also Nos. 748, 749,
    750, 751, 840.

784
BLESSED IS THE MAN

Blessed is the man who walks not
    in the counsel of the wicked,
nor stands in the way of sinners,
nor sits in the seat of scoffers;

but his delight is in the law
    of the Lord,
and on his law he meditates day
    and night.

He is like a tree
    planted by streams of water,
that yields its fruit in its season,
and its leaf does not wither.
In all that he does, he prospers.

The wicked are not so,
but are like chaff which the wind
    drives away.

Therefore the wicked will not stand
in the judgment,
nor sinners in the congregation
of the righteous;

for the Lord knows the way
of the righteous,
but the way of the wicked
will perish.
—*From Psalm 1, R.S.V.*

The Lord, strong and mighty,
the Lord, mighty in battle!
Lift up your heads, O gates!
and be lifted up, O ancient doors!
that the King of glory may come in.

Who is this King of glory?

The Lord of hosts, he is the King
of glory!
—*From Psalm 24, R.S.V.*

785
THE EARTH
IS THE LORD'S

The earth is the Lord's
and the fulness thereof,
the world and those who dwell
therein;

for He has founded it upon the seas,
and established it upon the rivers.

Who shall ascend the hill
of the Lord?
And who shall stand in his
holy place?

He who has clean hands and
a pure heart,
who does not lift up his soul
to what is false,
and does not swear deceitfully.

He will receive blessing from
the Lord,
and vindication from the God
of his salvation.
Such is the generation of those
who seek him,
who seek the face of the
God of Jacob.

Lift up your heads, O gates!
and be lifted up, O ancient doors!
that the King of glory may come in.

Who is the King of glory?

786
THE NEW LIFE

What shall we say, then?
Should we continue to live in sin
so that God's grace will increase?

Certainly not!
We have died to sin—
how then can we go on living in it?
For when a person dies,
he is set free from the power of sin.

Since we have died with Christ,
we believe that we will also
live with him.
For we know that Christ has
been raised
from death and will never
die again—
death will no longer rule over him.

And so, because he died, sin has no
power over him;
and now he lives his life in fellow-
ship with God.
In the same way
you are to think of yourselves
as dead, so far as sin is concerned,
but living in fellowship with
God through Christ Jesus.

Sin must no longer rule in your
mortal bodies,
so that you obey the desires
of your natural self.

Nor must you surrender any part of
   yourselves to sin to be used for
   wicked purposes.

Instead, give yourselves to God,
as those who have been brought
   from death to life,
and surrender your whole
   being to him
to be used for righteous purposes.
Sin must not be your master;
for you do not live under law
but under God's grace.

What, then? Shall we sin,
because we are not under law
   but under God's grace?
By no means!

Now you have been set free from sin
and are the slaves of God.
Your gain is a life fully dedicated
   to him,
and the result is eternal life.

For sin pays its wage—death;
but God's free gift is eternal life
in union with Christ Jesus our Lord.
                —*From Romans 6, T.E.V.*

787
CHRISTIANITY
IN PRACTICE

Let love be genuine; hate what is evil,
hold fast to what is good;
love one another with brotherly
   affection;
outdo one another in
   showing honor.

Never flag in zeal, but aglow with
   the Spirit,
serve the Lord.

Rejoice in your hope, be patient
   in tribulation,
be constant in prayer.

Contribute to the needs
   of the saints,
practice hospitality.
Bless those who persecute you;
bless and do not curse them.

Rejoice with those who rejoice,
weep with those who weep.
Live in harmony with one another;
do not be haughty,
but associate with the lowly;
   never be conceited.

Repay no one evil for evil,
but take thought for what is noble in
   the sight of all.
If possible, so far as it depends
   upon you,
live peaceably with all.

Beloved, never avenge yourselves,
but leave it to the wrath of God;
for it is written,
"Vengeance is mine, I will repay,
   says the Lord."

No, "if your enemy is hungry, feed
   him;
if he is thirsty, give him drink;
for by so doing
you will heap burning coals upon
   his head."

Do not be overcome by evil,
but overcome evil with good.
                —*From Romans 12, R.S.V.*

788
LOVE

Though I speak
   with the tongues of men
   and of angels,
but have not love,
I have become as sounding brass
   or a clanging cymbal.

And though I have the gift
   of prophecy,

and understand all mysteries
*   and all knowledge,*
and though I have all faith,
so that I could remove mountains,
but have not love,
I am nothing.

And though I bestow all my goods
    to feed the poor,
and though I give my body
    to be burned,
but have not love,
it profits me nothing.

Love suffers long and is kind;
love does not envy;
love does not parade itself,
is not puffed up;

does not behave rudely,
does not seek its own,
is not provoked,
thinks no evil;

does not rejoice in iniquity,
but rejoices in the truth;
bears all things,
believes all things,
hopes all things,
endures all things.

Love never fails.
But whether there are prophecies,
    they will fail;
whether there are tongues,
    they will cease;
whether there is knowledge,
    it will vanish away.

For we know in part
*   and we prophesy in part.*
But when that which is perfect
*   has come,*
then that which is in part will be
*   done away.*

When I was a child,
    I spoke as a child,
    I understood as a child,
    I thought as a child;

but when I became a man,
I put away childish things.

For now we see in a mirror, dimly,
but then face to face.
Now I know in part,
but then I shall know just as I also
*   am known.*

And now abide faith, hope, love,
    these three;
but the greatest of these is love.
            —*From 1 Corinthians 13, N.K.J.V.*
            (A New Testament canticle.)

789
GROWING IN CHRIST (SANCTIFICATION)

Since you have been brought back to
    true life with Christ,
you must look for the things
that are in heaven, where Christ is,
sitting at God's right hand.

Let your thoughts be on heavenly
*   things,*
not on the things that are
*   on the earth,*
because you have died,
and now the life you have is hidden
*   with Christ in God.*

But when Christ is revealed—
    and he is your life—
you too will be revealed
    in all your glory with him.

That is why you must kill
*   everything in you*
that belongs only to earthly life:
fornication, impurity, guilty
*   passion,*
evil desires and especially greed,
which is the same thing as wor-
*   shipping a false god;*
all this is the sort of behaviour
that makes God angry.

And it is the way in which you
      used to live
when you were surrounded by
      people doing the same thing,
but now you, of all people,
must give all these things up:
getting angry, being bad-tempered,
spitefulness, abusive language
      and dirty talk;
and never tell each other lies.

*You have stripped off your old
      behaviour with your old self,
and you have put on a new self
which will progress towards
      true knowledge
the more it is renewed
      in the image of its creator;*

and in that image there is no room
for distinction between Greek
      and Jew,
between the circumcised or the
      uncircumcised,
or between barbarian and Scythian,
slave and free man.

*There is only Christ:
he is everything and he is in every-
      thing.**
                    —From Colossians 3, Jerusalem.

_____

* May be joined with No. 812 for a longer
   passage.

790
THE CHILDREN OF GOD

See what love the Father has
      given us,
that we should be called children
      of God;
and so we are.
The reason why the world does not
      know us
is that it did not know him.

*Beloved, we are God's
      children now;*

*it does not yet appear what
      we shall be,
but we know that when he appears
      we shall be like him,
for we shall see him as he is.
And every one who thus hopes
      in him
purifies himself as he is pure.*

Every one who commits sin
      is guilty of lawlessness;
sin is lawlessness.
You know that he appeared to take
      away sins,
and in him there is no sin.

*No one who abides in him sins;
no one who sins has either seen him
      or known him.
Little children, let no one
      deceive you.
He who does right is righteous,
as he is righteous.*

He who commits sin is of the devil;
for the devil has sinned from
      the beginning.
The reason the Son of God appeared
was to destroy the works of the devil.

*No one born of God commits sin;
for God's nature abides in him,
and he cannot sin
      because he is born of God.*

By this it may be seen who are the
      children of God,
and who are the children
      of the devil:
whoever does not do right
      is not of God,
nor he who does not love his brother.

*For this is the message which you
      have heard from the beginning,
that we should love one another.*
                    —From 1 John 3, R.S.V.

791
SET YOUR MIND ON GOD'S KINGDOM

"No servant can be the slave of
   two masters;
for either he will hate the first and
   love the second,
or he will be devoted to the first and
   think nothing of the second.
You cannot serve God and Money.

*"Therefore I bid you put away
   anxious thoughts about food
   and drink to keep you alive,
   and clothes to cover your body.
Surely life is more than food, the
   body more than clothes.*

"Look at the birds of the air;
they do not sow and reap and store
   in barns,
yet your heavenly Father
   feeds them.
You are worth more than the birds!

*"Is there a man of you who by
   anxious thought can add a foot
   to his height?
And why be anxious about clothes?*

"Consider how the lilies grow
   in the fields;
they do not work, they do not spin;
and yet, I tell you,
even Solomon in all his splendour
   was not attired like one of these.

*"But if that is how God clothes the
   grass in the fields,
which is there today, and tomorrow
   is thrown on the stove,
will he not all the more clothe you?*

"How little faith you have!
No, do not ask anxiously,
'What are we to eat? What are we
   to drink?
What shall we wear?'

*"All these are things for the heathen
   to run after, not for you,
because your heavenly Father
   knows that you need them all.*

"Set your mind on God's kingdom
   and his justice before everything else,
and all the rest will come to you
   as well."
                    —*From Matthew 6, N.E.B.*

792
THE PATH OF LIFE

You, O Lord, are the portion of my
   inheritance and my cup;
You maintain my lot.

*The lines have fallen to me
   in pleasant places;
Yes, I have a good inheritance.*

I will bless the Lord who has given
   me counsel;
My heart also instructs me in the
   night seasons.

*I have set the Lord always
   before me;
Because He is at my right hand I
   shall not be moved.*

Therefore my heart is glad, and my
   glory rejoices;
My flesh also will rest in hope.

*For You will not leave my soul
   in Sheol,*
Nor will You allow Your Holy One
   to see corruption.*

You will show me the path of life;
In Your presence is fullness of joy;
At Your right hand are pleasures
   forevermore.
                    —*From Psalm 16, N.K.J.V.*

———
* The grave.

CHRISTIAN LIFE, JOY AND PEACE

793
HAPPY ARE ALL WHO FEAR THE LORD

Happy are all who fear the Lord,
who live according to his will.

*You shall eat the fruit of your own
labours, you shall be happy and
you shall prosper.*

Your wife shall be like a fruitful vine
in the heart of your house;
your sons* shall be like olive-shoots
round about your table.

*This is the blessing in store for the
man who fears the Lord.*

May the Lord bless you from Zion;
may you share the prosperity
of Jerusalem all the days
of your life,
and live to see your children's
children!

Peace be upon Israel!
—*From Psalm 128, N.E.B.*

———
*Children *in R.S.V. and other versions.*

794
WISDOM

Happy the man who discovers
wisdom, the man who gains
discernment:

*gaining her is more rewarding than
silver, more profitable
than gold.*

She is beyond the price of pearls,
nothing you could covet is her
equal.

*In her right hand is length of days;
in her left hand, riches
and honour.*

Her ways are delightful ways, her
paths all lead to contentment.

*She is a tree of life for those who
hold her fast, those who cling to
her live happy lives.*
—*From Proverbs 3, Jerusalem.*

795
THE CHRISTIAN LIFE

"Blessed are the poor in spirit,
for theirs is the kingdom of heaven.

*"Blessed are those who mourn,
for they will be comforted.*

"Blessed are the meek,
for they will inherit the earth.

*"Blessed are those who hunger and
thirst for righteousness,
for they will be filled.*

"Blessed are the merciful,
for they will be shown mercy.

*"Blessed are the pure in heart,
for they will see God.*

"Blessed are the peacemakers,
for they will be called sons of God.

*"Blessed are those who are
persecuted because of
righteousness,
for theirs is the kingdom of heaven.*

"Blessed are you when people insult
you, persecute you and falsely
say all kinds of evil against
you because of me.
Rejoice and be glad,
because great is your reward
in heaven,
for in the same way they persecuted
the prophets who were before
you.

"You are the salt of the earth.
But if the salt loses its saltiness,
how can it be made salty again?
It is no longer good for anything,
except to be thrown out and tram-
pled by men.

"You are the light of the world.
A city on a hill cannot be hidden.
Neither do people light a lamp
    and put it under a bowl.
Instead they put it on its stand,
and it gives light to everyone
    in the house.

"In the same way,
let your light shine before men,
that they may see your good deeds
and praise your Father in heaven."
    —*From Matthew 5, N.I.V.*

————

JOY AND PEACE: See also Nos. 743,
748, 757, 758, 784, 796, 807, 811,
818.

796
HOPE AND COMFORT

Do not be afraid, for I am with you;
stop being anxious and watchful, for
    I am your God.
I give you strength, I bring you help,
I uphold you with my victorious
    right hand.

The eye of Yahweh is on those
    who fear him,
on those who rely on his love,
to rescue their souls from death
and keep them alive in famine.

It is by faith and through Jesus
that we have entered this state
    of grace
in which we can boast about looking
    forward to God's glory.

But that is not all we can
boast about;

we can boast about our sufferings.
These sufferings bring patience, as
    we know,
and patience brings perseverance,
and perseverance brings hope,

and this hope is not deceptive,
because the love of God has been
    poured into our hearts by
    the Holy Spirit which has
    been given us.

May the God of hope
bring you such joy and peace in
    your faith
that the power of the Holy Spirit
will remove all bounds to hope.
    —*From Isaiah 41, Psalm 33, and*
        Romans 5, 15, Jerusalem.

————

HOPE AND COMFORT: See also Nos.
    726, 729, 745, 782.

797
MEDITATION

This book of the law
shall not depart out of your mouth,
but you shall meditate on it
    day and night,
that you may be careful to do
according to all that is written in it;
for then you shall make your way
    prosperous,
and then you shall have
    good success.

I have laid up thy word in my heart,
that I might not sin against thee. . . .
I will meditate on thy precepts,
and fix my eyes on thy ways.

I will delight in thy statutes;
I will not forget thy word. . . .
I revere thy commandments,
    which I love,
and I will meditate on thy statutes.

I remember thy name in the night,
O Lord,
and keep thy law. . . .
Oh, how I love thy law!
It is my meditation all the day.

Thy commandment makes me wiser
than my enemies,
for it is ever with me.
I have more understanding than all
my teachers,
for thy testimonies are my
meditation.

I rise before dawn and cry for help;
I hope in thy words.
My eyes are awake before the
watches of the night,
that I may meditate upon thy
promise.

Let the words of my mouth and the
meditation of my heart
be acceptable in thy sight,
O Lord, my rock and my redeemer.
—*From Joshua 1 and*
Psalms 119, 19, R.S.V.

798
PRAYER

"When you pray, do not imitate the
hypocrites:
they love to say their prayers stand-
ing up in the synagogues
and at the street corners
for people to see them.
I tell you solemnly,
they have had their reward.

"But when you pray,
go to your private room
and, when you have shut your door,
pray to your Father who is in that
secret place,
and your Father who sees all
that is done
in secret will reward you.

"In your prayers do not babble as
the pagans do,
for they think that by using
many words
they will make themselves heard.
Do not be like them;
your Father knows what you need
before you ask him."

"If you forgive others their failings,
your heavenly Father will forgive
you yours;
but if you do not forgive others,
your Father will not forgive your
failings either."

"Ask, and it will be given to you;
search, and you will find;
knock, and the door will be opened
to you.

"For the one who asks always
receives;
the one who searches always finds;
the one who knocks will always
have the door opened to him.

"Is there a man among you who
would hand his son a stone
when he asked for bread?
Or would hand him a snake when he
asked for a fish?

"If you, then, who are evil,
know how to give your children
what is good,
how much more will your Father in
heaven
give good things to those who
ask him!"
—*From Matthew 6 and 7, Jerusalem.*
(The Lord's Prayer is No. 834.)

———

MEDITATION AND PRAYER: See
also Nos. 804, 834.

799
DO NOT WORRY

Do not worry about the wicked,
do not envy those who do wrong.
Quick as the grass they wither,
fading like the green in the field.

*Trust in Yahweh and do what
    is good,
make your home in the land and live
    in peace;
make Yahweh your only joy
and he will give you what your
    heart desires.*

Commit your fate to Yahweh,
trust in him and he will act:
making your virtue clear as the light,
your integrity as bright as noon.

*Be quiet before Yahweh,
    and wait patiently for him,
not worrying about men
    who make their fortunes,
about men who scheme
to bring the poor and needy down.*

Enough of anger, leave rage aside,
do not worry, nothing but evil can
    come of it:
for the wicked will be expelled,
while those who hope in Yahweh
    shall have the land
    for their own.

*A little longer, and the wicked will
    be no more,
search his place well, he will
    not be there:
but the humble shall have the land
    for their own
    to enjoy untroubled peace.*
    —*From Psalm 37, Jerusalem.*

800
UNION WITH CHRIST

"I am the true vine,
and My Father is the vinedresser.

*"Every branch in Me that does not
    bear fruit,
He takes away;
and every branch that bears fruit,
He prunes it,
that it may bear more fruit.*

"You are already clean
because of the word which I have
    spoken to you.

*"Abide in Me, and I in you.
As the branch cannot bear fruit
    of itself,
unless it abides in the vine,
so neither can you,
unless you abide in Me.*

"I am the vine, you are the branches;
he who abides in Me, and I in him,
he bears much fruit;
for apart from Me you can
    do nothing.

*"If anyone does not abide in Me,
he is thrown away as a branch, and
    dries up;
and they gather them,
and cast them into the fire,
and they are burned.*

"If you abide in Me,
and My words abide in you,
ask whatever you wish,
and it shall be done for you.

*"By this is My Father glorified,
that you bear much fruit,
and so prove to be My disciples.*

"Just as the Father has loved Me,
I have also loved you; abide
    in My love.

"If you keep My commandments,
you will abide in My love;
just as I have kept My Father's
commandments,
and abide in His love."
—From John 15, N.A.S.B.

FAITH AND TRUST: *See also No. 698.*

801
I WAITED PATIENTLY FOR THE LORD

I waited patiently for the Lord;
he turned to me and heard my cry.
He lifted me out of the slimy pit, out
of the mud and mire;
he set my feet on a rock and gave me
a firm place to stand.

He put a new song in my mouth, a
hymn of praise to our God.
Many will see and fear and put their
trust in the Lord.

Blessed is the man who makes the
Lord his trust,
who does not look to the proud, to
those who turn aside to
false gods.

Many, O Lord my God, are the
wonders you have done.
The things you planned for us
no one can recount to you;
were I to speak and tell of them,
they would be too many to declare.

"To do your will, O my God,
is my desire;
your law is within my heart." . . .
I do not hide your righteousness in
my heart;
I speak of your faithfulness and
salvation.
I do not conceal your love and your
truth
from the great assembly.

Do not withhold your mercy from
me, O Lord;
may your love and your truth
always protect me.
—From Psalm 40, N.I.V.

802
GUIDANCE

Blessed are those whose way
is blameless,
who walk in the law of the Lord!
Blessed are those who keep
his testimonies,
who seek him with their whole heart.

Put false ways far from me;
and graciously teach me thy law!
I have chosen the way of
faithfulness,
I set thy ordinances before me.

Lead me in the path of thy
commandments,
for I delight in it. . . .
Turn my eyes from looking
at vanities;
and give me life in thy ways.

Thy word is a lamp to my feet
and a light to my path.

Good and upright is the Lord;
therefore he instructs sinners
in the way.
He leads the humble in what is right,
and teaches the humble his way.

All the paths of the Lord are
steadfast love and faithfulness,
for those who keep his covenant and
his testimonies.

Your ears shall hear a word behind
you, saying,
"This is the way, walk in it,"
when you turn to the right or when
you turn to the left.

I will instruct you and teach you the
way you should go;
I will counsel you with my eye
upon you.

"When the Spirit of truth comes,
he will guide you into all the truth;
for he will not speak on his
own authority,
but whatever he hears he will speak,
and he will declare to you
the things that are to come."
—*From Psalms 119, 25, Isaiah 30,*
Psalm 32, and John 16, R.S.V.

———

GUIDANCE: *See also Nos. 716, 721, 724,*
726.

803
PRAISE IS RIGHTFULLY YOURS

Praise is rightfully yours,
God, in Zion.
Vows to you must be fulfilled,
for you answer prayer.

All flesh must come to you with
all its sins;
though our faults overpower us,
you blot them out.

Happy the man you choose, whom
you invite to live in your courts.
Fill us with the good things of your
house, of your holy Temple.

Your righteousness repays us with
marvels, God our saviour,
hope of all the ends of the earth and
the distant islands.

Your strength holds the mountains
up, such is the power that
wraps you;
you calm the clamour of the ocean,
the clamour of its waves.

The nations are in uproar,
in panic those who live at the ends
of the world,
as your miracles bring shouts of joy
to the portals of morning
and evening.

You visit the earth and water it,
you load it with riches;
God's rivers brim with water
to provide their grain.

This is how you provide it:
by drenching its furrows,
by levelling its ridges,
by softening it with showers,
by blessing the first-fruits.

You crown the year with
your bounty,
abundance flows wherever you pass;
the desert pastures overflow,
the hillsides are wrapped in joy,
the meadows are dressed in flocks,
the valleys are clothed in wheat,
what shouts of joy, what singing!
—*From Psalm 65, Jerusalem.*

———

THANKFULNESS: *See also Nos. 702,*
711, 712, 723, 728, 869.

804
A PRAYER OF CONFESSION

"Lord God, you are great, and we
honor you.
You are faithful to your covenant
and show constant love to
those who love you
and do what you command.

"We have sinned, we have been evil,
we have done wrong.
We have rejected what you com-
manded us to do
and have turned away from what
you showed us was right.

"We have not listened to your
    servants the prophets,
who spoke in your name to our
    kings, our rulers,
our ancestors, and our whole nation.

"You, Lord, always do what is right,
but we have always brought dis-
    grace on ourselves. . . .
You are merciful and forgiving,
although we have rebelled
    against you.

"We did not listen to you, O Lord
    our God,
when you told us to live according
    to the laws
which you gave us through your
    servants the prophets. . . .
You did what you said you would do
    to us and our rulers. . . .
O Lord our God, we have not tried to
    please you
by turning from our sins or by
    following your truth."

"O Lord our God, you showed your
    power by bringing your people
    out of Egypt,
and your power is still
    remembered.
We have sinned; we have
    done wrong."

"Listen to us, O God; look at us and
    see the trouble we are in
and the suffering of the city that
    bears your name.
We are praying to you because you
    are merciful,
not because we have done right.

"Lord, hear us. Lord, forgive us.
Lord, listen to us, and act!
In order that everyone will know
    that you are God, do not delay!
This city and these people
    are yours."
                    —From Daniel 9, T.E.V.

805
HUMILITY

If you have any encouragement
    from being united with Christ,
if any comfort from his love,
if any fellowship with the Spirit,
if any tenderness and compassion,

then make my joy complete
    by being like-minded,
having the same love,
being one in spirit and purpose.
Do nothing out of selfish ambition
    or vain conceit,
but in humility consider others
    better than yourselves.

Each of you should look not only to
    your own interests,
but also to the interests of others.
Your attitude should be the same
as that of Christ Jesus:
Who, being in very nature God,
    . . . made himself nothing.

And being found in appearance
    as a man,
he humbled himself
and became obedient to death—
even death on a cross! *

Therefore, my dear friends, . . .
continue to work out your salvation
    with fear and trembling,
for it is God who works in you
to will and to act according
    to his good purpose.

Do everything without complain-
    ing or arguing,
so that you may become blameless
    and pure,
children of God without fault in a
crooked and depraved generation,
in which you shine like stars in the
    universe.
                —From Philippians 2, N.I.V.
_____

* Philippians 2:6-11 is No. 842.

806
ARISE, SHINE

Arise, shine out, for your light
    has come,
the glory of Yahweh is rising on you,
though night still covers the earth
and darkness the peoples.

Above you Yahweh now rises
and above you his glory appears.
The nations come to your light
and kings to your dawning
    brightness.

Lift up your eyes and look round:
all are assembling and coming
    towards you,
your sons from far away
and your daughters being
    tenderly carried.

At this sight you will grow radiant,
your heart throbbing and full;
since the riches of the sea will
    flow to you,
the wealth of the nations come
    to you.

Though you have been abandoned,
and hated and shunned,
I will make you an eternal pride,
a joy for ever and ever.

    —*From Isaiah 60, Jerusalem.*

807
THE LORD'S WORK

The Spirit of the Sovereign Lord
    is on me,
because the Lord has anointed me
to preach good news to the poor.

He has sent me to bind up the
    brokenhearted,
to proclaim freedom for
    the captives
and release for the prisoners,

to proclaim the year of the
    Lord's favor
and the day of vengeance of
    our God,
to comfort all who mourn,

and provide for those who grieve in
    Zion—
to bestow on them a crown of
beauty instead of ashes,
the oil of gladness
instead of mourning,

and a garment of praise
    instead of a spirit of despair.
They will be called oaks of
    righteousness,
a planting of the Lord
    for the display of his splendor.

I delight greatly in the Lord;
my soul rejoices in my God.
For he has clothed me with
    garments of salvation
and arrayed me in a robe of
    righteousness,
as a bridegroom adorns his head
    like a priest,
and as a bride adorns herself with
    her jewels.

For as the soil makes the sprout
    come up
and a garden causes seeds to grow,
so the Sovereign Lord will make
    righteousness and praise
spring up before all nations.

    —*From Isaiah 61, N.I.V.*

808
DOING GOOD TO ALL

Brothers, if someone is caught
    in a sin,
you who are spiritual
    should restore him gently.
But watch yourself,
or you also may be tempted.

Carry each other's burdens,
and in this way
you will fulfill the law of Christ.

If anyone thinks he is something
    when he is nothing,
he deceives himself.
Each one should test his own actions.
Then he can take pride in himself,
without comparing himself to some-
    body else,
for each one should carry his
    own load.

Anyone who receives instruction
    in the word
must share all good things with his
    instructor.

Do not be deceived:
God cannot be mocked.
A man reaps what he sows.

The one who sows to please
    his sinful nature,
from that nature will reap
    destruction;
the one who sows to please
    the Spirit,
from the Spirit will reap eternal life.

Let us not become weary in
    doing good,
for at the proper time
we will reap a harvest if we do
    not give up.

Therefore, as we have opportunity,
let us do good to all people,
especially to those who belong
    to the family of believers.
        —*From Galatians 6, N.I.V.*

809
CHRISTIAN DUTIES

Now we ask you, brothers, to respect
    those who work hard
    among you,

who are over you in the Lord
and who admonish you.
Hold them in the highest regard in
    love because of their work.

Live in peace with each other.
And we urge you, brothers,
warn those who are idle,
encourage the timid, help the weak,
be patient with everyone.
Make sure that nobody pays back
    wrong for wrong,
but always try to be kind to each
    other and to everyone else.

Be joyful always; pray continually;
give thanks in all circumstances,
for this is God's will for you in
    Christ Jesus.

Do not put out the Spirit's fire;
do not treat prophecies with
    contempt.
Test everything. Hold on
    to the good.
Avoid every kind of evil.

May God himself, the God of peace,
sanctify you through and through.
May your whole spirit, soul and body
be kept blameless at the coming of
    our Lord Jesus Christ.
        —*From 1 Thessalonians 5, N.I.V.*

810
WORK AND DUTY

Let our people learn to apply them-
    selves to good deeds,
so as to help cases of urgent need,
and not to be unfruitful.

They are to do good,
to be rich in good deeds,
liberal and generous,
thus laying up for themselves a
    good foundation for the future,
so that they may take hold of the life
    which is life indeed.

I desire you to insist on these things,
so that those who have believed
    in God
may be careful to apply themselves
    to good deeds;
these are excellent and profitable
    to men.

We must all appear before the
    judgment seat of Christ,
so that each one may receive
    good or evil,
according to what he has done in
    the body.

Fear God, and keep his commandments;
for this is the whole duty of man.

For God will bring every deed into
    judgment,
with every secret thing,
whether good or evil.
> —*From Titus 3, 1 Timothy 6,*
> *2 Corinthians 5, and Ecclesiastes 12, R.S.V.*

LOVING SERVICE: See also Nos. 743,
    787, 795, 813, 814, 844.

811
PEACE

How wonderful it is, how pleasant,
for God's people to live together in
    harmony!

By the authority of our Lord
    Jesus Christ
I appeal to all of you, my brothers,
to agree in what you say,
so that there will be no divisions
    among you.
Be completely united,
with only one thought and
    one purpose.

So then, we must always aim at those
    things that bring peace

and that help strengthen one
    another.

The wisdom from above is pure
    first of all;
it is also peaceful, gentle,
    and friendly;
it is full of compassion
and produces a harvest of
    good deeds;
it is free from prejudice and
    hypocrisy.

And goodness is the harvest
that is produced from the seeds
the peacemakers plant in peace.

Strive for perfection;
listen to my appeals;
agree with one another;
live in peace.

And the God of love and peace will
    be with you.
> —*From Psalm 133,*
> *1 Corinthians 1, Romans 14,*
> *James 3, and 2 Corinthians 13, T.E.V.*

812
CHRISTIAN RELATIONSHIPS

You are God's chosen race,
    his saints;
he loves you, and you should
    be clothed
in sincere compassion, in kindness
    and humility,
gentleness and patience.

Bear with one another; forgive each
    other as soon as a
    quarrel begins.
The Lord has forgiven you;
now you must do the same.

Over all these clothes, to keep
    them together
and complete them, put on love.

And may the peace of Christ reign in
  your hearts,
because it is for this that you were
  called together as parts
  of one body.
Always be thankful.

Let the message of Christ, in all its
  richness,
find a home with you.
Teach each other, and advise each
  other, in all wisdom.
With gratitude in your hearts
sing psalms and hymns and
  inspired songs to God;

and never say or do anything
except in the name of the Lord Jesus,
giving thanks to God the Father
  through him.*
  —*From Colossians 3, Jerusalem.*

———

* May be joined with No. 789 for a longer
  passage.

———

LOVE FOR ONE ANOTHER: See also
  Nos. 713, 732, 787, 790, 805, 808,
  809, 813, 827.

813
LORD, WHO MAY DWELL IN YOUR SANCTUARY?

Lord, who may dwell in your
  sanctuary?
Who may live on your holy hill?

He whose walk is blameless
and who does what is righteous,
who speaks the truth from his heart
and has no slander on his tongue,

who does his neighbor no wrong
and casts no slur on his fellow man,
who despises a vile man
but honors those who fear the Lord,

who keeps his oath even
  when it hurts,

who lends his money without usury
and does not accept a bribe against
  the innocent.

He who does these things
will never be shaken.
  —*From Psalm 15, N.I.V.*

814
THE REQUIREMENTS OF GOD

With what shall I come before
  the Lord
and bow down before the
  exalted God?
Shall I come before him with
  burnt offerings,
with calves a year old?
Will the Lord be pleased with thou-
  sands of rams,
with ten thousand rivers of oil?
Shall I offer my firstborn for my
  transgression,
the fruit of my body for the sin
  of my soul?

He has showed you, O man, what is
  good.
And what does the Lord require of
  you?
To act justly and to love mercy
and to walk humbly with your God.

Who is a God like you,
who pardons sin and forgives the
  transgression of the remnant of
  his inheritance?

You do not stay angry forever
but delight to show mercy.
You will again have compassion
  on us;
you will tread our sins underfoot
and hurl all our iniquities into the
  depths of the sea.

Return, O Israel, to the Lord
  your God.

Your sins have been your downfall!
Take words with you
and return to the Lord.
Say to him:

"Forgive all our sins
and receive us graciously,
that we may offer the fruit
of our lips."

"I will heal their waywardness
and love them freely,
for my anger has turned away
     from them."
> —From Micah 6 and 7,
> and Hosea 14, N.I.V.

_____

OBEDIENCE: See also Nos. 763, 775,
789, 791, 800, 822, 828.

815
WATCHFULNESS

Only be careful,
and watch yourselves closely
so that you do not forget the things
     your eyes have seen,
or let them slip from your heart as
     long as you live.
Teach them to your children
and to their children after them.

Be careful not to forget the cove-
*   nant of the Lord your God*
*   that he made with you;*
do not make for yourselves an idol
in the form of anything the Lord
*   your God has forbidden.*

So then,
just as you received Christ Jesus
     as Lord,
continue to live in him,
rooted and built up in him,
strengthened in the faith as you
     were taught,
and overflowing with thankfulness.

See to it that no one takes you
*   captive through hollow and*
*   deceptive philosophy,*
which depends on human tradition
and the basic principles of this
*   world rather than on Christ.*

Be self-controlled and alert.
Your enemy the devil prowls around
     like a roaring lion looking for
     someone to devour.

Resist him,
standing firm in the faith,
because you know that your
*   brothers throughout the world*
are undergoing the same kind of
*   sufferings.*

So then, brothers, stand firm
and hold to the teachings we passed
     on to you,
whether by word of mouth or
     by letter.

"Be on guard! Be alert!
You do not know when that time
*   will come."*
"What I say to you, I say to every-
*   one: 'Watch!'"*
> —From Deuteronomy 4, Colossians 2,
> 1 Peter 5, 2 Thessalonians 2,
> and Mark 13, N.I.V.

816
PREPARATION FOR
CHRIST'S COMING

You know very well that the day of
     the Lord
will come like a thief in the night.
While people are saying, "Peace
     and safety,"
destruction will come on
     them suddenly,
as labor pains on a pregnant woman,
and they will not escape.

But you, brothers, are not
*   in darkness*

*so that this day should surprise you
    like a thief.*
*You are all sons of the light
    and sons of the day.*
*We do not belong to the night
    or to the darkness.*

So then, let us not be like others, who
    are asleep,
but let us be alert and self-controlled.
For those who sleep, sleep at night,
and those who get drunk,
    get drunk at night.

*But since we belong to the day,
let us be self-controlled,
putting on faith and love
    as a breastplate,
and the hope of salvation
    as a helmet.*

For God did not appoint us to
    suffer wrath
but to receive salvation
    through our Lord Jesus Christ.
He died for us so that,
whether we are awake or asleep,
we may live together with him.

*Therefore encourage one another
and build each other up,
just as in fact you are doing.*
        —*From 1 Thessalonians 5, N.I.V.*
———
WATCHFULNESS: See also No. 747.

817
CHRISTIAN WARFARE

Finally, build up your strength
    in union with the Lord
and by means of his mighty power.
Put on all the armor that God
    gives you,
so that you will be able to stand up
    against the Devil's evil tricks.

*For we are not fighting against
    human beings*

*but against the wicked spiritual
    forces in the heavenly world,
the rulers, authorities, and cosmic
    powers of this dark age.*

So put on God's armor now!
Then when the evil day comes,
you will be able to resist the
    enemy's attacks,
and after fighting to the end,
you will still hold your ground.

*So stand ready,
with truth as a belt
    tight around your waist,
with righteousness as your
    breastplate,
and as your shoes the readiness to
    announce the Good News
    of peace.*

At all times carry faith as a shield;
for with it you will be able to put out
    all the burning arrows shot by
    the Evil One.
And accept salvation as a helmet,
and the word of God as the sword
which the Spirit gives you.

*Do all this in prayer,
    asking for God's help.
Pray on every occasion, as the
    Spirit leads.
For this reason keep alert and never
    give up;
pray always for all God's people.*
        —*From Ephesians 6, T.E.V.*
———
*CHRISTIAN WARFARE: See also No.
    840.*

818
WHEN THE LORD BROUGHT BACK THE CAPTIVES

When the Lord brought back the
    captives to Zion,
we were like men who dreamed.

Our mouths were filled with
laughter,
our tongues with songs of joy.

Then it was said among the nations,
"The Lord has done great things
for them."
The Lord has done great
things for us,
and we are filled with joy.

Restore our fortunes, O Lord,
like streams in the Negev.

Those who sow in tears
will reap with songs of joy.
He who goes out weeping,
carrying seed to sow,
will return with songs of joy,
carrying sheaves with him.
—*From Psalm 126, N.I.V.*

819
I CRY ALOUD TO THE LORD

I cry aloud to the Lord;
I lift up my voice to the Lord
for mercy.
I pour out my complaint before him;
before him I tell my trouble.
When my spirit grows faint
within me,
it is you who know my way.

In the path where I walk
men have hidden a snare for me.
Look to my right and see;
no one is concerned for me.
I have no refuge;
no one cares for my life.

I cry to you, O Lord;
I say, "You are my refuge,
my portion in the land
of the living."
Listen to my cry,
for I am in desperate need;

rescue me from those who
pursue me,
for they are too strong for me.

Set me free from my prison,
that I may praise your name.
Then the righteous will gather
about me
because of your goodness to me.
—*From Psalm 142, N.I.V.*

820
TITHES AND OFFERINGS

"'All the tithe of the land,
whether of the seed of the land
or of the fruit of the tree,
is the Lord's.
It is holy to the Lord.'"

"Will a man rob God?
Yet you have robbed Me!
But you say,
'In what way have we robbed You.'
In tithes and offerings.

"You are cursed with a curse,
For you have robbed Me,
Even this whole nation.

"Bring all the tithes into the
storehouse,
That there may be food in
My house,
And prove Me now in this,"
says the Lord of hosts,
"If I will not open for you
the windows of heaven
And pour out for you such blessing
That there will not be room enough
to receive it.

"And I will rebuke the devourer
for your sakes,
So that he will not destroy the fruit of
your ground,
Nor shall the vine fail to bear fruit
for you in the field."

"And all nations will call
you blessed,
For you will be a delightful land,"
Says the Lord of hosts.

—From Leviticus 27
and Malachi 3, N.K.J.V.

821
GENEROSITY

See that you . . . excel
in this grace of giving. . . .
For you know the grace of our Lord
Jesus Christ,
that though he was rich,
yet for your sakes he became poor,
so that you through his poverty
might become rich.

If the willingness is there,
the gift is acceptable according to
what one has,
not according to what he does not
have.

Remember this:
Whoever sows sparingly will also
reap sparingly,
and whoever sows generously
will also reap generously.

Each man should give what he has
decided in his heart to give,
not reluctantly or under compul-
sion,
for God loves a cheerful giver.

And God is able to make all grace
abound to you,
so that in all things at all times,
having all that you need,
you will abound in every good work.

Now he who supplies seed to the
sower and bread for food
will also supply and increase
your store of seed
and will enlarge the harvest
of your righteousness.

You will be made rich in every way
so that you can be generous on every
occasion,
and through us your generosity will
result in thanksgiving to God.

This service that you perform
is not only supplying the needs of
God's people
but is also overflowing in many
expressions of thanks to God.

Because of the service by which
you have proved yourselves,
men will praise God for the
obedience
that accompanies your confession of
the gospel of Christ,
and for your generosity in sharing
with them
and with everyone else.

And in their prayers for you their
hearts will go out to you,
because of the surpassing grace
God has given you.
Thanks be to God for his indescrib-
able gift!

—From 2 Corinthians 8 and 9, N.I.V.

STEWARDSHIP: See also No. 700.

822
OUR DAILY WORK

The Lord God took the man
and put him in the Garden of Eden
to work it and take care of it.

Six days you shall labor and do all
your work.

"By the sweat of your brow
you will eat your food."

The sleep of a laborer is sweet,
whether he eats little or much.

Whatever your hand finds to do,
do it with all your might.

We gave you this rule:
*   "If a man will not work, he*
*   shall not eat."*

If anyone does not provide
    for his relatives,
and especially for his immediate
    family,
he has denied the faith
and is worse than an unbeliever.

Never be lacking in zeal,
but keep your spiritual fervor,
serving the Lord.
    —*From Genesis 2, 3, Exodus 20,*
    Ecclesiastes 5, 9, 2 Thessalonians 3,
    1 Timothy 5, and Romans 12, N.I.V.

823
TEMPERANCE

Teach what befits sound doctrine.
Bid the older men be temperate,
    serious,
sensible, sound in faith, in love,
and in steadfastness.

Bid the older women likewise
*   to be reverent in behavior,*
not to be slanderers or
*   slaves to drink;*
they are to teach what is good,
and so train the young women
to love their husbands and children.
        . . .
Likewise urge the younger men
*   to control themselves.*

Wine is a mocker, strong drink
    a brawler;
and whoever is led astray by it
    is not wise.

Who has woe? Who has sorrow?
Who has strife? Who has
*   complaining?*

Who has wounds without cause?
Who has redness of eyes?
Those who tarry long over wine,
those who go to try mixed wine.

Do not look at wine when it is red,
when it sparkles in the cup
    and goes down smoothly.
At the last it bites like a serpent,
and stings like an adder.

Every athlete exercises self-control
*   in all things.*
They do it to receive a perishable
*   wreath,*
but we an imperishable.

For the grace of God has appeared
    for the salvation of all men,
training us to renounce irreligion
    and worldly passions,
and to live sober, upright, and godly
    lives in this world,

awaiting our blessed hope,
the appearing of the glory
Of our great God and Savior Jesus
*   Christ.*
    —*From Titus 2, Proverbs 20, 23, and*
        1 Corinthians 9, R.S.V.

824
HEALTHFUL LIVING

My dear friend,
I hope everything is going happily
    with you
and that you are as well physically
    as you are spiritually.

Your body, you know,
is the temple of the Holy Spirit,
who is in you since you received
*   him from God.*
You are not your own property;
you have been bought and paid for.
That is why you should use your
*   body for the glory of God.*

Whatever you eat, whatever
you drink,
whatever you do at all,
do it for the glory of God.

There is no need to worry;
but if there is anything you need,
pray for it,
asking God for it with prayer and
thanksgiving,
and that peace of God,
which is so much greater
than we can understand,
will guard your hearts and your
thoughts,
in Christ Jesus.

Finally, brothers,
fill your minds with everything
that is true,
everything that is noble,
everything that is good and pure,
everything that we love and honour,
and everything that can be thought
virtuous or worthy of praise.
—*From 3 John, 1 Corinthians 6, 10,*
and Philippians 4, Jerusalem.

HEALTH AND WHOLENESS: See
also No. 711.

825
OUR CIVIC DUTIES

Everyone must submit himself
to the governing authorities,
for there is no authority
except that which God has established.

The authorities that exist
have been established by God.
Consequently, he who rebels
against the authority
is rebelling against what God
has instituted,
and those who do so will bring
judgment on themselves.

For rulers hold no terror for those
who do right,
but for those who do wrong.
Do you want to be free from fear
of the one in authority?
Then do what is right
and he will commend you.

For he is God's servant to do you
good.
But if you do wrong, be afraid,
for he does not bear the sword for
nothing.
He is God's servant,
an agent of wrath to bring punish-
ment on the wrongdoer.

Therefore, it is necessary
to submit to the authorities,
not only because of possible
punishment
but also because of conscience.

This is also why you pay taxes,
for the authorities are God's
servants,
who give their full time
to governing.
Give everyone what you owe him:
If you owe taxes, pay taxes;
if revenue, then revenue;
if respect, then respect,
if honor, then honor.

Let no debt remain outstanding,
except the continuing debt to love
one another,
for he who loves his fellow man
has fulfilled the law.
—*From Romans 13, N.I.V.*

826
FAMILY LIFE

Love the Lord your God
with all your heart
and with all your soul
and with all your strength.

These commandments that I give
    you today
are to be upon your hearts.

Impress them on your children.
Talk about them when you
        sit at home
        and when you walk along the
        road, when you lie down and
        when you get up.

Children, obey your parents in the
    Lord, for this is right.

"Honor your father and mother"—
        which is the first commandment
        with a promise—
"that it may go well with you
and that you may enjoy long life on
    the earth."

Fathers, do not exasperate
    your children;
instead, bring them up
in the training and instruction of
    the Lord.
                —From Deuteronomy 6
                and Ephesians 6, N.I.V.

827
THE CHRISTIAN HOME

Never have grudges against others,
or lose your temper, or raise your
        voice to anybody,
or call each other names,
or allow any sort of spitefulness.

Be friends with one another,
    and kind,
forgiving each other as readily as
    God forgave you in Christ.

Try, then, to imitate God,
as children of his that he loves,
and follow Christ by loving as
        he loved you,
giving himself up in our place
        as a fragrant offering
        and a sacrifice to God.

Among you there must be not
    even a mention
of fornication or impurity in any of
    its forms, or promiscuity:
this would hardly become the
    saints!

There must be no coarseness,
    or salacious talk and jokes—
all this is wrong for you;
raise your voices in thanksgiving
    instead.

You were darkness once,
but now you are light in the Lord;
be like children of light.

Sing the words and tunes of the
    psalms and hymns when you are
    together,
and go on singing and chanting to
    the Lord in your hearts,

so that always and everywhere
you are giving thanks to God who is
    our Father
in the name of our Lord
    Jesus Christ.
                —From Ephesians 4 and 5, Jerusalem.

828
YOUTH

Remember your Creator
    in the days of your youth,
before the days of trouble come
and the years approach when
        you will say,
"I find no pleasure in them."

Even a child is known by
    his actions,
by whether his conduct is pure
    and right.

How can a young man keep his
    way pure?
By living according to your word.
I seek you with all my heart;

do not let me stray from your
    commands.

My son, do not forget my teaching,
but keep my commands in
    your heart,
for they will prolong your life
    many years
and bring you prosperity.

Let love and faithfulness never
    leave you;
bind them around your neck,
write them on the tablet of
    your heart.
Then you will win favor and a
    good name
in the sight of God and man.

Trust in the Lord with all your heart
and lean not on your own under-
    standing;
in all your ways acknowledge him,
and he will make your paths
    straight.

Praise the Lord, O my soul,
and forget not all his benefits. . . .
He satisfies my desires with
    good things,
so that my youth is renewed like
    the eagle's.
            —From Ecclesiastes 12, Proverbs 20,
                Psalm 119, Proverbs 3,
                and Psalm 103, N.I.V.

829
A NOBLE WIFE

Who can find a virtuous wife?
For her worth is far above rubies.

The heart of her husband safely
    trusts her;
So he will have no lack of gain.
She does him good and not evil
All the days of her life.

She seeks wool and flax,
And willingly works with her hands.
She also rises while it is yet night,
And provides food for her house-
    hold,
And a portion for her maidservants.

She girds herself with strength,
And strengthens her arms. . . .
She extends her hand to the poor,
Yes, she reaches out her hands
    to the needy.

Strength and honor are her
    clothing;
She shall rejoice in time to come.
She opens her mouth with wisdom,
And on her tongue is the law of
    kindness.

She watches over the ways of her
    household,
And does not eat the bread
    of idleness.
Her children rise up
    and call her blessed;
Her husband also, and he
    praises her.
            —From Proverbs 31, N.K.J.V.

830
MARRIAGE

The Lord God said,
"It is not good for the man to
    be alone.
I will provide a partner for him."

The Lord God then built up the rib,
which he had taken out of the man,
into a woman.
He brought her to the man, and the
    man said:

"Now this, at last—
bone from my bones,
flesh from my flesh!—
this shall be called woman,
for from man was this taken."

*"For this reason a man shall leave
his father and mother,
and be made one with his wife;
and the two shall become one flesh.*

"It follows that they are no longer
two individuals:
they are one flesh.
What God has joined together,
man must not separate."

*Be subject to one another
out of reverence for Christ.*

Wives, be subject to your husbands
as to the Lord;
for the man is the head
of the woman,
just as Christ also is the head of
the church.

*Husbands, love your wives,
as Christ also loved the church
and gave himself up for it, to
consecrate it,
cleansing it by water and word,
so that he might present the church
to himself
all glorious, with no stain or wrin-
kle or anything of the sort,
but holy and without blemish.*

In the same way
men also are bound to love
their wives,
as they love their own bodies.
In loving his wife a man
loves himself.
For no one ever hated his own body:
on the contrary, he provides and
cares for it.
—*From Genesis 2, Matthew 19,
and Ephesians 5, N.E.B.*

LOVE IN THE HOME: See also Nos.
793, 827.

Canticles and Prayers

831
THE SONG OF MOSES
AND OF ISRAEL

"I will sing to the Lord,
For He has triumphed gloriously!
The horse and its rider He has
thrown into the sea!

*"The Lord is my strength and song,
And He has become my salvation;
He is my God, and I will
praise Him;
My Father's God, and I will
exalt Him.*

"The Lord is a man of war;
The Lord is His name.

*"Pharaoh's chariots and his army
He has cast into the sea;
His chosen captains also
are drowned in the Red Sea.*

"The depths have covered them;
They sank to the bottom like a stone.

*"Your right hand, O Lord,
has become glorious in power;
Your right hand, O Lord,
has dashed the enemy
in pieces.*

"And in the greatness of Your
excellence
You have overthrown those who
rose against You;
You sent forth Your wrath
which consumed them like
stubble.

*"And with the blast of Your nostrils
The waters were gathered together;
The floods stood upright
like a heap;
And the depths congealed in the
heart of the sea.*

"The enemy said, 'I will pursue,
    I will overtake,
I will divide the spoil;
My desire shall be satisfied on them.
I will draw my sword,
My hand shall destroy them.'

**"You blew with Your wind, the sea
    covered them;
They sank like lead in the mighty
    waters.**

"Who is like You, O Lord,
    among the gods?
Who is like You, glorious in holiness,
Fearful in praises, doing wonders?

**"You stretched out Your
    right hand;
The earth swallowed them.
You in Your mercy have led forth
    The people whom You have
    redeemed;
You have guided them in Your
    strength
To Your holy habitation.**

"The people will hear and be afraid;
Sorrow will take hold of the inhabi-
    tants of Palestina.
Then the chiefs of Edom will
    be dismayed;
The mighty men of Moab,
Trembling will take hold of them;
All the inhabitants of Canaan will
    melt away.

**"Fear and dread will fall on them;
By the greatness of Your arm
They will be as still as a stone,
Till Your people pass over, O Lord,
Till the people pass over
Whom You have purchased.**

"You will bring them in and
    plant them
In the mountain of Your
    inheritance,
In the place, O Lord, which You
    have made

For Your own dwelling,
The sanctuary, O Lord, which Your
    hands have established.

**"The Lord shall reign forever
    and ever."**
        —*From Exodus 15, N.K.J.V.*

832
OUT OF THE DEPTHS

Out of the depths I have cried to
    You, O Lord;

**Lord, hear my voice!
Let Your ears be attentive
To the voice of my supplications.**

If You, Lord, should mark iniquities,
O Lord, who could stand?

**But there is forgiveness with You,
That You may be feared.**

I wait for the Lord, my soul waits,
And in His word I do hope.

**My soul waits for the Lord
More than those who watch for the
    morning—
I say, more than those who watch
    for the morning.**

O Israel, hope in the Lord;
For with the Lord there is mercy,
And with Him is abundant
    redemption.

**And He shall redeem Israel
From all his iniquities.**
—*From Psalm 130, N.K.J.V. (De Profundis)*

833
HOLY, HOLY, HOLY

"Holy, holy, holy is the Lord of hosts;
The whole earth is full of His glory!"

"Hosanna!
'Blessed is He who comes in the
     name of the Lord!'

"Blessed is the kingdom of our
     father David
That comes in the name of the Lord!

"Hosanna in the highest!"
—From Isaiah 6 (the Sanctus)
          and Mark 11, N.K.J.V.

834
THE LORD'S PRAYER

Our Father which art in heaven,
Hallowed be thy name.
Thy kingdom come.
Thy will be done
     in earth, as it is in heaven.
Give us this day our daily bread.
And forgive us our debts,
     as we forgive our debtors.
And lead us not into temptation,
     but deliver us from evil:
For thine is the kingdom,
     and the power,
     and the glory, for ever. Amen.
—From Matthew 6, K.J.V.

835
THE SONG OF MARY *

"My soul magnifies the Lord,
And my spirit has rejoiced in God
     my Savior.

"For He has regarded the lowly
     state of His maidservant;
For behold, henceforth all genera-
     tions will call me blessed.

"For He who is mighty has done
     great things for me,
And holy is His name.
And His mercy is on those who
     fear Him
From generation to generation.

"He has shown strength
     with His arm;
He has scattered the proud in the
     imagination of their hearts.
He has put down the mighty from
     their thrones,
And exalted the lowly.

"He has filled the hungry with
     good things,
And the rich He has sent
     away empty.
He has helped His servant Israel,
In remembrance of His mercy,
As He spoke to our fathers,
To Abraham and to his seed
     forever."
—From Luke 1, N.K.J.V.

———

* Commonly called The Magnificat.

836
ZACHARIAS' PROPHECY *

"Blessed is the Lord God of Israel,
For He has visited and redeemed
          His people,
And has raised up a horn of salvation
     for us
In the house of His servant David,
As He spoke by the mouth of His
          holy prophets,
Who have been since the
     world began,

"That we should be saved from
     our enemies
And from the hand of all
     who hate us,
To perform the mercy promised to
     our fathers
And to remember His holy
     covenant,
The oath which He swore to our
     father Abraham:

"To grant us that we,
Being delivered from the hand of
     our enemies,

Might serve Him without fear,
In holiness and righteousness before
    Him all the days of our life.

**"And you, child, will be called the
    prophet of the Highest;
For you will go before the face of the
    Lord to prepare His ways,
To give knowledge of salvation to
    His people
By the remission of their sins,
Through the tender mercy·
    of our God,**

"With which the Dayspring
    from on high has visited us;
To give light to those who sit in
    darkness and the shadow
    of death,
To guide our feet into the
    way of peace."
                —*From Luke 1, N.K.J.V.*

------

*Commonly called The Benedictus.

837
SIMEON'S PRAYER*

"Now, Master, you can let your
    servant go in peace,
just as you promised;
because my eyes have seen
    the salvation
which you have prepared for all the
    nations to see,
a light to enlighten the pagans
and the glory of your people Israel."
            —*From Luke 2, Jerusalem.*

------

*Commonly called The Nunc Dimittis.

838
PAUL'S DOXOLOGY

Oh, the depth of the riches
    of the wisdom and knowledge
    of God!

How unsearchable his judgments,
and his paths beyond tracing out!

**"Who has known the mind
    of the Lord?
Or who has been his counselor?"**

"Who has ever given to God,
that God should repay him?"

**For from him and through him
    and to him are all things.
To him be the glory forever! Amen.**
            —*From Romans 11, N.I.V.*

839
SPIRITUAL WISDOM

We speak wisdom among those
    who are mature,
yet not the wisdom of this age,
nor of the rulers of this age,
who are coming to nothing.

**But we speak the wisdom of God in
    a mystery,
the hidden wisdom which God
    ordained before the ages
    for our glory,
which none of the rulers of
    this age knew;
for had they known,
they would not have crucified
    the Lord of glory.**

But as it is written:
"Eye has not seen, nor ear heard,
Nor have entered into the heart
    of man
The things which God has prepared
    for those who love Him."

**But God has revealed them to us
    through His Spirit.
For the Spirit searches all things,
yes, the deep things of God.**

For what man knows the things of a
    man except the spirit of the man
    which is in him?

Even so no one knows the things of
God except the Spirit of God.

Now we have received,
not the spirit of the world,
but the Spirit who is from God,
that we might know the things
that have been freely given
to us by God.

These things we also speak,
not in words which man's
wisdom teaches
but which the Holy Spirit teaches,
comparing spiritual things
with spiritual.

But the natural man does not
receive the things of the
Spirit of God,
for they are foolishness to him;
nor can he know them,
because they are spiritually
discerned.

But he who is spiritual judges
all things,
yet he himself is rightly judged
by no one.
For "Who has known the mind of the
Lord that he may
instruct Him?"

But we have the mind of Christ.
—*From 1 Corinthians 2, N.K.J.V.*

840
THINGS SEEN
AND UNSEEN

We do not lose heart.
Even though our outward man
is perishing,
yet the inward man is being renewed
day by day.

For our light affliction,
which is but for a moment,
is working for us a far more exceed-
ing and eternal weight of glory,
while we do not look at the things
which are seen,
but at the things which are not seen.

For the things which are seen are
temporary,
but the things which are not seen
are eternal.
—*From 2 Corinthians 4, N.K.J.V.*

841
THE PLAN OF
SALVATION

Blessed be God the Father of our
Lord Jesus Christ,
who has blessed us with all the
spiritual blessings of heaven in
Christ.

Before the world was made, he
chose us, chose us in Christ,
to be holy and spotless, and to live
through love in his presence,
determining that we should become
his adopted sons, through
Jesus Christ
for his own kind purposes,
to make us praise the glory of his
grace,
his free gift to us in the Beloved,
in whom, through his blood, we
gain our freedom, the forgive-
ness of our sins.

Such is the richness of the grace
which he has showered on us
in all wisdom and insight.

He has let us know the mystery of
his purpose,
the hidden plan he so kindly made
in Christ from the beginning
to act upon when the times had run
their course to the end:
that he would bring everything
together under Christ, as head,

everything in the heavens and
   everything on earth.

And it is in him that we were claimed
   as God's own, chosen from
   the beginning,
under the predetermined
   plan of the one
who guides all things as he decides by
   his own will;
chosen to be, for his greater glory,
the people who would put their
   hopes in Christ before he came.

Now you too, in him,
have heard the message of the truth
   and the good news of
   your salvation,
and have believed it;
and you too have been stamped with
   the seal of the Holy Spirit
   of the Promise,
the pledge of our inheritance
which brings freedom for those
   whom God has taken
   for his own,
to make his glory praised.
   —From Ephesians 1, Jerusalem.

842
ON THE INCARNATION*

Christ Jesus, . . . being in the
   form of God,
did not consider it robbery
   to be equal with God,
but made Himself of no reputation,
taking the form of a servant,
and coming in the likeness of men.

And being found in appearance
   as a man,
He humbled Himself
   and became obedient
   to the point of death,
even the death of the cross.

Therefore God also has highly
   exalted Him and given Him the

name which is above
   every name,

that at the name of Jesus
   every knee should bow,
   of those in heaven,
   and of those on earth,
   and of those under the earth,

and that every tongue should
   confess
that Jesus Christ is Lord,
to the glory of God the Father.
   —From Philippians 2, N.K.J.V.

_____

*This is perhaps the earliest Christian
   hymn.

843
IN PRAISE OF CHRIST

He is the image of the invisible God,
   the first-born of all creation;

for in him all things were created,
   in heaven and on earth,
   visible and invisible,

whether thrones or dominions
   or principalities or authorities—
all things were created through him
   and for him.

He is before all things,
and in him all things hold together.
He is the head of the body,
   the church;
he is the beginning,
   the first-born from the dead,
that in everything he might be
   pre-eminent.

For in him all the fulness of God
   was pleased to dwell,
and through him to reconcile
   to himself all things,
whether on earth or in heaven,
making peace by the blood
   of his cross.
   —From Colossians 1, R.S.V.

844
THE INCARNATE WORD

Something which has existed since
    the beginning,
that we have heard,
and we have seen with our own eyes;
that we have watched
and touched with our hands:
the Word, who is life—
this is our subject.

That life was made visible:
we saw it and we are giving our
    testimony,
telling you of the eternal life
which was with the Father
    and has been made visible to us.

What we have seen and heard
we are telling you
so that you too may be in union
    with us,
as we are in union
with the Father
and with his Son Jesus Christ.

We are writing this to you
    to make our own joy complete.
        —*From 1 John 1, Jerusalem.*

The following are also New Testament
prayers and canticles:
No. 708—The Song of Moses and the Lamb.
No. 732—Jesus' Prayer for His Disciples.
No. 745—Paul's Song of Assurance.
No. 749—A Song of Triumph.
No. 788—Love.

CALLS TO WORSHIP

    The Bible has many calls to worship. As these calls are heard, the worshiper is awed by the holiness of God and moved to respond with a sense of wonder. It is entirely appropriate to vary the form of the call, which may be extended by the pastor, worship leader, choir, or the congregation.

    Various responsive or antiphonal forms could be used. Some of the calls presented here in responsive form can also be made by an individual or the congregation, and those printed for one voice or unison can be done responsively.

    The worship leader may choose to use only a portion of the printed call. Other Scripture texts and additional sources will be found to vary the call to worship. In any case, the call to worship should generate a sense of the immediacy of God and the vibrancy of worship.

845
Psalm 29:1, 2, N.K.J.V.

Give unto the Lord, O you
    mighty ones,
Give unto the Lord glory
    and strength.
Give unto the Lord the glory due to
    His name;
Worship the Lord in the beauty
    of holiness.

846
Psalm 42:1, 2, T.E.V.

As a deer longs for a stream
    of cool water,
so I long for you, O God.
I thirst for you, the living God.
When can I go and worship in your
    presence?

847

Psalm 43:3, 4, N.I.V.

Send forth your light and your truth,
let them guide me;

**let them bring me to your
holy mountain,
to the place where you dwell.**

Then will I go to the altar of God,
to God, my joy and my delight.

**I will praise you with the harp,
O God, my God.**

848

Psalm 47:5-7, Jerusalem.

God rises to shouts of acclamation,
Yahweh rises to a blast of trumpets,
let the music sound for our God,
let it sound,
let the music sound for our King,
let it sound!
God is king of the whole world:
play your best in his honour!

849

Psalm 48:9-11, 14, T.E.V.

Inside your Temple, O God,
we think of your constant love.
You are praised by people
everywhere,
and your fame extends over all
the earth.
You rule with justice;
let the people of Zion be glad!

**This God is our God forever and
ever;
he will lead us for all time to come.**

850

Psalm 52:8, 9, N.I.V.

I trust in God's unfailing love for
ever and ever.
I will praise you forever for what you
have done;
in your name I will hope, for your
name is good.
I will praise you in the presence of
your saints.

851

Psalm 57:9-11, N.K.J.V.

I will praise You, O Lord, among
the peoples;
I will sing to You among the nations.

**For Your mercy reaches unto the
heavens,
And Your truth unto the clouds.**

Be exalted, O God, above the
heavens;
Let Your glory be above all the earth.

852

Psalm 63:1-5, adapted.

O God, You are our God.
Earnestly we seek You today.
Our souls thirst for You,
our whole being longs for You.

**Because we have seen You in
the sanctuary
and beheld Your power and glory,
we can respond.**

Lord, Your love is better than
life itself,
and we declare that our lips will
glorify You.

**We will praise You as long
as we live,
and in Your name we will lift up
our hands to do Your work.**

Lord, we will be satisfied if
   You feed us,
and we will now sing praises to
   Your name.

853

Psalm 65:1-4, Jerusalem.

Praise is rightfully yours,
   God, in Zion.
Vows to you must be fulfilled,
for you answer prayer.

*All flesh must come to you
   with all its sins;
though our faults overpower us,
you blot them out.*

Happy the man you choose,
   whom you invite to live
   in your courts.

*Fill us with the good things
   of your house,
of your holy Temple.*

854

Psalm 67:1, 2, 4, 7, Jerusalem.

May God show kindness and bless us,
and make his face smile on us!
For then the earth will acknowledge
   your ways
and all the nations will know of your
   power to save.

*Let the nations shout and
   sing for joy,
since you dispense true justice to
   the world;
you dispense strict justice
   to the peoples,
on earth you rule the nations.*

May God bless us, and let him
   be feared
to the very ends of the earth.

855

Psalm 89:8-11, 13-15, T.E.V.

Lord God Almighty, none is as
   mighty as you;
in all things you are faithful, O Lord.

*You rule over the powerful sea;
you calm its angry waves. . . .
Heaven is yours, the earth also;
you made the world and
   everything in it.*

How powerful you are!
How great is your strength!
Your kingdom is founded on righteousness and justice;
love and faithfulness are shown in all
   you do.

*How happy are the people who
   worship you with songs,
who live in the light of your
   kindness!*

856

Psalm 92:1-5, Jerusalem.

It is good to give thanks to Yahweh,
to play in honour of your name,
   Most High,

*to proclaim your love at daybreak
and your faithfulness all through
   the night
to the music of the zither and lyre,
to the rippling of the harp.*

I am happy, Yahweh, at what you
   have done;
at your achievements I joyfully
   exclaim,

*"Great are your achievements,
   Yahweh,
immensely deep your thoughts!"*

857

Psalm 95:6, 7, K.J.V.

O come, let us worship and
   bow down:
let us kneel before the Lord
   our maker.

For he is our God;
and we are the people of his pasture,
and the sheep of his hand.

858

Psalm 96:8, 9, K.J.V.

Give unto the Lord the glory due
   unto his name:
bring an offering, and come into
   his courts.
O worship the Lord in the beauty
   of holiness:
fear before him, all the earth.

859

Psalm 98, R.S.V.

O sing to the Lord a new song,
for he has done marvelous things!
His right hand and his holy arm
   have gotten him victory.

The Lord has made known
**   his victory,**
he has revealed his vindication
**   in the sight of the nations.**

He has remembered his steadfast
   love and faithfulness
to the house of Israel.
All the ends of the earth have seen
   the victory of our God.

Make a joyful noise to the Lord, all
**   the earth;**
break forth into joyous song and
**   sing praises!**

Sing praises to the Lord
   with the lyre,
with the lyre and the sound
   of melody!
With trumpets and the sound
   of the horn
make a joyful noise before the King,
   the Lord!

Let the sea roar, and all that fills it;
**   the world and those who**
**   dwell in it!**
Let the floods clap their hands;
let the hills sing for joy together
**   before the Lord, for he comes**
**   to judge the earth.**

He will judge the world with
   righteousness,
and the peoples with equity.

860

Psalm 99:5, N.K.J.V.

Exalt the Lord our God,
And worship at His footstool;
For He is holy.

861

Psalm 100:2-5, N.I.V.

Serve the Lord with gladness;
come before him with joyful songs.
   . . .
Enter his gates with thanksgiving
and his courts with praise;
give thanks to him and praise
   his name.
For the Lord is good and his love
   endures forever.

862

Psalm 107:31, 32, K.J.V.

Oh that men would praise the Lord
   for his goodness,

and for his wonderful works to the
children of men!
Let them exalt him also in the
congregation of the people,
and praise him in the assembly of the
elders.

863

Psalm 117, N.E.B.

Praise the Lord, all nations,
extol him, all you peoples;
for his love protecting us is strong,
the Lord's constancy is everlasting.
O praise the Lord.

864

Psalm 118:24-26, T.E.V.

This is the day of the Lord's victory;
let us be happy, let us celebrate! . . .
May God bless the one
who comes in the name of the
Lord!

865

Psalm 118:19-21, N.I.V.

Open for me the gates of
righteousness;
I will enter and give thanks to
the Lord.

**This is the gate of the Lord
through which the righteous
may enter.**

I will give you thanks, for you
answered me;
you have become my salvation.

866

Psalm 122:1; 118:24, R.S.V.

I was glad when they said to me,
"Let us go to the house of the Lord!"

**This is the day which the Lord
has made;
let us rejoice and be glad in it!**
(Both are excellent as separate
Calls.)

867

Psalm 134, T.E.V.

Come, praise the Lord, all
his servants,
all who serve in his Temple at night.
Raise your hands in prayer
in the Temple,
and praise the Lord!
May the Lord, who made heaven
and earth,
bless you from Zion!

868

Psalm 135:1-3, N.E.B.

O praise the Lord.

**Praise the name of the Lord;
praise him, you servants of
the Lord,
who stand in the house of the Lord,
in the temple courts of our God.**

Praise the Lord, for that is good;
honour his name with psalms,
for that is pleasant.

869

Isaiah 12:4-6, T.E.V.

"Give thanks to the Lord!
Call for him to help you!
Tell all the nations what he has done!
Tell them how great he is!

**"Sing to the Lord because of the
great things he has done.
Let the whole world hear the news.**

"Let everyone who lives in Zion
shout and sing!
Israel's holy God is great,
and he lives among his people."

870

Isaiah 42:10-12, Jerusalem.

Sing a new hymn to Yahweh!
Let his praise resound from the ends
of the earth,
let the sea and all that it holds sing
his praises,
the islands and those who
inhabit them.
Let the desert and its cities raise
their voice. . . .
Let the inhabitants . . . shout from
the mountain tops.
Let them give glory to Yahweh.

871

Isaiah 55:6, 7, N.I.V.

Seek the Lord while he may
be found;
call on him while he is near.
Let the wicked forsake his way
and the evil man his thoughts.
Let him turn to the Lord,
and he will have mercy on him,
and to our God, for he will
freely pardon.

872

Isaiah 63:7, Jerusalem.

Let me sing the praises of Yahweh's
goodness,
and of his marvellous deeds,
in return for all that he has done
for us
and for the great kindness
he has shown us in his mercy
and in his boundless goodness.

873

Jeremiah 29:12, 13, Jerusalem.

When you call to me, and come to
plead with me,
I will listen to you.
When you seek me you shall find me,
when you seek me with all
your heart.

874

Habakkuk 2:20, K.J.V.

The Lord is in his holy temple:
let all the earth keep silence
before him.

875

Matthew 11:28-30, Jerusalem.

"Come to me, all you who labour and
are overburdened,
and I will give you rest.
Shoulder my yoke and learn
from me,
for I am gentle and humble in heart,
and you will find rest for your souls.
Yes, my yoke is easy and my
burden light."

876

*Matthew 18:20; John 4:23, 24,
Jerusalem.*

"Where two or three meet in
my name,
I shall be there with them."

**"The hour will come—in fact it is
here already—**
**when true worshippers will wor-
ship the Father in spirit
and truth:**

"that is the kind of worshipper
the Father wants.
God is spirit,
and those who worship
must worship in spirit and truth."

877

Hebrews 4:14, 16, T.E.V.

Let us, then, hold firmly to the faith
    we profess.
For we have a great High Priest
who has gone into the very presence
    of God—
Jesus, the Son of God.

Let us be brave, then,
    and approach God's throne,
where there is grace.
There we will receive mercy and
    find grace
to help us just when we need it.

878

Hebrews 10:19-22, N.E.B.

So now, my friends, the blood of
    Jesus makes us free
to enter boldly into the sanctuary
by the new, living way which he has
    opened for us. . . .
We have, moreover, a great priest set
    over the household of God;
so let us make our approach
in sincerity of heart and full assur-
    ance of faith.

879

Hebrews 10:23-25, N.I.V.

Let us hold unswervingly to the hope
    we profess,

for he who promised is faithful.

And let us consider how we may
    spur one another on toward
    love and good deeds.

Let us not give up meeting together,
as some are in the habit of doing,
but let us encourage one another—
and all the more as you see the Day
    approaching.

880

Revelation 22:17, N.E.B.

"Come!" say the Spirit and the bride.

"Come!" let each hearer reply.

Come forward, you who are thirsty;
accept the water of life,
a free gift to all who desire it.

    The first verse, and often the first
several verses, of the following
Scripture Readings are also excellent Calls to Worship. Their use will
significantly expand the variety and
range of choice in Calls to Worship.

    Nos. 696-703, 705-707, 711, 712,
714, 715, 718, 723, 728, 751, 755,
780, 803, 807. Reading No. 708,
either in its entirety or by verses, is an
excellent Call.

WORDS OF ASSURANCE

One of the greatest joys of the Christian life is the knowledge that Christ has died for our sins, that we who believe are forgiven, and that God constantly cares for us. The Bible contains rich promises assuring us of God's love and willingness to forgive. These words of assurance enhance our joy in worship and increase our sense of worth as daughters and sons of God.

Words of assurance can be used after prayer, particularly prayers of confession, or they may well be incorporated into a prayer. They can be especially meaningful in the communion service.

An appropriate introduction to these passages can be a phrase such as "Hear the word of the Lord" or "Hear the words of Scripture." Some may choose to conclude the promise with a statement such as "The grace of our Lord Jesus Christ be with us all."

881

Job 19:25-27, N.K.J.V.

"I know that my Redeemer lives,
And He shall stand at last on
    the earth;
And after my skin is destroyed,
    this I know,
That in my flesh I shall see God,
Whom I shall see for myself,
  And my eyes shall behold, and
    not another."

882

Psalm 55:22, R.S.V.

Cast your burden on the Lord,
and he will sustain you;
he will never permit
    the righteous to be moved.

883

Psalm 68:19, 20, Jerusalem.

Blessed be the Lord day after day,
the God who saves us and bears
    our burdens!
This God of ours is a God who saves,
to the Lord Yahweh belong the ways
    of escape from death.

884

Isaiah 1:18, 19, N.I.V.

"Come now, let us reason together,"
    says the Lord.
"Though your sins are like scarlet,
they shall be as white as snow;
though they are red as crimson,
they shall be like wool.
If you are willing and obedient,
you will eat the best from the land."

885

Isaiah 41:10, Jerusalem.

"Do not be afraid, for I am with you;
stop being anxious and watchful,
    for I am your God.
I give you strength, I bring you help,
I uphold you with my victorious
    right hand."

886

Matthew 6:14, T.E.V.

"If you forgive others the wrongs
    they have done to you,
your Father in heaven will also
    forgive you."

887

Psalm 103:8-12, Jerusalem.

Yahweh is tender and
    compassionate,
slow to anger, most loving; . . .
he never treats us, never
    punishes us,
as our guilt and our sins deserve.
No less than the height of heaven
    over earth
is the greatness of his love for those
    who fear him;
he takes our sins farther away
than the east is from the west.

888

Matthew 7:7, 8, N.E.B.

"Ask, and you will receive;
seek, and you will find;
knock, and the door will be opened.
For everyone who asks receives,
he who seeks finds,
and to him who knocks, the door will
    be opened."

889

Romans 8:1, N.K.J.V.

There is therefore now no
    condemnation
to those who are in Christ Jesus,
who do not walk according to
    the flesh,
but according to the Spirit.

890

I John 1:9, K.J.V.

If we confess our sins,
he is faithful and just to forgive
    us our sins,
and to cleanse us from all
    unrighteousness.

891

I John 2:1, 2, N.I.V.

If anybody does sin,
we have one who speaks to
    the Father
in our defense—Jesus Christ, the
    Righteous One.
He is the atoning sacrifice
    for our sins,
and not only for ours
but also for the sins of the
    whole world.

892

I John 5:11-13, Jerusalem.

This is the testimony:
God has given us eternal life
and this life is in his Son;
anyone who has the Son has life,
anyone who does not have the Son
    does not have life.
I have written all this to you
so that you who believe in the name
    of the Son of God
may be sure that you have
    eternal life.

893

I John 5:14, 15, N.I.V.

This is the assurance we have in
    approaching God:
that if we ask anything according
    to his will,
he hears us.
And if we know that he hears
    us—whatever we ask—
we know that we have what we
    asked of him.

———

Additional valuable Words of Assurance are: Nos. 871, 873, 875, 877, and 878 in the Calls to Worship.

OFFERTORY SENTENCES

Returning our tithes and giving our offerings is a genuinely rewarding part of worship. In addition to providing the means for the continuation and growth of the Lord's work, we symbolize our faithful stewardship of all that is His, as well as the giving of ourselves to the Lord. Using scriptural commands and invitations for the offering call lends an authenticity and spiritual tone to that part of worship. The following passages provide an example of the type of scriptures that can be used.

894

1 Chronicles 29:11-13, N.I.V.

"Yours, O Lord, is the greatness
    and the power
and the glory and the majesty and
    the splendor,
for everything in heaven and
    earth is yours.

**"Yours, O Lord, is the kingdom;
you are exalted as head over all.**

"Wealth and honor come from you;
you are the ruler of all things.

**"In your hands are strength
    and power
to exalt and give strength to all.**

"Now, our God, we give you thanks,
and praise your glorious name."

895

Psalm 50:10, 11, 14, T.E.V.

"All the animals in the forest
    are mine
and the cattle on thousands of hills.
All the wild birds are mine
and all living things in the fields.
Let the giving of thanks be your
    sacrifice to God,
and give the Almighty all that
    you promised."

896

Psalm 54:6, N.I.V.

I will sacrifice a freewill offering
    to you;
I will praise your name, O Lord,
    for it is good.

897

Psalm 56:12, 13, Jerusalem.

I must fulfil the vows I made
    you, God;
I shall pay you my thank-offerings,
for you have rescued me from Death
to walk in the presence of God in the
    light of the living.

898

Psalm 96:8, T.E.V.

Praise the Lord's glorious name;
bring an offering and come into
    his Temple.

899

Proverbs 3:9, N.E.B.

Honour the Lord with your wealth
as the first charge on all your
    earnings.

900

Malachi 3:10, R.S.V.

"Bring the full tithes into the
storehouse,
that there may be food in my house;
and thereby put me to the test, says
the Lord of hosts,
if I will not open the windows of
heaven for you
and pour down for you an overflowing blessing."

901

Matthew 5:16, R.S.V.

"Let your light so shine before men,
that they may see your good works
and give glory to your Father who is
in heaven."

902

Romans 12:6-8, N.I.V.

We have different gifts,
according to the grace given us.
If a man's gift is prophesying,
let him use it in proportion to
his faith.
If it is serving, let him serve;
if it is teaching, let him teach;
if it is encouraging, let him
encourage;
if it is contributing to the needs of
others, let him give generously;
if it is leadership, let him
govern diligently;
if it is showing mercy, let him
do it cheerfully.

903

2 Corinthians 8:3-5, R.S.V.

They gave according to their means,
and beyond their means, of their
own free will,
but first they gave themselves
to the Lord.

904

2 Corinthians 8:9, Jerusalem.

Remember how generous the Lord
Jesus was:
he was rich, but he became poor
for your sake,
to make you rich out of his poverty.

905

2 Corinthians 9:6, 7, N.E.B.

Remember: sparse sowing,
sparse reaping;
sow bountifully, and you will
reap bountifully.
Each person should give as he has
decided for himself;
there should be no reluctance,
no sense of compulsion;
God loves a cheerful giver.

906

2 Corinthians 9:13-15, N.E.B.

Many will give honour to God
when they see how humbly you
obey him
and how faithfully you confess the
gospel of Christ;
and will thank him for your liberal
contribution
to their need and to the
general good. . . .
Thanks be to God for his gift
beyond words!

---

*See also Scripture Reading Nos. 820
and 821 for additional offertory passages.*

BENEDICTIONS

The use of Scripture in pronouncing the benediction provides majesty, beauty, and dignity—God's own Word blesses the congregation. Especially if the service is begun with a scriptural call to worship, the spiritual benediction adds balance and brings worship full circle.

The selections that follow enable worship leaders to avoid repetition and also present a choice of benedictions to correlate with the worship theme of the day. Some of the selections are doxologies that can be used effectively at other times in addition to the closing of worship.

From time to time the entire congregation can participate in pronouncing the benediction with appropriate pronoun changes. Other scriptures may be adapted as benedictions to build a unified worship service.

907
Genesis 31:49, N.K.J.V.

"May the Lord watch between
    you and me
when we are absent one
    from another."

908
Numbers 6:24-26, N.I.V.

"'"The Lord bless you
    and keep you;
the Lord make his face shine
    upon you
and be gracious to you;
the Lord turn his face toward you
and give you peace."'"

909
Joshua 1:9, N.I.V.

"Be strong and courageous.
Do not be terrified; do not
    be discouraged,
for the Lord your God will
    be with you
wherever you go."

910
Psalm 19:14, N.K.J.V.

Let the words of my mouth and the
    meditation of my heart
Be acceptable in Your sight,
O Lord, my strength and
    my redeemer.

911
Isaiah 60:1, 19, N.I.V.

"Arise, shine, for your light
    has come,
and the glory of the Lord rises
    upon you."
"The Lord will be your
    everlasting light,
and your God will be your glory."

912
Romans 15:13, N.I.V.

May the God of hope fill you with
    all joy and peace as you
    trust in him,
so that you may overflow with hope
by the power of the Holy Spirit.

913

2 Corinthians 13:14, R.S.V.

The grace of the Lord Jesus Christ
and the love of God
and the fellowship of the Holy Spirit
be with you all.

914

Ephesians 3:20, 21, Jerusalem.

Glory be to him whose power,
    working in us,
can do infinitely more than we
    can ask or imagine;
glory be to him from generation
    to generation
in the Church and in Christ Jesus
for ever and ever. Amen.

915

Jude 24, 25, Jerusalem.

Glory be to him who can keep you
    from falling
and bring you safe to his glorious
    presence, innocent and happy.
To God, the only God,
who saves us through Jesus Christ
    our Lord,
be the glory, majesty, authority
    and power,
which he had before time began,
now and for ever. Amen.

916

Philippians 4:8, 9, R.S.V.

Finally, brethren, whatever is true,
whatever is honorable, whatever
    is just,
whatever is pure, whatever is lovely,
whatever is gracious,
if there is any excellence,
if there is anything worthy of praise,
think about these things.
What you have learned and received
and heard and seen in me, do;
and the God of peace will be
    with you.

917

1 Timothy 1:17, K.J.V.

Now unto the King eternal,
immortal, invisible, the only
    wise God,
be honour and glory for ever
    and ever. Amen.

918

Philemon 3, K.J.V.

Grace to you, and peace,
from God our Father and the Lord
    Jesus Christ.

919

Hebrews 13:20, 21, N.I.V.

May the God of peace,
  who through the blood of the
    eternal covenant
brought back from the dead our
    Lord Jesus,
that great Shepherd of the sheep,
equip you with everything good
    for doing his will,
and may he work in us what is
    pleasing to him,
through Jesus Christ,
to whom be glory for ever and ever.
    Amen.

920

2 Peter 3:18, N.E.B.

Grow in the grace
and in the knowledge of our Lord
    and Saviour Jesus Christ.
To him be glory now and for
    all eternity!

TOPICAL INDEX OF HYMNS AND READINGS

Entries in italics refer to Scripture Readings

TOPICAL INDEX

TOPICAL INDEX

781

TOPICAL INDEX

TOPICAL INDEX

TOPICAL INDEX

TOPICAL INDEX

787

SCRIPTURAL INDEX OF
WORSHIP AIDS

789

SCRIPTURAL ALLUSIONS IN HYMNS

The letter a *following a hymn number indicates stanza 1; the letter* b *indicates stanza 2, et cetera;* r *indicates refrain.*

Indexed by Scripture Reference

Reference	Hymn
23:1, 3	513b
23:2	197b
	537a
	537b
23:2, 4	192c
	513c
23:2, 4, 5	104b
23:3	500c
	546b
23:4	208a
	508a
	537c
	546c
23:5	493r
	546d
23:6	1c
	104c
	197d
23:6	546e
23:6, 5	244a
24:1	92a
	641d
24:7	176b
	202r
	226a
24:8	243a
24:10	18e
25:3	666a
25:5	482a
25:11	535b
26:8	344a
27:1	469c
	470a
	515a
27:1-3	339a
27:3	553b
27:4	395a
27:5	525r
27:8	478b
27:10	499c
27:11	553c
27:14	339b
28:9	690a
29:2	90c
29:11	84a
30:5	6d
	37d
	348c
31:3	335c
32:7	238c
33:6	86a
33:8	3a
33:9	97a
	276a
33:20	187c
34:1, 6, 7	37a
34:7	49c
	52c
	57b
34:10	37b
34:15, 19	37c
36:5	100b
36:6	21b
36:7	1b
	489b
36:8	236d
36:9	242a
	334a
	489d
37:3	279r
37:5	519b
40:2	541c
42:1	113a
	271a
42:2	113b
	239a
42:5	113c
42:8	324d
42:11	1a
43:4	76c
	247c
45:26	240b
46:1	29c
	489b
	506a
	528d
46:2	239b
46:10	461a
	497c
46:16	109b
48:14	325d
	517c
	553a
	560a
	690a
51:1, 2	297a
51:3, 9	243b
51:5-7	297b
51:7	318r
51:10	318d
	323a
51:10-12	297c
51:12	191d
51:13-15	297d
51:17	301b
	398b
52:8	185d
	279a
52:9	243c
	550c
53:1	53a
55:6	242c
55:22	298b
	485r
	666a
57:10	666a
59:9, 11	83a
59:16	183r
59:17	645c
60:4	621d
61:1	517a
61:2	525a
62:7	525c
62:8	74c
	499c
	524d
63:3	110c
65:2	668a
65:12, 13	649c
71:1	535a
71:16	618c
72:8	227a
72:11	227c
72:12, 13	227d
72:15	227b
72:17, 19	227e
72:19	474a
73:25	569d
76:2	236d
77:19	107a
79:9	514a
81:1	12a
81:10	326c
84:1-5	62
	319a
85:1	649a
85:6	341r
85:10	192b
87:3	423a
88:9	486a
89:13	482c
	519d
89:14	114a
89:26	494b
90:1	103a
90:2	103c
90:4	103d
91:2	529b
91:4	529a
91:5, 6	49c
91:10	529c
91:14	529r
92:5	5e
94:16	618a
95:1-6	63
95:4, 5	7b
95:6	557a
96:1	22b
96:1-3	89a
96:2	340a
96:2, 3	250a
96:5, 6	89b
96:7-9	89c
96:8	341a
96:10	250b
96:11, 12	12b
96:12	213b
97:1	10a
	92c
	221a
	210b
97:8	
98:1	19a
	33a
98:1-3	13a
98:3	33b
98:4	125a
	173a
	639a
98:4-6	33c
98:4-7	13b
98:4, 6	9a
98:5, 6	19b
98:5-8	125b
98:7	213
98:7, 8	19c
98:7-9	33d
98:8	213b
98:8, 9	13c
98:9	19d
	125d
99:9	30a
100:1, 2	16a
100:1, 3	82a
100:3	16b
	82b
	7c
100:4	16c
	82c
100:5	16d
	82d
	337a
103:1	173d
103:3	370a
103:3, 4	298b
103:4	68b
103:9	4b
103:11	189b
103:13	101a
103:14	4c
	83d
103:19	622c
103:17	84b
103:20	4d
104:1	86r
104:1-3	83b
104:2	536a
104:3	84a
104:10	83c
104:14	88b
104:24	88b
104:27	88c
104:30	95b
104:33	462r
105:3	423d
106:2	105a
106:4	191a
106:48	663a
	664c
107:25	88c
107:28	85a
116:1, 2	684a
116:12	562d
118:14	22a
118:24	681a
119:10	326a
119:11	603d
119:18	60a
119:19	45a
119:57-59	273a
119:60	273b
119:105	192c
	272c
	274a
	275a
	595c
	621a
	676a
119:137	84c
119:173	667a
121:1, 2	102a
121:3, 4	102b
121:4	29b
	49b
	101d
121:5	57c
	606d
121:5, 6	102c
	528b
121:7, 8	102d
125:2	513a
126:2	269c
126:2, 3	559a
126:3	341c
126:5	358c
126:6	366d
	369c
	430a
130:5	495r
136:1	106a
	112a
136:3	106b
136:7	112b
136:25	112c
136:26	4a
	112d
137:31	85d
138:2	70a
139:7	88c
139:12	49b
139:18	498a
139:23	567b
141:2	48a
142:5	108d
143:8	685a
143:9	187b
143:11	522a
144:2	11b
145:10	94a
145:15, 16	561a
146:2	321c
147:1, 8	35a
147:4	98a
147:7	563a

SCRIPTURAL ALLUSIONS IN HYMNS

Ref	Hymn
11:15, 17	59c
12:30	639d
13:26	220a
13:32	511d
13:33	604c
	605b
13:35	207a
13:37	610c
14:12, 15	399a
14:15	397a
14:22	399b
14:22, 23	397c
14:23, 24	399c
14:24	295a
14:26	32c
14:32, 15, 17	491b
15:13	188c
15:17	154c
	283b
	321b
15:17-20	165c
15:47	317b
16:15	340a
	354d
	431c
16:15, 16	378a
16:17	378b
16:19, 20	378d

LUKE

Ref	Hymn
1:32	429c
1:35	24b
1:46-48	31a
1:49	24a
1:49, 50	31b
1:51-53	31c
1:54, 55	31d
1:68	529a
1:78	128a
2:3, 4	333b
2:4	135a
2:5	544a
2:5, 7, 13, 8	141a
2:7	24b
	120a
	121c
	124a
	133a
	136a
	140a
	143a
	360b
2:7, 5	149a
2:7, 13, 11	127a
2:7, 15	150a
2:8	118a
	119b
	129b
	142b
2:8, 9	121a
	139a
2:8-10	127b
2:8-14	144a
2:9	128a
2:10	120b
	139b
2:10, 11	119a
2:11	120c
	143d
	647c
2:11, 12	129c
	139c
2:11, 13, 14	135b
	143b
2:12	139d
	142d

Ref	Hymn
2:12, 14	122b
2:13	121b
	126b
	129a
	139e
	140b
	142a
	408c
2:13, 14	152a
2:13-15	122a
2:14	23c
	129d
	130a
	132b
	139f
	142r
2:15	138b
2:15, 11	142c
2:17	121r
2:25	70c
	204a
2:29-32	67a
	682a
2:35	298c
2:37, 39	255a
2:40	543b
	650b
	653c
2:51	149c
3:2-4	373a
3:6	255c
3:15	204a
4:1, 2	152b
	148b
	150b
4:16	380d
4:18	255b
	374c
	578b
6:38	562e
	576c
7:38	572b
7:34	187a
7:44	398b
8:1	442a
8:25	561b
8:35	480a
9:16	686a
9:20	555d
9:23	317d
9:58	140c
	152b
10:35	365c
10:39	244b
	590b
12:35	597b
12:36	597c
12:37	202c
	597d
13:29	442c
14:21	212d
14:23, 17	368c
14:27	76d
15:4	192a
	255a
	361a
15:5	197c
15:6	108a
15:18	280r
15:18, 20	296a
17:5	45d
	69c
	488c
	494a
17:20	619b

Ref	Hymn
18:16	653d
18:37	569a
19:6	114b
19:10	272a
	370b
	373a
19:41	364c
	586b
21:10, 11	213d
21:25	202b
	212b
	439c
21:25, 26	594c
21:27	253c
	438a
21:28	202c
	601c
21:28, 27	594e
21:36, 28	451b
22:19	396d
22:19, 20	410a
22:31-34, 61	491a
22:42	510c
22:44	280b
	281c
	402c
22:48	402d
22:51	567c
22:53	172b
23:11, 33	140d
23:33	144c
	159b
	288a
	491b
23:33, 53	152c
23:42	336b
23:46	280b
23:53	175b
23:56	317c
24:6	144c
	148d
	150f
	152c
	172c
24:6, 7	175c
24:29	46a
	50a
24:32	17e
	46b
	214a
24:50	176d
	415a
24:51	176a

JOHN

Ref	Hymn
1:1	261b
	555b
1:3	232b
1:9	72a
	233a
1:11	188b
1:14	119b
	132c
	141b
	188a
	276b
	489c
	637a
1:26	194b
1:29	298a
	433d
	540b
1:49	118r
1:51	462b
2:2, 9	145b

Ref	Hymn
3:7	122c
3:8	270b
3:16	78a
	164e
	341a
	572b
4:10	371a
	677a
4:14	242c
	460a
	465b
	489d
4:14, 15	493a
4:35	357a
	358a
	359a
	582b
4:38	226a
4:42	255a
5:25	177d
6:14	238d
6:31	65b
6:32	493r
	516b
6:33	167c
6:35	409c
6:37	313a
	318a
	523b
6:38	134a
	301a
6:44	477c
6:48	242c
	408a
6:51	261c
6:63	271c
	286a
	447b
	593b
6:68	486a
8:10	177b
8:11	521c
8:12	46c
	234a
	247b
	465c
8:32	17e
	140d
	204a
	343r
	396e
	585d
	654b
8:36	117b
	621c
9:1-41	188d
9:4	375a
	548c
9:25	371a
10:10	290a
10:11	361b
	555a
10:14	55a
10:15	192c
10:16	59b
	61c
	65a
	361c
	371b
10:27	549b
10:28	549a
10:30	30d
	117d
12:12, 13	413b
	34b

Ref	Hymn
12:21	245a, 494a
12:24	175a
12:26	259c, 331c
12:32	362d, 371a, 585a, 615d
13:1	196r, 396a, 577a
13:4	396c
13:4, 5	411b
13:5	397b
13:13	575c
13:14	401c, 406b
13:15	401a
13:34	69b, 266a, 634c
13:35	652r
14:2	321d, 430c, 431a, 437c
14:2	464a, 577d, 633a
14:3	213a
14:6	247a, 373c, 388b
14:9	234a, 261b
14:16	70c, 71b, 257a, 260d
14:17	650c
14:18	167b, 477b
14:27	397d, 471a
15:4	409c
15:5	18b, 295a
15:10	482b, 513a
15:11	69d
15:12	352a
15:13, 14	352b
15:14	396d, 400c, 411c
15:16	352c, 578c
15:17	352d
16:7	148d
16:8	511c
16:13	245b, 347d, 642a, 680c
16:33	239c, 514c
17:10	421e
17:17	412d
17:21	401b, 410b, 492d, 587b, 637d, 654b
17:23	655d
19:2, 13, 30	148c
19:17	288c
19:18	158a
19:23	455c
19:30	157c, 163a
19:34	300a, 332a
19:42	158c
20:1	487a
20:7	171a
20:9	158d
20:16	487b
20:19	170d
20:20	169a
20:21	578a
20:22	34c, 191b, 683b
20:25	158b
20:27	223b, 521d
20:28	238d
21:15	285b
21:17	236a, 321a

ACTS

Ref	Hymn
1:9-11	228
1:11	417b
2:1	382b
2:2	263b, 267a
2:3	264a, 270d
2:17	264e
2:24	169b
2:36	618a
2:46	259b, 403a
3:1	478a, 501a
3:14	489c
3:19	195a, 417c
3:26	293a
4:12	253a, 254r, 646a
5:31	433d
7:48	347b
8:37	486f
9:34	196c
10:34, 35	585c, 588a
10:36	229e
10:38	363b, 387b
10:43	116c
10:37	276d
11:17	521b
12:7, 9	198c
15:11	522b
17:25	21c
17:27	405a
17:28	365b

ROMANS

Ref	Hymn
1:16	457r
2:4	521c
2:12	412b
3:10	496a
5:5	214a
5:8	188a
5:10	299d
	335b, 412d
5:11	177c, 335a
5:16	341a
5:20	109a, 489d
6:4	332c
6:6	332b
6:11	198d
6:14	290b
6:23	180r
7:6	634a
8:1	198d
8:9	260r
8:15	468c
8:16	276e, 462a
8:17	468r
8:21	396e
8:22	201a, 439c, 617a
8:26	492a, 680b
8:28	387c
8:30	412d
8:34	290b
8:38, 39	186d
10:13	242b
11:33	320a
12:1	318b, 556b, 634a
12:3	511b
12:10	353b
13:11, 12	202a, 594a, 614a
14:7	541a
15:12	408c
15:13	260a, 268b
16:20	128a

1 CORINTHIANS

Ref	Hymn
1:7	621b
1:24	94c, 111c, 115b
1:30	177a, 547b
2:9	210c, 320c, 420c
2:10	413c
3:11	348a
3:12	353a
3:16	3b, 45b, 204b, 226d, 257d, 268d, 347b, 547b, 642b, 353d
5:8	
5:15	164a
6:19	193c, 316b
6:20	239a, 348a, 545a
9:26	609b
10:4	516b
10:10	593r
10:11	276c
10:13	539c
10:31	591a, 678a
11:24	402b
11:26	402a, 409a, 409b, 411d
12:4	363a
12:12	349b
12:20	316d
12:25	346e
12:31	589a
13:1, 2	81a, 589b
13:3	589c
13:4	589d
13:4-7	81b
13:8	589e
13:8, 13	81c
13:12	206b
13:13	589f
14:15	680a
15:4	170b
15:43	419c
15:52	174a, 216a, 220b, 418a, 419a, 438b, 448a
15:55	50d, 166b, 171b, 172e
15:57	42c, 335e, 343c, 377b, 578a
16:22	200r

2 CORINTHIANS

Ref	Hymn
1:3, 4	395b
3:5	483r
3:18	191d, 500b
4:5	61c
4:6	274d, 411a
4:17	629e
5:7	67b, 515c
5:14	362r
5:15	359b, 475b
5:17	191d
5:19	110b, 584b
6:1	582a
7:4	622a
7:5	313c
8:9	468b
9:14	109c, 334c
12:9	582c
12:9, 10	568a
12:10	578c
13:4	184a
13:8	647r
13:11	65r
13:14	30d, 659a

SCRIPTURAL ALLUSIONS IN HYMNS

SCRIPTURAL ALLUSIONS IN HYMNS

Indexed by Hymn Number

66.   See 65
67. a. Luke 2:29-32
    b. 2 Cor 5:17
        1 Pet 1:19
68. b. Gen 8:22
        Ps 103:4
69. a. 1 Pet 1:16
    b. John 13:34
    c. Luke 17:5
    d. John 15:11
70. a. Ps 138:2
        148:2
    b. Matt 9:36
        Ps 148:12
    c. Luke 2:25
        John 14:16
71. a. Dan 7:22
    b. John 14:16
    c. Matt 6:10
72. a. Gen 1:16
        John 1:9
    b. Phil 2:9, 10
    c. 1 Tim 1:17
73. a. Rev 4:8
    b. Rev 4:10, 8
        5:11
    c. Ps 18:11
        Ex 33:20
        Ps 18:30
74. a. Isa 48:18
    b. 1 Pet 5:6
    c. Ps. 62:8
    r. Isa 26:3, 4
76. a. 1 John 4:8
    b. 1 John 1:5
    c. Ps 43:4
    d. Luke 14:27
77. c. 1 John 4:18
78. a. John 3:16
    b. Isa 49:26
    c. Isa 49:10
    d. Rev 5:13
    r. Jer. 31:3
79. a. Jer 31:3
        Eph 3:19
    c. John 3:16
80. b. John 3:16
81.   1 Cor 13:1-13
82.   Ps 100:1-5
83. a. Ps 59:9, 11
        Dan 7:9
    b. Ps 104:1-3
    c. Ps 104:10
    d. Ps 103:14
84. a. Rev 19:6
        104:3
        29:11
    b. Ps 103:17
    c. Ps 119:137
    d. Matt. 6:13
85. a. 1 Tim 1:17
        Job 38:11
        Ps. 107:28
    b. Matt 14:25
        Mark 4:38, 39
    c. Gen 1:2
    d. Ps 137:31
86. a. Ps 33:6
    c. 1 Pet 2:24
    d. 1 Thess 4:16
    r. Ps 104:1
87. a. Gen 1:1, 3

    b. Heb. 1:1, 2
    c. John 1:14
        15:20
88. a. Gen 1:9, 6, 16
    b. Ps 104:14
        Gen 1:24, 25
        Ps 104:24
    c. Ps 107:25
        104:27
        139:7
89.   Ps 96:1-9
90. a. Heb 1:3
    b. Jas 3:17
    c. Ps 29:2
    d. John 14:9
        4:34
91. a. Rev 19:1
92. a. Ps 24:1
    c. Ps 97:1
93. a. Matt 6:26, 30
    c. Gen 8:22
    d. Mark 7:37
    r. John 1:3
94. a. Ps 145:10
    b. Gal 6:14
    c. 1 Cor 1:24
    d. Rev 5:12
95. b. Ps 104:30
96. a. Ps 19:1, 4
    c. Ps 19:3
97. a. Ps 33:9
    b. Eph 1:9
    c. Gen 1:27
    d. John 8:32
98. a. Gen 15:5
        Ps 147:4
99. a. 1 Pet 5:7
        Ps 17:8
    c. Phil 4:19
        John 15:16
    d. John 13:25
100. a. Lam 3:22, 23
        Jas 1:17
        Mal 3:6
    b. Ps 36:5
    c. Isa 55:7
        John 14:27
        Matt 28:20
101. a. Ps 103:13
    b. Isa 40:11
    c. Rom 8:38, 39
    d. Ps 121:4
    e. Job 1:21
102.   Ps 121:1-8
103.   Ps 90:1-4
104.   Ps 23:1-6
105. a. Ps 106:2
        1 Kgs 3:14
106. a. Ps 136:1
    b. Ps 136:3
        Rev 19:6
    c. John 3:16
107. a. Ps 77:19
        Nah 1:3
    b. Eze 34:26
    e. Prov 15:19
108. a. 1 Chron 17:16
        Luke 15:6
    b. Eph 1:7
    d. Ps 142:5
109. a. Rom 5:20
    b. Ps 46:16

    c. 2 Cor 9:14
110. a. 1 Pet 1:3
    b. Eccl 11:7
    c. Ps 63:3
    d. Prov 4:18
111. a. Rev 19:6
    b. John 1:14
    c. 1 Cor 1:24
    r. John 5:14
112. a. Ps 136:1
    b. Ps 136:7
    c. Ps 136:25
    d. Ps 136:26
113.   Ps 42:1-5
114. a. Ps 89:14
    b. Luke 19:6
    c. Eph 3:18, 19
115. a. Isa 7:14
    b. 1 Cor 1:24
    c. Hag 2:7
116. a. Rev 22:13
    b. Rev 7:11
    c. Dan 7:14
117. a. John 8:36
        Phil 2:7
    c. Rev 1:7
        20:8
    d. John 10:30
118. a. Luke 2:8
    b. Matt 2:2
    d. Matt 2:9
    e. Matt 2:11
    r. John 1:49
119. a. Luke 2:10, 11
    b. Luke 2:8
        John 1:14
    c. Matt 2:1, 2
        Hag 2:7
    d. Mal 3:1
120. a. Matt 2:2
        Luke 2:7
    b. Luke 2:10
    d. Luke 2:11
121.   Luke 2:7-17
122. a. Luke 2:13-15
    b. Isa 9:6
        Luke 2:12, 14
        Matt 1:23
    c. Mal 4:2
        Phil 2:7
        John 3:7
123. a. Matt 2:1, 2
    b. Matt 2:11
    c. Matt 2:11
    d. Matt 6:14
124. a. Luke 2:7
125.   Ps 98:4-9
126. b. Luke 2:13
    c. Prov 23:26
127. a. Luke 2:7, 13
    b. Luke 2:8-10
128. a. Luke 1:78
        2:9
        Rom 16:20
    b. Phil 2:7
        Matt 1:23
129.   Luke 2:8-14
130. a. Luke 2:14
131. a. Isa 11:1
    b. Matt 1:23, 21
132. a. Matt 2:11
    b. Luke 2:14

    c. John 1:14
133. a. Luke 2:7
        Matt 2:11
    b. Matt 2:2
134. a. John 6:38
        Phil 2:7
135. a. Luke 2:4
    b. Luke 2:11, 13
    c. Ps 149:4
    d. Eph 3:17
136. a. Luke 2:7
    b. Heb 2:15
137. a. Matt 2:1
    b. Matt 2:11
    c. Matt 2:11
    d. Matt 2:11
    e. Rev 19:1
138. a. Matt 2:2
    b. Luke 2:15
139.   Luke 2:8-14
140. a. Luke 2:7
    b. Luke 2:13
    c. Luke 9:58
    d. John 8:32
        Luke 23:11, 33
    e. Rev 3:20
141. a. Luke 2:5, 7, 13
    b. John 1:14
    c. Matt 2:12
142.   Luke 2:8-14
143. a. Luke 2:7
    b. Luke 2:13, 14
    d. Matt 2:2
        Luke 2:11
144. a. Luke 2:8, 10
    b. Matt 2:23
    c. Luke 23:33
        24:6
145. a. Matt 2:1, 2
    b. Matt 3:13
        John 2:2, 9
146. a. Matt 19:14
    b. Mark 10:16, 14
147. a. Mark 9:2
    b. Mark 9:4
    c. Mark 9:7
    d. Rev 1:11
148. a. Eph 3:18, 19
    b. Luke 4:2
    c. John 19:2, 13
        16:7
    d. Luke 24:6
149. a. Luke 2:7, 5
    c. Luke 2:51
    e. Matt 24:30
150. a. Luke 2:7, 15
    b. Luke 4:2
    c. Matt 21:9
    d. Matt 26:36
    e. 1 Pet 2:24
    f. Luke 24:6
    g. Rev 2:27
151. a. Isa 63:3
152. a. Luke 2:13, 14
    b. Luke 4:1, 2
        Isa 53:3
        Luke 9:58
    c. Luke 23:33, 53
        24:6
153. a. Isa 9:6
    b. Rev 5:9
    c. Matt 26:39

154. a. Phil 3:8
     b. Gal 6:14
     c. Mark 15:17
     d. Matt 22:37
155.   See 154
156. a. Matt 27:29
157. a. Matt 26:36, 40
     b. Matt 27:9, 26
     c. John 19:30
158. a. John 19:18
     b. John 20:25
     c. John 19:42
     d. John 20:9
159. a. Gal 6:14
     b. Luke 23:33
     c. 1 Pet 3:18
     d. Heb 12:2
160. a. Matt 21:9, 5-8
161. a. Matt 27:45
     b. Matt 27:46
162. a. Gal 3:13
     b. Ex 3:14
163. a. John 19:30
        Ps 22:6
     b. 1 Pet 2:24
164. a. 1 Cor 5:15
     c. Eph 4:32
     e. John 3:16
        1 Pet 1:18
165. a. Isa 53:3
        63:1
        Rev 19:12
     b. Rev 3:21
        19:16
     c. Mark 15:17-20
        1 Pet 3:22
     d. Heb 1:6
166. a. Rev 19:1
     b. 1 Cor 15:55
     c. Acts 2:24
167. a. Rev 5:9
     b. John 14:18
        Acts 1:9
        Heb 13:5
     c. John 6:33
        Matt 11:19
168. a. Job 9:7, 9
     b. Matt 18:20
169. a. John 20:20
     b. Acts 2:24
     c. Rev 19:6
170. a. Ex 14:22
     b. 1 Cor 15:4
     d. John 20:19
     e. Rev 19:6
171. a. Matt 28:2
        John 20:7
     b. Matt 28:9
        1 Cor 15:55
     c. Rom 8:37
172. b. Luke 22:53
     c. Luke 24:6
     e. 1 Cor 15:55
        Rev 19:1
173. a. Ps 98:4
        Rev 19:6
     b. Matt 28:6
     d. Ps 103:1
174. a. 1 Cor 15:52
     c. 1 Thess 4:16
175. a. John 12:24
     b. Luke 23:53

     c. Luke 24:6, 7
176. a. Luke 24:51
     b. Ps 24:7
     c. Rev 3:21
     d. Luke 24:50
177. a. 1 Cor. 1:30
        Ps 3:3
     b. John 8:10
     c. Rom 5:11
     d. John 5:25
178. a. Matt 27:51
     b. Heb 7:25
     c. Heb 1:6
     r. Isa 53:3, 12
179. a. 1 Pet 1:18
     b. 1 Pet 2:22
     c. Heb 4:16
     d. Heb 4:15
     e. Isa 53:11
180. a. Matt 18:11
     b. 2 Cor 5:19
     r. Rom 6:23
        Heb 7:25
181. r. 1 Pet 5:7
182. a. Rev 1:18
183. a. Ps 9:2
        1 John 4:19
     c. Eph 3:18, 19
        Isa 1:18
     r. Ps. 59:16
184. a. 2 Cor 13:4
        Col 3:11
     b. Eze 36:26
     c. Rev 7:14
     d. Rev 4:10
     r. Isa 1:18
185. a. Jas 2:23
     b. Matt 5:45
     d. Ps 52:8
186. a. 1 John 4:19
        Hosea 11:4
     b. Matt 22:37
     c. Matt 28:18
     d. Rom 8:38, 39
187. a. Luke 7:34
     b. Ps 143:9
     c. Ps 33:20
     d. Col 1:14
188. a. Rom 5:8
        John 1:14
     b. John 1:11
     c. Mark 11:8, 9
        15:13
     d. John 9
     e. Matt 27:21
     f. Isa 53:3
189. b. Ps 103:11
     c. Phil 4:19
        Col 3:11
     d. Rev 22:1
     r. S.S. 5:10
190. a. 1 John 4:9
     b. Rev 1:5
191. a. Isa 57:15
        Matt 9:36
        Ps 106:4
     b. John 20:22
        Heb 4:9
        Rev 22:13
        Heb 12:2
     c. Mal 3:1
        Rev 4:8
        5:11, 12

     d. 2 Cor 5:17
        Eph 5:27
        Ps 51:12
        2 Cor 3:18
        Rev 4:10
192. a. Ps 23:1, 2
        Luke 15:4
        Prov 4:18
     b. Ps 85:10
        Matt 20:28
        Phil 3:7
     c. Matt 4:19
        Ps 119:105
        23:2, 4
        John 10:15
193. a. 1 John 4:19
     c. 1 Cor 6:19
     e. 1 Pet 2:21
194. b. John 1:26
195. a. Eze 34:26
        Acts 3:19
     b. 1 Kgs 18:41
196. b. 1 Tim 1:15
     c. Acts 9:34
     r. John 13:1
197. a. Ps 23:1
     b. Ps 23:2
     c. Luke 15:5
     d. Ps 23:6
198. a. Gal 2:20
     b. Phil 2:7
     c. Acts 12:7, 9
     d. Rom 8:1
        6:11
        Heb 4:16
199. a. Matt 26:29
        Rev 19:12
     b. Rev 19:16, 23
200. r. 1 Cor 16:22
201. a. Rev 22:20
        Rom 8:22
        Isa 9:6
     b. Matt 26:27
     c. Tit 2:13
202. a. Rev 14:6
        Rom 13:12
     b. Luke 21:25
     c. Luke 21:28
        12:37
     r. Ps 24:7
        Rev 5:12
        11:15
203. a. 1 Thess 4:14
204. a. Luke 3:15
        John 8:32
        Luke 2:25
        1 Tim 1:1
        Hag 2:7
     b. Matt 2:8, 2
        2 Pet 2:9
        1 Cor 3:16
205. a. Matt 25:21
     c. Matt 24:14
        25:5
        24:31
     d. Rev 21:4
        Isa 61:1
206. a. Rev 22:4
     b. 1 Cor 13:12
     c. Isa 40:45
     d. Rev 1:5
207. a. Mark 13:35
        Matt 13:26

     b. Matt 24:27
     c. 1 Thess 4:17
     r. Rev 6:10
208. a. Ps 23:4
     b. Rev 21:4
     r. Isa 66:18
209. a. Matt. 24:30
        1 Thess 4:17
     b. 2 Thess 1:8
        Matt 13:42
     c. 1 Thess 4:17
        Rev 21:4
        22:5
     d. 1 Thess 5:6
210. a. Isa 21:12
        Matt 25:6, 7
     b. Ps 97:8
     c. Rev 21:2
        1 Cor 2:9
211. a. Rev 1:7
        Matt 16:27
     b. Rev 1:7
     c. 1 Thess 4:16
        Rev 20:11
     d. Rev 22:12
212. b. Luke 21:25
     c. Matt 25:7
     d. Luke 14:21
     r. Gen 32:24
213. a. Isa 58:1
        John 14:3
        Ps 149:5
     b. Ps 96:12
        98:8
        Matt 24:30
        Rev 13:8
     c. Ps 98:7
     d. Luke 21:10, 11
     e. Rev 11:18
        Dan 12:4
214. a. Luke 24:32
        Tit 2:13
     b. Rom 5:5
215. b. Matt 24:30
     c. Matt 28:2
     d. Rev 22:4
216. a. 1 Cor 15:52
     b. 1 Thess 4:16
217. b. Rev 6:10
     d. 1 Thess 4:13
     e. Rev 22:4
     f. Rev 21:4
218. a. Mal 3:17
219. a. Rev 19:16
        1:14, 15
     b. 1 Thess 4:16, 17
     c. Rev 22:4
     d. Rev 22:16
        21:2
220. a. Mark 13:26
     b. 1 Cor 15:52
     c. 1 Thess 4:17
221. a. Ps 97:1
        Phil 4:4
     b. Rev 3:21
     c. Rev 1:18
     d. 2 Tim 4:1
222. a. Rev 5:11, 13
     b. Rev 11:15
        22:4
     c. 2 Pet 3:12
        Rev 19:1
        20:11

223. a. Rev 19:12, 16
     b. John 20:27
     c. Isa 9:6
        Rev 11:15
     d. Matt 28:9
224. a. Matt 6:33
     b. Matt 13:44-46
     c. Matt 13:33
        Mark 4:27
     d. Matt 13:32
        8:11
     e. 1 Pet 5:6
        Matt 5:3
        18:3
225. a. Hab 2:14
226. a. Ps 24:7
        Rev 19:6
        John 4:42
     b. Isa 45:21
        Heb 13:6
        Lev 8:9
     d. 1 Cor 3:16
     e. Eph 3:16
227.   Ps 72:8-19
228. a. Acts 1:9-11
     b. Rev 17:14
     c. Rev 3:21
229. a. Rev 4:10, 11
     b. Eph 2:5
     c. Rev 5:9
     d. Rev 5:13
     e. Acts 10:36
230. a. Matt 21:9
     b. Matt 21:8
     c. Phil 2:9
231. a. Mark 11:9, 10
     d. Matt 11:29
232. a. Phil 2:10, 11
     b. John 1:3
     c. Phil 2:8, 9
     e. Matt 16:27
233. a. John 1:9
        Mal 4:2
        2 Pet 1:19
     c. Prov 4:19
234. a. John 8:12
        14:9
     b. Eph 2:14
     c. 1 John 5:12
     d. 1 John 4:20
235. a. 1 Pet 2:6, 7
     b. Rev 21:2
236. a. John 21:17
     d. Ps 76:2
        36:8
237. a. Gal 6:14
     d. Col 1:20
238. a. S.S. 1:3
     b. Prov 18:14
     c. Ps 3:3
        32:7
     d. Ps 23:1
        Jas 2:23
        John 6:14
        Heb 7:26
        Matt 21:5
        John 20:28
239. a. 1 Cor 6:20
        Ps 42:2
     b. Deut 33:27
        Ps 46:2
     c. John 16:33

240. a. Mark 1:1
        2:10
        Phil 4:1
     b. Ps 45:26
     c. Heb 1:9
241. b. Mark 1:21
242. a. Ps 36:9
     b. Is 40:8
        Rom 10:13
        Matt 7:7
     c. John 6:51
        4:14
        Ps 55:6
243. a. Ps 24:8
        Isa 9:6
        Ps 6:9
     b. Ps 9:1
        51:3, 9
     c. Ps 52:9
244. a. Ps 23:6, 5
        Rev 5:9
     b. Luke 10:39
245. a. John 12:21
     b. John 16:13
     d. Phil 4:19
        Isa 9:6
246. a. Rev 5:12
     b. Rev 20:3
     c. Rev 14:1
     r. Rev 19:1
247. a. John 14:6
     b. John 8:12
     c. Ps 43:4
248. r. 1 John 4:1
249. a. Prov 23:11
        Isa 40:11
     b. 1 Pet 3:18
        Isa 53:4
     c. Rev 11:14
250. a. Ps 96:2, 3
     b. Ps 96:10
     d. Rev 1:5
251. a. Matt 28:6
     b. Tit 2:13
     c. Phil 4:4
     r. Matt 7:14
        Eph 3:17
252.   Rev 5:9-13
253. a. Acts 4:12
     c. Luke 21:27
254. a. Matt 9:12
     d. Rev 2:10
        1 Pet 5:4
     r. Acts 4:12
255. a. Heb 1:6
        Luke 15:4
        2:37, 39
        John 4:42
     b. Luke 4:18
        Matt 11:28
     c. Luke 3:6
     d. Matt 8:26
        Rev 11:15
256.   Rev 7:9-12
257. a. John 14:16
     b. Matt 3:11
     c. Eph 4:2
     d. 1 Cor 3:16
258.   Mark 1:5-11
259. a. Matt 18:20
        9:20
     b. Acts 2:46

     c. John 12:26
260. a. Matt 3:16
        Rom 15:13
     d. John 14:16
     r. Rom 8:9
261. a. Heb 1:1
     b. Heb 1:2
        John 1:1
        14:9
     c. John 6:63
263. a. Matt 3:11
     b. Acts 2:2
     c. Eph 3:16
     d. Heb 4:12
        2 Thess 3:5
264. a. Acts 2:3
     d. Ex 34:29
        Job 1:22
     e. Acts 2:17
265. a. Job 33:4
266. a. John 13:34
     c. Matt 22:37
     e. Matt 3:16
267. a. Acts 2:2
     c. Matt 3:11
     d. Matt 3:16
268. a. 1 John 2:8
     b. Rom 15:13
     d. 1 Cor 3:16
269. a. Matt 3:16, 11
     c. Ps 126:2
270. a. Matt 3:16
     b. John 3:8
     c. Joel 2:23
     d. Acts 2:3
271. a. Matt 14:19
        Ps 42:1
     b. Col 3:11
     c. John 6:63
272. a. Luke 19:10
     b. 1 John 4:18
     c. Ps 119:105
     r. Matt 7:14
273. a. Ps 119:57-59
     b. Ps 119:60
274. a. Ps 119:105
     b. Matt 5:16
     d. 2 Cor 4:6
275. a. Ps 119:105
        Prov 4:18
     b. 2 Pet 1:21
     c. Matt 9:36
     d. Rev 14:6
276. a. Ps 33:9
     b. John 1:14
     c. 1 Cor 10:11
     d. Acts 10:37
     e. Rom 8:16
277. a. 1 Tim 5:17
        1 Pet 5:7
278. a. Matt 5:1, 2
     c. Matt 7:21
279. a. Ps 52:8
     b. Isa 1:18
     c. John 14:6
     r. Ps 37:3
280. a. Matt 11:28
     b. Luke 22:44
        23:46
     r. Luke 15:18
281. a. Gal 2:20
        Eph 2:1

     b. Phil 2:7
     c. Luke 22:44
282. a. Rev 1:5
     b. Phil 3:21
     d. Jer 23:6
283. a. Rev 3:20
     b. Mark 15:17
        Isa 52:14
        Eph 3:19
284. a. Heb 7:25
     b. Matt 6:9
     c. Isa 61:10
     r. Jas 5:16
285. a. Matt 4:19
     b. John 21:15
286. a. John 6:63
     c. 1 Tim 4:10
        2:5
287. a. Matt 11:28
288. a. Luke 23:33
     b. Matt 27:29
     c. John 19:17
289. a. Eph 3:17
     b. Col 1:27
     r. Rev 3:20
290. a. John 10:10
     b. Rom 8:34
        6:14
        8:37
291. c. Rev 2:4
292. a. Matt 9:28
     d. Rev 22:4
293. a. Acts 3:26
     c. Heb 4:16
     d. Mal 4:2
294. c. Ps 119:164
     r. Rev 12:11
295. a. 1 Tim 1:15
        Mark 14:24
        John 15:5
     b. Eph 3:18, 19
     c. Col 3:11
296. a. Luke 15:18, 20
     d. Gal 2:20
     e. 1 John 1:9
        Isa 1:18
297.   Ps 51:1-15
298. a. John 1:29
        Isa 1:18
     b. Col 1:19
        Ps 103:3, 4
        55:22
        Matt 11:30
     c. Luke 2:35
299. a. Matt 6:12
     b. Matt 18:35
     c. Matt 18:24, 28
     d. Rom 5:10
300. a. Deut 32:4
        John 19:34
301. a. John 6:44
        1 Pet 2:4
     b. Ps 51:17
        1 John 1:9
302. a. Rev 1:5
     d. Rom 5:1
303. a. Isa 32:2
     b. Matt 27:36
     c. Gal 6:14
304. a. Heb 11:34, 36
     c. Matt 6:44
305. r. Matt 16:26

b.	Heb 1:11	409.	a.	1 Cor 11:26		Rev 5:10		1 Pet 2:11
	4:9		b.	1 Cor 11:26	d.	Ps 105:3		Tit 2:13
c.	Rev 21:4		c.	John 6:35		1 John 2:17		Rev 22:20
	7:9			John 15:4	424.	c.	Rev 21:19-21	b.	Eze 37:12
387. a.	Mal 4:2		d.	Rev 19:9			Eph 2:20		Rev 20:13
b.	Acts 10:38	410.	a.	Luke 22:19, 20	d.	Gal 6:14	c.	Luke 13:29
c.	Rom 8:28		b.	John 17:21	e.	Heb 11:16	d.	Rev 19:4
388. a.	Ex 20:9-11		c.	Tit 2:13	425. a.	Rev 5:11, 12		1 Pet 5:4
b.	Ex 20:8			Rev 22:5	b.	Rev 5:9	r.	Rev 22:12
	John 14:6	411.	a.	2 Cor 4:6		7:14	443. a.	Rev 21:25
	Rev 21:6		b.	John 13:4, 5		19:8	b.	Rev 21:4
c.	Isa 58:13		c.	John 15:14	c.	Matt 25:21	444. a.	Heb 11:13
	Eph 3:17			Matt 26:26, 27	d.	Jer 33:8		Rev 22:1
389. a.	Isa 58:13		d.	1 Cor 11:26	r.	Isa 6:3	b.	Rev 21:26
b.	Isa 6:3	412.	a.	1 Pet 2:22	426. a.	Rev 22:4	c.	Rev 21:23, 4
c.	Ex 20:8			Isa 1:18	b.	Rev 22:5	d.	Rev 20:15
390. b.	Job 38:7		b.	Rom 2:12	c.	Mark 10:45	f.	Rev 22:3
c.	Ex 31:13		c.	Rev 19:8	r.	Rev 5:13	445. a.	Heb 11:10
e.	Rev 7:9		d.	Rom 5:10	427. a.	Rev 21:16, 25	446. a.	Rev 21:1
391. a.	Isa 58:13			8:30	b.	Rev 21:21	b.	Rev 21:3
392. a.	Lev 23:32			John 17:17	c.	Rev 21:25, 1	c.	Rev 21:4
b.	Ex 20:9, 10		r.	Eph 3:19	d.	Rev 21:23	d.	Rev 6:10
c.	Gen 2:3	413.	a.	Heb 1:1	r.	Rev 21:4	447. a.	Eze 34:12
d.	Isa 66:23			Rev 2:8	428. b.	Isa 35:10	b.	Rev 7:12
393. a.	Ex 20:11		b.	Heb 1:1, 2	429. a.	Rev 21:2		John 6:63
d.	Gen 2:3			John 10:30		Ex 3:8	c.	Rev 21:21, 4
	Heb 4:9		c.	1 Cor 2:10	c.	Luke 1:32	d.	Rev 1:7
394. b.	Rev 12:17	414.		Gal 5:22, 23		Eccl 10:19		1 Thess 4:16
c.	Mark 2:28	415.	a.	Matt 28:18		Rev 3:5		Rev 22:20
	Isa 48:18			Luke 24:50	430. a.	Ps 126:6	448. a.	1 Cor 15:52
d.	Rev 22:14			Acts 1:9		Rev 21:2		Rev 21:6
395. a.	Ps 27:4		b.	Dan 7:9, 10, 13	b.	Rev 11:5	b.	Heb 10:23
b.	2 Cor 1:3, 4		c.	1 Thess 4:16	c.	Ps 16:11	r.	1 Thess 4:17
396. a.	John 13:1			Rev 1:7		John 14:2	449. c.	Rev 22:5
d.	John 13:4	416.	a.	Dan 7:10	431. a.	Rev 22:1	c.	Deut 3:27
	Luke 22:19			Matt 12:36		John 14:2	r.	Rev 20:4
	John 15:14			2 Tim 4:8	b.	Rev 22:2	450. a.	Rev 21:2, 21, 22
e.	John 8:32		b.	1 Pet 4:17		Rev 7:16	b.	Rev 22:2
	Rom 8:21		r.	Dan 5:27	c.	Mark 16:15	c.	Rev 4:4
397. a.	Mark 14:15	417.	a.	Rev 14:7	432. a.	Rev 22:1		7:9
b.	John 13:5		b.	Acts 1:11	433. d.	Isa 56:1	451. b.	Luke 21:36, 28
c.	Mark 14:22, 23		c.	Dan 12:13		John 1:29	453. a.	Rev 22:1
d.	John 14:27			Rev 3:5		Hag 2:7	c.	Rev 7:9
398. a.	Matt 26:26-28			Acts 3:19		Matt 24:30		21:21
b.	Ps 51:17		d.	Rev 14:1		Acts 5:31		22:2
	Luke 7:44			15:2	434. a.	Rev 21:21, 19	454. a.	Mark 8:38
	Matt 11:29	418.	a.	Heb 10:27	b.	Rev 21:4	b.	1 Thess 4:17
399. a.	Mark 14:12, 15			1 Cor 15:52		19:8	455. a.	Jer 31:3
b.	Mark 14:22		b.	Isa 25:9		Heb 12:23	b.	Rom 10:6, 7
c.	Mark 14:23, 24		c.	Rev 20:12, 13	c.	Rev 21:2	c.	John 19:23
400. c.	John 15:14			Matt 24:29	435. a.	1 Pet 5:1		Matt 14:36
401. a.	John 13:15		d.	Matt 25:34	b.	Eph 2:8	e.	Eph 4:6
b.	John 17:21	419.	a.	1 Cor 15:52	r.	Rev 22:4	456. a.	1 John 4:9
c.	John 13:14		b.	Isa 6:19	436. a.	Rev 21:25, 4	c.	Matt 11:28
402. a.	1 Cor 11:26			1 Cor 2:9	437. a.	Rev 21:4		Col 2:6
b.	1 Cor 11:24		c.	1 Cor 15:43	b.	Rev 21:23	457. d.	Matt 5:6
c.	Luke 22:44	420.	a.	Rev 21:4	c.	John 14:2	r.	Rom 1:16
d.	Luke 22:48		b.	Rev 21:19-21	438. a.	Luke 21:27	458. r.	1 John 4:17
403. a.	Acts 2:46		c.	Rev 22:2	b.	1 Cor 15:52	459. a.	Rev 21:2
404. a.	Gal 2:20			1 Cor 2:9	c.	1 Thess 4:17	460.	John 4:14
b.	1 Pet 1:21		d.	Phil 3:14	439. a.	Isa 21:11, 12	461. a.	Ps 46:10
405. a.	Acts 17:27			Rev 2:7	b.	Phil 3:14	c.	1 Thess 4:17
b.	Ex 16:15	421.	a.	John 17:10	c.	Luke 21:25	462. a.	Heb 1:14
	Isa 35:6		b.	Ps 18:26		Rom 8:22		Rom 8:16
406. b.	John 13:14		c.	2 Tim 4:8		1 Thess 4:16		Rev 1:5
408. a.	Rev 1:5		e.	Rev 21:21	d.	Rev 7:17, 14	b.	John 1:51
	Ps 3:3	422.	r.	Isa 51:11	440. a.	Tit 2:13	c.	Matt 24:42
	John 6:51	423.	a.	Ps 87:3	b.	Rev 20:4	r.	Ps 104:33
c.	Luke 2:13			Matt 16:18	c.	Rev 22:20	463.	Isa 26:3
	Rom 15:12			Isa 60:18		1 John 3:2	464. a.	John 14:2
d.	Heb 9:28		b.	Rev 22:1	441. a.	Tit 2:13	b.	Eph 6:16
	Rev 1:5		c.	Ex 13:21	442. a.	Luke 8:1	465. a.	Matt 11:28
				Rev 1:5				

	Isa 32:18	
b.	John 4:14	
c.	John 8:12	
466. r.	Phil 4:7	
467. a.	Matt 6:25	
c.	S.S. 8:6	
e.	Matt 26:56	
468. a.	Hag 2:8	
b.	2 Cor 8:9	
c.	Eph 2:12	
	Rom 8:15	
r.	Rom 8:17	
469. a.	Deut 33:27	
	Phil 4:7	
b.	Prov 4:18	
c.	Ps 27:1	
470. a.	Ps 27:1	
d.	2 Tim 4:9	
472. c.	Isa 35:10	
473.	Gen 28:11-18	
474. a.	Ps 72:19	
d.	Rev 17:14	
475. b.	2 Cor 5:15	
r.	Jer 46:11	
476. a.	Matt 11:30	
b.	1 Pet 5:7	
477. a.	Matt 11:28	
b.	John 14:18	
c.	John 6:48	
	Rev 22:1	
478. a.	Acts 3:1	
	Heb 4:16	
b.	Ps 27:8	
	1 Pet 5:7	
c.	Deut 33:27	
479. r.	Hab 2:20	
480. a.	Luke 8:35	
b.	Mark 1:16-18	
e.	1 Kings 19:11	
481.	See 480	
482. a.	Ps 25:5	
b.	John 15:10	
c.	Ps 89:13	
483. r.	2 Cor 3:5	
484. a.	1 Pet 2:7	
	Heb 11:13	
b.	Rev 4:3	
	22:4	
485. r.	Ps 55:22	
486. a.	Ps 88:9	
	John 6:68	
c.	Heb 12:2	
f.	Acts 8:37	
487. a.	John 20:1	
b.	John 20:16	
c.	Matt 28:10	
488. c.	Luke 17:5	
d.	1 John 4:7	
489. a.	Jer 31:3	
	Isa 32:2	
b.	Ps 46:1	
	Ps 36:7	
c.	Col 3:1	
	Acts 3:14	
	Isa 64:6	
	John 1:14	
d.	Rom 5:20	
	Ps 36:9	
	Rev 22:17	
	John 4:14	
490.	See 489	
491. a.	Luke 22:31, 32	

b.	Mark 14:32, 15	
	Luke 23:33	
c.	1 Pet 5:7	
492. a.	Rom 8:26	
d.	Eccl 9:10	
d.	John 17:21	
r.	1 John 3:2	
493. a.	John 4:14, 15	
r.	Ps 23:5	
	John 6:32	
494. a.	John 12:21	
	Luke 17:5	
b.	Ps 89:26	
d.	1 Thess 1:10	
495. r.	Ps 130:5	
496. b.	1 Kgs 7:48, 50	
497. b.	Ps 19:12	
c.	Ps 46:10	
498. a.	Ps 139:18	
d.	1 Thess 4:17	
499. a.	1 Pet 5:7	
c.	Matt 11:28	
	Ps 62:8	
	27:10	
500. a.	1 Pet 1:16	
b.	2 Cor 3:18	
c.	Ps 23:3	
501. a.	Acts 3:1	
	1 Pet 5:6	
b.	1 Pet 5:7	
502. b.	Prov 3:24	
d.	Isa 50:4	
503. a.	Mark 6:31	
504. a.	Neh 5:19	
505. r.	Jas 5:16	
506. a.	Ps 46:1	
	1 Pet 5:8	
b.	Jas 5:4	
c.	2 Pet 2:4	
d.	1 Pet 1:23	
	Dan 7:27	
507. a.	Gal 2:20	
b.	Matt 1:29	
d.	Heb 4:15	
508. a.	Ps 23:4	
b.	Prov 3:24	
r.	Isa 41:10	
509. a.	2 Tim 2:19	
	Heb 6:18	
b.	Isa 41:10	
c.	Isa 43:2	
d.	Isa 43:2	
e.	Heb 13:5	
510. a.	Isa 26:4	
	Matt 7:25	
b.	1 Pet 5:7	
c.	Luke 22:42	
d.	Heb 13:5	
511. a.	Tit 2:11	
b.	Rom 12:3	
c.	John 16:8	
d.	Mark 13:32	
	1 Thess 4:7	
r.	2 Tim 1:12	
512. c.	Matt 11:29	
d.	Col 3:11	
r.	2 Thess 2:16, 17	
	Matt 14:27	
513. a.	John 15:10	
	Ps 125:2	
b.	Ps 23:1, 3	
c.	Ps 23:2, 4	

514. a.	Ps 79:9	
b.	Matt 16:18	
c.	John 16:33	
515. a.	Ps 27:1	
c.	2 Cor 5:7	
d.	Col 3:11	
	Isa 49:26	
516. a.	Deut 32:12	
	Mark 7:37	
b.	John 6:32	
	1 Cor 10::4	
517. a.	Ps 61:1	
b.	Heb 12:28	
c.	Ps 48:14	
	Rev 21:4	
518. a.	2 Pet 1:4	
b.	1 Pet 1:23	
c.	Hos 11:4	
	Eph 6:17	
519. a.	Ps 3:3	
b.	Ps 37:5	
d.	Ps 89:13	
520. a.	Isa 9:6	
	Ex 33:22	
b.	Ps 16:8	
	Deut 33:25	
c.	Eph 3:19	
d.	1 Thess 4:17	
r.	Isa 32:2	
521. a.	1 Tim 1:15	
b.	Acts 11:17	
c.	Rom 2:4	
	John 8:11	
d.	John 20:27	
522. a.	Ps 143:11	
b.	Acts 15:11	
	Heb 6:19	
c.	Ps 18:18	
d.	1 Thess 4:16	
	Phil 3:9	
	Jude 24	
r.	Matt 7:24, 26	
523. a.	Rev 1:18	
b.	John 6:37	
c.	Matt 1:21	
d.	Matt 9:12	
524. a.	1 Pet 3:5	
	Hag 1:13	
b.	1 John 1:7	
d.	Ps 62:8	
525. a.	Ps 61:2	
c.	Ps 62:7	
r.	Ps 27:5	
526. a.	1 John 4:14	
	Matt 28:6	
r.	John 14:19	
527. a.	Ex 25:22	
b.	Heb 1:9	
c.	Heb 4:16	
528. a.	Deut 32:4	
	Isa 25:4	
b.	Ps 121:5, 6	
d.	Ps 46:1	
529. a.	Ps 91:4	
	Luke 1:68	
b.	Ps 91:2	
c.	Ps 91:10	
d.	Ps 91:14	
530. a.	Isa 48:18	
	2 Kings 4:26	
b.	1 John 1:9	
c.	Col 2:14	
d.	Rev 6:14	

531. a.	Matt 7:24, 25	
b.	Matt 7:26	
c.	Isa 28:16	
r.	Deut 32:4	
532. a.	Deut 33:25	
b.	Isa 9:6	
c.	2 Pet 1:4	
533. b.	Heb 12:11	
534. r.	Heb 6:19	
535. a.	Ps 71:1	
b.	Ps 25:11	
c.	Ps 31:3	
	Phil 4:19	
d.	Jude 24	
536. a.	Ps 104:2	
b.	Rev 11:18	
537.	Ps 23:2, 4	
538. a.	Neh 9:19, 20	
b.	Ps 18:2	
	Neh 9:19, 20	
c.	Jer 12:5	
539. a.	1 Pet 2:21	
	Matt 7:14	
c.	1 Cor 10:13	
	Matt 7:7	
r.	Rev 1:5	
540. a.	Matt 18:3	
b.	John 1:29	
c.	Phil 2:5	
d.	1 Pet 2:9	
541. a.	Rom 14:7	
b.	Isa 58:7	
c.	Ps 40:2	
542. a.	Mark 10:13, 16	
b.	Mark 10:14	
543. a.	Matt 18:2	
b.	Luke 2:40	
c.	1 Pet 2:21	
d.	Heb 13:5	
544. a.	Luke 2:5	
	1 Pet 2:22	
b.	Matt 19:14	
c.	Mark 10:16	
d.	1 Pet 2:2	
545. a.	Ps 23:1, 2	
	1 Cor 6:20	
546.	Ps 23:1-6	
547. b.	1 Cor 1:30	
	1 Cor 3:16	
548. a.	Ps 23:1	
b.	1 John 2:13	
c.	John 9:4	
549. a.	John 10:28	
b.	John 10:27	
c.	1 Pet 2:21	
550. b.	Eph 3:17	
c.	Ps 52:9	
551. b.	Mark 4:39	
c.	Isa 43:1, 2	
552.	See 546	
553. a.	Ps 48:14	
b.	Ps 27:3	
c.	Ps 27:11	
554. a.	Gen 5:24	
555. a.	John 10:11	
	Rev 17:14	
b.	John 1:1	
	Phil 2:7	
c.	Heb 3:1	
d.	Luke 9:20	
556. a.	Lev 23:10	
b.	Rom 12:1	

SCRIPTURAL ALLUSIONS IN HYMNS

557. a. Ps 95:6	579. r. 1 John 3:18	Matt 24:36, 32
b. Matt 13:25	580. a. Matt 5:16	d. Tit 2:13
Mark 4:28	581. b. Jas 2:17	Rev 2:25
c. Matt 13:41, 42	582. a. 2 Cor 6:1	Matt 25:21
d. Tit 2:14	b. John 4:38	Rev 3:21
558. a. Mark 4:27	c. 2 Cor 12:9	601. a. Isa 21:11
b. Matt 20:4	583. a. 1 Pet 2:3-5	c. Isa 21:12
25:40	b. 1 Pet 2:5, 9	Luke 21:28
c. Gal 5:22	c. 1 Pet 2:9, 10	602. a. Matt 25:21
559. a. Ps 126:2, 3	584. b. 2 Cor 5:19	Isa 25:9
560. a. Ps 150:6	585. a. John 12:32	Eph 3:18, 19
Gen 1:21, 25	c. Acts 10:34, 35	b. Rev 21:18, 21
Ps 48:14	d. John 8:32	c. Matt 16:27
20:5	586. b. Luke 19:41	Rev 7:9
Ex 13:21	587. a. Gal 3:28	Matt 25:21
b. Judg 5:20	b. John 17:21	d. Jas 1:12
Isa 40:26	c. Matt 6:9	603. a. Matt 26:41
Ps 148:9, 7, 12	588. a. Acts 10:34, 35	b. Eph 6:13
561. a. Ps 145:15, 16	b. Eph 2:14	d. Ps 119:111
b. Luke 8:25	c. Heb 6:6	604. a. Matt 24:36
Matt 6:11	589. a. 1 Cor 12:31	c. Mark 13:33
r. Jas 1:17	b. 1 Cor 13:1, 2	Matt 25:7
562. b. Deut 26:2, 3	c. 1 Cor 13:3	r. Matt 24:44, 30
d. Ps 116:12	d. 1 Cor 13:4	605. b. Mark 13:33
e. Luke 6:38	S.S. 8:6	c. Eccl 8:8
563. a. Ps 147:7	e. 1 Cor 13:8	Rev 3:11
564. b. Ps 16:11	f. 1 Cor 13:13	606. a. Josh 24:15
565. a. Heb 13:15	590. a. 1 John 1:7	d. Ps 121:5
566. a. Eccl 11:7	b. Luke 10:39	607. a. 1 Pet 5:10
567. a. Isa 64:8	591. a. 1 Cor 10:31	b. 2 Tim 3:13
b. Ps 139:23	Isa 43:15	608. a. 1 John 5:4
Isa 1:18	b. Phil 4:13	b. Eph 6:17, 14
c. Matt 6:13	592. a. Isa 21:11	c. Rev 3:5
Luke 22:51	c. Isa 9:6	r. 1 John 5:4
d. Eph 3:17	593. a. 1 John 4:14	609. a. 2 Tim 2:3
568. a. 2 Cor 12:9, 10	Heb 6:19	Rev 14:4
569. a. Luke 18:37	b. John 6:63	b. 1 Cor 9:26
b. Mark 9:24	r. 1 Cor 10:10	f. Rev 5:13
c. Prov 8:14	594. a. Jas 2:5	610. a. Eph 6:14, 16
d. Ps 73:25	Rom 13:11, 12	b. Eph 6:12
570. a. Gal 2:20	c. Luke 21:25, 26	c. Mark 13:37
c. Matt 12:36	d. 1 John 2:17	d. Isa 35:6
d. Phil 4:19	e. Matt 6:22	r. Josh 7:8
1 Thess 5:23	Luke 21:28, 27	611. a. Phil 3:14
571. r. Micah 5:8	595. a. Matt 25:6	c. Heb 12:1
572. a. Matt 22:37	b. Matt 25:5	Phil 3:13
b. Ex 32:29	c. Ps 119:105	d. Rev 4:10
Luke 7:38	Heb 13:5	612. a. 2 Tim 2:3
John 3:16	d. Matt 5:16	b. Jas 4:7
c. Mark 10:45	r. Matt 25:7	c. Eph 4:3, 4
Phil 2:8	596. a. Jer 6:16	d. Matt 16:18
r. Num 18:29	b. Dan 2:38-40	e. Rev 5:13
573. r. Isa 6:8	c. Dan 2:42, 44	613. a. 1 Tim 6:12
574. a. Gen 5:24	597. b. Luke 12:35	b. Heb 12:1, 2
d. Prov 4:18	c. Luke 12:36	c. 1 Pet 5:7
575. a. Matt 25:40	d. Luke 12:37	d. Mal 3:6
10:42	598. a. Matt 24:29	Col 3:11
c. Matt 5:16	25:7	614. a. Jer 51:12
John 13:13	b. Rev 7:14	Rom 13:12
576. c. Luke 6:38	4:10	b. Jer 51:11
2 Tim 6:17	c. Dan 2:44	c. 1 Pet 5:4
577. a. John 13:1	Rev 10:7	615. a. Matt 22:37
b. Matt 6:25	d. Dan 2:44	c. 1 John 2:14
c. Matt 20:6	e. Heb 7:25	d. John 12:32
d. John 14:2	r. Rev 22:12	616. a. Eph 6:10, 11
578. a. John 20:21	599. a. Matt 25:1-6	b. Eph 6:13
1 Cor 15:57	b. Rev 19:9	c. Eph 6:12, 18
b. Luke 4:18	c. Rev 4:10	617. a. Joel 3:9
c. 2 Cor 12:10	600. a. Rev 3:11	Rev 20:8
John 15:16	1 Thess 5:1	Rom 8:22
d. Matt 16:24	b. Matt 26:41	b. Eph 6:14-17
25:21	1 Thess 5:2	c. Eph 6:12
		d. Rev 12:12

e. Matt 25:21
618. a. Ps 94:16
Isa 13:2
Acts 2:36
b. Ex 10:11
c. Ps 71:16
Isa 31:3
Eph 6:13
d. Rev 2:10
619. b. Luke 17:20
c. 2 Tim 4:8
620. a. Josh 3:15
b. Rev 21:22
c. Rev 22:4
r. Rev 15:3
621. a. Jude 24
Ps 119:105
b. 1 Cor 1:7
Col 3:24
Jas 1:27
Ps 60:4
c. Lev 25:10
Rom 8:2
John 8:36
622. a. 2 Cor 7:4
Isa 58:11
b. Isa 11:9
Ps 103:19
623. a. Matt 8:19
c. Heb 4:15
d. Heb 11:37
r. Rev 1:5
624. r. 1 John 2:6
625. c. Phil 3:14
c. Eph 6:16
626. a. Rev 21:25
b. Eccl 9:10
c. Heb 5:2
d. Rev 21:4
r. 1 Pet 5:10
627. a. Ex 28:12
2 Tim 2:3
628. a. Gen 28:12
d. Rev 11:12
629. a. Heb 11:13
Matt 11:29
b. Matt 4:2
c. 1 Pet 1:6
d. 1 Pet 1:7
Gen 28:12
e. 2 Cor 4:17
630. a. Eph 2:6
b. Eccl 1:7
c. Phil 3:14
631. c. Isa 28:16
632. r. Rev 21:2
633. a. John 14:2
d. Phil 3:14
Rev 21:21
634. a. Rom 7:6
12:1
b. Matt 25:15
Mal 3:8
c. John 13:34
d. Matt 28:19
635. b. Matt 22:37
636. a. 1 Tim 6:17
b. Eph 2:13
Rev 22:3
c. Matt 25:14
9:35
637. a. John 1:14

806

	Eph 1:22	645.	a.	Isa 40:26	654.	b.	John 8:32
	b.	Matt 10:8		b.	1 Sam 7:12		17:21
	Hag 2:8		c.	Ps 59:17	655.	d.	John 17:23
	Isa 9:6		d.	Rev 21:25	656.	a.	Matt 19:6
	d.	John 17:21	646.	a.	Acts 4:12	658.	a.	Matt 19:6
	Matt 6:10		Eph 5:23	659.	a.	2 Cor 13:14
638.	a.	Matt 2:11	647.	a.	Matt 24:30	660.	a.	Eph 3:21
	b.	1 Chron 29:5		Isa 63:3	661.	a.	Rev 4:8
639.	a.	Ps 98:4		b.	Zech 9:14	662.	a.	Hab 2:20
	c.	Tit 1:7		Dan 5:27	663.	a.	Ps 106:48
	d.	Mark 12:30		c.	Luke 2:11	664.	a.	Ps 106:48
640.	a.	Eccl 3:11		r.	2 Cor 13:8	665.	a.	1 Chron 29:14
	Gen 1:28	648.	b.	Heb 11:14	666.	a.	Ps 55:22
	c.	Gen 2:8		Prov 3:17		16:8
	Matt 6:9	649.	a.	Ps 85:1		57:10
641.	a.	Gen 1:28		c.	Ps 65:12, 13		25:3
	b.	Eccl 3:11	650.	a.	Eph 3:15	667.	a.	Ps 119:173
	c.	Rev 11:18		b.	Luke 2:40	668.	a.	Ps 65:2
	d.	Ps 24:1		c.	John 14:17	669.	a.	Num 6:24-26
642.	a.	John 16:13	651.	b.	Eph 5:25	670.	a.	1 Chron 29:14
	b.	1 Cor 3:16	652.	r.	John 13:35	671.	a.	Heb 4:16
	Rom 12:1	653.	a.	1 Sam 1:27	672.	a.	Eph 5:18
	c.	1 Thess 5:23		b.	Matt 6:13	673.	a.	Gen 31:49
643.	a.	1 Tim 6:17		c.	Luke 2:40	674.	a.	1 Sam 25:6
	c.	Matt 6:13		d.	Luke 18:16		
644.	c.	Matt 10:8					

675. a. Num 6:24
676. a. Ps 119:105
677. a. John 4:10
678. a. 1 Cor 10:31
679. See 678
680. a. 1 Cor 14:15
b. Rom 8:26
c. John 16:13
681. a. Ps 118:24
682. a. Luke 2:29-32
683. a. John 20:19
b. John 20:22
684. a. Ps 116:1, 2
685. a. Ps 143:8
686. a. Luke 9:16
687. a. Hab 2:20
688. a. Gen 28:16
690. a. Ps 48:14
28:9
691. a. Ps 5:8
4:8
692. a. Hab 2:20
693. a. Isa 30:18
694. a. Ps 148:1, 2
695. a. Ps 148:1, 2

HYMNS SUITABLE FOR
SENTENCES AND RESPONSES

In addition to hymns listed under "Sentences and Responses" in the Topical Index, many others contain stanzas that can be used for calls to worship, invitations and responses to prayer, before or after the offering, or benedictions and "maranatha" ("the Lord is coming") sentences for the closing of worship. For the latter, all hymns listed under "Closing of Worship" in the Topical Index may also be used. The following is a partial list. The letter *a* following a hymn number indicates stanza 1; the letter *b* indicates stanza 2, et cetera; *r* indicates refrain.

Call to Worship

All people that on earth do dwell	16a
As pants the hart	113d
As with gladness men of old	123a, b
Before Jehovah's awful throne	82a
Come, all Christians, be	634a, d
Come, Christians, join to sing	10a
Come, Thou almighty King	71a
Give to our God	106a, b
God Himself is with us	3a
God is here	61a
God is love	349a, b
God is our song	22a, b
Good Christian friends, rejoice	173a
Holy God, we praise Your name	30a
Holy, holy, holy	73a
Joyful, joyful, we adore Thee	12a
Let all on earth their voices raise	89a

Let us with a gladsome mind	112a
Lord, in the morning	39a
Lord of creation	320a
Now that daylight fills the sky	42a, d
O come, let us sing	63a
O for a thousand tongues	250a
O God, unseen, yet ever near	405a, b
O love of God most full	77a
O praise ye the Lord	20a
O worship the King	83a
O worship the Lord	6a
Of the Father's love begotten	116b, c
Open now the gates of beauty	45
Praise, my soul, the King of heaven	4a
Praise the Lord, His glories	25a
Praise to the Lord	1a
Praise ye the Father	70a
Rejoice, the Lord is King	221a

Rejoice, ye pure in heart 27a
Sing praise to God 29a
Sing to the great Jehovah's praise 105a
This is the threefold truth 203a
When morning gilds the skies 43a, b

Invitation or Response to Prayer
As pants the hart 113a
Breathe on me, Breath of God 265
Draw us in the Spirit's tether. 259a
Eternal Love, we have no good 496a, b
Father, we thank You 566d
Forgive our sins .... 299a, d
Heavenly Father, bless us now 293a
Hover o'er me, Holy Spirit 260r
Lift up your heads 226e
Like Jesus 492a
Lord, in the morning 39a
Lord of creation .... 320b, c
O God, unseen, yet ever near. 405a, b
O love of God most full 77a
Open my eyes, that I may see 326a
Open now Thy gates of beauty 45
Prince of Peace, control my will 153a, c
Savior, teach me 193a
Spirit of God 266a
Still, still with Thee 498a
Tread softly 479a

Offering Response
All things are Thine 376a
As saints of old .... 556a, c
As with gladness men of old... 123c
Come, all Christians 634b
Come, sing a song of harvest. 562a, d
Lord of all good 635a
My Maker and my King 15
Son of God, eternal Savior 637b

Benediction/Maranatha
An upper room 397d
As Jacob with travel 628r
As with gladness men of old... 123d
Blest be the tie .... 350a, d
Breathe on me, Breath of God 265
Christ is coming 201a
Eternal God, whose power upholds 90d
Every flower that grows 550c
Father, lead me day by day ... 482a
Fight the good fight 613
Give to our God immortal praise 106d
God is love 349c
God, who spoke in the beginning 87c
God will take care of you 99a
Gracious Father, guard 621
Hail Him the King of glory ... 202c, r
How sweet are the tidings 442r
I want Jesus to walk with me.. 624a
Jesus, guide our way .... 553a, c
Lift high the cross 362a
Lift up your heads 226e
Lord of creation .... 320d, e
Lord of the boundless curves of 97g
Lord, whose love 363c
My song shall be of Jesus 244c
Now let us from this table rise 404b, d
O God, our help 103e
O love of God most full 77d
Sent forth by God's blessing ... 407a, b
Star of our hope .... 174a, e
That glorious day is coming ... 209a
The church has waited long ... 217d
The King shall come 215e
The Lord is coming 200a
This is the threefold truth 203c
We have this hope 214

CANONS (OR ROUNDS)

Dona Nobis Pacem 471
Grant Us Your Peace 471
Hark, the Vesper Hymn Is Stealing 58
Let Us Praise the Name 14
Praise and Thanksgiving 563
Shalom 674

Hymns That May Be Sung as Canons
All Praise to Thee 53
Every Flower That Grows 550
Holy Spirit, Gracious Guest 589
How Firm a Foundation 509
My Shepherd Will Supply 104
Now That Daylight Fills the Sky... 42

HYMNS SUITABLE FOR YOUNG WORSHIPERS

Worshipers from preschool through junior high can enjoy learning to sing the great hymns of the church. These hymns then become lifelong companions and make it easier for the children and youth to be involved in the services of the church. The following hymns are recommended for family worship, school, Sabbath school, and choirs. The hymns marked with asterisks are suggested as suitable for young children.

AUTHORS, TRANSLATORS, AND SOURCES OF TEXTS

COMPOSERS, ARRANGERS, AND SOURCES OF TUNES

ALPHABETICAL INDEX OF TUNES

An indented entry is another name by which the tune at that number is known.

ALPHABETICAL INDEX OF TUNES

METRICAL INDEX OF TUNES

S. M.
(Short Meter - 6.6.8.6.)
Dennis 350
El Kader 15
Festal Song 117, 615
Garden City 217
Garelochside 597
Laban 605
No Sorrow There 443
Paraclete 265
St. Bride 519
St. Thomas 344, 372
Schumann 409, 670
Southwell 504
Trentham 390
United Man 419
Woolwich 488

S. M. with Refrain
I Hear Thy Welcome
   Voice 282
Marching to Zion 422
Marion 27

S. M. D.
(Short Meter Double - 6.6.8.6.6.6.8.6.)
Diademata 223, 616
Leominster 568
Terra beata 92

C. M.
(Common Meter - 8.6.8.6.)
Antioch 125
Arlington 609
Azmon 250
Beatitudo 323
Bedford 35
Benediction (Ledington) 667
Bishopthorpe 644
Cascadel 379
Chesterfield 611
Coronation 229
Crimond 552
Day of Praise 411
Detroit 299
Dove of Peace 400
Dundee 107
Dunfermline 649
Exhortation 440
Gräfenberg 267
Horsley 164
I Do Believe 486
Irish 63
Jeg er saa glad 586
La Sierra 179
Land of Rest 420
Lobt Gott ihr Christen 105
Maitland 328
Manoah 315
Martyrdom 113
McKee 62
Mear 39

Meditation 405
Morning Song 215, 576
New Britain 108
Northfield 533
Perry 399
St. Agnes 241, 269, 655
St. Anne 103
St. Botolph 585
St. Columba 639
St. Magnus 19, 199
St. Peter 238, 587
San Rocco 97
Serenity 455
Soll's sein 261
Stracathro 392
Twenty-Fourth 406, 681
Vandeman 77
Wetherby 273
Winchester Old 139

C. M. with Refrain
At the Cross 163
God Will Take Care of
   You 99
I Know Whom I Have
   Believed 511
I Would Be Like Jesus 311
Lead Me to Calvary 317
Near to the Heart of
   God 495
Never Part Again 449
New Jerusalem 446
No Other Plea 523
O, How I Love Jesus 248
Only Trust Him 279
Promised Land 620
The Cleansing Wave 332
There's Sunshine in My
   Soul 470

C. M. D.
(Common Meter Double - 8.6.8.6.8.6.8.6.)
Balm in Gilead 475
Carol 130
Clonmel 642
Forest Green 90, 168
Halifax 497
Hymn of Praise 564
Kingsfold 144, 465
Regwal 556
Resignation 104
There Is a Fountain 336
Varina 88
Welcome Guest 46

C. M. D. with Refrain
Faith Is the Victory 608

L. M.
(Long Meter - 8.8.8.8.)
Abends 242
Angelus 94

Beautiful Zion 450
Bluebonnet 278
Cannock 160
Canonbury 541, 548, 686
Conditor alme 72
Deus tuorum militum 404
Duke Street 82, 227
Dunedin 106
Gardiner 177, 355, 376
Gonfalon Royal 41
Hamburg 154
Hursley 502
I Want Jesus to Walk With
   Me 624
Infinite Love 148
Janice 410
Laurel 42
Maryton 574
McCabe 401
Melrose 588
Mendon 264
Old Hundredth 16, 694, 695
Ombersley 79
Park Street 17, 393
Pentecost 613
Puer nobis 333
Retreat 527
Rockingham Old 155
Russia 252
Suantrai 352
Tallis' Canon 53
Truro 182, 378
Trygare kan ingen vara 101,
   153
Wareham 174, 226
Woodworth 314

L. M. with Refrain
A Shelter in the Time of
   Storm 528
Hark! 'Tis the Shepherd's
   Voice 361
He Leadeth Me 537
Higher Ground 625
I Need the Prayers 505
I'm Going Home 437
Montrose 111
More About Jesus 245
The Solid Rock 200, 522
Watch, Ye Saints 598

L. M. D.
(Long Meter Double - 8.8.8.8.8.8.8.8.)
Contrast 434
Creation 96
Duane Street 441
Finally 417
Jerusalem 80
Sweet Hour 478

L. M. with Alleluias
Lasst uns erfreuen 2, 91,
   228

819

METRICAL INDEX OF TUNES

9.6.9.5. with Refrain
Wholly Thine 308

9.7.9.7.D.
What Did He Do? 180

9.7.9.7.D. with Refrain
I'll Go Where You Want Me
to Go 573

9.8.8.9.
Randolph 66
Surely, Surely 688

9.8.8.9. with Refrain
God Be With You 65

9.8.9.7. with Refrain
We'll Build on the Rock 531

9.8.9.8.
Communion 398
Dronfield 342
O Waly Waly 397
St. Clement 56

9.8.9.8. with Refrain
Ada 338
Redeemed 337
Turn Your Eyes Upon
Jesus 290

9.8.9.8.D.
Rendez à Dieu 13

9.8.9.8.8.8.
Wer nur den lieben gott 510

9.8.9.8.9.8.
Fragrance 28

9.8.9.12. with Refrain
Resurrection 526

9.9.8.10. with Refrain
In Times Like These 593

9.9.9.6.
Lois 270

9.9.9.6. with Refrain
Just When I Need Him 512

9.9.9.9.
Adelaide 567
Benediction (Froom) 690

9.9.9.9. with Refrain
Cover With His Life 412
Marvelous Grace 109
Sweet By and By 428

9.9.10.8. with Refrain
Does Jesus Care? 181

9.10.9.9. with Refrain
Blessed Assurance 462

9.10.9.10.10.
Morris 301

9.11. with Refrain
Sweet, Sweet Spirit 262
I'm a Pilgrim 444

10.4.10.4.10.10.
You Yangs 102

10.5.10.5. with Refrain
Gleams of the Golden
Morning 205

10.5.10.6. with Refrain
Hail Him the King of
Glory 202

10.7.10.7. with Refrain
Draw Me Nearer 306
I Shall See the King 426
Jesus Is Coming Again 213
Rise Up, Shepherd, and
Follow 138

10.7.10.7.8.7.10.7.
Janelle 81

10.8.10.8.7.7.7.10.8.
General Conference 214

10.8.10.9. with Refrain
Sound the Battle Cry 614

10.9. with Refrain
Gott ist die Liebe 78

10.9.10.8. with Refrain
Power in the Blood 294

10.9.10.9. with Refrain
I Must Tell Jesus 485
Leaning on the Everlasting
Arms 469
Nothing Between 322
Seeking the Lost 373
Will Your Anchor Hold 534

10.9.10.9.D.
Blott en Dag 532

10.10.
Pax tecum 463

10.10.4. with Refrain
Let Us Break Bread
Together 403

10.10.8.
Lobet und preiset 563

10.10.9.10.
Slane 547

10.10.10. with Alleluias
Sine Nomine 421

10.10.10.4.
Engelberg 32

10.10.10.7. with Refrain
There'll Be No Dark
Valley 208

10.10.10.9.5.
May God Be With You 673

10.10.10.10.
Crucifer 362
Eventide 50
Morecambe 266, 668
Morestead 31, 635
National Hymn 645
Sly Park 657

10.10.10.10. with Refrain
Look for the Waymarks 596
Moment by Moment 507
O Where Are the
Reapers 366
The Glory Song 435

10.10.10.10.10.
Old 124th 22

10.10.10.10.10.10.
Finlandia 461

10.10.11.11.
Hanover 256
Lyons 83

10.10.11.11. with Refrain
The Lord Is My Light 515

10.10.14.10.
Were You There? 158

10.11.10.11.
Slane 320

10.11.10.11. with Refrain
A Child of the King 468
Hold Fast Till I Come 600

10.11.11.6.
Christe sanctorum 234

11.7.11.7. with Refrain
Softly and Tenderly 287
The Savior Is Waiting 289

11.8.9.7. with Refrain
The Judgment Has Set 416

11.8.11.8.
Beloved 36

11.8.11.8. with Refrain
He Hideth My Soul 520

11.8.11.8.D.
O Brother Be Faithful 602

11.8.11.9. with Refrain
It Is Well With My Soul 530

11.10.11.10.
Atkinson 275
Bolton 570
Charterhouse 654
Consolation
(Mendelssohn) 498
Consolation (Webbe) 477

Eternal Love 496
Highwood 364
Noël Nouvelet 175
Northbrook 354
O Perfect Love 656
Pevensey 394
Rodman 594
Russian Hymn 84
Seventh and James 346
Wallog 641
We Would See Jesus 494
Welwyn 651

11.10.11.10. with Refrain
Give Me the Bible 272
Great Is Thy
   Faithfulness 100
O store Gud 86
So Send I You 578
Tidings 365
Under His Wings 529
Until Then 632

11.10.11.10.11.10.11.12.
Londonderry Air 255

11.11.9.
Day by Day, Dear Lord 689

11.11.11.5.
Cloisters 514
Flemming 70

11.11.11.9. with Refrain
Standing on the
   Promises 518

11.11.11.10. with Refrain
I'd Rather Have Jesus 327

11.11.11.11.
Anniversary Song
   (Marshall) 640
Cradle Song 124
Cranham 224
Foundation 509
Gordon 321
I Love Thee 236
St. Denio 21
Whitworth 353

11.11.11.11. with Refrain
Anywhere With Jesus 508
Hiding in Thee 525
Jacob's Ladder 628
Stand Like the Brave 610
To God Be the Glory 341
Whiter Than Snow 318

11.11.12.11.
Heavenly Music 452

11.11.12.11. with Refrain
For You I Am Praying 284

11.12.12.10.
Nicea 73

12.8.12.8. with Refrain
Bonnie Eloise 442
The Old Rugged Cross 159

12.9.12.9. with Refrain
In a Little While We're
   Going Home 626
Wonderful Peace 466

12.10.12.10.
Southampton 6

12.10.12.10.11.10. with Refrain
Praise Him, Praise Him 249

12.11.12.11. with Refrain
Bringing in the Sheaves 369

12.11.12.11.D.
The Ash Grove 560

12.12.12.6. with Refrain
We Know Not the Hour 604

12.12.12.7. with Refrain
It May Be at Morn 207

12.13.13.13. with Refrain
Don't Forget the
   Sabbath 388

13.11.13.11. with Refrain
Morning Trumpet 448

13.12.12.12.12.
Ubi caritas 349

13.12.13.7.6.
'Tis the Blessed Hour of
   Prayer 501

13.13.13.13.13.13.
Thaxted 648

14.14.4.7.8.
Lobe den Herren 1

15.11.15.11. with Refrain
When the Roll Is Called 216

15.15.15.6. with Refrain
Battle Hymn 647

INDEX OF TITLES AND FIRST LINES

INDEX OF TITLES AND FIRST LINES

INDEX OF TITLES AND FIRST LINES

INDEX OF TITLES AND FIRST LINES

INDEX OF TITLES AND FIRST LINES

INDEX OF TITLES AND FIRST LINES

INDEX OF TITLES AND FIRST LINES